Personality Theories:
guides to living

Nicholas S. DiCaprio

Department of Psychology
John Carroll University
Cleveland, Ohio

1974   W. B. SAUNDERS COMPANY
Philadelphia • London • Toronto

W. B. Saunders Company: West Washington Square
Philadelphia, Pa. 19105

12 Dyott Street
London, WC1A 1DB

833 Oxford Street
Toronto, Ontario M8Z 5T9, Canada

Personality Theories: Guides to Living   ISBN 0-7216-3055-3

Last digit is the print number: 9   8   7   6   5   4   3   2   1

Preface

The purpose of this text is to present the *distinctive features* of the major theories of personality and their implications for everyday living. In my reading of the original sources, I discovered exciting ideas about personality and living, which I found to be vitally applicable to myself. Most of the personality theorists were also personality therapists who had to deal day after day with the sufferings of human beings. They were persistently confronted with the task of understanding and changing deviant or personally disturbing behaviors. The problems, like the patients, were varied and diverse. Theorizing about the nature of individual behavior—its development, growth, and change—had to meet the acid test of practical utility. Could the theory help to explain the behavior? Could it serve as a guide to alleviating the problems of living? Did the theory spell out what is normal, or ideal, for man? These are vital issues not only for the personality theorist, but for everyone. Our own image of man, our own personality theory, can be expanded and improved through a knowledge of the theories of others.

The original sources were written not for students but for professionals in the field. The problem is to find a way of preserving the richness of ideas and the freshness of approach of the theorists. Existing secondary sources that digest the personality theories usually attempt to accomplish other goals, such as summarizing the research suggested by the theories or presenting historical background and biographical material. Still others offer extensive critical evaluations of the theories and intricate comparisons of the subtle differences among them. The richness of meaning and explanatory power of the theories are not conveyed. There simply is not enough time and space to accomplish all the goals of the ideal course or textbook; thus the beginning student, dazzled by a host of academic issues which have little interest or value for him, may not recognize that the theorists were, above all, dealing with living human beings with personality problems. One of my objectives is to remedy this situation by highlighting the rich and vital thinking of the outstanding personality theorists and the implications of their work to life and its questions.

This text might be characterized as a *distinctive themes* approach to personality study. It deals with the perennial concerns of mankind, as portrayed by highly trained and perceptive students of human nature. The most powerful postulates of each theory are elaborated extensively, and each theory is viewed from its own particular perspective. Emphasis is given to those themes which foster knowledge of individual behavior and have a direct bearing on effective living. Like the outstanding themes of a symphony or the memorable arias of an opera, each theory is identified by one or more powerful constructs. Such constructs have wide explanatory scope and increase our insight into human nature, because they can be related to the ordinary problems of ordinary people.

The text is organized topically, so as to treat the major aspects of personality and living — development, learning, motivation, conflict, and especially models of the good life. But it is also designed to be flexible. Taken singly, the chapters are self-contained; thus, their arrangement may be tailored by the instructor. One might sample a chapter from each section and focus on the last section, which treats ideal models of living. Some theorists appear in two sections because their contributions are distinctive in more than one topical area; thus the two Freud chapters, the two Allport chapters, and the two Maslow chapters may be considered as single units. Some chapters may be assigned for outside reading and given only summary treatment in class.

Each chapter follows a similar format, beginning with an overview of the theorist and the theory, then developing the theorist's outstanding theme. A critical evaluation of each theorist's concepts is included, as are chapter summaries, suggested readings with brief descriptions, and bibliographical references. In some chapters, significant terms are defined and distinctive quotations from primary sources are included. The Insights sections at the end of each chapter offer practical applications of the theories to real-life situations. Instructors who wish to stress the relationship of the theories to problems of living and to promoting effective living may decide to concentrate on these sections.

Several influential theories have not been included because of space limitation and because they are not as applicable to a functional orientation as those that are. Constitutional and the factor analytic approaches are notable examples. While several major viewpoints are represented, it should be noted that the humanistic approach has been most influential in the personality field to date; thus, these theories have been given greater weight. Theories that apply to abnormal behavior have been balanced by those that deal with normal or ideal behavior.

This text is appropriate for courses in adjustment as well as those in personality theory. It is also suitable for courses in individual psychology, as opposed to those courses which emphasize a highly biological and experimental orientation. Obviously, ancillary reading should be encouraged when students have the requisite ability and interest. No background in general psychology is required, however, for the content is life-oriented and not overly technical. The six sections are introduced with the necessary principles of general psychology, so that the treatment of the theories can be easily grasped. The text can thus be useful to anyone planning to enter a profession dealing with individual behavior — not only in the field of psychology but also social work, nursing, the ministry, and teaching. In brief, it should be of value to anyone interested in the growth and adaptive processes of human life.

Acknowledgments

Many hands, hearts, and minds played a part in the preparation of this book. Special gratitude is due Dr. Morton Bloomberg, who worked laboriously over every chapter and made significant improvements throughout the manuscript. His personal involvement was a source of inspiration to me. To Mark Savickas, a former student, I owe a dept of appreciation for stimulating new insights when the going got rough. I would also like to thank Professors Robert Kaplan, University of California, San Diego, Martin Moss, Wright State University, James Calhoun, State University of New York at Stony Brook, and Robert Singer, University of California, Riverside, for their reviews and valuable suggestions.

Mr. Baxter Venable, Psychology Editor of the W. B. Saunders Company, did the usual editorial work, but I am especially indebted to him for devoting an entire work week to going over the manuscript with me. Mrs. Marie Low, my copy editor at Saunders, was also most patient and helpful.

Mrs. Esther Murphy patiently and diligently typed and retyped hundreds of manuscript pages and devoted many Sunday afternoons to proofreading and editing. She became a personal part of the project. A faculty fellowship award from John Carroll University and a scholarship grant from the Cleveland Sight Center gave me a much needed sabbatical to work on the book. The following persons also helped me in important ways and deserve my gratitude: Cleo B. Dolan, Marian Shapiro, Kerry Slattery, Madge Snyder and her wonderful volunteers, Mrs. Ada Harrison, Betty Daniel, and Anita Brown, my student assistant. To Rita, my wife, I am indebted not only for help throughout, but also for the many hours I had to spend working on the project instead of being with her and our children, Paul and Laureen.

I dedicate this work to the memory of my father, who did not have the benefit of formal schooling.

NICHOLAS S. DiCAPRIO

Contents

Chapter 6

S-R, COGNITIVE, AND SOCIAL LEARNING THEORIES: *Dollard and*
Miller, Bandura and Walters, Rotter

Part IV

HUMAN MOTIVATION

Chapter 7

HUMAN NEEDS: *Henry Murray*

Chapter 8

Chapter 9

Part V

PART I

The Meaning of Personality Theories

The beginning student thinks of psychology as the study of people. He takes a psychology course with the hope that he will learn about himself and others. But after he is dazzled with a discussion of the scientific characteristics of psychology, he finds that he is learning instead a multitude of discrete generalizations and such precise topics as the principles of perception, motivation, and learning. He is of course encouraged to apply such knowledge to himself and his friends, but what he set out to know (himself and others) seems to be lost in the great array of principles, postulates, and hypotheses to which he is exposed. What he really wants is to learn about *the single person and himself.* What he wants is a course in personality, which for our purpose may be taken as *the scientific study of the individual.* The concepts and principles proposed by the personality theorists presented in this book should aid him in attaining his objective.

In studying another person or ourselves, we may apply knowledge about perception, learning, motivation, and development, but we need to find a way of *characterizing* the distinctive quality of the particular individual, what G. W. Allport (1961) termed *patterned individuality.* John is certainly like many other people in some ways, and quite similar to some people, but nevertheless, he has his own particular identity, his own style of life. We are quick to sense when John is or is not himself. The major task of the student of personality is to *characterize* John's behavior. To put it simply, we should be able to form a model of John, or any other individual, so that the characteristics of the model parallel the actual characteristics and processes that take place in the person who is being represented. Studying the model should enable us to learn about the person it represents.

We form *images or conceptions* of people, including ourselves. These conceptions may be only approximately correct, and certainly, quite incomplete. A particular trait may be overweighted and we might overlook many important qualities (Kelley, 1967). What we find depends upon a theory of personality, either our own or someone else's. We may think of people in terms of rather limited categories: they are bright or dull, generous or stingy, attractive or unattractive, pleasing or not pleasing to us. Our particular theory of personality guides us in observing the behavior of ourselves and others, and helps us to interpret what we observe. It includes certain assumptions about the nature of man, such as that all people are selfish or that people are really out to hurt you if they can, or that everyone wants to be at the top. We also have our own interpretation of what is desirable and undesirable behavior. One may value competitiveness and judge another or himself by the amount of this dimension he displays. A second may value considerateness of others, and judge himself and others accordingly. We tend to be quite categorical in our judgments: our thinking runs along lines of either/or, without allowing for intermediate states. We describe people with single terms; e.g., a grouch, a nice guy, a real sport, a passivist.

If our theory of personality has few categories, we are likely to have a distorted conception of the personality we are studying. If we simply classify people as emotional or unemotional, we of course miss the richness and complexity of the range of emotions possible to them. A complex thing such as personality can be represented only by means of a complex set of concepts and principles, although complexity in itself is not necessarily a desirable thing.

One might ask: "Why do we need a theory of personality?" He might point out that we can learn about ourselves and others simply by observing what behaviors occur in specific situations. What does Mary do when she is around boys? What does John do when he does not get his way? What does Harry do when there are other people he likes near him? If we can ask these questions, why should we bother to fathom something as difficult to study as "personality"? The answer is that personality may be considered an important locus of *causes* and *determinants* of behavior. Knowing the make-up and operations within the personality assists us in understanding behavior in a way that knowledge of isolated situations cannot. I may discover that John is consistently in a bad mood on rainy days, and so conclude that his behavior is affected by the weather. On a particular rainy day, I find that John is in an exhilarated mood, and when asked why, he says he just feels good.

In brief, there are two basic types of causes or determinants: *situational* and *personality* (Raush, Dittman, and Taylor, 1959). It is useful to discover what a person does in particular situations, but knowledge of the personality variables increases the likelihood that we can have a correct picture of the causes of behavior. Knowing that a person has a trait of talkativeness can help us to understand his behavior in a variety of different situations. Frequently, however, his actions are more strongly determined by internal or personality variables than by situational ones. Just as we need some means of characterizing environmental variables—visual, auditory, and tactile stimuli—so also we need some means of characterizing what takes place in the personality—learning, motivation, emotions, conflict, change, and the like.

The present text is organized according to the major topics in personality study. The topics represent what are assumed to be the significant factors and events that take place in personality. Thus we will consider theories concerned with personality development, with learning, with conflict, with motivation, and finally with ideal models of living. Through these theories we will attempt to understand what happens within personality when it is growing and functioning normally or abnormally. We accept that personality is something real and describable, that it grows and changes, and that its working principles can be understood.

The make-up and operation (or *dynamics*) of personality must be inferred from behavior. If our intention is to explain all significant behaviors which characterize someone, particularly with respect to his identity as a person, then we are dealing with a theory of personality. In its simplest form, a theory of personality is a *construct,* proposed to represent the make-up and operation of individual character. It is a hypothetical postulate, formulated when definitive knowledge is lacking.

When we do not know the causes operating behind any event, we may begin our investigation by guessing at them. If something occurs, we seek to understand the causes. If we look for a book on the bookshelf where we had last placed it and do not find it, we begin to question why. In an analogous manner, we seek to understand the causes of behavior. If we cannot account for behavior by means of external causes, we may look to personality, or internal variables. A person who believes that others are plotting against him when this is not the case may be assumed to have a paranoid trend within his personality. Proposing this explanation would account for his abnormal behavior and would also lead us to look for other manifestations of the paranoid trend. If there are other expressions of paranoia, our construct acquires greater support. We become more confident in our predictions concerning his behavior in specific circumstances.

Suppose we have two friends: one works hard to gain our attention, while the other seems not to care. How can we account for the difference? One way is to propose that the one friend has a much stronger *need for affiliation* (need to be with people) than the other friend. We assume that this need has specifiable effects on our friend's behavior. We look for other manifestations of the need because it enables us to explain behavior which we could not otherwise explain. Of course, someone else might suggest a different construct: perhaps one friend seeks our attention because he is more insecure than the other. This alternative explanation could be further tested, and it might account for the difference in the behaviors of the two friends better than the first construct. Thus we can see that although personality constructs are initially used to explain isolated actions, they must be verified in other behaviors. Any proposed construct, such as a trait of generosity, accounts for past and present behaviors and also predicts future behavior. This fact allows ample opportunity for validation of the hypothesis. If one knows something about another person, his past, present, and future will be revealed to some extent because personality variables have stability.

Many personality theories will be discussed extensively throughout the book, but one point should be kept in mind. Not everything about a person is worth knowing, or at least, is equally pertinent. That Mary has a habit of letting her toenails grow too long, or that John prefers cream and sugar in his coffee, or that Nelly likes to have tea and crumpets in the middle of the night, may tell us little about these people. We could catalog hundreds, perhaps thousands, of things about a person that would still reveal little about him. Some constructs deal with the central aspects of personality, while others are concerned with the peripheral. Following Leon Levy (1970) we might think of personality as *components of identity*. Whatever constructs we use to characterize a person, they should represent some aspect or aspects of his identity. This means that the constructs should be capable of depicting the stability and consistency as well as the changeability of the person.

It will soon become obvious to the reader that there is no all-encompassing theory of personality, and perhaps, as Levy believes, there never will be. The various theories of personality have a *range of convenience* (Kelly, 1955), which means that *they apply best to certain aspects of personality*. For instance, Erikson's theorizing focuses upon the *development* of personality. Murray's theorizing concentrates on *motivation*. Freud dealt a great deal with *conflict*. The focus of each theory is well defined and each theorist offers his most valuable insights in a particular area of personality study.

As we shall see when we discuss the nature of personality theories more thoroughly, a personality scientist may use a theory to help him explain or bring together what is already known in a particular area, but the theory may also give him ideas that he can test. For example, Freud, as we shall see, divided the personality into three systems: the id, the ego, and the superego. The ego is the administrator of the personality; the id represents impulses or drives; the superego represents conscience or restraining forces. One might think of the effect of a weak ego upon personality control. Other questions may arise: How can the ego be strengthened? What happens when another component, such as the superego, dominates the personality? Do neurotics have weaker egos than normals? Should the ideal of personality growth be to have a strong ego or rather to balance the three components of personality? We have noted only a few ideas for research that Freud's concepts have suggested. The scientific usefulness of a theory may be judged by the number of such testable ideas that it inspires.

What can theories of personality do for one who simply wants to improve his life? They should help him to a better understanding of himself and of those with whom he associates. Furthermore, many of the theories offer us a view of man in his ideal state. A theory may explicitly or implicitly characterize the model of the good life. In this sense, a particular personality theory offers us a guide to living. It provides the goals of personality growth and functioning we should strive to attain. Several of the theories deal almost exclusively with ideal human existence. Many of the personality theorists were also personality therapists; thus they were concerned with the restoration of healthy growth and functioning. Frequently they theorized about the abnormal conditions of their patients and also about the ends which they sought to attain with the therapeutic concepts and techniques they employed. Knowing both the ideal states for man and the means of accomplishing them should assist us in living more effectively and in perfecting our own capabilities. We can attempt to accomplish these ends by applying the concepts and techniques proposed by the personality theorists presented in this book.

CHAPTER 1

Introduction to
Personality
Theories

CONTENTS OF THEORIES OF PERSONALITY

Usually there are three types of propositions in a theory of personality: (1) *assumptions*, (2) *postulates*, and (3) *definitions*.

ASSUMPTIONS

Assumptions are *general principles about man's nature which cannot be tested*. They are the philosophical underpinnings of a personality theory. Some theorists do not state them explicitly, but there are always underlying premises. Some examples of basic assumptions are: The only real purpose of life is to reduce psychobiological tensions. All motives are reducible to seeking pleasure and avoiding pain. Personality grows normally if appropriate conditions are present. Man is ultimately selfish. Self-control is the ultimate measure of maturity. Man, by nature, is evil. In using a theory of personality, we should be aware of the underlying assumptions, because the total orientation of the theory depends upon these assumptions. There is a distinct difference between a theory which assumes man's capacity for self-control and one that denies it.

As we have indicated, in our own theory of personality, whether applied to ourselves or to others, the basic assumptions are often unknown or unconscious. We are nevertheless influenced by them. We might have the implicit assumption that true happiness is a state of great joy, which once attained by the fortunate will continue forever. We will judge our own behavior and that of others according to this assumption, and of course, our judgments will produce serious distortions. In like manner, we may value ourselves according to status, attractiveness, accomplishments, and other similar things, but be unaware that we are doing so.

6

POSTULATES

Postulates are the *proposed laws or principles* of a theory. They are of two types: those which embody *empirical generalizations,* and those which represent *constructs.* (We will devote more time to this aspect of the theories than to any other because postulates are a theory's *major components.*) An empirical generalization is a proposition that summarizes a relationship between two or more variables. An example is the frustration-aggression hypothesis, which states a cause-effect relationship between frustration and aggression (Dollard et al., 1939). To apply this hypothesis we would have to be clear about the meaning of both frustration and aggression. There are many ways of expressing anger, ranging from open attack to self-injury, and there are also many forms of frustration. This postulate tells us that whenever we observe anger, hostility, or destructiveness in ourselves or others, we have an indication that some goal or need is being blocked or frustrated. Conversely, if we know that we are being frustrated in our desires and needs, we can be quite certain that tendencies toward aggression are activated. We might even suspect that some of our transitory symptoms such as fatigue, headache, nervousness, or depression are indirect expressions of these tendencies.

A hypothetical construct is a more general statement than an empirical generalization (MacCorquodale and Meehl, 1948). It cannot be directly translated into a testable hypothesis like the aggression-frustration hypothesis. Let us consider an intriguing principle, one proposed by C. G. Jung: what a person appears to be is often just the opposite of what he really is. A warm, friendly, loving person in our casual contacts may really be masking strong antisocial, unfriendly, selfish tendencies. So long as our contacts with him are superficial, these qualities do not emerge. Our picture is quite different from that of those who really know him. In like manner, an apparently unimpressive, plain, drab individual is often quite the opposite when we come to know him well. A person who has vivid, exciting dreams may, in fact, live a very empty waking life. There are many other applications of this principle. Jung observed its occurrence often enough to propose it as a postulate, though obviously there are some people who appear to be just what they really are. Other principles in Jung's theory help us to identify signs which tell us if a person is what he appears to be or is masking his real self.

Postulates that are empirical generalizations *summarize* what has been *discovered* through observation and experiment. There is frequently considerable agreement regarding the validity of empirical generalizations: anxiety produces distortions in perception; repression blocks thinking; conflict interferes with action; behavior is acquired through imitation, and so on. To account for or explain the empirical generalizations we need postulates that are hypothetical constructs. The constructs are the *proposed* or *tentative* explanations, the *determinants within the personality.*

In the absence of true explanations, there may be much disagreement concerning the constructs that are used to account for the empirical generalizations. For example, Freud proposed the construct of the id as a means of representing man's primitive personality—selfish, antisocial, impulse-driven. The widespread prevalence of destructive and antisocial behavior could be accounted for by an id not under proper control of the ego. Maslow proposed the construct that such antisocial behavior is the result of frustrated needs. Jung proposed the construct of the shadow, of unperceived evil tendencies in oneself, to account for the same behavior. Following a strict behavioristic view, Skinner argues that Freud's construct of the unconscious and other similar fictions were convenient explanations for behavior that Freud could not explain. He holds that it is unenlightening to propose that a current behavior problem is caused by an unconscious early traumatic experience which was never properly worked through. Constructs such as these make up the major postulates of personality theories. To validate a construct, it is necessary to demonstrate that it can be applicable to a variety of behaviors.

The thoughtful student may question the necessity of having so many theories of personality, since there would seem to be only one set of laws and not twenty or more. It should be noted that the postulates which make up theories of personality fall far short of meeting the requirements of established principles and laws of behavior. A postulate must be tested and found applicable to specific behaviors, to become a law. Until we have better methods of studying personality phenomena, and accumulate more dependable knowledge, it is possible to propose many different models of personality. As more knowledge is gained, the theories should decrease.

DEFINITIONS

The purpose of a definition is to *identify the behaviors which the concepts represent.* Theorists usually tell us what the terms of a theory mean, but their definitions vary in detail and precision. If the terms of the definition are vague and general, it is never clear whether a particular behavior may or may not be included in the scope of the definition. We are all familiar with the woman who complains that her husband does not love her because he never acts sentimentally or romantically towards her. But he gives her his pay check, lets her buy anything she wants, takes her where she wants to go, comes home for dinner every night, and respects her freedom to do whatever she pleases. From a behavioral standpoint, he does love her very much, but his definition of love is different from hers. Apparently she does not realize that he is "acting out" his love for her in tangible ways. She is interested in verbal expressions of love.

To make definitions precise, many psychologists have adopted the policy of using *operational definitions.* An operational definition is one which stipulates the *behaviors which are covered by the concept,* and *the manner in which the behaviors are measured* (Stevens, 1939). In order for the concept of love to be meaningful, it would have to be reduced to specific behaviors. To define it in abstract emotional terms might be satisfactory for the poet and the lyricist, but each person would have his own interpretation of the meaning. Such usage could not promote scientific inquiry.

Scientific investigators must agree on the precise meaning of terms. Consider the problems associated with defining such terms as patriotism, fidelity, self-awareness, sociability, security, self-hatred, philosophy of life. Unless the theorist tells us exactly how he intends to measure such concepts behaviorally, we would never know whether the terms had the same meaning for us as they do for him.

TYPES OF CONSTRUCTS

As we have noted, constructs are inferred from observable behavior, and are attempts to account for or explain that behavior. A construct is operationally defined if the theorist specifies the behaviors to which the construct applies. For example, Freud's concept of the id has no meaning unless the behaviors which are expressions of the id are designated. Whatever the nature of the construct, there must be some way to translate it into actual behavior; otherwise the construct will have no explanatory value. If a theorist proposes the construct that the major governing principle of the personality is the tendency toward self-actualization, he must demonstrate how this tendency is expressed in actual behavior, and what happens when it is blocked or distorted.

We might briefly consider the types of constructs that personality psychologists use to describe and explain the make-up and functioning of personality. Some constructs refer to existing entities. Others deal with the operation of these entities. Some constructs refer to long-standing or enduring features of personality, while others depict temporary and transitory conditions.

Contents Versus Function

If we examine the contents of a toolbox, we might want to know the names and descriptions of each of the tools we find, and then we may wish to know what each tool does. Here we have a distinction between content and function. Personality theorists have used constructs in both ways. Freud, for example, discussed the contents and functions of his three conscious and unconscious realms of the psyche.

Processes

Many constructs deal with processes; a governing principle such as Adler's striving for superiority or Rogers's principle of self-actualization represents a process. Processes encompass functions and include more, namely, interrelationships among personality components.

Trends

Another popular use of constructs is to designate a long-standing trend within the personality. A trend represents an enduring theme or tendency, such as an optimistic or pessimistic orientation. A strong sense of inferiority may be an enduring trend. One's style of life consists of a number of trends.

Dispositions

Constructs depicting dispositions suggest that there is a readiness within personality to organize perception, thinking, feeling, and responding in a certain manner. The response to a situation may be understood only if the existing dispositions are known. For instance, a person may become extremely upset in a situation that does not provoke the same reaction in others because he has a disposition of social unacceptability.

States

Constructs are used to identify emotional states such as anxiety, psychological disequilibrium, regression, and the like. The construct depicts a temporary state of the personality that of course is inferred from behavior.

Events

Constructs are used to name events that take place in the personality, such as having an insight, erecting a defense mechanism, coping with a stress situation, and many others. Again, it should be recalled that whatever the nature of the construct, there must always be some behavior that defines the construct. Personality theorists have not always been diligent in specifying the behaviors covered by their constructs.

EVALUATION OF PERSONALITY THEORIES

A personality theory can be judged by its utility in *describing, explaining, predicting,* and *controlling* the behavior of a particular individual or group of individuals.

DESCRIPTION

When we describe personality, we answer the *"what question."* What is the person doing? What are all the things he can do? What types of experiences does he have? We must be able to describe what we are studying before we can do anything else. Behavior is often described by terms which are designated *traits*. A trait applies to several "ways of acting." Moreover, several traits may be associated, so that we can designate these clusters as *types.* Both the trait and the type concepts are descriptive labels. They name and designate behaviors, but do not account for them.

We might look at an example of a descriptive scheme, proposed by Erich Fromm. Fromm divides people into five types, according to life orientation: the receptive, the exploitive, the hoarding, the marketing, and the productive. Each of these is defined by a number of traits. We might consider the marketing type, which he believes is a product of a capitalist society. It is significant that he considers both negative and positive traits for the type. The positive traits are (Fromm, 1947, p. 116):

sociable	intelligent	purposeful
experimenting	adaptable	able to change
undogmatic	tolerant	youthful
efficient	witty	forward looking
curious	generous	open-minded

The negative traits are:

relativistic	indifferent	inconsistent
overactive	silly	childish
tactless	wasteful	without a future or past
intellectualistic	opportunistic	without principle and values
undiscriminating		

Our economic system has fostered the development of these specific traits, but not everyone reacts to societal pressures in the same way. Thus each positive and negative trait should be defined by specific behaviors. Though Fromm, unfortunately, does not do this, the marketing type is nevertheless recognizable; it describes many people. We need to have concepts which describe the phenomena of personality, and each personality theorist usually provides such descriptive concepts, although in some cases they are quite vague.

Often we may think that we are explaining behavior, whereas we are simply naming or describing various behaviors. An example is the defense mechanisms. They provide significant insights into an important aspect of ego functioning, that of protecting or defending against threat, disappointment, failure, and other psychological hurts. To protect ourselves against failure, we make excuses, blame others, minimize the value of what we seek, divert our attention by means of substitute activities, and deny our real interest or involvement.

Typical constructs that personality psychologists use to describe the kind and causes of behavior are: needs, traits, types, roles, intentions, sentiments, habits, dispositions, tendencies, trends, ego functions, thoughts, images, and desires. We might think of these as the *contents* of personality. At the level of behavior, there are many categories of responses: reflexes, conditioned responses, operant responses, motor responses, and so on. We may of course name specific behaviors such as walking, talking, eating, singing, working, writing a letter to John, and the like, and study these behaviors as they relate to situational and personality variables. The point is that before we can hope to explain, or do anything else, we must discriminate and name the various things we wish to study.

EXPLANATION

Generally speaking, to explain means to identify causes; thus we will consider the possible causes of behavior, and especially those which are relevant to the personality psychologist. If we observe a child running along the street crying, we may go to him and attempt to discover the explanation. We find that the cause is that the child is lost. We may find that certain people make us uncomfortable, but we cannot specify the cause. The explanation might be the reawakening of an unpleasant experience from the past. Another possible explanation is that certain behaviors of others make us feel insecure. We may discover causes at different levels: we may, for instance, discover the characteristics in others that cause our insecurity; but we might also seek an explanation for the genesis of this sensitivity in ourselves. The types of causes depend upon the thoroughness of the analysis.

What are the various causes of behavior? The determinants of behavior are (1) environmental, (2) organismic, (3) genetic, and (4) personality.

Environmental Causes

The physical and cultural environment plays a widespread and continuous role in determining the form and operations of behavior. We need only to think of the pervasive influence of learning upon every facet of life. We are born into a culture, which imposes all sorts of demands and pressures. The culture not only presents us with the problems we are to solve, but also prescribes the acceptable solutions that are available to us. So important are environmental and situational causes that some psychologists, notably the learning theorists, have given preponderant weight to them.

Organismic Causes

Behavior is greatly influenced by physiological, biochemical, and other organismic determinants. Our moods, our capacity to carry on sustained work, our emotional reactivity, even our intelligence: practically everything that goes on in personality is influenced in important ways by organismic causes (Arnold, 1970). We could not understand the causes of behavior without considering the organismic influences. There are those (the reductionists) who hold that all psychological causes will ultimately be explained in biological terms. Most personality psychologists reject this idea, arguing that one can have explanations on different levels, each legitimate. Thus we can explain some behaviors from the standpoint of economic principles, others from geographical, and still others from personality variables. The fact remains that although behavior is in fact influenced by organismic determinants, and though some of the most enduring aspects of personality have a biochemical basis, for the personality psychologist the *major determinants of behavior are personality and situational variables.* We cannot, however, ignore the biological aspect of behavior.

Genetic Causes

There is no question that we are born with certain native equipment, and that we have potentialities and predispositions to grow in certain directions. Striking resemblances between parents and offspring are found in many variables. But in man the role of learning is so great, and the possible directions that behavior can take so plastic, that one has difficulty parceling out the direct influence of heredity. Nevertheless, we do know that genetic factors are major determinants of behavior.

Personality Causes

As we have noted, most personality theorists postulate the existence of causes within the personality. Their constructs refer to such entities as the self, needs, emotional states, cognition, and memory. Personality theorists do not deny the significant influence of the other behavior determinants; rather, they deal with their effect on the make-up and functioning of personality. Thus the environment influences personality, the biological determinants affect personality functioning; heredity fixes the limits of personality development.

The Correlational Approach

We may distinguish between the causal approach and the correlational approach as a means of explaining. We have considered the causal approach: relating behavior to environmental causes, to historical causes, to biological causes, to personality causes, to conscious or unconscious determinants. However, we may observe that certain behaviors are found together. A person who conforms to the demands of others may also be submissive and shy. One who feels dominant in relation to others may also be high on extroversion. Because personality has organization and structure, we can discover the factors that are correlated. Explanation frequently takes the form of identifying the network of interacting or coacting personality variables (Cronback, 1957).

EXPLANATORY FUNCTIONS OF THEORIES

The explanatory power of a theory refers to the number of behaviors it can account for, summarize, or synthesize. Obviously, some concepts are more powerful than others in that they cover a multitude of behaviors, yet remain specific in their application. Consider the postulate that all behavior is goal-directed. This principle is general enough to cover all behavior, but it does not help much in describing, understanding, or predicting specific behaviors. If we analyze the principle, it says that all behavior can be explained. This principle may have been useful when psychology was first getting under way as an experimental science, but it does not help us much now.

Roles

A powerful explanatory concept is provided by role theory. Much behavior may be brought together under the role concept. We will consider just a few ramifications here.

A role is a *culturally prescribed mode of behavior*. The culture prescribes a variety of roles based on such conditions as age, sex, status, social relationships, appearance, wealth, and vocation. We might consider a specific individual from the role standpoint: does he know his various roles, or does he suffer from "role confusion"? Each person has a variety of roles which he is expected to play out. A man may be expected to be receptive and obedient to his parents, even though he is himself a parent who demands such behavior from his children. He must be able to switch roles when the conditions are changed. If he does not carry out his roles as expected, he will run into problems: his parents may not seek his company, or his children may perceive him as ineffective.

Because each role is rather specific, a person may be thrown into a *role conflict*. A man may expect his wife to be submissive and receptive, and at the same time to run the home independently. The wife, in turn, may be caught in a role conflict because she cannot always discern when to be submissive and when to be aggressive.

A person may hate his roles; a man may not like the requirements placed upon him. He does not want to be what society forces him to be. There are many people who perform their roles grudgingly and perfunctorily. Others rebel against them and are imprisoned, committed to hospitals for the mentally ill, or regarded as inferior or eccentric. We might describe this type of person as a "role deviant." Of course, there are people who love their roles, identify with them, and use them as guides to living. If a person wishes to fit in with his various settings, he must learn the appropriate roles which are prescribed.

This brief treatment of the role principle should be sufficient to indicate its value as an explanatory concept. You can "make sense" of much of a person's behavior with it, and you can also understand a wide range of people (Sarbin, 1964). Knowing how a person views his roles is a means of getting to know him. We can, of course, use the role concept to understand our own behavior.

The Self

The self is a concept which is being used more and more by contemporary personality theorists. Consider some of the ways in which the concept of self is stated: self-hate, self-love, self-confidence, self-extension, self-esteem, the real self versus the ideal self, and so on. Many people really do not know much about themselves. They may be unaware of their most basic motives or attitudes. They are sometimes surprised at their own reactions. They may conceive of themselves in a certain way, and discover through harsh experience that they were mistaken. Sometimes these harsh experiences effect changes in self-conception, but more often, they lead only to further distortions.

The self may be evaluated: a person likes or dislikes what he really is. Low self-esteem is a condition, in many instances, of personality disturbance (Engel, 1959). Many people complain of lack of self-worth; they believe that other people would not like them if they revealed themselves.

In some people, the self-image may be formed as a reaction to the way the person has been treated. The self-image tells the person how he should behave to avoid trouble with others, or to please others. Quite often, this artificial self is quite different from the real self, which has to be suppressed. This condition causes serious disturbances in the structure of personality; the person does not become what he can be. Much of what he really is does not come to the surface. Like the concept of role, the concept of self is a powerful explanatory tool.

Needs

If we are concerned with the forces which "run" the personality, we might consider the important concept of need. Need theory is usually classified under the heading of motivation and has many basic applications in describing, explaining, and predicting behavior. Consider some of the obvious ramifications of need theory. Needs may be taken as *deficit states*, which can be eliminated or reduced by specific goal objects. In a state of need, an organism is *impelled to activity toward an appropriate goal*. But in man the need may be unconscious, or the goal unattainable, or one need may be in conflict with another. If we know some of these things about a person's needs, we have a means of describing, explaining, and predicting his behavior. Furthermore, if we know the behaviors which are typically used to satisfy needs and the specific goal objects which reduce the needs, we have still more to guide us.

A need may be so dominant that almost everything the person does is traceable to it. Achievement is so important to some middle-class Americans that their lives are completely organized around the satisfaction of this need (Veroff et al., 1960). A man may select his friends on the basis of the extent to which they can further his interests; he may arrange his leisure activities so that he can make the right contacts; he may, in fact, suppress or subordinate most of his other needs for the sake of achievement.

Knowing a person's needs, and their order of priority, tells us a great deal about him. If we also know his typical means of meeting his needs, we have still more to help us. If we can identify the major oppositions or conflicts among needs, we may be able to discover the sources of tension within his personality.

What we have said in regard to needs in general may be applied to ourselves. We can strive for understanding of ourselves through knowledge of our needs. For example, we might ask such questions as: What are the priorities of my needs? Are there important personal needs that are in conflict? Which of my needs are not being met as I would like them to be? What can I do to better fulfill my needs? There are many other aspects of need theory, but what we have said should be sufficient to highlight the potentials of this approach to personality study.

The Pleasure–Pain Principle

The pleasure–pain principle has been expressed in a variety of forms, but its essential feature is that man is motivated in everything he does to seek as much pleasure as possible, and at the same time, to avoid or minimize pain as far as he can. An important implication of this principle is that self-seeking is the motivation underlying all other motives. A drive, or need state, is experienced as tension, and the organism acts to remove the tension, no matter what its specific nature might be. A need to make money is a tension which can be satisfied only in a particular way. Conversely, other things are done solely for the pleasure they afford.

Selfishness is a most pervasive feature of human striving, and it appears in many disguises. Apparently generous acts may really be motivated by selfish concerns: a wealthy man creates a scholarship fund to honor his name rather than to help needy students. It may seem unflattering to consider self-interest the dominating force in man's life, but the frequency of its occurrence is a convincing demonstration of the validity of this point (Christie and Geis, 1970). Many aggressive people use the guise of doing good to victimize those over whom they have control. Thus some personality psychologists attempt to include all behavior under the scope of the pleasure–pain principle by stretching the meanings of pleasure and pain. Later we will consider the behaviors which simply cannot be covered by the principle, despite its significance.

We can see the operation of the pleasure–pain principle in our own lives by considering how much of our behavior is actually in the service of pressures, necessity, tension, and coercion. Much of what we do is strictly the outcome of tensions which we are trying to relieve, even though most people would prefer to increase their pleasure than merely to mitigate their stress.

PREDICTION

The most useful function of a theory is prediction. A theory should allow the user to predict events or relationships which may then be tested or verified by observation and experiment. Explanation is usually easier than prediction because theories contain general principles which can be stretched or interpreted to cover almost any behavior (Holt, 1962). It is much easier to explain phenomena or events after they have taken place than to predict them.

Freud observed rather frequently that his adult patients displayed a childish quality in certain areas of their lives. He finally concluded that these childish trends were fixations of desires and motives blocked or frustrated in early life. He proposed a principle to account for or explain this phenomenon: frustrated needs or desires of childhood remain in unaltered form throughout life. This principle seems to explain his repeated observations, but there are other ways of accounting for the same thing. What is needed is an experimental test of the postulate. We might think of an application of this principle in a contrived situation. We might, for example, predict that children who have received strict oral training will chew tasteless gum significantly longer than a matched group who have not been orally frustrated. We would have to operationally define and measure "oral frustration" in order to select our two groups. If the experiment were carried out, and the hypothesis received confirmation, we would have to conclude that Freud's postulate about childhood frustration is a useful guide from which to make predictions. Usually, one confirmation of a hypothesis drawn from a theory is not sufficient to establish a postulate as a principle of behavior. Many hypotheses must be derived and repeatedly tested. Probably the best test of a theory is its capacity for suggesting hypotheses which are confirmed. Hall and Lindzey summarize the predictive uses of a personality theory as follows:

First, and most important, it leads to the collection of *observation of relevant empirical relations not yet observed.* The theory should lead to a systematic expansion of knowledge concerning the phenomena of interest and this expansion ideally should be mediated or stimulated by the derivation from the theory of specific empirical propositions (statements, hypotheses, predictions) that are subject to empirical test. In a central sense, the core of any science lies in the discovery of stable empirical relationships between events or variables. The function of a theory is to further this process in a systematic manner. The theory can be seen as a kind of proposition mill grinding out related empirical statements which can then be confirmed or rejected in the light of suitably controlled empirical data (Hall and Lindzey, 1970, p. 12).

Another point about prediction: if we have confidence in our theories (confidence in a theory is gained through repeated confirmation of hypotheses derived from it) we can make predictions rather than ask questions. Instead of posing the question, "I wonder what would happen if I do such and such," we may make a presumption: "I'll bet that if I do such and such, I will get the results that the theory proposes." Prediction requires principles which have been demonstrated to have some validity. The first stages of science begin with questions, but as empirical knowledge is accumulated and useful theories are developed, predictions become possible. If we learn how to use rewards to influence behavior, we may specify the behaviors that will occur under the conditions of rewarding the experimenter sets up.

While theories suggest ideas that the scientist may test, they can also help us improve our lives by discovering the stable and the changing aspects of both our own personalities and those of others. For example, the need construct enables us to contrast stable and long-standing needs with short-term and transient ones—needs that play a part in much of the personality, and those which are highly circumscribed. Furthermore, if we can obtain a picture of the organization of needs for ourselves and others, we will increase our predictive ability. Ordinarily, personality changes gradually, and some aspects of it remain fairly constant throughout life (Baltes and Schaie, 1973). Knowing the enduring characteristics—temperamental traits, long-standing needs, styles of life, major goals and intentions—allows us to predict our own behavior and that of others.

CONTROL

A highly regarded formula for living is "Know, and then do." We are able to produce specified effects, if we have appropriate knowledge. The history of discovery is replete with examples of the relationship between knowledge and its real-life application (Oppenheimer, 1956). Knowledge gained from the esoteric concerns of scientists has often led to technological advances which have had practical significance in solving man's problems. Thus behavior control—not to be taken in a pejorative sense—is today effectively applied in a wide range of professions. The teacher uses knowledge of personality to foster learning in his students; marriage counselors use specialized techniques and knowledge of human behavior to promote insights in couples who are having marital difficulties; the psychotherapist and behavior therapist use psychological principles to modify behavior in people who are suffering from personality disturbances. As principles of behavior are acquired this control potential will increase, a factor which could present problems if behavior modification becomes too extensive (Lefcourt, 1973).

We may consider behavior control from the standpoint of the explanatory causes that we discussed previously. Consider the control of behavior through environmental manipulation. In many different settings, from the classroom to the mental hospital, from the prison to the work setting, the behavior of different types of people of all ages has been and is being controlled by the use of rewards and punishments. Many of the same principles of behavior control that have been used with animals are found to be successful with humans. Consider the possibility of controlling biological causes of behavior. A great deal of control has already been achieved through tranquilizing and psychoactive drugs. The possibility of altering genetic abnormalities is just beginning to open up. With respect to personality factors, the whole basis of counseling and psychotherapy is the ability to control or change intrapsychic variables such as self-image, attitudes, motives, and cognitions. A traditional therapist attempts to broaden his patients' insights into their abnormal behavior so that they are motivated to change their approach to life. The assumption is that changing the intrapsychic causes will alter behavior. Both conscious and unconscious determinants of behavior can be influenced or controlled.

Some of the same things that others can do to control behavior we can do for ourselves. We do have a certain amount of control over our environment: we have some vocational freedom, or choice in location of a home, or liberty in selecting companions. Through personal efforts we may gain increased environmental control. We can take advantage of discoveries in the biological sciences to promote our health. But probably the greatest control we have is over our own personality variables. Many people have demonstrated that they can quit smoking, or lose weight effectively, or get hard jobs done, and in general, take charge of their lives. We can alter our knowledge, our desires, our emotional reactions, even our interpretation of the past. And through the personality theories presented in this text, we can increase this self-control by learning about ourselves.

SYSTEMATIC AND HEURISTIC POWER OF THEORIES

The *heuristic* value of a theory lies in its *power to suggest testable hypotheses*. Note that we use the word "suggest" rather than "generate"; the difference is quite important. A theory *generates* a hypothesis when we can derive the hypothesis directly from manipulating the terms of the theory. This is termed *systematic derivation*. A theory *suggests* a hypothesis when we take a principle and apply it to actual behavior.

Most actual theories in psychology today do not provide a basis for making precise prediction. They suggest more often than they generate. The hypothesis might state that one condition will produce greater behavior than another condition. Just how different the two behaviors will be is not usually specifiable. Let us take a hypothesis which we might infer but not directly deduce from the postulates of role theory. Role theory *suggests* that people who know and carry out their expected roles have a better work history than those who are confused about their roles, or who hate them. To test this hypothesis, we would have to determine the means of measuring good and bad work history. We would also want to measure role awareness and role performance. Selecting a representative sample of workers, we could then administer our tests, or make our observations, or obtain a work history, and so on. It should be noted that there are many other ways of testing this same hypothesis. The more ways it is tested and the more often the hypothesis is confirmed, the greater is the support given the underlying theory.

Erikson proposes that there are eight stages of life, and each requires that the ego accomplish a certain task: for instance, a sense of trust, a sense of autonomy, of initiative, or of identity. The researcher might draw some inferences about each of the stages and test them. He might identify those who have not attained the goal set for a particular stage. He might study what happens to the ego accomplishments under stress. Allport proposed seven aspects of the development of the self, and again, one might draw inferences that could be tested experimentally. Rotter suggests that those who believe that they have control of their circumstances behave quite differently from those who believe that control is external to them. Much research has been generated by this proposal. A scientifically useful theory will stimulate research through its postulates. From a personal point of view a useful theory will actually engender self-knowledge and knowledge of others, as well as promote the art of living.

ONE THEORY OR MANY

Though some theorists attempt to cover all personality phenomena by a single set of principles, personality data are probably best explained by several theories which deal with specific topics rather than by a single all-embracing one.

The question of whether there could be a single, all-embracing theory of personality, which would render all existing theories obsolete, has been taken up by Professor Leon Levy (1970). Given the nature of a theory as an interlocking system of postulates, principles, and definitions which explain and predict behavior in general and the behavior of the individual in particular, Levy takes the position that *no single theory could accomplish such a task*. He holds that:

It is unlikely that a single comprehensive theory of personality could ever be formulated to account for all the phenomena within the domain of personality. There are surely relationships between many of these phenomena, but there is no reason to believe that they are all governed by a single set of principles, and that they could all be encompassed by a single theory of personality. Nor is there any reason why the field of personality would not be well served by the formulation of a number of personality theories (in contrast to theories of personality) each concerned with accounting for a limited range of phenomena within the domain of personality. This indeed appears to be what has been happening, and it seems both strategically and scientifically sound (Levy, 1970, p. 440).

PERSONALITY THEORIES AS CONCEPTUAL PICTURES

In this section we will develop the following proposition: Theories of _personality are personal interpretations of man's individual and common psychological nature_ and _are not_ established principles or laws of behavior.

A theory of personality may be viewed as a "conceptual picture" of personality. Like any other picture, a personality theory should capture the essence of what it represents. If it does, we ought to be able to learn about personality from the theory which represents or pictures it. There must be a correspondence between elements of the picture (theory) and the actual determinants of man's nature. But just as a painting communicates the view of the painter, so a representation of anything as complex as personality is not simply an exact copy. A personality theorist gives us a portrait, a conceptual picture which is his own invention and embodies his interpretation of personality. Another artist depicting the same scene could alter the perspective. Yet if the picture is too one-sided or distorted in other ways, its usefulness as a scientific tool is reduced. Some believe that Freud's extreme stress on sexuality as a motivational force in personality is an example of a distorted picture of man.

It should be noted that a theory not only prescribes what is salient in personality, from one expert's point of view, but also prevents the user from seeking fruitless avenues. It keeps him from making errors and wasting time and effort. Hall and Lindzey describe this function of a theory in a quaint manner as follows:

Another function which a theory should serve is that of *preventing the observer from being dazzled by the full-blown complexity of natural or concrete events.* The theory is a set of blinders and it tells its wearer that it is unnecessary for him to worry about all the aspects of the event he is studying. To the untrained observer any reasonably complex behavioral event seems to offer countless different possible means for analysing or describing the event and indeed it does. The theory permits the observer to go about abstracting from the natural complexity in a systematic and efficient manner. Abstract and simplify he will, whether he uses a theory or not, but if he does not follow the guidelines of an explicit theory the principles determining his view will be hidden in implicit assumptions and attitudes of which he is unaware. The theory specifies to the user a limited number of more or less definite dimensions, variables, or parameters which are of crucial importance. The other aspects of the situation can to a certain extent be overlooked from the point of view of this problem. A useful theory will detail rather explicit instructions as to the kinds of data that should be collected in connection with a particular problem. Consequently, as might be expected, individuals occupying drastically different theoretical positions may study the same empirical event and share little in the way of common observations (Hall and Lindzey, 1970, p. 14).

THEORIES REPRESENT TYPES OF PEOPLE

This writer proposes the hypothesis that each of the outstanding theories of personality depicts some portion of the population and describes that segment better than other models do. That is to say, each model reflects not only the personality of the theorist who proposes it, but also the people who resemble the theorist. This view assumes that people can be grouped or typed according to similarities — an assumption which does, in fact, receive both empirical and experiential support (Peterson, 1965). If the hypothesis is correct, one should be able to select a theory of personality that fits him — one which describes, explains, and predicts his behavior better than the others. He may use the theory to help him identify explicitly the goals of fulfillment, of maturity, of self-actualization, or whatever the theorist designates as the ideal personality.

Many (but not all) personality theories propose a number of types of people. Usually there are several abnormal types and at least one that is considered normal or even ideal for man. The types, of course, reflect the biases of the theorist, and we find wide differences in what is considered both abnormal and ideal. Yet, as the sections of this text demonstrate, there are classes of theories, and within each class there is considerable resemblance. Again, the author's hypothesis about individual differences in the applicability of the theories is relevant; if the theories depict different types of people, the ideals of personality development and functioning should also vary. We will encounter such ideal types as the genital personality, the fully functioning personality, the self-actualized personality, the mature personality, the productive personality, and the individuated personality. In some of the theories, we will need to draw out personality types because they are not detailed.

USES OF PERSONALITY THEORIES

Let us see how personality theories may actually be used to guide us in studying behavior. Consider the following situation: Suppose you are given the assignment of interviewing someone for an hour in order to "get to know" the person as thoroughly as possible. You are pretty much limited to interview procedures; you cannot use drugs, or place the individual under severe stress. What types of information would you seek? What types of information would tell you most about the interviewee? There are a variety of possibilities open to you, not all equally valid and useful in yielding information. You may soon feel at a loss as to how to select the proper approach. Let us consider some of your options.

Is it better to study the person as he now is, or would it be more profitable to study his past? Since everyone has plans to a greater or lesser degree, would it be helpful in your diagnosis to learn about these? Everyone copes with stress, and it may prove valuable to identify the particular ways in which the person deals with frustrations, disappointments, failures, and threats to the ego. Everyone has needs, and these determine many behaviors; thus, it would seem that a knowledge of needs would be the best way of getting to know a person. Everyone is forced to play out certain roles, and maybe you had better focus on your subject's knowledge of roles, performance of roles, and conflicts among various roles. It should be possible to identify a person's major traits, and this approach might give you what you are seeking. The answer is not easy and you cannot use all these approaches. It may have occurred to the reader that some of the approaches include others: the trait and role approach, and perhaps the need approach, could accomplish the same result by different avenues. Again, a theory of personality will serve as a guide.

USES OF A SINGLE THEORY VERSUS SINGLE CONSTRUCTS

We might pose the question: How can we use theoretical concepts to explain behavior? We can take two viewpoints on this issue: We can attempt to *rely exclusively on a single theory and use all of its components and their complex interrelations to explain what we observe.* An example of this approach is to take a comprehensive theory, such as Freud's, and explain what we observe within the framework of that theory. The second approach is to *use principles from all the theories, using each concept to do a specific job.* This approach is termed *eclectic:* it involves taking the best from each theory, or taking what is needed from each. There are some serious disadvantages and limitations to the practice of using theoretical principles without considering their whole context.

It will be recalled that ideally a theory of personality is a network of interlocking, logically coherent postulates representing actual processes of personality. The theory is a model of personality, so that we can learn about personality through the study of the model. To understand the nature of a theory of personality, we should understand two basic principles of behavior: that behavior is *multidimensional,* and that behavior is *multidetermined.* To say that behavior is multidimensional means simply that there are always several behaviors happening at the same time—weighing opposing tendencies, considering the consequences of behavior, choosing between alternatives. We must take account of all these behaviors if we wish to understand or explain a given cross-section of behavior. A theory must provide principles to help accomplish this task, and usually a single principle is insufficient. To say that behavior is multidetermined means simply that several causes are responsible for a given cross-section of behavior. Again, more than one theoretical principle is usually required to provide an adequate explanation. Using a single principle limits the "explanatory power" of the theory.

Let us consider a simple example of the use of a principle taken from a theory and its modification when used with other principles taken from the same theory. After observing a persistent weakness and inferiority in man, Alfred Adler proposed the principle that much behavior is a *striving for power or superiority* over others. This principle certainly seems to account for a great deal of behavior. It helps to explain the conduct of a pathological liar who repeatedly lies about such innocuous things as his age, what kind of gifts he received, or even what he ate for supper. What about the kleptomaniac, the one who steals apparently just for the fun of it? Is this not a way of gaining superiority over others? What about the person who always wishes to get an exemption, the one who thinks the rules simply do not apply to him? Is this not a way to gain privileged status? Adler postulated another principle, *social interest,* the strength of which he believed varies from person to person. This principle holds that there is an innate social responsiveness in everyone, but it has to be nurtured by those who have charge of the growing child. This social interest principle interacts with and significantly alters the innate motive for power. One in whom the social interest is strong will still strive for superiority, but he will work for self-perfection and the welfare of others. His power motive will be directed to promoting social living and continual self-improvement. If we considered only the power motive, we might be able to account for the behavior of the pathological liar, the kleptomaniac, and the person who always wishes to be favored, but we would have difficulty with the "normal" person who does not display this motive in obvious ways.

We will not discuss Adler's theory in detail here, but one more postulate will make our point clear: the principle of the *style of life.* Adler held that each child develops, by the age of five or six, a style of life, by which he meant a characteristic way of perceiving, evaluating, thinking, feeling, and acting that becomes fixed. Later developments produce elaborations and extensions of this style of life but not changes in direction. A child who is slow moving, easy-going, and optimistic at age five will continue to possess these traits throughout his life, even though he may vary his circumstances greatly. Knowing the style of life helps us group a person's many behaviors into a coherent picture. The style of life brings together the specific direction which the striving for superiority takes, the strength of social interest, the individual sensitivities and weaknesses, the manner of dealing with frustration, and other traits central to the nature of the person. We have seen that several interacting principles increase the explanatory power of a theory. For the most comprehensive description, explanation, and prediction, all the elements of a theory should be used.

Rather than grasping a total theory of personality, the reader will probably follow the eclectic approach: he will acquire concepts and principles from the various theories. Such concepts and principles can be useful in describing, explaining, and predicting our own behavior and that of others. It will be recalled that the theoretical principles were meant to be functional by those who proposed them. The student of personality should be better off with them than without them.

PRINCIPLES TO REMEMBER

We have been considering some of the ways in which personality has been represented. Each theory will confront the student with new terms to master. Keeping some of the following principles and suggestions in mind may assist you in understanding and remembering the various theories.

1. A theory is a functional tool which should help you to describe, explain, and predict behavior. Without the theory you would have difficulty deciding what to look for in yourself and others. Remember, we all have a theory of personality, whether we know it or not.

2. Theories of personality are conceptual portraits of man's psychological nature. Each theorist gives us a different portrait. Usually, the theorist focuses on a particular aspect of personality and of living, such as development, motivation, conflict, fulfillment; thus the theory is at its best when it is applied in the manner in which the theorist used it.

3. Principles taken from a theory can be used to describe, explain, and predict behavior, but single principles are usually insufficient for the task. Because personality is *multidimensional* and *multidetermined* the principles which represent it must also be *multifaceted*. The operations of the components of personality simply cannot be brought together under one principle. All the components of a theory should be employed for the greatest scope of coverage.

4. Theories of personality reflect the personality make-up of the theorist who formulated them. They also may be applied to specific types of people who resemble the theorists. Thus we might identify one person as a Freudian man, another as a Rogerian, still another as an

Allportian, with the understanding that these highly complex human beings are like other people.

5. Many theories provide an ideal model or type of personality as well as nonideal types. The theory tells us what a well-developed and fully functioning person is. It also tells us what happens when the requirements for ideal development and functioning are not met. Some theories are not specific in detailing this information, but often it can be derived from the theory.

6. Theories usually provide statements about human nature in general as well as the ways of living of real people that we encounter.

7. Theories of personality often consider what is characteristic of a person as well as what is distinctive.

8. The theory may provide for a comparison among people and it may also account for the particular complex of variables within a single individual. Both types of data are essential for a complete knowledge of personality make-up and functioning.

SUMMARY

1. A course in personality theories might be thought of as the scientific study of the individual case. But while the major focus is on the characterization of the distinctive qualities of the individual, similarities and differences among people are also considered.

2. We form images or conceptions of ourselves and others, and these are our own personality theories. Such theories may be quite general with little formal structure, or they may follow one of the standard personality theories, containing many terms and postulates. All theories have a specific focus, or range of convenience, and thus apply better to one specific range of phenomena than to others. Theories are personal constructions which reflect the biases, preconceptions, and preferences of the theorist. Thus theories vary in their validity and utility.

3. Personality is considered by many to be an important internal locus of determinants or causes of behavior which can only be inferred, not observed directly; thus we can use theories of personality to suggest what the determinants might be. We are interested in what takes place both in the environment and in the personality itself. The personality psychologist deals with such processes as learning, motivation, conflict, development, and personality change. The make-up and operations of personality are presented in the form of constructs. Personality constructs are first used to explain a specific behavior, but they must be verified in other behaviors. Some constructs deal with peripheral aspects, while others deal with the central aspects of personality.

4. A personality theory may be considered a conceptual tool because it can aid thinking about the nature and operation of personality. A theory of personality hypothetically explains one's identity as a person when definitive knowledge is lacking.

5. There are three types of propositions which make up personality theories: assumptions, postulates, and definitions. Assumptions are general principles about man's nature which may or may not be explicitly stated. They are the philosophical underpinnings of a theory, and are usually not verifiable by empirical test. Postulates are the proposed laws or principles. They may express empirical generalizations, which are propositions summarizing many related observations. Postulates that state a construct attempt to explain the empirical generalizations; thus constructs are the types of causes that are supposed to occur in personality. There are many theories of personality because one can usually conceptualize things and events in more than one way, and because the postulates of such theories are only tentative explanations. They cannot approach established laws until they have been tested repeatedly and found applicable to specific behaviors. By definition is meant the specification of the behaviors designated by the terms in question. Operational definitions are used to anchor the constructs to measurable behaviors.

6. Constructs deal with both enduring and transitory features of personality. Some of the major types of constructs are those depicting contents, functions, processes, trends, dispositions, states, and events. Constructs may embody characteristics of all people (core tendencies and characteristics) or characteristics unique to the individual (peripheral characteristics and types).

7. The postulates of personality theories can be used in four ways: to describe, to explain, to predict, and to control personality. Description is naming, categorizing, and identifying the structures and operations of personality—answering the "what" question. To explain means to discover causes. The causes of behavior are environmental, organismic, genetic, and personality-determined. Historical explanations, favored by the learning theorists, involve the tracing of causes in the history of the organism—answering the *how* question. Explanations that deal with motives are called dynamic, and answer the *why* question. The correlational method of explanation identifies clusters of traits or tendencies. For the personality scientist, a personality theory should suggest ideas or hypotheses that can be tested. From the standpoint of mental health, a personality theory should enable its user to discover the enduring and changeable features of his personality. Knowledge of the enduring features promotes prediction of behavior. Control of personality implies the ability to bring about personality change. Formal techniques and concepts which are used to promote personality change are known as psychotherapy and behavior modification. The notion of control, as applied to oneself, means self-knowledge and self-management.

8. Personality theories may be considered from the perspective of their systematic and heuristic functions. Ideally, a theory should provide the necessary terms and postulates to enable direct deduction of testable hypotheses. No theory in the area of personality does this, but theories do have a heuristic function, which means that they suggest ideas for the researcher to translate into experimental hypotheses. From a personal point of view, theories of personality should point the way to the good life by specifying the ideals of living and the means of attaining them.

9. Ideally, a personality theory should be a map of personality, but existing theories are really personal interpretations. They reflect the personality make-up of the theorist, and probably apply as well to a portion of the population that resembles him. A theory tells us what is significant and worth examining, and what is unimportant or trivial.

10. One may attempt to describe and understand personality with a single theory as a guide, or one may use constructs taken from several different theories. A single construct may apply to only a delimited range of behaviors. Because behavior is complex and the outcome of many causes operating at the same time, using all the constructs of a theory usually increases explanatory power. But the eclectic approach, which involves selecting what is considered the best from a number of theories, may provide still greater explanatory power. Some commonly used explanatory constructs are the self, roles, needs, the pleasure–pain principle, and traits.

REFERENCES

Arnold, M. Perennial problems in the field of emotion. *In* Arnold, M., ed., Feelings and Emotions. New York: Academic Press, 1970. Pp. 169–85.

Baltes, P. B., and Schaie, K. W., eds. Life-Span Developmental Psychology: Personality and Socialization. New York: Academic Press, 1973.

Christie, R., and Geis, F. L. Studies in Machiavellianism. New York: Academic Press, 1970.

Cronback, L. J. The two disciplines of scientific psychology. Am. Psychol. *12*:671–84, 1957.

Dollard, J., Doob, L. W., Miller, N. E., Mowrer, O. H., and Sears, R. R. Frustration and Aggression. New Haven: Yale University Press, 1939.

Engel, M. The stability of the self-concept in adolescence. J. Abnorm. Social Psychol. *58*:211–15, 1959.

Fromm, E. Man for Himself. New York: Holt, Rinehart and Winston, 1947.

Hall, C. S., and Lindzey, G. Theories of Personality, 2nd ed. New York: John Wiley and Sons, 1970.

Holt, R. R. Individuality and generalization in the psychology of personality. J. Pers. *30*:377–404, 1962.

Kelley, H. H. Attribution theory in social psychology. *In* Levine, D., ed., Nebraska Symposium on Motivation. Lincoln: University of Nebraska Press, 1967. Pp. 192–238.

Kelly, G. A. The Psychology of Personal Constructs. New York: W. W. Norton and Company, 1955.

Lefcourt, H. M. The function of the illusions of control and freedom. Am. Psychol. *28*:417–25, 1973.

Levy, L. H. Conceptions of Personality: Theories and Research. New York: Random House, 1970.

MacCorquodale, K., and Meehl, P. E. On a distinction between hypothetical constructs and intervening variables. Psychol. Rev. *55*:95–107, 1948.

Oppenheimer, J. R. Analogy in science. Am. Psychol. *11*:126–35, 1956.

Peterson, D. R. The scope and generality of verbally defined personality factors. Psychol. Rev. *72*:48–59, 1965.

Raush, H. L., Dittman, A. T., and Taylor, T. J. Person, setting, and change in social interaction. Hum. Rel. *12*:361–78, 1959.

Sarbin, T. R. Role theoretical interpretation of psychological change. *In* Worhcel, P., and Byrne, D., eds., Personality Change. New York: John Wiley and Sons, 1964. Pp. 176–219.

Stevens, S. S. Psychology and the science of science. Psychol. Bull. *36*:221–63, 1939.

Veroff, J., Atkinson, J. W., Feld, S. C., and Gurin, G. The use of thematic apperception to assess motivation in a nationwide interview study. Psychol. Monogr. *74*:xb.12, Whole No. 499, 1960.

PART II

The Formation and Development of Personality

In this section we will examine one of the most basic approaches to the study of personality: the developmental. The developmental approach studies personality from the standpoint of its formation and growth throughout the life span. Let us consider the assumptions behind this approach. At any given point, personality is the end product of its previous history. Further, the acquisitions of the past continue to be active in the contemporary personality configuration to a great degree.

While most personality psychologists would accept the past of the organism as one of the causal determinants of contemporary personality, they disagree widely about the extent to which the present continues the past. At one extreme is Freud's position, which views personality as formed by the age of five or six and later development as a mere elaboration and extension of the trends developed in the formative years. *One's early life sets the pattern for his present,* and no matter how removed from basic self-seeking one's present behavior may appear, it can always be reduced or traced back to selfish infantile motives. At the other extreme, Allport conceived the adult personality as *functionally autonomous of its childhood personality.* The major interests and intentions of the adult have only a historic connection with childhood behavior. They are neither derivative of earlier motives nor reducible to infantile trends. There are many intermediate positions on this issue, of course. Without taking sides, we will consider some pertinent aspects of the developmental approach to the study of personality.

Throughout life, there are striking developmental changes in each aspect of personality. Consider the development of emotions: there are surely great differences between the emotional life of the child and that of the adult. The only emotion one finds in an infant is diffuse excitement (Bridges, 1932). The infant is either tranquil or in distress during the first few weeks of postnatal life, and no matter what circumstances prevail, no other emotion occurs. As the potential for emotion unfolds, both the number of emotions and the range of situations giving rise to them increase.

29

TABLE II-1   DIFFERENTIATION OF EMOTIONS

Age (months)	Positive Emotions	Negative Emotions
Birth	Diffuse excitement	
1		
2	Delight	Distress
5		Anger
		Disgust
7		Fear
	Elation	
8		
	Affection for adults	
12		
15		Jealousy
	Affection for children	

The newborn infant experiences only a generalized and undifferentiated state of excitement. As he grows older, increasingly complex emotional states, both positive and negative, emerge. (Adapted from K. M. B. Bridges, Emotional development in early infancy. *Child Development* 3:324–41, 1932. Reprinted in Morse and Wingo, 1962.)

Like so many other aspects of personality, emotional growth is quite rapid during the early years and decreases gradually with age, though some change continues throughout life. The calmness and serenity of the "wise old man" are in sharp contrast to the highly volatile emotions of youth. Certainly a major alteration has taken place through the years.

Following the history of emotions we can discover other differences: the emotions of a child are easily aroused and reach a high intensity quite readily, only to subside just as rapidly. The emotions of the adult are finely graded, with intense emotions reserved for "big" occasions. The child is incapable of certain feelings: harboring a grudge, or letting resentment smolder. Even love and hate are quite shallow in a child. Emotional attachments are easily broken or changed, while adults, of course, are capable of long-term emotions which are deeply felt. In fact, one may judge maturity by studying emotional development: do the subject's emotions resemble those of a child or those of a mature adult? Control over emotions is another aspect which changes with personality growth; the child's emotions are quite freely expressed, whereas the adult learns to control or disguise his true feelings.

Much more may be said about the differences between the emotions of the child and those of the adult, but the point is that every aspect of personality—motivation, perception, cognition, volition, attitudes, and even the self—has a typical course of development. The course of development of each component may be followed in a representative sample of children. We can determine what is normal and what is abnormal, and then we may learn something of the causes of both normal and abnormal development. We can focus upon environmental conditions (such as child-rearing practices) which promote or hinder development. Indeed, the developmental approach to personality study can provide hard data about man not obtainable in any other way.

DEVELOPMENTAL STAGES VERSUS GROWTH THROUGH UNFOLDING

In keeping with the purpose of the text, namely, to highlight distinctive themes from outstanding personality theorists, we will begin our investigation of personality theories by considering the views of Freud, Erikson, and Allport on personality development. Freud and Erikson hold that personality develops in fairly distinct stages. Each stage involves a rather complete organization of the personality, with new problems and needs to face. While each stage builds upon the achievements of the preceding stages, each also is fairly distinct in its make-up. In Freud we see the formation of personality fixed early in life, by five or six years of age, while in Erikson we find stages of personality growth throughout the entire life cycle. The difference between the two theories is quite significant: Freud termed his stages of development psychosexual, while Erikson designates his stages psychosocial.

A view which is at variance with the stage approach is the growth model, which holds that personality grows unremittingly through progressive differentiation and integration. There is a continuing change due to maturational growth and learning, with new functions slowly developing, and these elements are integrated within the existing structure through processes of steady transformation. If development proceeds normally, existing functions usually are transformed or superseded by new ones. The adult is not a grown-up child, but distinctly different, requiring different concepts and principles to distinguish him from the earlier personality. Allport's views on the development of personality will be taken as an example of this type of theorizing.

CHAPTER 2

Stages of Development

Sigmund Freud

**Sigmund Freud (1856–1939)
(Courtesy of National Library
of Medicine.)**

BIOGRAPHY AND OVERVIEW

Sigmund Freud was born in 1856 in Freiberg, Moravia, and died in London in 1939. With the exception of three years in Moravia and his last year in London, he lived 80 years in Vienna. He received his medical degree on March 31, 1881 after spending eight years in medical school, where he specialized in neurology and the treatment of nervous disorders (Shur, 1972). During the year 1885, Freud studied hypnosis and the treatment of hysteria with Charcot in Paris. The following year he entered private practice as a nerve specialist, concentrating in a field relatively neglected in Vienna, the treatment of neurosis. Three years later he joined with Josef Breuer to publish *Studies on Hysteria* (1895), his first ideas as an explorer of the unconscious. Though Freud always praised his co-author for the development of the cathartic procedure, the talking cure for hysteria which Breuer had originated with the famous case of Anna O. (1880–1882), he later broke with him because Breuer preferred a more physiological explanation for neurosis to his own emphasis on sexual etiology (Freud, 1914).

Freud extracted his theory of infantile sexuality from the free associations of his neurotic patients and from his own systematic self-analysis, which he began in 1897 (Shur, 1972). In trying to resolve his inner conflicts and free his patients of neurotic symptoms, he began to see that the symptoms were distortions and exaggerations of phenomena all men experienced. His theories of psychosexual development, childhood experiences, and the Oedipal complex were founded almost exclusively on the analysis of adults, since he had little opportunity for direct observation of children (Freud, 1914).

32

In 1900, Freud published *The Interpretation of Dreams.* This work laid the foundation for his new psychology. While the psychologists of his day investigated the conscious mind, Freud probed the deeper layers — the unconscious which he believed contained the hidden urges, wishes, and impulses behind behavior. With the publication of three works in 1905, he shocked Vienna with his psychosexual theory of development. He spent the rest of his life embellishing and revising his psychoanalytic theory into two main thrusts: developmental and interactive. The interactive component, to be examined in a later chapter, deals with motivation, conflict, and the structure of personality. The developmental aspect, dealing with the course of development, continuity in growth, and the unfolding of sexual instincts, will be the major focus of this chapter.

FIXATIONS AND TRAIT FORMATION

While attempting to understand and treat the personality disturbances, Freud was struck by the frequency with which he found a certain childish quality in his patients (Freud, 1914). Intellectual endowment or attainment seemed to have little to do with the appearance of the primitive trends: even his bright patients displayed childish traits when he got to know them. A highly intelligent, well-educated woman, apparently mature and poised in early meetings, would soon manifest emotional reactions and childlike needs which seemed to be totally out of character. The repeated occurrence of these phenomena perplexed Freud very much and led him to the hypothesis that such trends were *fixations* from earlier life which the patient had not outgrown. The inconsistent elements could be explained as partial blocking or debilitation of specific personality traits rather than as complete stunting, since the patient was an adult in many respects. Certain traits and reactions from an earlier life period, normally replaced by more mature traits and reactions, continued to be active in personality, usually producing a disruptive effect. Freud finally came to the conclusion that the *childish trends became permanent features* of the adult's personality. In fact, in many patients they were the major determinants of personality. One could trace large segments of behavior to them: the choice of mate, vocational preferences, recreational interests and activities, even character features such as orderliness, promptness, optimism and the like.

Freud became more and more convinced that the major traits of personality were established early in childhood, and that subsequent personality development was merely an elaboration of these traits (Freud, 1917). He held this principle to apply to normal as well as to abnormal development. In the abnormal person, persisting childhood traits create many difficulties because they are often expressed directly in their primitive forms, and in a socially disapproved manner. The normal person possesses early childhood traits in a more moderate degree and finds ways of expressing them that are acceptable to himself and others. A person may, for instance, have a lifelong interest in oral activities which is expressed in different forms at various periods of his life. As a child he may have enjoyed sucking his thumb or biting his finger-nails; as a teen-ager he may have enjoyed eating excessively; as an adult he may enjoy reading about and preparing exotic foods; and as an old man he may join a wine-making club. The oral interest may become a dominant force in his life, so that it is behind most of his motivation. To sum up, a particular form of pleasure-seeking may become permanently imprinted in the person-ality make-up as a result of certain early experiences which interfered with normal growth.

ARRESTMENT OF GROWTH

What could cause an arrestment of growth so early in life? Freud came to the conclusion that there are two basic causes: _excessive frustration_ and _excessive in-dulgence_ (Freud, 1917). If the child's needs are either frustrated too much or indulged too much, a particular aspect of his personality is totally stunted or hindered in some degree. An excessive need might be created as the result of the stunting of growth; this process Freud termed _fixation_ (Freud, 1917).

In normal development the needs of early life are expressed in socially approved rather than in primitive forms. The acquisitions of each stage of development do in fact carry over to the next stage, but in normal growth they support and enhance the newly emerging patterns and do not obstruct them. The point is that under conditions of excessive frustration or excessive in-dulgence, motives may acquire a high level of value and interfere with growth. These intense motives compete with the motives which should pre-dominate in the subsequent stage of development. The child who has learned to use obstinacy and negativism as a means of getting his way with his parents may run into difficulties if he uses the same techniques with his playmates. His fixation at the negativistic stage prevents later, more socially effective modes of adaptation from developing. A child who persists in obtaining oral gratifi-cation by means of thumbsucking not only encounters social disapproval but actually fails to acquire acceptable ways of obtaining oral satisfactions appro-priate to his age.

The principle of the fixation of needs as a result of excessive frustration or in-dulgence explains much adult behavior which otherwise seems quite incom-prehensible. A temporary reverting to earlier forms of behavior or more primitive types of responses occurs rather frequently, and Freud recognized this phenomenon in his concept of _regression_ (Freud, 1900). Through fixation, however, the infantile quality becomes a permanent feature of personality: it is, in a real sense, a distinguishing character trait.

Given this view of the formation of personality, we can see how Freud could place so much stress on the early years of life, the so-called formative years when the foundations of personality are laid down. Every personality psychol-ogist accepts the significant influence of the early years, during which the most basic learning takes place, but Freud went one step beyond; he held that the structure of personality was permanently set through the child's experiences, particularly his frustrations and pleasures. Traits formed during this period are quite resistant to change. In fact, as the child develops, many conditions increase the growth and potency of the early traits: selectivity of perception, sheer repetition, fear of change, unwillingness to give up certain pleasures, and so on.

All of us know people who seem to enjoy things and activities more appropriate to an earlier period of life. The older boy who can only play and get along with younger children is an example. Another example is the father who enjoys his son's toys as much as the boy does. It seems that if we do not get enough of what we want at a particular time, the desire lingers and is never really satisfied. The following case may illustrate this point: A young wife devoted a great deal of her time to reading about the latest bridal fashions. She avidly read every magazine article on the topic she could find. She watched every program on television which focused on newly-weds. She had always wanted a large colorful wedding, but her husband and his family were opposed to it for financial and other reasons. She reluctantly went along with a small and informal wedding, but the unfulfilled need continued to be a source of influence over her conduct for many years, even though it led to behavior considered somewhat juvenile by her friends and probably by herself.

Another example of the persistence of a need, far beyond the time when it is appropriate, is the perpetual flirt. A certain amount of responsiveness to the other sex is a healthy quality at all ages from adolescence on, but the middle-aged Don Juan and the inexhaustible philanderer who dream continually of an all-consuming romantic involvement are abnormal.

Freud assigned a prominent role in his theory to the concept of unconscious motivation. Although behavior throughout life is traceable to needs, the individual ordinarily is not aware of the true needs behind his behavior. These ideas will be further developed in the discussion of conflict in Freud's system. The point is that much adult behavior is in the service of unconscious needs engendered in childhood.

ROLE OF CHILD-REARING PRACTICES IN TRAIT FORMATION

The parents are the most important influence during the first few years of the child's life. Gradually other people and institutions play a part as well. Do's and dont's are increasingly evident, and these are supported by a variety of sanctions: the giving or withdrawal of love, criticism and punishment, rejection and exclusion, and a host of others. It is not surprising that so much attention has been given to child-rearing practices by Freudians (e.g., Josselyn, 1948).

Parents and other authorities have the serious responsibility of helping the child learn the important lessons of living without receiving either too much indulgence or too much frustration during the training process. They must work for his welfare so that he can take over his own life, a process which occurs gradually over many years. One does not have to stretch the imagination to see how a particular mode of living, created by the behavior of the parents toward their child, might become habitual. During the first year of life, when the receptive mode of dealing with the world is dominant, an over-indulgent parent could produce a fixation of that mode in the child. If the child is given little opportunity to experience frustration, or to learn gradually to use his own resources to secure what he wants—if everything is given to him without any conditions—the child will probably acquire a deeply in-grained dependent and receptive orientation to life. He may develop a strong habit of expecting things to be given to or done for him.

REGIONS OF THE BODY AND STAGES OF DEVELOPMENT

Freud proposed the novel hypothesis that stages of personality development were caused by or at least were associated with the prominence at different times of various regions of the body such as the mouth, the anus, and the genitals (Freud, 1905). Specific pleasures resulting from the satisfaction of the needs occurred when the specific region became prominent. In the process of satisfying his needs the child encounters the significant people in his life and experiences healthy gratification, or frustration, or indulgence.

CHARACTER TYPES

Fixation at a particular stage of development produces what Freud (1925b) calls a character type, which is manifested through a syndrome of traits. A character type may be interpreted as a personality type. A syndrome of traits is a particular pattern of interrelated traits. We may speak, for instance, of the oral character type and also of oral traits. There are even specific varieties of oral character types, depending upon when the fixation occurred during the oral stage (Goldman-Eisler, 1948).

Freud believed that everyone could be described by one or more of the character types with the clusters of traits included under each (Freud, 1917). The specific traits may exist in pathological form and constitute an abnormal condition in the personality. An example is one of the anal character types, which is often manifested in extreme forms of three highly disruptive traits: stubbornness, stinginess, and orderliness. Traits and trait clusters are also found in people who are normal, but they are not dominating factors in personality; in fact, they become an integral part of the life style. Only when the traits become the major determinants in the life style do they constitute a personality disturbance.

WHY PSYCHOSEXUAL STAGES OF DEVELOPMENT?

Freud termed his stages of development psychosexual because he assigned a significant role to the sexual instincts in the development and formation of personality (Freud, 1917). For Freud, the best way to understand the meaning of sexuality, particularly in infancy and childhood, is to equate it with *any sensual pleasure.*

The infant soon undergoes a pattern of growth: physical, intellectual, emotional, motivational, and the like. Focusing on this growth, Freud theorized that *needs and motives* were the driving forces in personality. At varying periods during early infancy and childhood, specific needs related to specific zones of the body (the mouth, anus, and genitals) become prominent. In adults these areas are of course the locus of sexual pleasures and tensions, but Freud attributed their sexual aspect to children as well. In fact, he equated pleasure with sex: the child seeks to produce as much pleasure as possible, even though, to be sure, his sexual enjoyment is rudimentary and merely experienced as pleasurable sensations. If, as Freud (1925a) proposed, pleasure-seeking is the major motive of life, and if whatever provides pleasure is sexual, then sexuality is the general major motive of life, together with the survival motive. The survival motive applies to the total organism, whereas pleasure-seeking applies to personality. The development of personality consists of the growth or unfolding of the sexual instincts. At first these instincts are separate, but gradually they become integrated and focused in the mature sexual act.

On the basis of the particular zones of the body which become the focuses of sexual pleasure, Freud delineated four psychosexual stages of development: oral, anal, phallic, and genital. Between the phallic and genital stages is a latency period which is not a psychosexual stage of development (Freud, 1917). The first year is the oral stage, the second year the anal, the third through the fifth years the phallic, the sixth through the twelfth the latency period, a time of integration. Finally, at puberty, the child reaches the genital stage, which will continue through adulthood. Maturity of personality is attained with full genitality.

Freud came to believe that an infant, during the oral stage, actually derives sexual pleasure from such activities of the mouth as sucking, chewing, biting, and spitting out. Later, during the anal stage, the child obtains sexual pleasure from holding in or expelling fecal matter, and even from playing with it. Still later, the genital zone becomes a source of pleasure and concern, and the child derives sexual pleasure from observing and manipulating his own genitals; his curiosity may extend to observing and touching the genitals of others. Finally, sexuality reaches its mature form in adolescence and young adulthood, and occupies an important place in heterosexual love. If you find the foregoing discussion of childhood sexuality difficult to understand, you are not alone. No less a psychiatrist than C. G. Jung, who was at first a devoted disciple of Freud, broke with the master on this very point: he could not see sexuality in the unorthodox manner that Freud conceived it (Jung, 1933).

For our purposes, the point to keep in mind is that during childhood, *certain regions of the body take on*, at a particular time, *a prominent psychological significance*, and each region comes to be the source of new pleasures and new conflicts. What happens, with respect to both the pleasures and the conflicts, molds the personality. Much of the early learning of the child is prompted by needs of the major zones of the body, and such learning relates significantly to the art of living and to the manner of meeting these needs.

THE ORAL STAGE

During the first year of postnatal life, the major source of pleasure-seeking and, at the same time, of conflict and frustration, is the mouth. The child's enjoyment of sucking, chewing, biting, and vocalizing is soon restricted by those who care for him (Freud, 1903). His mother becomes upset when he sucks his thumb, or bites into his toys, or vocalizes instead of going to sleep, or plays with his food by spitting it out instead of eating it. He is expected to conform to his mother's demands concerning oral activities, and to move gradually in the direction of oral self-management. He is criticized and punished if he does not conform, and praised and rewarded if he does. His independence is proscribed, so that he must operate within certain limits: he must eat three meals a day and at the times when the rest of the family eats, and he must follow the same manners they follow. It should be noted that during the oral stage, the child is not motivated by pleasures of other zones of the body. He is not at all concerned with excretory functions, nor do his genitals occupy his interests; only oral activities are prominent.

During the oral period, the child first encounters the power of authority in his life, an authority which limits his pleasure-seeking activities. As we noted earlier, Freud believed that the manner in which the needs are satisfied or frustrated determines the formation of specific traits which mold the personality in particular ways. Such generalized traits as pessimism or optimism, determination or submission, are engendered by *the interaction of child-rearing practices and the constitutional make-up of the child*. Freud believed that no matter how complex, or intelligent, or educated the person becomes, the general orientation, established early in life, is always manifest.

Principal Oral Modes

Oral modes of activity vary even during the oral stage, so that a distinction may be made between early and late oral modes. In order of appearance, the principal oral modes are sucking, biting, spitting out, chewing, and shutting the mouth so that nothing can be put in. There is thus a developmental sequence from *passive incorporation* (breast-feeding), through *active participation* (biting and chewing), to *rejection* (closing the mouth). At any point in this developmental sequence, a fixation, or fixations, may materialize. Consider the mother who enjoys nursing her baby so much that she has him in the feeding position practically all the time. The result might be that the infant becomes fixated at the earliest oral mode, that of incorporation. Throughout life he may be passive and dependent, optimistically expecting to receive nurturance from a bountiful, undemanding, all-caring source. The early nursing experience may have been so enjoyable as to engender a naively optimistic, even Pollyanna view of life—a belief that everything will always turn out wonderfully and happily. If the mother were grudging in her care of the child and caused him to experience deprivations of needs, a trait of dependence, interacting with envy and resentment of the good things of others, might also develop. Freud (1905) saw a close connection between orality and this trait of dependency.

Oral Traits

Freud and several of his followers have detailed some other traits of the oral character (Maddi, 1972). They are presented in bipolar form, with the right end of the continuum suggesting the product of fixation due to frustration, and the left the result of fixation due to indulgence. Neither extreme promotes optimal functioning, and if an extreme form of the trait is a dominant force, it constitutes a persistent pathological trend, a factor which hinders development and functioning. An intermediate position on the continuum, incorporating some elements of the two extremes in moderate form, promotes growth and functioning. The pairs are:

optimism	pessimism
gullibility	suspiciousness
manipulativeness	passivity
admiration	envy
cockiness	self-belittlement
	(Maddi, 1972, p. 271).

One way to identify a person is to select an outstanding pivotal trait which determines much of what he does. In his analysis of different types of traits, Allport (1961) called this pivotal characteristic the cardinal trait. It is the most outstanding thing about an individual, and by it we know him as greedy, jealous, optimistic, gullible, generous. We will consider some recognizable oral types that are identified by outstanding oral traits.

Oral Types

Optimism-Pessimism. Though most of us tend toward either one or the other of these oral types, some people are generally pessimistic or optimistic, no matter what happens to them. In such instances we might suspect a strong oral fixation. Consider your own attitudes in this respect; do you feel that the world is a friendly place in which you fit fairly comfortably? Do you regard the future without much fear, and expect to obtain your share or more of the good things in life? Do you have a basic sense of faith, hope, and trust that good things and loving people rather than tragedies and unfriendly people will be a part of your existence? Whenever things look bleak do you find that you can somehow pull yourself together and muster hope for a better tomorrow? If your answer is yes, you exhibit the general trait of oral optimism, the expectation of an eternal flow of good things. While it would seem that optimism is a highly desirable quality for effective living, its extreme form may lead to carefree indifference and lack of adequate preparation for potential dangers.

If you find that you are fundamentally dissatisfied with present circumstances and, in fact, have difficulty specifying what you really want, if you view the future as being frightfully uncertain, and if you feel that you are highly vulnerable to a variety of imagined misshaps, then you fit the description of the extreme oral pessimist. This is especially true if you appreciate the fact that your circumstances do not actually warrant a pessimistic attitude. Some other manifestations of pessimism are finding everything difficult — even the simplest undertaking provokes a great deal of fear and anxiety — and always dwelling on the worst aspects of a situation and expecting the worst outcome, even though it is the least likely.

Impatience and Unrealistic Expectations. These traits describe the person who is chronically dissatisfied with things as they are, with others, and often with himself. They stem from a sense of mistrust, the result of early need frustration, and from a disturbance in the self-assertive attitude during the latter phases of the oral stage. There is a persistent desire to have more than one presently has. The person is impatient with others because they do not meet his expectations and aggressively hostile because he cannot mold them to his liking.

Envy. This trait is caused by frustration of needs during the receptive mode of the oral stage. There is a persistent longing for more than one's share of life's material goods; there is suspiciousness and resentment of the reported good fortune of others. The trait of envy, aside from its origin as an oral fixation, is culturally produced in capitalistic societies such as our own, where everyone is promised an equal opportunity to secure the "good" things of life while only a few really succeed in doing so. The envious person, no matter what he has, views the lot of others as superior to his own. Although a moderate amount of envy is a positive motivating condition, if it is the dominant trait in a person's life, it can become a major source of torment, anxiety, resentment, self-depreciation, discouragement, and smouldering hostility.

THE ANAL STAGE

Freud designated the second major stage of personality development the *anal stage* (Freud, 1917). The reader may find this a curious, almost bizarre label, but his purpose was to highlight dramatically the major source of concern and activity for the child. While oral needs continue to be active, by this time the child has worked out some of the problems associated with the oral period. Certainly the oral concerns are not as prominent in this next stage as they were previously; anal concerns take over. The anal stage extends from about 18 months to about three and one half years, roughly the period of toilet training. The child seems actually to derive pleasure from the build-up, retention, and expulsion of fecal matter, pursuits which soon bring him into conflict with the authorities in his life. Again the fixation principle is applied: overindulgence or excessive frustration of needs in the process of toilet training may produce lasting traits of personality.

The mother has many things going for her: she can punish and criticize the child; she can bribe him with promised incentives; she can praise and cajole him. But the child, too, has his weapons: he can assert his independence of his mother's control by uncooperativeness; he can refuse to maintain regularity by soiling himself; he can become highly negativistic and obstinate, so that his mother gives up the venture of training him. This is an important time in the child's development because his ego is undergoing some major modifications in the direction of autonomy and independence.

There is a fine line between encouraging and assisting the child to become a conforming and cooperative member of society, and stunting or distorting the growth of his ego by too much control. The child needs to assert his ego in order to grow effectively and fully, but he also needs guidance and direction. Many parents react quite strongly to the negativism and stubbornness of their children, so common in this period, and incorrectly interpret these reactions as serious defiance. Negativism, at least in Western cultures, is a necessary step in the growth of the ego and should be handled without a great deal of negative emotionality.

Often the element of competition enters into toilet training: the mother's friends have already trained their children, or at least they claim they have, and her child is the last one. She may attempt to show her superiority as a mother by striving for unusually early training success, and any failure of her child is interpreted as her own failure. The child may assert his independence, even if he is maturationally ready for training, by refusing to go along with her game. Consider his point of view for a moment: up to a certain point he was given all the freedom in the world in respect to elimination, but with the institution of toilet training, another source of pleasure has become subjected to controls from outside. He is suddenly expected to conform to standards which he neither desires nor sets; he must give up his source of pleasure, and do so voluntarily. A conflict arises between his pleasure-seeking activities and the people who pressure him to limit or forego them. It should be borne in mind that the desires of his parents are also important to him, a factor which adds to his conflict and which can be used effectively by his parents in promoting toilet-training. Of course, parents can lose this power over their child by treating him harshly and cruelly. If he is beset on all sides with demands and controls, he may eagerly take to activities where he has some say, and in this assertion of independence lies the seed of permanent opposition between the child and his mother, and in fact, between the child and any authority.

Depending upon whether there is too much adult frustration or indulgence of the child, the traits which develop may reflect *compliance, overcompliance,* or *defiance*. During the anal period, the child is learning some basic orientations to life, namely, holding on to things and letting them go (Adelson and Red-mond, 1958); these orientations may become distorted or exaggerated into obstinacy, compulsive orderliness, stinginess, or untempered generosity. Consider how the personality trait of overvaluing one's accomplishments is formed. A mother who tends to overvalue what her child produces anally will probably overvalue any other accomplishment, even though it is quite miniscule. Her overvaluing may continue for a long period. The child may come to overvalue all his activities if his mother, in her zeal to motivate him to perform, fusses excessively over what he does. It is the overvaluation of anal products, however, which initially engenders the personality trait, according to Freud. At the other extreme, a mother may delight in trapping or tricking her child by catching him at the right time, or in simply keeping him to the task until he performs. Such practices may engender traits of depression, psychological emptiness and loss, and insecurity. These traits may manifest themselves in excessive hoarding or accumulating, or in compulsive trends.

A person who overvalues his performance may become a creative person, a good producer; or he may constantly seek praise and approval for meager performances and minor achievements. Whether the traits are favorable or unfavorable for growth and healthy functioning depends upon constitutional variables (inborn predispositions) as well as on conditions of training.

Anal Traits

Several bipolar traits have been identified as anal traits by psychoanalysts. All have their origins during the anal period, and all express, in one way or another, the tendencies of giving or withholding. To repeat, anal traits may be understood in terms of compliance, overcompliance, or defiance. The extreme forms of the traits are abnormalities, while moderate degrees of the traits are productive of healthy growth and functioning. An individual may possess a trait which is so all-encompassing that he is identified by it, as was noted with the oral types.

stinginess	expansiveness
constrictedness	acquiescence
stubbornness	messiness
orderliness	tardiness
rigid punctuality	dirtiness
meticulousness	vagueness
precision	(Maddi, 1972, p. 273).
overgenerosity	

All these anal traits apply to a greater or lesser degree to everyone, because they are necessary to meeting the requirements of living in a social group.

THE PHALLIC STAGE

The phallic stage occurs from about three to five or six years of age. The genital organs become a prominent source of pleasure during this period. Curiosity about the body may begin much earlier; the child at some point encounters his hands and feet with amazement. He may even discover his genital organs quite early, but they do not become objects of concern and interest until the phallic period, when the tensions and pleasures of this zone of the body are much more intense. The child now begins to notice and comment upon the differences between men and women—that boys and girls dress differently (Thompson and Beutler, 1971); his concern increases significantly if he notices anatomical differences. He becomes more curious about sexual dissimilarities as he begins to experience sexual tensions. But his curiosity is quite diffuse because he does not know, unless he observes directly, the actual differences between the male and female sex organs.

The maturation and learning processes combine to differentiate the roles of the sexes during this stage. Little girls learn to be coquettish and to display flirtatious behavior, and little boys learn to take on the role of the male with a display of toughness, arrogance, and other masculine qualities.

As in the oral and anal stages, a conflict develops between the child's curiosity about the use of his genitals for pleasure, and his parents' interest in his sexual modesty. In Freud's day, which was dominated by Victorian ideas about the evils of sex, there were many taboos, and a great deal of mystery surrounded the sexual act. It was regarded as animalistic, a part of man's lower nature to be brought under strict control. Masturbation, for instance, was severely disapproved, and a child might be humiliated and punished for engaging in what was considered a vile practice. Freud found sexual disturbances in a large number of his patients, a fact which led him to the conclusion that the disturbances originated in the phallic stage when the child began to experience sexual tensions and desires, which were at first directed, he believed, to the parent of the opposite sex. The manner of dealing with the child's sexual concerns had much to do with the formation of the disturbing traits (Freud, 1914).

In our day fewer parents hold to Victorian sexual mores, but the emergent liberal attitudes present problems of their own. Children cannot avoid broad exposure to sex information, and especially to the portrayal of sex as something exciting and tantalizing. The media are saturated with allusions to sex. Try as they may, parents and teachers cannot prevent children from overemphasizing sexuality. It may be recalled that permissiveness can be as detrimental as excessive restrictiveness to important needs. Indulgence as well as frustration produces arrestment and disturbance of development. The mother who, fascinated by her little boy's interest in sexual matters, acts seductively by encouraging the child to compete with his father for her affections, may content herself with the belief that she has a liberal attitude toward sex, but only at the expense of the child, who may develop unfavorable personality traits.

Oedipus Complex

One of Freud's most controversial proposals is the Oedipus complex, with its accompanying castration anxiety (Freud, 1917). Its intricacy permits only the briefest discussion here. Taken from the Greek myth of Oedipus Rex, who unknowingly slew his father and married his mother, the complex refers to the sexual attachment which a boy purportedly develops for his mother during the phallic stage. At the same time, the boy views his father as a rival for his mother's affection. Mixed or ambivalent attitudes exist toward a father who on the one hand is feared because he can remove the offending organ, the source of castration anxiety, and on the other is respected and revered as a model of manhood, superior to the child. If development is normal, the child gives up his amorous desires for his mother and strives instead to take on the masculine role by patterning himself after his father. His affection toward his mother then loses its sexual aspect. By accepting the father's masculinity, the boy's superego undergoes its final development and embraces a positive ego ideal. But if either parent creates too much frustration or overindulges the child by not providing appropriate training and knowledge during this crucial period, serious fixations with long-term consequences may occur. The child may fail to accept the masculine role, or his conscience may be stunted. He may have difficulty relating to women his own age, being comfortable only with older women. He may overvalue his sexual prowess and assume an arrogant, egotistic attitude in his dealings with women of any age. Other traits which may develop during this period are discussed in a later section.

Electra Complex

During this period, the little girl undergoes a similar process, the Electra complex, but with some important differences (Freud, 1905). Freud believed that a little girl takes her father as a sex object and views her mother as a rival. It should be remembered that her sexual interests and feelings are still quite rudimentary, by no means having the intensity or directness of the emotional and physical love which characterizes the sexual drive of an adult. If a girl discovers that she lacks a penis, the relationship with her mother is further complicated because she blames her for the loss. At the same time, she also loves her mother and a conflict ensues which, unlike the Oedipus complex in a boy, is never completely resolved—a condition which Freud held had profound effects on the emotional life of a woman. The major pathological trait developed at this stage is "penis envy," undervaluing the feminine role and overvaluing the masculine. Freud believed that he traced many disturbances in female sexual functions, such as frigidity and dysmenorrhea, to the conflicts of the phallic stage. As with a boy, mishandling of the training during this period will engender pathological trends in the personality of a growing girl.

Traits of the Phallic Stage

During the phallic stage the child's circle of contacts gradually widens to include significant people outside the family: playmates, teachers, policemen, clergymen, and many more. The child must learn to take his place with other children, to give in at times to the demands of others, and to assert his own claims when others threaten to violate his rights. As might be expected, the traits that develop during this stage are related to the nature of the child's growth and to the types of problems and lessons which are to be learned. In both normal and abnormal form, they involve *self-assertion, self-feelings,* and *relationships with others.* There is also the dimension of narcissism versus object involvement: the degree to which interest and energy are invested in the self or in other people and things (Freud, 1914). The traits listed below are some of the outstanding ones developed during the phallic period.

vanity	self-hatred
pride	humility
blind courage	timidity
brashness	bashfulness
gregariousness	isolationism
stylishness	plainness
flirtatiousness	avoidance of heterosexuality
chastity	promiscuity
gaiety	sadness

(Maddi, 1972, p. 276).

If development during this period is normal, that is, if there is a proper balance between gratification and control, with neither too much frustration nor overindulgence, the child should acquire a moderate degree of both aspects of the trait dimensions. The pairs of traits are in balance if both tendencies are present. For example, a certain amount of dissatisfaction with one's self is a prerequisite for self-improvement; at the same time, a good measure of self-regard offsets the negative effects of self-dissatisfaction and, in fact, also contributes to self-improvement through a sense of pride. Consider some other traits of this period which are in proper balance. In relations with others, a person will be neither overly haughty nor unduly self-effacing. He will yield and conform to the expectations of others for the sake of harmony, but will protect his rights when they are threatened. He will strike a balance between unrealistic and hopeless perseverance at a task on the one hand, and fearful and premature withdrawal on the other. He will be neither so other-directed as to reckon his worth through the appraisal of others, nor so self-sufficient as to deny his social needs and obligations.

THE LATENCY PERIOD

The period from approximately six to twelve years, during which preparations for the next important stage gradually take place, was named by Freud the latency period. Freud maintained that this period involves the consolidation and elaboration of previously acquired traits and skills, with nothing dynamically new emerging (Freud, 1917). The child continues to grow quite rapidly, but his growth patterns follow the lines established in earlier stages. Significant new interests and needs await the marked physiological, psychological, and social changes occurring during adolescence, when new sources of pleasure, hence new conflicts and frustrations, come to the fore. Thus, Freud had little to say about the latency period. It did not represent a genuine psychosexual stage.

THE GENITAL STAGE

The genital stage begins with puberty and constitutes the last significant period of personality development. The term "genital" may be somewhat puzzling; it derives from the outstanding feature of this period as Freud saw it, the emergence and full unification and development of the sexual instincts. In the earlier psychosexual stages, certain zones of the body are the loci of sexual tensions and pleasures. Some confusion may arise concerning the difference between the pregenital phallic stage and the genital stage itself because the sex organs are involved in both. In the phallic stage, sexuality is primitive and rudimentary, primarily self-centered, while in the genital stage, sexuality attains maturity and becomes heterosexual. Each zone is autonomous, but with the maturation of sexual instincts, the genital organ becomes the major source of sexual tensions and pleasures, and the other organs are ancillary.

Again, in order to obtain a proper perspective on this stage, we should keep in mind the broad interpretation of sex which Freud held. By the term "sexual" he meant many different activities, including both social interactions with the same sex and heterosexual contacts; even fear of being sexually assaulted is a "sexual outlet." For Freud the term "genitality" was equivalent to maturity.

Genitality, in a narrow sense, involves sexual potency and orgasm. Various disturbances in both of these aspects of sexual functioning accompany psychological disorders, and Freud frequently found such disturbances in his patients. But genitality, in a broader sense, is more than sexual potency. For a man, it means competence and mastery in a wide range of activities: vocational, recreational, and social. Many abilities and traits are needed for potency, as Freud saw it. Genitality in a woman also involves more than orgastic potency; she must be capable of standing on her own feet, of responsiveness to men, and of capability in certain feminine attributes such as emotional warmth, motherly concern, and creativity. We must conclude, therefore, that to Freud genitality was masculinity and femininity fully developed, an equivalent to what others have called personal maturity. We perceive an individual who has these genital traits and abilities as living effectively, even without reference to the Freudian personality theory.

What things occur in the adolescent period to produce new pleasures and new frustrations? Sexual interests increase markedly in vigor and intensity, and are focused on members of the opposite sex; there are new problems which result directly from the increased role of sex. The adolescent finds social disapproval and the prohibitions of his own conscience conflicting with his intense heterosexual desires. There is also the fear of pregnancy, and the still prevalent view that premarital intercourse is an unacceptable way of dealing with sex. In a sense, the genital stage fosters not new traits but rather the full integration and utilization of earlier traits. In order to develop successfully in the genital stage, the traits acquired in previous stages must be present in the proper proportion and form. Any fixations in development will hinder subsequent growth; thus, each stage builds upon the preceding ones. As the number of traits increases, there is an integration of the new and the old. Difficulties in one stage predispose the individual to have still greater difficulties in subsequent stages.

To sum up, immaturity according to Freud is characterized by the uneven development of certain traits: mature in some, less mature in others, and highly immature in still others. Maturity, then, is the harmonious blending and balance of all the pregenital traits properly developed.

Two defining attributes that begin to develop during the genital stage, and come to fruition with maturity, are the ability to love and the ability to work. Each of these requires the healthy development of the traits of the earlier stages of personality growth. According to Freud, to be able to love and work effectively, one should have the oral trait of optimism but not carefree indifference or recklessness, the anal trait of perseverance but not unyielding obstinacy, the phallic trait of self-confidence, but not blatant brashness and self-overvaluation. He should be courageous without being callous and insensitive, orderly without being compulsive, sociable without being self-effacing. In short, he must possess all the traits of the pregenital and genital stages in moderate amounts. Through work and love, he can best satisfy his most basic and most human needs. The mature person, according to Freud, accommodates himself to the demands of his culture, does his share to maintain it, and functions within its limits: laws, taboos, and standards of conduct. Instead of unlimited self-fulfillment, he satisfies his needs in socially approved ways. Freud's ideal man, then, might be described as a social conformist.

It should be noted that genitality represents a fairly high level of personality growth and functioning, presupposing normal development in all the previous stages, with the major lessons of life learned well. The genital person is viewed as a fully developed individual who has resolved, as far as possible, the opposing tendencies in his personality. Everyone carries into adulthood some fixations from the past, for ideal child-rearing has not yet been established.

One more point deserves mention: what genitality is not. Genitality does not mean sexual promiscuity. Freud's objection to the Victorianism of his time was simply to the view of sex as something evil in man, something to despise or merely tolerate. He felt sex should be treated indifferently, as just another aspect of life; in fact, he accepted procreation as the only proper object of the sex act, strange as this may seem to many people who have the erroneous idea that he was liberal in sexual matters. If he overemphasized the role of sex in personality development, it was because he wanted to counterbalance the negative view of sex as something evil and unnatural.

TABLE 2–1   CHARACTERISTICS OF FREUD'S PSYCHOSEXUAL STAGES OF DEVELOPMENT

Age	Stage	Source of Pleasure	Traits
First 18 months	Oral	Mouth, lips and tongue: sucking, chewing, eating, biting, vocalizing	Optimism – Pessimism Impatience Envy Aggressiveness
18 months to 3½ years	Anal	Anus: retention-expulsion control, toilet training, cleanliness	Stinginess Obstinacy Compulsive orderliness } anal retentive Meticulousness Cruelty Destruction } anal expulsive Messiness
3 to 5 or 6 years	Phallic-Oedipal	Genital organs: body curiosity about self and others	Relatedness with others Assertiveness Self-regard Gregariousness Chastity
6 to 12 years	Latency	Sensory-motor: pleasure from knowledge, skill, building, peer group interactions	Differentiation (elaboration of pre-latency traits) Social learning Conscience development
Puberty	Genital	Heterosexual contacts and productiveness	Harmonious blending of pre-genital traits (fullest capacity for love and work)

CRITIQUE OF FREUD

REACTION AGAINST INFANTILE SEXUALITY

Many people, including professional psychologists and psychiatrists, find Freud's ideas on infantile sexuality quite out of touch with reality. What actually does happen? It is conceded by some experts that Freud's views apply to a minority of cases in which a family could be described as abnormal. If you consider sexuality in a broad sense, as maleness and femaleness, the picture is clearer. A little girl of three is still a feminine creature, and has a feminine personality which is appealing on some level to her father. The father, in turn, having a masculine personality, is naturally appealing on some level to his daughter. As a matter of fact, the father plays a significant role in helping his daughter become a woman. The same notions also apply to the relationship between a mother and her son; she normally has a special attraction for him and he for her, again based on sex, taken in the broad sense as gender differences. Each parent plays an important role in the sexual development of the opposite-sexed child because each parent possesses, by virtue of his own gender, a particularly direct understanding which the other does not have. The little boy wants to help his mother with the grocery bags because his father does that. The little girl may want to cook for her father because she wishes to imitate her mother, but not necessarily replace her, as Freud maintained. A little girl of four came to her parents' bed one morning and announced boldly as she lay down next to her father that she wanted to go to bed with daddy, and that mommy could sleep in the baby's bed. One could be easily misled into a sexual interpretation, and as a matter of fact, her parents were a bit surprised by what the child had said. Actually the child was indicating that she, too, wanted to be a grownup and do what her mother did — to reverse things for once and put her mother in the place of the child. There is no reason to add a sexual component to a phenomenon which can be accounted for by other general principles, perhaps by the principle of identification, according to which the child takes on the qualities of an adult. Identification as a principle of learning is extremely important, especially during the first years of life (Sears, 1957). The child wants to be like an adult, and consciously or unconsciously patterns his behavior upon that of the adults in his life.

FAILURE TO CONSIDER CHANGES IN ADULT PERSONALITY

A most serious objection to Freud's psychoanalytic theory of development is his lack of interest in the alterations in personality beyond the genital stage. Significant new problems, frustrations, and even needs emerge as a person approaches middle age (Tuddenham, 1959), and still more profound are the changes of old age. Even if we restricted significant developmental dynamics

to the unfolding of the sex drive, surely there are important changes which
follow upon the diminution or cessation of so important a drive in middle and
old age. What happens to the personality of a man or woman when this function begins to wane? With major goals accomplished at the approach of middle age, there is often (as Carl Jung pointed out) a striking reorientation in the
form of an intense concern for a meaningful philosophy of life (1933). If an
individual progresses normally, he has accomplished much of what he set out
to do by the age of 35 or 40, but the "urge" for life continues. A great deal of
energy which was previously utilized for the pursuit of basic needs becomes
available for cultural and spiritual pursuits. Some of Freud's followers, notably Erikson (1968), have recognized this shortcoming in his work and have
proposed theories to take account of the personality changes following adolescence. Erikson, who delineates eight stages in the life cycle, will be discussed in
the next chapter.

REJECTION OF FREUD'S STRICT DETERMINISM

Freud has been criticized for his adherence to a strict determinism with respect to personality development and self-improvement. He believed, as do
his followers, that the structure of personality is formed and fixed in childhood. The vast changes which take place as a result of learning and maturation are considered a mere elaboration of the earliest themes. Thus, whether a
person is gullible, envious, self-assertive, vain, or compulsive, his character
is not altered by subsequent experiences. Even when he is old enough to
perceive the desirability of making changes in his personality, everything
about him has already been formed, including the ego itself. In the Freudian
view, personality is fixed from the standpoint of both its structure and the
role which the self or ego can take in bringing about changes.

INSIGHTS FROM FREUD ON PERSONALITY
DEVELOPMENTS

Freud, like his disciples, believed he could trace habitual attitudes and
practices to the early years of life; for example, he believed that he
could trace work habits to the toilet training experience. Keeping in
mind that toilet training is a most significant event in the early life of a
child, consider some of the traits that might develop as a consequence
of toilet training experiences: (1) Cooperation with the mother's expectations by doing what is expected promptly and thoroughly. You can
think of a person who always does what is expected of him, without objection or complaint. (2) Resistance to the mother's expectations by
obstinacy, procrastination, defiance, soiling, or carrying out the task
when the mother does not desire it. Could a habit of procrastination be
an expression of a generalized resistance to coercion? A person may
put off what he knows he should do because he unconsciously resists
any form of obligation or demand placed upon him by others. In a
sense, then, the toilet training experience is a work experience for the
child. He is expected to carry out certain tasks, and the parent who has

rewarding or punishing power over him is analogous to the boss. The two may work harmoniously together, or there may be a great deal of friction. These early experiences set the pattern for subsequent associations.

What arguments can we give in support of Freud's views on the development of lifelong traits? We might consider: (1) The importance of first learning in establishing prototypes for later experiences: early learning makes the strongest impression, has no competitors, and becomes the basis of subsequent learning. (2) The interaction of constitutional predispositions and the effects of training: some children have stronger oral, anal, or phallic interests than others, and training which requires them to give up specific pleasurable activities may produce especially strong conflicts between the child and the authority figures in his life. (3) Early training as "work experience" for the child: early attitudes toward work are difficult to change.

It would seem that if we could identify traits which are essential for effective living and attempt to acquire these traits in the appropriate degree, we would have a model with which to compare our present behavior and toward which we could strive. A promising beginning in this direction is provided by the traits associated with Freud's stages of development. We might look at the various bipolar dimensions, recognizing that each represents a potential problem area. Perhaps some of us cannot be objective enough to view ourselves in such a detached manner; thus we would not be able to perceive our traits without assistance from a professional therapist. But most of us are aware of many of our traits, both desirable and undesirable.

Consider each of the traits with respect to whether it serves or hinders adjustment (see Table 2–2). For example, consider the bipolar traits of vanity—self-hate. We should possess enough vanity or self-love to withstand assaults to the ego and to strive for autonomy in decision-making, but at the same time we should have enough self-hate or self-dissatisfaction to strive for continual improvement. One offsets the other. One without the tempering effect of the other would create problems. Each bipolar trait dimension should be examined from the same point of view: a moderate amount of each component of the bipolar dimension is necessary for optimum functioning.

In this section we have considered some potential applications of several of Freud's basic concepts of personality development. Freud dealt with the real-life problems of his patients, and it should be possible to apply his ideas to ourselves. His concepts and methods were meant to be functional. He used them as guides in his efforts to alleviate the difficulties of both his patients and himself. Freud believed his investigations demonstrated that early needs become enduring features of the personality. Personality development consists primarily of increasing the ways of satisfying these early needs. In primitive form, infantile needs would make civilized life impossible. Their satisfaction requires their sublimation into suitable outlets. The means of need gratification must be socially acceptable as well as acceptable to the self, and thus each society provides many of the necessary outlets.

In keeping with Freud's notion that needs may be sublimated, consider some of your deepest desires and the manner in which these might be expressed freely. A person who has a strong need for directing or instructing others will encounter a great deal of frustration if he attempts to satisfy this need in his personal relationships with his friends, but he

TABLE 2–2   TRAITS OF PSYCHOSEXUAL STAGES OF DEVELOPMENT

	Abnormal	Normal	Abnormal Zero (Absence of Trait)	Normal	Abnormal
Oral Traits	optimism	(←——————————→)			pessimism
	gullibility	(		)	suspiciousness
	manipulativeness	(		)	passivity
	admiration	(		)	envy
	cockiness	(		)	self-belittlement
Anal Traits	stinginess	(		)	overgenerosity
	constrictedness	(		)	expansiveness
	stubbornness	(		)	acquiescence
	orderliness	(		)	messiness
	rigid punctuality	(		)	tardiness
	meticulousness	(		)	dirtiness
	precision	(		)	vagueness
Phallic Traits	vanity	(		)	self-hate
	pride	(		)	humility
	blind courage	(		)	timidity
	brashness	(		)	bashfulness
	gregariousness	(		)	isolationism
	stylishness	(		)	plainness
	flirtatiousness	(		)	avoidance of heterosexuality
	chastity	(		)	promiscuity
	gaiety	(		)	sadness
Genital Traits	sentimental love	(		)	indiscriminate hate
	compulsive work	(		)	inability to work

The ideal personality should possess each of the above pairs of traits to a moderate degree. There must be a proper balance between opposing traits. Lack of balance among the traits constitutes a less than ideal personality. Abnormality in a personality may be determined in three ways: (1) possession of a trait to an extreme degree, (2) lack of the trait altogether, (3) imbalance between pairs of traits.

may satisfy it openly as a teacher, guidance counselor, lawyer, judge, or business consultant. A person who enjoys finding fault in others may give free expression to this tendency through the profession of literary critic.

Freud also offers us a useful method of identifying our fixated traits through his principle of regression. Regression is the opposite of sublimation: it generally means reverting to less mature forms of behavior under stress. When frustration is experienced, earlier and more direct forms of need gratification may override and replace current sublimated outlets. Thus, whenever regression takes place, one's traits may be experienced in their more primitive form. Observing our reactions to stress can thus be a valuable method of gaining self-knowledge because we will see our personality structures more directly. A talkative person becomes more talkative; a timid person becomes even more timid. An optimist may resort to magical or unrealistic thinking when he cannot solve his problems. If we find relief from tension through eating, smoking, or drinking, under stress these activities are intensified. Under extreme pressures, we may even discover traits which we did not previously perceive in ourselves. Many people have reported gaining insights into their deepest motivations during critical times. Selfishness, for instance, is often revealed when survival is in jeopardy.

SUMMARY

1.   The major traits of personality are established in childhood and subsequent personality development is merely an elaboration of these traits.

2.   On the basis of the particular zones of the body which become the focuses of sexual pleasure, Freud conceived four psychosexual stages of development: the oral, the anal, the phallic, and the genital.

3.   Each psychosexual stage has specific needs and gratifications which are significant. Specific traits are formed during each stage as a result of the manner in which the needs are gratified or frustrated.

4.   Fixation, a stunting of growth, is attributable to two basic causes: excessive frustration and excessive gratification. The frustrated or indulged needs of early childhood tend to remain as major determinants of personality.

5.   Freud has been criticized for his lack of interest in the alterations of personality beyond the genital stage of development.

SUGGESTED READINGS

Freud, Sigmund. The Interpretation of Dreams, 1900. Standard Edition 4–5.
　　Freud always considered this his capital work. It laid the foundation for his new psychology. May be considered as autobiography in disguise.

Three Essays on the Theory of Sexuality, 1905. Standard Edition 7:125–245.
　　This work on infantile sexuality caused great outrage in Vienna at the time of its publication.

Totem and Taboo, 1913. Standard Edition 3:1–161.
　　In this work, Freud traced the evolution of civilization and religion in human societies.

Introductory Lectures in Psychoanalysis, 1916–1917. Standard Edition 15–16.
　　A systematic exposition of psychoanalysis up to this date, garnered from Freud's lectures at the University of Vienna from 1915 to 1916.

The Future of an Illusion, 1927. Standard Edition 21:3–56.
　　One of the sharpest criticisms of religion ever published.

REFERENCES

Adelson, J., and Redmond, J. Personality differences in the capacity for verbal recall. J. Abnorm. Social Psychol. 57:244–48, 1958.
Allport, G. W. Pattern and Growth in Personality. New York: Holt, Rinehart and Winston, 1961.
Bridges, K. M. B. Emotional development in early infancy. Child Dev. 3:324–41, 1932.
Erikson, E. H. Identity: Youth and Crisis. New York: W. W. Norton and Company, 1968.

Freud, S. Instincts and their vicissitudes. *In* Collected Papers. London: Hogarth Press, 1925. Vol. 4 (6).

Freud, S. Some character types met within psychoanalysis work. *In* Collected Papers. London: Hogarth Press, 1925. Vol. 4 (9).

Freud, S. The Standard Edition of the Complete Psychological Works. London: Hogarth Press, 1963.

    Studies on Hysteria, 1895 (with Josef Breuer). Vol. 2.

    The Interpretation of Dreams, 1900. Vols. 4–5.

    Three Essays on the Theory of Sexuality, 1905. Vol. 7, pp. 125–245.

    On the History of the Psychoanalytic Movement, 1914. Vol. 14, pp. 7–66.

    On Narcissism: An Introduction, 1914. Vol. 14, pp. 67–102.

    Introductory Lectures on Psychoanalysis, 1916–1917. Vols. 15–16.

    An Outline of Psychoanalysis, 1940. Vol. 23, pp. 141–207.

Fromm, E. Man for Himself. New York: Holt, Rinehart and Winston, 1947.

Goldman-Eisler, F. Breastfeeding and character formation. *In* Kluckhohn, C., Murray, H. A., and Schneider, D. M., eds. Personality in Nature, Society, and Culture. New York: Alfred A. Knopf, 1948. Pp. 146–84.

Josselyn, I. M. Psychosocial Development of Children. New York: Family Service Association of America, 1948.

Jung, C. G. Freud and Jung–Contrasts. *In* Modern Man in Search of a Soul. New York: Harcourt, Brace and World, 1933.

Maddi, S. R. Personality Theories: A Comparative Analysis, rev. ed. Homewood, Illinois: Dorsey Press, 1972.

Morse, W. C., and Wingo, G. M. Psychology and Teaching. Chicago: Scott, Foresman and Company, 1962.

Sears, R. R. Identification as a form of behavioral development. *In* Harris, D. B., ed., The Concept of Development. Minneapolis: University of Minnesota Press, 1957. Pp. 149–61.

Shur, M. Freud: Living and Dying. New York: International Universities Press, 1972.

Thompson, S. K., and Beutler, P. M. The priority of cues in sex discrimination by children and adults. Dev. Psychol. 2:181–85, 1971.

Tuddenham, R. O. Constancy of personality ratings over two decades. Genet. Psychol. Monogr. 60:3–29, 1959.

CHAPTER 3

The Cycle of Life

Erik Erikson

Erik H. Erikson (1902—)

BIOGRAPHY AND OVERVIEW

Erik Homberger Erikson was born on June 15, 1902, in Frankfort, Germany, of Danish parentage. His father abandoned his mother before his birth and she subsequently married a pediatrician. Young Erikson was a gifted artist and resisted his stepfather's pressures to follow in his footsteps. After finishing high school, he left home and traveled across Europe. A schoolmate invited him to come to a training school for lay psychoanalysts in Vienna. Erikson took his friend's advice and studied under Anna Freud and August Eichorn, becoming one of the first psychoanalysts to deal with child psychiatry, even though he did not have a medical degree. He came to the United States when Hitler took over Germany. Henry A. Murray, whose ideas will be considered in a subsequent chapter, gave him his first home in this country at the Harvard Psychological Clinic. He also took an appointment on the staff of the Harvard Medical School, although he had only a high school education. He was called the "Ph.D. in nothing" by a fellow analyst. He was the exception; and of course, he turned out to be the outstanding psychoanalyst of them all.

Erikson's novel views on childhood developed through research on infantile neurosis at the Yale School of Medicine, where he held the position of Research Assistant in Psychoanalysis from 1936 to 1939. From 1939 to 1951, he was a research associate at the Institute of Child Welfare, and later he became Professor of Psychology at the University of California, Berkley. During the years 1951 through 1960, he was a senior consultant at the Austen-Riggs Center and professor at the University of Pittsburgh School of Medicine. Since 1960, he has been Professor of Human Development and Lecturer on Psychiatry at Harvard University.

COMPARISON OF ERIKSON AND FREUD ON DEVELOPMENT

Erikson acknowledges that Freud's theory of personality development has influenced his own. Thus it might be instructive to compare the two theories (Erikson, 1963). (See Table 3–1). Like Freud, Erikson views development from the standpoint of fairly distinct stages, but he proposes eight stages compared to Freud's four. For Freud, genitality, or maturity, is attained in young adulthood, and apparently once attained, continues throughout the adult years until the decline brought about through the aging process. Erikson covers the adult years by four stages; thus one major difference is that Erikson sees personality as changing and developing for a much longer period than does Freud.

Personality development for Freud is based on the manner in which the child's sexual needs are dealt with (it should be recalled that "sexual" means pleasurable sensations of the mouth, anus, or genitals). Overgratification or undergratification produces trait fixations. Erikson, on the other hand, does not attempt to account for the genesis of specific traits, but rather delineates *ego attainments.* For instance, in the period of early life Freud specified oral traits such as envy, gullibility, suspiciousness, cockiness; Erikson proposes a single general attainment, or the lack of it: trust versus mistrust. If personality develops normally, there are eight such attainments, each necessary for healthy development and functioning. On the definition of normality Freud and Erikson again part company. Whereas Freud viewed normality as essentially the absence of abnormality, Erikson describes the healthy personality in its own terms. His concept of normal development is positive rather than negative.

Freud's developmental theory has been termed psychosexual; Erikson's is called psychosocial. Thus while Freud attempted to explain the manner in which specific traits of personality are formed through his instinct theory, Erikson views the person from the standpoint of his sociocultural environment. The conditions of a culture may produce similar traits in all the members; all may be mistrusting, for example. Freud dealt more directly with the individual's needs and with the manner in which these are managed by those who care for the child. Erikson considers the major task of each period of life, and relates success or failure to the development of ego strength.

PSYCHOSOCIAL DETERMINANTS

It soon becomes apparent that Erikson's theory of personality takes in a broader area than does Freud's. Erikson encompasses aspects of personality development which he feels Freud hardly covered at all, or did not stress sufficiently (Erikson, 1963). In formulating his own theory of development, he does not deny the validity of Freud's psychosexual stages. Rather he builds on them through his emphasis on the social determinants of personality growth.

TABLE 3-1 A COMPARISON OF THE DEVELOPMENTAL STAGES OF FREUD AND ERICKSON

Freud's Sexual Stage	Erikson's Mode	Descriptive Verb For Mode	Outcome of Successful Resolution (Freud)	Outcome of Unsuccessful Resolution (Freud) (Fixation)	Outcome of Successful Resolution (Erikson)	Outcome of Unsuccessful Resolution (Erikson)
Oral	Incorporative (1) Incorporative (2)	To get To take	Smooth movement to anal stage	High degree of dependency	Sense of trust	Sense of mistrust
Anal	Retentive Eliminative	To hold on To let go	Smooth movement to phallic stage	Obsessive-compulsive characteristics	Sense of autonomy	Sense of shame and doubt
Phallic	Intrusive	To explore, make, or intrude	Smooth movement to latency period and genital stage	Hysterical characteristics and Oedipal conflicts	Sense of initiative	Sense of guilt
Latency						
Genital			Capacity for love and work			

(Reprinted from *Childhood and Society*, 2nd ed., by Erik H. Erikson. By permission of W. W. Norton & Company, Inc. Copyright 1950, © 1963 by W. W. Norton & Company, Inc.)

His thinking is strongly influenced by the main concepts and assumptions of the psychoanalytic school. He has been innovative in his own right, however, and has introduced many new ideas, particularly with respect to the role of the ego in personality. Because of this, he has earned for himself the title of "ego psychologist."

Erikson holds that major conflicts in early life are caused only in part by the frustration of the sex instincts; many conflicts result from the clash between the child's nonsexual needs and desires and the expectations and limitations of his culture (Erikson, 1963). Because there is throughout life a total inter-action between a person and his environment, personality growth and change cannot be restricted to the first 20 years. Erikson thus divides the life cycle into eight stages: four to cover the years up to approximately age 20 and four more to include the rest of life. Each of the stages is distinct and unique, with par-ticular problems and needs, as well as new cultural expectations and limita-tions. As the ego and superego (conscience) increase in importance, a person may set goals and limitations for himself, of course. But *each stage presents the individual with a major task to be achieved,* such as the development of a sense of basic trust in the environment and in the self, a sense of autonomy, or a sense of industry (Erikson, 1963).

THE EFFECTS OF CULTURE ON DEVELOPMENT

Every organism, including man, has a genetically determined nature which is manifested in growth in an orderly fashion. The course of development is remarkably similar among members of a given species, and can be predicted quite confidently for a particular individual. But although growth occurs within the organism, only certain environmental conditions can make it possi-ble, for every organism requires some form of nutrition.

What might be called schedule of development, which specifies the sequence of changes, is quite similar from child to child, although the particular time of a particular activity may vary considerably with each child. In other words, each child goes through the same steps in growth, but the time at which they occur varies. Many a young mother consults books on developmental norms to see whether her child is doing what the average child in his age group is doing. These averages are based upon actual observation of large represent-ative samples of children at specific ages.

Consider the development of speech, one of man's most complex activities. At a certain point a child begins to imitate the sounds he hears; the ability to imi-tate sounds undergoes a gradual change, from simple vowel sounds to conso-nants, to complex vowel-consonant combinations. In fact, all the sounds of all the languages of men are gradually evolved through maturation of the child's speech patterns.

INTERACTION OF THE PERSONAL AND THE SOCIAL

The specific sequence of the various speech sounds, although the sounds occur at different times for each child, is quite orderly and predictable. The equipment for learning language is within the child (Chomsky, 1968), as is also the motivation to learn to talk, but the language which the child actually learns is that of the social group of which he is a part. Here again we see the inextricable interaction between the personal and the social. As a matter of fact, virtually every aspect of personality development and functioning is the joint product of individual endowments and cultural influences. While growth is ostensibly an organismic process, human psychobiological development is impossible without the geographical and sociocultural conditions within which growth takes place. Humans have a long childhood and for civilized man, the growing-up period is protracted. Many experiences, both painful and pleasurable, can alter the psychobiological development during this period (Erikson, 1963).

Each culture prescribes standards which the authorities in the culture impose on its members; parents are the earliest authorities, or cultural representatives, for the child. Because cultures differ widely on what is acceptable and unacceptable behavior, each culture produces frustrations and conflicts, thereby engendering specific personality traits in its members. It will be recalled from the discussion of Freud's principle of fixation that specific frustrations and conflicts, as well as specific areas of indulgence, engender specific personality traits. Following this view of fixation, Erikson (1968) believes that particular personality types may be associated with various cultures.

CULTURAL CHANGES

Cultural and physical-geographical conditions have such a pervasive influence upon the course of development that the total orientation of a people — what is worthwhile, ethical, and moral — is established by such external conditions. The powerful role of culture is manifested when there is a sudden alteration in cultural patterns, as in the case of many American Indian tribes who were brought under the influence of American education, institutions, and norms. Often the people who are the victims of such transformations are divested of cultural supports — particularly the young, who are caught between the demands, values, and practices of two divergent systems. The beliefs and practices of the primitive societies are quite opposite to the prescriptions of the imposed culture, and many new problems are created by the clash of the old and the new. In several generations adaptation may occur, but at the present time the lot of the majority of American Indians is extremely dismal.

We can look to our own life situations for other examples of the influence of cultural and environmental forces. Growing up involves a continuing series of adjustments, for the world outside the home is certainly quite different from immediate family circumstances. Everyone has to learn how to get along with other children, with adults, and with authority figures. The school environment places further adjustive demands upon us. As we move up the grades, there are increasing requirements: for independence, for initiative, for industry, for self-definition. In a sense, the new requirements compete with the old habits, and like the Indians, we may have difficulty accepting the new and shedding the old. In the early stages of a new environment, we may long for our earlier circumstances because they are familiar and we have learned to deal with them. The ability to accommodate oneself to changing circumstances is a mark of maturity, Erikson believes (1968).

THE EIGHT STAGES OF LIFE

As we discuss Erikson's eight stages of life, keep in mind that each stage, if successfully encountered and lived through, adds something to the ego. As the child grows, there are changes in potentialities and abilities, but there is also increased vulnerability to injury. Learning to do more for himself, the child increases his susceptibility to frustrations and conflicts. And although the successful attainment of a particular achievement — for instance, a sense of trust — prepares him to live effectively, he may easily "backslide" or regress. Yet this principle of risk also offers hope. If a crisis is not resolved successfully at the appropriate stage of development, later experiences can provide a second chance: a trustworthy teacher, for example, can undo the psychological damage done by cruel or inattentive parents. At the same time, an achievement mastered at the appropriate stage may prepare the growing child to take on the tasks of the next stage; thus it will have an even greater likelihood of becoming a continuing influence on his personality.

GENERAL CHARACTERISTICS OF THE EIGHT STAGES

To Erikson, the same problems recur throughout life. He distinguishes between the *immature* phase, the *critical* phase, and the *resolution* phase of these universal problems (1968). For example, a child is confronted with the problem of self-identity (who he really is); so also is the adolescent, the young adult, the middle-aged person, and the elderly individual. The identity problem is not as acute for the child as for the adolescent or young adult; therefore the problem is in its *immature* phase. On the other hand, the problem of autonomy (asserting independence) is in the critical phase at the age of two. During adolescence, the search for identity reaches the *critical* phase because, at this time, a variety of conditions such as sexual maturity, parental and other expectations, and approaching adult status strongly bring out the need for self-definition, the so-called identity crisis. *By crisis, Erikson does not mean overwhelming stress, but rather a turning point in the life of the individual, when a new problem must be confronted and mastered.*

TABLE 3-2 ERICKSON'S EIGHT PSYCHOSOCIAL DEVELOPMENTAL CRISES

	1	2	3	4	5	6	7	8
VIII								INTEGRITY vs. DESPAIR
VII							GENERATIVITY vs. STAGNATION	
VI						INTIMACY vs. ISOLATION		
V	Temporal Perspective vs. Time Confusion	Self-Certainty vs. Self-Consciousness	Role Experimentation vs. Role Fixation	Apprenticeship vs. Work Paralysis	IDENTITY vs. ROLE DIFFUSION	Sexual Polarization vs. Bisexual Confusion	Leader- and Followership vs. Authority Confusion	Ideological Commitment vs. Confusion of Values
IV				INDUSTRY vs. INFERIORITY	Task Identification vs. Sense of Futility			
III			INITIATIVE vs. GUILT		Anticipation of Roles vs. Role Inhibition			
II		AUTONOMY vs. SHAME, DOUBT			Will to Be Oneself vs. Self-Doubt			
I	TRUST vs. MISTRUST				Mutual Recognition vs. Autistic Isolation			

To understand the table, one should bear in mind that there are eight major critical points in life. These crises are depicted by the intersection of the vertical and horizontal lines at the capitalized words. Where several items appear on a single vertical line, those items falling below the intersection are to be interpreted as the premature forms of the crises and those falling above the intersection as the later forms of the crises. (Adapted from *Identity: Youth and Crisis*, by Erik H. Erikson. By permission of W. W. Norton & Company, Inc. Copyright © 1968 by W. W. Norton & Company, Inc.)

The *resolution* of those conflicts and problems associated with each period of life helps to make normal development possible. Failure to attain specific achievements, when it is crucial to do so, results in a carry-over of problems and necessarily impedes efforts to solve the new problems of the following stages. The young adult who fails to establish a firm sense of identity during adolescence cannot form an intimate association with others; thus he may experience difficulties in his marriage, in his work, and in his recreational activities because he cannot relate with others in a satisfying way. The eight psychosocial tasks associated with Erikson's stages of life are quite general, and each influences the whole orientation to life (see Table 3–2).

Major Problems Are Conflicts

During each stage of life, according to Erikson (1963), an individual is confronted with a major problem *which is really a basic conflict*; it remains a recurrent problem throughout life, although it may take a different form at various periods. For instance, the lifelong dependence upon the external environment and the necessity of trusting one's ability to deal with it creates a conflict, trust versus mistrust. No one can ever establish a perfectly secure life situation. The sense of trust or mistrust thus determines the manner in which one faces life. Erikson says that there are other basic conflicts which are problems throughout life (1963). We will discuss these in detail later. To get a first impression of them, however, consider some of the basic decisions one must make: How much independence should he have? How hard and how long should he work for what he wants? How much of himself should he give to others?

STAGE ONE, FIRST YEAR OF LIFE: TRUST VERSUS MISTRUST

During the first year of postnatal life, the infant faces his first major challenge, the outcome of which has a profound effect on all later developments, Erikson believes (1963). The infant is torn between trusting and mistrusting the things and people in his environment. A sense of trust develops if his needs are met without too much frustration. A trustful environment also determines development of trust in one's self; self-confidence. A sense of trust is manifested in faith in the environment and optimism about the future. A sense of mistrust is revealed through suspiciousness, inwardness, and fearful and anxious concern with security. The child who has achieved a basic sense of trust views his surroundings as predictable and consistent.

During early life, the nature of the infant requires that he receive appropriate satisfaction of his basic needs — especially the need for mothering — because he himself can do little to meet them. His orientation is incorporative: he relates to his environment by receiving. There is no other time, except under certain conditions of illness and aging, when helplessness is so complete. A child's needs must be satisfied not only at the proper time but in the proper amount. Failure in either respect may result in a variety of disturbances. We can experience this feeling of infantile helplessness during highly traumatic moments, as after the sudden loss of a loved one.

A child must also regulate himself to his mother's schedule or there will be conflict between them. How can a mother help to create a sense of trust in her child? Erikson offers the following suggestions:

Mothers create a sense of trust in their children by the kind of administration which in its quality combines sensitive care of the baby's individual needs and a firm sense of personal trustworthiness within the trusted framework of their community's life style. This forms the very basis in the child for a component of the sense of identity which will later combine a sense of being "all right," of being oneself, and of becoming what other people trust one will become. Parents must not only have certain ways of guiding by prohibition and permission, they must also be able to represent to the child a deep, almost somatic conviction that there is a meaning in what they are doing. In this sense, a traditional system of child care can be said to be a factor making for trust, even where items of that tradition, taken singly, may seem arbitrarily or unnecessarily cruel, or lenient (Erikson, 1968, p. 103. © 1968 by W. W. Norton & Co., Inc.).

Erikson believes that if the relationship between mother and child is mutually satisfying, the child apparently receives a sense of "inner goodness" through a harmonious interaction with his mother, which does not have to be continually reaffirmed (1968). It seems essential that the child experience security in need gratification through warm and consistent care from those who minister to him. The mother whose care for her child harmonizes with his needs engenders in him a sense of being *acceptable*, of being *good* and *lovable*, and these are the essential ingredients of the sense of basic trust. The person who has a sense of basic trust feels at one with himself and with others; he feels "good and all right," and acceptable to those around him. He can be himself and likes to be himself. If his sense of trust is unusually well developed, he acquires the virtue of abiding hope.

Many children lacking trust display a great deal of disturbance if their mothers leave even for a short while. A sixteen year old boy who had always been kept at home near his mother could not bear her absence for more than a few hours. He would whine and mope and constantly question her whereabouts when she did not return from a shopping trip or a visit when he expected her. His dependence on her was extreme, and she, in turn, overprotected and "overmothered" him because she was having difficulty with her older children and husband.

The sense of basic trust is never attained permanently, and in fact, even early in life, undergoes a severe test. The helpless infant orients to his environment, at first almost exclusively by incorporating and receiving. But he soon learns to assert himself by resisting, accepting, or rejecting what is offered to him. As his needs increase and his knowledge and abilities grow, his relationship with his surroundings takes a more active turn; instead of having an exclusively incorporative and receptive orientation, he begins to participate actively by using his increased knowledge and skills in exploring, manipulating, and grasping the things he needs or wants. Taking or actively getting rather than receiving and accepting become the child's major modes of orientation to his environment before he is two years old. By asserting himself, he comes into conflict with the people in his world who have power over him. His sense of trust may be shaken, because at this stage his mother may begin to lose her "motherly" feelings toward him as Fromm has demonstrated (1947).

STAGE TWO, ONE TO THREE YEARS: AUTONOMY VERSUS SHAME AND DOUBT

With the development of perceptual and muscular skills, the child gains increasing autonomy of action. Two modes of dealing with his surroundings, although previously existing in primitive form, become dominant ways of coping: holding on to things and letting them go. This necessary step in growth may put the child in conflict with the significant people in his life. It marks clear assertion of the ego, and often his demands are directly opposed by others. Furthermore, because of the immaturity of his psychological faculties, he lacks discretion in the use of these modalities. He may resist the demands of his parents by obstinate tenacity; in toilet training, he may refuse to cooperate with his mother's wishes; indeed, he may generalize this approach to all of his dealings with others. He may also "let go" in hostile and aggressive ways, creating friction and conflict. And his immaturity may make him extremely vulnerable to feelings of shame and doubt.

Because the child has not yet learned to avoid certain situations, such as his mother's bad moods, he easily becomes the victim of her displaced aggression. He may make the same mistakes over and over through ignorance, and his parents may interpret this as defiance. Struggling to meet the demands of his environment, and encountering frequent failures, frustrations, and rebuffs, he may develop a sense of self-doubt. One result may be the development of obsessional and compulsive trends: he may doubt his own abilities and thus limit his participation in life to fixed and rigid routines. He may do only what is safe and what fits within the limits set by his authorities. At the other extreme, he may develop aggressive and hostile tendencies and react negatively to all external and internal controls. The need to overcome self-doubt may be so strong as to engender a rebellious and self-assertive orientation which overrides the effects of parental rewards, so that parental approval is not valued as highly as the reward which accrues from self-assertiveness. The child may actually develop a hatred of his parents and generalize it to any authority figure and to restriction of any kind: rules, standards, laws. His self-esteem is bolstered not by conformity to cultural expectations but by negativism. Overconformity with blocking of impulses and the total lack of respect for regulation and control are two of the extreme disturbances caused by a sense of self-doubt; there are many others as well.

In addition to a sense of self-doubt, a child may develop a sense of shame which persists throughout his life. Shame results when the ego is exposed and defenseless in the face of unfavorable or unflattering scrutiny. It is an undesirable form of self-consciousness, an injury to self-esteem, produced by the censorship and disapproval of others; thus, it is caused by outside evaluations rather than by self-evaluations, which may stem from conscience and be experienced as guilt, and which occur in the next stage of development. Before conscience develops sufficiently, guilt is not possible, but shame may be felt quite early.

A child is small and inferior in relation to those who have power over him; he thus has a tendency to undervalue himself and, at the same time, to overvalue those who have this authority. If parents, teachers, and older children downgrade and belittle his accomplishments, he may feel worthless, dirty, and evil, and begin to believe that what he does or produces is of no value. Here, we can see the foundations of a profound sense of self-doubt and inferiority. Many parents encourage such feelings because they are impatient with their child's level of accomplishment; they either continually berate the child for doing things badly, or are forever pushing him into things which are beyond his capabilities. Sometimes the child may react in an opposite way; he may flout all authority or callously disregard the interests and rights of others. Which reaction occurs depends upon the nature of the child and on the methods which are used to shame him.

As conscience begins to take shape, it exerts control over behavior. It exercises this control through self-rewards and self-punishments expressed as pride and self-hate. Guilt, which is the result of a poorly developed conscience, also promotes self-doubt; whatever is done is deemed unworthy. Conscience provides a source of inner controls and a model for desirable conduct; if one obeys these, one can avoid a great deal of doubt and guilt. Why don't some individuals use their consciences in this manner? The reason is that the urge for autonomy competes with the voice of conscience. We can see the effects of this conflict between conscience and autonomy in such traits as willfulness, cooperativeness, conformity to expectations, and rigidity in decision-making. These traits (which make such a difference between a satisfying life style and one which leads to dissatisfaction, unhappiness, and a feeling of being trapped) thus have their origins during the stage when autonomy is a crisis.

Before conscience is developed, the culture usually provides an all-important code of laws to regulate the child's conduct and to assist him in attaining a limited measure of autonomy while avoiding doubt and shame. Other subtle guidelines—tradition, customs, mores, folkways, taboos—help the child to know what he should or should not do to be acceptable as a member of the culture. Justice on the institutional level, and fairness on the individual level, ensure the protection of rights and guarantee a certain degree of equality of autonomy for all. The individual, if development is normal, gradually acquires a knowledge of his rights and limitations and even of his privileges, if he happens to have advantages over others. He also learns his obligations.

Just as the parents' own sense of trust is communicated to their child and affects the development of his sense of trust, so their degree of autonomy affects the conditions for the development of his autonomy. A parent who values conservative conformity can hardly expect development of individualism in his child. A fearful, anxious mother may have such an influence over her child that these traits will become enduring features of the child's orientation to life.

In brief, some very basic attitudes are formed during the second stage of development, when the need for autonomy creates a crisis. The formation of these attitudes depends upon how successfully the crisis is resolved, and on how well the ego fares. If a person develops a sense of autonomy to an unusual degree, he will demonstrate the virtues of courage, self-control, and will power (Erikson, 1965).

STAGE THREE, THREE TO FIVE YEARS: INITIATIVE VERSUS GUILT

During the ages from about three to five, the need for autonomy takes a more vigorous form; it becomes more coordinated, efficient, spontaneous, and goal-directed. In this period, the major accomplishment of the ego, according to Erikson (1963), is a sense of initiative, and failure in this task is experienced as guilt. If self-doubt and shame are the result of failure in acquiring a sense of autonomy, a profound and enduring sense of guilt and unworthiness is the result of failure in acquiring a sense of initiative. The capacities and abilities which were maturing during the stage of autonomy continue to mature; but the efforts at autonomy now take on greater activity and direction: undertaking, attacking, planning. The child can do essential things effortlessly — walking, running, and picking things up — which previously he struggled to do; thus, energy can be used more efficiently. In fact, his energy level is greater, and he can work and play at things for longer periods of time. Because he can do so many more things, failure at a task can easily be forgotten as he quickly turns to something else (Erikson, 1956).

Here is what Erikson thinks about the stage of initiative, while offering some pertinent observations regarding all the stages of development:

There is in every child at every stage a new miracle of vigorous unfolding, which constitutes a new hope and a new responsibility for all. Such is the sense of the pervading quality of initiative. The criteria for all these senses and qualities are the same: a crisis, more or less beset with fumbling and fear, is resolved, in that the child suddenly seems to "grow together" both in his person and in his body. He appears "more himself," more loving, relaxed and brighter in his judgment, more activated and activating. He is in free possession of a surplus of energy which permits him to forget failures quickly and to approach what seems desirable (even if it also seems uncertain and even dangerous) with undiminished and more accurate direction (1963, p. 255. © 1950, 1963 by W. W. Norton & Co., Inc.).

Following the Freudian notion of infantile sexuality, Erikson (1963) holds that the attempt at developing a sense of initiative takes on a sexual aspect, although rudimentary in character at first. A boy is supposed to become sexually interested in his mother and actively engage in primitive courting. More broadly, the boy derives pleasure from male aggressiveness and feats of conquest. He is curious, active, and intrusive. In a girl, sexual initiative turns to modes of "catching," aggressive forms of snatching, or making herself attractive and endearing. Erikson describes the sexual aspect of the striving for initiative as follows:

This then is the stage of the "castration complex," the intensified fear of finding the (now energetically erotized) genitals harmed as a punishment for the fantasies attached to their excitement. Infantile sexuality and incest taboo, castration complex and superego, all unite here to bring about that specifically human crisis during which the child must turn from an exclusive, pregenital attachment to his parents to the new process of becoming a parent, a carrier of tradition (1963, p. 256. © 1950, 1963 by W. W. Norton & Co., Inc.).

In the preceding passage, the influence of Freudian concepts and principles on Erikson's formulations is quite apparent; again it should be clear that Erikson does not modify Freud's ideas as much as he extends them. In accepting such controversial concepts as the Oedipus and castration complexes, the incest motive, and the superego, he opens himself to the same criticisms that we have applied to Freud. Nevertheless, Erikson moderates Freud's ideas to an extent, bringing them more in line with conventional principles of child development by giving a strong place during this period to both the ego and social influences.

The efforts at initiative, like the strivings for autonomy, often bring the child into collison with powerful people who can make him feel guilty for intruding and asserting himself. The child competes for and desires things which adults regard as their prerogatives—to take the mother's attention from the father, in the case of the boy; to be favored by the father, in the case of the girl; to be included in adult conversations and concerns and to be given the privileges of adult status, in the case of both. If the parents are too harsh with the child and put him down for his interference in their activities, the child will develop a sense of guilt.

The sense of initiative is greatly influenced by the development of the *superego*. The superego (which will be discussed in more detail in a later chapter) consists of two components: *conscience* (internal regulations, rules, and taboos), and the *ego ideal* (internalized images and models of acceptable and laudable conduct). It is the part of the ego which supervises and watches over the active ego. It is the moral agent of personality, reflecting the values and norms, as well as the taboos, of the culture. These are communicated in a variety of ways to the child: by parents, by other children, by institutions and agencies of the society in which the child lives. The superego has the power to produce guilt in the ego if it does not follow the dictates of the conscience or live up to the prescriptions of the ego ideal. The guilt is felt as unworthiness, dissatisfaction with self, and often depression. With the development of the superego, then, the ego begins to receive inner censorship, in contrast to the sources which it experienced during the stage of autonomy.

In the early stages of the formation of the superego, some children are all too willing to restrict and punish themselves. Pathological trends may thus develop: chronic self-depreciation, compulsive overconformity, deep and lasting resentment resulting from failure to meet standards the way others do. When the superego persists in an infantile form, it hampers the free expression of the ego; hence the development of a sense of initiative is blocked and the fullest potentials of the ego are never realized. The ego must eventually lessen the tyranny and power of the superego by becoming strong and taking over the personality.

Erikson (1963) points out that while the superego can be a serious hindrance to personality development and functioning, with the appropriate training and experience it can become an important personal asset. If development is normal, the child is quite eager to identify with the important people in his life: parents, teachers, heroes, and other models of the culture. He is ready at this stage for the beginnings of cooperative ventures, and for rudimentary productive work. Such activities can strengthen his capabilities for meeting the requirements of the next stage, when new problems will be confronted.

STAGE FOUR, SIX TO TWELVE YEARS: INDUSTRY VERSUS INFERIORITY

With a basic sense of trust, an adequate sense of autonomy, and an appropriate amount of initiative, the child enters the stage of developing industry. The fantasies and magical ideas of childhood must give way to the task of preparing for acceptable roles in society. The child becomes acquainted with the "tool" world at home and at school. Play continues, but productive work and real achievements are expected. *Skills and knowledge are to be acquired:* whether they are taught in a formal school setting or in a field situation depends on the culture, but every culture provides some arrangement for the training of children.

The child of this age might be described as *an apprentice in the art of learning the tasks of adulthood.* The training period is usually quite lengthy in civilized societies because so much is expected of the individual. There are many possible ways of living with technology, but the best educational preparation has not yet been devised; Erikson criticizes the current educational system for being an independent culture, not really in tune with the requirements of living after schooling. Many others have argued the same point. Schooling seems more to deaden and stultify creativity than to enliven it; it fits everyone into a mold, which is not suitable for modern living in a complex society.

While learning before the age of six concentrates primarily upon such basic skills as talking, walking, dressing, and eating, the grammar school years widen these skills to include productive work, independent social living, and the beginnings of personal responsibility. The child learns to win rewards and praise by making and doing things which are more than facsimiles of real achievements. Erikson (1968) holds that if all goes well during the period between six and twelve, the child will begin to develop two important virtues: *method* and *competence.* Usually he is eager to be like an adult, and if he is not stifled in his efforts he will willingly meet the demands placed upon him. But if these demands are contrary to his natural tendencies (as they often are in formal education, when, for instance, he is expected to sit attentively for long periods of time) he will rebel and resist what Maslow called "the breaking of his psychological bones" (Maslow, 1968). What happens during this period if things go wrong? Erikson tells us:

The child's danger, at this stage, lies in the sense of inadequacy and inferiority. If he despairs of his tools and skills or of his status among his tool partners, he may be discouraged from identification with them and with a section of the tool world. To lose the hope of such "industrial" association may pull him back to the more isolated, less tool-conscious familial rivalry of the Oedipal time. The child despairs of his equipment in the tool world and in anatomy and considers himself doomed to mediocrity or inadequacy. It is at this point that wider society becomes significant in its ways of admitting the child to an understanding of meaningful roles in the technology and economy. Many a child's development is disrupted when family life has failed to prepare him for school life, or when school life fails to sustain the promises of earlier stages (1963, p. 260. © 1950, 1963 by W. W. Norton & Co., Inc.).

And again: but there is another, more fundamental danger, namely, man's restriction of himself and constriction of his horizons to include only his work to which, so the book says, he has been sentenced after his expulsion from paradise. If he accepts work as his only obligation, and "what works" as his only criterion of worthwhileness, he may become the conformist and thoughtless slave of his technology and of those who are in a position to exploit it (1963, p. 261. © 1950, 1963 by W. W. Norton & Co., Inc.).

STAGE FIVE, ADOLESCENCE: IDENTITY VERSUS ROLE DIFFUSION

The "search for identity" is a commonly used expression which has become associated with Erikson's work. Erikson (1968) holds that the search for identity, although an ever-present concern throughout life, reaches a crisis point during adolescence when many significant changes in the total person, but especially in the self, take place. In the highly specialized technological society of Western cultures, the adolescent period is quite long because the preparations for independent adult status are greater than in simpler societies. The result is that the young person is caught in an identity problem: still a child yet with adult needs, still dependent yet expected to behave independently, sexually mature yet unable to satisfy his sexual needs, he does not know who he really is. In Western societies adolescence is a period of storm and turmoil. The adult world has difficulty defining the adolescent's roles, and so does the adolescent himself.

Many young persons resort to the formation of their own subculture, which is often quite different from and even antagonistic to the prevailing culture. This subculture may satisfy to some degree the adolescent's need for identity, but it does not deal with other needs which may be met only by taking on an approved role in the cultural mainstream. A political activist who believes in the equality of all men, whether they work or not, may run into difficulty meeting the requirements of life in our society if he does not engage in some kind of gainful employment. Every society sets up certain prototypes of work for both sexes, and those who deviate too much from these will encounter disapproval, censure, and even imprisonment.

It will be recalled that for Erikson ego identity is inner continuity or inner sameness; it may be taken simply as a core ego role which is acceptable to the individual and to the circle of people who are important to him. The nature of the social circle varies considerably throughout life but attains an extremely sensitive level during adolescence. Like every other aspect of personality, the search for identity follows a developmental course, with adolescence as the high point, but with another peak late in life as one faces the termination of his existence. The failure to attain a sense of identity Erikson (1963) terms *role diffusion.*

The sense of identity may be considered from a measurement point of view: it may occupy a point on a continuum from extreme role confusion at one end to a firm sense of identity at the other. In actuality, a fixed point does not describe accurately the fluid state of so complex a phenomenon as ego functioning; a better picture is a range of identity feelings which vary with both internal and external conditions.

A brief look at the history of the search for identity may help to highlight the place which this aspect of ego development holds in the growth of the child. The earliest attempts at establishing a sense of identity are based on achievement: the child is praised and rewarded for doing certain things, such as drinking from his cup, riding his bicycle alone, or doing his homework without assistance. The earliest achievements thus relate to personal management and play activities. With respect to the latter, Erikson (1968) makes the interesting point that in civilized societies such achievements have no bearing on adult work, except in a highly superficial way. Though during the stage of industry the child does learn to do many things which adults do — reading, writing, and ciphering — these accomplishments are still in the realm of training and contribute nothing to the well-being of the home. The formation of the child's sense of identity may be adversely affected: he may experience feelings of inferiority because he cannot help realizing that his play activities are just play, and that being an adult is a far more desirable status. In primitive cultures, on the other hand, the play activity of the child is integrated with the work of survival. The little boy learns to fish for fun, but his catch is eaten by the members of the family. He does not have complicated toys to play with, so tools associated with work activities are used for play.

During the adolescent years, the matter of achievement becomes highly critical, and often the young person feels that he is not much good at anything. He is judged by his achievements, and he judges himself by them. There are many areas of achievement and the standards are quite high. As a matter of fact, idealism colors much of what the young person strives for, and often his achievements fall far short of his expectations and there is disappointment and disillusionment. He may blame society, but usually he has a haunting notion that he himself is ultimately to blame. Thus achievement must enable him to find a place within his social group; he must learn how to dress and act in the definitive way which the group approves. Often the standards, although strictly maintained, are not clearly specified, and for some they are not readily discernible. These young people go through a particularly trying ordeal, experiencing rejection and censorship but remaining in the dark as to the reasons.

Erikson (1968) points out that the formation of a sense of identity in a complex industrialized society confronts the young person with other peculiar problems. The young person is bewildered; his knowledge of what is available is vague, and his opportunities for trying out different life styles are limited. Not really knowing what direction to take, he must venture along a particular path with many uncertainties and unknowns clouding his journey. There are inequities in class membership, unequal opportunities, different values, and various deviations from the mainstream culture. For example, a child growing up in a family where the only source of income is a welfare check, and in which the father has never held a steady job, surely has poor models after which to pattern his own sense of identity. From the foregoing discussion, it should be clear that the formation of a sense of identity is a highly complex process taking place over a long period, and frequently the individual is a victim of circumstances which he cannot control but which engender role diffusion and confusion.

Erikson relates the formation of a sense of identity to the necessity of selecting and successfully carrying out a vocation, but he also assigns a role to religion or philosophy of life:

Man, to take his place in society, must acquire a "conflict-free," habitual use of a dominant faculty, to be elaborated in an occupation; a limitless resource, a feedback, as it were, from the immediate exercise of this occupation, from companionship it provides, and from its tradition; and finally, an intelligible theory of the processes of life which the old atheist, eager to shock to the last, calls a religion (1968, p. 150. © 1968 by W. W. Norton & Co., Inc.).

Adolescence is the last stage of childhood. The adolescent process, however, is conclusively complete only when the individual has subordinated his childhood identifications to a new kind of identification, achieved in absorbing sociability and in competitive apprenticeship with and among his age mates. These new identifications are no longer characterized by the playfulness of childhood and the experimental zest for youth: with dire urgency they force the young individual to choices and decisions which will, with increasing immediacy, lead to commitments "for life." The task to be performed here by the young person and by his society is formidable. It necessitates, in different individuals and in different societies, great variations in duration, intensity, and ritualization of adolescence. Societies offer, as individuals require, more or less sanctioned intermediary periods between childhood and adulthood, often characterized by a combination of prolonged immaturity and provoked precocity (1968, p. 155. © 1968 by W. W. Norton & Co., Inc.).

If the process of attaining a sense of identity is successful, the individual has the conviction that he had to become the way he is, that there is no other possible way for him to be; further, he must feel that society sees him this way. Such a conviction implies that he feels integrated, at one with himself, and comfortable in relation to his physical and social surroundings (Erikson, 1968). This total sense of identity is an ideal which no one attains completely or achieves once and for always. Most people feel accepted and self-accepting in some aspects of their lives, and partially or totally rejected in others. Furthermore, personality integration is always a matter of degree; everyone has divergent trends within himself, dissociated aspects of personality which behave like separate personalities and elements which seem totally foreign. With respect to the course of development of a sense of identity, Erikson says:

From a genetic point of view, then, the process of identity formation emerges as an evolving configuration—a configuration which is gradually established by successive ego syntheses and resyntheses throughout childhood. It is a configuration gradually integrating constitutional givens, idiosyncratic libidinal needs, favored capacities, significant identifications, effective defenses, successful sublimations, and consistent roles.

The final assembly of all the converging identity elements at the end of childhood (and the abandonment of the divergent ones), appears to be a formidable task . . . (1968, p. 163. © 1968 by W. W. Norton & Co., Inc.).

In his attempts to attain a sense of identity, the youth experiences both *role confusion* and *role diffusion*, particularly toward the end of adolescence when earlier conflicts are intensified and the urgency of taking on a stable role is greatest. The adolescent "plays" with different roles, in the hope of finding one that "fits" (Erikson, 1956). The defenses of the ego during this time are quite fluid, and such role experimentation may give the impression that a serious disturbance exists in the personality, despite the fact that the only means the young person has of dealing with inner and outer stresses is the trial and error use of coping and adapting mechanisms. At this time the sense of role diffusion, or lack of identity, is the greatest; when a sense of identity is achieved, it is experienced as a sense of well-being, as Erikson points out: "An optimal sense of identity . . . is experienced . . . as a sense of psychosocial well-being. Its most obvious concomitants are a feeling of being at home in one's body, a sense of 'knowing where one is going,' and an inner assuredness of anticipated recognition from those who count" (1968, p. 165).

Role diffusion may be best understood as a reappearance, in the form of hindrances, of some of the problems encountered in growing up. The problem of basic trust, for instance, becomes in adolescence a distrust of time, a time confusion. There may be a fear of the passage of time and an uncertainty about the future.

As the adolescent approaches young adulthood, the requirements of social relationships become a necessary feature of living. Being a functional member of a group and being able to establish close affiliations with individuals of both sexes are now important tasks. The youth who does not have a firm sense of identity usually has difficulty forming both these human relationships. Because he is unclear about his own roles and changes them repeatedly, he is hard to know and understand; and because he is misunderstood, he cannot establish satisfying alliances with others. He may resort to earlier solutions to this problem; he may adopt an attitude of isolation, or he may assume a hostile, aggressive role, or he may allow himself to be dominated.

We have given more attention to the sense of identity than to any of the other psychosocial stages because this period is so crucial in the development of personality. Failure to attain a healthy sense of identity has greater adverse effects on subsequent personality growth and functioning than do the other psychosocial achievements. Erikson ascribes two highly important human virtues, devotion and fidelity, to the attainment of a healthy sense of identity. Without a firm sense of identity, a person cannot be loyal to anything or anyone. Erikson himself has much more to say about identity than any of the other achievements; in fact, he has devoted an entire book, *Identity: Youth and Crisis* (1968), to this topic.

STAGE SIX, YOUNG ADULTHOOD: INTIMACY VERSUS ISOLATION

Social interactions are significant all through life, but during young adulthood they reach a crisis point. Most people have a profound longing to relate intimately to a member of the opposite sex, and marriage is the usual means by which this need is gratified. If the basic requirement or task of a particular stage is successfully accomplished, it becomes a major source of activity and pleasure in the next stage. The adolescent who struggles with his problems of identity approaches social relationships fearfully, with more displeasure than pleasure, but if he settles his identity problems, his social interactions also improve. As a young adult he meets the challenges of social interactions with competence, genuinely enjoying his social relationships, the intimate as well as the casual ones.

Intimacy in human relationships presupposes other important achievements, and thus many are incapable of realizing it. One cannot form an intimate relationship without a basic trust in another. Then, too, an intimate relationship is built upon the secure autonomy of the parties; a person who stands on his own two feet can give more than the dependent, helpless individual who wants only to receive. A sense of industry enables the independent partner to show his love in a tangible way by competently doing things for his mate. A sense of identity provides him with a stable ego role, a healthy capacity for fidelity, and a well-defined set of values and priorities.

Erikson accepts Freud's idea that one of the marks of maturity (or what Freud called genitality) is the ability to love. To truly love requires qualities such as compassion, sympathy, empathy, identification, reciprocity, and mutuality. Compassion is the feeling of tenderness toward another and the desire to help. Sympathy means feeling pity for the other. Empathy is a feeling of sharing an experience. Identification is becoming as one with the other. Reciprocity means to take the position of the other person and accept his views and feelings ("to wear his shoes"). Mutuality means wanting what the other desires to give and giving what the other desires to receive. These are the social aspects of personality without which intimacy cannot occur.

Consider marriage as an example of an intimate relationship; if a marriage is to be successful, each partner must feel toward the other the emotions noted above. There must be mutuality and reciprocity; each must want what the other has to give, and in turn, be able to give what the other wants or needs.

Each gives up some of his own desires for the sake of the desires of the other. Compassion, sympathy, empathy, and identification serve to smooth over the rough spots and the natural differences between man and woman, as well as adding richness to the relationship. These social feelings and emotions are quite apparent in the sex act, which is but one facet of the intimacy associated with marriage. Erikson summarizes the joint participation of the partners in the sex act as follows:

Genitality consists of the capacity to develop orgastic potency which is more than the discharge of sex products in the same sense of Kinsey's "outlets." It combines the ripening of intimate sexual mutuality with full genital sensitivity and with a capacity for discharge of tension from the whole body. This is a rather concrete way of saying something about a process which we really do not yet quite understand. But the experience of the climactic mutuality of orgasm clearly provides a supreme example of the mutual regulation of complicated patterns and in some way appeases the hostilities and potential rages caused by the daily evidence of the oppositeness of male and female, of fact and fancy, of love and hate, of work and play. Such experience makes sexuality less obsessive, and sadistic control of the partner superfluous.

Before such genital maturity is reached, much of sexual life is of the self-seeking, identity-hungry kind; each partner is really trying only to reach himself. Or it remains only a kind of genital combat in which each tries to defeat the other (1968, p. 137. © 1968 by W. W. Norton & Co., Inc.).

By the term genitality, Erikson means more than a biological tension, as is evident from his description of it; it involves the total person and a complex interaction between the two partners; it brings the couple together in a way that nothing else can. Erikson (1968) believes that many aspects of masculinity are offensive to a woman, and the same applies with respect to feminine qualities for a man. Sharing genital pleasure is one means of dealing with the oppositeness in the partners; each needs the other for his needs to be satisfied.

Failure to establish satisfying intimate relationships often leaves the person with a deep sense of isolation and estrangement. While he may be able to carry on with his work and maintain some semblance of intimacy in superficial relationships, he may also experience a profound feeling of emptiness and loneliness. Most human beings seem to have a strong need for love, and an equally strong need to love. If these needs are not met, there is a haunting sense of incompleteness. Other reactions to failure in the need for intimacy include stereotyped social roles, such as always being sarcastic, always being the clown, or chronically submitting to the will of others.

In stressing the role of intimacy during young adulthood, Erikson does not say much about the other major task of this period, namely preparing for and working competently in a vocation. Everyone has the obligation to find some place in life, and this usually means some kind of acceptable work role. Perhaps Erikson believes that the need for intimacy overshadows the need for a vocation at this stage, particularly since work becomes the dominant concern of the next stage, that of generativity versus stagnation. Erikson (1968) ascribes two important virtues to the person who has successfully dealt with the problem of intimacy: affiliation (forming friendships), and love (profound concern for another).

STAGE SEVEN, MIDDLE ADULTHOOD: GENERATIVITY VERSUS STAGNATION

Freud held that along with the ability to love, the ability to work effectively is a mark of maturity. Erikson (1963) seems to agree with both requirements, love and work, and he delineated a stage of life which he terms *generativity* to describe the requirement of sustained, productive work and caring. The period is the middle years from about 25 to 45. It is usually the period of greatest productivity in life; one establishes himself in his vocation, brings up his family, and secures a favorable reputation in his community. In a group of elderly people who were asked to select the period of life which afforded them the greatest happiness, this was the period selected most often. It is the time when the individual reaches full physical, psychological, and social maturity. Vigorous functioning requires the achievements of earlier periods. One has most to give during these years, a fact quite apparent in the rearing of a family, which demands the utmost in generosity.

The care of a child demands an unqualified giving of oneself. While some parents may use their children to satisfy abnormal needs, the majority of parents do not have children for selfish reasons. Erikson makes the point that parents need children quite as much as children need parents. There are marriages in which children are not desired, and many men and women seem to do quite well without either spouse or children. The fact remains, however, that under the right conditions, having children adds a dimension to life for which there can be no substitute. There is indescribable joy in being a part of the growth of a child from infancy through adulthood. Seeing him undergoing the same stages of development as the parent adds a richness and meaning to life which cannot be had in any other way. What can substitute for the joy a father experiences when his son takes his first job? What a sense of pride a mother derives from taking her own baby to the doctor for the first time, or from enrolling him in nursery school, or witnessing his graduation from college, his marriage, his first-born child! There are many instances in a child's life which provide his parents with the deepest pleasures, but both parents need a high degree of maturity if such joys and pleasures are to be realized. There are sorrows, frustrations, and disappointments, and many parents make a terrible mess of parenthood. A clinical psychologist remarked that most parents he has dealt with disliked or hated their children. Allowing for the fact that this clinician dealt only with abnormal people in his professional work, the fact remains that among all kinds of people there is a great deal of disharmony in the parent-child relationship.

This stage of life has not been explored very extensively, and there are many questions to be answered. For instance, should the rearing of children be the primary concern of the mother? Or should the father take a more active part in directing the lives of his children? Is the home environment really the best place for rearing children? Which takes precedence, the children or the husband-wife relationship? Why do so many parents complain about their children, and children about their parents? What physical, psychological, and social changes take place during this period, and what can go wrong, and why? Why should this period, which has been reported to be the happiest, actually be so unhappy for so many?

Failure to attain generativity (taking this in the broadest sense as productivity and creativity in all spheres of life) Erikson designates *stagnation*. A sense of stagnation is a personal impoverishment. The victim may feel that life is drab and empty, that he is merely marking time and getting older without fulfilling his expectations. The person who stagnates does not effectively use what he has; he does not make his life interesting or zestful. He may become apathetic and complain of chronic fatigue, or there may be a chronic grumbling and resentment. Many homemakers complain that their lives are quite dull and dreary, that they are confined and trapped with children all day long, and that they have to do menial tasks. Many men complain that their jobs, which may have been exciting for the first two or three years, are dull and monotonous, and that life is a perpetual merry-go-round, with nothing very interesting to do. These are instances of the failure to use personal abilities to make life an ever-creative flow of experiences.

Even the most routine work can be done in a way to bring pleasure, if one uses his ingenuity. To be able to work productively and creatively requires the attainment of all the achievements of the previous stages, and it is no wonder that many people fail in the matter of generativity; they fail because they are not fully prepared to deal with their life situation during this period. It appears that the problem of the meaning of existence is one of the major concerns of our day, when existence itself is so precarious. The generative person finds meaning in utilizing his knowledge and skills for their own sake; usually he enjoys his work and does it well. Erikson (1968) attributes two very important virtues to the person who has attained generativity: production (working creatively and productively) and care (working for the benefit of others).

STAGE EIGHT, LATE ADULTHOOD: EGO INTEGRITY VERSUS DESPAIR

The eighth and last stage of life in Erikson's schema spans the years from forty-five or fifty to death. Ego integrity, which is the major task of this period, implies a full unification of personality, with the ego as the major determining force. This stage has the potential for a great deal of initiative. Its two virtues are directedness and purposiveness. Although Erikson has not really detailed this stage, it would seem to resemble Jung's idea (1964) of the individuation process and Rogers' ideas (1961) on "fully functioningness."

Lacking a clear definition, I shall point to a few constituents of this state of mind. It is the ego's accrued assurance of its proclivity for order and meaning. It is a postnarcissistic love of the human ego—not of the self—as an experience which conveys some world order and spiritual sense, no matter how dearly paid for. It is the acceptance of one's one and only life cycle as something that had to be and that, by necessity, permitted no substitutions: it thus means a new, a different love of one's parents (1963, p. 268. © 1950, 1963 by W. W. Norton & Co., Inc.).

The prospect of the termination of life results in a great deal of torment for many people. The aging person experiences difficulties ranging from physical aches and pains, to apathy and loss of interest in things and people, to feelings of uselessness, isolation, and despair—the term that Erikson uses to sum up all these problems. Erikson does not believe that the last period of life need be bleak and terrifying for everybody; it is not for those who have successfully accomplished the tasks of the preceding stages. For example, one needs trust that he has lived a good life and trust also that death will not be a terrifying experience; in fact for those who believe in an afterlife, death will be the threshold of a new kind of existence. Autonomy is needed to face the problems of this period with self-reliance. Initiative and industry are necessary to change circumstances that can be changed. The sense of identity is the most vital asset because the ego is valued as the most important facet in one's personality. Having attained rich friendships and having worked productively and successfully, a person feels no regrets or lingering desires for the things of his youth. Thus, in a sense, each achievement prepares one for the final task of life: the ability to face the prospect of death with no despair and with the feeling that one's life has been complete, lived the way it had to be.

Many elderly people report that they are not terrified at the thought of their own deaths. Having lived their lives fully, they do not long for perpetual existence on earth. It is as if each period were lived fully at the time, and no needs remained to haunt them. The feeling can be compared to consuming the various courses of a large meal: after one has eaten soup, he loses his taste for soup and wants something else. If one has had a satisfactory childhood, a successful career, a good marriage, and a family that is grown and independent, the pleasures of life have been experienced and there is not much more that a person could ask for.

It would be Pollyanna thinking to suppose that the greatest mystery of life could be faced without fear. Every new venture, no matter how well prepared one is, is approached with fear and hesitation. Consider the first day at school, the first day at work, the wedding day, the day the first child comes home, and many many more. Each major undertaking in life challenges the ego strength, and death probably presents the greatest of all challenges. However, each stage also provides the ego with greater strength and readies it for the challenges of the next stage. Those who find death totally incomprehensible and terrifying have failed in the previous accomplishments of living.

A summary of Erikson's eight stages of development is provided in Table 3–3.

CRITICAL EVALUATION

Erikson's ideas on personality development have been favorably received by some child psychologists because his concepts are amenable to testing (e.g., Mehrabian, 1968). For instance, he specifies both normal and abnormal ego development for each stage of personality growth. He details specific traits which can be translated into measurement procedures. He makes his concepts

TABLE 3–3 SUMMARY OF ERIKSON'S EIGHT STAGES OF LIFE

Success Brings	*Failure Brings*

1st Stage
Early Infancy
(birth to about one year)
(corollary to Freudian oral sensory stage)

Basic Trust and Trust in Self vs.	*Mistrust of Things, People and Self*
Result of affection and gratification of needs, mutual recognition.	Result of consistent abuse, neglect, deprivation of love; too early or harsh weaning, autistic isolation.

2nd Stage
Later Infancy
(about ages one to three years)
(corollary to Freudian muscular anal stage)

Autonomy vs.	*Shame and Doubt*
Child views self as person in his own right apart from parents but still dependent.	Feels inadequate, doubts self, curtails learning basic skills like walking, talking, wants to "hide" inadequacies.

3rd Stage
Early Childhood
(about ages four to five years)
(corollary to Freudian genital locomotor stage)

Initiative vs.	*Guilt*
Lively imagination, vigorous reality testing, imitates adults, anticipates roles.	Lacks spontaneity, infantile jealousy "castration complex," suspicious, evasive, role inhibition.

4th Stage
Middle Childhood
(about ages six to eleven years)
(corollary to Freudian latency stage)

Industry vs.	*Inferiority*
Has sense of duty and accomplishment, develops scholastic and social competencies, undertakes real tasks, puts fantasy and play in better perspective, learns world of tools, task identification.	Poor work habits, avoids strong competition, feels doomed to mediocrity; lull before the storms of puberty, may conform as slavish behavior, sense of futility.

(*Table continued on opposite page.*)

quite explicit: there is no question, for example, that trust is the first major task of the ego, that autonomy is the second major task, that initiative is the third, and so on.

Erikson's theory has also been favorably received because it covers stages beyond adolescence and allows for social determinants. But the later stages are not clearly delineated and are barely more than named. Thus the theory is incomplete. Furthermore, since Erikson's early stages closely parallel the four stages proposed by Freud, they are subject to some of the criticisms that have been applied to such Freudian concepts as the Oedipus complex and the formation of the superego. The particular order and relative importance of significant problems have perhaps engendered the most discussion; following Freud, Erikson gives the greatest weight to the early years while Allport, who

TABLE 3-3 SUMMARY OF ERIKSON'S EIGHT STAGES OF LIFE *(Continued)*

Success Brings	*Failure Brings*

5th Stage
Puberty and Adolescence
(about ages twelve to twenty years)

Ego Identity vs.	*Role Diffusion*
Temporal perspective	Time confusion
Self-certain	Self-conscious
Role experimenter	Role fixation
Apprenticeship	Work paralysis
Sexual polarization	Bisexual confusion
Leader—followership	Authority confusion
Ideological commitment	Value confusion

6th Stage
Early Adulthood

Intimacy vs.	*Isolation*
Capacity to commit self to others, "true genitability" now possible, *Lieben und Arbeiten*—"to love and to work"; "mutuality of genital orgasm."	Avoids intimacy, "character problems," promiscuous behavior; repudiates, isolates, destroys seemingly dangerous forces.

7th Stage
Middle Adulthood

Generativity vs.	*Stagnation*
Productive and creative for self and others, parental pride and pleasure, mature, enriches life, establishes and guides next generation.	Egocentric, nonproductive, early invalidism, excessive self-love, personal impoverishment, self-indulgence.

8th Stage
Late Adulthood

Integrity vs.	*Despair*
Appreciates continuity of past, present, and future; acceptance of life cycle and life style; has learned to cooperate with inevitabilities of life; "state or quality of being complete, undivided, or unbroken; entirety" (Webster's Dictionary); "death loses its sting."	Time is too short; finds no meaning in human existence, has lost faith in self and others, wants second chance at life cycle with more advantages, no feeling of world order or spiritual sense, "fear of death."

Adaptation of chart "Erikson's Eight Ages of Man's Ego Development" (data condensed from Erikson: *Childhood and Society*, 2nd Ed., Norton, 1963) in *Interpreting Personality Theories*, 2nd ed., by Ledford J. Bischof (Harper and Row, 1970).

will be discussed next, maintained instead that new dimensions of self, such as the adult conscience which normally supersedes the child's conscience, alter the personality significantly.

INSIGHTS FROM ERIKSON'S PSYCHOSOCIAL STAGES OF DEVELOPMENT

BASIC ACHIEVEMENTS

We all have difficulty setting goals and standards for ourselves. Without help from others, we may become confused about what is normal and abnormal behavior. Even the experts differ on ideal standards of development. We may look to Erikson's model of development for guidance. It will be recalled that he attempts to identify key conflict areas which everyone faces during the course of growth. Each conflict confronts the ego with a challenge, a major task to be achieved. Mastery means that the ego has gained strength, while failure means that the ego will be still more vulnerable to the increasing demands placed on it in later stages.

We can view Erikson's developmental tasks in the same way we viewed Freud's psychosexual traits: as basic lessons of living. Erikson specifies the favorable traits which are associated with successful mastery of the lessons, and he also tells us the general traits which result if they are not learned well. He sets before us the problem areas and a model for effective living. Knowing what is desirable in personality growth, we should be able to utilize the resources of the ego to promote the desirable traits. We will consider some psychological principles which may help the reader to strengthen his ego along the lines suggested by Erikson. Repeated application of the principles is the only way to benefit from them. The reader is encouraged to invent or find other principles.

Note: We will consider only five of Erikson's eight developmental conflicts because these are most directly relevant to the readers of this text. It should also be noted that the principles given to promote Erikson's ego accomplishments are not necessarily his principles.

TRUST VERSUS MISTRUST

Every one of us must live his life without having full control of his destiny. Most of us do not realize how little control we really have. Yet most of us are somehow able to function adequately because, according to Erikson, we have a basic sense of trust. It will be recalled that the basic sense of trust is apparently established early in life, which suggests that those who did not acquire it in early life may have particular problems with matters of security and self-confidence. Nevertheless, Erikson is not to be understood as proposing a fatalistic view of development—that early mistakes cannot be undone—but as implying that early mistakes make later problems more difficult to handle. Personality change, though difficult, is always possible.

There are matters in everyone's life over which there is no control, and others which can be brought under control, totally or in part. To deal with the former, we should practice the habit of suppression. In this context, suppression means the immediate cessation of thought. There are a number of good ways to get an idea out of consciousness. The present writer (1970) has developed a variety of techniques termed Verbal Satiation Therapy which are designed to reduce the intensity of unwanted ideas. Briefly, key anxiety words and phrases are repeated rapidly, or distorted through mispronunciation or by spelling or misspelling the words to oneself. The unwanted ideas may be projected on a screen or simply written out on cards to be viewed until the satiation effects occur. They may also be recorded on tape and replayed rapidly.

Another way to reduce the intensity of unwanted ideas is to have pleasant images which can be used for counteracting unpleasant thoughts. We should practice forming such images and use those which are particularly vivid. We may suppress a thought simply by thinking of something else, or we may use the technique of saying the word "stop" when we have unwanted thoughts. Some people find that engaging in vigorous activities such as running, scrubbing the floor, or taking a brisk walk serves as a distraction. The habit of not thinking about something can be cultivated as any other habit. It should be noted again that we are referring to matters over which we have no control; a habit of suppression can be highly maladaptive when we refuse to face problems which we can and should solve.

Regarding those matters over which we have control, there are times when even these should be put out of mind, as when we are merely worrying and stewing over our problems. However, Erikson holds that rationality is man's greatest tool; thus, the best way to deal with most problems is to reason out a solution and follow through with a plan of action. Once a plan is worked out, the total project should be broken up into small steps. Work inhibition is more readily overcome through small, easy steps than through large and difficult ones. Work toward the completion of a project can be promoted by a series of subgoals, each of which has a deadline. The best way to begin a term paper is to set a deadline for the selection and delineation of a topic. The next step is to take note cards, and this task also should have a deadline. The outline, the first draft, and the final draft should be scheduled with deadlines. We should keep these four words in mind when dealing with problems: project, plan, schedule, and goal.

The old adage "Take one day at a time" is relevant to promoting a sense of trust. We should cultivate the habit of dealing with problems as they arise, letting tomorrow take care of itself. We should also learn to cooperate with the inevitables; if there is a job to be done, begin with the idea that it will get done, then do something about it, even if it is only the most elementary step.

AUTONOMY VERSUS SHAME AND DOUBT

Like the sense of trust, the achievement of a basic sense of autonomy is critical early in life, and there may be a long history of self-doubt and self-depreciation. This problem of the ego involves matters of compliance and resistance to authority. The ability to cooperate and compete is directly related to feelings of autonomy.

We cannot attain a sense of autonomy simply by asserting a desire for independence. Autonomy is based upon achievements. The status of being independent of the control of parents, teachers, and other authorities may be quite appealing to a young person, but merely asserting that one is grown-up does not in itself justify the rights of independent status. Rights are always associated with obligations. To be truly autonomous, we should be able to "pay our own way." All living involves instrumental acts. We must be willing and able to work for what we seek.

Three major areas of personality growth are particularly troublesome in our society. First, intellectual judgments and decision-making relating to personal matters must be taken over from external authorities. As young people, we should learn to tolerate the frustration resulting from the conflict between our natural desire to depend on others and our equally strong urge to do things our own way. The resolution of this conflict is absolutely essential to the attainment of a sense of autonomy. Secondly, we should develop an increasing immunity against others' threats to our self-esteem. One of the most distinctively human attributes is the ability to value one's self. Yet though we can both know and value the self, we can also disparage it. Everyone has a long history of being judged by others: parents, teachers, and peers. It is quite easy to base self-esteem on the opinions of others. We surrender a great deal to another when we give him that power. The locus for self-esteem should be internal, primarily a personal matter. Thirdly, there should be a gradually increasing independence of emotional ties to others, such as childish dependence on parents. We may be overly dependent on the support of a friendship, or on the affiliation with a gang. We should never be so dependent on something or someone that the loss of the relationship would be intolerable.

Here are some suggestions that may assist the reader to achieve a sense of autonomy. First, cultivate the habit of self-respect. Your own opinion about yourself should be given the greatest weight in the choice of a course of action. Secondly, be willing to continually make resolutions, even if you break some of them. A resolution can motivate behavior in a particular direction. Thirdly, fear of making mistakes is normal, but mistakes should only be dreaded when one does not profit from them. Fourthly, be willing to work for what you get, and do not be misled by the good fortune of others to wallow in self-pity, or to excuse yourself from effort. Fifthly, consider a sense of autonomy one of your major goals in life, and like other important values, give it a high priority.

INITIATIVE VERSUS GUILT

A sense of initiative results from a balance between self-assertiveness and respect for the rights and needs of others. Self-interest requires that action be taken to meet our needs, but how far to go in the matter of self-seeking is a continuing problem for many people. The child is both rewarded and punished for self-assertive behavior; thus, one may experience a sense of guilt about himself as a worthwhile person.

A sense of initiative might be promoted by following some of the suggestions for achieving autonomy, for initiative is really an active form of autonomy. Guilt is ultimately the product of one's own conscience, and conscience can be brought under the control of the ego. Consider the following suggestions: First, examine your conscience periodically to determine if it is developing properly. Many people carry the child's conscience into adulthood. As we have noted, conscience can be either a terrible hindrance or a helpful guide to living. Proper development is not easy to specify, but conscience should become more conscious, more under control of the ego, and more flexible with age. The conscience should provide values and goals which can be worked out. Secondly, convince yourself that no one has a greater claim to life than you. A popular song expresses this sentiment well: "You are a child of the universe; you have a right to be here." Thirdly, be spontaneous, even though it may offend some people. A spontaneous person is expressing his real self, and that is the best self to be. Fourthly, learn to translate desires into instrumental behavior and to get started with the things you have to do. Take pride in the things that you have accomplished.

INDUSTRY VERSUS INFERIORITY

Every society demands that its members learn certain competencies. Every adult is expected to perform some kind of work. Certain skills are valued and win for the possessor acclaim as well as material wealth. Those who possess the prized skills in abundance are accorded high status and are encouraged to regard themselves as worthy and superior to others who do not have great skills, or who have not achieved the valued goals. The unskilled may be treated as inferior, and they are taught to regard themselves in an unfavorable light.

Here are some suggestions for promoting a sense of industry: First, consider a skill as a valuable possession and strive to acquire it. It is an important asset in the world of changing fortunes, Secondly, recognize that one of the richest sources of pleasure for a human being is the perfecting of skills. A performer may work to the day he dies to improve his skills, though even a first-rate musician, artist, or scientist seldom attains complete perfection. Thirdly, remember that not everyone can be a great pianist, artist, philosopher, or scientist, but everyone can perfect skills, even if they are modest ones. Fourthly, realize that good work on any job level is usually highly regarded. You can always count on winning favor by good work. A habit of doing a job well and promptly is a valuable asset. Fifthly, do not forget that a social skill is just as much a skill as an art or craft, and it can be learned. Social skills may make the difference between a happy and successful life, and one which is empty and stressful.

IDENTITY VERSUS ROLE CONFUSION

Adolescence is the time when the problem of self-definition, or as Erikson terms it, the identity crisis, is most critical. There is an intense need to answer the questions "Who am I?" and "What is the real me?" In early life, at home and at school, young people are exposed to an idealized presentation of values. Because of the powerful influence of authority figures and because of immature cognitive powers, they uncritically take over (introject) the values they are taught. But as symbolic processes develop (the ability to think about things and to evaluate them), they frequently re-examine their childhood values—an examination which often produces what Erikson (1956) terms a *psychosocial moratorium.*

Erikson has used the term psychosocial moratorium to designate some very puzzling behaviors in late adolescence and young adulthood. In its purest form, the moratorium is an *abrupt change* in the direction of behavior. For instance, a high school student who has indicated to everyone that he plans to attend college may decide at the last minute that he does not want to go. Instead, he may join the Peace Corps, take a job, or simply do nothing for a while. This apparently irresponsible attitude is easily misinterpreted by parents and teachers as laziness, defiance, or an out-and-out personality disorder. But Erikson has a different view; he believes it is a normal response to the stresses and strains of growing up. The psychosocial moratorium offers an unusual opportunity for close scrutiny of one's values. When the young person resumes his previous activities, he often has a better chance of achieving his goals.

For the many who cannot literally "drop out," there are more subtle reactions. A young person in college may begin drinking regularly, or turn to drugs, or join an extremist group and devote all his time to its affairs.

He may lose the incentive to do his assignments, perhaps even failing a semester, or his grades may drop sharply, or he may simply experience boredom and fatigue a good bit of the time.

The dissatisfaction and role confusion of adolescence (or of later stages) can be replaced by a sense of identity if five principles are kept in mind. First, one can best acquire a sense of identity by anticipating a period of confusion about and reexamination of accepted values (psychosocial moratorium), and then becoming intensely involved with something. A vocation, a career, a marriage, an affiliation with an organization can serve to establish an acceptable ego role.

Secondly, the young person should select his models, his interpreters of the culture, with great care. Quite often young people select models from other young people who are just as confused as they are. One way to tell a good possible model is to notice your own reactions to the person. Some people are therapeutic and produce positive emotions in those who interact with them; others produce unfavorable reactions such as depression, gloom, and bitterness (Jourard, 1963).

Thirdly, though the values of others can certainly be taken over and learned from, ultimately they must be internalized, made a matter of personal conviction. Values need to be reflected upon, to be made the object of one's highest critical and decision-making powers. They must become a part of the personality structure through the exercise of the ego's rational processes, not through automatic conditioning and unconscious mechanisms. An essential ingredient of the sense of identity is the formation of an adult conscience, as contrasted with the authoritarian conscience of a child (Allport, 1961; Erikson, 1968).

Fourthly, one should use his intellectual abilities to become increasingly aware of himself. He should be able to describe his conception of himself. An adult can usually describe himself more completely and accurately than a child, but many people never achieve self-knowledge (Schachtel, 1962).

Fifthly, fatigue, boredom, inability to work, and uncertainty about goals are products of identity confusion. Warring elements within the personality create a dissipation of energy. As one does establish a sense of identity, he begins to function more efficiently.

SUMMARY

1.   Erikson builds on Freud's psychosexual stages, but with an emphasis on the social determinants of personality growth.

2.   Erikson holds that major conflicts in early life are only partly caused by the frustration of the sex instincts. Many conflicts result from the clash between the child's needs and desires and the expectations and limitations of his culture.

3.   Erikson does not view the ego as the helpless servant of basic drives or the puppet of an all-powerful environment, but rather as an agency within personality which mediates between and coordinates the needs of the organism with the demands of the environment.

4.   Erikson divides life cycles into eight stages, with each stage confronting

the individual with a major developmental task. The eight stages are basic trust versus mistrust, autonomy versus shame and doubt, initiative versus guilt, industry versus inferiority, identity versus role diffusion, intimacy versus isolation, generativity versus stagnation, and ego-integrity versus despair.

5. Each of these stages presents the individual with a developmental crisis—a turning point in life when a new problem must be confronted and mastered. Mastery adds a dimension of increased strength to the ego, while failure makes it more vulnerable.

SUGGESTED READINGS

Erikson, Erik H. Young Man Luther: A Study in Psychoanalysis and History. New York: W. W. Norton and Company, 1962.
  A psychohistorical analysis of a noteworthy religious figure.

Childhood and Society, 2nd ed. New York: W. W. Norton and Company, 1963.
  Erikson's first book—a classic. He introduces the eight stages of life, along with his concept that the "identity crisis" of the young has become a national concern.

Insight and Responsibility. New York: W. W. Norton and Company, 1964.
  A collection of Erikson's essays.

The Challenge of Youth. Garden City, New York: Doubleday—Anchor, 1965.
  Erikson discusses fidelity and diversity in youth.

Identity, Youth, and Crisis. New York: W. W. Norton and Company, 1968.
  In this book Erikson again takes up the eight stages of life, applying many of his concepts to ethnic and social groups.

Evans, R. I. Dialogue with Erik Erikson. New York: Harper and Row, 1967.
  Erikson talks about his theory and about some misinterpretations of his work.

REFERENCES

Allport, G. W. Pattern and Growth in Personality. New York: Holt, Rinehart and Winston, 1961.
Bischof, L. J. Interpreting Personality Theories. New York: Harper and Row, 1970.
Chomsky, N. Language and Mind. New York: Harcourt Brace Jovanovich, 1968.
DiCaprio, N. S. Essentials of verbal satiation therapy: A learning theory based behavior therapy. J. Counsel. Psychol. 17:419–24, 1970.
Erikson, E. H. Ego identity and the psychosocial moratorium. In Witmer, H., and Kotinsky, R., eds., New Perspective for Research. Washington: U. S. Department of Health, Education and Welfare, 1956. Pp. 1–23.
Erikson, E. H. Identity and the life cycle. Psychol. Issues 1:18–164, 1959.
Erikson, E. H. Childhood and Society, 2nd ed. New York: W. W. Norton and Company, 1963.
Erikson, E. H. Youth and the life cycle. In Hamachek, D. E., ed., The Self in Growth, Teaching, and Learning: Selected Readings. Englewood Cliffs, New Jersey: Prentice-Hall, 1965. Pp. 325–37.
Erikson, E. H. Identity: Youth and Crisis. New York: W. W. Norton and Company, 1968.
Fromm, E. Man for Himself. New York: Holt, Rinehart and Winston, 1947.
Jourard, S. M. Personal Adjustment, 2nd ed. New York: The Macmillan Company, 1963.
Jung, C. G. Man and His Symbols. New York: Doubleday and Company, 1964.
Maslow, A. H. Toward a Psychology of Being. Princeton: Van Nostrand, 1968.
Mehrabian, A. An Analysis of Personality Theories. Englewood Cliffs, New Jersey: Prentice-Hall, 1968.
Rogers, C. R. On Becoming a Person. Boston: Houghton Mifflin, 1961.
Schachtel, E. G. On alienated concepts of identity. In Josephson, E., and Josephson, M., eds., Man Alone: Alienation in Modern Society. New York: Dell, 1962. Pp. 73–83.

CHAPTER 4

Child Versus Adult Personality

Gordon W. Allport

Gordon W. Allport (1897–1967)

BIOGRAPHY AND OVERVIEW

From the beginning of his professional career, Gordon Allport was daring enough to follow his own line of thinking in psychology. While other psychologists were studying man with methods and concepts used for the study of animal behavior, Allport held strictly to the view that man alone is the proper object of psychology. For this reason he has been termed a humanistic psychologist, although the term is not used in a flattering sense by some of his detractors. Allport was equally insistent on a strict differentiation between normal and abnormal, between mechanical and living systems, and (of special relevance to this chapter) between child and adult. He held that the concepts and principles which explain child behavior cannot be applied to the adult personality.

Allport reacted against a strong emphasis on the all-powerful role of the unconscious in the life of the normal person. He held that the normal person knows pretty well what he is doing and what he wants to do. His study was directed to the unique individual. For Allport (1961), *the psychology of personality is the science of the individual case.* While the main thrust in psychology was to discover principles of behavior common to all mankind, or at least to a definable group of people, he held that each person is highly unique and can be understood only through discovery of the principles of his own behavior. Allport did of course accept general behavior principles as a valuable aid, but the individual was to be the object of direct study, so that the psychologist might discover how these principles applied to him, if they did at all.

Allport was born in 1897 in Indiana but grew up in Cleveland, Ohio. He did his undergraduate work at Harvard, not in psychology but in philosophy and economics, receiving his B.A. in 1919. He then went to Robert College in Istanbul to teach sociology and English. He returned to Harvard to complete a Ph.D. in psychology in 1922. During the next two years he studied in several famous European universities and during that time visited with Sigmund Freud. Though he later taught at several American colleges, he was at Harvard from 1930 until his death in 1967.

Allport was primarily a college teacher but his activities were wide and varied. He wrote about a dozen books, many research papers, reviews, introductions for the works of others, and monographs on specialized topics. His style of writing is a delight to read: he writes clearly, concisely, and above all, with the intent to communicate. A beginning student of personality would do well to begin his study with Allport.

In this chapter we will consider the developmental views of one of the pioneers of humanistic psychology. Allport examined the major dimensions of personality and showed the sharp differences between the model of the child and the model of the adult. He accepts the importance of principles of *drive-related learning* (such as conditioning) for the child, but he finds these highly inadequate for the adult, for whom cognitive and personally relevant learning is more important. Another striking difference which Allport sees between the adult and the child is in the integrity of the *proprium,* or self, which attains its full development only in early adulthood. He delineates seven aspects of the proprium which we will discuss in the next section.

In addition to significant changes in the self, Allport posits striking changes in cognitive and motivational functions. While the major motivating determinants in a child are unlearned drives, with development, intentions which are products of learning become the major motivating forces. Another important explanatory concept associated with Allport is the principle of *functional autonomy* This principle is an attempt to account for the radical shift in motivation which takes place if personality development is normal: the motives of the adult are of a different order from those of the child. A fifth major Allportian concept, that of the *trait* or personal disposition, also explains the differences between the child and the adult personality. With personality development, personal dispositions increase in number, in complexity, and in relationship to one another. A sixth major point is his distinction between the child and the adult conscience. If development is normal, there is a significant modification in conscience, according to Allport: the "ought" conscience of the adult is totally different from the "must" conscience of the child.

THE DEVELOPMENT OF SELF

Because personality is so complex there are a number of ways in which its growth and development may be viewed. We might focus upon the development of needs related to significant zones of the body—oral, anal, phallic, and genital — as do the psychoanalysts. We might view the developing personality with respect to success or failure in achieving the dimensions of ego strength associated with stages of development, as does Erikson. We might follow the development of cognition, as does Piaget. Other approaches include studying the development of competence (White, 1948), and relating skills with growth stages (Havighurst, 1953) and with increasing social maturity (the Vineland Scales, Doll, 1965). We might, of course, take any dimension of personality, such as emotion, perception, or cognition, and study the changes that take place, specifying what is normal and deviant, and so on. Personality psychologists, because of their interest in the integrated functioning of the single individual, and their belief that all aspects of personality are interactive in development, have in general concentrated on global approaches rather than on specific dimensions. One of the most challenging of the global approaches is the study of the evolution of the self. Gordon Allport has done more with this topic than any other personality theorist, but he also considers the changes which take place in other specific dimensions of personality: learning, cognition, motivation. We will begin by considering his views on the various ways in which the self is experienced, describing some characteristics of each life period associated with the self-experiences. Then we will take up his other developmental concepts.

THE PROBLEM OF THE SELF

The concept of the self has created many difficulties for the psychologist who wishes to follow the concepts and methods of science in his study of man (Wylie, 1968). Why the self should be such a problem, so much so in fact that many psychologists have even denied its existence, is an extremely puzzling phenomenon to Allport. The subjective experiences of self cannot be doubted: they are existential facts. Allport holds that to question their existence is absurd; to inquire into their genesis, their development, and their various roles in personality can promote fruitful scientific knowledge. To deny the existence of the self because of the difficulties encountered in its study is contrary to the spirit of inquiry which has led to so much progress in the various departments of science. But why should the notion of self as a determining factor in personality present so many difficulties? The problem is that once the self has developed, it becomes a source of spontaneous activity and control which appears to mediate between antecedent conditions and behavior. In other words, the major problem is that the self seems to be a primary cause of behavior, different from other causes. Whatever the problems are, Allport believes that we should acknowledge the self as the central core of personality.

In doing away with the self, some psychologists have adopted what Allport calls a quasi-mechanical explanation of behavior. For example, they have defined learning as the formation of links or connections between stimuli and responses. The self does not play a part in the process. One simply sets up certain conditions, and learning must take place. But to Allport this is not the case: he believes (1961) that several people, similar in learning ability, may be exposed to the same conditions and demonstrate a striking difference in actual absorption of knowledge. What is learned is affected greatly by the degree of relevance of the material to the self. One may read over a poem a hundred times, but without the intent to learn, the poem will not be memorized. As we shall see, intentions constitute significant aspects of the self. Mere exposure, or even many repetitions, does not produce mechanical learning. Learning is influenced by attention, concentration, motivation, perceived value: factors which are related to the self.

PASSIVE ATTENDING, TASK INVOLVEMENT, EGO INVOLVEMENT

Consider the operation of the self in the following example. Suppose you were singing Christmas carols with a group of your friends, and one of them jokingly remarked that your singing was pretty awful. If you do not value your singing talent very highly, the remark would be considered humorous, and your sense of pride would not be called into play. But if you secretly nourish the idea that you are and might someday be recognized as a great singer, your self would be greatly affected. Self-relevance is a significant variable which must be taken into account to understand learning, motivation, development, and practically everything else in personality. The greatest threats are those which are directed toward the self. The best way to insult a person is to criticize his self, particularly in matters of social effectiveness and roles.

In analyzing the role of activity in learning, Allport (1961) notes that *attention,* which is in part determined by the self, is a necessary condition for learning. Attending is an activity with both cognitive and conative elements. Passive attending is not as effective in promoting learning as what Allport calls *task involvement*—active participation in the learning of the task. Learning is facilitated by such active participation: if one reconstructs or rehearses material during and after learning, the material will be learned with greater understanding and retention. A more complete participation in the learning process—deliberate memorizing, taking notes, rephrasing the ideas in one's own language—enhances the learning significantly. Thus while task involvement is much more conducive to learning than is passive involvement, because the person is participating more fully, *self-involvement* is more effective still.

Ego-involved participation may be considered participation based on interest. Interests bring into play the deepest levels of motivation. A student may be ego-involved in learning a foreign language because he is corresponding with a pen-pal who knows the language. Another student may devote the same amount of time to studying, but with only superficial ego involvement: because he is learning just to pass the course, he has little sense of purpose and does not learn well. In ego-involved learning, the outcome of the learning meets an important need and the learning is instrumental in attaining the goal. Participation without ego involvement does not call into play motives of the self. Thus the method of learning, though important in facilitating learning, does not tell the whole story: more crucial is the *type* of involvement.

The popular adage "Where there is a will there is a way" supports the case for ego involvement. One can see this principle in many areas of life. The boy who is failing the sixth grade because he cannot remember his spelling words or his history dates knows the batting average of every baseball player, a feat that would stagger his teacher. The teen-age girl who cannot even remember the homework assignment, let alone have enough motivation to do it, can learn the words to the latest hit song after only one hearing. Many high school boys are accused of being remarkably lazy or unmotivated, yet the problem is rather that they are motivated in different ways from those expected by their parents and teachers. They may not be ego-involved by the subjects or methods taught in school, but let them find a job where they can become ego-involved and the motivation factor will soon be evident. Many apparent high school failures later turn into vocational successes (McClelland, 1973).

When the self is "switched on," then the total relation between the individual and his activities is different: more intense, more significant, and more consequential. If the self exerts such influence on personality, it cannot be ignored simply because its study presents some problems. Better knowledge of the self may help to solve some of these problems. The self is highly complex when it is fully developed; tracing this development should foster understanding.

Allport delineates at least seven different self-experiences, each maturing at a different period during the first 20 years of life. These are: (1) bodily self, (2) self-identity, (3) self-extension, (4) self-image, (5) self-esteem, (6) self as rational coper, and (7) propriate strivings. Yet he cautions that the self should not be equated with the whole of personality; in fact, it is not even as broad as consciousness. At times it does not occupy the foreground of attention, as when one is so absorbed in a task that he loses his sense of self and is temporarily unconcerned with pride, conscience, and identity. At other times, consciousness of self may be extremely acute. The teenager at his first dance may feel painfully aware of himself: he notices everything he says and does; he worries about his appearance and manners. Ordinarily, however, the self is not so prominent.

SELF-EXPERIENCES

It should be understood that when Allport uses the term *self*, he refers to experiences of the self (the self as known and felt), not the self as agent or knower. As a matter of fact, he has invented a new term to stand for self-experiences, the *proprium*, which he distinguishes from the self, traditionally considered the active agent in personality (Allport, 1961).

Before his self begins to develop, however, the child must pass through the *sensorimotor stage,* which covers approximately the first 18 months of life. During this period, experiences "happen" to him. No mediational process intervenes between sensory inputs and response outputs. His behavior is controlled by impulses on the one hand and external stimuli on the other. He is stimulus bound, unable to interpose an evaluational process between an impulse or an attractive stimulus and reaction to them. The self does not yet play a part in his behavior.

1. The Bodily Self

Recurring organic sensations (which the infant perceives as belonging to himself when his memory has developed to a certain level), as well as frustrating encounters with objects, eventually lead to the formation of a sense of *me* as distinct from other things: this is the bodily self (Allport, 1961). It is not the total self because it is constituted only of sensations of the body. Under normal circumstances the bodily self is not experienced, but under certain conditions such as illness or injury it stands out. Some experiments on the effects of reduced sensory stimulation, which even produced psychotic-like states, indicate the vital role that the continuing flow of bodily sensations plays in normal functioning. The bodily self becomes salient during the growth period, when the child is quite alert to the changes in his own body. He may feel inferior because he is smaller, or weaker, or larger than others.

When sexual concerns become acute, they are accompanied by an increased attention to appearance, and this of course includes the bodily self. Many young people view themselves as puny, clumsy, fat, ugly, or the like. One young woman related the following experience to a counselor. At a dance she attended, most of the students were freshmen in college, and there was a marked timidity among the young men to ask girls to dance. The men congregated on one side and the girls on the other. Gradually some of the men began to come over to the girls' side and single out the most attractive ones. "They would look you over like you were a side of beef," the young woman remarked. She was quite large and felt that she was unattractive and cowlike. Rather than being an inconspicuous personality underpinning, her sense of bodily self was an ever-present torment. She was always aware of her "ugly me," and it created a serious disturbance in both her self-experiences and her interpersonal relationships. Because she felt physically unattractive, she drew the unhappy conclusion that she was a worthless person.

2. Self-Identity

Different from the bodily self is the sense of self-identity, the awareness of continuity or inner sameness (Allport, 1961). It is the awareness of the self as the core of personality. In other words, self-identity involves the sense of self which is ordinarily described as the "I," the ego. Despite the many changes which take place from infancy to old age, there is a perception of continuity.

When one awakens in the morning he is immediately aware of his identity, as the same person who went to bed. These observations may seem rather obvious, but the attainment of the sense of identity, as Erikson has so ably portrayed, is a difficult matter indeed. Identity is acquired gradually with many hazards, and some never have a firm sense of it.

Assigning a name to a child establishes a point of reference. Furthermore, holding him responsible for what he does — rewarding and punishing certain behaviors — fosters the experience of being an active agent. The child soon learns that his parents and siblings and everyone else for that matter have names and that they too are accountable for their conduct. He learns various pronouns which further delineate the self-identity. But because the sense of identity is unstable in the child, his grasp of these pronouns is at first quite tenuous. He may on occasion refer to himself by the pronouns "he" and "me" instead of "I," or he may take on the identity of an animal, and even become angry if others do not accept him as such. Allport holds that the "I" is more strongly configurated in Western cultures because such conditions as competition, striving to be superior, and personal responsibility for one's fate are imposed on the growing child. In other cultures individual identity is not so sharply experienced. The individual is a more integral part of his social group: his tribe, his clan, his family. The respect for individual identity is also reflected in many cultures in the strict laws and severe penalties attendant upon such practices as detraction and calumny.

3. Self-Esteem

As the sense of identity begins to take shape, a new self-experience becomes apparent during the second or third year of life: self-esteem (Allport, 1961). It is manifested in the efforts of the child to become acquainted with his surroundings, and may be equated with pride. When a child struggles valiantly to get something off the table and fails repeatedly, he may express his disappointment in crying, but success when it comes is a great event, and he may exclaim with laughter and glee. He tells everyone he meets of his feat and is willing to demonstrate it again and again.

Allport holds that negativism in the child is one of the earliest manifestations of self-esteem. As the child asserts himself effectively, he develops a positive self-valuation. Allport (1937) states that about 50 per cent of children in our culture display negativistic behavior from about 18 months until the age of four, although in some negativism in one form or another continues throughout life. The child makes a great discovery when he learns to say "no"; he finds a means of asserting his ego. Rewards and punishments may fail to modify his behavior because this need for ego assertion now outweighs the consideration of consequences. Thus, although a child is consistently praised and rewarded for certain behaviors and criticized and punished for others, he may persist in following his own line of activity, irrespective of what his parents or teachers do. This point is quite significant in child rearing and has too often been overlooked. The self-righteous grandmother who is amazed and horrified by the negativistic behavior of her grandchildren has forgotten that her own children displayed the same behavior. She finds fault with her daughter for allowing this kind of behavior to occur because she does not realize that a certain amount of negativism is a necessary condition for the development of a healthy self-esteem. Too much smothering or subjugation of the child's will can permanently hamper both his initiative and his pride in his accomplishments.

4. Self-Extension

Between the ages of four and six, two other dimensions of self-experience are prominent: self-extension and self-image (Allport, 1961). Self-extension is what a person values. For healthy people, it embraces a wide range of objects and people and its scope generally increases with age. One of the earliest manifestations of self-extension is ownership; a child may learn early by hard experience what is his and what is his parents'. If there are several children in the family, he must also learn that he cannot have all the toys, because some belong to his brother or sister. Another factor that fosters self-extension is the discrimination between significant people and the mass of mankind. The child of three or four begins to learn that his parents and relatives are related to him in a way that others are not. This process is aided by the special favors which family members bestow on him. With age the child's interests broaden to include his football team, his church, the welfare of his city and his country. In fact, we can learn a great deal about a person from a knowledge of his extended self: as Allport points out, "A man is what he loves" (Allport, 1961, p. 122).

The child of four to six is quite egocentric; he perceives and interprets the events of his world from his own frame of reference. He thinks the sun follows him, or that the store should be open on Sunday because he wants to get a toy, or that other people experience what he is experiencing, so he does not have to explain what is going on in his subjective world. Some people never outgrow this early egocentric orientation, and their friendships are characterized by a one-sided expectation: to receive without giving, to be understood without understanding. A major contributor to such developmental failure is pampering the child by catering to his whims. If the world revolves about the child and exists only to serve his needs, then the naturally primitive egocentric self will not have the opportunity to incorporate the concerns of others. Egocentric self-extensions are signs of immaturity which need to be replaced by what Allport (1961) terms *reciprocity*. Reciprocity means taking the point of view of another, recognizing its legitimacy and value, and accepting his right to hold it. More will be said on this point when we consider Allport's ideas on maturity.

5. Self-Image

The self-image refers to the image of the total personality, including the bodily self and the sense of identity. Roughly, it may be taken as one's self-conception. In this respect it differs from self-identity, which refers to the self or ego exclusively. Yet like self-identity, self-image is to a great extent the product of the roles in which the child is cast. If he happens to be small and weak he may be treated as if he were an invalid. Gradually he will form a self-image which corresponds to the role expectations of significant others: he will begin to think of himself as physically inadequate and helpless. Sometimes the formation of an unfavorable self-image is unavoidable. If a child has a physical impairment, he will perceive differences when he compares himself with his schoolmates. Other children may of course treat him with scorn and rejection, and the fact that he cannot compete on the same level will also affect his self-image.

Like other aspects of the self, the self-image is a slowly evolving process. At first it is vague and ill defined, having no elements of what one wants to be or should be — no notion of a perfected self. But as conscience becomes a salient feature of personality, and as the child begins to acquire the capacity to project into the future, the self-image broadens to include not only an approximate image of the real self, but also images of potential selves. There may be a failure in development of these aspects of self. One may have only vague notions of what he is, what he wants to be, or what he should be, and as a result, his orientation to life may lack direction. His growth will be limited, for one cannot change unless he has some ideal self-image as a goal. As we shall see when we discuss the "must" versus "ought" conscience, failure in development of the self-image can result in a protraction of the childhood conscience into adulthood.

6. The Self As Rational Coper

Between the ages of six and twelve, the child becomes aware of his growing intellectual powers. He begins to know and sense that he can solve problems, and that some children are better at it than he is. While in school, of course, his efforts at certain intellectual tasks are either rewarded or punished, and this factor helps to highlight his growing awareness of the ego as an active problem-solving agency.

During this period the child is fond of word games, puzzles, codes, and riddles. He forms relationships outside the home with other children his age, and there is a continual testing of skills, including intellectual ones.

Two trends which often compete with each other are active during this period: the child needs to test and assert his ego but he also needs the support which comes from conformity. It is a moralistic and legalistic period in which rules acquire sacred power over the child (Allport, 1961). Children in Western cultures have a penchant for following prescriptions as a result of identification with authorities, including those at home and at school, but especially those in their peer group. The child does not want to be different from others he respects, and he is not yet ready to question the authorities in his life, as he does after age twelve. But he begins nevertheless to sense his own rational powers, which will be pressed into service during adolescence when he first critically examines his inherited beliefs and values. It should be noted that self-identity is an awareness of the self as an object and subject of experiences, whereas a sense of self as rational coper is the experience of self as an active agent.

In growing up, every child encounters situations in which others are superior to him, yet many people appear capable of maintaining a healthy self-regard. This problem has not been studied extensively, but it would seem that continual belittlement of the child by the significant people in his life could engender a profound sense of inferiority involving several aspects of the self. If the parents treat the child as though he were clumsy and inept, or show no regard at all for his rights, he may acquire a sense of inadequacy which has little to do with his actual ability. Many people whom the world considers successful feel terribly inferior, belittling their accomplishments because they either set impossibly high standards for themselves or always compare themselves unfavorably with others. The mature person is able to live with the superiorities of others without suffering inferiority feelings, and his aspirations are in harmony with his achievements. Why should someone else's superiorities affect an individual's appraisal of himself? This occurs for many reasons, not the least of which is our society's tremendous stress on competition and winning, and on being better than anyone else. These of course are cultural products, not inherent to man. At any rate, the awareness of self as a rational coper is a significant self-experience which can contribute, depending on the circumstances, either to the enrichment of self or to its impoverishment.

7. Propriate Striving

As we follow development from age twelve on, we of course encounter the second greatest period of change, adolescence. During this period a new dimension of self-experience emerges; the projection of goals and long-term objectives. Allport (1961) calls this aspect of the self *propriate striving*; a term he uses to indicate that all aspects of self are involved in the process of striving for goals—bodily self, self-identity, self-extension, self-image, and self as rational coper. As the individual attains adult status, he must take over more and more of his own affairs. He is held responsible for choosing a vocation, for selecting a marital partner, and in general, for working out a life plan. In order to do these things, he must consider the future. He must try to work out goals on the basis of current potentialities, interest, and available facilities.

"Must" Versus "Ought" Conscience. A significant aspect of propriate functioning is the growth and operation of conscience. Conscience may be thought of as an internal indicator of right and wrong conduct which becomes active when behavior violates accepted standards or values. The values may be imposed by others, by what Fromm (1947) calls the authoritarian conscience and Allport (1961) the "must" conscience; or they may arise from the developed self, from what Fromm calls the humanistic conscience and Allport the "ought" conscience. The degree to which the self is developed is one of the factors determining whether the individual is governed by a "must" or by an "ought" conscience. The growing child is at first controlled largely by external authorities who have the power to punish and reward behavior. These authorities determine the standards which the child must meet. His fear of rejection and punishment makes him obey. As he begins to take over his own life, that is, as the proprium develops and propriate strivings come to the fore, he begins to set his own standards. He formulates what Allport terms a "preferred style of life" which greatly influences his goals and plans. Conscience is then a matter of success or failure in fulfilling the goals. He does many things because they will fulfill his ambitions, and he also avoids doing certain things because they distract him from his objectives. When he slips, he feels guilty. There are still "musts" in addition to "oughts," but now they become matters of rational consideration: I must go to class rather than sleep if I want to become a lawyer, or a doctor, or whatever. The anticipated consequences, rather than fear, determine behavior: the gas tank *must* be filled or the consequences are uncomfortable.

Whether a person remains on the level of the "must" conscience, dominated and controlled by fear, or attains the level of the "ought" conscience, motivated by long term objectives and the preferred style of life, depends upon the nature of his self-development, which in turn depends upon many conditions. There is not an automatic change from the "must" to the "ought" con-

TABLE 4-1   EVOLVING SENSE OF SELF

Self-Experience	Age	Identifying Characteristics
1. Bodily self	From 18 months	Sense of "bodily" me Configuration of bodily sensations Normally not experienced
2. Self-identity	From 18 months	Awareness of continuity: inner sameness Self as core of personality The "I": ego
3. Self-esteem	From 2 to 3 years	Equated with pride: self-love Capable of self-evaluation Basic influence in life style Manifested by negativism, egoism
4. Self-extension	From 4 to 6 years	Sense of ownership: possession Expands with age Equation of "me" and "mine"

5. Self-image	From 6 to 12 years	Early Form:
		    Conception of total person
		    Conception of one's self
		Mature Form:
		    Potential self: What one wants to be
		                    What one should be

6. Rational coper	From 6 to 12 years	Sense of self as a doer and problem solver Sense of competence Submission to external rules and regulations
7. Propriate striving	From 12 years	Projection of stable goals and long-term objectives Beginnings of "ought" conscience Formulation of personal values

science, and many people remain stuck with the "must" conscience of childhood, never enjoying the benefits which the "ought" conscience confers
(Kohlberg, 1969).

To sum up: Allport views the self as a complex aspect of personality, gradually evolving and exerting a greater and greater influence over behavior. In
the adult, if it has developed normally, it is the major internal or subjective
source of behavior. Usually it is not experienced unless there is something
wrong. A single behavioral act, however, may involve all the various self-experiences. During special circumstances, such as mental stress or physical suffering, the self is experienced quite acutely. Allport highlights this point by an
example:

> Although the seven aspects of the proprium do seem to evolve at successive stages of
> life, I do not mean to imply that they function separately. In our daily experience sev-
> eral, or even all aspects coexist. Suppose you are facing a difficult and critical examina-
> tion. No doubt you are aware of your high pulse rate and of the butterflies in your
> stomach (bodily self); also the significance of the exam in terms of your past and future
> (self-identity); of your prideful involvement (self-esteem); of what success or failure
> may mean to your family (self-extension); of your hopes and aspirations (self-image);
> of your role as the solver of problems on the examination (rational agent); and of the
> relevance of the whole situation to your long range goals (propriate striving). The
> propriate functions are the foundations of consistency within personality—they make
> for stable attitudes, intentions, and evaluations (Allport, 1961, p. 137).

ALLPORT'S DEVELOPMENTAL PRINCIPLES

Allport accepts such conventional developmental concepts and principles as
heredity, physique, temperament, and intelligence. He considers these the
underpinnings of personality. Once they attain their mature status, they
remain personality constants throughout life. He also accepts maturation as a
continuing factor: as a result of growth activity, many changes occur which
are not dependent, except in a supportive way, on environmental forces. We
will now consider some of Allport's more unique developmental principles:
functional autonomy, personal dispositions, principles of learning, and intentions.

COGNITIVE AND PERSONAL LEARNING VERSUS
CONDITIONING

Early in life, *cognitive and perceptual sets* (predispositions to perceive or respond
in a certain way) are formed and begin to play a significant role in the child's
visions of the world. By the time adulthood is attained, the perceptual and
cognitive sets have become important determining tendencies which intervene between the environment and personal reactions to it. A child may develop early in life a pessimistic outlook and interpret everything in the light of
this general set. If we arrange situations to promote the learning of principles

of mental health through conditioning, we might find that he still responds primarily on the basis of his pessimistic set. A mother's promise may fail to promote learning in another child because he has a cognitive set of expecting his mother not to follow through. Thus the learning which is predicted by the reinforcement theorist does not occur because the cognitive set may so alter the nature of the reinforcement that it is no longer reinforcing for the individual.

Insight is another cognitive process which plays an increasing role in the development of the child. The term "insight" here means more than the psychiatric sense of self-awareness or knowledge of one's own motives. *Cognitive insight* is *the formation of a conceptual representation of an event.* The growing child attempts to cognize or make some meaning of the events about him. Allport cites the case of a little girl of three who was found by her mother turning on the gas cock of the kitchen stove. The mother mildly slapped the child's hand as she said, "No, you mustn't do that." According to principles of conditioning, the sight of the stove should thereafter be a sufficient condition to cause the child to avoid it. If a neutral stimulus occurs at the same time as a painful stimulus, the neutral stimulus acquires some of the properties of the painful stimulus. Thus, the pain in this instance should be transferred to the neutral stimulus, the sight of the stove, which originally attracted the little girl. The next day, however, the mother again observed the child playing with the gas cock. When she approached her daughter, the girl put out her hand to be slapped. Apparently, she had put together a sequence of events; she was cognitively structuring incoming information, rather than simply responding in a quasi-mechanical manner as specified by principles of conditioning. Instead of being a passive recipient of circumstances, she was actively organizing the impressions she received. Generally, this activity increases with age. One continuously cognizes his world within a subjective frame of reference.

Three basic orientations characterize the individual's progress from childhood to adulthood, Allport believes (1955). At first, the child is almost totally dependent on his environment; then, gradually, as his psychological abilities mature and a great deal of learning takes place, he grows in autonomy and independence. Finally, having reached adulthood, he takes responsibility for his own life. These changes are characterized by an increase in cognitive activities, such as insight.

INTENTION

Some of Allport's major ideas are brought out by his use of the term *intention* to signify motivation which is usually conscious, contemporary, blended with cognition, and future-oriented. For Allport, intention is roughly synonymous with interest. "Intention is a much-neglected form of motivation, but one of central importance for the understanding of personality. It enables us to overcome the opposing of motive and thought. Like all motives, intention refers to what the individual is trying to do. There are, to be sure, immediate and short-run intentions (getting a glass of water, brushing off a fly, satisfying any drive); but the term has particular value in pointing to the long-range dispositions in personality (Allport, 1961, p. 223).

Allport's concept of intention brings out some important features of motivation: (1) The major motivating and cognitive aspects of life are consciously experienced. (2) The cognitive and emotive factors are fused into an integral unit. (3) Although the intention exists in the present it has future orientation: we can learn about the type of future the person is trying to bring about. Most people do not continually relive the past but rather work toward goals that may be realized in the future. (4) Intention implies the persistence of tension, which is a natural condition of all long-term motives. The distant goal exerts enough tension to keep the person at his task, or training, or whatever it takes to attain it. (5) Intentions are focal points in the personality which bring many subordinate motives together. Identifying major intentions helps us to understand many subsidiary trends.

Intentions Versus Drives

As applied to adult motivation, then, the concept of intention implies a close relationship between the present and the future. Intentions are an important part of an individual's present life style and self-image, but they point also to his future self, to the more perfect and ideal self which he hopes ultimately to be. Allport holds that knowledge of a person's intentions provides insights which other aspects of his personality do not. We may know a person's aptitudes, but without knowing his intentions we have no way of knowing which of those aptitudes he is going to develop. Since no one employs and perfects all of his potentialities (some are preferred over others) we cannot know which are propriate and which are not simply by knowing aptitudes.

It is generally agreed that radical changes in cognition and motivation occur as the child grows up, but theorists disagree considerably as to the nature of these processes. They also differ on the extent to which past or early motives are active in present behavior, on the degree of consciousness involved in motivation, on the relation of present motives to past ones, and on the role of the future in cognition and motivation. Thus some psychologists, such as Henry Murray (1938), have attempted to approach personality through need motivation: if we know basic needs we can comprehend and predict behavior. Others, rejecting the future orientation of intention theory in favor of a theory which stresses the influence of the past upon the present, have tried to reduce all motivation, both in the child and in the adult, to basic physiological drives.

Yet needs, like abilities, are often subordinated to intentions. A student may have a strong need to marry, but if he also has the intention of finishing college, the intention will override the need. We might argue that intention is equivalent to need, but Allport disagrees because he believes that intention includes cognitive as well as conative elements. He also finds the drive theory one-sided, with too much emphasis on tension reduction. In man, when a physiological drive is satisfied, interests begin to dominate the scene. Consider curiosity and the desire to play: they do not satiate. One can see this even in the play behavior of a child: if he loses interest in one toy, he does not stop playing; he finds some other toy. Drive psychology and emphasis on childish needs stress the tendencies to conserve, to adapt, to deal with tensions, but they ignore spontaneous activity, growth, and expanded outreach, so characteristic of normal behavior in both child and adult. The sick or immature person may be driven by his drives—caught up in excessive eating, drinking, sexual activity—but the normal, mature person puts these in their place and does much more. Drive motivation accounts for the essentials in man but not for the priceless unessentials. An individual who gradually grows toward an acceptance of marriage and family responsibilities could hardly be satisfying a basic, physiological drive, or any motive remotely associated with drives.

FUNCTIONAL AUTONOMY

Allport says: "Functional autonomy regards adult motives as varied, and as self-sustaining, contemporary systems, growing out of antecedent systems, but functionally independent of them" (Allport, 1961, p. 227). The principle of functional autonomy holds that an activity is motivational in its own right: it does not stem from another motive except itself. A musician makes music because he enjoys doing so: he may take a reduction in salary to take a job where he can play his instrument. An investment broker may continue to invest, even when he has enough to retire. The musician may work for money through necessity, but his principal motive is to make music, because this is the activity which he finds self-sustaining and motivational in its own right.

Functional autonomy may be contrasted with sublimation. A sublimated behavior can be traced to an unacceptable motive and represents a disguised outlet for that motive. A sadistic child who enjoys torturing insects may find a sublimated outlet through dissecting animals, during his premedical training. His dedication to his vocation of surgeon could also be explained as a sublimation of his sadistic needs. Allport does not deny the mechanism of sublimation, but he argues against the view that all adult motives and behaviors are sublimations. The dedicated surgeon may be fulfilling a self-image that includes the core role of healer. He obtains satisfaction by exercising his skills and applying his knowledge. He is not playing out childish needs but rather has worked out a style of life that is being expressed in part in his work as a surgeon. In other words, his motivation is functionally autonomous.

The principle of functional autonomy also holds that an activity which is in the service of a motive can itself become motivational. What begins as an activity performed out of necessity may come to fit into the propriate sphere and may hence become a strong autonomous motive. A man may work hard for money, and when he has more than enough to retire, he may continue working for other motives such as prestige, feeling useful, companionship, or because he hates to stay at home. But in order to be autonomous the motive to work must not be reducible to any other motive. Actually, any particular behavior is the outcome of a blend of many motives, some of which may be autonomous in varying degrees. Of course, some early motives may also continue to be active in the total pattern operating at any given time.

Suppose we ask the man in the preceding example, "Why do you continue working when you have enough money to retire comfortably?" and he replies, "Because I like to work." Allport would argue that this motive for working is functionally autonomous or self-sustaining. But as a psychologist he would also wish to carry his analysis beyond the man's superficial explanation by asking: "Why do you like to do it? How did you come to like to do it?" He believes we should attempt to relate the motive to the rest of personality, and especially to the proprium, which is the explanatory principle for autonomous motives. As we shall see, there are independent behavioral units that do not involve the proprium, but which are nevertheless functionally autonomous, to which Allport gives the name *perseverative functional autonomy*. But major functionally autonomous motives, such as intentions, may be explained in terms of one's style of life, which is made up of self-image, propriate strivings, self-extensions, adult conscience, temperament, and so on. It should be noted that the style of life may be either a continual reliving of the past, or it may have evolved, through learning and the fullest use of the capabilities of the ego, to the mature adult status. Within the developed personality, including the developed proprium, lies the explanation of the major functionally autonomous motives.

Perseverative Functional Autonomy

Allport (1961) distinguishes between propriate and perseverative functional autonomy as follows: Both refer to self-sustaining activities, not tied to more basic motives. Propriate functional autonomy, however, applies to general systems of motivation, intentions, or interests which are important aspects of the self and involve such functions of the proprium as the self-image, self-esteem, and self-extension. In perseverative functional autonomy, on the other hand, activities are repeated even though they have no connection with the proprium. Briefly, perseverative functional autonomy involves relatively isolated behaviors such as compulsions, whereas propriate functional autonomy might encompass a major life goal.

An example of perseverative functional autonomy is a habit that continues after it is no longer functional. A boy may let his hair grow long because he wants to be like the other members of his group. He comes to like long hair for itself and keeps the hair style even when he is no longer a part of the group. Circular mechanisms are also examples. A little child often repeats some activity, such as pounding his spoon on his dish, over and over again. The pounding appears to fascinate him and each performance of the act trig-

gers an additional performance. Some compulsive practices which seem to
have no adaptive significance fit this category. Perseveration may also result
from long-continued practice of some activity. Even though the justification
for the act no longer exists, the person may continue it. An example is the obsessional recall of test items after a test is taken. Again, familiarity and routine
lead to perseveration when familiar ways of doing things acquire motivational
strength and are preferred over novel ways. The familiar way acquires a value
over and above its utility value. These are examples of perseverative functional autonomy because they involve relatively isolated activities which have
their own motivation.

Propriate Functional Autonomy

It will be recalled that with the development of the proprium the motivational
picture changes. Though the process occurs gradually, the change in motivation is quite marked. Allport offers a colorful analogy to bring out this point.
A ship mired in the mud may be gradually lifted by the tide until it is afloat.
The change which is taking place is imperceptible, but the outcome is completely different from both the original state and each of the intermediate
stages. In like manner, the proprium gradually evolves as the child grows: it
plays a major role in his adaptation to the environment, but it comes to have
an autonomous existence and manner of functioning, and becomes a major
controlling force in the personality. Many behaviors serve only the proprium,
and are in no sense except historically tied to past needs, problems, or expectations. We will consider some processes which are involved as a motive or behavior becomes functionally autonomous. We will also consider the matter of
the unity of personality.

1. Organizing the Energy Level.   Allport (1961) suggests that drive-related
activity does not in fact exhaust the available supply of energy for most people, and that free-floating energy must be utilized in some kind of motivated
behavior. When drives are efficiently satisfied, more energy is available for
functionally autonomous motives. Propriate functions put this energy to work
if development has been normal.

2. Principle of Mastery or Competence.   Doing a thing and doing it well are
very different. The motive to do things well may be considered a functionally
autonomous motive because it goes beyond what is essential. A person may acquire competence in mastering things: he can produce the types of effects he
desires (White, 1959). Seeking to develop competence in knowledge and skills
does not serve drives but rather helps to fulfill an evolving self-image. Allport
(1961) believes that one of the ways that we can judge an individual's level of
maturity is by determining the degree to which his motives are functionally independent of his earlier needs and drives. A developed personality which has
been motivated primarily by drives cannot be mature. It necessarily must be
deficient in its fullest potential for growth. Only with the evolution of the
proprium does the personality attain anything that resembles full maturity.
The next three points will bring this out more clearly and attempt to explain
the unity of personality.

3. Abilities Often Turn to Interests. The exercise of abilities may attain motivational significance and serve as the basis for the acquisition of abiding interests or long-term intentions. We have here one possible explanation for the principle of functional autonomy: a developed ability has its own motivation. The use of abilities is similar to the notion of competence, but the motivation to be competent is concerned more with the product of abilities than with the sheer use of them. A carpenter may be highly motivated to build a fine cabinet, unsurpassed by others, but he may not necessarily love building it. Interests, nevertheless, are often formed around a particular ability or talent. A person who has musical talent is likely to develop an interest in making music, partly because the skill comes easily for him. He delights in using his skill and perfecting it, without any other apparent reason than the pleasure it provides. There may also be an element of challenge, as he attempts to perfect his musical skill. Allport (1961) points out that the driving force behind genius, except in a minority of cases, could hardly be financial reward, public acclaim, or power. On the contrary, many great men have had to suffer rejection, poverty, and even humiliation in the pursuit of a passionate interest. The use of one's talents may be a ruling passion around which the total life style is organized (see Crutchfield, 1973). A scientist may devote his entire life to his work, and even his leisure time may be filled with activities related to his dominant interest. Not everyone has abilities or talents which become the source of such compelling passions, but everyone has some abilities which can and do become the focal point of interests. We tend to enjoy doing what we can do well.

4. Acquired Interests and Values Have Selective Power. The various ways of expressing an interest are quite congruent in that they have the same meaning for the individual. Interests thus exert an integrating influence in personality: many behaviors may be traced to a particular interest. The question of units of personality (Allport, 1958) is partly answered by the idea that propriate interests bring together many personality aspects. Another aspect of an interest is its selective force: by knowing a person's interests, we can specify activities which are likely or unlikely to occur. An interest is like a magnetic core which holds many subsidiary trends and behaviors under control.

5. Self-Image and Life Style Are Organizing Factors. Interests constitute a significant ingredient of the proprium. Because of the central place of the proprium in the adult, it may be concluded that one's major interests reveal his life style. Interests are gradually evolved and become functionally autonomous motivational systems. An integrated style of life with interests as core motivational units gradually assumes an increasing role as the major determinant of personality growth and functioning. The evolving self-image, which is another significant component of the proprium, points out the main directions of development and is functionally autonomous in adulthood.

Allport succinctly summarizes several key aspects of functional autonomy in the following passage.

The principle of functional autonomy holds (1) that . . . motives are contemporary, that whatever drives must drive now; that the "go" of a motive is not bound function-

ally to its historical origins or to early goals, but to present goals only; (2) that the
character of motives alters so radically from infancy to maturity that we may speak of
adult motives as supplanting the motives of infancy; (3) that the maturity of personality is measured by the degree of functional autonomy its motives have achieved; even
though in every personality there are archaisms (infantilisms, regressions, reflex
responses), still the cultivated and socialized individual shows maturity to the extent
he has overcome early forms of motivation; (4) that the differentiating course of learning (reflecting ever more diversified environmental influence), acting upon divergent
temperaments and abilities, creates individualized motives. The dynamic structure of
every personality is unique, although similarities due to species, culture, stages of
development, climate, may produce certain resemblances (1940, p. 545).

Such concepts as intention and the principle of functional autonomy reflect
processes which, according to Allport, undergo marked changes in the course
of development. In fact, we could not appreciate the important changes which
take place without understanding these principles. We will now take up one
more basic concept of Allport's theory, the trait concept.

TRAITS: BASIC UNITS IN PERSONALITY

For Allport (1961), the trait is the most elementary component of personality:
it is the basic building block, analogous to the molecule of chemistry and the
cell of biology. By knowing the basic units of personality, we can trace the
changes that take place in these units as development occurs. For instance, if
we take the trait as the basic unit, we can discover three trait aspects, each of
which may be changed under appropriate conditions: (1) a core disposition,
(2) a specifiable range of stimuli which set off the disposition, and (3) a specific
range of responses which express the disposition. Thus by understanding the
basic units of personality and their specific nature, and by knowing the
changes (both normal and abnormal) which take place, we should be able to
predict and control both our own behavior and that of others.

COMMON TRAITS VERSUS PERSONAL DISPOSITIONS

The most usual way of describing personality is by means of trait terms. For
instance, we might describe Mary as friendly, conservative, outgoing, thrifty, a
bit selfish, and the like. Adjectives are commonly used as trait names: Allport
found as many as 18,000 trait terms in the unabridged dictionary (Allport and
Odbert, 1936). But not all the adjectives we use really tell us much about the
make-up of personality. If a man describes his girl as sweet, we have not really
learned much about her because the term sweet (or others like it – great, wonderful, lovely, sharp, and so forth) is an evaluative word which reflects a value
judgment rather than a trait of personality. Allport estimates that there are
about 4500 single words which do represent trait labels that can be useful in
depicting personality. This figure does not include descriptive phrases such as
lover-of-truth, hater-of-affectation, middle-of-the-roader, dyed-in-the-wool,
capitalist, and the like. Such descriptive phrases come closer to depicting traits

as they actually exist in personality, and with this point Allport (1961) makes a sharp distinction between what he terms common traits and individual traits or personal dispositions. This distinction will become clearer as the discussion proceeds, but for now the difference is that *a common trait is an abstract dimension by which many people may be compared and assigned a value,* whereas an *individual trait or personal disposition is a representation of a trait as it actually exists in a particular individual:* it does not apply to anyone else.

Common Traits

The common trait does not really exist in any particular individual; it is an abstract approximation of the individual trait. The basis of common traits is the similarities among people. As a part of an organized society, each person is exposed to certain values, institutions, and taboos. The majority of people are subjected to the same learning experiences, and they may be measured with respect to specific behaviors. Consider the matter of responsibility: the great majority of children in Western cultures are trained to take responsibility for themselves. Certain behaviors are used as indicators of the degree of responsibility the child has attained: turning in work on time, doing all that is expected, beginning a task without being told. A great many traits on which a large number of people can be compared have been identified, such as level of aspiration, degree of neuroticism, introversion-extroversion, and the like. For instance, one might measure by means of a standardized test how well a particular person compares with other people on these and similar traits and assign him a centile score which reveals the standing of his performance in relation to a large number of other people who have taken the same test. Such standings can be quite useful to a counselor: a personality trait profile might be used to advise a student not to pursue medicine because his trait pattern is quite unlike that of the typical physician.

Yet traits as they exist in the individual are quite complex because they involve a great variety of different behaviors and are triggered by a wide range of different stimuli. Neither the range of behaviors which are expressive of individual traits nor the range of stimuli which set off the core disposition is revealed by the centile standing of a person on a particular trait dimension. In other words, knowing a person's centile score on a common trait dimension is only a crude beginning in the task of understanding the nature of the trait as it exists in the individual. Then, too, each trait interacts with all other traits within the same individual, and is altered by that fact. Suppose that Mary falls at the eightieth centile on a test of dominance; we might conclude that Mary is quite dominant compared with other people her age. Suppose that Jean also scores at the eightieth centile on the same test; we might be tempted to interpret her score as being identical with Mary's, and to view her as the same in dominance standing. But such an interpretation is erroneous because Mary's dominance may not be expressed in the same way as Jean's, or elicited by the same situations. Mary's qualities of dominance, like Jean's, interact with everything else in her personality. Dominance is not expressed in the same way by an introvert as by an extrovert, by the highly intelligent person as by the mentally retarded, by the self-lover as by the self-hater. A number of trait scores on a test profile cannot faithfully represent the unique configuration of qualities making up the individual personality. Allport (1961) believes that this "patterned individuality" can be better approached through individual traits.

Secondary, Central, and Cardinal Traits

Secondary traits are relatively specific in relation to the range of effective stimuli and responses. They are on the periphery of personality, and are quite independent of other traits. Examples are the preference for chocolate to vanilla ice cream, beef to chicken, sandwiches to full meals, and so on. There are hundreds of such relatively isolated traits. They can be easily altered because they are not propriate. Furthermore, to know such traits does not tell us very much about a person. Knowing that John prefers tea to coffee does not tell us much about the major forces in John's life. Central traits are different: knowing fully a central trait tells a great deal, because much behavior is covered. In other words, knowing some things about a person (central traits) tells us considerably more about other aspects of personality than knowing certain other things (secondary traits).

Some examples of central traits are generosity, neatness, thriftiness, promptness, and industriousness. If one of these becomes dominant in personality, it becomes a cardinal trait. The cardinal trait is the one around which a great deal of behavior is organized. The individual may be identified by it. Often we use a single trait name to describe a person, and this may be taken as his cardinal trait.

Personal Dispositions

Much of what has been said of common traits applies also to personal dispositions because, after all, common traits are approximations of individual traits. Allport defines a personal disposition as "a generalized neural-psychic structure peculiar to the individual with the capacity to render many stimuli functionally equivalent and to initiate consistent or equivalent forms of adaptive or stylistic behavior" (1961, p. 373).

By "equivalent forms of behavior" Allport means the various ways of expressing the core tendency. Suppose that a certain girl is considered "motherly" by her friends. They would have identified this personal disposition by specific behaviors, since a trait is inferred from the repetition of behaviors having the same meaning. We could verify the existence of the disposition by observing her under a variety of circumstances, looking for these behavior congruences. She loves to feed and care for small animals; she brings home any stray dog or cat she finds; she enjoys sending get-well cards; she likes to host parties; she loves to prepare meals for her family. If we knew her better we could specify even more behaviors associated with her core disposition of mothering, and we could give more specific details of the way she responds. Allport's own

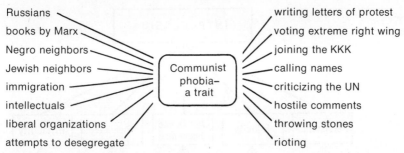

Figure 4–1   Generality of a trait. The range of a trait is determined by the equivalence of stimuli that arouse it and by the equivalence of responses that it provokes. (From G. W. Allport, *Pattern and Growth in Personality.* Holt, Rinehart and Winston, 1961.)

example of a man who has a phobia against communism (Fig. 4–1) further demonstrates the operation of equivalent forms of behavior.

Consider the core disposition for a moment: we can see that it involves a motivational force. If the motherly girl underwent some drastic biochemical changes, the core tendency would no longer act as a motivator and she would not display the motherly behavior, or at least the intensity would be greatly diminished. A personal disposition may be so powerful that it appears to become active spontaneously, but Allport disavows this idea; he believes that there is always a triggering stimulus. The stimulus may be difficult to identify, or because the core tendency is so powerful and pervasive, it may be triggered by minimal stimuli, or by almost any stimulus. A person who is driven to talkativeness may respond in a great many situations with an outpouring of verbal utterances. It seems that anything will set him off. Many neurotic symptoms fit this picture; the person manifests the symptom in a wide range of situations.

A personal disposition, then, has the capacity to render stimuli *functionally equivalent.* This means that many stimuli or situations are capable of setting off the disposition, to a greater or lesser degree. The disposition remains in a latent condition until an appropriate situation activates it. Just as we inquired into the range of responses which express a disposition, so also may we inquire about the range of stimuli which are functionally equivalent, which have the same meaning for the individual. A person who has an aggressive disposition may display various aggressive responses in a variety of situations, such as when an underdog is being beaten, or whenever he must deal with an authority figure, or in any competitive situation, or with any stranger. Only an exhaustive knowledge of him will bring out the many situations which activate his aggressive tendency. Thus we can see from Allport's view of an individual trait that a great deal of information must be obtained if we are to recognize the trait as it exists in the individual. A single adjective label is the barest beginning; there must be information about the various responses which express the disposition as well as about the range of situations in which the disposition becomes active. Then too, a particular trait always occurs with

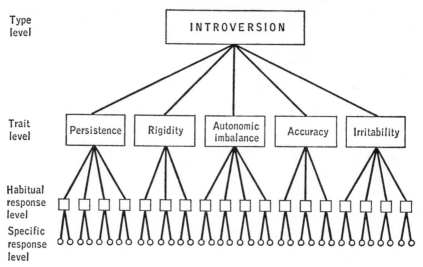

Figure 4–2   Various levels of a general trait. (Adapted from H. J. Eysenck. The organization of personality. *J. Pers. 20*:103, 1951. Copyright Duke University Press.)

other traits, and the picture becomes quite involved, as Allport sees it (Fig. 4–2).

Personal Dispositions Versus Habits.   Allport (1961) has held to the view that the personal disposition is the basic structural unit of personality. The popular Stimulus-Response approach is that the habit, defined as a measurable response to a measurable stimulus, is the irreducible unit; traits are categories invented for the purpose of classifying habits and have no real existence of their own. The S-R psychologist would argue that many habits may have similarities but they are nevertheless distinct. Little Mary learns to wash her hands and face as soon as she gets up in the morning, and gradually this becomes a habit. Then she learns to comb and brush her hair, another distinct habit. She learns to change her clothes, a third habit that bears some similarity to the other two. Allport believes that although during the process of learning each habit is at first distinct and separate, as the self-image and the life style begin to take shape the habits are gradually subsumed under a personal disposition, or better, the habits are expressive of a personal disposition of cleanliness. As she grows up, still other habits will be integrated into this core disposition of cleanliness: she will inspect her clothes for cleanliness and keep her room and things neatly. New habits will enter the sphere of existing dispositions and her personality will acquire more and more stability and unity with age. Hence, traits are more truly descriptive of Mary than single habits.

Now there may be some inconsistencies: Mary may have the disposition of personal cleanliness, but her room may be constantly in disarray. Allport (1966) holds that there is never total consistency, even in the best of lives.

The inconsistencies should be studied because they reveal a good deal about a person's course of development. Why does Mary, who is so meticulous about her person, neglect her room? We have already suggested one explanation of inconsistencies: sometimes there are opposing dispositions in the same personality.

Consider another example of the priority of traits over habits. A certain individual has the disposition of being polite which is expressed, among other ways, in being a good listener. In conversation, instead of worrying about putting in his piece, he listens carefully and asks many questions. But he finds that questioning causes one particular friend displeasure, so when he is with this friend he contributes his own ideas more actively. For the sake of the disposition to please others he alters his habit of listening and asking questions. Thus not only is concentration on the habit level inefficient; it may also mislead the observer to perceive inconsistencies in behavior where there are none. The man in question was being polite although his behavior was quite different when it was altered for the friend. A trait involves at least two habits, but there are usually many more than two, and new habits are formed within the existing framework of dispositions.

SOME CAUTIONS ABOUT TRAITS

To summarize: a trait never occurs alone; many determinants are always simultaneously active. The effects of a trait can often be detected by consistencies in behavior. We can usually identify important goals and purposes which reveal a trait. Repeated observations are necessary in order to observe the consistency produced by a trait. A particular trait may be blocked or inhibited by an opposite trait, but we can usually discover the conditions under which each is dominant.

Another difficulty with traits is that we must rely upon observable behavior to make inferences, and our observations may be incorrect. For example, it may appear that a person is friendly because he likes us, whereas his real motive is to get us to like him so that he can use us for some purpose. Here we are dealing with a pseudo trait; self-seeking rather than friendliness is the true trait.

Another difficulty is that we may think we know a core disposition when in fact we have identified only a surface expression of the trait. For instance, we may think that a friend is thrifty when he is actually suffering from a trait of compulsive hoarding. Thriftiness is only one manifestation of the hoarding trait. The difference in this case is between a *phenotypic trait*, which is a behavioral manifestation of a trait, and a *genotypic trait*, which is the core disposition itself.

To identify a trait we can use an application of the scientific method. The first step is to make many observations, the second to draw a tentative inference to explain the observations, the third to test again the inference by further checking the observations, and the fourth to revise the inference if necessary. Unfortunately, one rarely has the opportunity to carry on such a complete analysis.

A word more should be said about the question of consistency in personality. A knowledge of propriate strivings will usually provide a key to the central dispositions. We might look for firmly held convictions, long-term goals, and enduring stylistic expression. It should be noted that goals are much more revealing than the means which are used to attain them, because the means can vary considerably. Stylistic forms of expression are also remarkably stable over time. The major problem in getting to know the central dispositions is the lack of sufficient opportunity to make observations, and the necessity of observing under many different circumstances.

The Continuous Flow of Behavior and Convergence

There are two other factors which add to the difficulties of describing personality, and Allport covers these under two principles: the principle of the continuous flow of behavior, and the principle of convergence.

By continuous flow of behavior Allport means that during the waking state some behavior is always occurring. Although there are periods of ebb and flow, behavioral units are not discretely divided. One activity merges with the next and overlaps it, and later it may become dominant again.

By the convergence principle Allport means the multiple determination of behavior—that many currents are active at the same time. Yet whatever consistencies there are in personality may be attributed to the operation of traits, and in fact traits are inferred from congruence among behaviors. Inconsistencies may also exist because within the same individual there may be divergent trends: Mary may be both an angel and a devil. We must try to understand the conditions when one or the other prevails.

CRITICAL EVALUATION

Allport has been highly influential in the field of personality, and in fact, has voiced the problems which are major concerns in the field. As we noted earlier, he has persistently criticized the stress in American psychology and psychiatry on the irrational and unconscious determinants of behavior. Principles and methods appropriate to the study of psychologically sick people have been applied to the normal individual, creating a distorted model of normal personality. For example, Allport (1953) holds that the information obtained through the popular projective tests (Rorschach Ink-Blot Test and Thematic Apperception Test) is not substantially different from what one can get simply by asking the person to tell about himself. At best, the projective tests are not necessary to understand the normal person; at worst, they give a distorted picture by overemphasizing irrational and unconscious behavior patterns.

Allport has criticized many other current trends in psychology, proposing what he believes are more fruitful approaches. As we have seen, he finds serious difficulties with the attitude that a number of centile standings derived from psychological tests gives an accurate picture of personality. Thus he has contributed his own test of the single individual: the famous Allport-Vernon-Lindzey Test of Values (*Study of Values*, 1960). Through this test he attempts to measure six major value dimensions which he considers adequate descriptive units of personality. His ideas about traits, values and personal dispositions, his principle of functional autonomy, his distinction between the "must" and the "ought" conscience, his stress on intentions and propriate strivings in the adult, and his emphasis upon the central role of expressive behavior have also provided psychologists with ways of understanding the single individual.

Nevertheless, Allport's ideas have not garnered many disciples who continue to develop and test them. He himself admits that he has not conducted enough research to support his theories, many of which are simply untested hypotheses. Furthermore, he has focused his theorizing primarily on the personality rather than on social and other environmental factors. He recognizes the influences of environment in his treatment of the place of culture, situation, and roles, but exactly how these forces interact with his conceptualization of personality is never considered (Allport, 1960). On the basis of these and other criticisms not presented here, Allport's theory will probably continue to diminish in influence. We might infer, from the spirit of the following quotation, that Allport himself would have accepted this conclusion, for he appreciated the fact that his theory was merely a rough first approximation of an adequate model of man:

How shall a psychological life history be written? What processes and structures must a full-bodied account of personality include? How can one detect unifying threads in a life, if they exist? The greater part of my own professional work can be viewed as an attempt to answer such questions through piecemeal and stepwise research and writing. If my theoretical writing exceed in bulk my output of research, it is because of my conviction that significant, not trivial, questions must be posed before we lose ourselves in a frenzy of investigation (1968, p. 377).

The kinds of questions with which Allport was concerned are difficult to answer, but at the same time they are most relevant to the goal of depicting adequately the single case — his cherished ideal.

INSIGHTS FROM ALLPORT'S THEORY OF PERSONALITY DEVELOPMENT

ADAPTIVE AND STYLISTIC TRAITS

Every behavior may be viewed from two aspects, adaptive and stylistic. Adaptive behavior has a purpose: it accomplishes something; it may be termed coping. An adaptive act points toward some goal, and it may be judged as to whether or not the goal is accomplished, or to what degree

I.

II.

III.

Figure 4–3 Stylistic behavior demonstrated through excerpts from musical manuscripts of three renowned composers. (From W. Wolf, *The Expression of Personality*. Harper, 1944.)

it is. A person may be writing a letter to a friend, eating an apple, buying a book or simply laughing, coughing, or crying. Adaptive behavior consists of the "what" of a person's behavior, whereas stylistic behavior deals with the "how," the manner in which an adaptive act is carried out. Allport described stylistic behavior as "adverbial." We can learn about a person from both aspects of behavior, but probably stylistic behavior tells us more about underlying personality dispositions. Figure 4–3 displays stylistic behavior through excerpts from musical manuscripts of three renowned composers.

Consider a child answering a question on a test: he answers either correctly or incorrectly, and we learn something about his knowledge. But his *manner* of answering may tell us a great deal more of significance about his personality. We might learn whether his answer is superficially given, or deliberated and considered thoroughly. It may be vague, confused, and delivered hesitatingly, or presented confidently, with clear demonstration of understanding. To the astute observer, the stylistic expression will reveal things which the person may attempt to cover up; he may be so occupied with the coping aspect of his behavior that he does not pay attention to his manner of expressing it. A smiling

Figure 4–4 Expressive movements of personality may be reflected in jumping postures. P. Halsman photographed the three college professors above, describing the jump to the left as "impressive," the jump in the center as "explosive joy," and the jump to the right as "modest simplicity." (Copyright © 1959 by P. Halsman.)

face may be accompanied by a harsh manner of speaking. Other expressive behaviors include posture, gait, gestures, and facial expressions (See Figure 4–4). By studying stylistic behaviors one can learn about enduring temperamental traits, ingrained early habits, and strongly held attitudes.

The following differences between coping and expressive (or stylistic) behavior should be helpful in promoting knowledge both of others and of self. (1) Coping is purposive and specifically motivated; expressive behavior is not. (2) Coping is determined by the needs of the moment and by the situation; expressive movement reflects deeper personal structure. (3) Coping is formally elicited; expressive behavior is spontaneously "emitted." (4) Coping can be readily controlled (inhibited, modified, conventionalized); expressive behavior is hard to alter and often uncontrollable. (A change in our style of handwriting can be kept up for only a short time.) (5) Coping usually aims to change the environment; expressive behavior aims at nothing, though it may incidentally have effects (as when our manner of answering questions during an interview creates a good impression and lands us the job). (6) Typically coping is conscious, even though it may employ automatic skills; expressive behavior generally lies below the threshold of our awareness (Allport, 1961, p. 463).

PROMOTING HEALTHY SELF-EXPERIENCES (PROPRIATE FUNCTIONS)

According to Allport's view of man, a fully developed and well-functioning self is an essential feature of mental health. Allport discusses the seven dimensions of self from a developmental standpoint, but he does not tell us directly what steps to take to promote normal or healthy self-development. We will attempt to extract some suggestions from his writings.

Bodily Self. Allport observes, as have many others, that a healthy body is usually necessary for a healthy mind. Furthermore, a healthy body is not experienced acutely as is an unhealthy one. Sensory deprivation studies (Bexton, et al., 1954; Heron, et al., 1956) indicate that a minimal level of sensory stimulation is required for healthy living. Certainly the absence or reduction of normal stimulation causes serious personality disturbances, even symptoms that resemble severe mental illness. We might conclude, therefore, that healthy functioning demands a variety of stimuli. We should give expression to our curiosity, vary our circumstances frequently, learn to enjoy sensory experiences. Varied experiences not only add spice to life; they are absolutely essential for healthy living. Monotonous surroundings and activities may produce restlessness, fatigue, irritability, and boredom. Thus the sense of the bodily self may be enhanced by maintaining physical health and by ensuring a variety of sensory experiences.

Self-Identity. The sense of identity is the continuing awareness of being the same person. It is felt most strongly when we are fulfilling interests and attaining goals. Valued possessions strengthen the sense of identity. The number and quality of the possessions are not as important as is the value attached to them. We often speak of an original idea, for example, as "my baby." Allport refers to this aspect of the sense of identity as "extension of self." We might hypothesize that the more complete the involvement of the self with people and things, the firmer is the sense of identity. By implication, having well-defined goals and values would enhance identity. This hypothesis and others regarding the conditions necessary for self-identity are discussed in a recent paper by Waterbor (1972).

Self-Esteem. Self-esteem means self-love or self-pride. It is also roughly synonymous with Erikson's sense of autonomy. Self-esteem is promoted by doing things in one's chosen manner, by conforming to one's own ideals and proposed goals. The artisan takes great pride in his work. In a sense, it is an extension of him, and he enhances his self-estimation from its value. Self-esteem is thwarted when one is required to conform to the expectations of others. The negativism or rebelliousness of adolescence is a manifestation of the frustrated urge for self-esteem. "I may do it all wrong, but I want to do it my way" is the motto of many teen-agers. Sheer rebelliousness and protest against the established values and institutions may temporarily promote self-esteem, but genuine pride in self requires actual accomplishments. One way to acquire self-esteem is to discover what you are good at and work to perfect that skill. Creativity also makes for self-pride.

The sense of self-esteem is one of the most significant aspects of subjective life. Without it, personality development and functioning are seriously impaired. It is greatly promoted by adhering to conscience, but the conscience must be the adult conscience which consists of realistic ideals or "oughts." Many people dislike themselves and spend their lives wishing they were someone else. One of our major tasks is to come to terms with ourselves, recognizing and valuing what we are and perceiving what can and cannot be changed. While many people believe strongly that they are unlovable, Allport holds that the human being is so complex and unique that every individual is attractive to at least some people. Most psychotherapists who deal with the problem of personality change hold that low self-esteem is cured not by a radical change in personality but rather by perfecting what is there: eliminating some undesirable trends and improving others.

One other aspect of self-esteem is significant; namely, the role which others play in determining it. Allport agrees with G. H. Mede that the self is in large measure the product of others' expectations, the so-called "looking glass self." For many people self-esteem is tied exclusively to external opinion: what others think is valued more highly than self-knowledge. We surrender important power to others when we allow our self-esteem to be dependent on their evaluation. Although no one can fully escape the influence of others' opinions, ultimately the major focus of self-esteem should be within the individual.

Self-Extension. We have already suggested that participation in ego-relevant activities fosters a sense of self-identity. The sense of self is increased through self-extensions. What counts in life are the things that are valued by the self: vocation, family, home, knowledge, and skills. Some people, however, are deficient in self-extensions because they are preoccupied only with themselves. Learning to value our possessions — whether they be things, people, or personal attributes — can promote the sense of self-extension, and like all the other attributes of self, foster healthy living.

Self-Image. The concept one has of himself (self-image) is in early life largely the product of the various ways he is regarded by others. Gradually the self-image begins to be shaped by the person himself. It expands to include what one wants to be and what one ought to be. This latter expansion of the self has much to do with the development of the adult conscience, as Allport defines it. For the adult the "ought" conscience is an indicator that he has violated his preferred life style; it is a functional aspect of personality which serves to promote healthy living.

You might consider the following in regard to enhancing your self-image: First, do you have an adult conscience? How much of the "must" conscience is still active in your life? Your activities should be primarily governed by your own goals and values, not by what others dictate to you. When you must do things, you should know the reasons for the musts. Secondly, have you given your goals an order of priority? Do you know what things really count to you, and what are secondary or unimportant? Can you identify what is desirable and undesirable in your life? One cannot be everything he might want to be. Certain directions should be taken. A diffuse scattering of energy will result in failure on all levels. Thirdly, do you have an idea of your "perfected" self? Is it realistic and attainable, based on current performance? Fourthly, how many of your current activities are done out of fear, without much understanding of their purpose? What can you do to make present activities more meaningful? Interest does not always come naturally from external sources. It may result from a change of attitude. One may experience a college program as boring or view it as a series of unfolding episodes, each class becoming like a scene in a play, with new ideas, questions, and challenges continually opening up.

Self as Rational Coper.   It will be recalled that this aspect of self refers to the experience of the self as a problem solver. To promote the sense self as a doer, one might apply the suggestions given for Erikson's stages, particularly those relating to autonomy, initiative, and industry. Here are some other suggestions for promoting the sense of self as rational coper: First, can you specify the areas in which your talents lie? What can you do to increase your knowledge and skills? Secondly, do you know how to approach a problem? Can you work out a plan that is a workable guide? Thirdly, what happens when you do not attain your goals or solve your problems? Can you immediately rule out unworkable alternatives before you actually get started? Do your plans include alternative courses of actions if your path of progress is blocked? For security purposes, the space scientists built in backup systems. Can you see how you can apply the same approach in your problem-solving efforts?

Propriate Striving.   The latest development in the self is the projection of long-term goals. The self undergoes a major modification with the formulation of such stable intentions. A number of points should be kept in mind, however. Values can be a personal matter. They can and should be modified with changing life circumstances. From time to time, goals should be examined and compared with performance. Allport maintains that working toward goals which are propriate not only is an essential ingredient of maturity but affords man meaning and purpose in life. It should be noted clearly that goals need not be grandiose, idealistic, or culturally valued. One may strive simply to perfect his life, to rear his children properly, to do a good job in his work, and for other similar non-spectacular ends. A life without long-term goals is devoid of the richest human experiences.

NO ONE RIGHT WAY

Allport offers a challenging observation about the style of living one strives for. He recognizes that there are preferred cultural models which are held up as attractive to the young person, but adopting one of them does not necessarily promote better psychological health. Being an extrovert, a high achiever, or socially popular is not intrinsically more adaptive than being the opposite of these: one is not more successful, more likeable, or more effective as an extrovert than as an introvert. Each person has a unique personality, and while there may be resemblances among people, everyone's style of living is unique. One should examine all aspects of the proprium and strive to make it the major determinant of his behavior, rather than attempt to change his personality to suit a cultural model.

SUMMARY

1. The raw materials of personality are physique, temperament, and intelligence. These must be considered as constants in the development of personality.

2. The basic pattern of growth is contained within the genetic code, and maturational processes take place if appropriate conditions are present.

3. For man, learning plays a highly significant role, although the limits of learning are conditioned by the inherent nature of the personality as well as by environmental circumstances. Quasi-mechanical explanations of learning, such as classical and instrumental conditioning, account for only a small part of the total learning in man. Allport suggests two other levels of learning related to the development of the proprium: cognitive and personal learning.

4. With development the proprium begins to emerge, and it acquires an increasingly determinant role in the growth and functioning of the personality. The proprium evolves gradually, and if the course of development is normal, it attains maturity in early adulthood. Allport delineates seven aspects of the proprium, which develop at different periods during the first 20 years of life: bodily self, self-identity, self-extension, self-esteem, self-image, self as rational coper, and propriate striving.

5. The cognitive and motivational functions in personality undergo major changes, so that the adult status is qualitatively different from the earlier forms. One difference, for instance, is that the motives of the child are closely related to physiological drives, while the primary motivational forces in mature adults have little to do with drives, being instead embodied in intentions.

6. With development, cognition and motivation become more and more inseparable, as the proprium takes over the major directing role in personality.

7. Another stabilizing aspect of personality is the development of traits. Central traits hold together a great number of learned responses which have a common function for the individual. Many situations are perceived as functionally equivalent as a result of the core disposition of central traits.

8. As the traits grow, the personality becomes more differentiated and integrated: the adult personality is strikingly different from that of the child, and the connection with the past is historical, not functional.

9.   Long-term goals and intentions, which do not even exist in the child, guide the adult and give direction to living.

SUGGESTED READINGS

Allport, Gordon. Personality: A Psychological Interpretation. New York: Holt, 1937.
>   This book established Allport as a pioneer in the field of personality theory. He outlines the major areas of the personality field, weaving in his own theory of the person.

Becoming: Basic Considerations for a Psychology of Personality. New Haven: Yale University Press, 1955.
>   This short book presents Allport's views on the ideal state for man. It discusses the nature and evolution of the self, the requirements for maturity, the social aspects of behavior, and the future orientation of the individual.

Personality and Social Encounter. Boston: Beacon Press, 1960.
>   This volume contains a selection of essays which are neither "technical nor popular." Allport contends they were written "either to amplify the theory of personality contained in my *Personality: A Psychological Interpretation* or to express my concern with topical problems in social psychology."

Pattern and Growth in Personality. New York: Holt, Rinehart and Winston, 1961.
>   Allport presents his last major statement of his theory in this book. He stresses the uniqueness of each individual and introduces his concept of the personal disposition, which he considers the basic unit of personality make-up. The book is highly readable and is suggested for the beginning personality student.

The Person in Psychology: Selected Essays. Boston: Beacon Press, 1968.
>   This book is a collection of writings emphasizing Allport's humanistic approach to psychology.

REFERENCES

Allport, G. W. Personality: A Psychological Interpretation. New York: Holt, Rinehart and Winston, 1937.

Allport, G. W. Motivation in personality: Reply to Mr. Bertocci. Psychol. Rev. 47:533–54, 1940.

Allport, G. W. The trend in motivational theory. Am. J. Orthopsychiatry 23:107–19, 1953.

Allport, G. W. Becoming. New Haven: Yale University Press, 1955.

Allport, G. W. What units shall we employ? In Lindzey, G. W., ed., Assessment of Human Motives. New York: Holt, Rinehart and Winston, 1958. Chapter 9.

Allport, G. W. The open system in personality theory. J. Abnorm. Social Psychol. 61:301–10, 1960.

Allport, G. W. Pattern and Growth in Personality. New York: Holt, Rinehart and Winston, 1961.

Allport, G. W. Traits revisited. Am. Psychol. 21:1–10, 1966.

Allport, G. W. The Person in Psychology: Selected Essays. Boston: Beacon Press, 1968.

Allport, G. W., and Odbert, H. S. Trait names: A psychological study. Psychol. Monogr. 47:1–171, Whole No. 211, 1936.

Allport, G. W., and Vernon, P. E. Studies in Expressive Movement. New York: The Macmillan Company, 1933.

Allport, G. W., Vernon, P. E., and Lindzey, G. Study of Values, 3rd ed. Boston: Houghton Mifflin, 1960.

Bexton, W. H., Heron, W., and Scott, T. H. Effects of decreased variation in the sensory environment. Can. J. Psychol. 8:70–6, 1954.

Crutchfield, R. S. The creative process. In Bloomberg, M., ed., Creative Theory and Research. New Haven: College and University Press, 1973. Pp. 54–74.

Doll, E. Vineland Social Maturity Scale. Circle Pines, Minnesota: American Guidance Service, 1965.

Fromm, E. Man for Himself. New York: Holt, Rinehart and Winston, 1947.

Havighurst, R. J. Human Development and Education. New York: Longmans, Green and Company, 1953.

Heron, W., Roane, B. K., and Scott, T. H. Visual disturbance after prolonged perceptual isolation. Can. J. Psychol. *10*:13–16, 1956.

Kohlberg, L. Stage and sequence: The cognitive-developmental approach to socialization. *In* Goslin, D. A., ed., Handbook of Socialization Theory and Research. Chicago: Rand-McNally Company, 1969. Pp. 347–480.

McClelland, D. C. Testing for competence rather than for "intelligence." Am. Psychol. *28*:1–14, 1973.

Murray, H. A. Explorations in Personality. Fair Lawn, New Jersey: Oxford University Press, 1938.

Waterbor, R. Experiential bases of the sense of self. J. Pers. *40*:162–79, 1972.

White, R. W. The Abnormal Personality. New York: Ronald Press, 1948.

White, R. W. Motivation reconsidered: The concept of competence. Psychol. Rev. *66*:297–333, 1959.

Wylie, R. C. The present status of self theory. *In* Borgatta, E. F., and Lambert, W. W., eds., Handbook of Personality Theory and Research. Chicago: Rand-McNally, 1968. Pp. 728–87.

PART III

Learning Theories of Personality

We noted in the first chapter that we can describe, explain, and predict a person's behavior by using such constructs as roles, needs, traits, the self, and other so-called agents within personality. Take the trait approach, for instance: we can describe and understand a person's behavior if we know his traits. This statement implies a great deal. Some traits are dominant and highly significant in much of what the person does. Other traits are quite specific and are of little consequence in his life. A given behavior is the product of more than a single trait, as a rule. Traits give rise to responses, and we would have to know the range of responses that expresses a particular trait for an individual. Traits are also set off by certain stimuli, and again it is necessary to determine the range of stimuli which sets off each trait. The formation of traits, the responses which express them, and the stimuli which activate them are ultimately a matter of learning.

We have already seen how Freud's theory of personality structure makes extensive use of three components within personality: the id, the ego, and the superego. Whether one is dominated by his impulses (id), or faces up to the demands of reality (ego), or is overly controlled and self-limiting (superego), and much else of significance is explained in terms of the three structures. In describing and explaining personality it is perhaps helpful to think of the doings of the id, the ego, or the superego, but the learning theorist would argue that it might be better to deal directly with the behaviors which are covered by such labels. One approach we will discuss, that of Dollard and Miller, does in fact translate Freudian concepts into the terms of learning. But other learning theorists have abandoned the reliance on agents within personality.

Those who espouse a learning conception of personality tend to focus on the external aspects of behavior, on the causes and consequences of behavior which are observable. This view has been called the "empty organism" approach. The label is somewhat misleading, as B. F. Skinner, one of its proponents, argues. The point is not that the organism is empty but that we cannot know it from the inside, only from the outside. Thus the concern of the personality psychologist, according to the learning approach, should be with the conditions that relate to the *acquisition*, the *maintenance*, and the *change* of behavior, and these conditions are *environmental*, not personality factors.

In general, the learning theorists have attempted to account for the phenomena dealt with by the traditional personologists in terms of the principles of learning that have been discovered in the animal laboratory. They believe that the same requirements promote learning in both animals and man. Once we understand the principles that govern learning, these can account for a wide range of specific contents. In other words, the learning theorist is much more concerned with the "how" of personality than with the "what." As we have suggested, there are striking differences among the learning theorists, from Skinner who avoids inference concerning intrapsychic or organismic variables, to Rotter who proposes needs, expectancies, and goals—constructs that resemble intrapsychic agents. Perhaps the learning theorist is more sensitive to the empirical anchoring of his concepts than are those who postulate agents within personality. The learning theorist may ask: how did these agents come about, what behaviors do they effect, and what sets them off? Agents are really only verbal labels for specific classes of behaviors.

A learning psychologist might argue that he provides us with the concepts and principles by which all behavior can be described and understood. It is left up to us to apply these to specific behaviors. A carpenter could instruct us in the various ways we might fasten one thing to another: gluing, nailing, screwing, wedging, and so on. He might show us how to cut various angles in different types of wood, and point out the proper tools to use. What we do with our knowledge is up to us. Similarly, the learning psychologist specifies the conditions necessary for learning to take place and for personality change to occur, but we must apply this knowledge in specific instances. Still, it would be extremely helpful, as we noted in the introductory chapter, to have a picture of man that could tell us what to look for. Principles of learning alone do not constitute a conceptual picture of personality, in the strict sense.

There are two general models that psychologists use to describe and explain behavior: the S-R (stimulus-response) and the S-O-R (stimulus-organism-response) models. In the S-R model, the response is assumed to be instigated directly by the stimulus, as in the case of reflexes. A signal can trigger off fear without any apparent mediating process if the signal has been paired with a pain-producing event. In the S-O-R model, the stimulus causes a reaction in O, the organism, which then effects the response. The signal may not produce a fear response, unless one perceives that it could lead to danger. For our purpose the O is equivalent to personality variables, the intrapsychic agents.

Learning theorists may be categorized by means of the S-R and the S-O-R models. The S-R theorists minimize the acquisitions or agents of personality; the S-O-R theorists make provision for them and represent them in learning terms. The S-O-R theorists are really no different from the personality psychologists who propose agents within personality. The O variables of the learning psychologist are more closely tied to empirical terms, but the agents of personality of the traditional theorists can be defined operationally in many instances. We have less to guide us when we are not given the O variables or the agents within personality.

Of all the theorists we are considering, Skinner probably assigns the greatest role to external variables as the major determinants of personality. Skinner's concepts do not fit either of our two models because he concentrates on the formation of responses, not from the organismic or stimulus aspects, but from the *consequences that the responses produce.* But interestingly, Skinner (1953) takes the trouble to define in learning terms the agents within personality that Freud proposed, though it should be noted that as a learning theorist, he could not have inferred their existence.

Many theorists believe that personality exists as potentialities until these are actualized through learning and other processes. Yet while learning plays a significant role in the actualizing of these potentialities, it does not *create* them. We are referring to species-specific potentialities. Learning can take place only within the conditions that are present in the organism's nature. Consider the nature of man: could a person not have a self-concept, or not be capable of perceiving the future, or not be able to evaluate his own behavior? Learning certainly plays a part in the manner in which these processes develop, but it neither creates nor obliterates them. We all have a self-image, but it may take an almost infinite form. We all have some form of conscience, some form of awareness of ourselves, of the future, and so on. In brief, we are arguing that the learning approach does not disqualify the intrapsychic approach. It is clear that many personality theorists have not followed operational definitions in proposing their constructs, but that is the fault of the personality theorists, not of the approach. It would seem that we could begin with agents of personality, derived from careful observation of behavior, and trace their development, applying principles of learning. Having the agents of personality gives us a framework for dealing with the personalities we actually encounter. If we had a knowledge of the directions that learning could take, based on the species-specific potentialities of man, we could have much more control of the learning process than we now have. We know that certain species condition to different stimuli more readily, and we know that certain kinds of learning appear to be peculiar to man.

We will begin with Skinner's reinforcement theory because it is the least involved with intrapsychic constructs, and then we will consider the theories of Dollard and Miller, Bandura and Walters, and Rotter, all of whom allow for intrapsychic variables as well as social determinants.

CHAPTER 5

Reinforcement Theory

B. F. Skinner

B. F. Skinner (1904——)

BIOGRAPHY AND OVERVIEW

The concepts and work of B. F. Skinner are exerting a profound influence on many areas of contemporary psychology. Skinner is a strong advocate of behaviorism, and he has developed operant reinforcement procedures which he and his students have applied to many aspects of behavior control in a variety of settings. His reinforcement concepts and procedures have been used to modify behavior among institutional psychotics, in penal and correctional institutions, in business and work environments, in schools and other instructional settings, and in individual psychotherapy (Goodall, 1972).

Skinner is probably more influential today than any other psychologist. Several journals carry only operant conditioning studies, and an entire division of the American Psychological Association, with more than a thousand members, is devoted to the experimental analysis of behavior. There are many psychologists who identify themselves as Skinnerian, while several graduate schools offer programs in behavior modification, leading to a Ph.D.

Skinner was born in 1904 in Susquehanna, Pennsylvania. He received a Ph.D. in psychology from Harvard in 1931. He worked in Professor Crozier's biology laboratory as an assistant until 1936, when he received his first teaching appointment at the University of Minnesota. In 1938 his first major book was published, *The Behavior of Organisms*. He remained nine years at Minnesota, and after a brief period at the University of Indiana, he went to Harvard to teach. He has remained there ever since, winning many honors and awards both in psychology and outside the field, and becoming one of the outstanding figures in the behavioral sciences.

124

To obtain a preliminary picture of the application of Skinner's reinforcement procedures, let us contrast his approach with two others, a "loving" approach and a "punitive" approach, in dealing with the behavior of retarded children. The basis of the loving approach is that children should be influenced to behave in socially approved ways by means of suggestions supported with demonstrations of respect and concern. But workers in the field report that the love and tenderness method does not always instigate the type of behavior they desire. A negative child does not become cooperative just because he is treated kindly. Under the punitive approach, the children are threatened with punishment if they do not behave according to the wishes of the school authorities. This method is something like: "If you want to get along in this place, you'd better follow the rules." Yet even when punishment is actually used, in many instances the desirable behavior does not occur.

In contrast to these two approaches, Skinner uses rewards (*positive reinforcement*) to strengthen prescribed behaviors. When the prescribed behavior is rewarded by tokens that can be redeemed for a variety of goods, privileges, and exemptions, the degree of behavior control that can be achieved is amazing. The children will perform many tasks for the tokens that they simply would not do under either the loving or the punitive conditions. Using rewards to modify behavior has been applied effectively in many other settings as well (e.g., Ayllon and Azrin, 1965). Skinner and his students maintain that they can control the behavior of humans as effectively as they can the behavior of animals. Simply, the principle is that reinforcement raises the frequency with which behavior occurs: organisms do what pays off.

Another feature of Skinner's approach is his concern with the consequences of behavior. Although he recognizes the importance of behavior which is elicited by stimuli, he is more concerned with operant behavior which is emitted and strengthened by a reinforcer under the influence of a behavior engineer (Skinner, 1938). He is greatly interested in controlling the behavior of the individual. Many psychologists deal with the behavior of groups of subjects and concentrate upon behavior prediction. Skinner, in contrast, holds that it should be possible to control and engineer the behavior of every individual organism, if the appropriate conditions are known and applied.

Before we discuss Skinner's ideas, the reader may find the following terms and definitions helpful in understanding his concepts and methodology.

PRINCIPLES AND CONCEPTS

1. *Primary reinforcers* are those which satisfy certain biological needs and which are reinforcing to all forms of animal life. A primary reinforcer does not depend upon previous conditioning for its reinforcing power.

2. Objects or events repeatedly paired with primary reinforcers may acquire reinforcing properties themselves, thus becoming *secondary reinforcers.*

3. During *operant learning,* behavior is emitted by the organism. This behavior increases in frequency if followed by positive reinforcement.

4. *Respondent behavior* is any behavior which is reflexive.

5. Any event or stimulus that increases the strength or probability of the behavior it follows is called a *reinforcer.*

6. The process of removing *reinforcement* until behavior returns to low levels is called *extinction.*

7. If a given behavior serves either to terminate or to avoid a particular stimulus, that stimulus is said to be *aversive* and such behavior is maintained through *negative reinforcement.*

8. A neutral stimulus (such as paper) may take on reinforcement properties (such as money) when paired with other reinforcing agents, thus becoming a *conditioned reinforcer.*

9. By occurring in contiguity with aversive stimuli, neutral stimuli may become *conditioned aversive stimuli.*

10. *Generalization* occurs when an organism emits a response originally conditioned to one stimulus, to other stimuli having properties in common with the conditioned stimulus.

11. In *discrimination* learning, an organism restricts its responses to a narrow range of stimuli.

12. *Shaping* is a procedure of differentially reinforcing successive approximations, carried out step by step, until the desired behavior is achieved.

13. The best schedule for initially strengthening a behavior is a *continuous reinforcement* schedule, under which reinforcement is given after every emitted response.

14. *Intermittent schedules* of reinforcement are more effective in maintaining behavior once higher rates of responding have been established.

SKINNER'S VIEWS ON PERSONALITY CONSTRUCTS

Most of the personality theorists we are considering view personality as a real structure that can be depicted in terms of constructs such as traits, needs, values, habits, style of life, sentiments, the self, id, ego, superego, and the like. Knowledge of these components and their interactions will assist in accomplishing the aims of a science of personality, namely, to describe, to explain, to predict, and to control the behavior of a single individual. Yet many personologists also believe that behavior must be viewed as the product of an interaction between internal personality structures and environmental factors. Knowledge of either alone is insufficient to accomplish the aims of personality science, for the personality variables must be inferred from behavior and environment: they cannot be approached directly.

In the science of behavior, Skinner believes, personality variables are really only verbal labels for specific behaviors. Dependency, for instance, is a term that stands for certain types of behaviors in relation to certain types of people. It is not something that exists in the personality structure as a trait. The behaviors designated as dependency have something in common and substitute for one another; they may result in similar consequences; they occur in specifiable types of situations; but they do not emanate from a personality structure which can be called dependency. A knowledge of the behaviors designated as dependency, according to Skinner, is better promoted by learning the reinforcement history of the behaviors classified as dependent than by attempting to learn about the nature of the supposed trait and its interactions with other purported traits in the personality. A practical control of the "dependency" behavior can occur only when consequences of such behavior are altered (Skinner, 1953). Personality constructs appear to increase our knowledge of the determinants of behavior, but they are merely fictions — carryovers from psychology's mentalistic past (Skinner, 1971).

ACTIONS DETERMINED BY CONSEQUENCES OF BEHAVIOR

As we have suggested, a simple but most powerful guiding principle of Skinner's brand of behaviorism is that behavior is determined and maintained by its consequences. An animal or human can be controlled by those who possess reinforcers. Just as a rat can be trained to press a bar, jump over a fence, run a maze, turn to the right, fight with other rats, and perform other adaptive or unadaptive behaviors, so people are much more under the control of reinforcers than they think. Control does not necessarily mean conscious control exerted by a person or group, though of course it can be carefully planned and executed. It refers to the influence of environmental consequences upon what we do. One of Skinner's (1953) major contributions is his elaboration of the countless ways in which man's power of self-determination is under environmental control.

Everyone knows that in order to get certain results we have to take certain steps, that is, perform instrumental acts. "Instrumental acts" are the means to a goal. A behavior becomes an instrumental act if it leads to reinforcement. Furthermore, reinforced behavior tends to be repeated. The effects of reinforcement accrue only to that behavior which secures it, and do not strengthen behavior that is not instrumental (Skinner, 1963). Much of our behavior has been acquired through trial-and-error success. By success, we mean that certain behaviors have attained the status of instrumental acts; they have become means to reinforcers.

In his program for behaviorism, Watson (1914) suggested that the environment affects behavior, but he placed the emphasis on the determining power of situation. His S-R position stressed the power of the impinging stimulus and the plasticity of the person who simply reacts to the pressure of the stimulus. No doubt much behavior is molded by the events in a person's life, but reaction is not the only property of the organism. Thus Watson's S-R model is one-sided because it takes account of reaction only. Even the simplest organism behaves. In Skinner's approach to the study and control of behavior, behaving, rather than reacting, is studied. Behavior produces changes in the environment which may in turn change behavior. No doubt Watson perceived the fact that the consequences of behavior will influence the behavior that produced the consequences, but his preoccupation with the "molding" power of the environment led him to study this aspect alone. It soon became apparent that this model of behavior study was inadequate. By emphasizing the response aspect, Skinner comes much closer to controlling behavior. The environment selects behavior.

RESPONDENT AND OPERANT BEHAVIOR

Skinner has made an important distinction which should help us to understand the nature of conditioning: the difference between respondent and operant behavior. Respondent conditioning is the substitution of one stimulus for another in producing an already existing response. The same response is made to a different stimulus; thus, the learning which takes place in respondent conditioning increases the effects of the environment, that is, the number of stimuli that will elicit a response. A child may burn his hand with a lighted match, and as a result of the painful experience, may acquire an avoidance response to unlighted matches. Here a neutral stimulus, one which has produced no effect, acquires some of the properties of the lighted match. We will discuss this type of conditioning more thoroughly, but for now, the reader should bear in mind that responses are not increased through respondent conditioning; only the stimuli with which responses are already associated are increased. In operant conditioning, responses are modified. Native responses are organized in a great many different designs. Simple finger movements may be learned in many complicated patterns. In one sequence, the child drinks from a cup; in another pattern he eats with a fork; in another he learns to dress himself. The same responses can be used for countless instrumental acts. As we noted previously, the specific movements (the learned habit, or sequence of habits) depend upon the consequences. These may be arranged by an experimenter who wishes to engender the particular habits, or the consequences may occur in an unplanned manner (natural reinforcements and punishments).

A good way to remember the difference between the two forms of behavior is that in respondent conditioning, the stimulus *elicits* a response, whereas in operant conditioning, a response is *emitted* without a stimulus necessarily being present.

RESPONDENT CONDITIONING

The term "conditioning" has become associated with Ivan Pavlov (1927). Pavlov was a physiologist studying digestion, not a psychologist of learning, but his work with respondent conditioning has been extremely influential in theories of learning. Aside from all the technical jargon involved in describing conditioning, the process may be simply described as *stimulus substitution learning:* a neutral stimulus acquires some of the properties of a natural stimulus by being paired with it. A natural stimulus is one which produces a response in the absence of learning. All organisms have certain native reflexes which enable them to adapt to their environments. A reflex is made up of a response pattern that is elicited by a delimited range of stimuli. Examples of reflexes are eye blinking, avoidance of pain, pleasurable responses to certain stimuli, and the like. The range of stimuli capable of setting off such responses may be increased by pairing neutral stimuli with the natural stimuli. When the neutral stimulus acquires the property of producing a response that was elicited only by the natural stimulus, respondent conditioning has taken place.

The following facts are significant in respondent conditioning: (1) The conditioned stimulus (CS) has become an effective stimulus, and elicits a conditioned response (CR). (2) The natural stimulus is termed the unconditioned stimulus (UCS) because one does not have to be conditioned to respond to it. (3) The unconditioned response (UCR) is the natural reflex response, the unlearned response.

Having considered the basic elements of respondent conditioning, we may apply the concept to actual situations. But first a word should be said about the nature of the conditioned response. To say that in respondent conditioning a neutral stimulus substitutes for a natural stimulus in producing a response, implies that the response to the new stimulus is the same as that to the original unconditioned stimulus. The conditioned response is not the same; it is more in the nature of a lesser or greater fraction of the original response. It resembles the original response, but it may be weaker, or only a part of it. When the child was burned by the lighted match, he experienced a complex pattern of pain and fear in quick succession. The conditioned response to the sight of the unlighted match is not the same as the unconditioned response to the lighted match which burns the hand. The child now experiences fear of the unlighted match, but it is not of the same intensity, and furthermore, he does not experience pain. Again, a man may associate a particular perfume with a particular girl, but the scent of the perfume does not substitute for the girl nor elicit in him the same responses as her presence would do. Yet some fraction of the response is elicited, and it is extremely valuable to know this fact. The girl might be considered the natural stimulus to which many unlearned responses are made, and the perfume is the conditioned stimulus, which acquired some of the properties of the natural stimulus.

Suppose you would like to impress a certain person; it would be expedient to engage in activities with that person which he likes. If he enjoys eating, his pleasant reaction to food may be transferred to you so that you become a "conditioned positive stimulus." The practice of exchanging pictures, rings, gifts, and mementoes utilizes the principle of respondent conditioning. Some of the responses associated with the object are attributed to the giver, and some of the qualities of the giver are transferred to the object. If the object is enduring (not immediately consumable or temporary), such as wearing apparel, a music box, or other relatively permanent items, the conditioning may persist a lifetime. For instance, every time a gift record is played, it reminds the listener of the giver.

Many of our reactions to stimuli in our environment are the products of conditioning. Sometimes we may actually recall the original conditioning event which produced the reaction, sometimes not. A person who is uncomfortable driving may vividly recall an accident that conditioned his fear. A man reports that he always finds himself getting anxious during meals: he uses this time of the day to do his worrying. Eating seems to be a conditioned stimulus for reviewing his problems. He recalls that it all began during lunch periods in elementary school. While eating their lunches, the children were not permitted to talk. It happened that during this period he was having difficulty with the teacher with whom he spent most of his day. Not being able to converse during the lunch period, he found himself worrying and fretting about his relationship with his teacher, whom he feared and disliked intensely. Eating became associated with these negative emotions. He has suffered from digestive problems, chronic loss of appetite, and anxiety during certain meals ever since. His awareness later in life of the probable cause of his stomach difficulties has not altered the disorder. What is needed to bring about a cure is deconditioning, or extinction of the conditioned responses. Some of the bodily changes that occur as the result of conditioning are extremely difficult to remedy. Extinction procedures for such reactions have not yet been developed.

Extinction

Experimental extinction of respondent behaviors is produced by presenting the learned or conditioned stimulus repeatedly without following it by the natural or unconditioned stimulus. A dog that has been conditioned to salivate to a bell will extinguish the salivation response if the bell is presented repeatedly without food being paired with it. The intensity of the salivation to the bell gradually diminishes until no response occurs. Many conditioned emotional responses gradually extinguish because they occur in the presence of conditioned stimuli alone (Jones, 1924). However, if the conditioned stimuli are again followed by the original painful experience, the conditioned responses will regain strength. Because of the recurrence of the unconditioned stimulus from time to time, many conditioned emotional responses last a lifetime. What we have said regarding the extinction of conditioned respondents also applies to the extinction of operants. If the operant is not followed by reinforcement, the likelihood of its occurrence begins to weaken. An operant is extinguished when its occurrence has returned to its pre-conditioning level. The bar-pressing of a rat in a Skinner box will gradually decrease if reinforcement is not given.

We have noted that the man who had difficulty with eating would have to undergo extinction to be cured. His situation is highly complex because there are probably a multitude of conditioned responses that must be extinguished.

What are the stimuli? What causes the anxiety and worry? Is it the mere act of sitting down before a table to eat? Is it taking food in his mouth? Is it chewing and swallowing the food? Could it be a full stomach that serves as the conditioned stimulus? Probably the answer is that all of these, and others, are conditioned stimuli evoking the conditioned responses of fear, anxiety, anger, and hate. The extinction of unwanted conditioned responses is a major task of behavior therapy and behavior modification (Stampfl and Levis, 1967).

One method of extinguishing a conditioned response is to present the conditioned stimulus in mild forms or intensities. A child who fears water may be helped to overcome his fear by playing first in a small pool or pond where the water is shallow, then in a little larger one, and so on until he entirely extinguishes his phobia. Another method is to use counterconditioning: in order to prevent a child from developing a phobia of dentists, the child is brought for a visit, even though there is no work to be done on his teeth He may visit with the dentist, ride up and down on the chair, and look at some of the tools. It is assumed that through this procedure he will be conditioned with "pleasurable" responses which will later counteract, in part, his unpleasant reactions to the drill.

Aversive conditioning is also used as a counterconditioning procedure. A habit may be broken by making the consequences unpleasant. For instance, the craving for alcohol may be changed to an aversion by adding to the liquor substances such as Antabuse which produce nausea and vomiting. Assumedly the thought or sight of alcohol will then become a stimulus for an aversive response. However, it should be noted that this form of counterconditioning is not effective with everyone, for some people condition quite easily and extinguish slowly, while others condition slowly and extinguish easily. The English psychologist, Hans Eysenck (1965), has a theory of innate personality difference which attempts to account for these disparities in conditioning. There are certainly individual variations in the extent to which counterconditioning is effective in inhibiting a conditioned response.

OPERANT CONDITIONING

Operant conditioning is behavior that has been selected, sorted, and emphasized as a result of reinforcement. To understand clearly the nature of operant conditioning, we should keep in mind the important distinction between reaction or response on the one hand, and action or behavior on the other. The term "response" is often used synonymously with "behavior"; there is nothing wrong with this usage until we want to make a distinction between an action and a reaction. I react or respond to a doorbell ringing with a startle pattern, but when I go to the door I am behaving or acting. We have seen that in respondent conditioning one increases the range of stimuli that produce the same response; the conditioning does not alter the response but does alter the range of stimuli. In operant conditioning, behavior itself is altered: the conditioning results in an increase in the behavior repertory of the organism. If operant conditioning is successful, new behavior occurs. What is the nature of this "new behavior"? It may be simply a rearrangement of existing behavior, as was noted earlier.

The concept of emitted behavior will help to clarify the meaning of operant behavior. Emitted behavior is the observed random or spontaneous behavior of an organism which cannot usually be traced to specific stimuli (Skinner, 1938). If a rat is placed in a Skinner box, it will be active; its behavior is emitted behavior because there are no stimuli that can be identified as causing its actions. When the rat in its course of activity presses a bar in the box, a pellet drops which it eats. Something happens to the pattern of behavior as a consequence of the reinforcement, the food pellet: the emitted behavior of bar-pressing is strengthened. The rat begins to press the bar more frequently, gets more food, and presses more often. Once reinforcement begins, then, behavior starts to come under the control of the reinforcing stimulus, the food. The rat's actions become much less random. Time is now largely spent in regular and predictable bar-pressing.

The differences between respondent and operant conditioning are summarized in Table 5–1.

TABLE 5–1   PARADIGMS FOR RESPONDENT AND OPERANT CONDITIONING

A. Respondent Conditioning:

UCS _____ UCR

CS + UCS _____ UCR

CS _____ CR

In classical conditioning, an unconditioned stimulus (UCS), such as a tap to the knee, elicits the unconditioned response (UCR) of a knee jerk. A conditioned stimulus (CS) may then be paired with the UCS repeatedly until the CS, such as a bell, elicits a knee jerk in the absence of the UCS.

B. Operant Conditioning (Skinner Box):

$$
S \text{_____} \begin{cases} R_1 \text{ Exploring} \\ R_2 \text{ Scratching} \\ R_3 \text{ Grooming} \\ R_4 \text{ Defecating} \\ R_5 \text{ Urinating} \\ R_6 \text{ BAR-PRESSING: operant response} \end{cases}
$$

Total stimulus situation: Skinner box
Occasioning stimuli: Hunger stimuli
Discriminable stimulis: Sight of bar

In operant conditioning, the organism emits a variety of behaviors, but once the behavior desired by the experimenter is emitted, it is immediately reinforced. Upon subsequent emissions of the desired behavior such reinforcement causes an increase in frequency of this behavior. The paradigm above depicts the exploratory behavior of a rat in a Skinner box. There is a total stimulus situation within the box which includes the walls, lever, water tube, eating dish, etc. The rat thus has many things to act upon. In this total situation, a variety of responses are possible, as listed above. But only when bar-pressing occurs does the rat receive any reinforcement, usually consisting of a food pellet. Occasioning and discriminable stimuli signal and guide behavior, but do not elicit it.

CONTINGENCIES OF REINFORCEMENT

The term "contingency" may be defined as "dependence upon." To say that reinforcement is contingent upon a specific operant behavior means that it depends upon the occurrence of some specific operant behavior. An individual is not reinforced unless he acts appropriately. Let us consider a typical situation: John asks Mary for a date, and she accepts. He has now asked her ten times, and each time she has accepted. The operant behavior is John's invitation for a date. Mary's acceptance is the reinforcement. The schedule of reinforcement may be described as total; she has accepted every time. As we have noted, contingency implies a relationship in which there is mutual dependence; in this instance John's behavior depends upon Mary's, and Mary's behavior is influenced by John's. Obviously, Mary cannot reinforce behavior which John does not emit. But when John does emit behavior, Mary can influence future behavior by her reinforcement power.

After reinforcing John's invitations by accepting a number of dates, Mary may suddenly stop accepting. John will continue asking her for a while, but eventually the operant behavior of asking will be extinguished. However, the contingency (the relation of behavior and reinforcement) may not be all or none; Mary may choose to refuse from time to time. This type of reinforcement is known as partial or intermittent reinforcement, in this case, "playing hard to get." Mary wants to keep John's rate of responding high and to use her reinforcement power to best advantage. Animals can be made to work quite hard for smaller and smaller reinforcements, and there are parallels in human behavior. Work output is generally better on a piece rate than by hourly pay. Commissions can be highly motivating even if their occurrence is highly unpredictable; the salesman may emit a great deal of behavior for modest reinforcements. Gambling is another example: a few wins may sustain many tries. Skinner (Ferster and Skinner, 1957) has given names to the contingencies (the specific manner in which the reinforcement is related to operant behavior), such as fixed and variable interval schedules, fixed and variable ratio schedules.

SCHEDULES OF REINFORCEMENT CONTROL BEHAVIOR

That reinforcement can influence behavior has been known for a long time, but Skinner has demonstrated the intricate ways in which reinforcements can be used (see Fig. 5–1). Specific schedules of reinforcement have characteristic rates of responding associated with them. In the fixed interval schedule, the reinforcement is based on time, not on the behavior of the subject. In contrast, ratio reinforcement schedules do depend on the behavior of the subject, in that the subject can increase the likelihood of reinforcement by emitting more responses. Skinner and his collaborators have demonstrated the capability of such schedules in controlling the behavior of animals. The observer is impressed by the orderliness of the behavior that is being manipulated. Much of the same control has been demonstrated with humans.

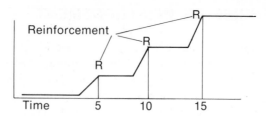

FI (Fixed Interval): Reinforcement occurs after a determined amount of time, such as every 5 minutes. Reinforcement is provided at these time intervals despite the organism's responses or lack of responses. A cumulative record of FI responding typically reveals a scalloped graph. Pauses occur after reinforcement and responding increases as the end of an interval approaches. When one is expecting an important letter, the checking of a mail box may be on an FI schedule. The rate of checking the mailbox increases greatly just before the mailman arrives. After his arrival, behavior ceases abruptly, then increases again just before his next scheduled arrival.

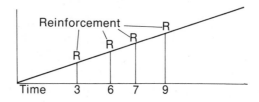

VI (Variable Interval): Reinforcement occurs after varying quantities of time. In one period, reinforcement may occur after 3-6-7-9 minutes successively. VI reinforcement results in sustained responding at a low rate.

Figure 5–1   Fixed Interval, Variable Interval, Fixed Ratio, and Variable Ratio responses.
Illustration continued on opposite page.

Consider some practical instances of behavior under the various schedules of reinforcement. The fixed interval schedule, so commonly used, produces low levels of responding. A weekly salary is an example. Unless the worker gets into trouble, the salary is paid no matter what he does. Many supervisors complain that their workers are lazy, but Skinner would argue that the difficulty lies instead in the fixed interval schedule of reinforcement. The same may be said of fixed salary increases. In some professions there is a guaranteed yearly increase in salary, according to a negotiated schedule. In such instances, merit has little to do with the salary increments. Another fixed interval schedule that may produce unfavorable consequences is the practice of giving gifts to children on certain days of the year. Ordinarily, the child does nothing to deserve the gifts. Could this practice foster the development of faulty expectations regarding the nature of the good life? One more example is the welfare program: what does it do to a person to receive doles regularly without doing anything to receive them, except being unable to work?

Consider the difference in behavior under a fixed and a variable interval schedule in the case of regularly scheduled tests and those unannounced. Let

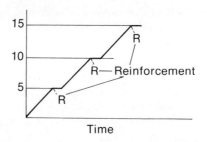

Cumulative Number of Responses

Time

FR (Fixed Ratio): Reinforcement occurs after a fixed number of responses. FR-5, for example, means reinforcement is given after every 5th response made by the subject. FR schedules result in high and stable rates of responding with a pause immediately after each reinforcement is given. Factory piecework (workers paid after a fixed number of items are produced) is an example of an FR schedule.

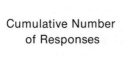

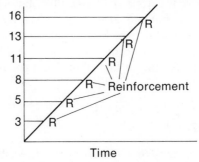

Cumulative Number of Responses

Time

VR (Variable Ratio): Reinforcement comes after varying numbers of responses. For example, reinforcement in one FR schedule may come after the 3rd then 5th then 8th responses, repeating the pattern of 3-5-8. Variable ratio schedules result in high steady rates of responding. Gambling devices such as slot machines employ the principle of variable ratio scheduling.

Figure 5–1 *Continued.*

us regard testing as an aversive stimulus and the preparation as a form of avoidance behavior. (Many students study primarily to avoid failing tests.) When the tests are regularly announced, the studying behavior increases just before the tests and drops right after. In the unannounced schedule, the behavior is steady because one must be prepared for each class, lest he experience unwanted aversive consequences.

In ratio reinforcement, the behavior of the subject can influence the occurrence of the reinforcement. In a piece-rate program of paying, the worker's output can augment and speed the salary rate. Even if the piece-rate requirement is increased, the worker's behavior can still influence the reinforcements. An example of an effective ratio schedule is the merit increase, if it is truly based on work output rather than on other aspects of working. Sometimes schedules may be combined, as when one receives both a fixed base salary and a commission.

Operant behavior is not only "built up" by means of reinforcers; the strength and frequency of the operant behavior also depend upon the way the reinforcer occurs, the particular schedule. Thus reinforcement both builds behavior and sustains it after it is formed. The question of the maintenance of behavior is highly crucial in many aspects of life. Behavior can be sustained with remarkably sparse reinforcement if the appropriate schedule of reinforcement is followed (Jenkins and Stanley, 1950). In general, one begins with total reinforcement, and gradually less and less is used, while more and more behavior is required of the organism for the same reinforcement. In the building of behavior, reinforcements are given at first for partial responses, even for incorrect responses, simply because they move in the direction of the correct response. Reinforcement is such a powerful factor in controlling behavior that it can be used to shape learning. We will look at this most important aspect of operant conditioning in a moment, but now let us return momentarily to John asking Mary for a date. We have seen that John has to emit behavior before it can be reinforced by Mary, but what causes John to emit the appropriate behavior? Mary can play a part by providing a *discriminable* or noticeable stimulus which may serve as an *occasioning* stimulus; in other words, she may give John a hint. But John has to be able to discriminate the meaning of the hint, or he will not emit the behavior that Mary wishes to reinforce.

SHAPING

Shaping is a term that is associated especially with Skinner's procedures for operant conditioning. It is roughly synonymous with the "method of successive approximations"—behavior modification, behavior engineering. Shaping behavior means building behavior patterns, or operants, by means of reinforcement of partial or graded responses. Undifferentiated behavior is molded gradually in an ordered series of steps which increasingly approximate the desired behavior pattern (Ferster and Skinner, 1957). A rat in a Skinner box will eventually learn to depress the bar that causes a pellet of food to drop into the food dish. It may be said that the operant response of bar-pressing is formed by the natural contingencies of the Skinner box; the hungry animal learns the response simply because it is active and eventually depresses the bar accidentally. But it is possible to shape the bar-pressing operant with the use of the method of successive approximations.

Bar-pressing behavior is far from a simple reflex response. The animal has to orient toward the bar, move in its direction, approach it, and press the bar with enough pressure to activate the mechanism. It is only because the Skinner box precludes many competing responses, and because it is so arranged that bar-pressing is a likely behavior, given the nature of a laboratory rat, that the operant behavior can be learned without any prompts and assists from the experimenter. By reinforcing behavior that more and more approximates the final pattern, the process of building up the operant is greatly speeded. The rat is reinforced first whenever he turns in the direction of the bar, then when he advances toward it, then only when he approaches the bar, then only when he touches the bar, and finally only when he depresses it. Shaping procedures not only hasten the process of building operants, but may also be used to produce operants that would never occur under natural contingencies or conditions. Skinner has been able to get pigeons to play ping-pong, dance with each other, peck for hours at a time on a switch, and engage in many other unpigeon-like behaviors. He has successfully regulated the speed, the strength, and the pattern of responses.

Shaping is a common experience among people in everyday life. A parent utters a word; his child attempts to imitate it; the parent reinforces the partially correct (approximate) response by saying "good"; he then repeats the correct version of the word. Some parents insist on the correct version before giving a reinforcement. Skinner (1957) suggests that they would obtain better results if they reinforced approximations of the exact word. It might be objected that reinforcing wrong responses makes those responses more likely to occur than the proper response. Many children are, in fact, reinforced for "baby talk" and carry this to adulthood, because the parents are apparently reinforced by such talk and, in turn, reinforce it in their children. But to say that reinforcing approximations is reinforcing wrong behavior misses the whole point of shaping. Reinforcement should be given only when the approximations progressively resemble the final form; thus, reinforcement is not given for approximations that have already been reinforced. Finally, only the correct word or phrase is reinforced. Instead of perpetuating "baby talk," the method of successive approximations is an excellent way of eliminating such incorrect verbal forms.

Skinner and many others have used operant procedures in education. Skinner (1968) is one of the pioneers in the field of teaching machines and programmed instruction. The learner proceeds, in a short time, through a series of graded steps, from a low level of performance or knowledge to almost complete mastery of a particular skill or subject. Many of the principles discovered in the animal laboratory are used. For example, the learner's behavior is shaped; the material is presented in small chunks. He may be given prompts to foster correct responses. Incorrect responses are undesirable because they can also be learned, and will interfere with the recall of correct ones; thus, in a well-developed program these are kept to a minimum by having the learner advance one small step at a time. He is informed by the machine each time his answer, which is filled in, matches the one given in the program. This knowledge of being correct is the reinforcer. Complicated sequences of ideas are graded, so that the learner proceeds systematically, going on to the next step only after he has mastered the one on which he has been working. The program is designed to shape the behavior of the learner, using principles of operant conditioning.

DIFFERENTIAL REINFORCEMENT

A variation on shaping is the technique of differential reinforcement (Skinner, 1953). This means selective reinforcement and extinction — reinforcing only desired behaviors and not others. Not only do certain operants acquire greater strength by this procedure, but others are weakened. Suppose that a friend whom you like very much emits both sarcastic and nonsarcastic behavior. Given the notion that you have "reinforcing power," it should be possible to shape your friend's actions. You would like to increase the occurrence of nonsarcastic behaviors and decrease the sarcastic ones. You can reinforce with approval, laughter, smiles, praise, or attention when he displays behavior which you prefer, and remain silent, turn away, interrupt, or change the subject when he is acting sarcastically. You are using differential reinforcement, and if you have reinforcement power over your friend, his behavior will be modified. It should be noted that Skinner advises against the use of punishment to eliminate the unwanted behavior. As we shall see, punishment does not automatically eliminate undesirable conduct and may in fact provoke worse behavior. The unwanted behavior should be ignored or extinguished by other nonpunitive methods.

Some recent work in the area of biofeedback conditioning has demonstrated the powerful role of differential reinforcement in promoting the control of organic processes by the individual himself. The traditional notions of self-control may have to undergo drastic changes. It has been possible to control physiological functions such as heart rate, digestive activities, the contraction and expansion of blood vessels, and even electrical brain activity. A typical procedure is to allow a subject to hear a signal which goes on when the heart rate drops several beats per minute. The signal informs the person that his heartbeat has slowed slightly, but this signal may be set so that it goes on only if the rate is several beats less than the previous setting. As a rule, there is a signal that matches the heartbeat all along, and a different signal that is heard when the rate of heartbeat drops. By this procedure, subjects have been able to reduce their heart rate as much as 15 beats per minute.

Such work offers the hope that one may be able to control moods, motivation, and even temperament with his own behaviors. A device known as an alpha sensor makes an audible signal when the alpha waves in the brain are present. The device is attached to the head, and the person listens for the signal that tells him that the brain activity is characteristic of relaxation. The alpha increases gradually in intensity and frequency as the alpha rhythm of the brain predominates. It takes some time to acquire the ability to keep the signal on, but it can be done. Subjects who have learned this technique report that they experience profound relaxation when the alpha rhythm emerges (Nowlis and Kamiya, 1970). The feedback of the alpha sensor provides the differential reinforcement that shapes the operant behavior. Even though the person does not know what behavior produces the particular brain wave, he is able to emit the behavior upon request.

Reinforcement is such a basic concept for Skinner that his entire psychology may be described as "reinforcement psychology." To sum up, operant conditioning occurs only if there is a reinforcement following an emitted response.

Shaping is the systematic use of reinforcers to produce a response by reinforcing approximations of that response. Scheduling refers to the timing, patterning, and amount of reinforcement. The basic principle of Skinner's psychology is that behavior is formed and maintained by reinforcers. We have already said some things about reinforcers and reinforcement, but the process is so universal that certain further ideas should be considered. We will look at positive and negative reinforcers, punishment and aversive procedures. If reinforcers play such a significant role in living, we ought to know what they are, how they can best be used, and what consequences occur when they are not used properly. Most of us prefer to be reinforced rather than punished, and Skinner (1971) believes that punishment to form or change behavior is used much too often. A highly significant fact about punishment is that it is an unpredictable, and often ineffective, means of controlling behavior. On the other hand, reinforcement increases the likelihood of the desired behavior. It would seem that those who have control of the behavior of others should take this difference into account. These ideas will become clearer as we discuss reinforcement.

POSITIVE REINFORCEMENT, NEGATIVE REINFORCEMENT, AND PUNISHMENT

POSITIVE REINFORCEMENT

Reinforcement, whether positive or negative, is ultimately an individual matter, but because of similarities among people, we can identify typical reinforcers. The broadest classification is the division of positive reinforcers into *unlearned* and *learned*. These classes are also termed *primary* and *secondary*, *unconditioned* and *conditioned*. Organismic requirements are clear cases of primary reinforcement: food, water, sexual object, rest, activity, curiosity. There are some obviously learned reinforcers such as money, awards, medals, and honors. There are also reinforcers—such as affection, approval, and attention—which Skinner (1953) calls *generalized conditioned reinforcers*, by which he means that they are learned reinforcers that can reinforce many different behaviors. Food is reinforcing to someone who is hungry or who has a craving for it, but praise, approval, attention, and affection can reinforce a great variety of behaviors. For instance, some people will do almost anything for attention, approval, or affection. It is significant to note that many of these generalized reinforcers are within the power of all of us to give. In other words, we have the power to pay attention to someone, to praise, to approve of his responses, to give affection (Rheingold et al., 1959). As we noted earlier, the manner of giving reinforcers (when, how much, and what type) is a critical factor in behavior control and modification.

Conditioned Reinforcers

We discussed respondent and operant conditioning as if they were totally distinct processes. While they are different, they frequently occur together. When behavior is successful in securing reinforcement, certain aspects of the reinforcing situation may become eliciting stimuli for emotional responses. These emotional responses may be either negative or positive. A child writes a good paper and receives praise from his teacher. Skinner considers praise to be a learned reinforcer, but there are those who would argue that it is a primary psychological reinforcer. Let us take this position. The praise is accompanied by a grade, or a per cent value. If this is repeated a number of times, the grades or per cent standings acquire the status of conditioned reinforcers; they are reinforcing in their own right, at least for a time. It is argued that such conditioned reinforcers must be strengthened from time to time with primary reinforcers, or they will extinguish; the grades must be supported by teacher or parental approval if they are to control the child's behavior. But the conditioned reinforcers have remarkable reinforcing power. Our lives are controlled by them much more than we suspect (Wilson and Verplanck, 1956), and one who wishes to take over his own life must identify them as a first step.

The author conducted an informal experiment with his two children with conditioned reinforcers. Paul, who is ten, and Laureen, who is eight, were told that they were going to receive points for certain jobs around the house. A chart would be provided for the points, but they were responsible for recording their own points. The rules were simple: certain jobs such as wiping the table and emptying the rubbish would earn specified points. Other jobs could earn points; they had to choose the job and submit it for evaluation. Nothing was said about the "pay off" for all this work. The first evening both children scurried about doing a variety of chores and assigning themselves the points. They continued doing jobs which they did not like to do for several days, despite their waning enthusiasm for the program. About the fourth day, Paul began grumbling about the prize, but the subject was quickly changed. A prize was never mentioned. About the sixth day, Laureen wondered what would happen if she won, and what constituted winning in any case. Again the question was simply evaded. The children continued working for the points, although at a diminished rate, for about three weeks, until finally a reinforcer was given to each of them.

This home experiment demonstrates the remarkable reinforcing power of something as unrewarding as points. Competition may have played a part, parental encouragement may also have contributed, but these factors were minimized as much as possible. Simply earning empty points was reinforcement enough to get the children to do things they disliked doing. We might consider how much we do for flattery, for status, for approval, to get ahead of others, to have more of certain intangibles such as better grades, awards, honors. Many conditioned reinforcers are the unpaying aspects of a culture: for instance, the tremendous amount of work that is performed for secondary reinforcements by volunteers (Skinner, 1953).

NEGATIVE REINFORCEMENT

Negative reinforcement occurs when behavior removes an unpleasant or aversive stimulus (the term "stimulus" is to be taken in a broad sense). The removal of the unwanted stimulus reinforces the behavior which accomplishes that feat. We will take up punishment separately, but for now it should be kept in mind that punishment adds something unpleasant to behavior in order to weaken or eliminate it, whereas negative reinforcement is designed to strengthen avoidance or escape behavior by adding something unpleasant which the behavior can remove (Skinner, 1972). Good attendance as a means of avoiding the final examination is an example of negative reinforcement: the unwanted final exam may be avoided. In this case, the behavior eliminates an unwanted aspect of a situation, and the outcome is highly desirable. Not every instance of negative reinforcement is so clear-cut, and frequently some punitive elements remain, as we shall see. Another example of negative reinforcement is the reduction of a prison term by good behavior. The prisoner's behavior does not obtain anything directly, as in the case of positive reinforcement, but it does give him the opportunity to secure positive reinforcement by reducing his sentence. Still other examples are the reduction of the number of periods in school by the earning of a certain grade average, and the lowering of a fine if the offender attends safety classes.

The examples of negative reinforcement that we have presented may be viewed as variations upon positive reinforcement, because when the unpleasant aspects are totally removed by the behavior, the person is free to seek other reinforcements. Yet many other cases fitting the pattern of negative reinforcement are more like punishment than reward: instances of avoiding the consequences of threats are of this type. An employee works in order to avoid the consequences that his boss might produce—being fired, being given an undesirable job, losing a promotion. This type of aversive control is often effective and is probably the most frequently used method of behavior engineering. Children avoid the punishment of their parents by conforming to their demands and expectations. Students avoid the power of the teacher by fulfilling the requirements of the course, no matter how irrational and distasteful they may be. There is no question that avoiding threats is reinforcing to a degree, but it is weak in many instances and may have unpleasant by-products (Brady, 1958). One of the problems with negative reinforcers is that their consequences are unpredictable; sometimes they are effective and sometimes not. The worker may stop working after a period of time, unless he is threatened anew by the boss. The boss has to keep a close watch and check on his employee. The inclination not to work, or to do other things, competes with the work activities; it is suppressed by the power of the boss, which must take the form of a continuous threat. The employee's behavior at best avoids the boss's power, but it does not eliminate it; therefore a punitive element remains. The good behavior really does not obtain anything for the worker, as is the case with positive reinforcement. Thus it seems to this writer that most instances of negative reinforcement are really instances of punishment, or at least an admixture of negative reinforcement and punishment.

CONSEQUENCES OF NEGATIVE AND POSITIVE REINFORCEMENT

Let us contrast positive and negative reinforcement. A father might get his son to study his lessons by offering him a positive reinforcer such as the use of the family car Saturday evening, or he may use a negative reinforcer by threatening an earlier curfew. In both instances the father may get results, but the consequences of positive reinforcement are much more desirable than those of negative reinforcement (Skinner, 1971). Threatening punishment may induce emotional responses in the son: the boy may become antagonistic toward the father; he may not come home on time in the evenings; he may talk back to his father; he may actually refuse to follow his father's wishes; he may even deliberately fail in his studies as a means of retaliating. One thing is clear: behavior that produces positive reinforcement tends to be repeated, whereas behavior that simply avoids a threatened punishment will not necessarily be sustained and, in fact, other undesirable behaviors may occur. Behavior which is punished is subject to the same conditions as negative reinforcement, and the unwanted by-products may be even more serious. Since one cannot avoid punishment, the emotional responses may be intense.

One point should be clear: in his criticism of punishment, Skinner does not advocate using positive reinforcers to prevent unwanted behavior. Rather, he advocates use of positive reinforcers to promote certain desirable behaviors, and use of methods other than negative reinforcement and punishment to eliminate undesirable behavior. What do you do with undesirable behavior, if you do not use negative reinforcers and punishment? There are alternative methods of behavior modification: extinction (not paying attention to the behavior), satiation (allowing the person to engage in the behavior until he tires of it), changing circumstances (e.g., distracting a child or changing the subject), promoting counteracting behavior, and simply allowing forgetting to take place (Skinner, 1953). Children are often controlled by threats of punishment; the mother follows the child about with a constant flurry of "nos" and "no-nos." Skinner advises the harassed mother to remove the objects she wishes to preserve until the child reaches the age when he is no longer interested in them. The child who has an intense interest in the telephone may be punished or threatened a hundred times, but he still continues to play with the phone when his mother is not around. Better to let him play with the phone until he tires of it, until he is satiated with it, than to engage in aversive control. We could go on with such examples, but the point should be clear: negative reinforcers and punishment are not the only ways to prevent or block unwanted behavior and promote desirable behavior.

PUNISHMENT

Punishment occurs when behavior is followed by an unpleasant consequence, or when behavior causes a desirable thing to be withdrawn. The purpose of punishment is to stop or change undesirable behavior. A child who has wandered off from home may be punished by being confined to the house for a period of time, or his mother may display strong disapproval and direct hostility. The purpose is to protect the child, but it may not be effective. Punished behavior is not necessarily eliminated (Estes, 1944); instead, the punished one may find other ways to secure what he wants. The child who is punished for wandering off has not been changed by the punishment. If he was trying to find his friend's house, he may persist in his desire to seek out his friend. Perhaps the mother should seek the cause of the child's wandering and deal directly to change it. For instance, she may instruct him to ask for help in getting to his friend's house.

Punishment, then, may stop or block behavior, but it does not necessarily change the cause of the behavior. The punishment builds up fear, but gradually the fear extinguishes if the person avoids the punishment, and eventually the behavior that was originally punished will recur. Imprisonment punishes the criminal and engenders fear, among other emotions. The fear persists at a sufficient intensity after imprisonment to block the antisocial behavior for a while, but it may diminish so that antisocial behavior again emerges. Some ex-convicts do not commit crime again; it may be that while the fear prevented them from committing crime, they became involved in other activities such as work, family, religion, and so on. The finding of these new interests should not be left to the ex-convict; it should be engineered by rehabilitation experts (Skinner, 1971). If punishment is not the answer to crime, then what is? Skinner would argue that rehabilitation is better than punishment, and that prevention, by reinforcing socially acceptable behavior, is better than treatment.

Like negative reinforcement, punishment may produce unfavorable by-products. The prisoner comes to hate society even more after imprisonment. His resentment may induce him to seek still more devious ways of expressing his hatred and bitterness. A person with a prison record is discriminated against; thus many conditions make return to crime the only way open to him. The identification of a child with his parents may also be greatly disturbed by repeated punishment (Mischel and Grusec, 1966). The positive reinforcing power of the parents wanes in the process. The same notion may be applied to husband and wife relationships: a nagging, complaining, critical mate will induce negative emotions in the other spouse, and these will counteract any positive reinforcers that are used.

If punishment is to be used in blocking behavior, it should be informative: it should communicate the notion that the behavior is undesirable. A parent informs a child by disapproval. The purpose is best accomplished by mild punishment, and many of the undesirable consequences are thus avoided. But Skinner, in general, prefers the use of positive reinforcers to foster behavior. Drivers should be reinforced for driving safely, not just punished when they do not. Children should be rewarded when they are behaving well and not just attended to when they misbehave. Misbehavior may become their only means of getting attention. In Table 5–2 the characteristics of positive and negative reinforcement are summarized and compared. Punishment is also considered.

TABLE 5-2 CHARACTERISTICS OF REINFORCEMENT AND PUNISHMENT

Positive Reinforcement	Negative Reinforcement	Punishment
1. Produced by instrumental behavior	1. Consists of the removal of unwanted consequences	1. Used to weaken behaviors, but frequently ineffective
2. Increases the probability of a particular instrumental response	2. Strengthens instrumental avoidance behavior	2. Consists of following instrumental responses by an unpleasant consequence, or removing one that is desired
3. Increases the intensity of a particular instrumental response	3. Strengthens instrumental escape behavior	3. Suppresses behavior, but does not necessarily weaken it
4. Sustains instrumental responses that have been learned	4. Increases the behavior that removes it	4. May instigate other instrumental responses that accomplish the same goal (being caught stealing during the day instigates stealing at night)
5. Elicits respondent emotional behaviors that induce approach behavior (enthusiasm, zest, encouragement, joy, excitement, pleasure)	5. Resembles positive reinforcement when instrumental responses remove certain aversive consequences (shortening a prison sentence by good behavior; receiving reduced work load as reward for good work)	5. May result in conditioned emotional responses (ulcers, chronic headache, resentment, and other psychosomatic processes; anger, hatred, fear, anxiety, distrust)
	6. Resembles punishment when instrumental responses simply prevent punishment (performing a job to avoid punishment by the boss; cleaning one's room to prevent mother's nagging)	6. May result in avoidance or escape behaviors (active avoidance: learning what to do to avoid the punishment; passive avoidance: learning what not to do to avoid or escape from the punishment)
		7. If mild, may stimulate alternative behaviors

Note: Reinforcement strengthens, punishment weakens. Strictly speaking, punishment cannot be avoided: an angry parent who is motivated to punish his child will administer the punishment in spite of the child's cries, protests, and pleadings. If punishment can be avoided or escaped, then we are dealing with negative reinforcement.

CRITIQUE OF SKINNER

As we suggested in the introductory notes on Skinner, his concepts and methods are highly influential in contemporary psychology. More than those of any other contemporary psychologist, they are being applied in other fields as well. The greatest support for Skinner is the empirical validation that his techniques are receiving. Behavior is being modified and controlled in many settings, ranging from penal institutions to the classroom, from the athletic field to the consulting office, with white rats and graduate students, with retarded children and superior adults. Behavior engineering is a widespread phenomenon in our day, and it seems to be increasing in scope. But there are questions that are still not answered. How enduring are the changed behaviors? If one removes the reinforcers, the behavior extinguishes. If the deviant is reinforced for socially approved behavior, what will assure the continuation of the behavior, when the contrived reinforcers are removed? Regarding the long-continued use of contrived reinforcers, Skinner says:

You don't need to maintain a system of contrived reinforcers indefinitely. People get the impression that I believe that we should all get gumdrops whenever we do anything of value. There are many ways of attenuating a system of reinforcement. Certain schedules of reinforcement permit you to reduce the frequency of reinforcement steadily. But the main thing is to let the noncontrived reinforcers take over. The students who get prizes for doing their homework eventually discover the natural reinforcers of getting work done. They discover that they are learning something, possibly in contrast with their brothers and sisters in other classrooms, but in any case something which makes them more successful (Skinner, 1972, p. 130).

It is tempting for one who advocates a whole new approach to the total field, as Skinner does, to explain everything with concepts which apply adequately to only a part of the total. Skinner attempts to relate concepts of operant conditioning to self-management, with the individual being both the controller and the controlled. He makes this distinction between the controlled self and the controlling self in order to demonstrate that personal management of behavior (what was traditionally called will power) can be brought within the framework of reinforcement theory. The controlling self can act as the behavior engineer and map out a program of behavior modification and control. One can institute a set of contingencies for himself. For example, certain desirable activities (positive reinforcements) may be made contingent upon certain behaviors; thus one may allow himself a trip to the snack bar only if he studies a given amount of time, or some indulgence such as buying a new record as a reward for studying hard for a test.

It is doubtful that Skinner can legitimately claim this form of self-control under his notion of behavior engineering. While it is true that one can be taught specific techniques of self-management, the application of these techniques requires an element of personal striving. Furthermore, one may create his own methods of self-control. How can this be explained behavioristically? After one has worked out a plan with all the behaviors and reinforcements specified, one may simply not be able to carry it out. It is a common observation that all the good intentions in the world may not be sufficient to guarantee that they will be executed. Saint Paul says: "The spirit is willing, but the flesh is weak." It would seem that Skinner is outside of his domain when he delves into self-management, even though he attempts to relate it to past reinforcement schedules. Why one person can carry out a personally developed program of self-management and another cannot remains an unanswered question. Perhaps one can more vividly sense the consequences of his behavior than the other. Then, too, how can the various schedules of reinforcement which have been found to be so effective in controlling behavior be applied to oneself? In any case, it seems likely that a different conception of man and different techniques will be required to promote better self-management.

Further, operant reinforcement theory seems limited to explaining learned behaviors that are chiefly under the control of reward and punishment. Skinner, despite active attempts, has not been particularly successful in accounting for cognitive behaviors such as concept formation, and thinking, or for the acquisition of language. He is also unable to account for learning by observation (imitation). The success of operant conditioning techniques should not lead us to assume that they explain all or even most of behavior.

However, when one broadens the concept of reinforcement to include contrived and natural, specific and generalized, extrinsic and intrinsic, other-imposed and self-imposed, the range of possible applications in human life is almost unlimited. There is no question that reinforcements play an enormous role in every aspect of living. It has always been so, but Skinner more than any other psychologist has refined the techniques of utilizing reinforcers for behavior management. Science is cumulative, and there is no reason why those who may have a different conception of man, such as the humanistic psychologists, cannot utilize and build upon the behavior modification procedures of Skinner. A model of man which allows for a certain degree of self-determination can incorporate Skinner's techniques and discoveries, even if not his general conception of humanity. It is unlikely that Skinner's technology will ever be replaced completely.

INSIGHTS FROM SKINNER'S REINFORCEMENT THEORY

EXAMPLES OF REINFORCEMENT

Skinner assumes that all behavior is established and maintained by reinforcers; thus if you observe a particular behavior, you should be able to discover the reinforcements that sustain it. Lack of behavior—apathy, laziness, and chronic fatigue—is indicative of low reinforcement levels. On the other hand, intense interest and dedication are indications of strong reinforcements. The reinforcers may be difficult to identify in a specific case, but by suitable observation, they can be found. Does a man spend his time in civic activities? Perhaps his reinforcers are public acclaim, honors, admiration by others. Does a mother spend time with her children, or does she do everything to get rid of them? Where do a person's payoffs lie? For what does he work the hardest and longest? Reinforcements are involved in every aspect of life: education, economics, leisure activities, work. Skinner gives us some advice on how to identify reinforcers:

We evaluate the strength of reinforcing events when we attempt to discover what someone is getting out of life. What consequences are responsible for his present repertoire and for the relative frequencies of responses in it? His responses to various topics of conversation tell us something, but his everyday behavior is a better guide. We infer important reinforcers from nothing more unusual than his interest in a writer who deals with certain subjects, in stones, or museums which exhibit certain objects, in friends who participate in certain kinds of behavior, in restaurants which serve certain kinds of food, and so on. The "interest" refers to the probability which results at least in part from the consequences of the behavior of taking an interest. We may be more nearly sure of the importance of a reinforcer if we watch the behavior come and go as the reinforcer is alternately supplied and withheld, for the change in probability is then less likely to be due to an incidental change of some other sort (1953, p. 74).*

Skinner has redefined many typical psychological concepts in operant conditioning terms. He has attempted to rid psychology of "explanatory fictions," as he terms them. These are concepts or constructs which Skinner believes are used to explain things they cannot explain. We might diagnose a personality disorder as low self-esteem, and institute therapy designed to bolster self-esteem. However, such vague terms do not help us either to treat the difficulty or to prevent it. Psychological entities such as traits, needs, sentiments, and feelings only add confusion, Skinner believes. What we need is to identify the reinforcers, and to do something about changing them. He contrasts his approach to the traditional one by considering some typical explanatory fictions:

The condition of low operant strength resulting from extinction often requires treatment. Some forms of psychotherapy are systems of reinforcement designed to reinstate behavior which has been lost through extinction. The therapist may himself supply the reinforcement, or he may arrange living conditions in which behavior is likely to be reinforced. In occupational therapy, for example, the patient is encouraged to engage in simple forms of behavior which receive immediate and fairly consistent reinforcement. It is of no advantage to say that such therapy helps the patient by giving him a 'sense of achievement' or improves his 'morale,' builds up his 'interest,' or removes or prevents 'discouragement.' Such terms as these merely add to the growing population of explanatory fictions. One who readily engages in a given activity is not showing an interest, he is showing the effect of reinforcement. We do not give a man a sense of achievement, we reinforce a particular action. To become discouraged is simply to fail to respond because reinforcement has not been forthcoming. Our problem is simply to account for probability of response in terms of a history of reinforcement and extinction (1953, p. 72).*

We do not have space to take up all of Skinner's reinterpretations of traditional topics in psychology, but to give the reader a flavor of his approach, we will take up the notions of self and self-control. No other concept has done more to foster the notion of an autonomous agent, or personality within personality, than the notion of the self. Skinner defines the self in terms of learned responses, primarily verbal. He believes that without a social community there would be no self. A behavioral approach to self-control does provide fertile soil for real control, both through the influence of others and by the individual himself

*Reprinted by permission of Macmillan Publishing Company, Inc.

(Skinner, 1953). Self and self-control need not be mystical subjects, Skinner believes, but only an experimental analysis of self-responses can foster knowledge and control. Self-control, like self-knowledge, is a learned response based on the prior reinforcement history; thus, people differ in both their self-concepts and the extent to which they are capable of controlling themselves.

SELF-CONTROL

Skinner believes that an experimental analysis of the behavior termed self-control should assist us in understanding the sense of freedom of decision-making that people experience. As long as one holds that there is an independent, autonomous will or self operating outside the laws of the material universe, we can do nothing about improving or strengthening the will (Skinner, 1971). It was assumed by some philosophers that the will is similar to a muscle, a "mental muscle" that could be strengthened through discipline and exercise. Thus, to strengthen your will, you can deny yourself things you like, force yourself to do things you dislike, and practice habits of punctuality, hard work, and clean living. These methods are generally not effective in promoting self-control, but Skinner might point out that when they are effective, it is because they lead to positive reinforcements or the avoidance of negative reinforcements. How is the self formed? The consequences of behavior change behavior. The self consists of certain learned responses resulting from the consequences of behavior as well as from the manner in which others relate to the individual.

MEANS OF SELF-CONTROL

Just as variables can be manipulated to influence the behavior of others, so also can we design conditions to manipulate our own behaviors (Goldiamond, 1965). A person who knows from past experience that he has a tendency to succumb to the flattery of a salesman can deliberately turn a deaf ear in such situations. If he adopts the policy of thinking over, for at least a day, any major purchase, even if there is a promise of a discount for signing on the spot, he will avoid a hasty decision that he may later regret. Reputable businessmen generally do not coerce their potential customers by offering discounts for immediate commitment. We can see here that susceptibility to flattery and the allure of a discount are definite variables that can be brought under self-control.

A person may also develop techniques to control his temper; he may, for instance, count to ten before responding while angry. As a rule, one should not write a letter when he is upset; or if he writes a letter, he should read it at a later time and then decide whether or not to send it. Many people have regretted the hasty words of criticism, or hate, or whatever they wrote in a state of anger. Unlike spoken words, the written can become a permanent record.

A person may have trouble waking up in the morning. Knowing this tendency, he may set two alarm clocks, with the second timed to go off 15 minutes after the first and located some distance from the bed. There are clock radios that have a snooze button that allows the sleeper a few minutes to wake up; if he does not, a loud buzzer sounds.

Some people find that they can control their tendency to spend money only by limiting the amount they take with them. One person said that he did not use charge accounts simply because it was so tempting to spend more than he could afford. Here is an example of a system of payment, a great convenience if used properly, that exerts control over the behavior of many. Skinner would point out that the aversive consequences are delayed: one does not pay until much later; thus the positive reinforcements of the purchase are not offset by the negative consequences. The misuse of charge accounts makes sense in terms of reinforcement theory. If one understands the dynamics of their use, he can take steps to guard against their dangers.

Suppose that one has some difficulty remembering things. There are many ways of controlling behavior to facilitate remembering. One may use the "displacement method": altering something he is bound to see. For example, he may displace the cover of the coffee pot, or place a cup upside down at his place at the table. The displaced thing will remind him of what he wants to remember. Or he may have a certain place where he puts things he wants to remember the next morning.

Any inveterate dieter could provide a host of procedures for self-control: he avoids certain foods by simply ruling them "illegal"; he deliberately selects foods that are not tasty; he may take small bites and eat slowly; he may tighten his belt so that he experiences aversive stimulation when he eats too much; he may not buy certain foods for his home; he may purchase garments only after he has lost weight. A number of organizations for weight control use these principles to counsel their members. The methods are supported by additional controls exerted by the group: censorship for those who violate the rules, mutual support, a definite program to follow. Many people respond well to group participation as a means of augmenting measures for self-control; witness Alcoholics Anonymous, Recovery, Weight Watchers, Gamblers Anonymous.

WHY SELF-CONTROL IS NOT ALWAYS EFFECTIVE

It may have occurred to the reader that measures for self-control are not always very successful. We will take up this point in more detail later, but for now it should be noted that the strength of the habit has much to do with whether or not controls are effective. Apparently, in some people overeating or the excessive use of alcohol produces such powerful reinforcements that they are unable to devise and implement self-control measures; thus they may enthusiastically attempt to control their intake, only to fall victim to self-deceiving mechanisms which also control their own behavior. In other words, they may utilize defense mechanisms to justify the very behavior they want to control: the dieter may refuse salad dressing for the sake of a rich dessert. So they fail, start over, fail again, and eventually lose confidence in themselves.

Skinner points out that frequently, natural aversive consequences are insufficient to control behavior; they have to be bolstered by additional reinforcers. He means that the natural consequences of our behavior are not always enough to alter it; other consequences must be added. A person who drinks excessively may experience repeated hangovers, but he continues the inordinate drinking. Skinner would argue that the natural consequences of his drinking apparently are not sufficient to change the behavior that caused it. Perhaps the reason is that there is a time lapse between the positive effects of the drinking and the aversive effects of the hangover. In any case, the natural aversive reinforcer in this instance would have to be augmented by other aversive consequences: losing his job or his mate, or a well-developed program of behavior control.

If a welder does not wear goggles, he is endangering his vision, but some welders who know this still will not wear goggles. The driver who passes another car on a hill is risking his life and threatening the lives of others, yet many drivers still insist on passing. Many people smoke even though there is possible danger to their health. In such instances, the possible consequences apparently do not change the behavior. The welder may go for weeks without an injury; the smoker may not experience the ill effects for years; the driver may pass many times without an accident. Other aversive reinforcers must be provided: the man who does not wear his goggles will get fired; the driver who passes on a hill risks a stiff fine; the smoker is warned by highly placed medical authorities. Such additional reinforcers are effective for many people, but there are still those for whom they are not effective. We can understand why when we re-examine the different consequences of positive and aversive reinforcement, as well as the reasons for the failure of punishment to control behavior. Skinner believes that risky behaviors could be more effectively controlled by using nonpunitive techniques for the undesirable behavior, and positively reinforcing desirable and compliant behaviors.

HINTS FOR SELF-CONTROL

Here are some questions which may help you to work out methods for self-control. First, what techniques can you use to alter your mood? Dress up, take a bath, read a favorite poem, go someplace. Secondly, how can you get yourself to do things you have to do but don't want to do? Establish objectives, work out a plan, schedule a timetable for completing each step. Thirdly, how can you break a habit? Avoid certain situations, practice weak forms of the habit: smoke a brand of cigarettes you don't enjoy, or touch, with gloves on, an animal you dread. You may counteract one emotion by its opposite. Fourthly, how can you overcome a symptom? You can tell yourself that the symptom is distressing but will not endanger health. If you feel fatigued when you have done nothing exhausting, you can simply endure the feeling of fatigue as a psychological reaction to an unpleasant life situation.

A student complained to a counselor that she was terrified at the prospect of giving a talk before a class. Without going into the origin of this intense phobia, the counselor asked her to tell him the animal she most respected, and the one she would choose to be if she had to choose. The girl was a bit perplexed, but she finally stated that she had always admired tigers. They impressed her as being self-contained and proud. The counselor suggested that she should imagine herself a tiger and practice at it. On the next occasion she was to give a talk, she should play-act the role of a tiger before the group and give herself fully to the role. As a matter of fact, the girl also had feelings of inadequacy in her social relationships, and she tended to avoid other people. The counselor advised her to use the tiger role procedure first with those with whom she felt comfortable, and then gradually with others who caused her to feel inadequate. During a subsequent interview, she reported to the counselor that she had applied the technique with success; her standing in relation to others had changed. She was taking a leadership role in her friendships. She was able to diminish her phobia of public speaking as well. This is an example of behavior control by opposing one pattern of emotions with an opposite pattern.

I once advised a young man who had an intense fear of talking in front of a class to experience anger at the group and at me. I asked the student if he disliked giving a talk, and the reply was "Very much." I responded, "You must hate those who inflict this requirement, or you should. At least give it a try." The student showed no signs of his phobia when he presented a project to the class; he actually appeared to have an air of confidence. He later revealed that he actually did experience anger at the students, and especially at me, though his anger was not apparent while he gave the talk. The two techniques described in the above examples are not Skinnerian, but they proved highly effective in modifying behavior. Both means of controlling behavior, suggested by others, could, of course, have been devised by the individuals themselves with the same effects.

WHERE DOES SELF-CONTROL ORIGINATE?

It is clear that not everyone knows the techniques for self-control that we have discussed. Quite probably, many would profit from an elaboration of these techniques. In rearing a child, parents and teachers inculcate such principles of self-control; when they do not, the child may lack self-control in significant areas of his life. It is also clear that we may work out our own strategies, and some of us do, but some who can, do not. Is there a will or agent that is influenced by instructions or previous experience? Skinner believes that self-control is a matter of behavior that is under the influence of the immediate or past environment. This view is clearly expressed in the following passage.

A man may spend a great deal of time designing his own life—he may choose the circumstances in which he is to live with great care, and he may manipulate his daily environment on an extensive scale. Such activity appears to exemplify a high order of self-determination. But it is also behavior, and we account for it in terms of other variables in the environment and history of the individual. It is these variables which provide the ultimate control.

This view is, of course, in conflict with traditional treatments of the subject, which are especially likely to cite self-control as an important example of the operation of personal responsibility. But an analysis which appeals to external variables makes the assumption of an inner originating and determining agent unnecessary (1953, p. 240).*

That self-control or self-management is subject to learning does not really make a case for determinism, any more than the provision of certain conditions causes the growth of a plant. Many very different trees may grow the same conditions of soil, moisture, and sunlight. As we noted in the critical evaluation of Skinner, one may be capable of setting objectives for himself, working out a plan of action, setting up a timetable, but in the end not be able or willing to follow it. Self-control involves more than knowing what to do. Like other personality variables, it is subject to wide individual differences, and quite probably certain personality variables not yet discovered will help us to understand this process. Undoubtedly instruction for self-control can be more effective than is now the case, as the following observations will demonstrate.

---

*Reprinted by permission of Macmillan Publishing Company, Inc.

Consider the question of teaching a child self-reliance. Parents and teachers control the child's behavior through their power to administer positive and aversive reinforcement. Mother makes sure that the child gets to school on time, and the teacher makes sure that he works when he gets there. Both mother and teacher issue verbal commands, and support their requests and commands with threats of punishment, if need be. The child eventually learns to tell time and to get off to school without being told. In a study hall, he works on a project that has been assigned. If we analyze his behavior, we can see that the environment is still the effective cause. He comes to depend on the clock rather than on his mother. Having been punished by his parents for being late, he uses the clock to avoid such punishment. At school he works on the assigned project rather than reading comic books because his environmental history has reinforced such behavior.

Whether or not techniques of self-control will be learned and utilized depends upon the previous history; if there have been prior reinforcements for utilizing techniques of self-control, then these will be used. Behavior which in the past has avoided aversive consequences will also tend to acquire strength. Thus, those who take control of themselves have been reinforced either positively or negatively for doing so. Skinner portrays the controlling influence of the environment and environmental history as follows:

Dependence on things is not independence. The child who does not need to be told it is time to go to school has come under the control of more subtle and more useful stimuli. The child who has learned what to say and how to behave in getting along with other people is under the control of social contingencies. People who get along together well with mild contingencies of approval and disapproval are controlled as effectively as (and in many ways more effectively than) the citizens of a police state. Orthodoxy controls through the establishment of rules, but the mystic is no freer because the contingencies which have shaped his behavior are more personal or idiosyncratic. Those who work productively because of the reinforcing value of what they produce are under the sensitive and powerful control of the products. Those who learn in the natural environment are under a form of control as powerful as any control exerted by a teacher.

A person never becomes truly self-reliant, even though he deals effectively with things. He is necessarily dependent on those who have taught him to do so. They have selected the things he is dependent upon and determined the kinds and degree of dependencies (they cannot therefore disclaim responsibility for the results) (1971, p. 91).*

SKINNER AND THE GOOD LIFE

Skinner has not confined his thinking to the rat in the Skinner box. He has wanted to do more than design better teaching devices, for his thinking extends to a utopian society (Skinner, 1948). Unlike other psychologists such as Rogers, Allport, Jung, and Fromm, he has not defined an ideal human state from the standpoint of personality make-up and functioning. He has concentrated on an ideal environment.

Skinner seems to believe that a man is largely what his environment makes of him. The astronaut in space traveling to the moon is a very different person from the dirt farmer in the Bible Belt who is barely eking out a living from the soil. The difference between them is due largely to the environments in which

---

*© 1971 by B. F. Skinner. Reprinted by permission of Alfred A. Knopf, Inc.

they live. Certainly, heredity plays a determining part as the raw material which the environment molds, but the fact remains that heredity cannot operate independently. Assuredly, man is what he is by virtue of his native potential, but the moldability of man is so great that his environment determines what he becomes. Aristotle could not transcend the limitations of his environment. Because he lacked a vast amount of knowledge he could not have devised a space program.

Skinner, through his behavior engineering, has induced behaviors in animals which have never occurred in the history of the species; he has used a behavior technology to do so. Man's superiority has been expressed in a highly complex world that is largely of his making. The world, however, is in dire trouble; science and technology have created almost as many problems as they have solved. Man himself remains one of the greatest.

The natural and biological sciences have faced many of man's ills, such as disease, the overcoming of food shortages, and in general, the control of nature. But pollution, population explosion, poverty, war, and a host of other hardships, many of them man-made, are very much with us. Skinner believes that even with the knowledge we now possess, life could be much less aversive and, in fact, more fulfilling.

Perhaps Skinner does not attempt to specify what ideal existence is on an individual level because he does not yet know all the possibilities of a technology of human behavior. His methods and concepts have been used only on specific problems such as behavior modification, behavior therapy, programmed instruction, and teaching machines. There are many other areas where traditional methods could be replaced by Skinner's. Many parents do not do a good job of bringing up children; many educational practices are highly punitive, and for the most part, foster a distaste for learning. Economics is geared toward unwholesome competition, and industry and business still resort to aversive controls. Many people simply do not like their work. Life, in general, is much more stressful than present knowledge and technology warrant.

Skinner, speaking through Frazier, the main character of *Walden Two*, offers a program for a benevolent control of behavior through the use of positive reinforcers. By their nature, positive reinforcers promote the operant responses that are required to secure them. The one who seeks them may be controlled willingly. Many persons forego pleasures for the sake of money reinforcement that they obtain through their work. The designers of the society can use behavior technology to foster certain values and behaviors, but this poses many problems regarding what those values should be and who will determine them. Frazier says:

Now that we know how positive reinforcement works, and why negative doesn't, we can be more deliberate, and hence more successful in our cultural design. We can achieve a sort of control, under which the controlled, though they are following a code much more scrupulously than was ever the case under the old system, nevertheless feel free. They are doing what they want to do, not what they are forced to do. That's the source of the tremendous power of positive reinforcement—there's no restraint and no revolt. By a careful cultural design, we control not the final behavior, but the inclination to behave, the motives, the desires, the wishes. The curious thing is that in that case the question of freedom never arises (Skinner, 1948, p. 218).

Skinner believes that what is needed is to engineer the environment so that behavior is brought under control. Some people, for example, should not procreate, but they do not have enough self-control to regulate themselves. The worker should be controlled by positive reinforcements rather than by aversive means. Many personality theorists hold that the model man is a responsible, contributing member of society who pursues his own interests within the limitations of the rights of others. But Skinner (1971) holds that freedom and responsibility assume the existence of an autonomous man within the person. This view, he believes, is hopeless and even fatalistic. The environment determines behavior; change and improve the environment, and desired behavior will occur. The hope of man lies in the judicious control of the environment, so that social, responsible, productive behavior is promoted in the members of society.

SIGNIFICANT QUOTATIONS FROM SKINNER

Skinner is a strong advocate of applying scientific techniques to the study of human behavior, yet he remains aware of the implication:

The possibility is offensive to many people. It is opposed to a tradition of long standing which regards man as a free agent whose behavior is the product, not of specifiable antecedent conditions, but of spontaneous inner changes of course. . . . To suggest that we abandon this view is to threaten many cherished beliefs—to undermine what appears to be a stimulating and productive conception of human nature. The alternative point of view insists upon recognizing coercive forces in human conduct which we may prefer to disregard. It challenges our aspirations, either worldly or other worldly. Regardless of how much we stand to gain from supposing that human behavior is the proper subject matter of a science, no one who is a product of Western civilization can do so without a struggle. We simply do not want such a science (1953, p. 7).*

Science is a willingness to accept facts even when they are opposed to wishes. . . . The opposite of wishful thinking is intellectual honesty—an extremely important possession of the successful scientist (1953, p. 12).*

Many oppose Skinner for advocating the control of human behavior through manipulations of the environment. According to Skinner, man is already controlled:

Behavior comes to conform to the standards of a given community when certain responses are reinforced and others are allowed to go unreinforced or are punished. . . . What a man eats and drinks and how he does so, what sort of sexual behavior he engages in, how he builds a house or draws a picture or rows a boat, what subjects he talks about or remains silent about, what music he makes, what kinds of personal relationships he enters into and what kinds he avoids—all depend in part upon the practices of the group of which he is a member (1953, p. 415).*

---

*Reprinted by permission of Macmillan Publishing Company, Inc.

Refusing to accept control, however, is merely to leave control in other hands (1953, p. 439).

Some psychologists have stressed permissive child-rearing practices as the best method of fostering personality growth. Skinner takes an opposing view:

Permissiveness is not . . . a policy; it is the abandonment of policy, and its apparent advantages are illusory. To refuse control is to leave control not to the person himself, but to other parts of the social and non-social environments (1971, p. 84).*

There are weak and strong forms of control, and the weak (under which Skinner includes suggestion, propaganda, teachers' praise, encouragement, offering a bargain, and similar means of influence) are preferred and condoned by those who advocate freedom and responsibility because it appears that these values are best preserved and attained by such methods. But Skinner argues that weak forms of control are often supported by subtler and unrecognized forms of control such as the prior reinforcement history. He says:

The freedom and dignity of autonomous man seem to be preserved when only weak forms of nonaversive control are used. Those who use them seem to defend themselves against the charge that they are attempting to control behavior, and they are exonerated when things go wrong. Permissiveness is the absence of control, and if it appears to lead to desirable results, it is only because of other contingencies. . . . Various ways of changing behavior by changing minds are not only condoned but vigorously practiced by the defenders of freedom and dignity. . . . A person who responds in acceptable ways to weak forms of control may have been changed by contingencies which are no longer operative. By refusing to recognize them, the defenders of freedom and dignity encourage the misuse of controlling practices and block progress toward a more effective technology of behavior (1971, pp. 99–100).*

Skinner asks the question: "What happens when controls are not present and a minimal level of survival is possible, as with welfare programs?" He says:

When the control exercised by others is thus evaded or destroyed, only the personal reinforcers are left. The individual turns to immediate gratification, possibly through sex or drugs. If he does not need to do much to find food, shelter and safety, little behavior will be generated. His condition is then described . . . as anomie . . . the lack of something to believe in and be devoted to. . . . These terms all seem to refer to feelings or states of mind, but what are missing are effective reinforcers of all kinds (1971, p. 118).*

Regarding a controlled or engineered environment for man, Skinner says:

The struggle for freedom and dignity has been formulated as a defense of autonomous man rather than as a revision of the contingencies of reinforcement under which people live. A technology of behavior is available which would more successfully reduce the aversive consequences of behavior, proximate or deferred, and maximize the achievement of which the human organism is capable, but the defenders of freedom oppose its use. The opposition may raise certain questions concerning

---

*© 1971 by B. F. Skinner. Reprinted by permission of Alfred A. Knopf, Inc.

"values." Who is to decide what is good for man? How will a more effective technology be used? By whom and to what end? These are really questions about reinforcers (1971, p. 125).*

Skinner views the relation of man and his environment as a continual interaction, but man has great potential to construct his own environment so that many aversive elements are absent:

An experimental analysis shifts the determination of behavior from autonomous man to the environment — an environment responsible for both the evolution of the species and for the repertoire acquired by each member. . . . But environmental contingencies now take over functions once attributed to autonomous man. . . . It is the autonomous inner man who is abolished. . . . He is indeed controlled by his environment, but we must remember that it is an environment of his own making. The evolution of a culture is a gigantic exercise in self control (1971, pp. 214–215).*

SUMMARY

1.   Skinner has made major contributions to the field of learning, especially in the use of reinforcement procedures in operant conditioning. He has long held the view that specific behaviors can be established and maintained by particular types of consequences. Behavior may be engineered by arranging certain contingencies; i.e., by making certain reinforcements dependent upon prescribed behaviors.

2.   Skinner makes an important distinction between respondent conditioning and operant conditioning. In respondent conditioning a neutral stimulus, such as a bell, is paired with a natural stimulus, such as food. After repeated pairings of the neutral and natural stimuli (conditioned and unconditioned stimuli), the conditioned stimulus (the bell) will produce the same response (salivation) that is elicited by the unconditioned stimulus (the food). Respondent conditioning accounts for the learning of many emotional responses to neutral stimuli in one's environment. In operant conditioning, the correct instrumental behavior is learned as a result of the reinforcement which follows it. The frequency and intensity of operant or instrumental behavior depend upon the particular schedule of reinforcement.

3.   By schedules of reinforcement is meant the manner in which the reinforcement occurs. Common schedules are total reinforcement (reinforcement following each correct response); interval reinforcement (reinforcement following a given time interval); ratio reinforcement (reinforcement for specific numbers of responses); extinction (operant behavior without reinforcement).

4.   Shaping is a term which refers to establishing operants by reinforcing partial or graded responses. During the shaping process, behavior is molded gradually in an ordered series of steps which increasingly approximate the desired pattern of behavior.

5.   Skinner's concepts and methods of behavior modification and control are receiving wide application in many diverse fields. They are replacing the

traditional punitive and "care" methods. Behavior control techniques are being used with retardates in institutional settings, with psychotics in hospital wards, in penal and correctional institutions, in ordinary classroom settings to obtain student cooperation, in the area of programmed instruction and teaching machines, and in behavior therapy with people suffering from personality disorders.

6. Differential reinforcement is a procedure of selectively reinforcing certain behaviors and extinguishing others through nonreinforcement. In biofeedback autonomic conditioning the learner can perform correctly as a consequence of differential reinforcements; a signal reveals when the correct response is being made. This procedure permits the acquisition of control over organic processes.

7. Positive reinforcement increases the frequency and intensity of emitted or operant behaviors. Negative reinforcement also increases the occurrence of behaviors such as escape and avoidance. Punishment is intended to weaken behavior and consists of following behavior by an unpleasant or aversive consequence. Skinner holds that punishment does not necessarily weaken behaviors and recommends that unwanted behaviors be eliminated by other procedures such as extinction, distraction, satiation, and counterconditioning. Punishment often produces undesirable side effects.

8. Reinforcements may be primary (unlearned) or secondary (learned or conditioned); specific or general (water versus praise).

9. Skinner rejects personality variables such as self, traits, and needs as being explanatory fictions. He relates behavior to environmental causes rather than to personality variables.

10. Skinner defines the concept of the self in terms of learned responses, primarily verbal. He holds that without a social community there would be no self.

11. According to Skinner, an experimental analysis of the behavior termed self-control would take into account the reinforcement history (learning history) which brought it about.

12. Skinner proposes two selves: one which controls, and one which is controlled. He maintains that the controlling self can institute contingencies of reinforcement, and thereby one can control or engineer his own behavior.

SUGGESTED READINGS

Skinner, B. F. The Behavior of Organisms. New York: Appleton-Century-Crofts, 1938.
    Presented here is a useful formulation of behavior in terms of the principles of conditioning. Selected experiments are used for illustrative purposes.

Science and Human Behavior. New York: The Macmillan Company, 1953.
    Topics include thinking, self-control, government and law, psychotherapy, group control, education, and many others.

Walden Two. New York: The Macmillan Company, 1948.
    Skinner constructs his utopia based upon the principles of behavior engineering.

Contingencies of Reinforcement: A Theoretical Analysis. New York: Appleton-Century-Crofts, 1954.
> Skinner restates his entire scientific position. He stresses the relevance of science in broad social problems.

Cumulative Record. New York: Appleton-Century-Crofts, 1968.
> A collection of Skinner's research papers, giving detailed analysis of experiments.

The Technology of Teaching. New York: Appleton-Century-Crofts, 1968.
> Here Skinner offers his views on how learning should be approached in the schools to optimize student potentials.

Beyond Freedom and Dignity. New York: Alfred A. Knopf, 1971.
> In this book Skinner questions the traditional views of freedom and responsibility and proposes instead an environmental control of behavior. He views the answers to man's problems in terms of a designed society in the hands of benevolent designers.

REFERENCES

Ayllon, T., and Azrin, N. H. The measurement and reinforcement of behavior of psychotics. J. Exp. Anal. Behav. 8:357–83, 1965.

Brady, J. V. Ulcers in "executive" monkeys. Sci. Am. 199(October, 1958):95–103.

Estes, W. K. An experimental study of punishment. Psychol. Monogr. 57:3, Whole No. 263, 1944.

Eysenck, H. J., and Rachman, S. R. The Causes and Cures of Neurosis. San Diego: Robert R. Knapp, 1965.

Ferster, C. B., and Skinner, B. F. Schedules of Reinforcement. New York: Appleton-Century-Crofts, 1957.

Goldiamond, I. Self-control procedures in personal behavior problems. Psychol. Rep. 17:851–58, 1965.

Goodall, K. Shapers at work. Psychol. Today 6(November, 1972):53–63, 132–38.

Jenkins, W. O., and Stanley, J. C. Partial reinforcement: A review and critique. Psychol. Bull. 47:193–234, 1950.

Jones, M. C. A laboratory study of fear: The case of Peter. Pedagog. Seminar 31:308–15, 1924.

Mischel, W., and Grusec, J. E. The model's characteristics as determinants of social learning. J. Pers. Social Psychol. 4:211–14, 1966.

Nowlis, D. P., and Kamiya, J. The control of electroencephalographic alpha rhythms through auditory feedback and the associated mental activity. Psychophysiology 6:476–84, 1970.

Pavlov, I. P. Conditioned Reflexes. London: Oxford University Press, 1927.

Rheingold, H. L., Gewirtz, J. L., and Ross, H. W. Social conditioning of vocalizations in the infant. J. Comp. Physiol. Psychol. 52:68–73, 1959.

Skinner, B. F. The Behavior of Organisms. New York: Appleton-Century-Crofts, 1938.

Skinner, B. F. Walden Two. New York: The Macmillan Company, 1948.

Skinner, B. F. Science and Human Behavior. New York: The Macmillan Company, 1953.

Skinner, B. F. Verbal Behavior. New York: Appleton-Century-Crofts, 1957.

Skinner, B. F. Operant behavior. Am. Psychol. 18:503–15, 1963.

Skinner, B. F. The Technology of Teaching. New York: Appleton-Century-Crofts, 1968.

Skinner, B. F. Beyond Freedom and Dignity. New York: Alfred A. Knopf, 1971.

Skinner, B. F. Will success spoil B. F. Skinner? (interview transcription) Psychol. Today 6(November, 1972):65–72, 130.

Stampfl, T. G., and Levis, D. J. Essentials of implosive therapy: A learning-theory based psychodynamic behavioral therapy. J. Abnorm. Psychol. 72:496–503, 1967.

Watson, J. B. Behavior: An Introduction to Comparative Psychology. New York: Holt, Rinehart and Winston, 1914.

Wilson, W. C., and Verplanck, W. S. Some observations on the reinforcement of verbal operants. Am. J. Psychol. 69:448–51, 1956.

CHAPTER 6

John Dollard
(1900—)

Neal E. Miller
(1909—)

S-R, Cognitive, and Social Learning Theories

Dollard and Miller, Bandura and Walters, Rotter

Albert Bandura
(1925—)

Julian B. Rotter
(1916—)

THE MANY APPLICATIONS OF LEARNING THEORY

Do we learn responses to situations, or do we learn information which can be used to guide our responses? Do we learn by responding, or respond after we learn? Furthermore, can the learning of man be understood through the principles of the animal laboratory, or is the nature of man so different from that of the lower animals that different principles are involved? Are man's abilities to cognize and interpret his world such that we cannot apply the principles of animal learning to human learning? What about the social aspects of man's learning: much important learning takes place in social contexts and involves social activities. Each learning theory tends to stress one aspect over others, yet we can learn something of value from each approach. Dollard and Miller (1941, 1950) use the S-R model to account for personality variables, but in doing so, they extend greatly the meaning of the stimulus and the response. Bandura and Walters (1963), without denying the value of other learning approaches, stress the imitative and observational aspect of learning. Rotter (1954, 1970) works in social variables which he believes the others have not dealt with adequately. The learning approach has an applied side, which is termed behavior modification or behavior therapy. We will consider the applied uses of learning concepts and principles in bringing about personality change.

159

THE S-R APPROACH TO PERSONALITY STUDY: DOLLARD AND MILLER

BIOGRAPHY AND OVERVIEW

The fantastic progress of knowledge is evident to anyone who is in touch with his world. In just a few years, we have seen the development of totally new fields such as space exploration, open-heart surgery, the computer, drugs for the treatment of the mentally ill, and many more. Our parents could scarcely dream of these developments. The high school student of today can solve problems which were not even known as problems a few years ago. He can solve them because he has *learned* to do so. Each generation passes on the knowledge of the preceding ones in addition to its own new discoveries. The achievements of great minds who may have studied and labored a lifetime can often be communicated easily to many who are willing to learn. Euclid's principles of geometry are taught to millions of tenth graders. But as Dollard and Miller point out, the principles of mental health have not been passed on from generation to generation. Many people are victims of poor mental health practices. They simply have not *learned* how to deal with frustration, how to get necessary work accomplished, how to cope with the irrationalities of life, how to moderate their ideals, how to live amicably with others. The discoveries in the fields of child-rearing, education, and self-management should be taught. What we have learned to do with the physical world all around us we can learn to do with ourselves. Better ways of dealing with needs and personal problems can be discovered and communicated. We already have much more knowledge than is being used to improve man's life.

The learning approach to personality study and improvement is one of the most optimistic personality theories. It holds that personality, normal or abnormal, is largely the product of learning. As one grows up he learns a multitude of habits, skills, attitudes, emotional responses, prejudices, and complexes. Neurosis and other abnormalities may thus be thought of as learned responses. One is not born neurotic, but acquires "bad habits" which can be accounted for by principles of learning. For Dollard and Miller, neurosis is a deficiency blocking the full use of the higher mental processes. Their optimistic note is that if neurosis is learned, then it can be unlearned by understanding and applying principles of learning. In this context, psychotherapy consists of teaching; the neurotic is the student who wishes to replace bad habits with good ones. Psychotherapy restores the higher mental functions and frees the patient of his symptoms so that he may have a clear and efficient mind.

Before being able to apply the insights of Dollard and Miller to himself, the reader must become familiar with terms such as drive, stimulus, response, reinforcement, drive-producing cues, primary and mediated generalization, discrimination, extinction, spontaneous recovery, cue-producing responses, primary and secondary reinforcement, inhibition of responses, competition among responses, and principles of conditioning. It is recommended that those who have not had any background in learning principles consult a chapter on learning in a standard introductory psychology text. The major principles and terms will be examined according to the S-R model followed by Dollard and Miller.

Some unique features of the theory of Dollard and Miller should be noted. The theory attempts to bring together (1) principles of learning that pertain to personality study, (2) social and anthropological findings, and (3) the clinical observations and concepts of psychoanalysis. Thus it is a full-bodied approach to the study of the individual. Many of Freud's clinical concepts and insights are translated into the S-R language, but Dollard and Miller offer some brilliant insights of their own in the process of clarifying psychoanalytic ideas.

John Dollard was born in 1900 in Wisconsin. He attended the University of Wisconsin, graduating in 1921. He subsequently obtained an M.A. and Ph.D. in sociology from the University of Chicago. He received instruction and experience in psychoanalysis at the Berlin Institute of Psychoanalysis. He has held a variety of academic appointments at Yale, including affiliation with the Yale Institute of Human Relations.

Neal E. Miller was also born in Wisconsin, in 1909. He received his B.S. from the University of Washington, his M.A. from Stanford, and his Ph.D. in psychology from Yale. He too has been associated with the Yale Institute of Human Relations, and like Dollard he took psychoanalytic training, but at the Vienna Institute of Psychoanalysis. In 1966 he ended his long affiliation with Yale to accept a position with Rockefeller University. He has received many honors in psychology, including election to the presidency of the American Psychological Association. His research interests are varied: he has worked with motivation, with conflict, and most recently in the exciting new area of autonomic conditioning, a field in which he is one of the pioneers.

The reader should keep one important point in mind in dealing with the content of this chapter, namely, that we will be using the concepts and principles of learning to describe and explain what comes under the heading of personality study—conflict, repression, the unconscious, development, personality dynamics, personality growth and change, and self-improvement. We can only touch on them in our summary. We will begin our discussion of Dollard and Miller by a consideration of the components of the learning process; we will then examine some of their important concepts and principles of learning; finally we will apply the S-R model to the major topics of personality.

COMPONENTS OF THE LEARNING PROCESS

According to the learning approach to personality study, learning occurs if there are the following: (1) cue, (2) response, (3) drive, and (4) reinforcement. If the telephone rings in your home, you normally answer it. The ringing telephone signals that answering is appropriate at this particular time; thus the ringing phone is a cue, a stimulus that directs responses. A phone might ring at a friend's house, but you would not answer it unless you had some reason to: the ring would not be a cue. At your own home, you have a motive, or drive, for answering the phone because the call may be for you. Answering the phone involves carrying out a series of responses, all of which must be learned through reinforcement. According to the learning theory espoused by Dollard and Miller, responses are reinforced (more likely to occur) if they produce drive reduction (if phone calls were never for you, the response of answering the phone would not be learned). Thus learning of responses is caused by drive reduction, and drive reduction means reinforcement. Miller and Dollard describe the learning process as noticing something, wanting something, doing something, and getting something (1941).

Drives

Strong stimuli that activate and energize behavior are considered drives by Dollard and Miller (1950). Any stimulus may acquire drive properties if it is intense. The ringing telephone, which we identified as a cue, also has drive properties because it produces annoyance. One hardly senses the temperature of a room when he is comfortable, but if the temperature is either too high or too low, it becomes a drive stimulus which impels the person to take action. Many pleasant stimuli become painful, and hence acquire drive properties, when they attain a high intensity. Drive stimuli may be external and internal. Hunger, thirst, pain, and sexual arousal are physiological states that generate internal stimuli which attain drive status from time to time. Dollard and Miller make a distinction between primary and secondary drives. *Primary* drives (unlearned drives) include the physiological drives of hunger, thirst, sex, and avoidance, while *secondary* drives (learned drives) are acquired in the process of satisfying primary drives. Important secondary drives are fear, guilt, and the desire for status. While we think of primary drives as being powerful determinants of responses, secondary or acquired drives or motives also energize responses. Strictly speaking, drives activate behavior, but do not direct or guide it. Cues serve the function of guiding and directing behavior to appropriate satisfiers.

Cues

Cues determine the form and direction which behavior takes. In S-R theory, learning is assumed to take place when a particular response is connected with a cue. There may be a series of responses to a series of cues, but the point is that learning consists of the formation of cue-response connections. The cues determine not only what responses will be made, but also when and where they will occur (1950). Responses are made only in the presence of cues; thus if either the appropriate cues are absent or the wrong cues are present, the correct response will not occur. Many behaviors which are described or explained by the personality psychologists as manifestations of personality structures, such as id, ego, and superego, traits, dispositions, sentiments, and the like, are explained by Dollard and Miller in terms of cue-response associations, as we shall see. Certain people may be cues for paranoid responses, as a consequence of previous experience or learning. The members of a particular race or religion may serve as cues for aggressive responses. One way of looking at learning is in terms of cue differences and similarities. If one is to associate a response with a situation, there must be cues that can be discriminated and to which the response may be attached. When many cues can be associated with a response, learning is rapid and retention may be good. One point should be clear: the stimuli produced by drives may also serve as cues, for example being hungry for a specific food. The words "stimulus" and "cue" are thus often interchangeable, although there are stimuli which are not cues. Cues are the informative aspect of stimuli.

Responses

In learning, the response is the other half of the cue-response association. In order for the response to be associated with the cue, there must be both drive and reinforcement. Reinforcement consists of drive reduction, as we noted previously. But how do responses occur that can lead to reinforcement? Dollard and Miller (1950) propose that there are response hierarchies which are innate. Given a cue and a drive, there is a series of responses that may occur. These responses vary in order of occurrence. For example, if a young child wants something to eat, his most likely response is to cry. If crying does not secure food, he may call his mother and ask for it; if that fails, he may actually go to the refrigerator and look for food. One of these responses may secure drive reduction (reinforcement). Thus its probability of occurrence in the hierarchy on the next occasion will be increased. If the child always gets food when he cries, the other responses in the hierarchy will never materialize. In a sense, then, learning might be thought of as the *rearranging* of response hierarchies. Thus there is a distinction between the *initial* response hierarchy and the *resultant* response hierarchy.

The concept of the response hierarchy might convey the erroneous impression that learning and actual behaving are a mechanistic running off of an ordered sequence of responses until the correct response is reinforced. Undoubtedly, much learning is of this type, but what is considered distinctively human (reasoning, problem solving, learning through imitation and identification, learning through instruction) cannot be covered by the response hierarchy concept. Dollard and Miller (1941, 1950) do encompass such forms of learning and behaving within the S-R framework. For instance, imitation, which plays a great part in human learning throughout life, obeys the principle of reinforcement. Parents, teachers, and other significant people in the life of a child eagerly reinforce imitative behavior; thus imitative behavior is important in satisfying primary drives. The tendency to imitate becomes a learned behavior that is generalized to many situations because it secures drive reduction.

Novel behavior, as in problem solving, can be accounted for in terms of cues which are produced by responses *(cue-producing responses)*, such as thoughts and images which can be covertly arranged and rearranged. Making a response also involves producing a cue. When I make the response of moving my arm out to the right of me, I experience a number of cues (visual, auditory, tactile) that tell me about my response. When I speak a word, a verbal response, I hear what I have said, which may suggest other words; thus I am being stimulated by my own response. Such cue-producing responses play an important part in thinking, problem solving, reasoning, generalizing, and discriminating (Kendler and Kendler, 1962). Our own responses can convey cues which not only tell us about the response we have made, but also serve as instigators of other responses. The concept of cue-producing responses can be used to describe and explain many phenomena that might seem outside an S-R approach.

Dollard and Miller have broadened the notion of stimulus to include more than energy impinging on sense organs, and that of response to man more than muscular movement. They distinguish among muscular, visceral, glandular, emotional, external and internal, and even verbal and attentional responses. In general, psychological phenomena are either stimuli or responses; thus both the stimulus and response concepts are central in the S-R model. All responses are capable of producing cue stimuli that can link them to other responses.

Reinforcement

Learning takes place (that is, responses and cues are connected) only if there is reinforcement, and reinforcement consists of drive reduction (1950). Learned responses that are not reinforced *extinguish*: they gradually weaken until the cue no longer produces a response. Often a person is confronted with a *learning dilemma* because present responses do not produce reinforcement. In the presence of a drive, new responses must be tried until one is capable of reducing the drive. Reinforcements may occur every time a response is made, but more typically they are *intermittent*. Learning is greatly influenced by the frequency, quality, and quantity of reinforcements.

GENERALIZATION AND DISCRIMINATION

We respond to similarities (generalization) and differences (discrimination) among objects, people, and events. In learning about ourselves and others, it is valuable to discover both processes. To facilitate our understanding of the process of generalization, Dollard and Miller (1950) make an important distinction between primary generalization and mediated generalization. *Primary generalization* means similarity of response as a result of the similarities of stimulus properties. High and low pitched bells might elicit the same response (although the low pitch would produce a less intense response and the time to respond might be longer, assuming the original learning was with the high pitched bell). _Mediated generalization_ is the labeling of stimuli by symbols or words; thus a variety of dissimilar objects may produce the same response. One may, for instance, label many different things as threatening (Lacey and Smith, 1954). In human psychology, verbal responses play an important role. We can see that the concept of mediated generalization can explain phenomena that primary generalization cannot. Many facts of interest to the personality psychologist and the clinician can be understood as faulty mediational generalization. Faulty categorization often causes maladaptive responses. In such instances therapy should concentrate upon promoting correct cue discrimination (Dollard et al., 1953).

There are two common forms of mediated generalization that lead to faulty adaptation: one involves considering dissimilar objects equivalent, such as regarding all superiors as punitive or inhuman; the other is carrying over past responses to current stimuli inappropriately, such as generalizing dependent responses from mother to wife. In therapy, these distorted forms of generalization are treated by correct labeling of situations. For example, while the wifely role may overlap with the maternal role, wife and mother are very different people. Agreeing with Freud, Dollard and Miller (1950) have observed that our present difficulties often result from responding to current events in ways more appropriate to earlier periods of our development. Again, proper discrimination by means of correct labeling is the method of treatment. Just as words can be the source of overgeneralization, they can also permit more precise discrimination by labeling things more exactly. All through life we are confronted with the task of forming correct categories and making appropriate distinctions among them.

INSTRUMENTAL VERSUS CUE-PRODUCING RESPONSES

An important distinction in Dollard and Miller's (1950) analysis of behavior is the difference between instrumental responses and cue-producing responses. Instrumental responses are easy enough to understand: they are responses that accomplish something for the individual. Drive or motive gratification usually requires the performance of an instrumental response. The food must be secured before it can be cooked, cooked before it can be eaten, and so on. Instrumental responses are the means by which goals are accomplished. The person may respond _directly_ to an external stimulus with an instrumental response. However, some responses (primarily verbal and imaginative) occur within the individual and have the function of producing cues that may be linked to other responses. These are _mediating_ cue-producing responses. In a sense, cue-producing responses may be thought of as responses that produce information. They may precede the instrumental response, enabling one to plan or even inhibit responding. One produces thought responses, evaluates his own thoughts by means of the cues they produce, and finally performs an instrumental response.

Dollard and Miller give the example of counting one's change to obtain information that will lead to the instrumental response of either putting money in one's pocket, giving some back, or asking for more. As we noted previously, all responses provide cues, but some responses, notably language, are primarily mediational or response-linking. When a stimulus produces a verbal response, a cue is also produced. The cue may in turn set off an emotional response. One may label something dreadful, and immediately experience strong fear.

The reader may not be accustomed to thinking of language as a response. Certainly talking involves muscular movements, which would be overt behavior. Even during silent thought some slight speech movements may be detected. Yet even without considering muscular movements, thoughts, ideas, and images behave like overt responses; hence they can be increased in strength, eliminated through forgetting or extinction, and competed with by other thoughts, ideas, or images. In man such responses may generate cues that can lead to other responses; thus Dollard and Miller can account for the so-called higher mental functions in man. They do admit, however, that being able to make appropriate verbal responses does not explain all aspects of thinking, reasoning, and problem solving. Still, knowing the language of a field of study can greatly assist one in dealing with the problems of that area. When we think, we are making cue-producing responses that can take the place of overt behavior (Berlyne, 1965). We can plan a course of action and work out alternatives, eliminating some, and in the process not perform a single instrumental act. The possibilities of adaptation and coping that this capability provides may be seen all about us. We may anticipate the future by arranging and rearranging ideational responses. The outcome of a course of action may be anticipated on the level of thought responses. Even something like self-awareness, which many humanistic psychologists believe is distinctively human, could be explained in terms of cue-producing responses. Thought responses produce cues which are experienced and which select other responses, and so on.

PRIMARY AND SECONDARY DRIVES AND REINFORCEMENTS

The following example should explain the operation of learned drives and reinforcers. A man enters a small office to be interviewed for a job. He begins to behave nervously and with evident discomfort. He asks that the door of the office be opened. His own behavior seems to be increasing his anxiety. Finally, he voluntarily terminates the interview, and of course does not get the job. He is puzzled by his conduct, just as the interviewer probably is, because neither perceives the current drive, cues, and reinforcement that sustained the apparently irrational fears and behaviors. The man's behavior would be described as claustrophobia, and if we took the trouble to investigate his life history, we would discover its origin. Perhaps as a child he was punished by being locked in a closet. His learned behavior is set off by specific cues and sustained by reinforcements. The behavior of requesting the door to be opened reduced drive stimuli (fear), and thus the phobic behavior was strengthened and continued.

Miller (1948) describes an experimental production of a phobia. A rat was placed in a box containing two compartments divided by a barrier with an opening door. The floor of one compartment contained a grid that could be electrified. With the door opened, a buzzer was sounded and followed by shock, and the animal ran to the other compartment. Subsequently he ran to the safe side upon hearing the buzzer alone. He had learned to fear the buzzer. It should be noted that while fear is unlearned, it becomes associated with particular stimuli through learning. Thus the fear which is attached to the buzzer is a *learned* or *secondary drive,* while the buzzer becomes a *secondary reinforcer,* a learned negative reinforcer.

In another experiment the rats had to learn to turn a wheel just above the door to open it. The buzzer sounded while the door was shut. Each animal learned to perform the instrumental response of turning the wheel to the sound of the buzzer. No further shock was needed. Other instrumental responses were learned by the animals when the previous responses were made ineffective by the experimenter's change of procedure.

Analysis of these experiments demonstrates that the rats were learning responses to cues that were neutral prior to learning. The drive was fear, which became associated with the cues of the box and the buzzer. Reinforcement consists of the reduction of fear. Fear may be thought of as a strong drive stimulus which, when reduced, is a form of reinforcement. A variety of instrumental responses were learned in Miller's experiments with fear reduction as the reinforcement, even when the shock was no longer administered.

In this experimental arrangement, one can observe the cues and the origin of the phobia. In the case of the man being interviewed, the cues, the drive, and the reinforcers were not known. The man's behavior appeared highly inappropriate and incomprehensible. The fear of the neutral cues is a learned drive.

Comparing the buzzer and the shock, the shock caused pain, which is a primary or unlearned emotional response. (Shock is a primary reinforcement because its termination will reinforce responses: that is, responses which turn off the shock are learned.) The buzzer is a secondary or learned reinforcer whose cessation is drive-reducing because fear is diminished. Instrumental responses that cause the buzzer to be turned off are strengthened. The rats in Miller's experiment learned instrumental responses for buzzer cessation alone, as they did for the shock alone.

Money may become associated with primary drive satisfaction, and thereby becomes a highly sought after learned or secondary reinforcer. The receipt of money for performing or learning certain responses can strengthen those responses. Looked at from another point of view, making money may be a drive which can instigate many instrumental responses. Dollard and Miller offer the following definitions of secondary drive and secondary reinforcement.

When, as the result of learning, previously neutral cues gain the capacity to play the same functional role in the learning and performance of new responses as do primary drives such as hunger and thirst, these cues are said to have *learned-drive value*. When as the result of learning, previously neutral cues gain the capacity to play the same functional role in the learning and performance of new responses as other reinforcements, such as food for a hungry animal, or water for a thirsty one, they are described as *learned reinforcements*. They may also be called learned rewards, or secondary reinforcements (1950, p. 78).

THE UNCONSCIOUS, THE UNLABELED, REPRESSION

Language is used by man to label things. We have names for persons, places, and things. The most complex events are labeled. Even complicated formulas which are expressed in letters represent words or phrases. Experiences that are unlabeled are equivalent to the unconscious, according to Dollard and Miller (1950). When we observe that unconscious processes can influence behavior directly, we mean that we can be influenced by behavior that is not under verbal control. Unconscious experiences do not come under the domain of the higher mental processes because these processes involve cue-producing responses such as thoughts and images.

Like other responses, the labeling process depends upon maturation and learning. Before language ability is acquired completely, significant experiences may take place that are either unlabeled or labeled incorrectly. Because language development is gradual, there are plenty of opportunities for distorted labeling of experiences. Early conflicts which were never labeled properly may continue throughout life without resolution because they are not under verbal control. One may be influenced by such conflicts, without being very clear about their nature.

It should be noted that even events that have been labeled correctly may be altered through repression and other forms of distortion. Repression in this context means the loss of the ability to use existing verbal labels so that such experiences are no longer under verbal control. Repression may also be thought of as a learned inhibition of responses (Dollard and Miller, 1950). In this sense, repression means not responding in the presence of certain cues. Thus not responding acquires the status of a learned response. But if we treat not responding like other learned responses, what are the reinforcements, the drive, and the cues?

According to Dollard and Miller, when an unpleasant emotion is instigated by verbal or other cue-producing responses, there is a drive state which, when reduced, is reinforcing. Whatever reduces the unpleasant emotion becomes a learned response. But not thinking, or avoidance of remembering painful experiences, is a response which is immediately followed by drive reduction

(reduction of the unpleasant experience). Thus, one might form a strong habit of not thinking of certain things. As soon as certain cues (internal, external) occur, the avoiding response immediately goes to work. Verbal and other cue-producing responses become unavailable in the operation of higher mental processes. For instance, a student may be so overwhelmed with anxiety when he begins to think about writing a term paper that he cannot work out a plan of action. He does not know how to begin. He may develop the habit of procrastinating as a means of reducing tension. Finally, he learns not to think about the term paper whenever anything reminds him of it. The likelihood of using the higher mental processes is greatly lessened by his avoidance behavior.

Dollard and Miller describe repression as being "stupid" about certain things. We are all reinforced for being logical and coherent; thus when we are not, repression may be at work. One may discover areas in which his own thinking is confused and unclear. Alternatives do not seem to be evident; there are gaps in knowledge, and the process of weighing the elements is hampered. One may find himself uncertain as to the exact date of a test. Is it this Friday or next? Bills that should be paid somehow never get paid on time. One easily forgets such matters as making out a will, or buying life insurance, or getting the oil changed in the car. A person may be quite alert and conscientious in certain aspects of his life, but surprisingly stupid about others. Such inconsistency suggests the operation of repression.

To return to verbal labels, one should be on guard to label things properly, or he may become a victim of repression. Even uttering anxiety-provoking words or sentences to oneself engenders emotional responses and may subsequently lead to repression. Simply mislabeling a situation can produce needless fear or anger. An acquaintance may be joking, but his remarks might be mistaken for criticism. One can gain control of his responses to a potentially disturbing situation by immediately labeling them as unimportant or silly. It can be seen that verbal labels play an extremely important role in all aspects of personality functioning.

S-R ANALYSIS OF CONFLICT AND REPRESSION

Conflict may be considered as competing or opposing responses that have the effect of inhibiting or blocking instrumental responses or overt behavior. Some of the most significant conflicts for man consist of the opposition between drives and competing inhibitory emotional responses such as fear and guilt. Typical conflicts are those between sex and fear and anger and fear. Goal responses which arise from some drives are blocked by fear. While repression hinders or blocks thought and other cue-producing responses, as we noted earlier, conflict impedes or blocks action. Failure to make the appropriate instrumental responses leaves drives unsatisfied; thus the drive stimuli (tensions) may continue or intensify. But the stimuli associated with the drive may activate the fear responses. Caught in a conflict, the person experiences frustration of the drive, and maybe even an intensification of it, plus the consequences of intense fear (Miller, 1951). The fear causes instrumental responses to be inhibited; thus the drive remains. In addition to the tension of the active drive and the condition of fear, there is still another source of tension and discomfort: the physiological concomitants of conflict such as hyperacidity, painful muscular tension, digestive difficulties, and other bodily reactions caused by high levels of psychological disturbance. Here is how Dollard and Miller describe conflicts:

Let us begin with fear, guilt, and other drives that motivate conflict and repression. Since fear seems to be the strongest and most basic of these, we shall simplify the discussion by referring only to it.

In the neurotic, strong fear motivates a conflict that prevents the occurrence of the goal responses that normally would reduce another drive, such as sex or aggression. This is called overt inhibition. It is produced in the following way. The cues produced by the goal responses (or even first tentative approaches to the goal) elicit strong fear. This motivates conflicting responses such as stopping and avoiding. The reduction in fear, when the neurotic stops and retreats, reinforces these conflicting responses. Because the conflicting responses prevent the drive-reducing goal responses from occurring, the drives (such as sex and aggression) build up and remain high. This state of chronic high drive is described as misery. At the same time, the high drives tend to evoke the approaches (or other incipient acts) that elicit fear. Thus the neurotic is likely to be stimulated by both the frustrated drives and the fear. Finally, the state of conflict itself may produce additional strong stimuli, such as those of muscular tension, which contribute to the misery (1950, p. 222).

Dollard and Miller point out that significant conflicts are formed early in life when the infant does not have the experiences and resources to cope with them. The child who cries as a reaction to a drive state may be ignored or punished by his parents. He may feel abandoned because he does not know that the punishment is temporary. He may not be capable of distracting himself by other activity. Unlike the adult who can assure himself that there will be better days, he is tied to the events going on around him; thus he is extremely vulnerable to frustration (Barker et al., 1941). He experiences forbidden drives fiercely, simply because he does not know what to do with them. Inhibiting emotions such as fear, guilt, and disgust may become associated with his important drives. Parents have the obligation to prevent such conflicts from developing and to keep drives from reaching high levels of intensity (Dollard and Miller, 1950). The child should be given full satisfaction of drives at first, and then as his own facilities develop, be encouraged to take care of his own needs. Unfortunately, conflicts engendered early in life, before the development of language, function unconsciously; they are not readily accessible to the higher mental processes.

Fear, guilt, disgust, and other inhibiting emotions associated with high drives also play a part in repression, as Dollard and Miller point out in the following passage.

Fear and guilt also motivate the repression of verbal and other cue-producing responses. The fact that certain thoughts arouse fear, motivates stopping them, and the reduction in fear reinforces the stopping. Repression is similar to overt inhibition except that it is a conflict that interferes with thinking instead of one that interferes with acting.

Since the verbal and other cue-producing responses are the basis for the higher mental processes, the repression of these responses makes a neurotic stupid with respect to the specific function of the responses that are repressed. One of the functions of the cue-producing responses is to aid in discrimination. When they are removed by repression, it is harder for the patient to differentiate the situations in which he has been punished from similar ones in which he has not. Interference with such discriminations greatly retards the extinction of unrealistic fears and thus helps to perpetrate the vicious circle of fear, repression, stupidity, lack of discrimination, and persistence of unrealistic fear (1950, pp. 222–224).

Symptoms result from conflict and repression. The symptoms are responses that temporarily relieve some of the tension. The tension relief is the reinforcement for the continued tenacity of the symptoms. For example, the avoidance responses of phobic persons reduce the tension of fear and thus are reinforced. The victim really *wants* his symptoms because things would be worse without them. Dollard and Miller discuss the nature of repression and symptoms as follows:

The stupidity in the areas that are affected by repression also tends to prevent the neurotic from finding adequate solutions to his problems and to cause him to do maladaptive things that contribute to his state of high drive or, in other words, misery. At the same time the misery tends to interfere with clear thinking and thus contributes to his stupidity. The high drives make it harder for him to stop and think. They over determine or, in other words, motivate certain thoughts so strongly that they occur in inappropriate situations. They produce preoccupation that distracts him from thinking clearly about other matters.

Both the fear and the drives that build up when their goal responses are inhibited by fear tend to produce symptoms. Some of these are unlearned physiological effects of the chronic state of high drive. Others are learned responses that are reinforced by the immediate drive reduction they produce (1950, p. 224).

INSIGHTS FROM DOLLARD AND MILLER ON SELF-CONTROL

SUPPRESSION

Dollard and Miller devote considerable attention to the notion of suppression because they believe it can be a significant adaptive device. Suppression is the *deliberate inhibition of responses,* the act of putting certain thought and emotional processes out of mind. Controlling *attention responses* is a key factor in bringing about suppression. When one wishes to attend to something, he blocks out other distractions, as when he turns off the television in order to read. One can control himself by deliberately controlling his attention. For example, a student will not purchase the evening paper so that he can concentrate on his studies.

Knowledge of the principles of learning can be used to promote suppression. One approach that is suggested by Dollard and Miller is to build *mental units* that can be called into action (1950). For example, one might remind himself that "the best time to begin is right now," or "the job won't get done unless I do it." In the case of a threatened impulsive outburst in an unpleasant situation, one can rehearse a sentence such as: "This is all just a part of the game," or "It's just a sick ego that he has." Any learned drive can be suppressed, whether it is an obsession with making money, or becoming popular, or achieving honors.

A strong affirmation of the goal which one wishes to achieve will begin to generate the competing responses that can inhibit the distracting ones. Actually making the appropriate responses, such as getting pen and paper to begin writing, will sometimes suffice to suppress the unwanted responses. Getting into a task more and more induces stimuli and responses that fix attention to the task and draw it away from stimuli and responses which interfere. Another way of suppressing unwanted responses is to set up a list of priorities and take them in order. If too much thinking is a problem, set a fixed amount of time for thinking and then begin to take action (close debate, as it were). We are often obsessed with the things we have to do because we fear that they won't get done unless we think about them, but thinking about so many things at one time may get nothing accomplished.

To be most effective, reinforcement should occur immediately following the response. This condition is not usually met. There is often a time gap between the application of the suppressive techniques and the attainment of the goal. Thus the suppressing responses receive little reinforcement. Dollard and Miller suggest that when the task is accomplished, one should rehearse some of the techniques used in producing the suppression of the distractions. One might say something like: "It was a matter of just getting down to business," or "I just decided to get started, and things started to happen," or "I kept thinking about the goal I wanted to achieve, and I was able to put everything else in the background." Perhaps this technique should be applied when the suppression appears to be taking over rather than at the completion of the task.

It should be clear that suppression is not always an easy process. Sometimes there are strong drives that cannot be met. These require a strong counterforce to suppress. Engaging in vigorous physical activity, changing the scene, moving away, and other similar activities may be required, but still the stubborn thoughts and feelings may recur. Sometimes temporary relief permits one to work out new approaches to old problems. A common mistake is the conviction that one should face and solve all his problems; there are many (some of man's greatest) that have no solution. A person may dwell on the problems he cannot solve, and neglect those he can. Of course, suppression is highly valuable in such instances. It plays its greatest role in helping a person to achieve the objectives he wishes to achieve. The point is that although complete suppression is not always possible, one should cultivate suppressing techniques to help him gain his objectives and deal with needless disturbances and distractions. Suppression is an absolute requirement for attaining self-control (Mischel and Ebbesen, 1970).

OVERT INHIBITION VERSUS OVERT RESTRAINT

As we noted, while in repression the responses are not under verbal control, in suppression the inhibited responses are; thus the former are not subject to the operation of the higher mental processes, while the latter are. Dollard and Miller (1950) make another important distinction with respect to inhibited responses: *overt inhibition* versus *overt restraint*. Overt inhibition involves the interference with or blocking of certain behaviors by unconscious competing responses. In overt restraint, instrumental responses are blocked by responses which are under verbal control. An inhibited person is one who cannot perform certain acts and knows that he cannot. One may know quite clearly that he suffers from work inhibition: he experiences much inner resistance when he sets out to do something. Another example of inhibition is the case of a sexually impotent man who experiences strong sexual desire but cannot perform the sex act.

In the case of overt restraint, the person sets up responses (primarily verbal) that prevent him from carrying out an instrumental response; an example is telling oneself not to be critical or insulting. Overt restraint, like suppression, is subject to the higher mental functions and can be extremely useful in coping with everyday problems. Overt inhibition is like repression, in that the source of the interference or blocking is not known to the victim. These conditions often require the intervention of psychotherapy. As problems are met, and labeling of experiences improves, inhibitions become weakened or unnecessary and may disappear.

SELF-STUDY

Dollard and Miller consider the challenging question of self-study and make some pertinent observations from which we may profit. They make a distinction between problem-solving and self-study. Everyone, to a greater or lesser degree, faces and solves problems of daily living, such as getting a watch repaired, arriving on time for work, keeping out of trouble with friends and associates. Self-study is self-observation or self-analysis. Self-analysis is undertaken when the self is experienced acutely, as when one feels chronically inferior, depressed, confused, or frustrated. Dollard and Miller point out that perhaps the normal person works out his repressions and faulty experiences as he goes along, without much fanfare. Self-study requires motivation, so if the person is not motivated, then perhaps he does not need it.

It is clear that many problems could be avoided by the application of rather obvious principles of mental health. One of the most frequent problem situations is the tendency to displace frustration-caused anger on innocent people (Miller and Bryebski, 1948). One may do this repeatedly without being fully aware of how irrationally he is acting. Social relationships are frequently hampered by bad moods, irritability, temper flairups, and the like. Being alert for this natural response to frustration is a good way of dealing with the displacements in a less damaging manner.

Another common affliction of our times is the tendency to blame ourselves for whatever goes wrong. We are taught from infancy that we can control our own destinies, and that if our plans do not work out as expected, we are somehow at fault. This myth causes many people to hold themselves accountable for things over which they have no control. We should build "mental units" (safeguards) that immediately rule out self-hatred, no matter what the circumstances are (Dollard and Miller, 1950). We might also look at our circumstances more closely and establish exactly what is and what is not under our personal control.

Many people agonize over physical unattractiveness and personal deficiencies which they cannot change. It should be possible to use suppression to deal with these matters. Often, problems associated with the self can be solved by using the higher mental processes. Sometimes the solutions are not discernible because strong drives are involved or emotions are active, but having previously worked out solutions that can be applied may overcome this difficulty in many instances. If we can use our abilities to solve physical problems, we certainly ought to be able to use them to deal with personal ones. Dollard and Miller suggest that self-study can be promoted through:

> "the identical activities which have been used during the course of formal therapy." The person stops to think instead of rushing into action. He attempts to see where blocks in association point and to decode dreams. He tries to trace vague anxieties to specific problem areas. He tests his reasoning for inconsistencies. He searches for missing units in his verbal series. In the privacy of his own mind, he will attempt to label irrational, emotional responses which he is making to persons in his real life. He will try at least to be clear with himself when he is at fault. He wants to act reasonably and therefore he must identify his unreasonable behavior.

> Undoubtedly, also, he consoles himself, as a therapist would console him. He assures himself there is no punishment for merely thinking. He affirms that he is free "to think anything." If he hits upon a solution of a problem, he then goes into action exactly as he was expected to do by the therapist. If he has been unreasonable, he tries to make amends. If he has been stupidly afraid, he tries responding despite his fear. In short, the mental activity of self study is designed to produce a more adaptive course of action in real life. It is not more brooding, or anxious self-preoccupation. Prolonged brooding is itself a symptom of mental malaise and not a positive use of the mind (1950, p. 437).

OBSERVATIONAL LEARNING: BANDURA AND WALTERS

A great deal of learning might be described as observational learning. We learn by observing the behavior of a model. Observational learning encompasses any type of *matching behavior,* such as imitation and identification. Simply observing the behavior of the model appears to be sufficient to promote learning, according to Bandura and Walters (1963). But how can observational learning be related to the principle of reinforcement, which, it will be recalled, states that responses are learned only if they are reinforced? According to Bandura and Walters, learning may occur both as a consequence of reinforcement and through modeling or observation alone.

In a new situation one learns what to do, or not do, through observing the behaviors of those who seem to know how to act. If you approach a friend and pour out your worries about your new job, he might advise you to keep cool and observe what the others are doing. There is no question that much human learning, and even that of the higher animals, consists of matching the behavior of others (Deutsch and Deutsch, 1966). Freud's notion of identification is really a type of observational learning. Freud held that the child learns the behaviors appropriate to his sex through his emotional involvement with the parent of the same sex. The little boy matches his behavior to his father's; the little girl imitates her mother. All through life, one has models to copy. Success or failure in many aspects of living in a culture depends upon observational learning. The culture deviant—the criminal, the neurotic, the malingerer—may be one who has failed to conform to role expectations. Such failure may arise from inadequate modeling: having the wrong models, or resisting the influence of models. Observational learning can be promoted as much by a deviant as by a prosocial model (Walters and Llewellyn Thomas, 1963), and the absence of appropriate models can result in deficiencies of behavior. The person may simply be unequipped to be a contributing member of his society.

LIFE VERSUS SYMBOLIC MODELS

Bandura and Walters (1963) distinguish between real-life and symbolic models. Under real-life models are included the agents of culture—parents, teachers, heroes, law enforcement authorities, sports stars. Symbolic models include verbal material, pictorial presentation (films and television), and written material (books and magazines). Numerous studies demonstrate that both real-life and symbolic models influence the behavior of observers. What children see on television does in fact affect their behavior (Murray, 1973). Bandura and Walters point out that the television productions may have greater influence than parental guidance because the direct portrayal of roles is more vivid than verbal instructions alone. The viewer of television and motion pictures is provided with lifelike scenes.

Anyone who has ever watched a highly emotional film can recall the strong feelings which he felt. This common experience has been studied in controlled experiments which demonstrated that even conditioned emotional responses can be produced by observational learning, without a direct experience of the pain, fear, or sorrow the actors were portraying. Presented with the same cues given to the performers, the subjects made the same responses (Bandura and Rosenthal, 1966). Thus instrumental responses, conditioned emotional responses, and even cognition may be acquired through observational learning; the learning may occur in the presence of real-life models or symbolic ones.

WHAT TYPES OF RESPONSES ARE ACQUIRED THROUGH OBSERVATIONAL LEARNING?

The specific responses that are subject to learning through imitation of a real-life or symbolic model are almost unlimited. The acquisition of aggressive responses has been studied most extensively, but dependency behavior, fear, sex-appropriate or -inappropriate behaviors, and others have also been studied. In general, behavior acquired through observational learning may be categorized under three headings: (1) the acquisition of new responses, such as the learning of aggressive responses from a model; (2) the strengthening or weakening of inhibitory responses, such as acquiring greater or less fear by observing the model's behavior in a fear situation; (3) stimulating already existing responses, such as practicing the piano longer after seeing a biography of a great musician (Bandura and Walters, 1963).

Acquisition of New Behaviors

Bandura and Walters (1963) cite many studies in which children exposed to a model behave more like the model as compared with a control group when presented with a test situation. In one experiment, the experimenter performed aggressive acts with a plastic doll — throwing the doll in the air, kicking it, hitting it with his fist, and pushing it over. When presented with a plastic doll shortly thereafter, the children who had witnessed the model's behavior performed many of the same behaviors. In the same test situation, children who had not witnessed the model's behavior did not engage in the aggressive acts.

Bandura and Walters (1963, Chap. 2) also cite studies which demonstrate that even generalized dispositions and tendencies, such as attitudes and personality traits, are the consequences of imitative learning. Children who were aggressive tended to have aggressive parents more frequently than children who were dependent in their orientations to problems. In various tasks children resembled parents. Undoubtedly, both observational learning and learning through reinforcement accounts for the similarities. Inherited constitutional dispositions played a part as well.

Observational learning appears to occupy a greater role than the learning psychologists have given it, Bandura and Walters believe (1963). There may be a complementary or conflicting interaction between observational learning and the subsequent reinforcement of the learned behavior. When new behavior is acquired through imitation, the consequences of performing the behavior may be either strengthened or weakened, depending on whether such behavior is reinforced or punished. A boy may acquire dependent behaviors through observation of his father at home, but such behavior may be either punished or reinforced by his peers at school. Perhaps the disparity between what might be expected through observational learning and the behavior that actually occurs is due to the overriding influence of the reinforcement consequences of the learned behavior (Liebert and Fernandez, 1970). For example, one daughter may be meticulous like her mother while the other daughter is careless.

Increasing or Decreasing Inhibitions

Bandura et al. (1969) demonstrated in an experiment dealing with snake phobias that observational techniques could actually lessen the snake phobia.

Subjects were divided into four groups, matched on fear of snakes. For one group, the live modeling group, the experimenter performed various activities with a live snake. He assisted the subjects in making some of the fear responses, such as touching the snake with gloves on. The second group, the symbolic modeling group, viewed a film which portrayed various scenes paralleling the live modeling performance. The subjects could work the projector, so that they could stop it or replay a scene. The members of the third group, the desensitization group, were presented with the same scenes verbally and were instructed to imagine them while they relaxed comfortably. The fourth group, the controls, was not exposed to any of the experimental conditions. The four groups were then tested on various approaches to a live snake. The three experimental groups showed a weakening of the snake phobia as compared with the control group, with the live modeling group showing the most approach responses. This experiment demonstrates that inhibitions can be weakened by observational techniques.

Inhibitions and phobias are learned through imitation. Children will pick up the phobias of their parents through observation of their behavior (Bandura and Menlove, 1968). A child might acquire a bug phobia, or a phobia of storms, simply by watching his mother's behavior in relation to the fear objects. The behavior of a leader can either strengthen or weaken the inhibitions of his followers. If the leader performs a daring feat, his behavior will induce his admirers to imitate him. Inhibitions related to sexual practices are often lessened in group situations. Those who might otherwise abstain from sexual intercourse may model their behavior after those who do participate in sexual activity, simply by observational imitation. The company we keep has much to do with the inhibitions we develop or lose.

Releasing Existing Responses

Bandura and Walters (1963) report several experiments in which the model's behavior appeared to "set off" behavior in the observer. The observer not only repeated some of the aggressive, dependent, or fear responses of the model, but also accomplished the same goals with his own behaviors. It frequently happens that those who imitate a model may exaggerate the model's behavior, as when religious fanatic carries out the precepts of his religion overscrupulously. Freud commented that he would hate to be a Freudian. He meant that his disciples were even more radical than he.

As we attempt to adapt and cope with the circumstances of our lives, we must rely on observational learning. Behavior is not always so neatly reinforced as in laboratory studies of animals, and mistakes may be fatal. We observe others, particularly those who are considered successful, to discover what should be done or avoided. To depend on natural reinforcements or punishments to guide us may subject us to many unnecessary hurts. Rather than being content to profit from our mistakes, we should try not to make them in the first place. From a practical standpoint, observational learning from the appropriate models can help us to avoid making costly errors.

ROTTER'S SOCIAL LEARNING THEORY

EXPECTANCIES

You are with a group of people who are discussing a topic you know very well. You would like to participate, but you are afraid that you will be ignored. Why? You are afraid to participate in group settings because in the past you have encountered repeated failures in such settings; thus you have formed an *expectancy* of being ignored in a group context. The expectancy was reinforced when it was confirmed; that is, whenever you thought you had failed in group participation. In the present situation, your *freedom of movement* (Rotter, 1954) is restricted because you expect to be ignored and thus avoid participating in the group. If we asked a cognitive social learning theorist such as Rotter "What is involved in learning?" his answer would be in part, "We learn a great number of expectancies about our world. Many of them help us to meet our needs and deal with our problems satisfactorily, but others cause us to restrict our participation, and to avoid many behaviors and situations that could enhance our lives."

Where do the expectancies come from? As we have already noted, expectancies are based on attempts to satisfy needs; that is to say, they are based on the *acquired probabilities of obtaining reinforcements* (Rotter, 1954). A man who has failed frequently in his requests for dates may develop a generalized expectancy that he will be rejected by women. His generalized expectancy will produce perceptual distortion, so that he is unable to discriminate between situations in which his probability of success is high and those in which it is low. He might simply follow a fixed pattern of avoidance and not ask any girl for a date. Many avoidances are based upon similarly generalized expectancies (Aronson and Carlsmith, 1962).

Another condition which instigates generalized expectancies is an event that is novel or not adequately labeled. For example, a man may respond to a woman he meets for the first time with generalized expectancies that may be highly inappropriate. As he gets to know her, his expectancies will become more specifically related to her actual behavior.. Resemblances between the situation or person and similar situations or people become the basis of response. For instance, expectancies derived from experiences with teachers may be applied in a work setting to one's first encounter with a supervisor.

Reinforcement Value

We have noted that the rate of occurrence of the reinforcement will influence the formation of expectancies. But the rate of hits and misses is not the only variable that must be taken into account in understanding learning and behavior, according to Rotter (1954): the *quality of the reinforcement,* the *reinforcement value,* is also a significant variable. If the reinforcement value of the goal object is strong, one may be driven to perform behavior even when the expectancy of securing the goal object is limited. Much irrational behavior can be accounted for as the vain pursuit of highly valued goals. A man may give up almost everything to gain status and wealth. He may tie himself to his profession to the neglect of his health and family, even when the attainment of prized goals is highly unlikely. In such instances we can see both the operation of modeling and the formation of false expectancies. Admiring someone who is attaining the prized goals may stimulate imitative behavior. "If George can do it, why can't I?" Such thinking obviously overlooks many important variables: fortunate circumstances, individual differences in talent, the sheer operation of chance factors that might favor one over another who has the same drive and ability.

Minimum Goal Level

Rotter (1954) introduces the concept of minimum goal level to bring out another important aspect of reinforcement value. The minimum goal level is the level of reinforcement which is considered minimal, below which reinforcement ceases or becomes aversive. A student may set the grade of A in a course as his minimum goal level, and consider anything below that unacceptable. He might be disturbed if his report card has even one B. When minimum goal levels are set unrealistically, one is bound to experience needless frustration. Too often goals are valued on the basis of their appeal rather than on their feasibility. We choose the goals that are glamorous and idealistic: a perfect marriage, an exciting job, all-loving and faithful friends, perpetual peak experiences, not being frustrated, disappointed, hurt, or misunderstood. Furthermore, the minimum goal levels that we are willing to tolerate are also set uncompromisingly high: if we cannot have perfection (the most, the best, the flawless), then we feel cheated, deprived, and frustrated. Goals and minimum goal levels must constantly be examined and brought into line with the possibilities for gratification.

A curious thing often takes place with respect to unrealistic goals and unwillingness to lower minimum goal levels: one may experience repeated failure (punishment), yet the goals are not altered. Sometimes in such instances the goal is actually intensified in value (Mischel and Masters, 1966). The behavior that results from the intensified value of the goal may be highly irrational and maladaptive. Persistent goal frustration may result in generalized irritability, displaced hostility, regression, self-hate, apathy, depression, neurotic avoidance, and obsessive and compulsive behaviors.

Meeting one's needs requires a realistic view of things. False expectancies may not only lead to needless frustration, but may also instigate behaviors that are injurious to the individual (Lewin et al., 1944). False expectations make living more difficult than it is. One should expect to be unhappy, disappointed, and hurt in a variety of situations. There is much unpleasantness in life—friends are not always what we would like them to be; we are not always treated justly; our circumstances change whether we like the changes or not; the world is not perfect, and neither are we. Expectancies should be constantly tested against reality. So much of our frustration and unhappiness stems from faulty expectations. A cynical person remarked that the first half of life involves building up faulty expectations, and the second half is spent in undoing them. While this statement is extreme, it points out the neuroticism of our culture. In the elementary school story books, there is usually a happy ending, or a silver lining for every cloud, or perpetual happiness and success for heroes. Movies and television portray glamorous ideas about love, marriage, and sex. In the school setting, vocations are presented in a glamorized manner. Even certain religions engender in their adherents false expectations of happiness if the precepts of the religion are followed. Happiness is conceived in terms of such unrealistic expectations as being at perfect peace with oneself, being tension and pain free, always being in control, and having one's prayers answered. As a result of faulty expectancies we strive for the wrong things and overlook the real possibilities for satisfying living (Bills, 1953).

Perceiving Precedes Responding

When Rotter states that perceiving precedes responding, he means that each individual responds to a subjectively meaningful world, a world as he interprets it. Perception is influenced by expectancies and the reinforcement value of the goals; thus behavior depends upon *perception, expectancy*, and *reinforcement value* (Rotter, 1954). In bringing about personality change, one can alter (1) his perception of particular events, (2) his expectancies, (3) the reinforcement value of goal objects, or (4) his behavior directly. Being a cognitive learning theorist, Rotter stresses the importance of subjective variables in producing change; thus behavior will change if one alters his perceptions, expectancies, or goals and goal values (Rotter, 1971). In psychotherapy or counseling, correct behaviors may be reinforced by the therapist, but in dealing with our own problems, the subjective variables would be more amenable to change.

INSIGHTS FROM ROTTER ON BEHAVIOR CHANGE

THE UNCONSCIOUS

The unconscious in Rotter's theory may be thought of as *expectancies that influence behavior but that are not in awareness.* A long-standing yet unperceived expectancy of failure may be active in a situation and instigate inappropriate behavior—behavior that the person himself does not understand. He may be aware only that he is behaving in an irrational or self-defeating manner, not of the expectancy that is determining this behavior. One may learn about his unconscious expectancies by letting his behavior reveal them.

One may also be unaware of his minimum goal levels and as a result suffer a host of unfavorable consequences (Rotter, 1954). He may experience a profound sense of inferiority, or of being a failure. His feelings are a puzzle to him because, logically, he ought to be self-satisfied. He may have many desirable attributes, and his life may not be so different from those of others. What he does not experience are the unrealistic goal levels that he has. Problems may also arise when the minimum goal levels are too low: the total pattern of striving and motivation may be generally depressed. Like knowledge of expectancies, knowledge of minimum goal levels may produce marked changes in the total personality, particularly if one makes genuine efforts to alter his minimum goal levels to accord with his circumstances. Minimum goal levels, whether conscious or not, play a significant role in all aspects of one's life. One's level of satisfaction (general state of happiness) is greatly determined by them. An ability to change minimum goal levels should be cultivated as one of the major principles in the art of living. Being willing to identify these levels is in itself a good first step; thus making the unconscious conscious is an ideal which applies to the notions of minimum goal levels and expectancies.

POSTPONING GRATIFICATION

Being able to forego immediate gratifications for the sake of potentially greater future satisfactions is certainly an important aspect of dealing with one's needs. In the same vein, if one is able to tolerate frustration and tension as he works toward his goals, he is more likely to actually attain them. There are wide individual differences on the variable of delay of gratification. Expectancies can play a part in the ability to delay gratification: an untrusting environment encourages the preference of immediate satisfactions to long-term ones. The choice between a lesser but immediate reward and a potentially greater but postponed reward has been studied in relation to many personality and situation variables (e.g., Bandura and Mischel, 1965; Klineberg, 1968; Mahrer, 1956). Many persons who are considered cultural deviants, such as criminals, neurotics, and psychopaths, seem unable to postpone gratification. Yet Rotter and his students have demonstrated that long-term expectancies can be promoted by providing the appropriate environmental conditions, and that one can alter his own expectancies.

LOCUS OF CONTROL OF REINFORCEMENT

Rotter's theorizing has led to the investigation of another important adjustive and coping variable: whether or not one expects to have control over his reinforcements. This dimension is referred to as *internal or external locus of control* (Rotter, 1966). We might think of it as a personality variable which takes a different form in each person. Many behaviors depend upon the amount of personal control the individual believes he has. When subjects were divided according to internal or external locus of control of reinforcements, significant variations were discovered in such important behaviors as risk taking, quitting smoking, willingness to participate in civil rights movements, time needed to make difficult decisions, success in influencing the attitudes of others, changes in reinforcement expectancies following success or failure in tasks, and other behaviors favoring the internal locus of control subjects (e.g., Davis and Davis, 1972). One's total orientation to life is influenced by this variable. Thus one should attempt to acquire a greater sense of control over his circumstances.

IMPLICATIONS OF SOCIAL LEARNING THEORY FOR PSYCHOTHERAPY AND SELF-IMPROVEMENT

We will briefly consider the implications for psychotherapy of Rotter's learning theory. As the following quotations demonstrate, the therapist or counselor helps his client to accomplish certain objectives. Many of these same objectives can be attained outside of therapy by one who is capable of dealing with himself and his situation in a problem solving manner.

The patient's difficulties are frequently seen from a problem solving point of view. As a result, there tends to be a greater emphasis on the development of higher-level problem solving skills, such as those of looking for alternative ways of reaching goals, thinking through the consequences of behavior, looking for differences or discriminations in life situations, turning attention in social situations to the needs and attitudes of others, and recognizing that one can exercise some control over one's fate by one's own efforts (1970, p. 235).

In place of the belief that experience changes people but little once they pass infancy and that only therapy can make major changes, a major implication of social learning theory is that new experiences, or different kinds of experience in life situations can be far more effective in many cases than those new experiences that occur only in a special therapy situation. . . .

Likewise, the opportunity for the patient to make environmental changes himself, such as changes in jobs, living circumstances, and social groups, should not be overlooked or discarded in favor of a belief that all his problems lie inside himself rather than in his interactions with the meaningful environments (1970, p. 238).

At the most general level, the implications of social learning theory are that psychotherapy should be viewed as a social interaction. The therapist helps the patient achieve a more satisfying and constructive interrelationship with his social environment. . . . There is no process special to psychotherapy and there is no need, even if it were possible, for the therapist to be a shadowy figure, or "catalyst." Rather, he is an active partner who utilizes learning principles, applied to a particular individual in a particular set of circumstances, to help that person achieve a better way of dealing with the problems of life (1970, pp. 238-239).

BEHAVIOR THERAPY

We are concerned with the application of personality theories to real-life problems. Certainly the learning theory approach to personality study has an important applied aspect. If personality is formed by means of learning, then it follows that personality change should fall under the scope of learning. The applied learning approach to personality change includes behavior modification or behavior therapy.

Behavior modification is the application of learning principles to promote behavior change which normally comes under the heading of learning. *Behavior therapy* covers techniques for the treatment of disturbed behaviors. To put it simply, behavior modification principles may be applied to the learning situations of normal people, while behavior therapy is used with those suffering from personality disorders. We have considered some of the uses of behavior modification techniques in our discussion of Skinner. We will now briefly discuss some applications of behavior therapy. The reader may have observed that some behavior modification techniques can, in fact, be used as behavior therapy, but the distinction is nevertheless useful.

We have already touched on the rationale or assumptions underlying behavior therapy in our discussion of the role of learning in the formation of and potential change in personality. An additional assumption is that disordered or deviant behavior should be the object of therapeutic focus. The traditional distinction between the cause of the disorder and its manifestations or symptoms is rejected by those who accept the learning approach. They hold that treating the symptoms is equivalent to treating the disorder (Eysenck and Rachman, 1965).

The traditionalist might consider excessive talkativeness as one of the symptoms of a sense of inferiority. The talkativeness is a means of compensating for, or covering over, the felt inferiority. To treat the talkativeness directly will not work, or if the treatment does diminish the symptom, another, such as withdrawal or shyness, might take its place. It is assumed that the treatment should focus on promoting self-accepting attitudes, so that the symptom becomes unnecessary. However, one major difficulty with this approach is that the causes are not easily identifiable. The therapist may resort to speculation about potential causes, basing his opinions upon one of the theories of personality. If he follows Freud, he may look for early traumas which are unconscious but whose effects cause the symptoms. If he follows Karen Horney, he may look for an idealistic self-image that creates unrealistic expectations of self and others. If he follows Fromm, he may look for the manifestations of an unproductive orientation to life. One thing is clear: the symptoms are much more apparent than are the causes, even if one accepts the distinction between them.

If a child does not know the rules of baseball, he might find himself being rejected by other children. The problem could spread to all aspects of his social relationships, and eventually he may begin to have difficulties in school. Teaching the child the rules of baseball, a relatively easy matter, could have changed his circumstances. When the problems have multiplied, as often happens because early difficulties usually go unrecognized, the treatment becomes more complex, but may still focus on disordered behavior. Improving any of the child's behaviors should generalize to other aspects of his life. (Rotter suggests that one might begin with the most recent problem area—the one which appears most directly treatable by behavior therapy—and then go on to the more difficult ones.) Improvement will make further improvement easier. Assisting the child with his school work may not help him learn baseball rules directly, but it will improve his status and eliminate some tensions.

Traditional treatment of personality disorders is termed psychotherapy or treatment of the psyche. The psyche may be taken to mean the personality; thus psychotherapy deals with personality disorders. The disorders may occur in many different ways: the personality may not have developed properly, or there may be repression and significant conflicts that produce anxiety and disordered behavior, or certain needs may be exaggerated, and so on. Many therapeutic techniques have been developed for treating the psyche: free association, dream analysis, interpretation, catharsis.

These traditional techniques are not utilized by behavior therapists, however. The behavior therapist, deriving his techniques from principles of learning, may point out that the whole self (the total personality structure) is seldom disordered; only specific behaviors are. A toothache, or a sprained ankle, can temporarily incapacitate the individual. He may be unable to do his work; his social contacts may be disturbed; he may experience a depressed mood. The whole person is affected, but the locus of disturbance is quite focalized. Analogously, an argumentative person may drive away potential friends and create difficulties for himself in all aspects of his life. Reduce the intensity of his aggressive behavior, says the behavior therapist, and his life situation will improve. Being argumentative causes conditions which are frustrating, and these in turn may increase his argumentativeness. Do something to lessen the disturbed behavior, and you should make its further use less necessary. Tranquilizing drugs may reduce the argumentativeness, but it may reappear unless the person has worked out ways of dealing with his aggressive tendencies. Sometimes while under the influence of the drug, a person can work out better means of confronting his problems; thus the tranquilizing drug may permit him to use his higher mental processes in dealing with his disturbed behaviors.

A great many specific techniques have been and are being developed for changing behavior. Such techniques are derived from principles of classical conditioning, from operant conditioning, and even from perceptual or cognitive learning. There is a host of new terms standing for new techniques: extinction, counterconditioning, deconditioning, aversion therapy or conditioning, reinforcement therapy, desensitization, satiation therapy, cognitive restructuring, observational learning, rational-emotive therapy, and others. The learning approach to personality study and change, although recent in origin, is already a strong competitor of the traditional psychotherapies (Paul, 1967). Bad habits can be changed, sensitivities reduced, new habits engendered, irrational responses eliminated, attitudes altered.

CRITICAL EVALUATION OF LEARNING APPROACHES TO PERSONALITY

We might begin by examining the differences between the S-R approach, as represented by Dollard and Miller, and the cognitive approach, represented by Bandura and Walters and Rotter. Let us take the situation of a man caught in the rain. The S-R theorist would analyze his behavior as follows: the rain causes discomfort (drive), and taking cover in a doorway reduces the discomfort, thus reinforcing the behavior of moving into a doorway when it is raining. The darkening sky becomes a cue which leads directly to finding a doorway. The cognitive theorist would argue that one learns expectancies, and that drives and reinforcers stimulate and direct behavior but are not directly involved in the learning process. The experience of being in the rain fosters the development of an expectancy that one will be wet when it rains.

Finding a shelter creates the expectancy that in a doorway one will remain protected from the rain. But what is the value of adding the cognitive elements, which after all are unobservable? One reason is that punishment, as well as reinforcement, can create expectancies: we can learn something about a situation from punishment. Another reason is that behavior appears much more flexible than the S-R approach allows: one might use any number of different shelters in avoiding the rain, even though they have never been tried in the past. Generalization does not explain this novel behavior as well as expectancy. Essentially, the two approaches accomplish different things: the S-R approaches better explain the learning of basic habits, while the cognitive theories better account for decision making and more complex behaviors.

For the most part, learning theories of personality are content-free; that is, they do not provide concepts that can be used to describe personality. If one wishes to compare people (between-subject differences) or the same individual on different dimensions (within-subject differences), he has no guidelines except the principles of learning. Learning theories are at their best when they deal with the *formation of personality* and with *personality change;* they are weak in dealing with the *structure* and *organization* of personality. There is an important difference between telling us *how* personality is formed through learning and telling us about the *nature* of the personality that is formed (the difference between process and contents). Knowing principles of learning does not help one to discover the patterned complex of attributes that constitutes a particular person. To know and characterize a personality one must know more than such learning principles as drive-reduction fosters learning, responses can be extinguished when they are not reinforced, learning is in part the formation of expectancies, present behavior is maintained by reinforcers, and so on.

Learning takes place within the limits of an organism that has a specific nature or species potential. There is great variation in what can be learned easily or with difficulty. Certain stimuli are more relevant for one species, or a particular member of that species, than others. Responses also vary according to the make-up of the organism. Furthermore, learning theorists have not considered the physiological, genetic, and social determinants as seriously as some believe they should.

The topics of the learning approaches to personality have probably been more fruitful than others because the learning theories are empirically oriented and more sophisticated in their construction. It should be borne in mind that the originators of the intrapsychic theories were more concerned with applying them to real-life people and to real-life situations than with deriving from them new ideas for research into man's behavior. Thus far it is difficult to distill what might be termed ideal human living from existing learning theories. Perhaps a learning theory by itself cannot provide a model of the ideal life, except in the empirical sense that what promotes health is what should be learned. This is a view which seems to be espoused by Skinner (1971).

SUMMARY

1.   The psychology of personality may be approached through the study and application of principles of learning. Each generation can and has acquired the achievements of earlier generations through learning. The learning theorist believes that man's personal problems are in large measure caused by faulty learning experiences. Faulty learning can be eradicated, or replaced by adaptive learning.

2.   In general, learning approaches to personality may be divided into the S-R and S-O-R models. Those who follow the S-R model tend to stress the learning of habits: they are concerned with the acquisition of responses. Those who follow the S-O-R model tend to stress the learning of cognitive processes and attitudes: they hold that responses are guided by knowledge.

3.   Dollard and Miller, who follow the S-R approach to personality phenomena, analyze the components of the learning process as cue, drive, response, and reinforcement. The cue is a stimulus that directs responses. Drive consists of a stimulus, or stimuli, that activate(s) or energize(s) the organism. Response refers to the behavior, learned or unlearned, that is set off by the drive and cue. Reinforcement occurs when the drive is reduced and the behavior which reduces the drive is strengthened.

4.   Responses to a situation occur according to an order of priority: this is termed a response hierarchy. Learning may be thought of as the rearrangement of the initial response hierarchy (resultant hierarchy). Response hierarchies may be innate or acquired through learning. Novel responses may be learned through imitation, which itself can become a generalized habit.

5.   Cue-producing responses are those which produce stimuli that are experienced. Such stimuli play an important role in selecting other responses; thus one might explain the operation of the higher mental processes in terms of cue-producing responses: thinking, planning, problem solving, and decision making.

6. We respond to similarities (generalization) and differences (discrimination) among objects, people, and events. Dollard and Miller distinguish between primary generalization (similarity of response to similar stimuli) and mediated generalization (responding to labeled stimuli which may be quite dissimilar). Words may be the source of faulty generalization or overgeneralization.

7.   Responses may be of many types: unlearned and learned, instrumental and cue-producing, overt and covert, muscular and verbal, produced directly by a stimulus or mediational. The higher mental processes may be viewed as mediational cue-producing responses.

8.   Drives and reinforcers are either unlearned (primary) or learned (secondary). We learn to value money, praise, status, and other cultural products. Many emotions become attached to a wide range of neutral stimuli through learning.

9.   The unconscious, according to Dollard and Miller, may be considered as experiences that are unlabeled. An experience which is not under verbal control does not enter the domain of the higher mental processes. Repression means the loss of the ability to use verbal labels. It also means a learned inhibition of responses—learning not to think about certain matters. Distorted labeling of events and experiences can be the source of much irrational behavior.

10.   Repression blocks thought, while conflict blocks action. Certain emotions, such as fear and anxiety, inhibit responses which serve drives; thus conflicts exist between drives and such inhibitory emotional responses.

11.   In S-R terminology, suppression may be viewed as the counteracting of unwanted responses by verbal and other mediating responses. One controls his attention responses to avoid distractions which may inhibit the attainment of his goals.

12.   Self-control and self-understanding can be learned. We can learn to solve our personal problems through self-knowledge, suppression, self-management, overt restraint, and other learned techniques.

13.   Bandura and Walters have stressed observational learning in the social context. We learn from observing the behavior of a model, without any apparent reinforcement. The consequences of the model's behavior, as well as of the learner's behavior, may determine whether or not the learned behavior will be continued, but the original learning is acquired through imitation or modeling. Reinforcement learning is not denied by Bandura and Walters, but they are more concerned with modeling.

14.   Bandura and Walters distinguish between real-life and symbolic models. Under real-life models are included the agents of culture, such as parents, teachers, heroes, law enforcement authorities, and sports stars. Symbolic models include verbal materials, pictorial representations such as television and films, and written materials such as books and magazines. Both types promote learning. Conditioned emotional responses, instrumental learning, and cognitive and perceptual learning may be acquired through observation.

15.   Observational learning may take the form of the acquisition of new responses, the learning or weakening of inhibitory responses, or the activation of already existing responses.

16.   Depending upon natural reinforcers and punishments to guide us may subject us to many unnecessary hurts. Observational learning of appropriate models can help us to avoid costly mistakes. Both prosocial and deviant behavior can be learned through observation; thus the types of models to which children are exposed make a great difference.

17.   For Rotter, who espouses a cognitive, social learning theory approach to personality, learning involves the acquisition of expectancies. Expectancies determine freedom of movement in the acquisition of goal objects. In a novel situation, generalized expectancies based on similar situations in the past may

cause highly inappropriate behaviors such as stereotyping people and prejudice. The reinforcement value of the goal object is an important factor in determining whether or not a particular behavior will occur. Even with low expectancy of attainment, highly valued goals may be pursued avidly.

18.   Rotter introduces the concept of minimum goal level to account for the
level of goal attainment which is considered minimum, and below which there
is lack of reinforcement. Minimum goal levels are often uncompromisingly
set.

19.   According to Rotter, behavior depends upon perception, expectancies,
and the reinforcement value of the goal object. In bringing about personality
change, one may change (a) his perception of particular events, (b) his expectancies, (c) the reinforcement value of goal objects, or (d) his behavior directly.
In psychotherapy or counseling correct behaviors may be reinforced by a
therapist, but in dealing with our own problems the subjective variables are
more amenable to change.

20.   The unconscious in Rotter's theory may be thought of as expectancies
that influence behavior but that are not in awareness. Making the unconscious
conscious is an ideal which applies to the notions of minimum goal levels and
expectancies.

21.   Rotter's theorizing has led to the investigation of (a) delay of gratification versus immediate acceptance of lesser goals, and (b) whether the individual believes he has an internal locus of control over his reinforcements or
whether the control is external to himself. These variables have been studied
in relation to a variety of behaviors, such as risk taking and decision making.

22.   The learning theory approaches to personality have important applications in behavior modification and behavior therapy. Maladaptive behavior is
assumed to be learned, and whatever is learned can be unlearned, or replaced
by more adaptive learning. Treatment should concentrate on the disordered
behavior directly, without searching for hypothetical causes. Behavior therapy may be contrasted with psychotherapy, which means in a literal sense the
treatment of the psyche.

23.   There are a great number of specific techniques for changing behavior
which have been and continue to be, developed. Such techniques are derived
from principles of classical conditioning, from operant conditioning, and
even from perceptual or cognitive learning.

SUGGESTED READINGS

Bandura, A., and Walters, R. H. Social Learning and Personality Development. New York: Holt,
    Rinehart and Winston, 1963.
        The authors hold that their theoretical approach is truly social because they are concerned
        with modeling or observational learning in social contexts. The book compares observa-
        tional and reinforcement learning, and relates these to self and others. Many research
        studies are presented. Implications for behavior therapy are elaborated, from both the re-
        inforcement and observational points of view.

Dollard, J., and Miller, N. E. Personality and Psychotherapy: An Analysis in Terms of Learning, Thinking, and Culture. New York: McGraw-Hill, 1950.
>   The learning approach is applied to Freudian concepts. Freud's therapeutic concepts and procedures, as well as his theory of personality, are translated into the terminology of learning. This is an excellent introduction to the learning approach to personality.

Miller, N. E., and Dollard, J. Social Learning and Imitation. New Haven: Yale University Press, 1941.
>   This is one of the earliest attempts to apply principles of learning to the phenomena of interest to the personality psychologist. One contention is that social behavior is learned through drive reduction or reinforcement. The higher mental processes are explained in learning terms. Imitative behavior is treated as any other reinforced behavior. The book is a good introduction to the learning approach to personality.

Rotter, J. B. Social Learning and Clinical Psychology. Englewood Cliffs, New Jersey: Prentice-Hall, 1954.
>   This book presents Rotter's social learning theory. It provides an introduction to the cognitive approach in learning. Rotter develops his concepts of expectancy, goal value, and minimum goal levels.

REFERENCES

Aronson, E., and Carlsmith, J. M. Performance expectancy as a determinant of actual performance. J. Abnorm. Social Psychol. *65*:178–82, 1962.

Bandura, A., Blanchard, E. B., and Ritter, B. Relative efficacy of desensitization and modeling approaches for inducing behavioral, affective, and attitudinal changes. J. Pers. Soc. Psychol. *13*:173–99, 1969.

Bandura, A., and Menlove, F. L. Factors determining vicarious extinction of avoidance behavior through symbolic modeling. J. Pers. Social Psychol. *8*:99–108, 1968.

Bandura, A., and Mischel, W. Modification of self-improved delay of reward through exposure to live and symbolic models. J. Pers. Social Psychol. *2*:698–705, 1965.

Bandura, A., and Rosenthal, T. L. Vicarious classical conditioning as a function of arousal level. J. Pers. Social Psychol. *3*:54–62, 1966.

Bandura, A., and Walters, R. H. Social Learning and Personality Development. New York: Holt, Rinehart and Winston, 1963.

Barker, R. G., Dembo, T., and Lewin, K. Frustration and regression: An experiment with young children. University of Iowa Studies in Child Welfare 18, Whole No. 386, 1941.

Berlyne, D. E. Structure and Direction in Thinking. New York: John Wiley and Sons, 1965.

Bills, R. E. A comparison of scores on the Index of Adjustment and Values with behavior in level-of-aspiration tasks. J. Consult. Psychol. *17*:206–12, 1953.

Davis, W. L., and Davis, D. E. Internal-external control and attribution of responsibility for success and failure. J. Pers. *40*:123–36, 1972.

Deutsch, J. A., and Deutsch, D. Physiological Psychology. Homewood, Illinois: Dorsey Press, 1966.

Dollard, J., Auld, F., Jr., and White, A. M. Steps in Psychotherapy: Study of a Case of Sex-Fear Conflict. New York: The Macmillan Company, 1953.

Dollard, J., and Miller, N. E. Personality and Psychotherapy. New York: McGraw-Hill, 1950.

Eysenck, H. J., and Rachman, S. The Causes and Cures of Neurosis. San Diego: Robert R. Knapp, 1965.

Kendler, H. H., and Kendler, T. S. Vertical and horizontal processes in problem solving. Psychol. Rev. *69*:1–16, 1962.

Klineberg, S. L. Future time perspective and the preference for delayed reward. J. Pers. Social Psychol. *8*:253–57, 1968.

Lacey, J. I., and Smith, R. L. Conditioning and generalization of unconscious anxiety. Science *120*:1045–52, 1954.

Lewin, K., Dembo, T., Festinger, L., and Sears, P. Level of aspiration. *In* Hunt, J. M., ed., Handbook of Personality and Behavior Disorders, Vol. 1. New York: Ronald Press, 1944. Pp. 333–78.

Liebert, R. M., and Fernandez, L. E. Effects of vicarious consequences on imitative performance. Child Dev. *41*:847–52, 1970.

Mahrer, A. R. The role of expectancy in delayed reinforcement. J. Exp. Psychol. *52*:101–05, 1956.

Miller, N. E. Comments on theoretical models: Illustrated by the development of a theory of conflict behavior. J. Pers. *20*:82–100, 1951.

Miller, N. E., and Bryebski, B. R. Minor studies in aggression: II. The influence of frustrations imposed by the in-group on attitudes expressed towards out-groups. J. Psychol. *25*:437–42, 1948.

Miller, N. E., and Dollard, J. Social Learning and Imitation. New Haven: Yale University Press, 1941.

Mischel, W., and Ebbesen, E. Attention in delay of gratification. J. Pers. Social Psychol. *16*:329–37, 1970.

Mischel, W., and Masters, J. C. Effects of probability of reward attainment on responses to frustration. J. Pers. Social Psychol. *3*:390–96, 1966.

Murray, J. P. Television and violence: Implications of the Surgeon General's research program. Am. Psychol. *28*:472–78, 1973.

Paul, G. L. Insight versus desensitization in psychotherapy two years after termination. J. Consult. Psychol. *31*:333–48, 1967.

Rotter, J. B. Social Learning and Clinical Psychology. Englewood Cliffs, New Jersey: Prentice-Hall, 1954.

Rotter, J. B. Generalized expectancies for internal versus external control of reinforcement. Psychol. Monogr. 80, Whole No. 609, 1966.

Rotter, J. B. Some implications of a social learning theory for the practice of psychotherapy. *In* Levis, D. J., ed., Learning Approaches to Therapeutic Behavior Change. Chicago: Aldine Publishing Company, 1970.

Rotter, J. B. Generalized expectancies for interpersonal trust. Am. Psychol. *26*:443–52, 1971.

Skinner, B. F. Cumulative Record. New York: Appleton-Century-Crofts, 1961.

Walters, R. H., and Llewellyn Thomas, E. Enhancement of punitiveness by visual and audiovisual displays. Can. J. Psychol. *16*:244–55, 1963.

PART IV

Human Motivation

The three chapters which comprise this section deal with human motivation. Chapter 7 covers the major ideas of Henry Murray who, more than any other psychologist, has developed the need approach. He has suggested a highly complex list of needs. He proposes a means of describing behavior by identifying its components in minute detail. Currently, he is placing more stress upon the major goals, which constitute the end states of needs. His catalog of needs will provide the reader with a comprehensive schema for ordering his own and others' behavior.

Chapter 8 will cover Abraham Maslow's famous concept of the need hierarchy. Disagreeing with Murray's schema, Maslow strove to bring out the *arrangement* of needs. He was concerned with the highest needs of man, those which he believed are distinctly human. Maslow held that one can identify the level of needs which are dominant in his life, and can thus obtain an indication of his level of functioning in respect to the fullest development and functioning possible, which Maslow termed self-actualization.

Chapter 9 considers the views of Alfred Adler on motivation. Adler is not ordinarily identified as a motivational theorist, but a close inspection of his views does in fact suggest that he was. He spoke frequently of man's inferiority as a motivating condition for a great variety of behaviors. He also introduced a second basic motivational principle which takes many forms: the struggle for superiority. His notion of social interest is another motivational concept. He espoused the principle of teleology, which holds that goals rather than drives determine behavior. One of his major proposals is that behavior is governed by guiding fictions, which are general values or goals. A person may be motivated to be a "good neighbor," a "hard worker," a "contributing member of his community," and the like. Adler termed such goals fictional because the person who is motivated by them has his own interpretation of what they are. Striving toward goals is certainly a motivational principle.

Each theorist has thus concentrated on a different approach to motivation, but the approaches are complementary rather than contradictory. We can learn something about motivation from each.

**TABLE IV-1   MOTIVATIONAL CONCEPTS OF MURRAY,
MASLOW, AND ADLER**

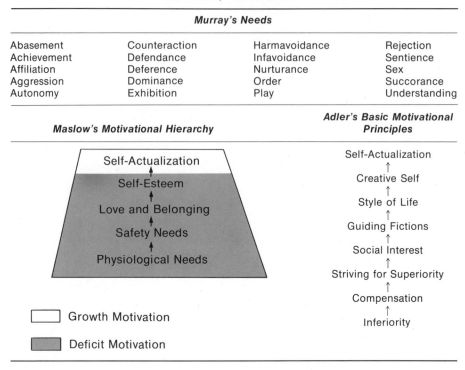

Murray's Needs			
Abasement	Counteraction	Harmavoidance	Rejection
Achievement	Defendance	Infavoidance	Sentience
Affiliation	Deference	Nurturance	Sex
Aggression	Dominance	Order	Succorance
Autonomy	Exhibition	Play	Understanding

Maslow's Motivational Hierarchy

Self-Actualization
↑
Self-Esteem
↑
Love and Belonging
↑
Safety Needs
↑
Physiological Needs

☐ Growth Motivation

▨ Deficit Motivation

Adler's Basic Motivational Principles

Self-Actualization
↑
Creative Self
↑
Style of Life
↑
Guiding Fictions
↑
Social Interest
↑
Striving for Superiority
↑
Compensation
↑
Inferiority

GENERAL RELATIONSHIPS OF MOTIVATION AND BEHAVIOR

As a first step toward gaining an appreciation of the central role of motivation in personality, the reader is asked to consider the relationships between motivation and behavior. The general aims of any form of inquiry are: (1) to know or comprehend causes or relationships, (2) to predict the future course on the basis of such knowledge, and (3) to manipulate and control events—to make things happen by altering conditions. One may look upon motivation from this frame of reference: to know, to predict, and to control. Knowledge of an individual's needs or motives will allow one to make sense of his behavior, to predict future courses of action, and to take steps to bring about certain effects through manipulation of motives.

UNDERSTANDING BEHAVIOR THROUGH NEEDS

Needs may be considered the source of behavior, active forces that get behavior going. One may think of a need as a lack or deficit, although some needs, such as sneezing, expiration, and elimination of wastes, involve excesses. Restless activity usually follows upon a need state. Sometimes by trial and error, but more often (after one has accumulated an extensive memory system) by recalling a habit, the correct activity or means is employed to secure the goal. When something interferes with this activity, as when the goal is unavailable, the tension continues and may even increase because of the frustration that occurs. The relation between need and habit becomes fixed, so that the need becomes linked to a certain means of satisfying it.

When cake mixes were first introduced on the market the reception was excellent. Contrary to some expectations, homemakers took to the ready-mixed cakes quite avidly. After a peak in sales, however, there was a rather steep decline. The quality of the cakes had not changed; therefore, the reason for the drop had to be either bad promotion or a change of attitude among the users. It turned out to be both. The difficulty seemed to be related to adding ingredients. In spite of the clearly written instructions not to add eggs and milk, many of the homemakers did just that; obviously a recipe that contains a double portion of eggs and milk will turn out not a fluffy sponge cake but something more like an overdeveloped pancake. Now why did homemakers, who are accustomed to following recipes, deliberately disregard or misperceive the instructions? Apparently some basic need was at work.

It turned out to be related to the nurturance need, which is expressed as caring, feeding, protecting, mothering, nursing, and in general, serving and assisting others. Being a wife and mother in western cultures is associated with cooking, and especially baking. The old song "Can She Bake a Cherry Pie, Billy Boy?" exemplifies this idea. But cake mixes required practically no effort at all and as the ads said, "Even your three year old could bake a perfect cake." The whole campaign seemed designed to take the "mother" out of the baking, and that apparently blocked the fulfillment of a basic need. In response, manufacturers of cake mixes changed their tactics: the mixes were made so the user could include eggs and milk, and the ads were changed to point up the extra free time that Mom could spend doing things with her children.

Here is an example of a frustrated need that led to a change of behavior—from using to not using cake mixes. Through knowledge of the problem, conditions were altered to influence behavior in the direction of again purchasing the mixes. This may be considered an instance of controlling behavior.

PREDICTING FUTURE BEHAVIOR FROM NEEDS

Murray cautions that prediction is a hazardous business, especially in matters of human behavior. The primary difficulty is the lack of all relevant information. The individual is so complex that knowledge of what is going on at any given moment is usually woefully inadequate. There are long-term and short-term needs; modes of expressing the needs are variable; goal objects of a particular need are varied; and usually many components are active and interactive at the same time. Then there is always the potential for change, which is difficult to estimate. The needs of one period of life drop out, or are changed, and new needs take their place. There is always the external environment, which can be neither fully predicted nor controlled. For example, one cannot predict the time of the loss of a loved one, and certainly such an event alters conditions radically enough to change some basic needs. All these factors make prediction of behavior a matter of probability and not certainty.

However there are factors that favor consistency, predictability, and stability. Needs, for example, do not change easily. A person with a strong need for achievement in athletics does not change objectives very readily or capriciously. If he does not succeed in one sport, he tries another. Even if he is disabled by an injury, his need for success in sports does not change: he may become a sports writer, or a sports commentator. The means of satisfying a need vary much more than the need itself. The goals of the need are also quite resistant to change, although they may vary.

Murray recommends that one should concentrate on *effects* (goals) of needs, that is, on what is actually accomplished as a result of the need. The means for bringing the effects about may vary greatly, and concentration on them may be misleading. An exhibitionistic person may find gratification by running for office in his school; later, in the business world, he accomplishes the same effect by being the "practical jokester." In both instances he is looking for attention; he is trying to produce the same effect. The need for exhibition is a basic component of his personality and continues to be active although his circumstances have changed. Knowing that he has this need, one may predict that it will be expressed in some manner.

Allport (1961) has something to contribute regarding the stability, or constancy, of personality. What he calls the raw materials or foundations of personality — physique, intelligence, and temperament — once stabilized, remain constant for the major part of life. Adequate knowledge of these factors is indispensable in making predictions.

Another important factor in favor of prediction is that humans are persistent in the face of obstacles and distractions. A certain goal is sought and the activity and the environment are structured to attain it. The weather changes and as a result of the need to avoid extremes of temperature, one turns on the furnace or the air conditioner. If the furnace does not function properly, then something is done about that. All these factors make for stability, order, and predictability.

CONTROLLING BEHAVIOR THROUGH NEEDS

The aim of science is not just knowledge or prediction but also the power to control events, to make things happen according to design. One may know about the change in seasons and be able to identify conditions that permit accurate prediction, but without the next logical step of controlling the conditions for the betterment of one's life, the knowledge is not functional. Through knowledge of needs and the conditions affecting them, the cake mix manufacturers were able to remedy a problem situation concerning their product and control the behavior of the consumer. On an individual level, everyone attempts to control the behavior of others by knowing and influencing their motives. A girl wears a certain type of perfume because her fiancé comments that he likes it. She hopes to enhance his need for her, and uses this means as one among many to accomplish this effect. If one possesses the power of satisfying another's needs, he can take control of the other's behavior, at least in a specific area.

The ability to satisfy needs is sometimes called reinforcement power. One can use his reinforcement power to bring about certain behaviors (Skinner, 1953). A teacher can use grades to influence the work habits of her students. A parent can use many reinforcements, including the child's need for love, to influence his behavior. If one can discover the needs of another, and can do things to satisfy them, he can control his behavior.

ACTIVE MOTIVES VERSUS MOTIVATIONAL DISPOSITIONS

An important distinction in understanding the role of motivation in behavior is the difference between an active motive and a motivational disposition. Behavior is the outcome of active motives, but not all of a person's motives are active all of the time. In fact, most of his motivational elements are merely dispositions, which may be set off by specific stimuli or activated by internal factors.

If a professor observes a student during a lecture day after day, he learns little regarding the student's major needs because the conditions are quite specific and only a few needs are active. The student wishes to pass the course; he pays attention in class, takes notes, and resists distractions. A powerful need may be inactive in the classroom situation because he has no possibility of satisfying it, or because the instigating stimulus does not occur. He may, for instance, be a poor sport in his competitive dealings with others, but this fact will not emerge in the classroom setting.

The motivational disposition can be observed only when it becomes active. This statement is rather obvious, but it has many important ramifications. In getting to know someone, we must rely upon observable behavior to make inferences about his need structure. However, comparatively few of his needs are active at any one time. Dispositions cannot be observed directly. Until the significant situations occur, many motivational dispositions will remain just that—a factor that impedes our knowledge of others.

Everyone in his own way has experienced repeatedly the ebb and flow, the arousal and satisfaction, the coming and going of drives, motives, and needs. Everyone has also recognized to a greater or lesser degree the differences in priority and generality of motivational states. When one is in serious pain, nothing else seems to matter except getting rid of the pain. The very essence of a person, his individual nature, what he really is, can be discerned through knowledge of his basic motives and desires. One's view of man's na-ture—whether one considers man basically evil or good or neutral, whether natural tendencies or cultural restrictions are seen as most productive of growth and healthy functioning, and many other basic issues—ultimately depends upon what he believes regarding the basic driving forces behind be-havior.

CHAPTER 7

Human Needs

Henry Murray

Henry Murray (1893——)

BIOGRAPHY AND OVERVIEW

Henry Murray (1938) coined the term "personology," which means *the scientific study of the total person.* He has introduced a large number of concepts to represent the factors which must be understood in describing, explaining, and predicting personality phenomena. His concepts encompass the personality, the environment, and the history of the organism. He takes a holistic view of man but at the same time strives for detailed understanding through a meticulous analytic approach. Murray views each person as highly complex and unique, and takes into account the totality of determinants. He has a bewildering list of factors from which one can draw to represent a single personality. He is known as a taxonomist — one who classifies and describes phenomena in a given field.

Murray has a varied background which has served him well in his work as a personologist. He was born in New York City in 1893 and graduated from Harvard in 1915, with a degree in history. He went on to Columbia in the School of Physicians and Surgeons and received a medical degree in 1919, graduating at the head of his class. He took an M.A. in biology from Columbia in 1920, and did some teaching at Harvard. For two years he trained as a surgeon in New York. He then went to England and studied biochemistry at Cambridge, receiving a Ph.D. in that subject in 1927. Up to this point he had no formal training in psychology or psychiatry, but he reports that as a physician he was highly concerned and curious about the psychogenic causes of his patients' disturbances. He actually visited the haunts of some of his sordid patients and began to learn psychology in the rough from dope addicts, prostitutes, sword swallowers, and gangsters (Murray, 1940).

197

While in Europe in 1925, he visited with C. G. Jung, whom he credits with kindling his total involvement in psychology. Murray was trained as a psychoanalyst between 1927 and 1943, when he was head of the new psychological clinic at Harvard. He had not been formally trained in academic psychology. Many well-known students were trained at the clinic, and a great deal of productive work took place there. *Explorations in Personality,* written by Murray and his collaborators and published in 1938, gives an account of some of the work — an intensive study of a small group of subjects. During the Second World War, Murray joined the Army Medical Corps and distinguished himself by his work in psychological assessment. He was charged with the task of identifying personnel who could handle secret and dangerous missions. After the war he returned to Harvard and remained there until his retirement in 1962.

A flavor of Murray's formulations can be seen in the following quotation, which highlights his view of man.

I can hardly think myself back to the myopia that once so seriously restricted my view of human nature, so natural has it become for me to receive impressions of wishes, dramas, and assumptions that underlie the acts and talk of everyone I meet. Instead of seeing merely a groomed American in a business suit, travelling to and from his office like a rat in a maze, a predatory ambulating apparatus of reflexes, habit, stereotypes, and slogans, a bundle of consistencies, conformities, and allegiances to this or that institution — a robot in other words — I visualize (just as I visualize the activity of his internal organs) a flow of powerful subjective life, conscious and unconscious; a whispering gallery in which voices echo from the distant past; a gulf stream of fantasies with floating memories of past events, currents of contending complexes, plots and counterplots, hopeful intimations and ideals. To a neurologist such perspectives are absurd, archaic, tender-minded; but in truth they are much closer to the actualities of inner life than are his own neat diagrams of reflex arcs and nerve anastomoses. A personality is a full Congress of orators and pressure-groups, of children, demagogues, communists, isolationists, warmongers, mugwumps, grafters, log-rollers, lobbyists, Caesars and Christs, Machiavellis and Judases, Tories and Promethean revolutionists. And a psychologist who does not know this in himself, whose mind is locked against the flux of images and feelings, should be encouraged to make friends, by being psychoanalyzed, with the various members of his household (1940, pp. 160–1).*

Murray expresses his objections to traditional academic psychology in the following statements.

At first I was taken aback, having vaguely expected that most academic psychologists would be interested in Man functioning in his environment. But not at all: almost everyone was nailed down to some piece of apparatus, measuring a small segment of the nervous system as if it were isolated from the entrails. I was in the position, let us imagine, of a medical student who suddenly discovers that all his instructors are eye, ear, nose, and throat specialists. The phenomena that intrigued me were not mentioned, since these were not susceptible to exact experimental validation, a standard that rules out geology, paleontology, anthropology, embryology, most of medicine, sociology, and divine astronomy. If my chief aim had been to "work with the greatest scientific precision" I would never have quit electrolytes and gases. I had changed because of a consuming interest in other matters, in problems of motivation and emotion. To try to work these out on human subjects was to become a literary or applied psychologist, a practitioner of mental hygiene, outside and looking in upon the real psychologists who, I concluded, were obsessed by anxious aims to climb the social scale of scientists

and join the elect of this day's God at any cost. What else could account for their putting manners (appliances and statistics) so far ahead of ends (importance of the
problems studied)? No matter how trivial the conclusions, if his coefficients were reliable, an experimenter was deemed pure and sanctified (1940, p. 154).*

In the majority of our personological formulations there are no provisions for creativity, no admitted margins of freedom for voluntary decisions, no fitting recognitions
of the power of ideals, no bases for selfless action, no ground at all for any hope that
the human race can save itself from the fatality that now confronts us (1962, p. 53).

EVIDENCE FOR THE EXISTENCE OF NEEDS

The most tangible aspect of personality is behavior. Surely there can be more
agreement on what a person *is* doing (and on the products of behavior) than
on *how* or *why* he does it. Because behavior is observable and measurable, the
most widely accepted definition of psychology is the science which studies behavior. To some psychologists, particularly the behaviorists, the "observables"
are stimuli, responses, and, potentially, the history of the organism. What
goes on within the person can only be inferred, not observed directly. Why
use some unobservable thing to explain that which can be observed, they
might argue. Would it not be better to deal with the tangibles only, since only
with them can one hope to get agreement?

Other psychologists have found behavioral explanations in terms of observables inadequate to account for what takes place, and equally insufficient for
making predictions. Except for relatively simple reflexes, a knowledge of the
stimulus does not give one enough information to specify the response which
may follow. To say it another way, responses are seldom predictable from a
knowledge of the stimulus alone. A man may almost always answer his telephone when it rings, but on a certain day, because he does not want to talk
with a certain person, he does not answer. This bit of knowledge might fall
under the heading of the "history" of the organism; if the man's unwillingness
to talk to his friend is known, his unusual behavior in relation to his phone
may be understood. However, the notion of the history of the organism
covers so much as to be practically meaningless as a working principle in
dealing with behavior. Murray (1959) has sought to develop working concepts
for classifying and understanding behavior and its causes, both environmental and intrapsychic. He places a great deal of stress on the personality as
a real structure with active forces: needs, abilities, and achievements.

THREE PHASES OF A NEED

The activities of the organism are usually divisible into three classes. There is
usually (1) a beginning state (a disequilibrium of some sort), (2) an activity
directed to changing the situation, and (3) an end state. Activities that are
blocked may be replaced with different activities, but the same end state is
sought. This latter point suggests the operation of a force within the personal-

*© 1940 by the American Psychological Association. Reprinted by permission.

ity that continues to act until the end state is attained, no matter which mode of activity is used.

One of the best proofs for the existence of needs is the degree of readiness of the organism to respond to the same stimulus situation at different times. Consider hunger as an example. When one has just eaten, even the most appetizing food may have no appeal. Sometimes, however, a person who has just eaten may still be enticed by a dessert. Most often, although there is no food present, a hungry person begins seeking it. Thus three states of a need may be distinguished: (1) an *inactive phase* in which no stimulus will arouse the need, (2) a *readiness phase* in which only certain stimuli will arouse the need, and (3) an *active state* in which the need impels the person to seek gratification, even without the presence of an appropriate stimulus.

While it is true that a man may not be thirsty until he passes a drinking fountain, or may not be hungry until he smells the odor of cooking food, the external instigation of behavior is not the whole of the motivational picture. To show the inadequacy of external causation of behavior, consider the man who strongly desires feminine companionship and actively seeks out the means of meeting appropriate mates. The strong need dominates the psychological environment entirely, and other matters may become subsidiary.

It should be pointed out that success at something may create a need, a factor indicating mutual interaction of internal and external causes. A person who finds that he has much more of an effect on others than he expected, although he never had a strong need to dominate or influence others, may acquire this need through the easy success of his efforts. Sometimes this is referred to as "tasting blood"; one does not acquire some needs until there is an encounter with a satisfier associated with them (Murray, 1938).

THE MEANING OF PRESS

Murray (1938) uses the term "press" to stand for stimulus or situation. He believes that the difficulty with the word stimulus is that its meaning is circular: a stimulus is whatever induces a response, and a response results from the action of a stimulus. One should be able to specify stimuli and situations without this circularity, Murray believes. *A press does something to or for a person.* A pretty blonde may be a highly positive press for a certain young man. Being in her presence sets off several basic needs. Her presence exerts pressure upon him. The notion of press is that the environment may force the person into certain postures or predicaments.

Consider the first day of classes: the professor announces that there will be several unannounced quizzes, certainly an oppressive situation. Then he mentions the lengthy term paper. Here is another press which surely affects the average student. There is a source of tension that he did not anticipate. The situation "presses" him in a certain direction which he otherwise might not have taken. The press does something to him; it makes him respond.

To arrive at significant press for yourself, consider what objects and people do, or can do, to or for you. A friend is critical, flattering, suspecting, admiring, envious, condescending. A parent may be dominating, restricting, punitive, loving, generous, frustrating. A toothache is painful, annoying, troublesome. The same press, of course, are interpreted differently by each person.

The need to pass a course requires fulfillment of all the requirements; thus the need is activated by the press and gives rise to certain activities which quiet the need, reduce the tension. It should be noted that needs may instigate behavior directly, without any apparent press. But needs will confer significance upon certain press more than others.

Just as needs tell us about the determining tendencies within the individual, so press provide us with knowledge of the environment. Specifically, we may discover which aspects of the environment are perceived as threatening, dangerous, favorable, helpful, and the like. A knowledge of needs would be insufficient without a knowledge of the significant environmental factors.

ALPHA AND BETA PRESS

Murray (1938) distinguishes between alpha press and beta press. Alpha press is what the object actually is, whereas beta press is the perception or interpretation of it. Obviously, we would have to know the beta press if we desired to secure a picture of the manner in which the environment affects a particular individual. Discrepancies and distortions between alpha and beta press can produce serious behavioral disturbance. A storm may be perceived quite differently by two people. One may seriously misinterpret the potential dangers, while the other may underrate the hazards. The manner in which a person views or interprets his environment is secured through knowledge of his significant press. Behavior is far better understood and potentially predicted from a knowledge of both needs and significant press (Murray, 1938).

GENERAL PRINCIPLES CONCERNING NEEDS

NEED EXPRESSIONS, VALUES, VECTORS

To say that a person has a strong achievement need does not really tell us much about him, because the need points only to his general orientation. Unless we understand his specific goals, knowing that he has a need for achievement is of little value. The goals are the concrete ways in which the need is expressed or satisfied. The goal gives the need substance, a tangible form. A person usually would not describe himself as having a strong need for achievement; there would have to be some specific goal or goals. He might want to earn more money than any of his friends, or possess the best-looking home, or attain recognition through athletic accomplishment. In addition to

TABLE 7-1   MURRAY'S LIST OF PRESS

1. Family Insupport
  Cultural Discord
  Family Discord
  Capricious Discipline
  Parental Separation
  Absence of Parent
    Father
    Mother
  Parental Illness
    Father
    Mother
  Death of Parent
    Father
    Mother
  Inferior Parent
    Father
    Mother
  Dissimilar Parent
    Father
    Mother
  Poverty
  Unsettled Home
	4. Retention, Withholding Objects
	
	5. Rejection, Unconcern, and Scorn
	
	6. Rival, Competing Contemporary
	
	7. Birth of Sibling
	
	8. Aggression
	    Maltreatment by elder male, elder
	      female
	    Maltreatment by contemporaries
	    Quarrelsome contemporaries
	
	9. Aggression--Dominance
	    Punishment
	
	10. Dominance, Coercion, and Prohibition
	
	11. Dominance--Nurturance
	    Parental Ego Idealism
	      Mother
	      Father
	    Physical
	    Econ, Vocation
	    Caste
	    Intellectual
	    Possessive Parent
	      Mother
	      Father
	    Oversolicitous Parent
	    Fears
	      Accident
	      Illness
	      Bad Influences

2. Danger of Misfortune
  Physical Insupport, Height
  Water
  Aloneness, Darkness
  Inclement Weather, Lightning
  Fire
  Accident
  Animal	

3. Lack or Loss
  of Nourishment
  of Possessions
  of Companionship
  of Variety	

Modified from C. Hall and G. Lindzey, *Theories of Personality,* 2nd ed. John Wiley and Sons, 1970, p. 181. Adapted from *Explorations in Personality,* edited by Henry A. Murray. Copyright 1938 by Oxford University Press, Inc. Renewed 1966 by Henry A. Murray. Reprinted by permission of the publishers.

goals associated with a need, there are specific means for attaining goals. Not every means of achieving is acceptable.

In the early formulation of his theory, Murray (1938) stressed the role of needs as determinants of behavior, but later he emphasized the "end states" of needs, which he terms *values* (Murray, 1951). Many needs may produce the same end state; that is, a particular value such as property, wealth, or fame may satisfy a number of needs. In like manner, Murray (1951) also classifies the diverse means of attaining values under a number of general headings, which he terms *vectors.* A behavior vector may comprise many acts, all of which have some specific direction or movement in common. Examples are locomotion, construction, acquisition, manipulation, and other similar general classes of activities.

Means, like goals, are highly specific. One may want wealth desperately, but he cannot steal to get it. One may seek recognition, but he will not step on another to attain it. Of course, some individuals allow themselves a wider range of means in accomplishing their goals. But even a criminal has certain means that are unacceptable to him: his code of ethics may preclude stealing from a friend.

Murray takes the position that man's personality is dynamic. A structure, although described as psychic, exists, grows, changes, and functions. It is *reactive* to circumstances in the environment, but it is also *proactive* through spontaneous inner activity (Murray, 1954). A ringing telephone may cause a person to do something to stop the annoying sound, but the same individual may produce sound on a piano as a result of an inner urge. Of specific relevance to the operation of personality are the goal-directed efforts that arise within the personality. The main driving forces are internal.

The happenings in a person's life are brought about by the individual. He makes things happen, and even the things that happen to him are interpreted within a framework of his needs. One man sees a plot of land as an unproductive empty field. Another becomes excited at the prospect of buying this piece of land and building a home for his family. The same situation has strikingly different significance to the two men, and the cause of the difference is within the personality of each: one does not need a home because he is not married, while the other has a strong need for it. Alter the need structure of a person and you alter his whole personality and its relation to his environment. Murray describes the role of needs in the following passage.

A need is a construct (a convenient fiction or hypothetical concept) which stands for a force . . . in the brain region, a force which organizes perception, apperception, intellection, conation, and action in such a way as to transform in a certain direction an existing, unsatisfying situation. A need is sometimes provoked directly by internal processes of a certain kind . . . but, more frequently (when in a state of readiness) by the occurrence of one of a few commonly effective press (environmental). . . . Thus, it manifests itself by leading the organism to search for or to avoid encountering or, when encountered, to attend and respond to certain kinds of press. . . . Each need is characteristically accompanied by a particular feeling or emotion and tends to use certain modes . . . to further its trend. It may be weak or intense, momentary or enduring. But usually it persists and gives rise to a certain course of overt behavior (or fantasy), which . . . changes the initiating circumstance in such a way as to bring about an end situation which stills (appeases or satisfies) the organism (1938, pp. 123–4).

OTHER PRINCIPLES

Before considering in detail the subjective and behavioral manifestations of the psychogenic needs proposed by Murray, we will discuss several additional principles relating to the dynamics of needs. These ideas will enable the reader to appreciate the scope of Murray's need matrix in describing, explaining, and predicting behavior. They are not ordered in any logical form or priority system.

1.   Behavior is not the sum of habits, but rather, habits are used to serve needs. They are the means by which needs are satisfied.

2.   Lack of flexibility in behavior — following rigid patterns, as in some elderly persons, and functioning predominantly on a concrete level, as in cases of severe brain damage — is an indication of abnormality.

3.   A need is a force that causes activity. It may be experienced as a tension, but the basis of the tension may not be known, and the appropriate goal also may not be known, as when a person feels depressed but does not know why. In most cases, however, both the need and the goal are in awareness: the person knows why he is disturbed and what he wants (Murray, 1938).

4.   The two major classes of needs are the *viscerogenic*, which relate to bodily functioning, and the *psychogenic*, which are qualities of the personality. The two classes are interdependent. Culture has the greatest influence on the psychogenic needs (Murray, 1954).

5.   Viscerogenic needs have a definite zone of the body that serves as the source of tension; the psychogenic needs are experienced without any particular localization: there is no bodily organ involved in feeling lonely. A "heartache" really takes place in the brain.

6.   Viscerogenic needs are rhythmical and cyclical: the needs come and go periodically as a result of the requirements of the living organism. Psychogenic needs are more dependent upon press or circumstances and do not occur in a set cycle. They also come and go, but the rhythm is not regular.

7.   The ease with which needs are satisfied is inversely proportional to their importance in personality. As Murray (1954) points out, air is the most urgent need of all, and yet as a need it plays an insignificant part in personality development and functioning. On the other hand, the need for sexual outlet, although not absolutely required for existence, is highly significant in personality growth and development.

8.   Needs may fuse and operate as virtually one motivational unit. Behavior is usually the outcome of a fusion of needs (Murray, 1938). One's work is satisfying because it involves being autonomous, achieving, affiliating with others, feeling dominant, and possibly many other needs. A man may fall in love with a woman because she satisfies a variety of needs. In her relationship with him she may assume such roles as a concerned mother, a working associate, a little sister needing care, even a rival to compete with. The more needs involved, the greater are the ties formed. The more compatible the needs of two people (and in general, similarities make for compatibility more than do differences, unless the needs of each are too extreme), the greater is the attachment.

9.   A need may be subsidiary to another need, as when an individual desires to befriend someone who has influence in the community (Murray, 1938). He needs the friendship, and may strive arduously to secure it. In this example, the need for friendship is subsidiary to the need to be superior or the need for recognition.

10. The satisfaction of a need is accompanied by positive affect: feeling or emotion. Dissatisfaction accompanies absence of need gratification. Murray (1954) distinguishes three types of satisfactions: (a) *activity pleasure,* associated with process needs, (b) *achievement pleasure,* associated with modal needs, and (c) *affect pleasure,* associated with effect needs. Activity, such as vigorous exercise or a brisk walk, in itself gives pleasure. Doing something competently gives pleasure. Certainly the attainment of a goal is pleasurable, particularly when it is highly valued. Affect pleasure derives from the relief of the tension of the need: all need states are held to be accompanied by tension. Removal of the tension is experienced as a pleasurable process.

EXAMPLES FROM MURRAY'S LIST OF NEEDS

Everyone is familiar with the viscerogenic needs. Although they are absolutely essential to the maintenance of life, they usually have little to do with the development and functioning of personality unless there is severe deprivation or excess; then the consequences are disastrous or even fatal.

A number of Murray's psychogenic needs will be discussed in order to demonstrate the power of this approach. The psychogenic needs, summarized in Table 7–3, are not usually a factor in survival but are essential for personality growth and functioning. The various behavioral manifestations or expressions of these needs will be given with actual examples of real situations. The material for this section is drawn largely from "Variables in Personality," Chapter 3 of Murray's *Explorations in Personality* (1938).

*n DOMINANCE**

The need to dominate others is manifested in a wide variety of forms. Subjectively, it may be experienced as a desire to control others, to lead, to persuade,

---

*The terms "n Dominance," "n Deference," and so forth are Murray's way of referring to the various needs. "n Deference," for example, may be read as "need for deference," "need to defer," and so on for all the needs listed here.

TABLE 7-2 MURRAY'S VISCEROGENIC NEEDS

Positive Needs (Initiated by Deficiency)	Negative Needs (Initiated by Tension Due to Secretion)	Negative Needs (Initiated by Tension Due to Excretory Pressures)	Negative Needs (Due to Harm)
n inspiration (oxygen)	n sex	n expiration (air)	n noxavoidance
n water	n lactation	n urination	(contamination,
n food		n defecation	noxious sub-
n sentience (sensation)			stances)
			n heat avoidance
			n cold avoidance
			n harmavoidance

TABLE 7–3 SUMMARY OF MURRAY'S PSYCHOGENIC (SECONDARY) NEEDS

Need	Definition
Abasement	To submit passively to external force.
Achievement	To accomplish something difficult.
Affiliation	To draw near and enjoyably co-operate or reciprocate with an allied other.
Aggression	To overcome opposition forcefully.
Autonomy	To get free, shake off restraint, break out of confinement.
Counteraction	To master or make up for a failure by restriving.
Defendance	To defend the self against assault, criticism, and blame.
Deference	To admire and support a superior.
Dominance	To control one's human environment.
Exhibition	To make an impression.
Harmavoidance	To avoid pain, physical injury, illness and death.
Infavoidance	To avoid humiliation.
Nurturance	To give sympathy and gratify the needs of a helpless object.
Order	To put things in order.
Play	To act for "fun" without further purpose.
Rejection	To separate oneself from a negatively cathected object.
Sentience	To seek and enjoy sensuous impressions.
Sex	To form and further an erotic relationship.
Succorance	To have one's needs gratified by the sympathetic aid of an allied object.
Understanding	To ask or answer general questions.

Modified from C. Hall and G. Lindzey, *Theories of Personality,* 2nd ed. John Wiley and Sons, 1970, pp. 176–77. Adapted from *Explorations in Personality,* edited by Henry A. Murray. Copyright 1938 by Oxford University Press, Inc. Renewed 1966 by Henry A. Murray. Reprinted by permission of the publishers.

to take charge of situations, to set a pattern or standard that others should follow. Usually the leader deliberately strives to dominate. He takes on responsibilities in order to be observed by those who can help him attain a position of authority. The common notion that leadership ability expresses itself naturally, and that the leader will emerge because of his superior endowment, is false (Carter and Nixon, 1949). The person who attains leadership has a strong need to be in a dominative role and organizes all his abilities to reach that goal.

Those who are dominant often manifest their dominance in their behavior, and freely report an unusual sense of self-confidence. They feel capable in relation to others. They do not shrink from those in authority or from those who hold highly respected positions. They indicate that they feel adequate to deal with most situations that confront them. Seldom do they experience feelings of inferiority, particularly in relation to other people. A not-so-obvious expression of the need to dominate, however, is the person who wishes to impose his desires or convictions on others. Such a person may lack the quality of reciprocity. Failure to see the world from the standpoint of others often results in overevaluation of himself.

n DEFERENCE

The need for deference is manifested in interpersonal relationships, such as ready compliance with the request of another out of high admiration. In general, it refers to willing acceptance of a subordinate position in relation to others (Lang and Lazovik, 1962). An individual who has a strong need for deference wants to work for, or be associated with, one whom he can admire and respect. A man is fortunate if he has a secretary who has an active need for deference, because her work in serving him fulfills a need. She derives great pleasure from his accomplishments and successes, and gains satisfaction from her work in promoting him.

The concept of the role model illustrates the operation of the deference need. The role model is an exemplar, one who is considered an ideal human, at least with respect to some attributes. Children often display a deferent attitude toward older children or adults. They are acutely aware of their insufficiencies and lack of perfection in comparison with older people. A child who is struggling with some problem is struck with a sense of awe by the older child or adult who solves the same problem with apparent ease. He may form a completely false image of the one who seems to do what he cannot do. Simply being near this great person satisfies something in him.

It may be instructive to contrast a deferent attitude with one of envy. The envious person dislikes and intensely resents the superiority of another. He may equate the achievements or advantages of the other with a lack in himself. The younger sister of an eight year old boy was home from school for a whole week. Throughout this period the boy complained bitterly that his sister was not really sick and that she was lying in order to stay out of school. He also complained that he was ill, and that no one was paying any attention to him. The last day of the week the girl was better, and the parents were deciding, in the presence of the children, whether she should go to school or stay home. The decision was that she would stay home one more day, at which point the boy shouted out, "Cheated again!" He believed that the supposed benefits that his sister was getting by staying home from school actually constituted a deprivation for him. This apparently strange interpretation also typifies the feelings of many adults. They perceive the superiorities or advantages of others as their own personal inferiorities and deficiencies. The other person is resented because he has more than the one who feels the envy. The basis of envy is probably a desire for superiority, as Alfred Adler would point out.

The deferent person, by contrast, actually derives satisfaction from the superiorities of others. He eagerly offers respect, admiration, and praise. He may undertake a campaign to elect his idol to office, or to promote him for an award. He takes great pride if the person receives the honor, especially if he was instrumental in bringing this about. While an envious person derives great pleasure from the defeat or injury of his superior rival, the deferent person delights in and actually desires the superiority of another. His need is fulfilled only in others' superiority.

Probably the purest form of the need for deference is devout religious surrender. The religious person offers prayers of supplication, praise, and adoration to a divine being. He believes that he is given special graces by being spiritually close to a personal God. He subordinates himself and becomes a part of the divine through his acts of deference. To love, serve, and obey are ideals that are espoused by the devout of almost all religions.

n AUTONOMY

The need for autonomy is manifested and experienced in the following ways: by resisting authority (anyone who has authority over the person is automatically seen as a threat); by resistance to being coerced (one cannot go along with something that others have suggested); by being independent; by being irresponsible or free of rules and regulations; by fighting against restrictions and constraints; by defying convention and ruling oneself in order to remain unattached and unobligated to others. One might describe a person with a strong need for autonomy as negativistic, independent, irresponsible, nonconformist, radical, willful, or stubborn.

Everyone at times experiences a sense of confinement and an overburden of regulations and restrictions. In conjunction with such feelings are the motives to be free and independent to do whatever one pleases. In a sense, a vacation is a means of accomplishing these things. One arranges for certain activities that are more in keeping with what he likes to do than with what he has to do (which is the normal state of things). The vacation activities satisfy many needs, among which the need for autonomy is of paramount importance to the individual.

There are countless tales and songs about the tall dark stranger who stole a pretty maiden's heart only to wander away because he had a "wanderlust." The sailor with a girl at every port is another example of the same theme. Many young people are so enchanted by the freedom that comes after school is finished that they do not want to marry and be "tied down" (Lantagne, 1958). This is usually a temporary state, however, since other needs combine to make marriage a very attractive thing.

The strength of the autonomy need may be appreciated through the many ways in which people seek to gratify it. The popularity of the hippy movement attests to the existence of this need (Adler, 1972). Some young people are lured by the total freedom and rejection of cultural forces that are espoused by such movements. They throw over the mores of their class and choose freedom and independence as their primary values. Money, status, fame — the goals traditionally sought by the young — are considered the deadening values of the "establishment" and are replaced by the goal of the greatest autonomy possible.

One could argue that the need for autonomy is a natural reaction against the cramping demands of society: the long confinement in school, the confusion over a career and acceptable life style, the conflicting demands of opposing values, and many other societal "ills." The young person does not like what he sees and what he is forced to do, and rebels against the system. The rebellion may range from a felt need (which is not acted upon) to escape the responsibilities that are placed upon him to an open attack on the institutions of the society.

The need for autonomy sometimes fuses with the need for achievement, with great resultant benefits for mankind. Scientists and men of genius who risk censure and rejection to pursue an idea which goes against the current are examples of the happy combination of the autonomy and achievement needs. Freud, who was rejected by the medical profession, continued to develop his radical ideas about the unconscious at the cost of professional security. In the end he became more famous than those who derided him, and many believe he made significant contributions to the study of psychology. The history of science and philosophy is replete with stories of men who gave up comfort, security, and even prestige to satisfy their need for autonomy.

In the lives of ordinary people, the need for autonomy takes over behavior. Everyone must face the independence-dependence conflict. As one grows up, more and more is expected of him. Choices, judgment, decisions are constantly confronting the individual. In the final analysis, he cannot turn to others for solutions. Others may give advice, but usually the final decision is left to the one faced with the task. In such instances the person is caught in a conflict between the need for autonomy and the fear of the consequences that autonomy may produce. Many shrink away from this situation, or develop symptoms of personality disorder. Even the strongest among us are often disturbed by the conflict. But in the end, the harsh call of necessity and the great urge for freedom and independence win out for most people, and they enjoy the benefits of autonomous living by taking control over and responsibility for their lives.

n AGGRESSION

The need for aggression is manifested objectively in behavior, and subjectively in the need to resist force, to fight and take revenge, to win over another forcibly, to attack and injure animals or humans, to oppose and deny the rights of a rival. The emotional aspects of the need for aggression include anger, irritation, annoyance, hatred, and yearning for revenge. A person with a strong need for aggression may be described as hateful, malicious, irritable, negativistic, ruthless, cruel, destructive, vindictive, critical, accusatory, abusive, domineering, harsh, and despotic.

One of the most perplexing aspects of human behavior is the amount of aggressiveness that exists. Man's inhumanity to man has for centuries puzzled the greatest minds. War and violence have played a conspicuous part in the history of man. At any one time there are a dozen or more trouble spots in the world with actual shooting wars that take a high toll of lives and leave many more to suffer permanent disabilities. No one can possibly estimate the extent of violence, murder, personal injury, and crime involving the injury of fellow men. In all the major cities of the United States the streets have become battle-grounds. One risks his life traveling alone after dark in many sections of the cities.

The daily newspapers are filled with tales of woe. A man is robbed and beaten mercilessly so that he is disabled for life. If one inquires into the motivation behind such behavior, he often finds an element that goes beyond the desire to steal. If the victim does not resist, as most do not, there is no justification for violence. The violence, the unprovoked attack, must serve a strong motive. The assailant demonstrates by his behavior that he has a need to see another human hurt. Often the need to injure actually seems to predominate, as when an individual is attacked by a gang and brutalized while his possessions remain untouched. The helpless victim wonders why this happened to him, and many great men have pondered the same question.

Freud (1926) became more and more convinced that the need for aggression is present in everyone to a greater or lesser degree. So pervasive is it that if it is not turned outward on other people or things, then it is turned inward upon the self, with many unpleasant consequences. Most people find acceptable outlets for their aggressive needs through their work, or in forms of recreation. The point is that the need to hurt is strong in some people and must be satisfied, just as must the needs to achieve, to affiliate, to express one's abilities, and so on. The acceptance of aggression as a need brings with it serious consequences, particularly if one assumes that everyone has this need. The control of aggression and the expression of it are among man's greatest problems.

There is a special fascination in sports that involve violence of the partici-pants: boxing, wrestling, hunting, and hockey. Even though there has been a persistent outcry against violent sports such as boxing, occasionally there is an outburst of interest among the public. Boxing has lost favor for a variety of reasons, but the vast interest that can arise spontaneously in a heavyweight title fight is difficult to account for. One might understand interest that was built up through many matches, but when interest is sparked by a single bout, there is the suspicion that some basic need for aggression is being satisfied in the spectators. It is estimated that 300 million people paid large sums to see the Frazier-Ali championship fight on closed-circuit television. There are few other events that have attracted such interest, and particularly interest requir-ing a high payment. It seems to be a matter of aggression waiting to be unleashed. If the fighters were engaged in a spelling bee, surely the audience would have been diminished considerably, because spelling bees ordinarily do not involve injuries to the contestants. The need for aggression, even if it is so diluted as to be satisfied merely through being a spectator of aggressive acts, must surely be a powerful need, and its prevalence is widespread.

Not everyone exhibits this need to the same degree, however. Anthropologists (e.g., Gorer, 1966) point out that certain cultures are characterized by a great deal of aggression among their members whereas others foster more benign traits. Women in general are less openly aggressive than men (Oetzel, 1966), but this may be due to cultural influences.

n NURTURANCE

A nurturant person is one who enjoys and strongly desires to do things involving the care of others. Some of the forms of expressing the need for nurturance are giving assistance to one who is helpless, guiding and assisting the weak, the hurt, the young, the lonely, the infirm. Other forms of expression include protecting, nursing, caring for, feeding, sympathizing with, and feeling pity, compassion, and tenderness.

What might go under the heading of nurturance is highly varied. A mother may have a nurturant attitude toward her baby. Although she receives little in return for her many sacrifices, she may devote most of her time and energy to caring for her child, especially if the child has an illness. If her nurturant need is strong, she does not regret or begrudge her sacrifice, even if it costs her many sleepless nights. On the contrary, she is at her best in this role. Being "motherly," at least in relation to her baby, satisfies a deep longing in her (Sears, Maccoby, and Levin, 1957). Strangely, she may feel and behave in a maternalistic way toward her baby but not feel the same impulse with respect to her older children (Fromm, 1947), a factor that may cause her to neglect them for the sake of the baby. Many persons have indicated a strong resentment of a younger brother or sister that dates back to the birth of the newcomer. All the mother's attention was directed to the baby, and the older child lost his position of dominance. Adler made a major point of this notion in his concept of family position and its effect on development.

This example suggests that the nurturance need can be quite specific. Some women may feel protective and motherly toward teen-agers, but not toward infants. Other women actually feel a maternal impulse for a grown man and may behave toward him as if he were a young child. There are men, of course, who seem to need this type of relationship; they may be described as having a need for succorance—a need to be taken care of, to be comforted and soothed, and to depend on someone. The marriage of a woman who has the need to nurture and a man who needs to receive succorance may be a good match. Each is satisfying the other's basic need: one complements the other; she wants what he provides and vice versa. Problems may arise when one of the partners expects or demands what the other is not motivated to give. A wife may want to lean on her husband for support and assistance in solving her personal problems, but he may not be willing or able to help her. In such instances a great deal of friction may be created.

To illustrate the varied expressions of the need for nurturance, one might consider some not-so-obvious outlets. For example, a woman may express her need to nurture by "mothering" stuffed animals. She may respond to them in a manner appropriate to a child. While such behavior is normal for girls and young women, it would represent at least a quirk of personality if not replaced by a more fulfilling outlet.

Consider the individual who loves to grow and care for plants: there is nothing so helpless and so totally at the mercy of external forces for survival as a plant. Plants can do nothing to secure their sustenance and alter their circumstances. From the standpoint of the nurturance need, no other thing can be as compliant and dependent. Even a child can resist his mother's efforts to mother him. As a matter of fact, as children grow (and this also applies to animals), they become more and more independent of the caring person. But plants cannot even secure water for themselves.

Pets are often objects of the nurturance need. To feel sympathetic and protective toward infant creatures is universal among humans, and absence of this feeling is considered by some psychologists to be indicative of faulty development (Maslow, 1968). However, the fascination of pets for humans is certainly a mystery. Perhaps a pet satisfies a number of needs: to dominate, to nurture, to feel superiority over something. Consider the relation of a dog to the one who cares for it. The dog gives itself completely to its master, irrespective of his status, appearance, and even style of life. Many a rejected soul has found some sense of identity and worth through a pet dog. An unfortunate young woman who suffered from facial deformities, poor vision, and an unattractive frail appearance, loved by no one, secured a guide dog to assist her in her work as a music teacher. Her personality underwent a remarkable change. Her dog was her constant companion. His response to her, and the care which she gave him, provided her with a whole new orientation to life. She behaved like a person who had met an exciting new friend. Everything about her improved—her work, her relationships with others, even her health. While many needs were undoubtedly satisfied, there is no question that her need for nurturance was greatly affected by her caring for the dog, which served her as a guide and companion.

n ACHIEVEMENT

The need to achieve may fuse with virtually all other needs. One individual may strive to achieve in order to gain power over others; another may seek success to prove that he is not inferior; still another may be driven to achieve because he feels insecure; and there are many, many other such fusions. According to Murray (1938), the basic elements in achievement are to do something well and to do it quickly.

Some specific ways to express the achievement need are: to master difficult situations; to control, manipulate, and organize physical objects; to overcome obstacles; to attain high standards; to rival and surpass competitors; to exercise one's talents and faculties; and, in general, to do things well (French, 1955). People in whom the achievement need is strong are described as ambitious, climbers, good scrappers.

The need for achievement has many people in its grip. So strong is it in some that the "what" of the achievement is not as important as the fact that some type of achievement has been attained. In such instances there is probably a fusion between achievement and dominance. Most often, however, the need for achievement is directed toward specific goals. Most persons do not want to achieve in all areas of their lives, but usually have specific directions that are significant to them. For one man the need to achieve takes the form of earning a large income; for another it is to hold an admired place; for another it is overcoming obstacles that others could not conquer. The reader may observe from these examples that achievement is almost always subsidiary to other goals but there are examples of achievement for its own sake, as we shall see.

Achievement is usually associated with culturally desirable goals such as financial security, status, power, and so on. The one who achieves has advantages over others. A variety of basic needs may thus be served by the achievement need.

Probably the purest forms of the achievement need are found in the inventor, the explorer, and the researcher, who strive to solve practical problems or to unlock nature's mysteries. Often such persons actually forego the use of their talents in certain directions that might guarantee them easy success in order to follow their interests, at the risk of total failure in the end. Many undoubtedly do fail in their pursuit of achievement in their own chosen way. Thus while the need for achievement is frequently socially oriented, it is not always so. The ego ideal, which may be considered in this context to be the image of the perfected self, is sometimes the basis of the need for achievement. *To be the perfected self involves the attainment of particular goals and the renunciation of other goals.* In the individual in whom the ego ideal is dominant, the achievement motive takes its purest form: the saintly man who gives up his own comforts in order to attain his cherished goals. Tradition holds that the greatest men are usually those who give up personal gains for the sake of ideals. If there is merit in this observation, we have an example of achievement for its own sake. The statement "no one can demand from me as much as I demand from myself" exemplifies the essential operation of the achievement need.

n ABASEMENT

The individual who has a need for abasement may passively accept criticism, blame, or punishment; he submits without a struggle to the demands of others; he gives up easily and surrenders and resigns himself to fate; he may readily admit his mistakes and failings and take defeat as a matter of course; he may seek out those to whom he can confess his sins; he wallows in self-criticism; he seeks and even enjoys pain, punishment, and hurt from others. The element of *self-depreciation* is always present in the person who has a need for abasement; the deferent person, in contrast, submits because he gains strength and importance through the superiority of another. Some of the emotions that go along with the need for abasement are guilt, shame, depression, helplessness, and despair. A self-abasing person is described as meek, humble, servile, submissive, spineless.

A college coed who thought herself extremely unattractive and unacceptable to men because she was somewhat overweight took an abasing attitude in her relations with others. When she spoke, she could hardly be heard because she spoke softly and swallowed her words. If someone wronged her, she would not stand up for herself. She met a male student who showed some interest in her, but her sense of inferiority led her to introduce him to her best girl friend. When she was asked about this rather strange behavior, she said that she really did not have much of a chance with him, and her friend was so much more worthy of him.

The element of self-effacement, or self-hate, is always a part of the picture in one who has a need for abasement, although its intensity may vary greatly. The following example illustrates the strength of self-aggression, and one might argue the presence of a masochistic trend. A young Air Force officer at a service club began to become disorderly and abusive after gulping down several drinks hurriedly. He walked up to the biggest man in the place and began to taunt him. The man did not want to fight and ignored him, but the officer continued his harassment. Finally the officer pushed the larger man, who then began to fight with him and caused severe injury. The officer had deliberately picked the fight; he did not even know the other man. He had a history of being destructive—committing needless violence as a means of venting his hostile feelings. He would also periodically impose many punitive restrictions upon himself, such as fasting or giving up drinking. On the evening of the fight, he was on a date with his girl friend at her apartment. They had engaged in some love play when he hinted that he wanted intercourse. She pushed him away, and he reacted by slapping her. Then he left angrily and went to the service club where he picked the fight. One obvious interpretation is that he was looking for punishment for having done something that was abhorrent to him.

n SEX

The need for sex, like the other needs, has many forms of expression. All forms of expression, however, have a sensual quality. For example, the need for sex is active when one enjoys looking at, touching, listening to, and being near a person of the opposite sex. (Some find members of the same sex more attractive than those of the other sex.) The need for sex varies in intensity from a constant preoccupation to an occasional sense of tension. The forms of expression and arousal are much more varied than most people imagine. An extensive treatment of the sex need is not possible here, but it might be mentioned that, as Freud held, this need constitutes one of the major problem sources for people in Western cultures. The problem, of course, is one of gratification.

One may look at the need for sex as an example of the subordination of one need to another. A man may have a strong aggressive need; he delights in hurting others, in making them suffer. The sexual need may be brought into service as a means of expressing his aggressive tendencies. Obviously, this type of situation is highly abnormal. Again, the need to care for someone may be the dominant need in a relationship, and sexual activity may be a means of satisfying that need. A woman may be very nurturant in relation to her husband. The sexual need is active in their relationship, but the need to nurture may be more potent. This emphasis on nurturance may cause difficulties when the first child is born if she finds greater satisfaction in caring for her baby and begins to ignore her husband. Many men complain that their wives change in relation to them with the birth of the first child. In such instances, an apparently good marital relationship is based on a strong need to nurture more than on affiliative and sexual needs.

n SENTIENCE

The need for sentience may be described as deriving pleasure from sensory and motor experiences, and feeling tensions when such experiences are not possible. All of the sensory modalities are sources of such tensions and pleasures — visual, tactual, gustatory, olfactory, and so on.

Many forms of psychotherapy have the aim of increasing sensory awareness. Gestalt Therapy, for example, consists in part of techniques that are designed to sharpen the client's awareness of his inner experiences — to make ideas and feelings *gestalten*, that is, definitely configurated and clearly perceived. In other words, the client is encouraged to become aware as much as possible of his inner and outer life. All this is done to aid him to know himself, and also to live more richly and fully.

Some individuals, such as those who truly enjoy art, or music, or vivid poetry, have an unusual need for sensory stimulation. The person who enjoys a good physical workout probably also has a need for sentience. Certainly there is an invigorating feeling produced by exercise. There is a heightening of activity, with accompanying feelings and sensations, and then the recovery and relaxation phase, with other pleasant sensations and feelings. Not everyone is willing to go to the trouble of finding an adequate facility for exercising, and the whole thought of physical activity is repugnant to many. They do not have a need for this type of sentience.

The recent popularity of drugs and the increasing use of alcohol (see Blum et al., 1969) certainly point out the pervasiveness of the need for sentience. Of all the reasons why people drink or take drugs, the alteration of consciousness (expansion, contraction, and all the many other paranormal states) is certainly one of the most compelling. A common expression among drug users is "taking a bad trip," which of course denotes an unpleasant experience.

Those who love the rustic beauty of the out-of-doors, who love to walk in the woods and look at the objects of nature, surely have a strong need for sentience. All the senses are stimulated in such natural settings. Man's most animalistic nature finds outlets in the primitive natural environment. But not everyone has this need, it appears, because some folks want little to do with outdoor life. The lures of the urban night life are far more attractive.

n EXHIBITION

One who has a strong need for exhibition may manifest it in a great variety of behaviors. Some of the commonest are: to make an impression; to be seen and heard; to excite, amaze, fascinate, intrigue, entertain, and shock; to try to create a reaction in others. The person with this need wants to be observed by others. He experiences tension when he is not noticed or when he is ignored. Many people deliberately dress in a manner that draws attention. Many engage in behavior that attracts the curiosity of others. A politician displays his wares to his audiences: he wants to be seen and heard; he wants to exhibit his competence by making promises and displaying his verbal talents. He has a need for public and individual attention from others. A man may undertake to write an autobiography for a variety of reasons: because he thinks that others want to know about his life, or maybe because he thinks that he has lived an unusual life. There are numerous reasons, but certainly the need for exhibition cannot be ruled out as a strong contributing force in many instances.

A certain degree of exhibitionism may be found in everyone under specific circumstances. The absence of this need, as in the person who has a strong need for seclusiveness, is probably abnormal. Some people have talents that make possible the satisfaction of exhibition tendencies. Others, finding repeated failure in their attempts to satisfy this need, may deliberately inhibit attempts at satisfaction and instead express an opposite need, such as seclusiveness, or take a hostile attitude toward other people. In one sense, aggressiveness toward others satisfies exhibition tendencies through the effects produced. Again, it can be seen that the desire to make an impression on others is one of the most powerful needs of man (Jones, 1964), and it has many acceptable as well as unacceptable forms of expression.

n PLAY

The need for play may take the form of pleasure-seeking as an end in itself. It may be described as activity for its own sake—activity pleasure. Among children it occupies a large portion of the waking hours, and appears to be a means of testing sensory and motor functions (Piaget, 1962). The play behavior of children is probably a fusion of several needs: sentience, dominance, achievement, understanding, and play. The small child explores the objects in his world by playing with them. He pushes and pulls, puts things together, builds and disassembles structures, and even breaks things, all for the sake of pleasure. Many adults play a great deal: bowling, golf, baseball, and so on.

Often there is the element of winning or losing, of competition with oneself or opponents. But in much play activity, such as hiking, rowing, sunbathing, and swimming, there is the element neither of competition nor of achievement.

n AFFILIATION

In general, the affiliative need means to seek companions, to work closely with others in a team effort, to be liked by those who are liked, to relate in an intimate manner to certain people, to be attractive to some people. The need varies markedly with different individuals, from those who crave the friendship of everyone they meet to those who are self-sufficient and make no effort to form friendships (McKeachie et al., 1966). Friendships are based on a variety of factors: one may simply like anyone who likes him; another searches out people who are inferior or dependent; another tries to befriend only those who are quite similar to him; still others strive to befriend dominant people. The history of the affiliation need in each person is quite significant in personality development. At three, one's need for affiliation is quite different from his need at twenty. At all ages, one of the major benefits of friendships is a sense of not being or feeling alone with one's problems. One's age mates usually have the same problems to deal with, and one finds support and actual solutions through contacts.

n REJECTION

When one turns away from someone considered inferior, or separates himself from certain groups or classes, or considers himself especially elite and superior, with a "better-than-thou" attitude, the need for rejection is determining his behavior. Such persons are often quite discriminating about the people they can like or accept. The qualities of humanness are not enough for them. Certain standards are demanded, and those who do not meet them are excluded as inferior or undesirable. The thinking and conversations of such people are permeated with an atmosphere of downgrading. One who has a strong need to reject others is intolerant: he is not willing to respect the right of the other to hold and value a different point of view. His general opinion is that most people are not worth listening to or bothering with. Consider this sentiment: "Few men are raised in our estimates by being very closely examined."

n SUCCORANCE

In general, succorance means to have one's needs taken care of by someone else. Other behaviors which come under the heading of the need for succorance are: to be loved, advised, protected, nursed, guided, consoled, forgiven, supported, encouraged, and sympathized or empathized with. One may picture, as an extreme instance of the need for succorance, one who is helpless, pleading, suppliant, begging forgiveness, crying for help. The element of dependence is frequently associated with a succorant tendency. The individual cannot stand on his own feet; he feels inadequate to deal with a situation and turns to others for help. But dependence is not always characteristic of one who thrives on being helped or cared for. A highly capable, self-sufficient woman may relate to the man she loves in a succorant manner: she may subordinate her ambitions for the sake of his. She desires to make him "feel masculine." She expresses appreciation and gratitude for the protection and care he wants to give her. He may have a need to nurture, and she has a need to receive the nurturance—a need for succorance. Actually, in real-life situations the roles vary: sometimes she cares for him, as when he is ill. Both of these needs are important aspects of human relationships. Giving love in a generous manner and receiving it with proper appreciation bind people together.

n HARMAVOIDANCE, n BLAMAVOIDANCE, n INFAVOIDANCE, n DEFENDANCE, AND n COUNTERACTION

Several needs relate to the fear of injury from other people and things, and also to the disapproval of one's own conscience. Harmavoidance deals with avoidance of injuries of all types; infavoidance refers to avoidance of failure. Defendance is an active tendency to protect oneself against threats to status, and counteraction refers to a renewal of effort as the result of failure.

One who has a strong need for harmavoidance is sensitive to any physical and psychological threat to his integrity. He wishes to avoid pain, physical injury, and death. Strong precautionary measures are taken, such as a strict special diet, avoiding certain foods because they are "poisonous," maintaining a strict regime of exercise, visiting a doctor frequently, reading and worrying about fatal diseases. Such a person may be described as timid, frightened, worrisome, hypochondriacal, sensitive, cautious, wary, prudent. A person dominated by this attitude has many fears: he thinks often of death with great horror; he fears animals such as snakes, dogs, cats; he worries about becoming ill and losing his status; he fears taking any risks that could involve injury. Some people believe that they need a great deal of rest and sleep to avoid becoming exhausted. Phobias are common: fear of dying in a fire, fear of hell, fear of being alone at night, and so on.

A need for blamavoidance appears to be related to living with other people who have the power to judge one's conduct. It involves avoidance of disapproval, censure, and punishment from others. This need to avoid certain behaviors exerts strong inhibitions and controls over activities that are detrimental to group living. When the controlling force is within the person, in the form of superego, the avoidant behavior is motivated by guilt. Specific forms of this need include avoiding blame, rejection, or loss of affection, and controlling selfish strivings, replacing them with socially directed behavior. Such expressions as "what would people say if they really knew me" exemplify the operation of this need. Some people cannot tolerate the idea that anyone disapproves of them. They wish to make a favorable impression on everyone, irrespective of position or closeness. Some even go so far as to value the opinions of others more than their own.

Infavoidance involves avoiding humiliation, embarrassing situations, and belittlement from others; quitting situations that are threatening; rejecting something new from fear of failing; feeling inferior; lacking self-confidence; feeling unworthy. Such a person may be described as sensitive, shy, nervous, passive. One who has a strong need to avoid failure is sensitive to any kind of failure. Failing in unessential matters is reacted to in the same way as are more significant shortcomings. Because failure of any sort is dreaded, there is a constant inhibition of action. If one does not seek much, he cannot be deprived or hurt (Birney, Burdick, and Teevan, 1969).

One has a need for defendance when he displays by his behavior an attitude of self-protection against criticism, blame, or any attack. This need is also operating in concealment, in self-justification, and in attempts to cover over a failure or to support one's course of action. A defendant individual may easily misinterpret the actions of others, finding insult where none was intended. Such people are quick to make excuses, cover up areas of weakness, and maintain a status of reserve. Sometimes even lying is used as a means of concealment and covering up. The individual may be so ready to assume a defensive screen that he does not make any effort to change the things he is defensive about, with the consequence that the defensive strategy becomes a fixed part of the personality. The blamavoidant person wants the good opinion of others so strongly that he is willing to make changes in himself; the defendant person does not do much changing.

The person who has a strong need for counteraction finds renewed motivation in the status of failure. He says, in effect: "I have been knocked down, but I won't stay down." Such persons typically strive to overcome weaknesses, to seek out obstacles to overcome. Pride and self-respect are highly significant to them. Counteraction is often manifested in a strong negative reaction to receiving aid: the person would rather do without than be helped or dependent on another. Such terms as resolute, determined, dauntless, adventurous, and prideful describe one who is dominated by this need. As a striking example of its power, one may think of the suffering hero, beset on all sides by limitations and difficulties, but nevertheless, through sheer willpower and self-sacrifice, gaining the victory for himself. Being a quitter is extremely distasteful to this type of person.

n ORDER

A need for order is manifested in behavior directed towards organizing the immediate environment. Some people have a compulsion to put things in order, to clean up, to arrange furniture and clothing neatly, to organize and systematize books and other possessions. The orderly individual experiences tension when his home or room is in a condition of disarray. He must "get the mess straightened out." Everything has a place and should be kept there. A need for orderliness is not easily learned by an adult, a factor that also appears to apply to most of the other needs. Many wives complain that their husbands are careless about their things, and despite persistent nagging the tendency to be slovenly does not change. An extreme tendency toward orderliness is a symptom of personality malfunction. A man or woman who is constantly cleaning and dusting because of an inordinate fear of dirt is an example. The behavior has a compulsive quality about it, and the home is kept too well to be livable and comfortable.

n UNDERSTANDING

Many philosophers and psychologists have puzzled over the question of the status of cognition in relation to motivation. Some have regarded cognition as the servant or tool of motivation. One has a need and uses cognitive functioning as a means of securing satisfaction. Some, however — Murray included — have taken the position that cognition meets the requirements of a need. One may seek knowledge for its own sake. Cognitive processes may be pressed into the service of needs, but they may also function as needs themselves.

The need for cognition may take some of the following forms: to analyze experience, to abstract, to discriminate among concepts, to define relations, to synthesize ideas, and to arrive at generalizations. One who has this need experiences tension related to intellectual pursuits. He thoroughly enjoys discovering new relationships; if he is a scientist, he may delight in seeing his hypotheses verified by his data. Some actual behavioral manifestations of the need for understanding are, according to Murray: the tendency to ask questions, interest in theory, the inclination to analyze events and draw generalizations, a zest for discussion and argumentation, a high premium on logic and reason, self-correction and criticism, the habit of stating opinion precisely, insistent attempts to make thought correspond to fact, disinterested speculation, and deep interest in abstract formulations such as science, mathematics, and philosophy. To pursue these activities, without any other intended end, exemplifies the operation of the need for cognition and understanding.

NEED-INTEGRATE AND THEMA

All the elements associated with a need become tied together; Murray (1938) calls this a need-integrate. The need-integrate includes the triggering stimulus (which he calls press), the deficit state (which is the need), the instrumental activity (which Murray terms *actone*), associated images and emotions, and finally, the particular goal or incentive which satisfies the need.

A thema is the conjunction of a press and a need (Murray, 1938). Certain objects, persons, or events (press) are highly significant for a person. Certain needs are dominant and pervasive. Themas refer to behavior, produced by a need, directed toward a particular object, person or event. Table 7–4 presents typical themas.

When a thema is the major determinant in one's personality, affecting all significant aspects of his behavior, it is termed by Murray "unity thema." Murray describes a unity thema as

a compound of interrelated-collaborating or conflicting-dominant needs that are linked to press to which the individual was exposed on one or more particular occasions, gratifying or traumatic in early childhood. The thema may stand for a primary infantile experience or a subsequent reaction formation to that experience. But whatever its nature and genesis, it repeats itself in many forms during later life (1938, p. 184).

PSYCHOLOGICAL TESTS BASED ON MURRAY'S FORMULATIONS

The Edwards Personal Preference Schedule is an assessment instrument which presents a profile of the subject's standing with respect to some of Murray's needs. The profile is presented on page 224, together with some sample items from the test.

Another important test which was inspired by Murray's ideas is the Thematic Apperception Test (Murray, 1943). The personality is described in basic themas, with special attention to the consistencies and conflicts among them. The purpose of this procedure is to stimulate literary creativity and thereby evoke fantasies that reveal covert and unconscious complexes. The test is based upon the well-recognized fact that when a person interprets an ambiguous social situation he is apt to expose his own personality more than the phenomenon to which he is attending (Murray, 1938). An example of one subject's interpretation of one of the picture situations and a clinical discussion of that interpretation follow:

Picture 16.   (A short elderly woman stands with her back turned to a tall young man. The latter is looking downward with a perplexed expression, his hat in his hands.)

Subject's interpretation: Mother and boy were living happily. She had no husband. Her son was her only support. Then the boy got into bad company and participated in a gang robbery, playing a minor part. He was found out and sentenced to five years in prison. Picture represents him parting with his mother. Mother is sad, feeling ashamed of him. Boy is very much ashamed. He cares more about the harm he did his mother than about going to prison. He gets out for good behavior but his mother dies. He repents for what he has done but he finds that his reputation is lost in the city. No one

(*Text continued on page 225.*)

TABLE 7-4 TYPICAL THEMAS

Need	Themas
Abasement	To submit passively to a motherlike person. To accept blame readily from a superior. To confess wrong-doing to anyone who will listen.
Achievement	To strive to earn a large income. To attain honors and awards through outstanding achievements. To rival and surpass associates.
Affiliation	To have a close friend. To please many people. To work closely with another, or on a team.
Aggression	To overcome the opposition of another who is perceived as a threat. To cause another to submit: to control, to obligate others. To demonstrate superiority over others by hurting them.
Autonomy	To resist any form of restraint or coercion from parents. To quit deliberately activities which are required by authorities. To express needs relating to desired objects freely and impulsively. To seek exemptions from rules.
Counteraction	To strive anew in the face of failure. To overcome humiliation by taking strong positive action. To seek constantly to overcome weaknesses in oneself. To seek obstacles and difficulties to surmount.
Defendance	To defend the self against any criticism from anyone. To conceal quickly or justify a misdeed or humiliation in relationships with one perceived as an inferior. To be vindictive toward anyone who interferes with strivings.
Deference	To admire and support an older sibling, parent, friend. To praise, honor, or eulogize a boss, teacher, hero. To yield eagerly to the influence of a friend, partner, parent. To imitate the example of a model such as one's boss.
Dominance	To control one's environment by making things suit one's plan. To influence or direct the behavior of friends, classmates, parents. To take charge of situations: leader, boss, director, persuader. To persuade, to restrain, to direct, to control others.
Exhibition	To make an impression on members of the opposite sex.

(Table continued on opposite page.)

TABLE 7–4 *Continued*

Need	*Themas*
	To fascinate, shock, entertain, intrigue people perceived as significant.
	To draw attention to oneself through appearance and behavior.
Harmavoidance	To avoid taking risks by a conservative approach to life.
	To take precautionary measures in any threatening situation.
	To worry excessively about the uncertainties of life.
Infavoidance	To maintain a high level of pride in relationships with others.
	To avoid failure in undertakings.
	To be especially sensitive to belittlement, scorn, and indifference of others.
Nurturance	To be attracted to babies, small animals, and helpless creatures.
	To rally for the underdog.
	To enjoy matchmaking, directing young people, giving support.
	To sympathize with, console, comfort one who is afflicted.
Order	To organize and plan a trip or program.
	To produce a balance or orderly arrangement.
	To work out a system in the midst of confusion.
Play	To enjoy pleasure-making through sports.
	To enjoy laughing and making jokes in company with others.
Rejection	To respond to some people with an air of superiority.
	To deliberately snub or exclude certain people.
Sentience	To need activities and people that promote sensual pleasures.
	To seek unusual experiences as a means of changing moods.
Sex	To be attracted by many sexual partners.
	To be preoccupied with erotic concerns.
	To be attracted by an older man or woman.
Succorance	To respond dependently to a motherlike person.
	To cling to any authority figure who demonstrates concern.
	To seek to be counseled, advised, consoled by a sympathetic friend.
Understanding	To ask questions of a knowledgeable person.
	To speculate about unknowns.
	To attempt to identify the causes of things and events.

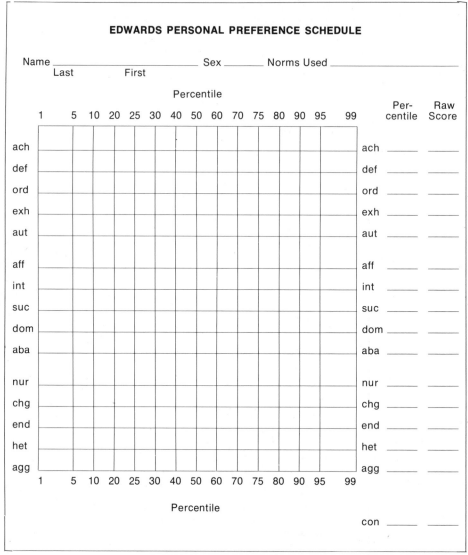

EDWARDS PERSONAL PREFERENCE SCHEDULE

Name _____ Sex _____ Norms Used _____
        Last   First

Percentile

| | 1 | 5 | 10 | 20 | 25 | 30 | 40 | 50 | 60 | 70 | 75 | 80 | 90 | 95 | 99 | | Percentile | Raw Score |

ach
def
ord
exh
aut

aff
int
suc
dom
aba

nur
chg
end
het
agg

con

ITEMS FROM THE EDWARDS PERSONAL PREFERENCE SCHEDULE

Alternatives		Items
A	B	A: I like to talk about myself to others. B: I like to work toward some goal that I have set for myself.
A	B	A: I feel depressed when I fail at something. B: I feel nervous when giving a talk before a group.

will employ him. He again meets bad companions and in despair he joins them in crime. However, he meets a girl with whom he falls in love. She suggests that he quit the gang. He decides to quit after one more hold-up. He is caught and sent to prison. In the meantime, the girl has met someone else. When he comes out he is quite old and spends the rest of his life repenting in misery.

The themas can be represented as follows [n = need, p = press]: pDominance: Bad Influence (externalization of blame) and nAcquisition: Robbery (Crime) → pAggression: Imprisonment (Punishment) and pLoss: Death of Mother (also as a punishment) → nAbasement: Remove and Dejection. The entire complex thema is then repeated with pRejection: Preference for Rival instead of pLoss: Death of Mother (Murray, 1938, pp. 536–539).*

CRITICAL EVALUATION

Murray's descriptive concepts and categories have been employed in a number of popular psychological tests. His concepts have been used as working tools by clinical psychologists, and he has developed theories to depict many aspects of personality. Not only has he suggested the key variables in personality study which should be assessed, but he has also given serious consideration to environmental factors. One who wishes to obtain a sense of the complexity and diversity of human behavior need only examine some of Murray's categories. One may become dazzled and bewildered by the variety and combinations of these descriptive categories: needs, emotions, modes, outcomes, impinging press, and many more. Murray's formulations of the motivational processes in man are his most outstanding contribution.

On the negative side is the criticism that Murray really only describes behavior and does not provide any explanatory concepts. Furthermore, there are overlapping concepts and categories: abasement and deference, nurturance. It is difficult to obtain an integrated view of a personality with Murray's system. He does appreciate this problem, and has introduced molar terms such as thema, unity thema, and need-integrate.

Although Murray is continually modifying his concepts, his system still has an unfinished quality about it. Thus, though his ideas have been fruitful in promoting research, particularly concerning the achievement and affiliation needs (Atkinson, 1958; McClelland, 1958), they have not been generally accepted by psychologists. His language is considered unscientific and poetic by many hard-core empiricists. Like other personality theorists, Murray is more concerned with the significance of the problems than with elegance of definition and precision of measurement. He speculates freely about all aspects of personality; thus he opens himself to criticism. Yet despite their shortcomings, his formulations have served as inspiration for many, and will continue to do so for some time.

---

*Note: This type of test is known as a projective test, because the subject projects his personal problems into the situation which is pictured.

INSIGHTS FROM MURRAY'S MOTIVATION CONCEPTS

PRACTICAL APPLICATION

Murray suggests that to use the need theory approach one should know all the needs quite well and be capable of identifying the active needs in a particular situation. Just as a physician keeps in the forefront of his mind symptoms of various diseases and can quickly link them with the cause, so also the individual using need theory should be aware of all the needs and their many behavioral and subjective manifestations and expressions. Murray includes questionnaires for each of the needs in his *Explorations in Personality* (1938). In going over the questionnaire related to the need harmavoidance, a student exclaimed to the author: "I never realized what a coward I am." He had long recognized that he feared a lot of things, but he did not realize how extensive his fears were and how much of his behavior was in the service of them. The questionnaire brought this point home to him quite vividly, and he was determined to act upon this new insight into his behavior.

One may read over the description of the needs with the view of discovering those most characteristic of himself. The next step may be a consideration of all the ways in which the needs are expressed in behavior. Include an evaluation of the effects you are seeking to accomplish; there should be a close relation between the needs and the effects. What happens when the needs are satisfied, and what happens when they are frustrated? Is there an unnecessary amount of frustration because the goals are beyond your capabilities, or are the needs too intense? This type of examination should enable you to discover areas of difficulty to work on. One can alter goals if they are unrealistic, or at least accept substitutes. The emotions associated with needs can be controlled. Even needs themselves can be moderated. A person who is extremely anxious about making friends may by that fact limit his opportunities. Controlling his anxiety should improve his social relationships. While awareness of a problem does not automatically solve it, ignorance is certainly a much less likely condition for solution.

In connection with need gratification, Murray subscribes to both tension reduction as a motivating force and generation of positive tensions (Murray and Kluckhohn, 1953). Some needs are associated with unpleasant tension, and we desire to rid ourselves of the tension. Examples are the viscerogenic needs. But some needs produce positive tension and their gratification is also pleasurable. Consider such needs as curiosity, appetite for certain foods, the desire to do something competently.

One more point about need gratification should be noted: Murray believes that we strive not for happiness directly, but rather to attain certain goals or values. Happiness is a byproduct of success in meeting our goals. A tensionless state provides pleasure of a sort, but the gratification of appetitive needs provides far greater pleasure. We should strive to gratify such needs more than the deficiency ones. According to Murray:

It is important to note that it is not a tensionless state, as Freud supposed, which is generally most satisfying to a healthy organism, but the process of reducing tension, and, other factors being equal, the degree of satisfaction is roughly proportional to the amount of tension that is reduced per unit of time. . . . A tensionless state is sometimes the ideal of those who suffer from chronic anxiety or resentment or a frustrated sex drive; but, as a rule, the absence of positive need-tensions—no appetite, no curiosity, no desire for fellowship, no zest—is very distressing. This calls our attention to the fact that the formula, tension-reduction of tension, takes account of only one side of the metabolic cycle. It covers metabolism, but not anabolism (which is the synthetic growth process by which tissues and potential energies are not only restored, but during youth, actually increased). The principle of homeostasis represents conservation but not construction. These considerations lead us to submit tentatively a more inclusive formula: generation of tension-reduction of tension. This formula represents a temporal pattern of states instead of an end state, a way of life rather than a goal; but it applies only to the positive need systems. The conservative systems that are directed toward withdrawals, avoidances, defenses, and preventions, are adequately covered by the reduction-of-tension formula (Murray and Kluckhohn, 1953, pp. 36–7).

As one technique for understanding oneself and others, Murray suggests that one begin with certain press and observe reactions to them at different times and under varying conditions. Consider your reaction to failure, making a lower mark on a test than you expected. Do you respond defensively by making an attempt at a justification? Do you seek a cause outside of yourself, such as blaming the test? Does the failure produce a depression, or are you motivated to change the situation? Reactions to specific press tend to become habitual. A person may always blame himself for failure, or he may habitually blame other people or things; or he may try to find a rational explanation and ascribe the cause to impersonal forces, and so on (Rosenzweig, 1943). Consider other situations such as reactions to the good fortune of a friend: are you pleased or envious? One can learn about his typical reactions from an examination of typical situations and responses to them. Murray calls these *dyadic relationships.*

"I know a person well when I am able to specify quite definitely his reactions to specific situations, or press. I know Mary well when I can say something regarding her typical situation-response patterns: Mary loves a surprise party; Mary dislikes a snob; Mary cannot tolerate being second best, and so forth." One can discover such dyadic relationships only by repeatedly observing the individual in a great variety of situations.

Another of Murray's ideas, which should assist in self-understanding, is his view of the complexity of the ego. Murray does not view the ego as a unitary agent as did Freud and many others. The ego is multidimensional; there are many aspects to it because there are divergent needs in the same person. It is more like a congress than a single agent. There are many factions, some of which are in diametric opposition. In a congress there are the liberals, the conservatives, the middle of the roaders, the radicals. The individual person may be conceived of in this manner. In making a decision, the conservative self says: "Don't be hasty to make a change; things are going quite well as they are." The liberal self says: "Let's do something exciting; who wants to just exist comfortably?" The conciliating self says: "Let's compromise; maybe we can take a longer vacation instead of moving away altogether."

Needs have much to do with the various aspects of the ego. Some needs are relatively unimportant in the activities of the ego. Whether one prefers sugar or cream or neither in his coffee does not cut across much of the personality. It plays no part in most decisions. Some needs are so dominant and pervasive, however, that they must be considered in virtually all personality functioning. They are constants in the personal equation. Just as in the congress certain factions carry more votes than others, so also in the ego certain needs dominate others and determine the direction of judgments and decisions. One can become acquainted with these various aspects of the ego through observation. Self-improvement may be thought of, in part, as changing the influence of certain needs, and strengthening others in their place. One may conclude, from the contents of this chapter, that the need-theory approach to personality study is powerful indeed and provides a highly useful frame of reference for conceptualizing personality data.

SUMMARY

1.   Knowledge of an individual's needs or motives will allow one to understand the other's behavior, to predict future courses of action, and to take steps to bring about certain effects through manipulation of motives.

2.   Needs may be considered the sources of behavior. All the elements associated with the need are called a need-integrate; this includes the triggering stimulus (press), the deficit state (need), the instrumental activity (action), associated images and emotions, and the goal or incentive which satisfies the need.

3.   Because Murray cautions that prediction of human behavior is a hazardous business, he recommends that one concentrate on effects of needs or goals. Therefore, if a definite effect is desired, certain behaviors will continue until it is attained. A certain goal is sought and the activity and the environment are structured to attain the goal. All these factors make for stability, order, and predictability.

4.   The ability to satisfy needs is called reinforcement power. If one discovers the needs of another, and does things to satisfy them, he can control his behavior.

5.   Behavior is the outcome of active motives; the motivational disposition can be observed only when it becomes active.

6.   A proof for the existence of needs is the degree of readiness of the organism to respond to the same stimulus situation at different times. Murray uses the term "press" to represent stimulus or situation; a press does something to or for a person. A positive press as well as a negative press produces a state of disequilibrium which is restored through appropriate activity. The goals are the concrete ways in which the need is expressed or satisfied.

7.   A thema is the conjunction of a press and a need. Themas refer to behavior, produced by a need, directed toward a particular object, person, or event.

REFERENCES

Adler, N. The Underground Stream. New York: Harper and Row, 1972.

Allport, G. Pattern and Growth in Personality. New York: Holt, Rinehart and Winston, 1961.

Atkinson, J. W. Motives in Fantasy, Action and Society. Princeton: D. Van Nostrand Company, 1958.

Birney, R. C., Burdick, H., and Teevan, R. C. Fear of Failure. New York: Van Nostrand-Reinhold, 1969.

Blum, R. H., Aron, J., Tutko, T., Feinglass, S., and Fort, J. Drugs and high school students. *In* Blum, R. H., et al., Students and Drugs: College and High School Observations. San Francisco, Jossey-Bass, 1969. Pp. 321–48.

Carter, L. F., and Nixon, M. An investigation of the relationship between four criteria of leadership ability for three different tasks. J. Psychol. *27*:245–61, 1949.

French, E. G. Some characteristics of achievement motivation. J. Exp. Psychol. *50*:232–36, 1955.

Freud, S. Inhibitions, Symptoms, and Anxiety. London: Hogarth Press, 1926.

Fromm, E. Man for Himself. New York: Holt, Rinehart and Winston, 1947.

Gorer, G. Man has no "killer" instinct. New York Times Magazine, November 27, 1966.

Hall, C., and Lindzey, G. Theories of Personality. New York: John Wiley and Sons, 1970.

Jones, E. Ingratiation. New York: Appleton-Century-Crofts, 1964.

Lang, P. J., and Lazovik, A. D. Personality and hypnotic susceptibility. J. Consult. Psychol. *26*:317–22, 1962.

Lantagne, J. E. Interest of 4,000 high school pupils in problems of marriage and parenthood. Research Quarterly of the American Association for Health, Physical Education, and Recreation *29*:407–16, 1958.

Maslow, A. H. Toward a Psychology of Being, 2nd ed. Princeton: D. Van Nostrand Company, 1968.

McKeachie, W. J., Lin, Y., Milholland, J., and Isaacson, R. Student affiliation motives, teacher warmth, and academic achievement. J. Pers. Social Psychol. *4*:457–61, 1966.

McClelland, D. C., Baldwin, A., Bronfenbrenner, V., and Strodtbeck, F. L. Talent and Society. Princeton: D. Van Nostrand Company, 1958.

Murray, H. A. Explorations in Personality. New York: Oxford University Press, 1938.

Murray, H. A. What should psychologists do about psychoanalysis? J. Abnorm. Social Psychol. *35*:150–75, 1940.

Murray, H. A. Thematic Apperception Test. Cambridge: Harvard University Press, 1943.

Murray, H. A. Some basic psychological assumptions and conceptions. Dialectica *5*:266–92, 1951.

Murray, H. A. Toward a classification of interaction. *In* Parsons, T., and Shils, E. A., eds., Toward a General Theory of Action. Cambridge: Harvard University Press, 1954. Pp. 434–64.

Murray, H. A. Preparations for the scaffold of a comprehensive system. *In* Koch, S., ed., Psychology: A Study of a Science, Vol. 3. New York: McGraw-Hill, 1959. Pp. 6–54.

Murray, H. A. The personality and career of Satan. J. Social Issues *28*:36–54, 1962.

Murray, H. A., and Kluckhohn, C. Outline of a conception of personality. *In* Kluckhohn, C., Murray, H. A., and Schneider, S. M., eds., Personality in Nature, Society, and Culture, 2nd ed. New York: Alfred A. Knopf, 1953. Pp. 3–52.

Oetzel, R. M. Classified summary of research in sex differences. *In* Maccoby, E. E., ed., The Development of Sex Differences. Stanford: Stanford University Press, 1966. Pp. 323–51.

Piaget, J. Play, Dreams and Imitation. New York: W. W. Norton and Company, 1962.

Rosenzweig, S. An experimental study of "repression" with special reference to need-perspective and ego–defense reactions to frustration. J. Exp. Psychol. *32*:64–74, 1943.

Sears, R. R., Maccoby, E. E., and Levin, H. Patterns of Child Rearing. Evanston, Illinois: Row, Peterson, 1957.

Skinner, B. F. Science and Human Behavior. New York: The Macmillan Company, 1953.

CHAPTER 8

Lower and Higher Needs

Abraham Maslow

Abraham Maslow (1908–1970)

BIOGRAPHY AND OVERVIEW

Abraham Maslow was born in New York in 1908. He received his B.A., M.A., and Ph.D. from the University of Wisconsin, ending his formal education in 1934. After teaching at Wisconsin, Columbia, and Brooklyn College, he went to Brandeis, where he became Chairman of the Department of Psychology. Maslow received many awards and honors, including election to the presidency of the American Psychological Association in 1967. He died in 1970 at the age of 62. Well liked by his students and colleagues, he had a profound trust in man's capacity to work out a better world both for mankind in general and for each individual. He risked professional censure to pursue his convictions. He was one of the pioneers of and major contributors to the so-called third force in psychology. The third force represents a humanistic approach to personality science, in contrast to the other two systems, behaviorism and psychoanalysis. Maslow's students, disciples, and supporters continue to promote his ideas and program. It appears that his influence on psychology will become greater as his ideas become more widely understood and disseminated.

As a humanistic psychologist, Maslow (1955) questioned the traditional assumption that pain avoidance and tension reduction are the major sources of motivation for man. He proposed instead that personality scientists examine man's strivings for growth, for happiness and satisfaction. He distinguished between *deficit needs* and *growth needs* or *metaneeds*. Deficit needs include physiological needs, safety needs, love and belonging needs, and esteem needs. The growth needs are encompassed by the general term *self-actualization*. Maslow held that the higher needs are as much a part of man's make-up as the

230

more rudimentary needs. Another of his important assumptions is that each person has an individual nature which has to be supported and encouraged. By concentrating only on the lower needs, some personality psychologists have taken the one-sided view that man is selfish, evil, antisocial, and animalistic by nature. Maslow believed that there are degrees of humanness, with functioning on the higher need levels representing the high end of the humanness dimension.

BASIC ISSUES IN HUMAN MOTIVATION

NEED SUPPRESSION AND DISTORTION

Maslow suggested that both the deficit (lower) needs and the growth (higher) needs are subject to distortion. Distortion of lower needs is strikingly evident in individuals suffering from psychophysiological disorders. A person may eat not to satisfy hunger but to relieve tension. Thus the basic hunger drive may be used as a channel or outlet for other motives, such as the desire for love, that have nothing to do with the need for food. This misuse of drives is harmful to the total economy of the organism, Maslow (1970) believed. The normal regulating mechanisms fail to operate properly, and as a result the drive fails to function adequately. The person who eats to relieve anxiety may neither receive nor know how to interpret the sensations indicating that food is necessary and also that enough food has been ingested (Young, 1944).

If the physiological drives can be severely distorted by faulty learning or misuse, the subtler needs are much more readily disturbed and misdirected by experience. The so-called virtues and noblest strivings of man – excellence, affectionate response, altruism, the creation of beauty, the discovery of truth, and the like – are not as powerful and fully structured as the typical physiological drives of hunger, thirst, sex, pain avoidance, and rest. Hence, they can be so modified and overridden by learning that they fail to function at all. In other words, a person may learn to like things that are contrary to his best interests, or to behave in a manner opposed to his growth needs. He may learn to be cold, unresponsive, and unaffectionate toward others, even though he has within his nature the need to express and to receive affection.

The maintenance of the higher needs demands a great deal of support from cultural influences. Current institutions and prevailing views of man's nature actually promote practices which suppress the highest needs of man, Maslow believed. If a child cries as a result of being hurt, his parents eagerly rush to help him, but if he expresses his inner feelings of well-being in a free and natural manner, he may be rebuked or punished for behaving "childishly." The guiding assumption here is that the child needs to be controlled. A further implication of this assumption is that when the child is behaving naturally, he is behaving badly.

Consider another example. In certain societies, maternal impulse seems nonexistent. Is there really a lack of maternal impulse in the women of these societies, or is there rather a disruption and destruction of the innate tendency by cultural practices? Whereas no culture can completely break down the hunger drive, certainly a need as weak in man as the maternal impulse can be easily negated and permanently suppressed. Instead of supporting the maternal tendency by rewarding maternal behavior in mothers, a culture may block the impulse by rewarding nonmaternal behavior. This situation prevails today in the United States and other Western countries. Motherhood, particularly in the middle and upper classes, is not given a high status. The implicit assumption is that almost every woman can be a mother, but not every woman can become a teacher, executive, politician, or the like. As a consequence, many mothers do not encourage their daughters to identify with the motherly role. A little girl may be brought up to dress as a woman and to identify with some of the superficial roles, but the role of homemaker may not be one of them. Even in a woman in whom the maternal impulse is strong, the allurements of being independent, earning money, holding a status position (all conventionally masculine values) may oppose the traditional maternal role of caring for the husband and children and block out the maternal tendency (Maslow, 1970).

This tendency may be distorted and manifested in peculiar forms. A woman hired a girl to care for her children and took a position as a teacher. She became intensely involved with her students and appeared to care more about them than her own children. Her friends noticed this peculiar behavior and criticized her for it. She was caught in a conflict between her maternal needs and her acquired values.

Some other growth needs which are weak and poorly formed are tenderness, affectionate behavior, and altruism. Many great thinkers have commented on the lack of such qualities in humans and on the prevalence, in fact, of the opposite qualities (hostility, selfishness, tendency to hurt others, jealousy, and envy). The prevailing Judeo-Christian view is that the individual is naturally selfish and even destructive of others, and socially oriented needs must be taught; they are not natural, but learned. Maslow held that the tender emotions and socially oriented needs are native to man, but they are weak and not as complete in their structure as the basic drives. They need support, and one way to support them is to satisfy the basic drives rather completely. If one is not concerned about the requirements for existence, he can allow his more humane impulses to surface (Maslow, 1970).

THE SURVIVAL VALUE OF NEEDS

The only inborn aspect of the total behavior necessary for meeting most needs of the organism is the feeling of tension or lack. The person must learn to find appropriate satisfiers and the means of securing them. The consequences of failing to satisfy certain (but not all) requirements are quite obvious: the person who does not obtain the proper nutrition suffers from some form of physical illness, or he may die. However, *some essential needs may go unheeded, and the consequences of not satisfying them may not be so obvious.*

The person who does not have affectional relationships with others will not die or suffer from malnutrition. The consequences of this lack of satisfaction of a basic human need are much more subtle, and not easily detected. One may experience unexplainable restlessness, general tension, and free-floating anxiety as a reaction to lack of love. Though survival is possible without such need gratification, the fullness of development and functioning may be severely hampered.

As so many others have done from a different frame of reference, Maslow advised that one should become acquainted with his real self and, in fact, with his entire organism. One should endeavor to identify the subtle impulses that may be contrary to cultural values, but that nevertheless are a vital part of his individual behavior. These impulses should be expressed in behavior, even if this requires going counter to the culture. In the long run, the benefits will be greater than those from blindly following the cultural ideals. Being a mother may be more satisfying, if the proper attitude is taken, than being a working wife. According to Maslow (1955), following prevailing practices and values may bring about certain apparently favorable results — wealth, power, prestige — but at the cost of fulfillment of one's individual nature. Again, one can learn to like what is not good for him.

The effects of taking certain drugs may be pleasurable but harmful to health: the momentary pleasure is inconsequential when compared with the detrimental influence on the person as a whole. Here is an instance of the discrepancy which has long been recognized: why is it that "everything man seems to want is either immoral, illegal, or fattening?" Yet Maslow indicated that for the person who is self-actualizing (he who is expressing his individual nature as fully as possible), doing what he wants to do is doing what is good for him. The self-actualizing person wants what his natural impulses or needs require. Gratifying wants (such as a craving for a drug) that are not impulse-driven may injure the organism. Hence, one gauge of successful living is the harmony between what is desired and what is good for the person. If what you want is what you need (or what you want to do is what you should do), then your motives and impulses can be trusted.

INSTINCTIVE VERSUS INSTINCTOID BEHAVIOR

Maslow (1970) made a valuable distinction between a *total instinct* and an *instinctoid tendency*, or *instinct remnant*, which should aid in understanding the difference between lower basic needs and higher basic needs. A total instinct involves all the elements of a behavioral act: perception of relevant stimuli, appropriate coping behavior, and selection of goals so that behavior terminates when they are attained. For instance, a sparrow does not have to learn how to build a nest, nor must it learn to discriminate among suitable and useless objects for its goal. In fact, it does not even learn the goal for which its activity is so well coordinated. All these elements, plus whatever emotions are experienced—if any—are a biological, genetic "given." Instinctive behavior is behavior not acquired through learning.

Man presents a difficult problem from the standpoint of instinctive behavior. There are no full-blown instincts in man. There are inborn reflexes and still more complex forms of behavior such as physiological drives. Even drives require for their satisfaction the learning of appropriate incentives, and instrumental behaviors for obtaining these incentives. The child surely does not instinctively know what is good or harmful; he must learn these things as a result of encounters with a variety of objects in his environment, or he must be told or shown. Figure 8–1 depicts the difference between a complete instinct and the instinctoid nature of man's higher needs.

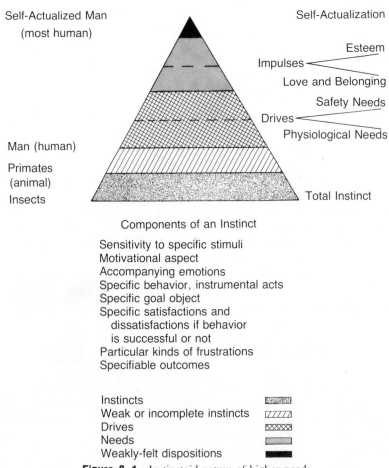

Figure 8–1 Instinctoid nature of higher needs.

Because of the apparent absence of inborn total instincts in man, some psychologists and others have assumed that man's behavior and experiences are entirely due to his learning. Maslow, however, believed that although man may not have a complete instinct in his make-up, he does have instinct remnants or instinctoid tendencies. A woman does not have a maternal instinct as do the lower animals in the sense that all the elements which are involved in bearing and caring for children are present without any learning, but she may certainly possess a strong impulse to tend and care for children. The point is that in the complex setting of civilized living this impulse or instinct remnant is not in itself sufficient to guide child-rearing behavior, but requires the support of correctly learned skills and attitudes, and the formulation of a philosophy of child-rearing (Caudill and Weinstein, 1969). Contrary to popular opinion, child-rearing is not a natural endowment of women. If all such qualities were simply a matter of doing what comes naturally, there would be no personality disorders.

A puppy does not have to learn to be a puppy; it "just is" one and behaves accordingly. In animals, the voice of impulse is strong, unmistakable, and clear. Only humans can choose to be what they are not, or not to be what they are. They can disregard their basic impulses and follow patterns of behavior that do not satisfy the requirements of their nature as humans. Maslow (1971) held that one of the major causes of psychological disorder is the loss of one's animal nature. A person may feel guilt for failing to live up to certain standards of conduct and may bend all his efforts toward meeting them even at the expense of denying some of his basic needs.

Every parent repeatedly experiences the selfishness and lack of concern for others so often displayed by his young children. Maslow certainly recognized these selfish tendencies, but he reminded us that the animal-like nature of children is often feared and distrusted without justification. He believed that allowing a child to express himself freely in an atmosphere of positive regard and acceptance, without overly rigid control and suppression of vital forces, is the best manner of teaching him (Maslow, 1970). The child has within his nature all the most human qualities. These do not have to be drummed in, but rather fostered and given free expression. For Maslow, the best approach to child-rearing is a great deal of gratification of all impulses, a minimum of restriction and control, and above all, a lack of punitiveness. However, unlimited gratification of needs does not guarantee healthy growth and functioning. Maslow appreciated the fact that a certain amount of frustration, disappointment, denial, and hurt play a part as well, but the child should not be exposed to these too soon. Exposure to frustration should be proportional to his capacity to deal with it (his "frustration tolerance").

In brief, man should learn to follow his instinct remnants more honestly and freely. This is Maslow's essential resolution of the conflict between instinctive and learned behavior: all the agents of the culture should support the instinctoid tendencies.

HIERARCHY OF NEEDS

As we have seen, Maslow held that the lower needs are more potent and take priority over the higher ones. A hungry man does not concern himself with impressing his friends with his daring and skills, but rather with securing enough to eat. A man whose life is threatened by a murderer does not experience a sense of pride, but seeks to escape by whatever means are at his disposal. When lower needs are taken care of, then the next higher needs make their appearance in awareness, and the person is motivated to deal with their gratification. Only when all of the lower needs are at least partially gratified can the person begin to experience the self-actualizing needs. The lower needs are themselves arranged in a hierarchy; in order of potency and priority, they are the physiological needs, the safety needs, the belonging and love needs, and the esteem needs.

SOME BASIC TERMS

In discussing human motivation in general, Maslow (1970) distinguished between a need and a motivation or desire. A need is a lack of something, a deficit state. By a motive he usually meant a conscious desire, a felt impulse or urge for a specific thing. One may have a hunger need and a motive or desire for a hamburger. The purpose of making this distinction is to point out the difference between basic ends and the specific means that are experienced. The individual may need food (an end) in a physiological sense, but experience hunger (a means) for a specific food. There are many more motives than there are needs. Two people may have the same need, for instance, for respect; one may attempt to achieve it by being an elder of his church, while the other may aspire to be the best salesman in his company. The term "appetite" is used in a sense similar to that of "desire." I can have an appetite for certain foods without experiencing the hunger drive. (Drive and need, in this context, are similar.)

PHYSIOLOGICAL NEEDS

The most potent needs of all, and yet the least significant for the self-actualizing person, are the physiological needs (Maslow, 1970). When these needs are deprived for a relatively long period, all other needs recede or fail to appear (Keys et al., 1950). Occasionally one hears of instances that seem to contradict this view; a religious man who starves himself to death, or a young woman who burns herself to death in moral protest. These are instances of higher needs that appear to function more powerfully than basic survival needs.

Maslow could have pointed out that some instances of "self-sacrifice" result from serious psychological disturbance. But it also appears to be a characteristic of the highest human needs that once a person has attained that unusual level of functioning, the consequences are so satisfying that lower needs are subordinated to higher ones, at least under temporary conditions. It would appear that prolonged deprivation of basic needs would eventually destroy the higher needs. The issue is not totally resolved, however.

Maslow proposed an interesting notion concerning the motivating powers of need-deprivation and need-gratification. Certainly one is motivated to do something about a deprived need. A man who is near starvation will do almost anything to secure food. Thus deprivation of a need is commonly used to instigate motivation. A parent may deprive his child of freedom, love, or respect in order to motivate him to do better in his school work, for instance. But consider the value of gratification as a better means of inducing motivation. Whereas the deprivation notion of motivation applies to the lower needs (if a person is hungry and eats enough to satisfy himself, the tension is relieved and the motivation ceases), the picture is different for the higher needs where gratification is usually a stimulant for further motivation. Gratification of basic needs renders them inactive, and hence the higher needs take their place. These higher needs are not satiated with gratification but rather increased in intensity. The person who learns the satisfactions of reaching out for others and of giving his love freely has no limit. The more he gives, the more he seems to have to give, and the greater is his motivation to give it.

SAFETY NEEDS

If the physiological needs do not constitute a serious problem for the person, then the safety needs become dominant forces in his personality. These include a variety of needs, all related to preserving the status quo—conserving and maintaining order and security. Examples of safety needs are the need for security, the need for stability, the need for order, the need for protection, and the need for dependency. Safety needs may take the form of fears: fear of the unknown, of chaos, of ambiguity and confusion. The person may fear loss of control over his circumstances, being vulnerable and weak, being unable to meet the new demands of life. Many people strongly desire structure, lawfulness, and to be under someone's direction (Adorno et al., 1950).

Although many adults complain that they want to be more independent in their work to do things their own way, when they are actually given this freedom they find it hard to accept. A large firm adopted the policy of giving new junior executives as much freedom as possible. The newly hired executive was told what his job was and to whom he was accountable, and then left pretty much on his own. There was no supervision or checking of his minute-to-minute activities. It soon became apparent that something was wrong, because many of the men were resigning within a period of three to six months. Their reason for quitting was not financial but a lack of structure; not having limits or standards by which to judge the adequacy of their work. Of course, the ones who left did not give these reasons, but rather found something wrong with the company practices. Some commonly given reasons were: "They don't really take much interest in what you do around here"; or "You get the feeling that you are never doing enough"; or "No one gives any real help in this company; you are given enough rope to hang yourself."

There is a tendency to overvalue the safety needs if these are not adequately met. Most people seem unable to get beyond the safety level of functioning (Maslow, 1970). They are security bound. This is reflected in the concern with building up large savings, overbuying of insurance, preferring a job with many fringe benefits. Uncertainty is not to be tolerated. Make the future as knowable as possible. The psychologically disturbed person may be so terrified of the unknown that he constructs rigid routines and standards for himself. He obsessively follows certain beliefs and compulsively carries them out. This is an extreme attempt to obtain a sense of security. While the normal person may prefer familiar events and circumstances, he does not need the crutch of total control over his world.

The question of security is particularly relevant for children. Not having a great deal of control over his surroundings, the child is frequently the victim of fear-producing situations. Maslow believed that children should be brought up in an environment that is somewhat protective and structured. They should be shielded from hurtful experiences until they have learned sufficient skills to cope with stress. The feelings of insecurity in childhood can be carried over into adulthood. Imposing a structured environment helps to promote security and healthy growth. Children seem to prefer being given direction because, after all, they cannot provide it for themselves. Permissiveness may place too much of a burden upon a child. If he is given too much freedom, he does not know what to do with it, and may use it to get himself into terrifying situations. Freedom and self-control should be given only in amounts that he can bear. A warm, accepting, yet structured atmosphere is the best climate for child-rearing.

Courage is a helpful attitude in dealing with feelings of insecurity. No one can take full control of his life and eliminate threats and fears, dangers and hurts, but each can take the attitude of faith in himself and meet most situations head-on. Such an attitude equips the individual to function in spite of the unknowns. Security obviously depends upon external circumstances, but not completely so, because there can never be full control of these events. A sense of safety is to a great degree a matter of attitude.

BELONGING AND LOVE NEEDS

Maslow (1970) included under the category of love and belonging needs a variety of socially oriented needs such as desiring an intimate relationship with another person, being an accepted member of an organized group, needing a familiar environment such as a family, living in a familiar neighborhood, and participating in group action as in working for a common end with others. These needs depend for their occurrence upon a certain degree of satisfaction of the physiological and safety needs.

The crowded living conditions of contemporary life seem to block the expression of love and belonging needs. Although people live close together in apartments and houses, they do not interact. Except in small rural communities, there is an unwritten taboo against getting too close to the neighbors. One hardly knows the name of the people next door, let alone socializes with them. Many people reveal that they feel alone and isolated, lonely though there are people all around them (Riesman, 1952).

The love and belonging needs take different forms throughout life. The child seeks a warm, accepting atmosphere with a great deal of physical demonstration and affection. The teenager wants love in the form of respect, being understood and appreciated. The young adult wants to be intimate with a loved one, to experience a great deal of emotional involvement. Mature love is an attraction to another based on valuing that other person as a person, as an end in himself. A less mature form of love, according to Maslow, is relating to others as a means of relieving loneliness, or of just having someone to become emotionally involved with. The highest form of love, which Maslow termed "B-love," is valuing another as he is without any desire to change or use him in any way; this was expressed by Maslow as loving the "being" of the other. He distinguished B-love from "D-love," which is based on a deficit need: one feels lonely and desires companionship; the companionship is sought as a means of relieving tension. If the relationship gives support, comfort, and security—as in going steady—rather than enabling one to value another person as an interesting, likable, pleasant friend or companion, then the person is being loved as a result of a deficit of some sort and not for himself.

The strength of the love needs is so great that, for many, thwarting of these needs is the major source of psychological disturbance. The nature of the disturbance depends upon the period of life when the need is frustrated. The elderly person may feel alone and cut off from the world. He may have lost most of his sources of human contact through death or the moving away of friends and family. This need for human contact is expressed in the increasing tendency among elderly people to form their own groups: golden-age organizations and the like.

At the other extreme, the infant who does not receive human love in a direct physical manner suffers from developmental retardation that is manifested in a variety of forms: physical, psychological, and social (Bowlby, 1952). Although he may have the best physical care, he will not develop properly unless he is also given tender loving care by a motherlike person. Whether the physical care is a matter of satisfying the infant's safety needs (children are particularly troubled by safety needs), or whether the desire for human contact is a rudimentary expression of the love and belonging needs, is not altogether clear. Probably both needs are involved. Unlike the adult, who needs both to give love and to receive it, the child seems to want more to be loved than to love.

The love needs are particularly evident during adolescence and young adulthood (Friedenberg, 1959). They vary from strong desires to have a "buddy" relationship with a member of the same sex, to being an accepted member of a closely knit gang, to the intimate, all-consuming passions of a romantic relationship with a member of the opposite sex. The concern with these needs is embodied in the lyrics of popular songs. A great percentage of these songs express in one way or another the powerful hold that love needs have and the hurt and fear produced by their frustration.

THE ESTEEM NEEDS

The esteem needs (Maslow, 1970) may be subdivided into two classes: (1) those relating to self-esteem, self-respect, self-regard, and self-valuation; and (2) those relating to respect from others; reputation, status, social success, fame, glory, and the like.

The concern with self-esteem, particularly regarding one's own evaluation of oneself, usually occurs in individuals who may be described as "comfortably situated." They are quite secure in the satisfaction of the lower needs. A carpenter who has established a sound reputation and does not have to worry about getting work may become quite discriminating about what type of work he accepts. He may accept only those jobs which can challenge his skills, rather than taking on routine work merely for the sake of earning money. The quality of his work is a matter of some concern to him; thus it fulfills a need for self-respect, a need to feel good about himself. The satisfaction of this need has an internal locus. His reasoning, although not explicitly expressed, may be as follows: "I am a competent judge of good carpentry, and this is certainly good work, and of course it is my work." Feelings of achievement, of competence, of meeting high standards of excellence in performance are not the concerns of the struggling beginner but the "extra touches" of the comfortable artisan (Gelfand, 1962).

Prior to attaining a level of prideful involvement in one's activities, one seeks the respect and assurance of others that one is a worthwhile person. Esteem is externally based before it becomes internally based. A man may buy a large home, not because he particularly likes one, but because having one is a status symbol in our culture. The home is a symbol of his importance; it represents him, so to speak. It serves as a visible, concrete object to announce his standing in the community. There are many similar status symbols that have the function of providing a tangible measure, usually for the benefit of others, of the position one holds. Such status symbols include clothing, titles, membership in organizations, location of home, type of automobile, and a variety of other easily and not-so-easily identifiable indicators of standing.

Another instance of the esteem needs is the need to feel superior to others. This need is gratified by conspicuous purchasing of items for the purpose of outdoing other people. Many women will not wear an outfit twice, particularly in the presence of the same people, because to do so would imply poor taste or a lack of financial resources. A man may not keep a new car more than a year, even if it is in good working condition, because to do so might create an unfavorable image of him. There are dozens of ways in which people attempt to prove their superiority. The person who is driven by this need wishes to feel more important than others and may go to any end to prove this importance.

As we shall see in Chapter 9, Alfred Adler, the great Viennese psychiatrist, believed that everyone has a need for superiority and that it must be brought under control. According to Adler, one should always avoid acting in a manner which brings out one's own superiority or others' inferiority. However, Coopersmith (1967) has noted that failure to gratify the need for respect, reputation, or adulation from others can produce widespread personality disturbance. The most frequent form of disturbance is a sense of inferiority, of being different from others, of being a misfit. The person experiences a sense either of guilt or of shame.

Needs related to respect from others—acceptance, admiration, and approval—vary in expression and intensity throughout life. What constitutes satisfactory respect in the life of the ten year old boy is certainly not the same as what constitutes respect for the teenager and young adult. Peer-respect may be defined by the ten year old as being feared or admired, whereas for the older individual, respect comes from being popular, having dates, being invited to parties. Although the intensity of the need for admiration and respect reaches a peak during young adulthood, there are people of all ages who sacrifice almost everything for glory and fame.

For many people, the intensity of the need for esteem from others diminishes in the middle years, and the need for self-regard becomes more significant as a force in personality (Jung, 1964). It may be that by that time in life, the person has tempered his needs for reputation by a realistic perception of their value, or it may be a matter of having learned to gratify these needs adequately. Probably both factors are involved. Maslow believed that sufficient gratification of the esteem needs lessens their dominating force in a person's life, thus enabling him to move in the direction of self-actualization.

SELF-ACTUALIZATION NEEDS

The self-actualizing needs are most difficult to describe because they are so highly unique and vary from individual to individual. In general, self-actualization means fulfilling one's individual nature in all its aspects, being what one can be (Maslow, 1970). The person who is talented in music must make music. He experiences tension if he does not. The carpenter who is retired itches to take up his tools and put them to use again. The man who enjoys nature wishes to spend much of his time in the wild. The motherly person is at her best when caring for someone, giving a party, ministering to someone who is sick. Not only is the type of activity the person desires to perform important as a means of meeting the end of self-actualization, so also is the manner of performing the activity. The artist has his own identifiable style and his particular manner of working, also identifiable by those who know him.

An essential aspect of self-actualization is freedom — freedom from cultural and self-imposed restraints. The self-actualizing person wants to be, and must be, free (Grossack, Armstrong, and Lussieu, 1966). He wants to be free to be himself. Generally, self-actualizing people are not revolutionaries, radicals, anarchists, or against their culture; they do not adopt any extreme movement, nor do they identify unquestioningly with the culture. They perform their cultural requirements out of a sense of duty but when such practices seriously interfere with self-actualization, they easily and freely react against them.

The lyrics of many popular songs express the desire for self-actualization: "I want to be free," "I want to be me," "I did it my way." These phrases imply the need for individuality and freedom from standards and superiors. Another popular expression is "doing my thing"; this also is an expression of the desire for individuality and freedom. We hear a great deal about the search for identity and the sense of alienation. While the young person may be having difficulty knowing who he really is, the older person may be questioning the meaning of his life. One suffers from a sense of alienation (being a stranger, feeling left out) and the other from existential anxiety (lacking meaning in living) (Frankl, 1963). In both cases we can see the frustration of self-actualizing needs.

Self-actualization is possible if the more basic needs are met to the degree that they neither distract nor consume all available energies. When a person is comfortable with his lower basic needs, he can more adequately experience and act upon his higher needs. Accepting this frame of reference, we can see that in order for a person to become self-actualizing, many preconditions must be satisfied. He should not have to worry about his survival requirements. He should be quite comfortable in his job and know that his skills are salable. He should feel accepted in his social contacts, from his marriage and family relationships to his work associations and organizational affiliations. He should feel respected by those who count with him. He should genuinely respect himself, feel a sense of competence, and possess a feeling of good will toward himself. Finally, he should attempt to know his preferences and tendencies, to give them a hearing, and to act to satisfy them.

Table 8–1 presents Maslow's Need Hierarchy.

THE NEEDS TO KNOW AND UNDERSTAND

Although Maslow did not assign the so-called cognitive needs a specific place in the need hierarchy, he definitely affirmed their status in man and even in animals (Maslow, 1970). The desires to know and understand are real motives that arise from basic needs. The normal human being cannot be passive about his world. He does not take things for granted but wants to know the causes. From the ponderings of the scientist to the "nosy" neighbor, we can see the

TABLE 8-1   MASLOW'S NEED HIERARCHY

5. Self-Actualization Needs
  Need to fulfill one's personal capacities
  Need to develop one's potential
  Need to do what one is best suited to do
  Need to grow and expand metaneeds: discover truth
                                              create beauty
                                              produce order
                                              promote justice

  4. Esteem Needs
    Need for respect
    Need for confidence based on good opinions of others
    Need for admiration
    Need for self-confidence
    Need for self-worth
    Need for self-acceptance

    3. Love and Belonging Needs
      Need for friends
      Need for companions
      Need for a family
      Need for identification with a group
      Need for intimacy with a member of the opposite sex

      2. Safety Needs
        Need for security
        Need for protection
        Need for freedom from danger
        Need for order
        Need for predictable future

        1. Physiological Needs
          Need for relief from thirst, hunger
          Need for sleep
          Need for sex
          Need for relief from pain, physiological imbalances

Note: The "actualization needs" imply activity whereas the lower needs imply the fulfillment of a deficit ("need to" vs. "need for").

powerful operation of the need to know. One does not have to learn to know, according to Maslow, because cognition is a basic need.

Satisfaction of the cognitive needs leads to the same consequences as satisfaction of the more usual needs, and likewise frustration of these needs is followed by disturbances in personality growth and functioning. Some disorders that occur as a result of cognitive frustration are a lowered zest for living, uninvolvement, and lack of curiosity. The marvelous and miraculous events pass by unnoticed. Like a child who has everything, the person may simply take what he has for granted and not value anything very much. Another common manifestation of cognitive distortion is the centering of concern inward, within the self. The self-centered person is not only denied a source of great pleasure from satisfying cognitive needs but also suffers harmful consequences as a result of lack of concern with this vital aspect of his life.

Maslow presented a classification of cognitive needs, again in the form of a hierarchy. For example, the need to know the world is more basic than the need to put events into some theoretical framework for the purpose of creating cognitive order. Certain other aspects of cognitive functioning are worth noting. One is the need to analyze—to discover the most basic components, to take things apart. One can see the operation of this need in early childhood. There is the need to experiment, to vary conditions in order to see what happens. The child says: "I wonder what will happen if I mix this liquid with this other liquid." Like so many other cognitive needs, this impulse is often blocked by parents and teachers. Still other cognitive needs are the desire to construct a system for the purpose of ordering events, the synthetic function of cognition, the need to explain events rather than simply to know them, the need to find meaning in one's life. There are probably others not included in this discussion, since our knowledge of the motivational aspect of cognition is still sketchy (Klein, 1970).

THE AESTHETIC NEEDS

Although little is known about the operation of the aesthetic needs (Maslow, 1970), their part in human life is quite significant, especially in the lives of specific individuals. Some people find disorder, chaos, ugliness, and the like quite intolerable. They crave the opposites of these qualities. The aesthetic needs include the needs for order, symmetry, and closure (the desire to fill in gaps in situations that are poorly structured), the need to relieve the tension produced by an uncompleted task, and the need to structure events (classify and systematize knowledge).

CRITICAL EVALUATION

Maslow's need hierarchy concept calls the attention of psychologists to the varying levels of motivation in man. Maslow repeatedly argued that psychology and psychiatry, and many other forces in society, conceive of man in terms of deficiency needs. Traditionally the higher needs were thought to be products of socialization. Maslow held that they are an inherent part of man's nature, but he also believed that gratification rather than suppression of lower needs is a prerequisite for the vigorous functioning of the higher needs. His view of man was optimistic, and it appears to open new vistas for research into vital human concerns.

Beyond emphasizing the necessity of gratifying needs, however, Maslow did not specify the particulars for dealing with them. Allport (1961) and Maddi (1965) have pointed out that there are numerous instances of high human achievement among those who have had anything but easy gratification of needs. Maslow might have responded that gratification is not the only, but rather the *best* way to deal with needs. Yet the experimental application of his

TABLE 8–2 MASLOW'S NEED HIERARCHY RELATED TO OCCUPATION

"In our society there is no single situation which is potentially so capable of giving some satisfactions at all levels of basic needs as is the occupation."—Ann Roe, *The Psychology of Occupations,* 1956, p. 31.

Needs	Work-Related Fulfillments
Physiological Needs	Earning money to secure the essentials for living: food, water
Safety Needs	Shelter: renting an apartment, buying a house Fringe benefits: pension, savings Clothing Personal property: furniture, car
Love and Belonging Needs	Working with a congenial group Being needed and welcomed by peers and superiors
Esteem Needs	Representing adulthood, independence, and freedom Feeling accomplishment, responsibility, and prestige Being valued by work associates
Self-Actualization Needs	Creative behavior Use of talents, pursuit of interests Productiveness

Adapted from A. Roe, *The Psychology of Occupations.* John Wiley and Sons, 1956, pp.31–35.

need hierarchy has yielded conflicting results: in some work settings, providing conditions which seem to gratify higher needs produced evident improvement in performance and employee morale (Marrow et al., 1967); however, in other settings there was no improvement (Hall and Nongaim, 1968). Table 8–2 presents a potential application of Maslow's need hierarchy to occupation.

INSIGHTS FROM MASLOW'S NEED HIERARCHY

In order to clarify the nature of needs and their interrelationships, several distinguishing characteristics of the higher and lower needs will be presented.

NEEDS DIFFER IN POTENCY AND PRIORITY

Some people mistakenly believe that the degree of fulfillment one attains is directly related to the extent of basic lower need gratification. Indulging the appetites for food and drink to great excess will not lead to fulfillment. To attempt to find contentment by compulsive satisfaction of physiological needs is to neglect significant aspects of one's nature. Moderation in lower need gratification is not simply a moralistic practice; it is dictated by the requirements of successful living.

THE HIGHER NEEDS ARE WEAK

A person cannot avoid his physiological lower needs for long but he can overlook, postpone, or even deny his higher needs all his life. Closely related to this lack of urgency is the difficulty of recognizing the higher needs. Many people have trouble mapping out a desirable life style for themselves. They can more easily identify what is wrong in their lives—what they dislike—than specify what they really want and like—what constitutes an ideal existence for them. The key to successful living, according to Maslow, is to recognize one's most personal higher needs and take steps to satisfy them, even if only in a small way at first.

LOWER NEED GRATIFICATION IS MORE TANGIBLE AND CIRCUMSCRIBED THAN HIGHER NEED GRATIFICATION

Although any food will do to eliminate hunger, the love of a loved one cannot be replaced. Furthermore, the amount of food or water or sexual gratification is limited, but the capacity to give love, to know, or to appreciate and value something is virtually unlimited. The higher needs, affording such a varied scope of gratification, should always provide motivation enough to make life interesting and exciting.

HIGHER NEEDS REVEAL MORE ABOUT A PERSON THAN LOWER NEEDS

Learning about the manner in which a person handles his need for food and other physiological drives reveals relatively little about him. One may eat much or little, slowly or rapidly, bland or spicy foods, only when he is hungry or often for pleasure, three times a day or also between meals. Aside from these rather insignificant bits of information, the basic physiological needs tell us little of value. Except when such needs are extraordinarily important in a person's life, as a result of severe deprivation or because they are gratified for neurotic purposes, they are relegated to a minor position and little attention is paid to them.

The higher needs have more generalized effects than the lower needs. A man's self-esteem, integrity, and honor may persist in his background and operate in much of his activity. Self-esteem affects the quantity and quality of his work. These needs are especially important in his social relationships. They also influence his recreational activities: being on the winning team may be a powerful motivation. Failure, and the fear of it, cut across many spheres of life and are very powerful motive forces. The esteem needs are behind fear of failure.

When higher needs are influential they are like constants in an equation. They play a part, and hence must be considered, in almost all significant behavior. Acceptance by others is another higher need that can become an important motive force. Consider how often the desire to be acceptable has affected your conduct. You dress in a manner that does not bring notice or criticism. You mind your table manners so as to fit in with others. In a thousand large and small ways, your conduct is regulated by the need to be acceptable. The consequences of not being acceptable to at least one other person are quite serious. Such an individual may become chronically ill. He may harbor a festering resentment and hatred of people who are popular. He may develop a sense of personal inadequacy. The point is that the higher needs are ultimately more important for total healthy functioning than are the lower needs (unless the latter are not properly gratified).

HIGHER NEED GRATIFICATION IS MORE REWARDING THAN LOWER NEED GRATIFICATION

The pleasure of an excellent meal, especially when one is hungry, is great, but it may be described as relief or comfort pleasure, relaxation, and the like. Usually, of course, the pleasurable experience is short-lived, and one again begins to experience hunger pangs. Satisfaction of higher needs leads to feelings of self-respect, self-love, self-satisfaction. Certain pleasurable experiences (the term is not to be interpreted as "sensual") are not possible without higher need gratification. What Maslow (1962) called "peak experience" is one such pleasure: the feeling of great joy at the birth of a child, or the marriage of a daughter, or graduation from school. Receiving an honor for one's work produces a sense of pride that has no substitute. Consider such emotional states as wonderment, awe, adulation, bliss, reverence, and exaltation. The gratification of the higher needs does not weaken with time. One may value such possessions for a lifetime. As a matter of fact, once an individual has experienced gratification of his higher needs, he cannot find substitutes for them through gratification of his lower needs, unless there is severe stress and consequent regression.

SIGNIFICANT QUOTATIONS FROM MASLOW

To the extent that growth consists in peeling away inhibitions and constraints and then permitting the person to "be himself," to emit behavior—"radiantly," as it were—rather than to repeat it, to allow his inner nature to express itself, to this extent the behavior of self-actualizers is unlearned, created and released rather than acquired, expressive rather than coping (1968, p. 39).*

B-lovers [love for the being of another person, unneeding love, unselfish love] are more independent of each other, more autonomous, less jealous or threatened, less needful, more individual, more disinterested, but also simultaneously more eager to help the other toward self-actualization, more proud of his triumphs, more altruistic, generous and fostering (1968, p. 43).*

B-love, in a profound but testable sense, creates the partner. It gives him a self-image, it gives him self-acceptance, a feeling of love-worthiness, all of which permit him to grow. It is a real question whether the full development of the human being is possible without it (1968, p. 43).*

The "good human being" can be defined only against some criterion of humanness. Also, this criterion will almost certainly be a matter of degree, i.e. some people are more human than others, and "good" human beings, the "good specimens" are very human. . . . A good human being (or tiger or apple tree) is good to the extent that it fulfills or satisfies the concept "human being" (or tiger or apple tree). . . . In exactly this same sense, we can pick the best specimens of the human species, people with all the parts proper to the species, with all the human capacities well developed and fully functioning, and without obvious illnesses of any kind, especially any that might harm

*© 1968. Reprinted by permission of D. Van Nostrand Company.

the central, defining, sine qua non characteristics. These can be called "most fully human" (1968, pp. 170–1).*

Now let me try to present briefly and at first dogmatically the essence of this newly developing conception of the psychiatrically healthy man. First of all and most important of all is the strong belief that man has an essential nature of his own, some skeleton of psychological structure that may be treated and discussed analogously with his physical structure, that he has needs, capacities and tendencies that are genetically based, some of which are characteristic of the whole human species, cutting across all cultural lines, and some of which are unique to the individual. These needs are on their face good or neutral rather than evil. Second, there is involved the conception that full healthy and normal and desirable development consists in actualizing this nature, in fulfilling these potentialities, and in developing into maturity along the lines that this hidden, covert, dimly seen essential nature dictates, growing from within rather than being shaped from without. Third, it is now seen clearly that psychopathology in general results from the denial or the frustration or the twisting of man's essential nature. By this conception what is good? Anything that conduces to this desirable development in the direction of actualization of the inner nature of man. What is bad or abnormal? Anything that disturbs or frustrates or twists the course of self-actualization. What is psychotherapy, or for that matter any therapy of any kind? Any means of any kind that helps to restore the person to the path of self-actualization and of development along the lines that his inner nature dictates (1954, pp. 340–41).

This inner nature is not strong and overpowering and unmistakable like the instincts of animals. It is weak and delicate and subtle and easily overcome by habit, cultural pressure, and wrong attitudes toward it. Even though weak, it rarely disappears in the normal person—perhaps not even in the sick person. Even though denied, it persists underground forever pressing for actualization (1968, p. 4).*

SUMMARY

1. Maslow questioned the traditional assumption that pain avoidance and tension reduction are the major sources of motivation for man. He proposed instead that personality scientists examine man's strivings for growth, for happiness and satisfaction.

2. Man has drives that are unlearned, unchanging, basic to his survival, and ever-present. Maslow suggested that man has within his nature tendencies toward growth, excellence, affectionate response, altruism, and the higher virtues.

3. Needs can be distorted through learning. Serious distortion of lower basic needs is strikingly evident in individuals suffering from psychophysiological disorders. The more subtle needs, also basic to man's nature, are much more readily disturbed and misdirected as a result of faulty experience.

4. Maslow made a valuable distinction between a total instinct and an instinctoid tendency. A total instinct involves all the elements of a behavioral act; these elements are biological or genetic. Although there are no full-blown instincts in man, there are instinct remnants or instinctoid tendencies. These, however, are not automatically expressed.

5. Maslow held that human needs are arranged in a hierarchy of potency and priority; the lower needs are more potent and thus take precedence over

the higher ones. Only when all of the lower needs (physiological, safety, love and belonging, esteem) are at least partially gratified can the person begin to experience the highest needs, the self-actualizing needs.

6. A need is a lack of something, a deficit state. A motive is a conscious desire, a felt impulse or urge for a specific thing. Deficit needs consist of a lack or deprivation which serves as the impelling force. Growth needs actually produce tension, but the kind experienced is positive.

REFERENCES

Adorno, T. W., Frenkel-Brunswik, E., Levinson, D. J., and Sanford, R. N. The Authoritarian Personality. New York: Harper and Row, 1950.

Allport, G. W. Pattern and Growth in Personality. New York: Holt, Rinehart and Winston, 1961.

Bowlby, J. Maternal Care and Mental Health. Geneva: World Health Organization Monograph, 1952.

Caudill, W., and Weinstein, H. Maternal care and infant behavior in Japan and America. Psychiatry 32:12–43, 1969.

Coopersmith, S. The Antecedents of Self-Esteem. San Francisco: W. H. Freeman, 1967.

Frankl, V. E. Man's Search for Meaning. New York: Washington Square Press, 1963.

Friedenberg, E. Z. The Vanishing Adolescent. New York: Dell, 1959.

Gelfand, D. M. The influence of self-esteem on rate of verbal conditioning and social matching behavior. J. Abnorm. Social Psychol. 65:259–65, 1962.

Grossack, M., Armstrong, T., and Lussieu, G. Correlates of self-actualization. J. Hum. Psychol. 6:37, 1966.

Hall, C., and Lindzey, G. Theories of Personality, 2nd ed. New York: John Wiley and Sons, 1970.

Hall, D. T., and Nongaim, K. E. An examination of Maslow's need hierarchy in an organizational setting. Org. Behav. Hum. Perform. 3:12–35, 1968.

Jung, C. G. Man and His Symbols. New York: Doubleday and Company, 1964.

Keys, A. B., Brozek, J., Henschel, A., Mickelson, O., and Taylor, H. L. The Biology of Human Starvation. Minneapolis: University of Minnesota Press, 1950.

Klein, G. S. Perception, Motives, and Personality. New York: Alfred A. Knopf, 1970.

Maddi, S. R. Motivational aspects of creativity. J. Pers. 33:330–47, 1965.

Marrow, A. J., Bowers, D. G., and Seashore, S. E. Management by Participation. New York: Harper and Row, 1967.

Maslow, A. H. Motivation and Personality, 1st ed. New York: Harper and Row, 1954.

Maslow, A. H. Deficiency motivation and growth motivation. In Jones, M. R., ed., Nebraska Symposium on Motivation. Lincoln: University of Nebraska Press, 1955.

Maslow, A. H. Toward a Psychology of Being, 1st ed. New York: Van Nostrand Reinhold, 1962.

Maslow, A. H. Toward a Psychology of Being, 2nd ed. Princeton: D. Van Nostrand Co., 1968.

Maslow, A. H. Motivation and Personality, 2nd ed. New York: Harper and Row, 1970.

Maslow, A. H. The Farther Reaches of Human Nature. New York: Viking Press, 1971.

Riesman, D. Faces in the Crowd. New Haven: Yale University Press, 1952.

Roe, A. The Psychology of Occupations. New York: John Wiley and Sons, 1956.

Young, P. T. Studies of food preference, appetite, and dietary habit: 1. Running activity and dietary habit of the rat in relation to food preference. J. Comp. Psychol. 37:327–70, 1944.

CHAPTER 9

Striving for Superiority

Alfred Adler

Alfred Adler (1870–1937)

BIOGRAPHY AND OVERVIEW

Man is a social being by nature, and is motivated more by social needs than by sexual drives. We are also conscious, not mainly unconscious. We are able to create our own destinies. We need not be the victims of primitive drives and an uncontrollable environment. We are self-conscious and capable of improving ourselves and the world around us. Our main concerns in life are a vocation, communal living, and love. These statements reflect some of the basic concepts of the great Viennese physician, Alfred Adler. They constitute a radical departure from Freudian psychoanalysis, and in fact became the ground on which the two great psychiatrists separated (see Table 9–1).

Adler was born in Vienna in 1870 and lived there until 1935, when as a result of a threat from the Nazi Regime, he moved to the United States. In 1895 he received a medical degree from the same university at which Freud had earlier studied medicine. Although he trained to be an eye specialist, he became a practicing psychiatrist. He learned of Freud and joined his movement. Freud was much impressed by Adler and appointed him the first president of the Vienna Psychoanalytic Society. It soon became apparent that Adler's views were more than an elaboration of the psychoanalytic approach; thus he was invited to state his position before the group in 1911. Subsequently, he was voted out of the association, but about one third of the members left with him. He formed a school of psychiatry of his own, which he named Individual Psychology. Adler was very concerned with the mental health of children and was instrumental in calling attention to child training. He established a child guidance clinic in Vienna and also instituted experimental classes for young children. He died suddenly in 1937, while on a lecture tour of Scotland.

TABLE 9–1 KEY CONTRASTS BETWEEN FREUD AND ADLER

Freud	Adler
Philosophical pessimism.	Philosophical optimism.
The individual divided against himself.	Essential indivisibility of the individual.
Predominantly antecedent determinants: the past.	Predominantly future outcomes determine behavior: goals, ends.
The ego is oppressed by the superego and threatened by civilization.	The individual tends to act aggressively toward the community.
Defenses of the ego. Impulsive need-driven behavior may occur when the defenses are not strong enough.	Styles of life characterized by aggression of the individual against other men. "Barricades" when active aggression has failed.
The infant has a feeling of omnipotence (hallucinatory wish fulfillment).	The child has a feeling of inferiority (relation of midget to giant).
Basic importance of libido (psychic energy), its fixations and regressions.	Symbolism of man's sexual behavior in relation to his struggle for superiority. Using sex in power plays.
Emphasis on relationship to father and mother, and Oedipus complex.	Emphasis on relationship to siblings and situations in the sibling set.
Neurosis is an inescapable effect of civilization and almost inherent in the human condition.	Neurosis is a trick of the individual to escape fulfilling his duties to the community.

Adapted from H. F. Ellenberger, *The Discovery of the Unconscious.* Basic Books, 1970, p. 627.

THE NATURE OF MAN'S INFERIORITY

Many great students of human nature have recognized human frailty and the profound sense of inferiority which seems to be so characteristic of man, but none has developed this theme as extensively as Adler (1927). Adler believed that man, unlike many other animals, is not equipped to survive as a solitary being. He does not have claws and sharp teeth to secure food and to defend himself. His senses are not as well attuned to the primitive state of existence; thus he would be an easy prey to predators. In order to survive, man had to band together into clans for mutual protection.

Consider the matter of temperature tolerance as an instance of man's frailty. In the course of a year the temperature may vary as much as 100 degrees, but most people find a range of 10 degrees comfortable. Some have difficulty adjusting to changes of three or four degrees. Thus in order to survive, man has had to exercise his ingenuity. He has had to build shelters with heating systems to protect against the cold. In the high temperatures of summer he has found relief through air conditioning. He has invented elevators and escalators to ease his burdens. He has invented refrigerators to preserve food and hundreds of gadgets and appliances to overcome one inferiority or another.

Adler, in brief, saw life as an uphill struggle from birth onward, with many skills to learn and many obstacles to overcome. In the course of the struggle the individual often experiences insecurity because of his inability to adapt to or cope with his situation. He expends much effort in bringing about security, and for the sake of preserving it, he also seeks a measure of reserve. This striving for security and "security plus" may lead to a one-sided development. The power-driven individual not only saves for a rainy day but also accumulates wealth in order to exert control over others. Wealth becomes synonymous with power.

Recognizing man's powerful struggle for survival, Adler early in his career viewed him as possessing an innate aggressive drive (Ansbacher and Ansbacher, 1956). Later he attempted to concretize this aggressive drive by proposing that it is a striving for power or superiority over others (Adler, 1930). To be strong and masterful and gain superiority is everyone's goal. Even women desire to be masculine because certain privileges relating to courting, marriage, and vocation are associated with masculinity (Adler, 1929). Adler could have predicted the movement of women's fashions toward more masculine apparel.

DEVELOPMENT OF NORMAL AND ABNORMAL STRIVINGS FOR SUPERIORITY

Adler held that man's prolonged state of inferiority exerts a profound effect upon his whole motivational system. The child, just as the adult, is always striving to improve his status. Everything significant that the child seeks is governed by a desire to overcome a profound sense of inadequacy. No matter what he accomplishes or acquires, there is always more. Life is not motivated by forces making for homeostasis or equilibrium, nor is it motivated by survival tendencies, nor is it driven by the lure of pleasure and the avoidance of pain. Adler (1930) believed that the main force behind everything man does, beyond the drive level of functioning, is the push to move from an inferior to a superior state, from minus to plus, from beneath to above. The urge for superiority takes many forms: insatiable craving to rule others in the power-driven psychopath, tyrannical wailing in the hypochondriac who controls everyone around her, energetic striving in the parent who wants to bring up his family to be contributing members of society. In thousands and thousands of ways, the human seeks to perfect his life.

The child has a vast number of things to learn. Before mastering something, he is inferior with respect to that particular thing. When he extends his sphere of activity outside the home in play with other children, a whole new source of inferiority situations is opened up. Certain standards of performance are expected, and the child who fails is dealt with harshly. As the child grows older he is brought more and more into the culture. Competition is everywhere. Games are played to win. Team against team, boy against boy, and girl against girl creates a climate of contention, of striving from an inferior status to that of superior or victor.

In school the child also encounters the signs and symbols of power. The teacher is an authority who has great influence over him. Grades and awards are given for superior performance. These awards are usually based on meeting certain requirements, regardless of how this is accomplished. In an atmosphere of continual evaluation and testing, great praise and honor are accorded those who meet the high standards of the test.

In his later years, Adler came to the conclusion that for those who are developing and functioning normally the striving for superiority is a search for self-perfection (Ansbacher and Ansbacher, 1964). This concept is similar to the notion of self-actualization proposed by Maslow and by Carl Rogers—the quality of being a fully functioning person, or at least of moving in the direction of actualizing one's potentialities. The person who has attained a high degree of superiority in the sense of perfecting the self can be considered individualized, mature, fully functioning, or self-actualized. Striving for superiority is a general human motive which is expressed in unique ways by each individual: being excused from rules, being cared for, gaining control of others, or being exempt from work. Perfecting oneself within the framework of a highly developed sense of social feeling is the healthiest expression of this striving for superiority, Adler (1939) believed. Social motives are just as much a part of human nature as the urge to be superior. To become active, however, they must be fostered and supported in the child by a tolerant and affectionate family climate. Without such encouragement, the harsher forms of superiority striving—aggressiveness and the desire for power over others—will predominate. These tendencies, characterized by selfish motives and lacking a sense of social feeling, are signs of abnormality.

UNREALISTIC EXPECTATIONS

One type of striving for absolute perfection is steadfast commitment to unrealistic goals. Such striving, often an abnormal expression of the struggle for superiority, may be harmful to personality growth and functioning if the expectations remain unfulfilled. A child may grow up with great hopes for success in school, only to experience a succession of failures. Young persons are easily trapped into looking everywhere for perfection. The young man wishes to find a perfect wife, not one who gets angry or is moody from time to time. Even the mature person searches for a car without a dent in it. Because it is so important to him he wants it to be perfect. We expect the significant events of life to be without the slightest flaw. But most aspects of living are ordinarily far from perfect; thus one who cannot make compromises or accept less than absolute perfection will suffer disillusionment and disappointment. The person who desires absolute perfection is really saying, by his behavior, that he is a superior being.

Probably the greatest source of unhappiness is failure to fulfill expectations. An unfulfilled expectation may have an additional element: a sense of personal responsibility for not being able to remedy it. Many expectations are by their very nature unfulfillable and thus inevitably lead to disillusionment.

Many young adults, for instance, approach marriage with the unrealistic expectation of finding a perfect marital partner with whom they can live in ecstasy. This is but one example of the numerous false promises that entice young people growing up in the American culture. All the media are saturated with the romance motif. When in fact these ideals are not fulfilled, the young people have a vague sense of responsibility for bringing the situation about. Frequently, the chronic dissatisfaction which pervades their marriage impels them to obtain a divorce and search separately for others who will meet their expectations of marital perfection. If the second marriages do in fact work out better than the first, the reason could be that their expectations have been tempered considerably by reality considerations; thus better choices were made and much less was demanded. Many enduring marriages exist with the partners feeling themselves to be the victims of an unjust fate. They overlook the real possibilities for a good marriage and instead resign themselves to the status of victims.

The striving for perfection is not limited to marriage but permeates all significant spheres of life. Most people, for example, have unrealistic expectations regarding vocation. A number of difficulties may arise: aspirations may be based on job status rather than on real abilities or interest. Medicine is selected by many young men because it offers so many apparent benefits. The man who expects his work to be challenging, exciting, worthwhile, and contributing to the betterment of mankind is bound to be disillusioned. Not that one's work cannot satisfy basic needs (indeed, many find work their major interest in life), but to expect from it total fulfillment or satisfaction of needs that should be met by other activities can lead only to self-pity or other abnormal reactions.

The clearest manifestations of the striving for perfection occur during adolescence. As he grows up, the child is faced with all sorts of demands. The culture prescribes how problems are to be solved. In fact, it even creates the problems for which it offers solutions. The young person may be indoctrinated into a number of systems: the etiquette system, the school system, the moral code. Being incapable of critical examination, and usually having no choice in such matters, he is instructed by rules and regulations. The dos and don'ts (even though they are arbitrary and sometimes blatantly irrational) acquire the sanction of sacredness. When the young person's critical abilities mature during adolescence, he scrutinizes these precepts because they have such a profound bearing on his style of living. In the free inquiring climate which prevails among the youth of our culture, nothing is sacrosanct. The young person questions his religion, his school, his political system, even his parents. All this questioning stems from the discontent engendered by a highly imperfect world. The young person says in effect: "I want to live a perfect life with complete happiness. I want perfect happiness for myself and everyone around me. Nothing short of perfection is acceptable. If I can't have it all, then I want none of it. There can be no compromise with perfection."

Young people do indeed have much to complain about. Imperfections abound in all institutions of their culture. Their own inner lives are fraught with turmoil. They have not yet settled on a firm sense of identity. They are not yet what they will become; thus many basic needs remain unsatisfied. They may feel alienated, outside of the main stream of things. They cry out for reforms; they do not want the establishment, but their suggested solutions are often grandiose and unworkable. They project their inner turmoil to the circumstances around them. They want fulfillment and a sense of meaning. Imperfections of all sorts are abhorred: war, racial discrimination, a polluted environment, poverty, the other ills of society. Along with all these social, economic, political, and religious changes, they desire a life of perfect happiness.

Not everyone goes through this stage of questioning and rebellion against the traditional to the same degree (Weiner, 1972). Most people question and react mildly, learning to make compromises and to accept less than perfection. The reason for the increased emphasis upon the rebellion of youth in the past few years is that young people have made themselves felt in tangible ways, not simply vocally. The striving for perfection is not a new phenomenon of our generation. It is just receiving more attention. This intensified competition fosters the striving for perfection — the belief that life can not only be better than it is, but perfect.

INFERIORITY AND COMPENSATION

Adler termed the strategy whereby one makes up for an inferiority *compensation*. Compensation helps to establish and preserve self-esteem. In the strict Adlerian sense, it means to make up for or to cover over a weakness (Adler, 1931). In a broader sense it may include such activities as eating sweets to relieve frustration, or gratifying one need in place of another which is thwarted. One may compensate for weakness by working diligently to overcome it, as for example when a stutterer works to conquer his speech difficulty and actually becomes an excellent speaker. This form of compensation, which is a manifestation of the striving for superiority, promotes healthy adaptation to life by the overcoming of a severe handicap. Such compensation might be designated *direct compensation*, because it involves a direct attack upon a weakness.

Other forms of compensation aim more to prove superiority over others than to perfect one's life. The person who masks a profound sense of inadequacy by a blustering manner or by monopolizing conversation is exhibiting a form of compensation which is maladaptive.

A subtler but also abnormal form of compensation is *overcompensation* (Adler, 1954). Overcompensation means attempting to convert a weakness into a strength, rather than accepting the weakness. The weakness is focused upon extensively, and sometimes appears to be a strong point in the person's life. This form of compensation may appear to be direct compensation because it seems to involve the overcoming of a handicap. The key to understanding overcompensation as a form of superiority striving, however, is to recognize that it involves lack of acceptance of self. The person cannot accept himself with the supposed weakness. Ordinarily the inferiority is an unalterable one, such as physique, limited talent in music, or poor sensory acuity. The behavior which constitutes the overcompensation is exaggerated: for instance, the unattractive girl who overdresses.

SAFEGUARDING TENDENCIES

Safeguarding tendencies are security measures or strategies for dealing with feelings of inferiority (Ansbacher and Ansbacher, 1956). The individual is constantly assailed by demands and pressures. These external requirements and his own needs lead to insecurity which is accompanied by anxiety, fear, anger, doubt, and other unpleasant affective states. Efforts are expended to deal with the internal or external demands when they occur, and even to anticipate them before they occur. Safeguarding strategies (in contrast to coping and adaptive procedures) may include: distorted or selective perception, prejudicial thinking, memory impairment, obstinacy, compulsiveness, general nervousness, depression, and in short, those behaviors and emotions which are considered symptoms of personality disorders. Certainly no one is free from safeguarding tendencies; everyone uses protective devices at times. But the normal individual uses them less often and in less exaggerated forms.

Adler has given an example of the safeguarding tendency in the adult nail-biter. He considered this continuation of an activity which is repeatedly criticized and blocked by parents and teachers an expression of the striving to be superior. The nail-biter has preserved his sense of integrity and independence by persisting in a habit which elicits strong negative reaction from others. The habit continues despite the pain it produces.

Again, a sickly individual may use his illness, whether real or self-induced, as a safeguarding measure. He cannot be expected to carry his share of responsibilities. He must be judged by more lenient standards, since after all he is ill, a condition which is not his fault. He enjoys not only the benefits of exemption from work but even a degree of superiority over those who grant him such privileges. In addition, illness can be used as a means of *excusing oneself* from participation in work activities. Just as others may apply less stringent standards for one who is ill, so the individual may evaluate himself in this way. He may continue to harbor great visions of the accomplishments he will someday achieve when his illness passes. A persistent illness preserves his self-esteem by keeping him out of battle and at the same time obviating the possibility of a test of his abilities. With these considerations in mind, it should not be surprising to find that many people are in a chronic state of illness. Usually this takes the form of vague aches and pains, digestive difficulties, or headaches. No treatment seems to bring about a cure, for unconsciously, the individual does not want to be cured. According to Adler (1927), his illness is a means of attaining a position of superiority: should he succeed despite his supposed sickliness, he is all the more worthy of glory because, as it were, "he accomplishes with one hand what others do with two." Adler termed the use of illness to control others the *weapon of weakness*.

FICTIONAL FINALISM: THE ROLE OF FICTIONAL GOALS

As we have seen, striving for superiority is a general motivation that takes concrete form as a striving toward a particular goal. Adler (1930) greatly emphasized the role of future goals in determining present behavior. Many aspects of present behavior can be understood only in terms of a guiding goal. With the knowledge of the guiding goal, all the elements of a behavioral unit are perceived as forming a coherent structure. This view has much in common with the Gestalt principle that the whole is different from the sum of its parts. Like the "whole" concept of Gestalt psychology, the guiding idea gives the parts a specific formal unity (Dreikurs, 1963). Frequently, a behavioral act begins with the projection of a goal, which is then followed by the specific behaviors to attain it. The behaviors would not make sense to an observer who did not possess knowledge of the goal.

Some form of striving is characteristic of all living things, but in man striving toward goals may be a conscious process, as when a young man wishes to marry a particular girl and works to win her affection. However, goal striving need not be conscious. A school boy may behave badly in class without really knowing what his purpose is. The astute teacher may understand the purpose perfectly well: the child may be wanting and striving to get attention directed toward him. Not being capable of or willing to earn it in the usual manner, he resorts to unruly behavior. The fact that the child is unaware (unconscious) of his goal does not alter the fact that his behavior is being subordinated to a goal. Taken in this sense, so-called unconscious motivation may lose some of its mystical elements. Unconscious motivation is simply motivation which one does not recognize (Adler, 1927).

Adler (1927) would have counseled one who wishes to understand the behavior of another to look for the goal which the person wishes to achieve or avoid. In therapy he would ask his patient: "Supposing that you did not have this ailment; what would you do?" The reply would usually reveal the particular thing the patient was avoiding: the hypochondriac, for example, would desire to work (Ellenberger, 1970). If one is fortunate enough to hit upon the dominant goal early in his investigation, he will find that the patient's life history, as well as his contemporary style of life, are logical outcomes of this goal. A little girl whose major goal in life is to be a wife and mother will orient her total psychological being to this end. As a little girl, she plays the role of wife and mother. As a teenager she loves to care for children. Her thinking, feelings, and reading, and practically everything she does, ready her for the goal of marriage and homemaker. Some of the major goals around which lives may be organized are: dominating others, leaning on others, withdrawing from the world, seeking wealth, craving fame, or desiring to be the most beautiful person in the world. Ultimately, there are as many guiding goals as there are people.

THE NATURE OF A FICTIONAL GOAL

In Adlerian psychology, all guiding goals are fictions (Adler, 1930). A fiction is not true or false, or right or wrong, but rather *useful or not useful*. It should serve the individual; it should have functional utility. If it does not serve him, then it should be discarded or modified. It may appear strange to say that an untruth may be useful, but an example will clear up this point.

Suppose you ask someone to name a friend. He says "John is my friend." You inquire further what it means to be a friend. He tells you that John thinks a great deal of him. They enjoy each other's company. They like to do things together. He may make the statement that John would do most anything for him. If you press him on this point, he might say that his friend would come to his rescue if he were really in need. It may happen, however, that John does not actually consider himself a friend. Then the belief which the individual has is objectively false: although he thinks John is his friend, he really is not. Yet his behavior toward John and the benefits he gains from believing that he has a true friend are genuine and valuable to him, even though they are based on a fiction. He may go on believing for years that John is his friend. He may go on, that is, until he puts the friendship to the test. He may be in serious need one day and call on "his friend" for help and to his dismay be turned down. This incident certainly should have some effect on his fictional belief. In fact, it might be sufficient to cause him to question his belief, and ultimately to change it. He now recognizes that he was operating under a delusion, a false conviction. The important point is that the fictional belief served a useful function, even though it might appear to solve problems by distortion of reality. Unlike the normal, the neurotic tenaciously clings to his beliefs even when they are demonstrably false. He refuses to see the evidence. This last point applies to psychotics even more.

Another example of a fiction which serves as powerful motivation for many Americans is the view that with much hard work and a little good luck, you can accomplish almost anything. Many people believe that work is the solution to all desires. If you want something seriously enough, you can get it by working hard. Yet there are many who work hard and never achieve their dreams. A graduate student who received poor marks complained that he worked hard throughout the semester. He had done a good deal of reading in his field. He could not understand why he was not doing well. He was reading in his field, but the trouble was that he was not reading his assignments. He wanted to read those things which interested him, not what was required to pass examinations. He was also operating under a delusion, following a useless fiction, that "reading is a sacred thing to do." This fiction has been fostered by well-meaning teachers. A physicist who devoted all his reading time to psychology would not be true to his professional obligation.

Fictions may take the form of ideals. An ideal by its very nature is never completely attainable. A teacher may desire to be excellent in her profession. To be excellent has no final limits. She can always learn more in her subject area. Certainly, she can spend more time than she does with students. She might be able to increase her preparation time, or at least increase her efficiency. The ideal can hardly be defined, let alone attained. Yet the striving for attainment is a genuine striving.

Some would hold that a belief in God is a guiding fiction which has proved valuable for man in general and for countless individuals. They hold that whether God really exists is not as important as that the belief is real. The effects produced by the fictional beliefs in God are identical to those produced by the real existence. Society as well as the individual profits from the belief.

Though much fictional thinking is useful for the person and may promote adaptive and coping behavior, some fictions are dangerous and harmful. The person who believes that power over others is a desirable thing may bend all his efforts to acquire this status. His behavior is guided by a false ideal, but it impels him toward the end of dominating those around him.

Under the influence of a guiding fiction, an individual may behave "as if" something exists or is in fact true (see, e.g., Vaihinger, 1925). Many people are convinced that their personal physician is genuinely concerned with them in a very personal way. However, they do not expect to test this conviction by attempting to socialize with him. It is as if they unconsciously knew that such a relationship could not occur. As we indicated earlier, favorable consequences may emanate from fictional beliefs. Believing that the doctor really cares is a sufficient incentive to hold one to a difficult diet, or to help him take distasteful medicine regularly. One woman who had an overweight problem would tell her friends that her doctor got angry with her when she got beyond a certain point, and before seeing him for her yearly checkup she would diet stringently. Again it should be noted that whether or not her physician was really concerned about her condition does not change the matter. Even if he were not really concerned, the fact that she believed he was kept her from losing control of a potentially dangerous situation. Her behavior was being controlled by a fictional goal, namely, to please her concerned physician. This same point may be applied to an attorney, the clerk at the store, a boss, clergyman, and anyone who serves the public. The individual who is able to engender in those he serves the conviction that he is genuinely concerned, whether he really is or not, has a valuable asset. It should be pointed out, however, that sham interest and concern is usually translated into overt behavior. It can be readily identified. The best way to induce in another the conviction that you are really interested is to cultivate genuine concern for him.

We should keep in mind that all perceptions and ideas we form are personal constructions. They frequently involve personal interpretations. This point may not be obvious with respect to simple objects such as a table, chair, or book, but it becomes quite relevant with more complex objects. Consider your interpretations of such complex concepts as greatness, love, goodness, joy, the good life, the successful parent, the serious worker, the patriot. The more abstract the ideas and beliefs are, the more fictional they are. In this sense "fictional" means personally interpreted. Our guiding goals are highly abstract; thus they are highly fictional in character. Nevertheless, there are both useful and harmful fictions.

GOAL OF LIFE

Adler spoke repeatedly of the "goal of life," as if a person has only one goal—a concept that may be confusing. Obviously a person has many, many everyday desires which set him to work toward goals. He wants to get married, buy a house, follow a career. Yet in each person there is usually one outstanding goal, conscious or not, which plays a dominant role in that person's life. It may be something like being a reasonable and likable sport, possessing more wealth than one's friends, being more attractive than anyone else, making an impression on everyone, being a good conversationalist. Sometimes the guiding goal is a secret ambition that is cherished and guarded from being discovered by others. Adler maintained that the neurotic individual usually harbors a secret ambition of being unique and extraordinary among men. He may act as if the secret ambition is being fulfilled. The point is that the concrete goals of life stem from a feeling of inferiority and can best be comprehended as expressions of the one ultimate goal of striving for superiority (Adler, 1927). They must also be interpreted through a knowledge of the person's *style of life*.

THE STYLE OF LIFE

Adler (1929) used the expression "style of life" to designate the unique configuration of characteristics identifying a person. Each style of life is unique, though the psychology of personality has not yet advanced to a point which permits adequate characterization of the unique individual. We cannot yet, so to speak, put a person on paper. While insisting on the uniqueness and complexity of styles of life, Adler in his description of them usually used general trait names, such as the power-driven individual, the optimist, the pessimist, or the seclusive orientation. He did, however, elaborate some traits which are less general but expressive of a dominant trait. For example, he described the optimistic style of life by characteristics such as courage, openness, social feeling, and so on. One can recognize a style of life much more easily than one can describe it.

The style of life is integrated, with all the components working together (Adler, 1931). Every major component has an effect on all the others. If a person is intelligent, a large portion of his behavior is influenced by this fact. In most things he does, although some behaviors are more affected by it than others, his intelligence plays a major role. A person who is egocentric often perceives, remembers, thinks, feels, and acts with a selfish attitude. Whether he is driving or playing cards or participating in a conversation, his egocentricity plays a part. Some components are more influential, more easily aroused, more central than others. In characterizing the style of life one can usually point to a single directional tendency which is the most central determinant. This, it will be recalled, is a guiding fiction.

EARLY ESTABLISHMENT OF THE STYLE OF LIFE

Like Freud, Adler (1931) held that the style of life is formed early, usually during the first five years. He pointed out that one can observe marked differences in infants right from birth. Some children are restless and easily agitated. They may have difficulty sleeping and eating. Others seem more attuned to the demands of living and demonstrate little disturbance in meeting their survival requirements (Thomas, Chess, and Birch, 1970).

The style of life becomes more complex, more unique, and more fixed with development. It includes elements which maintain and preserve it. As it is formed, all psychological processes are organized into habitual modes of perceiving, thinking, feeling, and behaving. An optimist remembers, reasons, judges, feels, and acts quite differently from a pessimist. If two individuals with different life styles experienced the same event and subsequently described what took place, the accounts would be radically different. There would be omissions and additions by both individuals that could be traced to the particular style of life. If an interpretation of the events were given, the disparity between the accounts would be still greater.

One major determinant of life style is the family environment in which the child grows. The earliest experiences are quite significant because everything is so new and unexpected. Consider such events as the first spanking, waking up cold and alone in the middle of the night, the first fall from the crib, mother and dad having a quarrel. Adler (1931) gave special weight to the position of the child in relation to brothers and sisters, *birth order*. Being the youngest boy with three older sisters must contribute something significant to the formation of a style of life, he would argue. Each of the many possible family configurations would exert a similarly enduring effect on its members. Other early influences are the temperament of the parents, their financial circumstances, and companions. Early attitudes, emotional responses, and expectations persist a lifetime.

Weak children, who often have to endure the hardship of being picked on constantly, may never get over the resultant feelings of profound inferiority in their relationships with others. They may develop forms of compensation which become characteristic. Their secret ambition may be to humiliate others, in order that they may prove their superiority. Their perceptions of events, their memories, their judgments, their emotions—all are exposed to the influences of the family atmosphere and early environment into which they are born.

Many great students of man have accepted the notion that infancy and childhood are the formative years, a period when basic habits are shaped. Certainly, more learning takes place during the first five years than during any other five-year period. Furthermore, the nature of the learning is unlike that of any other period. Children's learning is drive-related. They learn basic social skills and reactions. Their learning might be described as "gut level" learning. They learn to receive, to withhold, and to give. But Adler went beyond saying that the first five years are important formative years. He also held that the form of personality is *established* during the first five years (Adler, 1954). In other words, the basic structure is laid down and whatever modifications later occur are mere elaborations and extensions of the basic style of life.

While imprinting had not yet been discovered in Adler's day, the principles that have since been laid down (Hess, 1964) would tend to support the notion that certain time periods and appropriate experiences combine to produce learning which is quite resistant to change. Birds that mimic can be trained to utter sounds or vocalizations during a relatively brief critical period. Learning is rapid during this period but may not be possible after it. Extending this concept to childhood, early pleasurable and painful experiences (and probably attitudes, prejudices, and general orientation to life) are especially well learned and preclude being replaced by other experiences. It is certainly true, at least, that children have difficulty dealing with concepts and situations that have been blocked out of their previous experience. A child who has not been respected may not know how to respond to the regard of others, and may thereby frustrate their expression of regard to him. This same notion may apply to hurtful experiences. They foster faulty learning which interferes with later corrective learning.

STYLES OF LIFE AND STRIVING FOR SUPERIORITY

As Adler was fond of pointing out, some individuals react to their inferiority by developing a faulty style of living, while others distinguish themselves by superior achievements. The pampered child may find that he can rule his parents by making his demands conspicuously felt. The neglected child gains his superiority by withdrawing and becoming self-sufficient, although he grows up lacking social feeling, a handicap which hinders him in everything he does. The petted child wins a place of superiority through weakness. The sickly child gains his significance from the care that is given him. Adler held that in the lives of many great men one can find, if one searches diligently, either a physical or psychological inferiority which was especially difficult to bear.

Psychological inferiorities are just as powerful determinants of behavior as the more obvious physical inferiorities. A child who is adequately endowed

TABLE 9-2   THE SOCIALLY MATURE INDIVIDUAL

Respects the rights of others	Is courageous
Is tolerant of others	Has a true sense of his own worth
Is interested in others	Has a feeling of belonging
Cooperates with others	Has socially acceptable goals
Encourages others	Puts forth genuine effort

Meets the needs of the situation
Is willing to share rather than say
   "How much can I get?"
Thinks of "we" rather than just "I"

Adapted from D. Dinkmeyer, The "C" group: Integrating knowledge and experience to change behavior. An Adlerian approach to consultation. *Counsel. Psychol.* 3:63–72, 1971.

physically and mentally may aquire a terrible sense of inferiority as a result of adverse comparison with an older brother who is favored by the parents. He develops the secret goal of someday defeating and humiliating his brother and earning his parents' esteem, and this attitude may generalize to all people: he needs to have everyone's highest regards.

Children, according to Adler (1939), are not antisocial by nature. They have innate dispositions to respond with social feeling and interest, but they are also highly egocentric. Life in a community is social in almost every respect. They cannot avoid relationships with others. Success in satisfying individual needs is contingent upon success in dealing with social relationships. A warm, tolerant, supportive home atmosphere fosters the development of social feelings and social skills. Normal people want and value social relationships. They recognize that social interest is a criterion of social-emotional maturity (see Table 9–2). They accept the requirements of the culture and become contributing members. Abnormal people direct their motivation to egocentric goals and reject the culture. They are aliens in an enemy country.

Table 9–3 is a summary of the major Adlerian concepts. It depicts the differences between normal and neurotic strivings for superiority.

CRITICAL EVALUATION

Adler's concepts and principles have a wide-ranging explanatory scope. The principle of striving for superiority can be applied to many behavioral phenomena. His ideas do, in fact, highlight many major problems of life. The theory is a working tool for numerous therapists and counselors. It does serve in part the functions of describing, explaining, and predicting behavior. Adler has called attention to certain aspects of man's nature which were being neglected by the psychoanalysts: man's social nature, his conscious life, his self consciousness, his ability to construct a better world. He rejected the irrationalism of his day and stressed instead man's social nature and benign qualities.

TABLE 9–3 ADLER'S BASIC MOTIVATIONAL PRINCIPLES

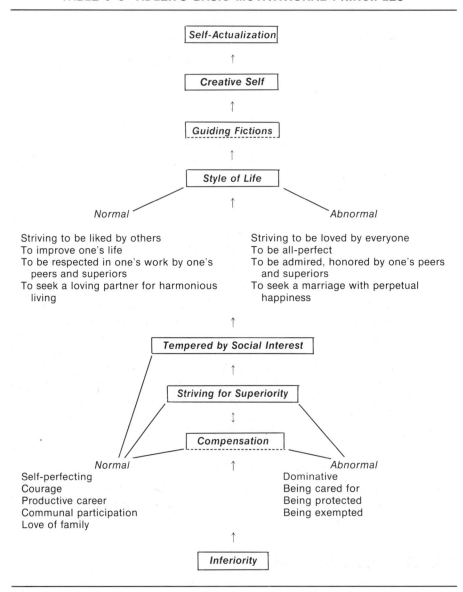

Adlerian theory has not dealt adequately with the matter of learning, although Adler did emphasize the role of learning in the formation of the style of life. Perhaps he felt that a learning theory was a matter that required the attention of specialists in the field. His theory has also been criticized on formal grounds. It is sketchy and quite general. One cannot relate its components in a systematic way. For example, how are social interest and feeling related to the various forms of striving for superiority? What are the specific determinants of a normal style of life? Of an abnormal style of life? How can one help to promote social feeling in an individual who has developed a faulty life style? Despite these shortcomings and criticisms, however, Adler's theory of personality has been a source of research ideas and therapeutic principles.

INSIGHTS FROM ADLER'S PRINCIPLE OF STRIVING FOR SUPERIORITY

Consider the many forms which strivings for superiority can take, both in yourself and others. Each person seems to have one goal which he is trying to live out. It may be something like: being liked by everyone, being a warm, friendly person, being always witty and clever, being quicker and smarter than anyone else, being a great lover. Although he may be unaware of the existence of a particular goal, his behavior makes the inference of the goal necessary. We need only observe his behavior in a variety of situations in order to become aware of his guiding goal. There are always quite specific goals, but there is usually one which is central.

Adler was fond of tracing behavior to the striving for superiority. There are many explanations for depression, but Adler in his characteristic fashion reduced it to thwarted feelings of superiority. A person feels depressed because he believes he deserves much more than he is getting. Although he may not experience the sense of superiority, his depressed state reveals it. Things should be better for him, and ultimately the explanation is that he deserves more than what prevails.

Why does a person become a pathological liar? The pathological liar may lie about the most trivial things. Some people love to deceive their listeners by making up lies. They gain a sense of superiority over those who cannot refute their fictions. The kleptomaniac (one who steals for apparent pleasure rather than from a desire for the object) is also demonstrating a striving for superiority, Adler believed. He is "pulling something off." He is "getting something for nothing."

There are those who constantly seek to gain an advantage over others through exemptions or privileges. Again, the superiority striving is evident: "If there are rules, they apply to the masses but not to me. If there is an obligation, it applies to ordinary people but not to me." The cynical person says by his behavior that nothing is good enough for him; thus nothing is worthwhile. The criminal is looking for an easy way of getting what others must work for. The cultural drop-out puts himself above the ordinary requirements of day to day living. Many forms of striving for superiority are maladaptive, and in the long run produce more difficulties for the individual. In his therapeutic work, Adler was vigilant for these abnormal forms of the striving for superiority. He found that many of his patients were trying to get away with doing less than their share of work. The neurotic, for Adler (1929), was a coward who used his illness as a means of exempting himself from the responsibilities that others had to take.

It takes courage to face up to the problems of living. It is more comfortable to watch a television mystery than to study one's lessons. It is easier to engage in recreation than to work. It is simpler to let someone else solve your problems than to do it yourself. But only by assuming one's responsibilities courageously can one live independently.

HOW WE CAN OVERCOME FEELINGS OF INFERIORITY

Many human emotions appear to stem from the desire to overcome a sense of inferiority. Consider such emotions as impatience and intolerance, envy and resentment, feeling snubbed, offended, and rejected, being avaricious or arrogant, and many other similarly negative emotions.

The inferiority which is such a pervasive part of our lives is accentuated by the fierce competition for the good things of life in our society. What can one do to overcome this profound sense of inferiority? Here are some thoughts.

1. Inferiority feelings may arise from repeated comparisons either with others or with mythical standards.

2. Instead of striving for a high level of self-esteem or egoism, one should strive for self-acceptance. In the process of maintaining a high level of egoism, one will frequently fall short and experience inferiority.

3. To have the most or the best may be far more than is necessary for a satisfying life.

4. Guiding fictions play an important part in producing a sense of inferiority. When one's goals are grandiose and fantastic, they serve only to hinder personality growth and functioning. Guiding fictions should foster healthy growth and functioning. Fictions should be constantly examined, and when they hinder adjustment and growth they should be altered.

5. One can deliberately create fictions which foster healthy functioning. For instance, an optimistic attitude toward the future sustains present activities better than does a pessimistic view. The fortunes of the future are not known; thus an optimistic approach is just as much a fiction as a pessimistic one. But the optimistic view is a better fiction than the other, so why not adopt it? One can arrive at other similar fictions in the same manner.

6. Adler has offered us an interesting way of identifying our major guiding goal in life. He termed the method "tracing the lifeline." Unlike Freud, who sought to uncover early repressed memories, Adler sought out early known memories. He believed that one could learn many highly personal matters through such earliest memories. He compared the earliest memories to one's attitudes and postures in current dreams; thus the "lifeline" consists of two poles, the significant events of the past and the manifestations of the guiding goal in the present. This method can reveal the deepest source of motivation for an individual. Often this motivation turns out to be selfish, grandiose, and impossible to attain.

7. Adler frequently found that his patients were operating on the useless side of life, and he encouraged them to change to a more useful way of living. His advice to his patients could be taken by everyone. So much of what we do is uselessly destructive, self-defeating, antisocial. We should look instead in the direction of growth, expanded outreach, courageous confrontation, social and family experiences, and the fulfillment of our native talents. In advocating usefulness and personal growth, Adler offered his own view of the ideal personality. A comparison between his well-adjusted man and Maslow's self-actualized man is provided in Table 9–4.

TABLE 9-4 IDEAL PERSONALITY
ADLER AND MASLOW

Objects of Concern	Adler's Well-Adjusted Man (Striving with Social Interest)	Maslow's Self-Actualized Man (Growth Motivation)
Self	Feelings of worth and value, courage and optimism	Acceptance of self, others, nature
Opinions of others	Independence of others' opinion	Independence, autonomy, detachment
Problems Outside Self	Overcoming common instead of private inferiority feelings	Focusing on problems outside oneself
Fellow Man	Being a fellow man, friend	Enriching interpersonal relationships and friendships
	Equal, cooperative footing with fellow man	Democratic, not authoritarian character structure
Mankind	Love of mankind	Identification with mankind
Realities of Life	At home in life, acquiescing in common advantages and drawbacks	Comfortable relations with reality, more efficient perception of it
Universe	Harmony with the universe, cosmic feelings	Oceanic feeling, mystic experience
Ethics	Religious and ethical feelings	Clarity in ethical norms and dealings, religious in a social-behavioral way
Esthetics	Better esthetic judgment. Improved mind, spontaneous social effort	Freshness of appreciation of beauty. Creativity, spontaneity in inner life, thoughts, impulses

Adapted from *J. Individ. Psychol.* 24:131–49, 1968.

8. Adler also advised us to look for a person's compensations. The particular means of striving for superiority, or the specific compensations the person seeks, reveal the nature of his felt inferiority. The belligerent individual may feel inferior about his adequacy as a male or female. The person who is always pleasant may be compensating for his strong antisocial tendencies. The compulsive person may be compensating for his tendency to be chaotic and disorganized. In any case, compensations reveal inferiorities.

COMBATING THE INFERIOR STATUS OF WOMEN

Adler wrote repeatedly of the inferior status of women. He wrote long before the current women's liberation movement, but many of his ideas are identical to those currently being proposed (e.g., Friedan, 1963). He deplored the inferior status of women and blamed the aggressive superiority of men for the roles in which women were cast. He felt that man forced inferior roles upon women so that they themselves could have advantages. Of the three major tasks of life—occupation, community, and love—women have traditionally been expected to partake of only the last.

There is no biological inferiority justifying the inferior status of women, Adler believed. Except for child-bearing, and some other qualities which characterize women, there are no differences between the sexes that favor men. While Freud stressed women's inferior status through his concept of penis envy, Adler rejected the notion that women are inherently inferior to men. He probably saw a complementary relationship between the two sexes (different but equal), with quite narrow definitions of differences. Men and women are much more alike than they are different, in his view.

Many women have rejected their own feminine identity, as Freud stated, and actively compete with men (Adler, 1927). The solution, Adler believed, is to give women much greater freedom of choice and opportunity to express themselves. In other words, the role prescriptions should be far more flexible than they were in Adler's day, and greater even than they are today.

USE AND MISUSE OF FICTIONS

An example of a useful fiction held to a greater or lesser degree by almost everyone is the belief in man's invulnerability to death. The ordinary activities of living would be impossible or greatly distorted if one constantly held in mind the thought of his own demise. All activities and strivings would pale into insignificance when viewed from such a perspective. Most people strongly cling to the fiction, although not clearly in consciousness, that they will enjoy a perpetual life. As a matter of fact, whenever something occurs—such as the loss of a loved one, or a serious injury in an automobile accident—which brings home quite vividly man's weakness and lack of real control over events, one begins to experience a vague sense of the fictional character of the belief he has been harboring. Often, in such instances, there is an acute anxiety attack. For most people day to day activity is most meaningfully comprehended in the framework of a guiding fiction of perpetual life, but even this fiction may take an unrealistic form. An example of the exaggeration of the fictional goal of living forever is the case of the person who is reckless and does not exercise adequate caution in driving, caring for his health requirements, or saving for a rainy day. Although he cannot verbalize his attitude, his behavior manifests the operation of this fiction. In this case also, if there occurs an event which intensifies his feeling of vulnerability, the operation of the fiction will decrease so drastically that he will experience a profound death anxiety. It may be seen from this example that fictions, although having no counterpart in reality, may vary in degree of usefulness; thus everyone's life is directed by fictional goals, but some are harmful and hinder adjustment while others serve it.

The person who suffers from a personality disorder formulates fictions that are not useful. In fact, because they are so vague, unrealistic, and impossible of attainment, they provide faulty objectives and lead to chronic inferiority and discontent. The young man does not strive simply to be a teacher, or even a good teacher, but the best teacher, the ideal teacher. He longs to be respected and admired by all. As a working fiction, this extreme ideal provides a highly inadequate goal model. He constantly experiences a crippling sense of inferiority and accompanying despair which impedes rather than fosters motivation. He always falls short of his ideal fiction. If the notion of a good teacher is difficult to define, the notion of an ideal teacher is still more nebulous and ill-defined. The neurotic's or psychotic's goals are tinged with the fantastic, the impossible, and hence are not even approached in actual accomplishment. The continual failure serves only to make the sense of inferiority more acute; consequently, means must be found to overcome the inferiority. These strategies may take the form of unhealthy compensations, defensiveness, hostility, cynicism, and a host of other protective devices.

TABLE 9-5   HEALTHY AND UNHEALTHY MANIFESTATIONS OF SAME GOAL

Active Constructive	*Active Destructive*

"Success"
Cute remarks
Seeks praise and
   recognition
Performs for attention
Stunts
Overambition
Impression of excellence
   (may seem to be an
   "ideal" student, but
   goal is self-elevation,
   not learning)
	"Nuisance"
	Show off
	Clown
	Restless
	Talks out of turn
	"The brat"
	Makes minor mischief
	Questions not for infor-
	   mation but for
	   notoriety
	Speech impediments
	Self-indulgence

> **Attention-Getting**
> The child's probable goal
> and his "faulty logic."

Passive Constructive	*Passive Destructive*

"Charm"
Excess pleasantness
   and charm
"Model" charm
Bright sayings, often
   not original
Little initiative
Exaggerated conscien-
   tiousness
"Southern belle,"
   (often the "teacher's
   pet")
	"Laziness"
	Clumsiness, ineptness
	Lack of ability
	Lack of stamina
	Untidiness
	Fearfulness
	Bashfulness
	Anxiety
	Frivolity
	Performance and read-
	   ing difficulties

Note: Although the active constructive traits would be most productive of healthy living according to Adler, one can still detect superiority strivings. (Adapted from D. Dinkmeyer, The "C" group: Integrating knowledge and experience to change behavior. An Adlerian approach to consultation. *Counsel. Psychol. 3:*63–72, 1971.)

TABLE 9–6   USEFUL AND HARMFUL FICTIONS

Normal Person	*Neurotic Person*
Alters his fictions when they are no longer useful.	Chooses his fictions on the basis of appeal rather than usefulness.
Moderates his fictions when they cause repeated frustration.	Clings to his fictions tenaciously, even when they produce hurt and frustration.
Has at least partial awareness of the unreality of his fictions.	Adopts fictions that are grandiose and idealistic.
Derives the benefits of certain of his fictions without putting them to the test, because he knows the difference between a hypothesis and a fiction.	Treats his fictions as if they were hypotheses to be put to the test, but responds irrationally to the outcome.
Careful to adopt fictions which will foster living when there is absence of knowledge about the proper course of action.	Frequently unconscious of his fictions and reacts to their failure with faulty adaptive responses rather than by changing the harmful fictions.
Willingly examines the effectiveness of his fictions.	Unwilling to examine his fictions with respect to their utility value.

Note: A hypothesis has value only if it is tested and confirmed. Before visiting the supermarket on Sunday, I may call to see if it is open. A *fiction* is useful or not: I believe that the people who run the supermarket are honest; thus I do not weigh and measure every item I purchase. If it is called to my attention that they are dishonest, I alter my fiction. However, some fictions (such as belief in divine providence) cannot be tested.

A person need not be conscious of his guiding fiction for it to be active. Adler believed that most people think that they are pursuing one end, whereas the real end is quite different. A woman may state that she likes to be friendly with everyone, but in fact her behavior may indicate that she is seductive of men and jealous of other women. Obviously, the individual is aware of some of his goals, but he may not be aware of his overriding goal, the one which is the pivotal point of his life and which subordinates all the others. Degree of awareness of goals is an indication of degree of normalcy.

To sum up, man's experiences are brought together in the form of fictions. Fictions are cognitive representations of events. They may be thought of as cognitive constructs, frames of reference which the person uses to depict the events of the world in a personal way. Unable to have an exact picture of things as they really are, we always structure our own ideas of them. These ideas are usually centered around a single major goal, or guiding fiction, which becomes the principal focus of our activity. A single guiding fiction may have both healthy and unhealthy manifestations (see Tables 9–5 and 9–6). Obviously, if the interpretations are completely false, behavior which is based on them will be highly maladaptive. For most people fictional representations are constantly in a state of flux to meet the requirements of reality.

SUMMARY

1.   Human behavior is largely motivated by striving for superiority to compensate for a sense of inferiority. Superiority may take the form of power over others or a striving for perfection and completion. The striving from inferiority to superiority takes concrete shape as a striving to attain a goal which is an ideal — such as being loved by all, being always self-controlled, being the most glamorous person, or being famous. The goal is a fiction because it cannot be attained, although it exerts much influence upon behavior.

2.   The goal, or guiding fiction, may be unrecognized, but its effects are manifest in the behavior of the individual. Behavior can be adequately explained only by inferring the existence of the guiding fiction. Since there are degrees of awareness of the goal, a large component of the unconscious for Adler is the motivation engendered by the guiding ideal. The weak, frail, helpless child may have the unconscious goal of ruling the family by requiring assistance and solicitude. The child's illness may be perpetuated if his goal is fulfilled by the other family members.

3.   The dominant goals in our lives may be thought of as the ultimate causes of our behavior. They may be considered organizing principles which are the root of most of our striving. A man who has the fictional goal of being superior to others may strive to gain this superiority through possessing a great deal of wealth. Everything he does which really counts with him flows from this basic motivation. His training is guided by this fiction; his actual career activities are directed to this end. Even his leisure pursuits are subordinated to his guiding fiction. Some of the typical fictions which motivate people are: financial security, vocational freedom, an all-embracing love relationship, a life of recognition, a life of perfect happiness.

4.   Given the nature of children, their early circumstances, and their fictional goals, consistent patterns of behavior are evolved which become fixed and characteristic of each individual. The enduring components of the personality constitute the style of life. Adler described the style of life with an analogy to a play: all the roles make a coherent picture with the plot as the guiding theme.

5.   Biological and environmental factors are not direct causes of behavior but are transformed by the style of life. One who has a high energy level may lash out at a world he sees as hostile, while another individual with a style of life permeated with strong social feeling converts his energy to family, vocational, and civic matters. Heredity and environment are molded according to the style of life.

6.   A major component of the style of life is the unique interpretation of the world and self which takes shape early in childhood and becomes increasingly pervasive with development. These interpretations are general orientations to life (Allport, 1961, calls them proceptive directions), such as pessimism or optimism, desire for power versus striving for personal perfection, a self-

directed approach to life versus a dependent clinging to others who are perceived as more powerful than oneself.

7. Each individual is so inextricably involved in a social context that personality cannot be considered apart from one's social environment. Social and historical information must be incorporated into any attempt to know a particular individual; data from psychological tests, such as scores on intelligence or interest tests, would be meaningless if taken alone because they would not reveal the style of life.

8. Social feeling, or social interest, is innate in man, not the result of repression and sublimation of selfish motives. Although innate, it must be nurtured by a favorable family climate. A family atmosphere which values competition at all cost and distrust of everyone may block the growth of social feeling in the children. Life is a balance between social feeling and personal advancement. Normalcy can be gauged by the degree to which the social considerations predominate over the selfish ones.

SUGGESTED READINGS

Adler, Alfred. Practice and Theory of Individual Psychology. New York: Harcourt, Brace and
    World, 1927.
        Adler presents a rather complete statement of his theory of personality in this book. He introduces such principles as "striving for superiority," "style of life," "creative self," "fictional finalism," and "social interest."

Science of Living. New York: Chilton, 1929.
        This is a highly readable account of Adler's basic principles, designed for the layman and intended as a book on mental health.

The Education of Children. Chicago: Henry Regnery Company, 1930.
        In this book Adler seeks to apply the principles of mental health to the school setting. He is guided by the view that formal education should include knowledge of and practice in the art of living. He also introduces his pioneer ideas on group counseling and family therapy.

The Problem Child. New York: G. P. Putnam's Sons, 1963.
        Adler presents clinical cases which comprise faulty life styles. He describes and explains these life styles in the light of his theory of personality.

Ansbacher, H. L., and Ansbacher, Rowena, R. The Individual Psychology of Alfred Adler. New
    York: Basic Books, 1956.
        Two devoted disciples of Adler have collaborated to bring together a series of excerpts from his original writings. Adler's theoretical thinking is represented in an evolutionary perspective.

REFERENCES

Adler, A. Practice and Theory of Individual Psychology. New York: Harcourt, Brace, and World,
    1927.
Adler, A. Problems of Neurosis. London: Kegan Paul, 1929.
Adler, A. Individual psychology. *In* Murchison, C., ed., Psychologies of 1930. Worcester, Massachusetts: Clark University Press. 1930. Pp. 395–405.
Adler, A. What Life Should Mean to You. Boston: Little, Brown and Company, 1931.

Adler, A. Social Interest. New York: G. P. Putnam's Sons, 1939.

Adler, A. Understanding Human Nature. New York: Fawcett, 1954.

Allport, G. W. Pattern and Growth in Personality. New York: Holt, Rinehart and Winston, 1961.

Ansbacher, H. L. Alfred Adler, individual psychology and Marilyn Monroe. Psychology Today III (February, 1970):42–5.

Ansbacher, H. L., and Ansbacher, R. R., eds. The Individual Psychology of Alfred Adler. New York: Basic Books, 1956.

Ansbacher, H. L., and Ansbacher, R. R., eds. Superiority and Social Interest. Evanston, Illinois: Northwestern University Press, 1964.

Dinkmeyer, D. The "C" group: Integrating knowledge and experience to change behavior. An Adlerian approach to consultation. Counsel. Psychol. 3:63–72, 1971.

Dreikurs, R. Individual psychology: The Adlerian point of view. In Wepman, J. M., and Heine, R. W., eds., Concepts of Personality. Chicago: Aldine Publishing Company, 1963. Pp. 234–56.

Ellenberger, H. F. Discovery of the Unconscious. New York: Basic Books, 1970.

Friedan, B. The Feminine Mystique. New York: Dell, 1963.

Hess, E. H. Imprinting in birds. Science 146:1129–39, 1964.

Thomas, A., Chess, S., and Birch, H. G. The origin of personality. Scientific American 223: 102–09, 1970.

Vaihinger, H. The Philosophy of "As If." New York: Harcourt, Brace and Company, 1925.

Way, L. Adler's Place in Psychology. New York: Collier, 1962.

Weiner, I. Perspectives on the modern adolescent. Psychiatry 35:20–31, 1972.

PART V

Conflict: Intrapsychic and Psychosocial

The first chapter of this section focuses upon conflicts resulting from the structures of personality as proposed by Freud: the id, ego, and superego. The personality structures will be considered from the standpoint of two major conflicts: those which exist between the individual and his environment (*psychosocial* conflicts), and those which exist within the individual himself (*intrapsychic* conflicts). Many theorists accept the significance of conflict in man's life, but none has given this aspect as much attention as did Freud.

In this section we shall also discuss the ideas of the brilliant psychiatrist, Karen Horney, on conflict. Like Freud, Horney delineated conflicts both within the person himself and between the person and his environment. She viewed the latter as caused by basic needs which the individual cannot deal with adequately. These needs may be grouped under three basic orientations to life: moving toward, moving away from, and moving against people. In the normal person the orientations are taken flexibly and in accordance with the prevailing situation and the momentary needs. In the case of the neurotic, one orientation becomes fixed, irrespective of its appropriateness to need gratification or to the existing situation. Horney's concept of the major internal conflict is centered upon the discrepancy between the *real self* and the *ideal self*. Freud had not elaborated the role of the ideal self, and Horney filled in this gap, although as will become evident, her thinking about personality was quite different from Freud's. We will consider some of her differences with Freud when we get to her chapter.

THE NATURE OF CONFLICT

A conflict exists when two or more incompatible motives, intentions, or goals are active at the same time. The specific nature of conflict involves the inability to satisfy opposing needs or to secure competing alternatives. One or more of the alternatives must be abandoned. Sometimes the alternatives are mutually exclusive: *to satisfy one excludes the possibility of satisfying the other*. In many conflict situations, all the alternatives are undesirable. In such instances, the choice is a matter of selecting the least undesirable course. Conflicts vary in degree of significance for the individual and also in duration. Some conflicts come and go because they are centered about a momentary situation; others endure a lifetime because they stem from the very nature of man, or from the relation of the individual to his environment.

If a basketball game you wish to attend occurs at the same time as a play you want to see, the result is a state of conflict. The conflict in this instance is not very important because nothing of real significance to your personality is at stake, and furthermore, the resolution of the conflict is not difficult. No matter which alternative you finally settle upon, you are going to be doing something you enjoy. Nevertheless, in order to cope with this relatively mild conflict you must make some sacrifice—forego some pleasure you would like to have. If the play will be scheduled at another time, you can attend the basketball game now and see the play later; thus you can accomplish both objectives. Strange as it may seem, some people have difficulty resolving even such a simple conflict as this one because they have not trained themselves to endure frustration, or because they have not learned to accept compromise.

Many conflicts are not so easily resolved, and the consequences of such conflicts may profoundly affect the whole course of personality development. Conflicts which are inherent in man's nature, such as the opposition of basic impulses by a rigid conscience, have widespread effects on personality growth and functioning. Such conflicts may be a source of personality malformation or chronic psychobiological disturbance.

FRUSTRATION

Conflicts, whether mild or severe, produce frustration. A knowledge of frustration is indispensable for an appreciation of the role of conflict in human life; therefore, we will touch upon this topic briefly. Frustration is experienced as a highly unpleasant state when basic needs are in conflict. Because frustration is experienced as tension, it serves as a motive state which instigates some sort of action to relieve the tension. The action is either directed toward elimination of the cause of frustration or simply endeavors to alleviate the tension. The conflicts which are rooted in man's very nature leave the person in a perpetual state of frustration if they are not properly resolved. Environmental obstacles and personal limitations may also produce frustration (Morgan and King, 1972), but *motivational conflicts* are its most important cause.

The nature of frustration is difficult to specify beyond the notion that it is a tension state. It consists of (1) a condition of deprivation, and (2) an inability to remove the source of frustration. Deprivation in itself is insufficient as a defining quality of frustration. An arctic explorer may be alone, but he is not lonely because he has chosen to forego companionship for the sake of his work. Being deprived of companionship is frustrating when the individual wishes to be with friends but cannot do so. The inability to remove the source of blocking is the major defining factor. The person remains helpless to do anything about the tension. Freud believed that under severe frustration a person is reduced to the helplessness of infancy, being totally at the mercy of forces over which he has no control. This feeling is revived when the person is under severe stress.

MOTIVATIONAL CONFLICTS

As we indicated previously, motivational conflicts may be divided into two general categories: psychosocial (conflicts between the person and his environment) and intrapsychic (conflicts which exist within the person himself).

An example of psychosocial conflict is the continual opposition between individual desires and actual punishment from the environment, or the threat of it. At first the child's self-seeking motives are blocked or diverted by the parents. Later this function is taken over by other agencies and institutions of authority: teachers, bosses, peers, legal and religious authorities. External pressures which block individualistic goals are always present. The unlimited good and welfare of the individual members of an organized group are sacrificed for the good of the whole. If every person acted only for himself without any organized controls, except those resulting from the brute force of others whose rights were being violated, human culture would not have developed or certainly could not survive. Each member of a society sacrifices some of his egoistic motives for the sake of the whole, and in the long run benefits a great deal, because his rights are also protected in the process, although he must necessarily experience a certain amount of need frustration. Law enforcement authorities, custom, tradition, and other social forces act to pressure group members to forego unlimited egoistic aims (Freud, 1930).

At every stage in life, there are constant pressures to lessen one's self-seeking demands; in addition, all members of society do not have equal possibilities for gratification. Some people are simply less gifted by nature; in other instances, unreasonable or uncontrollable circumstances block the fulfillment of goals. Racial prejudice is an example of such circumstances. It should be remembered that in the psychosocial conflict, the opposition exists between the individual acting in his own behalf and the restraining forces of his society. The purest form of this conflict applies to young children before the development of cognitive processes which enable them to anticipate external punishment. Normally the conflict pits the egoistic motive against the fear of, or motive to avoid, punishment. One is caught in the conflict between egoistic desire and potential reprimand; thus this conflict is really a motivational conflict.

Intrapsychic conflicts comprise opposing tendencies within the personality which are so basic that they are not eradicable. Most notable of these conflicts is the opposition between *drives* and *conscience.* The person has a strong desire to do a certain thing but conscience says no. He wavers between the strong desire, on one hand, and the equally strong proscription against it on the other. The conflict is internal; he may be described as a house divided against itself. Compromise as a means of resolving such conflicts leaves the person with some frustration because the opposing forces are vital aspects of personality. If the person allows his impulses outlet, the activity of conscience is intensified and the outcome is guilt and self-depreciation. The dictates of conscience are not easily dispensed with. These matters will be considered more extensively when we discuss the relationships among the three structures of personality—id, ego, and superego—proposed by Freud; for the present, an overview will suffice.

FOUR TYPES OF CONFLICT

We have divided conflicts into two major categories, namely, intrapsychic and psychosocial, but there are other schemas as well. We may delineate four types of conflict: *approach-approach, avoidance-avoidance, approach-avoidance,* and *double approach-avoidance* (see Table V–1).

TABLE V–1   FOUR TYPES OF CONFLICT

Type of Conflict	Number of Alternatives	Resolution	Situation Representatives
Approach-Approach	2	Choice of one or the other	+ ⟵— PERSON —⟶ +
Avoidance-Avoidance	2	Indecision, or choice of a third alternative, or vacillation, or choice between two negatives	– —⟶ PERSON ⟵— –
Approach-Avoidance	1	Ambivalence (liking and disliking the same object)	PERSON —⟶ + ⟵— –
Multiple Approach-Avoidance	2 or more	Indecision, or choice of a third alternative, or vacillation, or choice of one of the alternatives (weighing the sum total of positive features and negative features)	– —⟶ ⟵— – PERSON + ⟵— —⟶ +

Adapted from Norman L. Munn et al.: *Introduction to Psychology,* 2nd ed., p. 509. Copyright © 1969, Houghton Mifflin Company. Used by permission.

Approach-Approach Conflict

The approach-approach conflict consists of two equally attractive but mutually exclusive goals. If the goal objects are not only equally attractive but also motivationally significant for the individual, the conflict may be severe. Normally, however, the approach-approach conflict is not highly stressful. For one thing, whichever alternative is selected, the outcome gratifies a motive.

We have already given an example of this type of conflict in the case of choosing between the basketball game and the play. Another example is choosing between two sweater styles, when only one can be purchased. The pure form of this conflict is rare because there are usually negative elements in each of the alternatives.

Avoidance-Avoidance Conflict

In the avoidance-avoidance conflict one is caught between two or more negative choices. If the unattractive choices involve important motives and the choices are approximately equal in undesirability, then the conflict may be very intense. Although in some instances the person caught up in an avoidance-avoidance conflict simply escapes from the situation or refuses to choose an alternative, there are usually other "forcers" that pressure the individual to make a choice. A mother may confront her child with the delightful offer: "Either eat your spinach, or go to bed." Of course, the child wants neither alternative and would prefer to escape the conflict by going out to play, but the mother forces him to make a decision.

The avoidance-avoidance conflict can be extremely frustrating because the choices are plainly unpleasant. Consider the case of the girl who is faced with the choice of marrying someone she does not love, or risking the possibility of not meeting anyone else who is interested in her. There is no pleasant way of resolving her dilemma. In like manner the unfortunate worker who is given the choice between being fired or resigning has little consolation with either alternative. Although Freud did not use the same name for this conflict, he certainly recognized its crucial role in man's life. He held that many of man's difficulties are the result of continual opposition between conscience and impulse, or between external forces and basic drives. If the individual yields to the external forces or to his conscience, he continues to experience the tension of his unfulfilled drives. But if he satisfies his drives, he will come into conflict with the power of external authorities or his own conscience. The only realistic solution is some kind of compromise, but compromise would necessarily result in a certain amount of tension.

Approach-Avoidance Conflict

In the approach-avoidance conflict, the same goal has both positive and negative elements. The choice is difficult because the undesirable elements are not wanted, but they accompany the desirable ones. One may like certain things about his job—location, hours, pay—but he may strongly dislike his boss. He may be described as being in an approach-avoidance conflict regarding his job. We may both like and dislike the same thing to a high degree. A person may be highly attracted to someone of the other sex, and just as strongly repelled because of certain characteristics.

Psychologists have termed this particular state *ambivalence,* which means being attracted and repelled by the same object. A man may both like and dislike his wife, his mother, his boss—in fact, a great many things in his life. Seldom is anything completely the way we want it to be: thus one of the most basic lessons of mental health is to learn to accept the undesirable with the desirable.

Double Approach-Avoidance Conflict

This conflict is an elaboration of the approach-avoidance conflict in that two or more goal objects, each having both positive and negative features, are involved. A student may be attempting to choose between two colleges, each of which has some features he likes and some he dislikes. This is one of the commonest types of conflict encountered in real life, and like the approach-avoidance conflict, it necessitates accepting the undesirable with the desirable.

In the double approach-avoidance conflict, it is necessary to weigh the qualities of the alternatives carefully to make the best choice. The frustration resulting from the conflict itself may hamper the use of the cognitive processes (Dollard and Miller, 1950). Thus one is wise to seek the help of a disinterested party, such as a counselor or friend, if conflicts are very intense. The tension level increases with the severity of the conflict and makes the resolution more difficult. In dealing with conflicts, one should take steps to keep the tension as minimal as possible.

CHAPTER 10

Id, Ego, and Superego

Sigmund Freud

Sigmund Freud (1856–1939)

LEVELS OF CONSCIOUSNESS

CONSCIOUS, PRECONSCIOUS, AND UNCONSCIOUS

Freud began his medical practice in 1885, specializing in the treatment of the so-called nervous and mental disorders, which at that time were poorly understood. He heard about the work with hypnosis of the great neurologist, Charcot, in Paris. After receiving a grant from the University of Vienna, Freud spent several months observing the French doctors using hypnosis with neurotic patients. He was much impressed by their demonstrations. His abiding interest in the study of the unconscious was inspired by what he observed. The phenomenon of posthypnotic amnesia, for instance, puzzled him: a patient in a deep hypnotic trance would recall the events that took place in a previous hypnotic state, but he would be unable to recall the same events in the waking state. Then there was the phenomenon of posthypnotic suggestion: the patient would carry out a suggestion given during the hypnotic state even several days later; yet there was lack of awareness of the cause of his behavior. Furthermore, many of the symptoms which are commonly observed among neurotics could be induced by suggestion while an individual was in the hypnotic state. Deeply impressed by these phenomena, Freud began his medical treatment of neurotics by using hypnosis. Although he eventually abandoned the use of hypnosis and replaced it with his own psychoanalytic therapy, his interest in the dynamics of the unconscious, kindled by his early work with hypnosis, continued throughout his professional life.

TABLE 10–1　LEVELS OF CONSCIOUSNESS

Conscious	Preconscious	Unconscious
Awareness as a result of external stimulation or revived inner experiences	Latent memory arising spontaneously and deliberately or through association with current stimulation	Mental storehouse of past
Present moment of awareness	Between conscious and unconscious	Not bound by moral obligation or restriction
Awareness of identity	Filters between the conscious and unconscious	Ordinarily inaccessible

One of the cornerstones of Freud's system of concepts was his strong belief in the division of the psyche into different layers which at times oppose each other. What a person experiences consciously is only a small portion of his mental life and may in fact be a distortion of the true motives which exist unconsciously. Conflicting motives may create so much frustration for a person that they are made unconscious.

Obviously, one does not experience everything he knows at every moment; actually, momentary awareness constitutes a minute part of total possible recall and current stimulation. Thus Freud distinguished between the conscious and the preconscious systems on the one hand, and the unconscious on the other (see Table 10–1). Consciousness is the awareness that occurs as a result of external stimulation or the revival of inner experiences, or both in some combination. The preconscious consists of latent memories, which can be brought to consciousness deliberately, or which arise through association with current experiences. The largest and most significant realm of the mind is the unconscious system. In fact, Freud defined psychoanalysis as the *science of the unconscious.* Although the unconscious system is not experienced directly, it has profound effects on the contents and operation of conscious and preconscious activity.

THE MEANING OF THE UNCONSCIOUS

A great deal of controversy centers around the notion of the unconscious. Because Freud stressed its place in personality so strongly, and because his reputation is so outstanding, the topic deserves serious consideration. It should be pointed out, however, that Freud was not the first to recognize the unconscious, nor was he the only one to explore its operations. As a matter of fact, Carl G. Jung gave still more weight to the unconscious than Freud, and viewed it as playing a greater part in personality. Jung's views, nevertheless, are not as popular and widely known as Freud's.

One of Freud's earliest insights into the dynamics of motivation was that abnormal behaviors could be caused and sustained by hurtful early experiences which had apparently been forgotten. (This peculiar kind of forgetting he later termed *repression*.) The unpleasant experience was alive in the unconscious realm of the psyche and caused disturbances in consciousness and behavior. A wife or husband might have unaccountable difficulty with the sexual aspects of marriage as a consequence of a traumatic sexual experience in childhood. If one consciously experiences a powerful emotion, such as fear or guilt, it would be understandable that sexual activity or any other vital need might be disturbed. If one assumes that the same processes which occur consciously can also take place unconsciously, as Freud held (and assumes that these could be preserved by being made unconscious), the unconscious processes would serve the same functions as those experienced consciously. The significant difference is the element of *awareness:* one whose behavior and experience is under the influence of the conscious motive can at least take steps to alleviate the condition, whereas one who is under the influence of an unconscious motive can neither understand nor change his behavior. If I am unconsciously angry with a friend, I can do nothing to alter the situation, but unconscious anger may have many outlets, and these may have many peculiar manifestations: impulsive outbursts, inconsistent behavior, fluctuation of emotions.

In general, there are two meanings of unconscious: (1) unconscious as *unawareness* and (2) unconscious as a *layer of the psyche* (Freud, 1933). This distinction requires some elaboration. A man may have the habit of biting his lower lip when he is under stress, but not realize it until someone calls the matter to his attention. His mannerism could be considered unconscious in the first sense; his behavior lacks the quality of awareness. A child may defy his teacher for a reason which the child does not know, but to the trained observer the explanation for the defiance may be obvious: the child does not receive the attention he wants by ordinary compliance with regulations; thus he resorts to other measures. The purpose of his behavior is outside his awareness; the behavior may be said to be governed by motives of which he is momentarily unaware. He may come to "understand" his behavior if it is explained to him or if he spontaneously recognizes his motivation.

The first meaning of unconscious mental processes seems to lessen the mystery which the second meaning creates. According to this first view, there is no independent layer of mental activity which is inaccessible, only a lack of full cognition. Freud probably would have accepted the phenomena covered by the foregoing explanation, but he could have pointed to some striking but common experiences which he believed prove the existence of an unconscious mind which is independent of the conscious one.

Evidence for the Existence of the Unconscious Mind

According to Freud (1917), the unconscious has a life of its own. Among other things, it is made up of basic psychobiological motives which oppose conscious motives and thus produce the major conflicts of life. Freud held that we have unconscious thinking, unconscious wishes, and unconscious conflicts which may directly affect our behavior. They exert a great deal of influence upon conscious and preconscious mental activity. If the man who habitually bites his lip continues to do so even after he is made aware of his mannerism, the *meaning or purpose* of the habit is in the unconscious. Ordinarily he cannot discover this meaning or purpose. The example thus becomes an instance of the operation of the unconscious in the second sense: as an independent layer or level of the psyche having a life of its own.

Another source of evidence for the existence of the unconscious is "forgetting" which serves an obvious purpose. A person may completely "forget" an appointment until it is too late to meet it. Without using a great deal of analysis, it can be shown to the person that the "forgetting" deliberately kept him from the appointment because it was an unpleasant or threatening event (Glucksberg and King, 1967). The fact that the person later remembers the appointment indicates that the "forgetting" was only temporary, and hence not really forgetting. Missing the appointment, of course, does not really solve anything; hence one would suspect that the desires which were active to block the recall were not conscious and therefore were unconscious. The behavior of the person was in the service of an unconscious desire rather than a conscious one.

A variety of similar situations seem to point to the operation of unconscious motives and thoughts. Slips of speech (errors which express what the person really feels or believes) are also difficult to explain without invoking the concept of unconscious motives (Freud, 1901). Usually what the person has said turns out to represent true feelings which may have gone unrecognized because they were unacceptable to the person. A child might mistakenly announce to a counselor that he hates his parents because they are so good to him, when he meant to say that he loves them. His true feelings are expressed by the slip of speech.

Certain accidents may be the outcome of unconscious wishes to hurt oneself. The person who is "accident prone" (the victim of many accidents) is a good example of the operation of an unconscious self-destructive wish. Quite often there is an inconsistency in the person's behavior. He might be quite observant and cautious with respect to certain activities, but totally unreceptive and reckless in regard to others. Such discrepancies would be difficult to explain without assuming the operation of unconscious wishes. We can often detect unconscious motives, Freud believed, from observation of apparently careless behavior.

Something of the powerful control which the unconscious may exert is illustrated in the following example of a woman who probably had a strong self-punishing motive. A bright young woman had the habit of always misplacing her car keys. When she arrived home she would unload her packages and her keys at the first convenient place, and inevitably the keys were brushed onto the floor or into a remote corner. When she needed the keys, she would not be able to find them, and the search would cause her to become panicky about being late. Her friends and her husband advised her repeatedly to make a habit of putting the keys in a set place; but, strangely enough, she disregarded this advice. The husband asked a counselor about this strange behavior, and he was told to purchase four or five sets of keys which were to be placed at strategic points around the house. This simple solution turned out to be adequate, although at times she loses all but one set. From this example, one may gain some appreciation of the primitive nature of the unconscious. The strategy which the counselor suggested was actually a means of "outwitting" the interference of the unconscious. In this particular case, the woman had a poor image of herself because she was obese.

Freud pointed out the operation of unconscious motives in an unsuspected place: criminality. Commonly the criminal experiences guilt or remorse after the commission of a crime, but the occurrence of guilt before the crime, although not directly felt, may operate to lead the person to commit the crime as a form of self-punishment. In other words, the offender may commit the crime because like the young woman who lost her keys, he unconsciously wants to be punished. This strange interpretation needs to be demonstrated, of course, in any particular case. Freud pointed to the complete disregard of precautions in some cases of criminality.

Some people neglect matters of health in such a way as to suggest the operation of an unconscious desire to hurt themselves. An overweight person who has a serious heart condition may continue to overeat despite repeated warnings from his physician. Many people go on smoking cigarettes, even well-informed and otherwise responsible persons, despite overwhelming evidence of the harmfulness of this habit (Wolitzky, 1967).

For Freud, the most convincing evidence of the existence of the unconscious as an independent layer of the psyche was personality disorders. He held strongly to the principle of *psychic determinism*—that any psychological event has an adequate explanation or cause. Antecedent conditions must account fully for the event. With respect to symptoms, the application of this principle means that symptoms are explainable; they do not just happen. Furthermore, they have meaning for the person; they serve a purpose. If the purpose is not consciously recognized, then the symptom is serving an unconscious motive of which the person is unaware.

Freud (1925) arrived at the notion that symptoms serve, or stem from, the unconscious through cases similar to the following. A young woman came in for treatment complaining that she was unable to do her work at home because of paralysis of one arm. (A medical examination revealed no organic cause which could explain the mysterious symptom.) She was caring for her invalid father, who was a widower and had no one else to care for him. Because she would not forsake this obligation, her fiancé broke their engagement, and soon afterward the paralysis developed. Since there was no apparent physical weakness or conscious motivation causing the symptom, Freud came to the unorthodox conclusion that the symptom must be serving an unconscious motive. But what could that be?

He reasoned that consciously the girl could not accept herself as harboring hostility toward her father. She certainly could not injure him, at least not consciously. But in her unconscious motives, which were not bound by any sort of moral obligation or restriction, she desired the paralysis because it was a way of expressing her hostility. Because she now was also ill, she could not be expected to care for her father. In fact, she needed care herself. Her symptom also served the purpose of soothing her remorse over the loss of her fiancé. After all, had she married, she would now be unable to carry on the responsibility of a home; therefore, although the breakup was terribly painful, it happened for the best in the long run, she reasoned. The symptom was definitely related to the problems the woman had.

In this case we can readily perceive the operation of strong conflicts between powerful unconscious motives. The young woman could not deal with her conflicts consciously; thus she resorted to unconscious solutions which really were quite irrational because they did not solve her problems. She neither helped her father in his time of need, nor did she resolve her own difficulties. She wanted marriage and freedom, and in the end failed miserably at satisfying her needs. She tried to solve her problems in a primitive way, by getting sick herself. Admittedly, she was in a difficult situation, but her solution, which was largely unconscious, only gave her some relief from her conflicts and did not resolve them.

Many common symptoms were difficult to explain in Freud's day, and for that matter are still not explainable to everyone's satisfaction. They are especially incomprehensible to the one who has them. A compulsion is a fixed behavior pattern which is repeated again and again. The person who feels compelled to perform an act cannot understand the reason behind it. He knows only that the urge comes rather spontaneously and that if he does not carry it out, he experiences anxiety. He experiences the urge consciously, and he also experiences the tension consciously if he does not perform the activity, but what is not experienced on a conscious level is the motivation behind the compulsion. He is driven to perform something over and over, but he has no idea why. Many forms of behavior may become compulsions. A woman may spend all her time cleaning her home. The home may appear immaculate to others, but to her it is dirty and she must clean it. Another person may have a handwashing compulsion, and as a consequence wash his hands a hundred times a day, even to the point of damaging the skin. If there is not a conscious motivation for this behavior, there must be an unconscious one, Freud reasoned. Lack of knowledge on the part of the sufferer regarding the cause of the strange behavior does not mean that there is no cause.

One point which Freud (1933) made is that when a conscious motive or conflict is made unconscious, *it is preserved* and continues to affect behavior as if it were conscious. If one cannot discover the cause of his symptoms, presumably there is no way of eliminating them. Whatever maintains the symptoms continues to operate because the person cannot identify the cause.

Repression

In order to understand the unconscious and its operation, we should know something about the process of repression (Freud, 1914). By means of this process, the content of the unconscious is increased; that is, new material is added to the unconscious realm through repression. Repression may be described as an exclusion of material, an exclusion which is performed unconsciously. When conscious material is repressed, the person neither recalls it nor realizes that it is being repressed. The material may proceed from consciousness into the preconscious, where it is temporarily out of mind, and while it is in the preconscious, it may be thrust into the unconscious, the outcome of which is forgetting. Sometimes consciousness itself may be bypassed, as when an event is not perceived by the person but his behavior indicates that the experience is active unconsciously. An event may occur which is so disturbing that he represses its recall. He does not remember the event, nor does he recall the time or process of exclusion.

Repression may be contrasted with *suppression,* in which the person simply determines not to think about certain things. Unlike repression, the exclusion is a conscious process and the material is accessible. The person may recall the material whenever he wishes. Another important difference between suppression and repression is that external events may activate the suppressed material, but external events do not bring up repressed material. Certain circumstances may remind the person who has suppressed his problem that it still has not been solved, but in the case of a repressed problem, such events serve no reminding function. The problem continues because the person does not even recognize that he has one.

A repression often continues to be dynamically active. It influences the contents and operations of consciousness. Freud believed that a repressed motive, for instance, continues to press for expression into consciousness and behavior. The repressed material must be held back by counterforces. Sometimes these give way, and there is an impulsive outpouring of the repressed material. A man who represses his resentment for his boss might, under special conditions such as drinking too much at the office Christmas party, explode and viciously attack him. The drinking weakens the resisting forces which had kept the repressed hostility in check.

Repressed material may cause a person to do strange things as it seeks expression. Freud believed that *the symptoms of neurosis are the overt outlets of repression.* The compulsion, obsession, or phobia provides some outlet for the repressed material. A repressed hatred may even be converted to conscious feelings of tender love, but the love is superficial and really a sham which easily gives way to the true emotion. In order to get into consciousness, repressed material must be made acceptable to the ego. Some of Freud's greatest contributions to psychology relate to the numerous ways repressed material may be transformed so as to acquire this ego acceptance (Table 10–2).

TABLE 10-2 THE MOST IMPORTANT DIFFERENCES BETWEEN
PSYCHOTHERAPY AND BEHAVIOR THERAPY

Psychotherapy	Behavior Therapy
1. Considers symptoms the visible upshot of unconscious causes ("complexes").	1. Considers symptoms as unadaptive conditioned responses.
2. Regards symptoms as evidence of repressions.	2. Regards symptoms as evidence of faulty learning.
3. Believes that symptomatology is determined by defense mechanisms.	3. Believes that symptomatology is determined by individual differences in conditionability and autonomic lability, as well as by accidental environmental circumstances.
4. All treatment of neurotic disorders must be historically based.	4. All treatment of neurotic disorders is concerned with habits existing at present: the historical development is largely irrelevant.
5. Cures are achieved by handling the underlying (unconscious) dynamics, not by treating the symptom itself.	5. Cures are achieved by treating the symptom itself, i.e., by extinguishing unadaptive C.R.s and establishing desirable C.R.s.
6. Interpretation of symptoms, dreams, acts, etc. is an important element of treatment.	6. Interpretation, even if not completely subjective and erroneous, is irrelevant.
7. Symptomatic treatment leads to the elaboration of new symptoms.	7. Symptomatic treatment leads to permanent recovery, provided autonomic as well as skeletal C.R.s are extinguished.
8. Transference relations (neurotic responses, directed toward the therapist, which are fixations from the past) are essential for cures of neurotic disorders.	8. Personal relations are not essential for cures of neurotic disorders, although they may be useful in certain circumstances.

Adapted from H. J. Eysenck and S. Rachman, *The Causes and Cures of Neurosis: An Introduction to Modern Behavior Therapy Based on Learning Theory and the Principles of Conditioning.* Robert R. Knapp, 1965, p. 12. It should be noted that Freud's ideas about the unconscious are not accepted by all psychologists. Those (such as Eysenck and Rachman) who are involved with behavior modification and behavior therapy focus directly upon the behavioral disturbance, employing learning concepts and procedures to effect behavior change. They believe that Freudian psychotherapy is based on inconsistent theory and is derived from clinical observations which are made without necessary controls and experiments (see "Behavior Therapy," Chapter 6).

THE STRUCTURE OF PERSONALITY: ID, EGO, AND SUPEREGO

Freud conceived the personality as made up of warring systems which are continually in conflict with each other. The id represents the psychobiological urges; the ego represents the conscious agent or core of personality; the superego is the moral and social aspect of personality. Each system strives to dominate the personality as much as possible. The id would do away with considerations of reality and morality; the ego strives to be rational and realistic and to do away with tensions associated with needs; the superego seeks to eliminate im-

TABLE 10-3 COMPONENTS OF PERSONALITY

Id	Ego	Superego
Is the primitive part of the psyche	Is the "I" (self)	Has 2 functions: conscience and ego ideal
Comprised of inherited psychobiological instincts	Serves and controls the id	Is moral or cultural component of personality
Source of psychic energy	Administers the personality	Is primitive in the neurotic
"True psychic reality"	Uses the psychological faculties	Strives for moralistic and perfectionistic ends
Operates according to the pleasure principle; reduces tension	Distinguishes between objective and subjective	Promotes self-control
Controls reflex action and is characterized by primary process thinking	Obeys the reality principle	Inhibits impulses of the id
Is totally unconscious	Characterized by secondary process thinking	Is both preconscious and unconscious
	Is both conscious and unconscious	Opposes the id and ego
	Mediates between the id and the superego, and deals with the external	

pulses and to strive for moralistic or idealistic goals. But there is no doing away with any of the basic components of the personality. The only solution is for the ego to take over the personality and allow some expression to both the self-seeking motives of the individual and the social and moral restrictions imposed by external forces. We will discuss the component systems which Freud proposed as well as the interrelationships among them (see Table 10-3).

THE ID

The id is difficult to describe because we do not have direct access to it. It may be thought of as the most primitive part of the psyche, the *original personality*. It is the storehouse of psychic energy. It represents the psychological counterpart of biological needs: for every biological need there is a corresponding urge in the id which becomes active when the need does (Freud, 1933). As the need for food increases in intensity, for instance, the desire for food, which takes place in the id, also increases in intensity. At some point the intensity of the desire is great enough to be experienced in the ego as a tension state unless there is some force that opposes the desire. Thus the total process begins with a biological need which is experienced in the id (but not consciously, because the id is totally unconscious). The desire for food becomes consciously felt in the ego when the need in the body is of sufficient intensity.

To obtain an appreciation of the operation of the id, consider what happens when one is sleeping. During sleep, even though the operations of the ego and consciousness are greatly reduced, there is considerable activity (Webb and Agnew, 1973). The biological functions are active, though at a diminished level. The person moves about much more than one would expect. He digests his food and may actually become hungry enough to be awakened. If the skin becomes irritated by being in one place too long, the person changes position—all without awakening. The tension associated with the irritation is translated into movement, without mediation of the ego or consciousness. The same thing may happen with an irritation of the throat or nostrils: the person coughs or sneezes without the intervention of the ego. Thus it may be seen that the id may actually control bodily activity directly, but it may also be active enough to disturb the ego during sleep, as when a person wakes up hungry. The point here is that the id is or may be active all the time. One of its main functions is to communicate tensions which it cannot discharge directly into the ego, which is more capable of discharging them.

Besides wishes, which are representations of the biological needs, the id contains at least one other class of material: repressed ideas, impressions, or desires. Such material must be held in check by counterforces from the ego.

The id may be experienced as an unwanted impulse which intrudes into consciousness at the most unwelcome times. Impulses related to sex and aggression are commonly the most troublesome. The young man who is trying to concentrate on the lecture cannot get his mind off the red-haired girl in the front row. He may feel so tense and restless that he cannot keep his mind on the lecture. Anger may be provoked by another person to the point where one loses control and says things he never intended to utter. No effort by the ego at suppression will be effective against the power of the id impulses. There are ways of giving the impulses a disguised outlet. Anger may be expressed in the form of sarcasm or even in the form of wit. Yet no matter how the impulses are given outlet, the point is that the id is the main driving force in personality according to Freud.

The Pleasure Principle and Primary Process Thinking

The pleasure principle embodies the idea that man's most basic motivation is the pursuit of pleasure, primarily through the reduction of instinctual tensions. Freud (1917) believed that this principle governs the activities of the id. The id impels the person to seek immediate relief from tension whenever it arises. Tension arises when needs are active, and is reduced when they are gratified. Relief of tension was considered by Freud to be the major source of pleasure; thus the absence of need tension was in a sense the highest form of human existence for him. Later in life he came to the conclusion that some tensions are pleasurable and constitute a source of motivation, as when a person enjoys sensual experiences and activity for their own sake. When the id dominates the ego, the pleasure principle reigns, at the expense of realistic and moralistic considerations.

By primary process thinking Freud (1900) meant thinking which is fantastic, illogical, wish-fulfilling, and induced by strong unfulfilled motives of the id. Primary process thinking is highly personal, or autistic. It does not follow the rules of logic, reality, or common sense. When the ego is under the influence of the id, as when a person is sexually motivated, primary process thinking may replace realistic thinking, which is the proper function of the ego. The ego may construct a world of fantasy. The ordinary limitations of reality are suspended. Dreaming is an example of primary process thinking. Objects may substitute for people, or a part may stand for the whole. In a dream, cutting a person's hair may symbolize the act of killing him. Killing a bear may symbolize the killing of one's father, or the wish to do so.

It should be noted that the pleasure principle and primary process thinking take place in the ego, but are induced by the id. When the id urges are strong, the proper activities of the ego are pre-empted by primary process thinking and the pleasure principle.

Why The Id?

We might question the reason why Freud proposed the existence of the id, which was supposed to intervene between the biological needs and the rest of the personality. Why are such motives, or all motives, not experienced directly by the ego? The answer is that Freud repeatedly observed a discrepancy between the behavior of his patients and the conscious motives they reported. The motives simply did not account for the behaviors. A mother might believe that she is being a "good mother" by keeping her child away from the other children in the neighborhood whom she believes are "bad" and can hurt her child, when in fact the real motivation behind this behavior is contempt for the child. By not allowing the child to play with the other children, she is depriving him of the normal pleasures of infancy and childhood. She is, so to speak, "getting even" with him for making her a prisoner. The real motivation, which is totally unacceptable to her, has been disguised by the unconscious portion of the ego into a motive which is acceptable and even laudable. The motive of the ego is different from the motive of the id, although the ego motive is a *transformation* of the id motive.

Some modification in current psychoanalytic thinking regarding the role of the ego assigns motives to the ego proper (e.g., White, 1963), but the traditional Freudian view was that all motivations of the ego are derivatives of id motives and serve the id.

The *derivative* motive experienced in the conscious portion of the ego may have little resemblance to the *root* motive in the id. Motives which are especially disapproved by society (and by the superego when it develops) produce motive derivatives which are made acceptable to self and society. Freud (1930) held that the frustration of such disapproved motives as sex and aggression is an important cause of man's highest achievement, both on an individual and cultural level. Having to find new and better outlets for forbidden motives, man develops and vigorously utilizes the powers of the ego. However, if the derivative motives take the form of ego defenses and primary process thinking, personality growth and functioning is faulty and abnormal. To understand Freud's notion of the relation between the ego and the id, one should bear in mind that the *ego is the servant of the id which is its master.* Some of the id motives are experienced directly, but others are disguised, so as to be acceptable to the ever-watchful superego and the power of external authorities. As we shall see, the process of transforming or disguising forbidden id motives takes place in the *unconscious portion of the ego.*

THE EGO

The ego is the administrator of the personality. It runs the personality. It is what is ordinarily experienced as the subject and object of action—the "I" or self. Its main function is to take care of need satisfaction. The ego stems from the activity of the higher centers of the brain. Freud believed that a portion of the id becomes differentiated into a distinct part of the personality, the ego. All of the psychological faculties (such as perception, memory, judgment, reasoning, problem solving, decision making) are at the disposal of the ego. The ego can come to know and learn about the external world, for unlike the id, it is constantly in touch with the outside environment (Freud, 1933). The growing child must learn to obey the reality principle and engage in secondary process thinking. The ego grows in strength by drawing energy from the id. It does this by investing energy in object choices, interests, and activities. As the ego grows the id weakens.

The Reality Principle and Secondary Process Thinking

The ego operates according to the reality principle and by means of secondary process thinking. By the reality principle, Freud meant that the ego must take into account all pertinent facts in the process of satisfying needs. Often tension must be endured while an appropriate course of action is worked out. There are always obstacles and hindrances which have to be surmounted or overcome. Since direct pleasure seeking usually is not possible, there is continual conflict between the pleasure principle of the id and the operation of the reality principle of the ego. But the ego does in fact have the capabilities of securing need gratification: thus the reality principle gets better results. The reality principle is supported by secondary process thinking. By secondary process thinking Freud meant thinking which is correct. The person must perceive correctly, follow the rules of logic, learn natural laws. He must be in touch with the real world. Secondary process thinking conflicts with primary process thinking, and often primary process thinking wins out because it requires less effort and produces immediate relief of unbearable tensions. In the end, secondary process thinking alone serves the reality principle, which in turn must be obeyed if the person is to survive (Freud, 1911).

Conflicts Between the Id and Ego

We might picture the relationship between the id and the ego in this manner: the id is like a very successful but not very bright heir of a large fortune. With all his wealth, he has many wild and impractical desires. He wants to buy a boat and is talked into buying a luxury liner. He decides that he likes baseball, so he buys a whole team. All this gets him into serious debt. Finally he hires a very knowledgeable business manager. The business manager is like the ego, whose job it is to hold back the irrational id. The witless heir has the resources, but the manager must put them to good use. His job is to satisfy the desires of his boss without making him bankrupt or provoking his anger. The ego works in behalf of the id. When the id says: "I want it, and I want it right now," the ego replies: "I'll try to get it for you. Give me a chance to work out a plan. Will you accept a substitute, or would you be willing to take less than what you asked for?"

Freud believed that man is a pleasure-seeking creature at bottom. Everything he does represents an avoidance of pain or an attempt to generate pleasure. Reality is accepted only because of necessity, and a conflict between the pleasure and the reality principles is always present.

One of the main tasks of life is the "taming of the id" (Freud, 1933). If the ego did not limit the id, the person would always act selfishly and without regard for the rights of others. In fact, given only the id, survival could not take place. During infancy and childhood (when each person is strongly dominated by his id), those responsible for children do not expect them to manage their own impulses; rather, the expression of the id is controlled by external authorities. A parent does not permit a two year old to take charge of the money that he is given as a gift, nor does he allow the child to make decisions for himself regarding matters of daily living. The child is judged with the view that the ego has not yet taken over his personality.

As children grow older, more and more is expected of them. They are held accountable for impulse control. If they display anger toward their parents, they may be punished, whereas such behavior was not punished during an earlier period of their lives. When something is not available, older children are expected to accept that fact and not to cry about it. Gradually, but inevitably, they must take over the management of their impulses. The id always presses for gratification and pleasure, but the ego must face the harshness of reality and the consequences of unlimited and untempered gratification.

THE SUPEREGO

The superego consists of two important aspects of the personality: the *conscience* and the *ego ideal* (Freud, 1933). The conscience represents the *cultural prohibitions* (the "don'ts"), the ego ideal the *positive prescriptions* (the "dos"), both of which are internalized. To internalize means to take something and to make it an integral part of personality, as though it were one's own. The superego is the moral or cultural representative within personality. The ego must not only take rational steps to satisfy the demands of the id and at the same time meet the requirements of the external world, but it must also obey the prescriptions or requirements of the superego. Only certain modes of meeting needs are acceptable to the superego; even though a variety of means of meeting needs are permitted by the culture, the superego does not necessarily tolerate all of them. Dancing, for instance, is permitted by the culture as a means of bringing young persons together, but it is not acceptable to members of some religions. In this case the superego blocks a channel of need satisfaction which is open to the ego: the conflict is within the person, rather than between the person and his environment.

Ego Conscience and Superego Conscience

In order to appreciate the nature of the superego and its place in the personality as Freud conceived it, a distinction between what might be termed "ego conscience" and "superego conscience" is necessary. We learn principles of conduct which guide our behavior, and which we can more or less enunciate if we are pressed. A man knows that exceeding the speed limit is a violation of law, but he may disregard the law and speed one morning. If he is involved in an accident which he knows to be his fault, he may experience remorse over his actions. He may criticize himself for speeding. "If I hadn't been so selfish and disregarded the rights of others, the accident would not have happened. I am totally at fault, and I deserve to be punished." His reasoning in this matter may be as follows, although he may not go through these steps fully:

> "One who disobeys the law commits a wrong against society;
> I have disobeyed the law;
> Therefore I have committed a wrong against society.
> One who commits a wrong against society deserves to be punished;
> I have committed a wrong against society;
> Therefore I deserve to be punished."

One need not go through these steps explicitly in order to experience the remorse. In a sense, such behavior is not really conscience but realistic thinking. The reality principle requires the ego to keep the person out of trouble as the ego goes about meeting the requirements of the id. Obeying the law is one way of accomplishing this end. Many of the dos and don'ts which guide behavior are matters of secondary process thinking and the reality principle. The mature person gradually takes over the precepts of the superego conscience and exposes them to the scrutiny of the ego. In other words, if development is normal the controlling force in personality becomes more and more the ego. *Conscience becomes more and more conscious.* This point will have more meaning as we explore the functions of the superego further.

Like the id, the superego is unconscious, although it can produce conscious effects in the ego, such as guilt, remorse, and anxiety. It operates by forcing upon the ego certain prescriptions, such as "never think about sexual matters;

never get angry at one's parents; never be selfish; never be unloving." The person who harbors a strict superego is usually unable to verbalize its prescriptions, but he is nevertheless influenced by them. Just as the command of the superego is unconscious, so the reason behind the command is equally unknown to the person.

An example of the operation of the superego may make this last point clear. A man feels driven to work hard, and he does in fact work many hours and is merciless with himself. Although he is on a vacation which he rightly deserves, he feels ill at ease, tense, and restless. He cannot give any reasonable explanation for these feelings. He finds peace only when he is back at work. For a large segment of Western culture, the taboo against pleasure has been superseded by a taboo against low achievement and inferior status. To engage in recreation is to take time away from striving for success.

In brief, the primitive superego conscience says "thou shalt not," but it does not tell why not; just as a child is told to do something without knowing why, so the superego issues its commands without giving an explanation. A second point is relevant, regarding the strictness of the superego. When the superego issues a command, there are no exceptions. One must work all the time, or be generous and thoughtful all the time, or never have an immoral thought, and the like. However, in the mature adult the dictates of the superego conscience are ordinarily moderated or even disregarded altogether from time to time. In other words, the person learns how to adapt his code to his needs and circumstances. One usually works hard, but occasionally one deviates from this requirement and allows himself some relaxation and fun. The mature person works out a balance between work and play, egoistic and altruistic motives, and other dichotomies in his life.

Origin of the Superego Conscience

A brief account of the origin of the superego will aid in obtaining a clear notion of its place in the personality. At first the child's behavior is either impulsive or caused directly by the stimulus. As every mother who has to change diapers will agree, whenever tension is experienced the reaction is immediate. As one psychologist quipped, "The best characterization of kids is obtained by dropping the 'k.'"

The child responds directly to secure the desirable stimulus or to withdraw from an unpleasant one. If an expensive vase on the table attracts the child, he immediately tries to get it. Later, as the ego begins to master reality, the child may hesitate a bit while he weighs the consequences of his behavior, but frequently gives in to the impulse because he does not know what else to do with it. As the ego increases in strength and influence, rational thought processes intervene and the child spends more time deliberating before taking direct action (Grim, Kohlberg, and White, 1968). The ego learns to avoid punishment by identifying situations which are associated with it.

The superego conscience develops after the beginnings of the ego conscience. The ego conscience at first is the outgrowth of the need to avoid loss of love from the parents. The child avoids certain behaviors because they have been disapproved by his parents. Loss of love means deprivation of satisfactions, and even actual punishment. The controls are external to the child, and the primary force is fear of being apprehended and punished. The child fears the parents (or what they can do to him) and avoids situations which will cause their displeasure. At this time, the operation of conscience is a function of the ego and the reality of the authority which the parents possess. This form of conscience does not disappear with the coming of the superego conscience, but is always active. For example, one may obey traffic regulations only because one is afraid of being apprehended.

The second stage in the development of the superego involves an identification with the parents (Bronfenbrenner, 1960). By *identification* is meant making the characteristics of the parents an integral part of the personality. The little boy worships and admires his father, whom he perceives as a more perfect specimen of manhood than he is himself. He models his behavior after his father's in hopes of becoming the wonderful person he imagines his father to be. In every respect his father is superior to him. He is much larger; he can do so many wonderful things; and he holds a special place with mother, a fact which the child may resent. To be like father means to have what father has. His image of his father is glamorous, not marred by unfavorable comparisons. The earliest identification of the child with his parents is instrumental in forming the ego ideal, which appears to precede the development of the superego conscience.

The little girl also views herself as greatly inferior to her mother. Mother is a much more perfect specimen of womanhood. She has many privileges which the little girl would like to have, not the least of which is her special place with father. The little girl takes her mother as a model and identifies with her by taking on her characteristics.

Since parents can withdraw their love and punish the child, a part of the identification involves the internalization of this parental authority. A part of the ego, the dictates of the parents, later enters the realm of the superego by splitting off from the ego and becoming unconscious. In this role, the superego judges and prescribes the rules of conduct which the ego must follow in its work of meeting the demands of the id. Thus the ego has to contend not only with the requirements of reality but also with the demands of the superego, which constantly monitors it. Just as the child fears the authority of the parents because of their power over him, so the superego as the psychic representative of the parent is also feared because of its power. Violating the commands of the superego brings upon the ego guilt, anxiety, self-depreciation, and the desire for punishment.

The Ego Ideal

Freud (1914) did not have much to say regarding the nature of the ego ideal; other personality theorists such as Horney and Allport have developed this notion extensively. What is presented here regarding the ego ideal goes beyond what Freud said, but the topic will be developed in the context of Freudian ideas.

The ego ideal involves the incorporation within the child's personality of *positive prescriptions for conduct.* It represents within the child ideals of conduct which are dictates of the parents, and subsequently of other significant authority symbols: teachers, religious leaders, law enforcement authorities, the traditions, customs, and noblest practices of the culture, and in general whatever represents the embodiment of values, such as heroes. It is an idealized self which may be a distortion of the real self.

Like the imperatives of the superego conscience, the standards of the primitive ego ideal are either all or none. There are no in betweens: the child is either good or bad, moral or immoral, considerate or selfish. Normally these standards undergo changes with development. Ideal behavior at age five is certainly not the same as it is at twenty or sixty. Expectations change throughout the life cycle. But if the individual does not come to terms with the rigid nature of the infantile ego ideal — that is, if the ego ideal does not develop as it should — he may suffer anxiety and other serious consequences. Just as the primitive conscience stands as a tormenting taskmaster over the ego, so also the ego ideal which remains fixated at an early stage of development goads the ego to impossible aspirations and expectations.

Resolution of the Oedipus Complex

According to Freud (1924), a significant factor in the development of the superego is the manner in which the Oedipus complex is resolved. It will be recalled that the Oedipus complex involves the sexual attraction of the child for the parent of the opposite sex. At the same time, the parent of the same sex is both feared and hated. As a consequence of the fear, the child gives up the attachment and rivalry, and instead identifies with the parent of the same sex. The identification is much more intense than the early identification occurring before the Oedipus complex, which is supposed to manifest itself between three and five years of age. Important changes take place in the superego conscience and ego ideal if the resolution of the Oedipus complex is normal. Basic attitudes are formed: attitudes toward authorities, toward members of the same and opposite sex, toward acceptance of the roles which the culture prescribes, and many others. Failure to resolve the Oedipus complex may result in the carry-over of the early conflicts and attitudes to other significant people, a factor that hinders the process of socialization.

Advantages and Disadvantages of the Superego

The conscience and ego ideal, which comprise the superego, add a new dimension to personality which creates many conflicts. Not only must the ego contend with id impulses and external forces, but it must also follow codes of conduct which rigidly limit the means of satisfying needs. The impulses and the superego are directly opposed. In some instances the superego so controls the ego that most avenues of gratification are blocked. Thus man himself may hinder his possibilities of need gratification even more than the external world does. The superego may torment him mercilessly, set goals which cannot be attained, and produce guilt and feelings of unworthiness in the process. Unless one lessens the tyranny of the conscience and the unreality of the ego ideal, he will experience severe restrictions in every aspect of life. This necessary process can best be accomplished by strengthening the ego.

The superego, nonetheless, is a necessary condition for societal living. Given the nature of the id and ego, there is the necessity of a restraining force within personality, because external controls would not suffice to promote group life. The law of the jungle would hold, and "might makes right" would be the dominant principle of action. Man quite likely would have become extinct in this state. The superego, with the conscience and ego ideal, exerts a restraining force over the id-dominated ego. It assists the external forces of authority to promote societal living and the best climate for the fulfillment of the individual. However, Freud believed (1930) that even with all the controls, both external and internal, individual fulfillment is still more of a dream than a reality.

OTHER FUNCTIONS OF THE EGO

We have discussed the various forces in personality which must be integrated by the ego and the conflicts which arise in man's nature, as proposed by Freud. To round out the picture, a number of additional topics regarding ego functioning need to be touched on. These are anxiety, defense mechanisms of the ego, and the synthesizing and moderating role of the ego.

THE EGO AS MEDIATOR

The ego must constantly contend with three powerful forces: the *external environment*, the *id*, and the *superego*. Both the external demands and the id impulses are ever-present and increase with age. Somehow the ego must attempt to moderate the three competing forces. In the process it may become helpless and confused, especially if the external demands and the id impulses are diametrically opposed. It may experience anxiety or *psychic pain*. The solution is complicated by Freud's seemingly contradictory views that the ego is fundamentally the servant of the id and that id motives must often be disguised to be made acceptable to the ego. An important question arises: how are the unacceptable id motives to be disguised?

Like the ego itself, Freud attempted to resolve his dilemma through compromise. He held that a portion of the ego is unconscious and in touch with the id. It serves the id by effecting the motivational transformations. Thus the unconscious portion of the ego, unobserved by the superego, works to support the id. But the derivative motives (the disguised motives and substitute outlets) always gratify the id motives only partially. If the superego is moderated in its expectations of the ego, the outlets of the ego are more directly what the id motives require. On the other hand, if the id impulses and the superego demands are equally powerful, the ego resorts to defense mechanisms and secondary process thinking rather than to primary process thinking and problem solving.

ANXIETY

In attempting to get to the root of anxiety and for the purpose of describing its true nature, Freud (1936) proposed that the earliest and most powerful source of anxiety was birth itself. The fetus in the uterine environment enjoys a high degree of protection from external stimuli. With birth the environment changes radically, and the infant is open to a great variety of experiences, some of which are overwhelming. In such instances he feels small and helpless, unable to change the disturbing event. What is experienced as anxiety, in situations where the individual cannot cope with the stress situation, is a reawakening to some degree of this original form of anxiety.

Freud distinguished three types of anxiety: objective, neurotic, and moral. Each involves an unpleasant emotional state.

Objective Anxiety

For Freud (1933), objective anxiety was equivalent to fear. A real threat or actual danger is involved in objective anxiety. There is something definite which is the cause of the fear. If not too intense, the fear serves to stimulate the individual to some kind of action. The unpleasant emotional reaction is often a warning that there is a threat of danger. In this sense, objective anxiety is a preliminary to what is ordinarily considered fright.

Neurotic Anxiety

In neurotic anxiety, the ego is afraid of the id rather than of the external world. The fear thus arises from forces within the personality. The anxiety is produced by the threat of an id impulse breaking through the defenses which the ego has erected to keep it repressed. The fear is not so much of the impulses, but of the consequences which impulse gratification may produce. The ego senses the danger before it actually occurs, and experiences anxiety. The anxiety, of course, may assist the ego in dealing with the dangerous impulse. It intensifies the efforts of the ego to hold the impulse in check (Freud, 1933).

Moral Anxiety

Moral anxiety is caused by the superego. It is felt as guilt, self-depreciation, the desire for punishment, and some forms of depression. The ego experiences a sense of unworthiness, and this is often a chronic state. The more primitive and rigid the superego, the greater the intensity of the anxiety feelings (Freud, 1933).

Many people carry around an excess amount of guilt. They fret constantly over their worthiness and effectiveness. This overconcern about personal adequacy is given the name of insecurity. The insecure person suffers from a superego that has not been tempered in its severity. Either the superego conscience or the ego ideal or both continue in their primitive state and rage against the impulses of the id. As a consequence the person suffers moral anxiety. He finds the management of his impulses a terrible ordeal. He cannot deal with them because the restrictions against them are totally unyielding.

The Ego and Anxiety

It should be remembered that the three types of anxiety are experienced by the ego. Whether the anxiety is caused by (1) an impulse from the id which threatens to overwhelm the ego, (2) the superego, through its conscience, condemning the ego for thinking about or actually giving in to the id impulses, (3) the ego ideal condemning ego as evil, or (4) the overwhelming stress from the external environment, the fact remains that the ego is the victim.

The ego cannot remain passive when it experiences anxiety, irrespective of the type. In the case of objective anxiety, the cause of fear may be dealt with directly. The person may attempt to perceive the situation correctly, evaluate possible alternative solutions, and make a decision to follow a particular line of action. When he carries out his plan, more often than not the problem is solved and the anxiety associated with it passes. Anxiety as a warning signal serves the important function of preparing the person for appropriate coping or avoidance behavior. Sometimes appropriate action is not possible, and the anxiety continues to rage. In such instances the ego employs defense mechanisms, which deal *directly with the anxiety* rather than with the situation which produces it. In neurotic and moral anxiety, the danger is from within the personality. The ego usually has more difficulty dealing in a rational manner with these forms of anxiety, and much of its defensive strategy may be used to protect against the powers of these forces.

The reader may have observed that what was described as frustration in the early part of this chapter is almost identical to the meaning of anxiety as Freud saw it. The terms may be used interchangeably. It will be recalled that motivational conflict is the major source of frustration, or anxiety, for adults.

EGO DEFENSE MECHANISMS

Freud had much to say about the important role of defense mechanisms as means of dealing with the difficult situations which the ego confronts. The portion of the ego which is unconscious, and thus not so tightly constrained by the requirements of reality, acts to distort, disguise, and deny motives, perceptions, and other psychological contents. The ego develops strategies by which it protects itself against the oppressive forces of the id, superego, and external reality. It may simply deny any expression to the impulses of the id, or it may disregard external realities; in either case the consequences will be undesirable. The conscious ego is often not aware of the deception.

CRITIQUE OF FREUD'S SYSTEMS OF PERSONALITY

Freud has been criticized for many aspects of his theoretical conceptions. Relevant to this chapter are the criticisms on the unconscious and the structures of personality.

To many behaviorists, the notion of the unconscious appears to be an evasion of the obligation to explain phenomena which are difficult to explain. The unconscious is purported to be active in every person and at all times, but the evidence is far from conclusive (Eriksen, 1960). Those who are inclined to accept the existence of unconscious processes thus modify the position by holding that the normal person is much more conscious of his motivations, emotions, and judgments than is the abnormal, who may lack such knowledge to a remarkable degree.

Many also find the personality structures an artificial breakup of personality which has no value beyond the rather obvious one of conveying the place of conflict in man's life. As constructs the structures serve no useful purpose in the effort to discover principles of behavior. To simply label phenomena (as is done with concepts such as id, ego, and superego) gives the illusion of explanation, but in fact to remain at the level of description constitutes only the premature stage of science. However, analysts working in the field of therapy have reported that they find the concepts useful both in diagnosis and treatment. In any case, Freud's ideas on the unconscious and on the structures of personality have been extremely influential in the fields of personality theory and psychotherapy.

INSIGHTS FROM FREUD'S MENTAL MECHANISMS

EGO DEFENSE MECHANISMS

The major purpose of ego defense mechanisms is to reduce anxiety. In some instances a defense mechanism may also bolster the ego, but most of the strategies are protective (Table 10–4). The defense mechanisms reduce anxiety most effectively when they operate uncon-

TABLE 10–4 EGO DEFENSE MECHANISMS

Defense Mechanisms	*Identifying Characteristics*
Denial of Reality	Protecting self from unpleasant reality by refusing to perceive or face it Escapism: "not being in the mood," procrastinating, avoiding painful situations
Fantasy	Gratifying frustrated desires in imaginary achievements Conquering hero, suffering hero themes
Rationalization	Attempting to prove that one's behavior is "rational" and justifiable, thus worthy of self and social approval Sour grapes (debunking what you don't have); sweet lemon (exaggerating value of what you do have)
Projection	Placing blame for difficulties upon others or attributing one's own unethical desires to others Excuses of "bad luck" or "fate"
Repression	Preventing painful or dangerous thoughts from entering consciousness
Reaction Formation	Preventing dangerous desires from being expressed by exaggerating opposed attitudes and types of behavior and using them as barriers
Undoing	Atoning for and thus counteracting immoral desires or acts (repentance)
Regression	Retreating to an earlier developmental level involving less mature responses and usually a lower level of aspiration

Adapted from *Abnormal Psychology and Modern Life,* 4th edition, by James C. Coleman. Copyright © 1972 by Scott, Foresman and Company. Reprinted by permission of the publisher. Many of the mechanisms listed in the table were formulated by disciples of Freud; e.g. Anna Freud, *The Ego and the Mechanisms of Defense,* International Universities Press, 1946.

(Table continued on opposite page.)

sciously. One could not deliberately decide to excuse himself from an obligation without experiencing guilt feelings; but if this took place unconsciously, then the guilt would not occur. The mechanisms are learned: a person is not born with them. Blaming others is discovered by a child to be a means of avoiding the anxiety of being caught. Thus it may become an established strategy for dealing with anxiety.

Defense is accomplished by two means: self-deception and reality distortion. Through self-deception, one may deny or minimize certain unpleasant truths which one does not want to face. Through reality distortion one alters events to suit one's wishes. If the real events are not what one desires, they may simply be altered by overlooking certain aspects, by distorting some parts, and a variety of other techniques for making over what is actually present. It should be kept in mind that defense mechanisms are like pain killers: they reduce the pain of anxiety but they do not accomplish anything in the way of resolving the

TABLE 10–4 *Continued*

Defense Mechanisms	*Identifying Characteristics*
Identification	Increasing feelings of worth (self-esteem) by identifying self with person or institution of illustrious standing
Introjection	Incorporating external values and standards into ego structure so individual is not at their mercy as external threats "If you can't beat 'em, join 'em"
Compensation	Covering up weakness by emphasizing desirable trait or making up for frustration in one area by overgratification in another
Displacement	Discharging pent-up feelings, usually of hostility, on objects less dangerous than those which initially aroused the hostility Phobias
Emotional Insulation	Reducing ego involvement and withdrawing into passivity to protect self from hurt
Intellectualization (Dissociation)	Cutting off affective charge from hurtful situations or isolating incompatible attitudes in logic-tight compartments
Sublimation	Gratifying or working off frustrated sexual desires in nonsexual activities Finding acceptable outlets for unacceptable impulses
Sympathism	Striving to gain sympathy from others, thus bolstering feelings of self-worth despite failures "Tough breaks"
Acting Out	Reducing the anxiety aroused by forbidden desires by permitting their direct expression in behavior

conflict or solving the disturbing problem. Pain killers can be useful as temporary aids over rough spots, but if they are used in excess they can so warp the personality as to cause permanent damage. Then, too, defense is costly. If one assumes, as Freud did, that the amount of psychic energy is limited, then whatever energy is used for defense must decrease the amount available for more fruitful functions. A rigid, defensive, guarded person is usually so busy and occupied with his difficulties that he does not have much time or energy for anything else.

Rationalization. Rationalization means justification of one's behavior or desires. To rationalize is not to think rationally as the term implies, but rather to make conduct *appear* rational. If there is a conflict between an impulse and the conscience, then one might either rationalize away the restriction of conscience or deny the impulse; thus the conflict is lessened or eliminated altogether. If a young person has a strong desire to engage in forms of love-making which violate his moral code, he may weaken the force of conscience by a rationalization such as "everybody is doing it; it can't be so bad." The rationalization may succeed in lessening the force of conscience sufficiently to allow him to give way to the impulses. Many conflicts are resolved in this manner: one of the opposing forces is weakened by rationalization.

What is unacceptable behavior in others may be made quite acceptable to oneself by a bit of rationalizing. If another takes an unfair advantage he is a cheat, but if I do the same thing I may conclude that it is a matter of "good business practice." A fault in another makes him unworthy of my friendship, but a fault in me makes me "only human." Rationalization is used to dress up the flaws in oneself.

Projection.   One is projecting when one fails to see his own shortcomings, but instead perceives them in others. Like a projector which flashes an image upon a screen, the mechanism of projection causes the person to falsely see qualities in another. The gossip says more about himself than about the person he is maligning. One who feels a great deal of hostility toward others may through projection ascribe the hostility to them. Paradoxically, we are quick to see and condemn our own weaknesses in others (Putney and Putney, 1964). By doing so, we draw attention from our own failings.

Reaction-Formation.   In reaction-formation, a motive which conflicts with the ego ideal or a dictate of conscience is blocked by a conscious motive which is opposite in character. The conscious motive and feelings are diametrically opposed to the true but unconscious motives and feelings. Before the motive reaches consciousness it has been converted to its opposite. For instance, a husband who despises the power his wife exerts over him may consciously feel solicitous about her health.

Since the conscious motives and emotions are disguises, real feelings occasionally come to the surface explosively. More typically, the real motives and feelings find devious outlets which are acceptable to the censoring powers. A man who never forgets his wife's "important days" always manages to get her things which she does not want. He might bring her candy when she is on a diet, or buy her flowers that remind her of funerals.

Displacement.   If a man is irritable with his family because he harbors a hatred of his boss which cannot be openly expressed, his behavior toward his family may be described as a displacement. The mechanism of displacement involves substituting an available outlet of need gratification for one which is blocked.

Substitute objects inevitably produce anxiety. A boy strongly desires to make the football team but is rejected. He becomes a cheerleader instead, a move which could be considered a reasonable manner of dealing with his frustration. Suppose, however, that he occupies all his time with football. He attends all the practice sessions; he reads everything he finds about football; he talks about nothing else, and in general, he organizes his whole life around the sport. Here we may see the defensive nature of a displacement. What the boy really wants he cannot get, so he accepts a substitute. But the substitute leaves him chronically under tension; thus he goes to extremes in the substitute activity. A healthier strategy might be to engage in activities which will satisfy other basic needs.

There is probably no other mechanism which hinders social relationships as much as displacement. A popular song says: "You Always Hurt the One You Love"; we hurt the ones we love because they happen to be the ones we are near. We often take out our frustrations, bad moods, and anger on others unknowingly. Tension is an everpresent part of living, and the handling of tension is one of the major tasks of growing up.

Some people use others to play out their emotions. Their inner moods are directly reflected in their behavior: if they are in a good mood then all is well, but if they are in a bad mood all around them must suffer. The ones who suffer most are those who are victims by virtue of dependence. A child may be tormented by the moodiness of parents who lash out at him viciously. In such instances, the behavior of the child may have little to do with the parents' erratic outpouring of venom. There are many mean-spirited people full of resentment and hatred, who use subordinates as targets for their hostile emotions.

Sublimation.   Sublimation refers to a displacement which is socially and personally acceptable. The object which is selected to satisfy the forbidden motive is a substitute, but it and the means of securing it are tolerable and even commendable (Freud, 1920b). A man who hates a rival cannot attack him directly because the law and his own conscience prevent him, but he can channel the energy which the hostile impulse arouses into acceptable activities, and in the end accomplish the same objective. For instance, he may gain superiority over his opponent in some achievement: earning power, or marrying a more attractive wife. The point is that there are usually acceptable outlets, even for unacceptable motives.

Sublimations vary in degree of usefulness. Freud greatly emphasized the role of sublimation in healthy living. He believed that one should seek the best possible sublimation for his needs. A man who has lost his own children may dedicate his life to scout work or to helping wayward boys. A woman who did not marry may find great satisfaction in her work as a nurse. She may be extremely dedicated and care for her patients far beyond the call of duty. Her patients become substitutes for children and a husband. But other sublimating activities which a lonely woman might adopt are of questionable value, even though they are socially and personally acceptable. She might sublimate her desire to have children in caring for a pet poodle as if it were an infant. She might make clothing for it, bathe it often, and arrange to have it sleep in a special bed in her room at night. Or she might collect stuffed animals as a hobby, spending a great deal of time caring for them, reading about them, and obtaining them.

Whether or not the theory of sublimation is valid as Freud proposed it, there is something of value which everyone can learn from it. Whenever there is frustration there seems to be a buildup of tension, even more than one would expect. The manner in which the tension is utilized makes a great deal of difference in personality functioning. It may be directed toward hostile, aggressive ends; or it may be squandered in self-pity, worry, depression, and other maladaptive behaviors; or it may be used to promote rational activity. An angry person can accomplish a great deal if his anger is properly channeled. Emotions can add extra force to motivation. Thus what for many is a disturbance can be a source of great productivity for others.

THE SYNTHESIZING FUNCTIONS OF THE EGO

Given the nature of personality as Freud saw it, certain questions regarding its growth and functioning are in order. How can the ego reconcile the opposing forces within personality? What can society do, and what can the individual do for himself, to help the ego in its tasks?

Can child-rearing play an important part, since so much of the foundation of personality, according to Freud, is established during childhood? Can one who has experienced an unhealthy childhood do anything to rectify the damage? The following discussion about the healthy ego will not attempt to cover all these questions, but it aims to suggest some ideas which can aid the reader in dealing with them.

An important point to bear in mind is the principle of the *conservation of energy*, which Freud (1920a) believed applied to psychic energy as it does, of course, to physical energy. The principle holds simply that energy can be transformed, but it cannot be created or destroyed. The amount of psychic energy at any period of life is constant; what is used up in one kind of activity limits what is available for others. Therefore if the ego develops and becomes dominant, it takes over the energy from the id and superego. These are weakened and more easily managed by the ego.

How can the ego weaken the id and superego? Consider the superego first: the reasons behind much of what one does ordinarily are not known to him. Man is a "creature of habit": thus many activities continue long after the need which they served is no longer active. Habitual behavior is not usually accompanied by rational evaluation. One way of making the superego conscious is to examine from time to time one's basic values, aspirations, and standards of right and wrong conduct. Many people find that their beliefs begin to change as they examine them. The normal person certainly alters his superego as he grows up. He learns when to follow rules and when not to. He re-examines the role of authorities in his life. Many of his fictional dreams and hopes are toned down. He learns to make many adjustments and compromises with his superego. Both the superego conscience and the ego ideal become more and more functions of the ego. He comes to know what he wants and what steps must be taken to attain his objectives. He is also clearer about what is right and wrong. All this, of course, is a matter of degree: not everyone comes to terms with his superego, and many carry its primitive form with them for life. Here again the expression "knowledge is power" applies. *Knowledge of the superego conquers the superego.*

A child can be taught the habit of examining his assumptions and values as a matter of course. If the child is given increasing freedom to make decisions and to evaluate courses of action for himself, the ego gradually takes over. The opposite of this is an authoritarian approach, in which the parents make all the decisions for the child. The superego, by taking over the role of the parents, may also keep the ego under control and subservient. Even a very young child can be given some freedom of choice in the color of clothing, the type of food for meals, the time for a party. Giving the child an explanation of the reasons behind parental decisions also lessens the absolute force behind authority. The child should come to recognize that rules and laws make sense when you understand them. Authority for its own sake is the poorest basis for rules or laws. The parents' reasoning with the child should be on a graded basis, of course.

With respect to the id, Freud (1933) made the statement that "where the id is, the ego should be." He also on many occasions indicated that the main task of psychoanalysis is making the unconscious conscious. Knowledge of impulses does not eliminate them or reduce their strength in the same way that knowledge of the superego weakens its power.

But knowledge of impulses can aid in bringing the impulses under the reality principle and secondary process thinking of the ego. If one knows his impulses and experiences them without distortion, there is great probability that he can do something in the way of satisfying them. Incidentally, with all of his emphasis on sex, Freud did not advocate free expression; he believed that the purpose of sex is procreation and that its pleasure is incidental, and he made this point quite clearly. But disguised outlets for sex are dangerous to personality development and functioning. One must come to know his impulses before he can do anything to master them. Expression which is outside of awareness and not under voluntary control is potentially damaging and limits the effectiveness of the ego in obtaining gratification of needs.

Every culture provides some acceptable outlets for potentially dangerous impulses. Often the person must meet certain requirements, such as marriage as a means of satisfying the sexual outlet, and during the period of preparation tension is inevitable. However, life is made up of compromises and displacements, sublimations, and even of denial. The well-adjusted person has learned to moderate his desires, to conform to the established standards of the community, and in general, he "carries his load." Using his rational and logical powers as much as possible, he attempts to structure his life. He gives to charity because he feels that some others are more needy than he is. His earnings are sufficient to allow for a certain amount of gratification of his impulses. His impulses have been brought under control, and his superego, while not as rigid and strict as it was, still keeps him on the "straight and narrow." He has probably established a fair balance between superego and id.

Whether or not the reader believes that this is an ideal way of life, the fact is that many, if not the majority, fall far short of this "comfortable" style of living. Freud did not have great regard for the average man. He believed that most people never arrive at an adequate balance between impulse and control. Personality development, he believed, was usually one-sided. For most people, the impulses are dominant and must be held in check by persistent pressures from outside. Without the power of the law, and even more subtle pressures such as the presence of superiors, heroes, customs, and tradition, life would be impossible; man would destroy himself. On the other hand, there are many who suffer all their lives from a rigid, primitive, self-limiting superego which constantly torments them. They carry around a heavy load of guilt and self-depreciation. Their impulses are kept under strict control and restriction. They lack spontaneity, freedom to grow in accordance with their individual natures, and in general, fall far short of living a fulfilling life. There are those who have an overglamorous ego ideal and go through life chasing after rainbows and impossible dreams. They strive after the unattainable and in the process overlook what they have. The outcome is disillusionment and cynicism (Freud, 1930). Freud believed that the best solution is a balance among the opposing forces of personality.

The "perfect act," according to Freud, takes account of all the agencies within personality, as well as the pressures and exacting demands of the external world. The person may be described as enjoying inner harmony as well as concord between himself and his environment. The two conflicts which this chapter has been discussing, the psychosocial and the intrapsychic, are held at a minimum level. The bywords to personality functioning are moderation, the golden mean, conformity, compromise, and a degree of acceptance of conditions as they exist.

PARTICIPATION IN CAUSING AND CURING ILLNESS

Freud contended that the psychologically disturbed individual continually relives inappropriate conflicts and faulty emotional responses from his early history. The sufferer is not simply the passive victim of his neurosis, but rather actively sustains it. While he does not desire his illness, he is terribly afraid to make changes. His current defenses help him to function on a level which he does not like, but which he cannot give up because he has not worked out better methods of solving his problems. Two basic requisites for personality change are first, to truly want it, and second, to realize that you must be the agent that brings it about.

Giving up infantile conflicts and behavior will ultimately secure greater gratification and more satisfying social relationships, but there may be a feeling of helplessness and loss in the transitional state. Here are some practical suggestions. First, be sympathetic with yourself in the struggle to improve. This does not mean self-pity and excusing yourself from hard work. Sympathetic self-understanding means an appreciation of oneself as a combatant in a painful struggle which nevertheless must be waged. Secondly, re-examining old conflicts may help to dissipate the pent-up emotions which continue to cause current emotional responses. Thirdly, replace inappropriate models of ideal human figures with more realistic ones. One should see important figures differently at each stage of life: the heroes of childhood should be superseded by heroes more helpful to adult living. Fourthly, be willing to admit your mistakes. Self-disclosure has many therapeutic effects. If one is fortunate enough to have a sympathetic friend, the process of confession may produce good results. Fifthly, self-awareness and self-study will occasionally be punctuated with insights. In this context, the term insight means a clear awareness of truths about oneself. Such experiences are highly conducive to personality improvement and should be used to the best advantage.

Freud (1914) did not picture mature adulthood as a "turned on" state with continual exuberance and happiness, but rather as a never-ending battle with many hurts and sorrows, but also with great moments of joy and satisfaction. The grownup must learn to take less than he really wants, to work for what he desires, to be willing to suffer for what he most cherishes, to take charge of his own life, and to assume responsibility for his successes and failures. One should strive to meet life head-on, and to face the trials and frustrations of living with a sense of inner equanimity. Each person must ultimately stand alone and be the master of his own destiny. Truths about oneself and reality are often painful to bear, but self-deception and distortion of reality can lead only to madness and suffering.

Freud once said that the goal of his psychoanalytic therapy was to help his patients to be able to love and work. Although this goal may appear quite simple, much is implied in order that it may be achieved. In dealing with the sufferings of his patients, Freud sought to replace neurotic misery with the ordinary unhappiness of everyday living. And, we might add, as the misery diminishes the level of happiness increases.

Figure 10–1 depicts two characterizations of personality, the typical and the ideal, following Freud's model of personality. It should be noted that in this case of the ideal personality, the ego is the largest system and both the superego and the id are quite accessible to awareness.

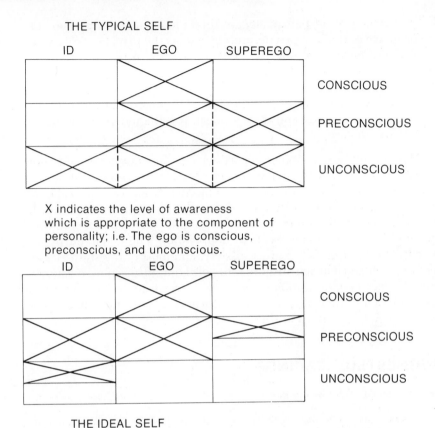

THE TYPICAL SELF

X indicates the level of awareness
which is appropriate to the component of
personality; i.e. The ego is conscious,
preconscious, and unconscious.

THE IDEAL SELF

Figure 10-1   Awareness levels associated with Freud's personality structures in the typical and in the ideal self. Note that in the ideal self the role of the unconscious is greatly diminished.

SUMMARY

1.   One of the cornerstones of Freud's system of concepts is the strong belief in the division of the psyche into different layers. Consciousness is the awareness which occurs as a result of external stimulation or the revival of inner experiences, or both in some combination. The preconscious consists of latent memories, which can be brought to consciousness deliberately, or which arise through association with current stimulation. There are two meanings of unconscious: (1) unconscious as unawareness, and (2) unconscious as a layer of the psyche.

2.   The most convincing evidence for the existence of the unconscious as an independent layer of the psyche is the personality disorders.

3.   Repression is the process by which the content of the unconscious is increased; it may be described as an exclusion of material, an exclusion which is performed unconsciously.

4. The structures of personality are three: id, ego, and superego. The id is the primitive part of the psyche, and represents the psychological counterpart of biological needs. It is governed by the pleasure principle and the primary process. The ego is the administrator of the personality and is experienced as the subject and object of action—the "I" or self. It acts according to the reality principle and secondary process thinking. The superego consists of two components: the conscience and the ego ideal. It is the moral or cultural component of personality.

5. There are various topics regarding ego functioning which should be noted. These are anxiety, defense mechanisms, and synthesizing functions of the ego. Anxiety can be divided into objective (equivalent to fear), neurotic (the ego is afraid of the id impulses rather than of the external world), and moral (caused by the superego and felt as guilt, self-depreciation, the desire for punishment, or some forms of depression). The major purpose of ego defense mechanisms is to reduce anxiety, and most of the strategies are protective. Such mechanisms include rationalization, projection, reaction-formation, displacement, and sublimation. The bywords to personality functioning are moderation, the golden mean, conformity, compromise, and a degree of acceptance of conditions as they exist.

SUGGESTED READINGS

Freud, Sigmund. The Psychopathology of Everyday Life. New York: New American Library, 1904.
> Freud expands his theories to include normal persons. He cites numerous examples of the instance of psychopathology in everyday life. He discusses lapses of memory, slips of speech, accident proneness, mistakes, and other similar forms of unconscious behavior. This is a good second book on Freud.

The Ego and the Id. London: Hogarth Press, 1923.
> This brief book presents Freud's earliest ideas on the systems within personality. The relationships between the ego and the id are extensively explored.

Civilization and Its Discontents. London: Hogarth Press, 1930.
> In this book Freud discusses the conflicts between the individual and society, and also the conflicts within the individual. An excellent treatment of the superego is presented. The book is an excellent supplement to this chapter.

Outline of Psychoanalysis. New York: W. W. Norton and Company, 1938.
> This was Freud's last book. It is brief and easier to understand than his other works. It was intended to be an introduction to psychoanalysis for the nonspecialist. It is the best source for a beginner in the study of Freud.

Fenichel, O. The Psychoanalytic Theory of Neurosis. New York: W. W. Norton and Company, 1945.
> The author is a disciple of Freud and presents an excellent coverage of the concepts and methods of psychoanalysis. He adheres closely to the Freudian concepts and methods.

REFERENCES

Bronfenbrenner, U. Freudian theories of identification and their derivations. Child Dev. *31*:15–40, 1960.

Coleman, J. C. Abnormal Psychology and Modern Life, 4th ed. Chicago: Scott, Foresman and Company, 1972.

Dollard, J., and Miller, N. Personality and Psychotherapy. New York: McGraw-Hill, 1950.

Eriksen, C. W. Discrimination and learning without awareness: A methodological survey and evaluation. Psychol. Rev. 67:279–300, 1960.

Freud, A. The Ego and Mechanisms of Defense. New York: International Universities Press, 1946.

Freud, S. The Problem of Anxiety. New York: W. W. Norton and Company, 1936.

Freud, S. The Standard Edition of the Complete Psychological Works. London: Hogarth Press, 1963.

> The Interpretation of Dreams, 1900. Vol. 5.
> The Psychopathology of Everyday Life, 1901. Vol. 6.
> Formulations on the two principles of mental functioning, 1911. Vol. 12, pp. 213–26.
> On the History of the Psychoanalytic Movement, Papers on Metapsychology, and Other Works, 1914, Vol. 14.
> Introductory Lectures on Psychoanalysis, 1917. Vols. 15–16.
> Beyond the pleasure principle, 1920. Vol. 18, pp. 7–64. (a)
> Group psychology and the analysis of the ego, 1920. Vol. 18, pp. 67–143. (b)
> The dissolution of the Oedipus complex, 1924. Vol. 19, pp. 173–9.
> Inhibitions, symptoms, and anxiety, 1925. Vol. 20, pp. 77–172.
> The Future of an Illusion, 1927. Vol. 21.
> Civilization and its Discontents, 1930. Vol. 21.
> New Introductory Lectures on Psychoanalysis, 1933. Vol. 22.

Glucksberg, S., and King, L. J. Motivated forgetting mediated by implicit verbal chaining: A laboratory analog of repression. Science 167:517–19, 1967.

Grim, P. F., Kohlberg, L., and White, S. H. Some relationships between conscience and attentional processes. J. Pers. Social Psychol. 8:239–52, 1968.

Morgan, C., and King, R. An Introduction to Psychology, 4th ed. New York: McGraw-Hill, 1972.

Munn, N. L., et al. Introduction to Psychology, 2nd ed. Boston: Houghton Mifflin, 1969.

Putney, S., and Putney, G. J. The Adjusted American: Normal Neuroses in the Individual and Society. New York: Harper and Row, 1964.

Webb, W. B., and Agnew, H. W., Jr. Sleep and Dreams. Dubuque, Iowa: William C. Brown, 1973.

White, R. W. Ego and reality in psychoanalytic theory. Psychol. Issues 3:1–210, 1963.

Wolitzky, D. Cognitive control and cognitive dissonance. J. Pers. Social Psychol. 5:486–90, 1967.

CHAPTER 11

The Real Versus the Ideal Self

Karen Horney

Karen Horney (1885–1952)

BIOGRAPHY AND OVERVIEW

Karen Horney was born in Hamburg, Germany, in 1885. The only child of a sea captain father, she distinguished herself as a pioneer in the field of psychiatry and was instrumental in eradicating the image that medicine was strictly a man's profession. She received her medical training at the University of Berlin. For 14 years she was associated with the Berlin Psychoanalytic Institute—from 1918 to 1932. She came to the United States in 1932 and became Associate Director of the Chicago Psychoanalytic Institute. In 1934 she moved to New York City and began a private practice. Her first major work, *The Neurotic Personality of Our Time*, was published in 1937 and was followed by four other books, the last published in 1950. Horney was a co-founder of the American Institute of Psychiatry. She died of cancer in 1952, at the age of sixty-seven.

Although trained in the Freudian tradition, Horney gradually became convinced that psychoanalysis was one-sided in its stress on the genetic and instinctive determinants of behavior (Horney, 1939). When she came to America, during the great depression, she came face to face with the powerful role of environmental forces—economic, social, and educational. In dealing with the problems of her patients, she found Adler's ideas and Fromm's stress on social forces more helpful than Freudian theory. Rather than being tormented by sexual fixations, a man might be struggling with problems associated with career, marriage, and setting feasible goals for himself. Horney believed that women were not by nature inferior to men, but were being treated as if they were. She disagreed with Freud about feminine penis envy—the need to be dominant and masterful. She demonstrated by her own

312

example that a woman could fulfill herself both in a profession and as a home-maker. She pursued an active career and brought up five daughters.

Unlike Freud, Horney (1937) did not accept the notion that conflict is inevitable; rather, she believed that it is acquired through the faulty training and expectations of the child. Her basic ideas regarding the formation of neurotic trends are:

1. The child is subjected to a stressful environment which produces *basic anxiety*.
2. A strategy is developed to cope with the stress.
3. Because the strategy reduces anxiety, it becomes highly significant for the individual. It actually becomes a need.
4. The strategy (or need) may be elevated to the status of a general orientation to life. It becomes *compulsive* and is *indiscriminately used*.

Some of the adverse conditions which foster the development of maladaptive strategies are: overdomination by parents, indifference, erratic treatment, lack of respect for the child's individual needs, lack of real guidance, disparaging attitude, too much admiration (or the absence of it), lack of encouragement and warmth from parents, too much (or too little) responsibility, overprotection, isolation from other children, injustice, discrimination, unkept promises, hostile atmosphere, quarrelsome parents, and so forth (Horney, 1945).

Under such conditions, the child becomes insecure and works out a strategy to alleviate his feelings of insecurity. One child finds that he can reduce his insecurity by compliance with his parents' requests, even though he must sacrifice his own wishes. Another finds that he can get what he wants by becoming hostile and aggressive, but that he must suppress his more tender emotions in the process. Still another discovers that aloofness and detachment work in her family setting, but that she has to hold back her own desires for self-assertion and love. In each orientation something is lost while anxiety-reduction is accomplished. The particular strategy becomes habitual and generalized as a total approach to life.

It is important to remember that Horney considered neurosis a matter of degree. Both healthy and unhealthy forces exist in all persons: "Neurosis, it must be said, is always a matter of degree — and when I speak of 'a neurotic' I invariably mean 'a person to the extent that he is neurotic.' For him awareness of feelings and desires is at a low ebb. Often the only feelings experienced consciously and clearly are reactions of fear and anger to blows dealt to vulnerable spots. And even these may be repressed" (Horney, 1945, p. 28). Horney (1942) identified ten neurotic needs and then later derived from these three orientations toward social relationships (Horney, 1945): *moving toward people, moving against people, and moving away from people*. These major orientations have normal and abnormal expressions. In her last formal statement of the theory Horney expanded the social orientations to encompass a wider scope, the total orientation to life. She named these general orientations (1) *self-effacing solution* (striving for love), (2) *expansive solution* (striving for mastery), and (3) *resignation* (striving for freedom).

TABLE 11-1 TEN NEUROTIC NEEDS

Neurotic Need	Specific Manifestations	Social Orientation	General Orientation to Life
Affection and approval	Wishes to please others and to live up to their expectations	Toward	Self-effacing (Compliant)
Dominant partner in life	Is a parasite and is afraid of being deserted and independent	Toward	Self-effacing
Power	Believes in the omnipotence of will, craves power for its own sake	Against	Expansive (Mastery)
Exploitation of others	Uses people for his own gain	Against	Expansive
Prestige	Bases self-evaluation upon the amount of public recognition he receives	Against	Expansive
Personal admiration	Wishes to be admired for the inflated picture he has of himself	Against	Expansive
Ambition in personal achievement	Wants and strives to be the best	Against	Expansive
Narrowly confined limits of life	Is undemanding, content with little, values modesty	Away from	Resigned (Detached)
Self-sufficiency and independence	Refuses to be tied down; desires total freedom	Away from	Resigned
Perfection and unassailability	Tries to make himself infallible	Away from	Resigned

Table 11-1 lists Horney's ten neurotic needs and briefly describes them. It also designates the social orientation and the general orientation to life associated with each need. Everyone may possess these needs, but in the neurotic person they are quite strong and generalized (Horney, 1937). Furthermore, one need usually predominates and becomes a compelling force. The needs develop as a consequence of the child's efforts to find solutions for disturbed social relationships. However, the solutions are irrational.

Although Horney focused almost exclusively on the neurotic aspects of personality, both her work as a therapist and her definition of neurosis as a matter of degree obviously demonstrate that she was interested in bringing about health and normality. To know what she considered normal, the reader must simply convert each quality to its opposite throughout the discussion of her theory of neurosis. A number of personality psychologists (e.g., Allport, 1961; Maslow, 1970) would oppose this approach and argue for a distinction between not being sick and being healthy. Yet despite Horney's influence by the physician's bias—to treat the sick rather than to promote optimal growth and functioning—her theory offers us many useful insights and guides to healthy living.

Life in a capitalistic system seems to hold out many benefits, but it also creates many stresses. One is tempted by "the good things"—status, power, wealth, and fame—with the expressed hope that everyone may have them, whereas in reality the competition is fierce and the attainment of great success is possible for relatively few. From the earliest period of life, the child is tantalized with a glamorous world of make-believe; television, newspapers, and magazines—indeed all the media, including parents, of course—portray the "beautiful people" who live the glamorous lives. One of the basic points Horney (1937) made regarding the relation of culture to personality growth is that the culture imposes the stresses which hamper growth and at the same time provides false solutions that are appealing and simple to follow. Such solutions are a mirage that can lead only to a chronically disordered personality. They take the form of an abandonment of the *real self* for the sake of pursuing an *idealized version of the self*. Many striking changes in personality development result from the rejection of the potentialities of the real self and the vain attempt to actualize the idealized or glamorous self. This is the theme that will be taken from Horney's work.

THE REAL SELF, THE IDEAL SELF-IMAGE, AND THE IDEAL SELF

We all confront the tasks of setting goals for ourselves and working out our aspirations toward a better life. We form an idealized self-image, which is the self we would like to be. We might think of this self-image as the conception of the perfected or ideal self. Yet there is always the danger of confusion between one's notions of his real self and of the self he would like to become. If in fact one adopts the idealized image of self as the real self, the basis for neurosis is established, in Horney's (1950) view. The distinction between the real self and the ideal self is blurred, and the person begins to distort reality.

Horney believed that there are many factors which promote a faulty conception of self. One needs an ideal self-image as an objective toward which to strive. But one's capacities and abilities are difficult to assess: it is quite natural to overestimate or even underestimate them.

Horney believed that one should constantly examine his ideal image of self and compare it with his actual achievements and performances. There should always be a fairly clear awareness of the difference between the real self and the aspired or ideal self. Ultimately, one should attempt to actualize his real self in order to perfect it. One should continually strive to insure a *close correspondence* between what one really is and one's conception or image of self.

Adequate functioning of the self presupposes a favorable environment, and especially the early environment. During this period of time the self lacks the resources and strength to administer the organism. This vital function is the major task of the parents; they make the decisions for the child. Gradually the self emerges as a source of control and growth, and inner controls are substituted for the outer forces.

Horney believed that the child has his own individual nature which must be given full freedom to develop. The deceptively simple key to liberating the forces of the self is self-knowledge (Horney, 1950). The individual, no matter how favorable his environment, will possess both constructive and destructive tendencies. The destructive tendencies may be dealt with by a punitive environment, by severe inner dictates of a harsh conscience, or by suitable learning. Horney favored the *outgrowing of the undesirable tendencies* as a result of learning, particularly learning about the self. To work at one's self is a requirement of liberating and cultivating the forces of the self.

For the self to unfold to its fullest, the child must be given opportunity in accordance with his inner potential. This requires warmth, encouragement, being a part of the family, respect of his rights, and even a certain amount of friction with those about him (Horney, 1950). When parents do not provide the appropriate atmosphere and ingredients to promote growth, the following development ensues: the child experiences insecurity or anxiety; he works out strategies to defend against the anxiety; these usually relieve only some tension temporarily and at the expense of the attainment of full growth. Basic anxiety is painful and adverse. It is difficult to describe. Horney (1937) defined it as the *feeling of being isolated and helpless in a world that is potentially hostile.* Feeling utterly helpless and alone in a life situation that one cannot master is certainly a terrifying state.

CLARIFICATION OF THE NOTION OF THE IDEAL SELF

The reader may find some confusion in the distinction between the real and the ideal selves as Horney used these concepts. At times she spoke as if there were *two selves.* For instance, she used the analogy of a civil war raging within the personality—a war between the real self and the ideal self. It may help to clear up the confusion to make a more detailed distinction between the real self and the self-image. Man is capable of reflecting upon his psychological and physical processes. One may know something and know that he knows. Just as one may form perceptions of objects in his world, so one may also form a perception of himself. The perception of self (we may call it a self-image) stands for the self. It is not the self, but a representation of it, just as a perception of an object is not the same as the object. The representation or image of self may or may not correspond quite well with the existing self. Thus "what I am" may or may not correspond with "what I think I am." A peculiar situation exists with respect to the causes of actual behavior when the self-image and the real self do not correspond.

One major source of motivation—if not the most important—centers about the self-image. If a person pictures himself as a great athlete, he will entertain fantasies of his great feats and subsequent acclaim. Many psychological activities will be organized around this self-image. Ultimately, he will act upon the image; he will try out for the football team, or whatever. The self-image sets expectancies, aspirations, or demands upon the real self.

The person who follows the dictates of his image of self and firmly believes that his representation of self is his real self creates problems for his real self. *The conflict between the ideal and the real self, which Horney took as the basis of neurosis, derives from a faulty representation of self that is acted upon.*

Multiple Conceptions of Self

Horney followed the simplest distinction with her notions of the real self and the self-image. The actual picture is much more complex, as Jourard (1963) has pointed out. One may have images of potential selves. Thus, in addition to the image of self, there may be an image or conception of the perfected real self. One might say: "I know what I want to be; I also know what I ought to be; and I know what my parents want me to be." One may also have an image or conception of what might be termed "the despised self." Horney did in fact bring out these various selves, or self-images, but she did not name them explicitly. Her major concern was with the discrepancies between the real or actual self and the idea of self which the person possesses.

MOVING TOWARD, AGAINST, OR AWAY FROM PEOPLE

Depending on the nature of the child—his learning experience, his temperament and abilities—and depending upon the nature of the parents, the child may react by acquiring a fixed behavior pattern. For instance, the child may find (1) that compliance with the parents (doing what they ask and demand) is the only way to keep anxiety away; (2) that aggressiveness and resistance to the wishes of the parents, if pursued long enough, will also get the desired results; or (3) that escape—keeping away physically—is the best strategy. These three trends can be summarized as moving toward, moving against, and moving away from people.

The compliant individual acquires needs, sensitivities, inhibitions, and even values that center about winning affection and acceptance by others. He desires to be saintly, good, perfect, a true friend. The aggressive person seeks to win the good things of life, to be in control of things and himself, to be a tower of strength and composure. The person who solves his problems by aloofness aims at detachment and inviolability. He desires total self-sufficiency. *Any one of these three directions can become the focal organizing principle which pervades the total personality of the neurotic* (Horney, 1945). *Any one of the three directions is a major limitation to growth.*

The three trends that Horney maintained become fixed styles of life are glorified by literature, drama, the parents, and in general by the carriers of the culture. Consider the individual whose major orientation is moving toward people: his idealized type is the saintly, selfless, noncombatant person who gets along with everyone and is loved and admired by all who know him. He is the real lover of mankind, a true humanitarian. This ideal is exemplified by the suffering hero who, despite great adversity and misunderstanding by others, emerges victorious in the end. His glory is all the greater because he is humble and courageous.

For the person who moves against people in his effort to secure safety for himself, the ideal image is also readily available. The conquering hero who is strong and masterful and willingly obeyed is an appealing model for the young child. Everything desirable — power, fame, wealth, and adulation — accrues to the strong, powerful individual.

The person who by temperament and circumstance takes a direction away from people has an idealized image too. Some of the most highly respected humans are the philosophers, the great theologians, the dedicated scientists — the great benefactors of mankind with enviable status — who live above the mundane and commonplace. Horney stated that the person who moves away from people "feels himself akin to a rare oriental rug, unique in its pattern and combination of colors, forever unalterable. . . . He takes extraordinary pride in having kept free of the leveling influences of environment and is determined to keep on doing so" (1945, p. 81).

THE ALIENATION FROM SELF

The process of alienation which Horney described as the central inner conflict is the total abandonment of the real self for the sake of the ideal self. The person who rejects his real self has lost touch with his greatest source of strength (May, 1953). Everyone confronts this conflict. In striving to improve the real self, an image of the perfected self is formed and used as a guide. The image may be unrealistic, or the person may believe that he is closer to being perfected than he really is. These matters are difficult to assess, and one can easily make mistakes. Figure 11-1 portrays the alienation process by pointing out the discrepancy that may exist between the conception of self and the real self.

Gradually the person *becomes his ideal self.* Being much more appealing than the real self, the idealized self is easily identified as real. To the frustrated child, the discovery of the ideal self is a momentous event because it opens up a variety of possibilities that previously did not exist. Then too, it offers the prospect of solving all his problems. The feelings of inadequacy, alienation from others, inner discord — feelings the child continues to experience — can be easily rationalized, for what he really has become, in his own view, is a wonderful, glorious person with extraordinary powers and endowments! Being his ideal self becomes a tantalizing prospect and is sought after ten-

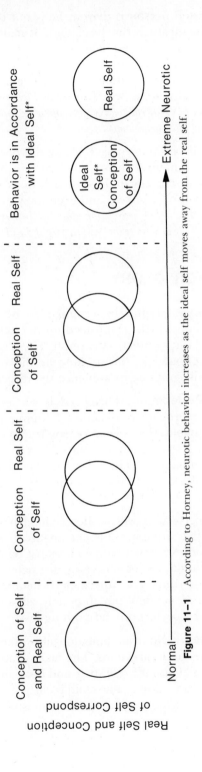

Figure 11–1 According to Horney, neurotic behavior increases as the ideal self moves away from the real self.

aciously. The frustrated person is driven; he is not the driver. So strong is identification with the ideal self that he clings to it at all cost. The biggest price he pays is neglect of the real potentialities he has. He chases after the talents and abilities he does not have. The great qualities attributed to oneself, even though they are unreal, flow naturally from the alienation of the real self and the identification with the ideal self. *Horney pointed out that the ideal self is the logical outcome of conditions during early development, and when it occurs, it is the beginning of a new line of development.*

In brief, the ideal self becomes more real for the person than the real self. Since there is always a natural thrust outward, toward self-expression, the person's life is changed radically in the direction of expressing the glamorous self. The real assets are overlooked, and eventually even demeaned, for the sake of the ideal qualities. *The search for glory is Horney's way of designating the abandonment of the real self to pursue the actualizing of the ideal self* (Horney, 1950).*

THE SEARCH FOR GLORY

The "search for glory" is regularly accompanied by three needs that take unique form in each individual: (1) the need for perfection, (2) neurotic ambition, and (3) the need for a vindictive triumph. These needs may vary in form of expression throughout life, but as long as the individual pursues the idealized self, they will continue to influence the direction of behavior.

1. The Need for Perfection.   This need is a logical implication of the desire for glory. The search for perfection is a common quest of youth, but in the course of development, the normal person learns to accept compromises and less than perfection—the good with the bad. When the ideal self is in control, imperfection is intolerable. The person *must* be perfect. As Horney says: "The neurotic is the Faust who is not satisfied with knowing a great deal, but has to know everything" (1950, p. 35).

The nature of the perfection will be determined by the direction toward which the individual has organized his personality: toward, against, or away from people. If he moves toward people, he must be not only morally good but saintly and without flaw. If he moves against people, he must be not only capable but most extraordinary: a superman. If he moves away from people, he must be not only independent but absolutely self-sufficient. Whatever the direction, there *must* be perfection and nothing less.

2. Neurotic Ambition.   Neurotic ambition also takes individual form on the basis of one of the three directions. The main component is excelling, or supremacy over others. This indiscriminate and insatiable urge to excel is part of the fabric of American culture. The child is early taught to be a good competitor. As one popular expression has it, "To win isn't everything, but to lose

---

*It should be noted that by *alienation* Horney did not mean cultural estrangement or rejection by others, which is a current meaning of the term, but rather the much more devastating process of the loss of the real self.

is nothing." The goals sought are grandiose and fantastic. They may be totally unrealistic and not at all in tune with the individual's potentialities. But the fact that they are lofty and highly desirable endows their pursuit with a sense of significance and urgency.

3. The Need for Vindictive Triumph.   This need manifests itself consciously as a desire to surpass and humiliate others. Despite the noble ideals, the neurotic experiences a great deal of misery. He does not really accomplish his goals, and thus the solution he adopts dooms him to continuous failure. He does not abandon the search for glory, however, as he *has rejected his real self.* Instead he becomes bitter and resentful of those who have power over him. He blames them for his problems and frustrations: the reason he lost his job was that the boss hated him; the teacher failed him because she did not like the truly bright students; someday those who have hurt him will appreciate his true worth—they will pay for what they have done to him.

NEUROTIC NEEDS AND VICIOUS CIRCLES

Neurotic needs lead to a condition that may be described as a vicious circle (Horney, 1937). The neurotic need creates conditions which intensify the need. To begin with, the need is unrealistic in that it cannot be satisfied, at least to the extent the person desires. *Because the need cannot be gratified completely, fear is always associated with its arousal. Fear becomes a regular component of all the neurotic's major needs. This fear, in turn, increases the intensity of the need.* The greater need instigates more intense fear, and greater effort is expended to gratify it; hence the vicious circle.

If a person seeks glory by means of domination—by being always the winner, the leader, the feared and respected one—he has a strong fear that these needs will be frustrated. As he inevitably fails (because the need to dominate admits of no exception), the fear associated with his desire to dominate is increased. Rather than decreasing the desire, he actually increases it and may go to extremes to ward off the fear. Thus a condition of insatiability may occur; he never gets enough power or control or respect from underlings. Because fear is associated with his needs, there is a compulsive quality about them: he is trapped. The neurotic is locked into a certain course by his needs, and the only real solution to his trapped existence is to return to his real self.

IMAGINATION AND THE SEARCH FOR GLORY

The normal person may have whimsical moments—daydreams—when he temporarily flees from harsh reality to an inner world of make-believe, but he is fully aware of this excursion into the unreal. He does not make decisions, plan, or take action on the basis of sheer daydreams; he does not live by them (Singer, 1966). While the normal person keeps in touch with reality, the neurotic distorts it, sometimes quite seriously. Horney pointed out that his imagination often soars into unlimited possibilities. For example, he believes that posing puzzling questions about life is sufficient to prove that he has great depth of personality and is different from the masses. Imagination goes to work to serve the ideal self, and this is largely done unconsciously. There begins to be an air of artificiality about the person. His relationships with others are superficial. Even his feelings, which are often displayed dramatically, are hollow and not genuine. Paradoxically, he agonizes and worries about things that he cannot change and overlooks those things that he should (Temerlin, 1965).

Since the attributes of the ideal self are grandiose and fantastic, the neurotic must have recourse to imagination to bring about the many distortions that support them. It is noteworthy that the ideal self emerges as a result of neurotic needs to relieve basic anxiety. Once it takes shape, the process of distortion must intensify. The glorious image of self *drastically changes the approach to life.* The neurotic who has lost the appreciation of reality renounces the ordinary means of obtaining gratification of his needs. He wants to be on the mountain without climbing it; work may become abhorrent to him, for his goals are so far beyond anything he can accomplish that other techniques must be substituted.

THE DEVIL'S PACT

Horney presented a vivid analogy, which she called "The Devil's Pact," to describe the process of alienation from the real to the ideal self. The basis of the pact is the *desire for greatness* and the equally strong desire for an *easy way out.* The despicable real self is renounced for the glorious ideal self. All one has to do is to give up the claim to the real self. This the neurotic does quite readily, for the real self is despised. The price to be paid is eventual hell for the total self, but there are moments of grandeur and the immediate expectation of relief from an unbearable life situation. The person sells his soul, the real self, for fabricated glory, the ideal self (Horney, 1950). Horney says:

I now saw gradually that the neurotic's idealized image did not merely constitute a false belief in his value and significance; it was rather like the creation of a Frankenstein monster which in time usurped his best energies. It eventually usurped his drive to grow, to realize his given potentialities. And this meant that he was no longer interested in realistically tackling or outgrowing his difficulties, and in fulfilling his potentials, but was bent on actualizing his idealized self. It entails not only the compulsive drive for worldly glory through success, power, and triumph but also the tyrannical inner system by which he tries to mold himself into a godlike being; it entails neurotic claims and the development of neurotic pride (1950, pp. 367–8).*

ATTEMPTS TO SUSTAIN THE GLORIOUS SELF-IMAGE

Horney delineated four methods by which the neurotic, often assisted by his imagination, seeks to maintain a godlike or glorious image of self: (1) *neurotic pride,* (2) *neurotic claims,* (3) *tyrannical shoulds,* and (4) *auxiliary protective strategies.*

---

*© 1950 by W. W. Norton and Co., Inc. Reprinted by permission.

1. NEUROTIC PRIDE VERSUS REAL PRIDE

Real Pride

Pride stems from an evaluation of self and takes the form of self-regard or self-love. The person who overvalues himself suffers from false pride, which Horney considered neurotic pride. Self-condemnation ultimately follows upon false pride. This undercutting of the self may range from misguided humility to a deep sense of personal inferiority.

A genuine pride requires a basic foundation in fact. A student, for instance, may be justly proud of his marks if he earns them honestly and has worked hard for them. Genuine pride, because it is grounded in fact, is not usually demonstrated in pompous displays. The person enjoys a deep sense of accomplishment and may experience a momentary elevation of self-esteem.

Neurotic Pride: Needs Become Virtues

To bolster the ideal self, neurotic needs may be transformed into virtues by means of distortion, rationalization, displacement, and compartmentalization. An appreciation of this process is vital if we are to understand the operation of neurotic pride. Not all neurotic needs are converted to virtues, only those that suit the dominant character structure. If an individual's primary reaction in human relations is one of compliance and submission, a giving in rather than an asserting of self, this compliant tendency will be transformed. As compliance is considered a sign of weakness in our culture, it cannot fit the idealized self-image. It thus becomes a sensitivity to the needs of others, a genuinely human desire to promote harmony. Conversely, the individual who is uncontrollably self-seeking and uses any method at his disposal to dominate over others may transform this basically selfish motivation by calling it competitive spirit, being a "good scrapper." He further justifies his unscrupulous behavior by reasoning that the loser has learned a lesson. Again, the person who pursues his activities in solitude, unable either to relate well to others or to deal with them by open competition, may glorify his conduct by holding that he is rejecting enslavement by the allurements of the world. He finds his fulfillment in self-sufficiency. He does not need "big happenings" to make him content.

Thus, under the influence of his dominant orientation to life, each person's particular weakness is easily touched up and converted from a flaw which he cannot accept into a highly prized virtue. Obviously such hypocrisy and sham ultimately hinder the development and functioning of the personality. No real change in behavior occurs with the transformation of the neurotic needs into virtues. If anything, the person is less equipped to deal with his problems, as he has converted weaknesses into presumed strengths by means of self-deception. Until the real self gains ascendance, the real potentials for growth will be overlooked.

Since neurotic pride is an exaggerated form of self-valuation, it sensitizes the one who possesses it to threat and injury to a remarkable degree. A slight irritation may provoke a strong and prolonged fear or rage reaction. The reasoning is something like this: "I am a very special person—how could you do this to me? It would be bad enough to do it to others, but to do it to me is absolutely despicable." The fear of injury is also reflected in the neurotically proud individual's rejection of situations that might provoke shame or humiliation, such as competing in sports, asking for a date, or giving a talk before a group. The pride system demands that such situations be *avoided,* not overcome. This may involve a general emotional suppression which inhibits the most alive portion of the personality. A rigid caution against spontaneous expression of thoughts and feelings may be adopted as a method of dealing with social relationships.

Often the very quality of which the neurotic is most proud is the one that needs the greatest change. He may flaunt his refusal to be pushed around, but he would do much better if he were not so driven to win every battle that the fear of losing deadens his personality.

The demands of the ideal self, with accompanying neurotic pride, convert existing needs into neurotic claims and imperfections of the self into impossible shoulds. We will now turn our attention to these claims and shoulds.

2. NEUROTIC CLAIMS

Neurotic claims—neurotic needs transformed by the imagination—involve the *groundless assertion of a right or title.* They are quite different from genuine needs in that an element of personal due is added. The neurotic says in effect: "I like and appreciate this very much and therefore, by that very fact, it should be mine."

Cultural practices often support the formation of neurotic claims. On Christmas, birthdays, and other holidays, children are showered with gifts and much attention. The statement "Christmas is really for children" exemplifies this practice. (A child who came from a large family with many unmarried members asked her mother, upon receiving a large number of gifts, "Why does everyone love me so much?") During infancy the child's main strategy, although obviously not consciously formulated, is to obtain gratification of his requirements on the claim of being helpless but very lovable. The child reared under conditions of pampering and indulgence readily claims all sorts of things solely on the basis of being a "glorious person." The tendency to idealize the self comes rather naturally, and thus this tendency should be restrained rather than encouraged by the parents. Usually restraint is achieved by requiring more and more from the child. He must eventually earn what he gets, develop his real abilities, and adjust to and master his environment.

A need that has been *converted* to a claim produces much more intense frustration than the same need not so transformed. Frustration is an unpleasant psychic state for all, but the person who has transformed his needs to claims considers it a direct affront and a cause for righteous indignation.

The Relation of Claims to Moving Toward, Against, or Away from People

Like most aspects of his search for perfection, the neurotic's claims are organized around his major direction in life. If he moves toward people (the self-effacing orientation) as a means of getting what he needs, his claim will take the form of expecting unqualified love. He must be constantly reassured of the love of the other. An example is the wife who expects her husband to call her several times a day from work. She may be obsessed with jealousy and nag him incessantly for supposed infidelity. The irony of such a situation is that the person who is claiming the devotion of his partner usually does not do anything to deserve the love. The love is demanded by the assumed qualities bestowed by the ideal self (Horney, 1950).

The person with the expansive orientation who manipulates people for his own ends (moving against people) claims that something should be his simply because it is available. Why should he not have the good things of life, since he knows others who possess them and are obviously inferior to him? The fact that those who possess the good things had to work hard and sacrifice a great deal is conveniently glossed over. He claims respect and allegiance from others on the basis of his assumed qualities of leadership and competence (Horney, 1950).

The detached person with the resigned orientation (moving away from people) does not seem to make claims. He wants to be left alone. But he does make at least one claim: not to be held responsible for ordinary obligations. This requirement may not appear to be a claim at all, but it is. He may object that as he criticizes no one and makes no demands of anyone, they should not criticize him. If he is reproved for not doing what is expected of him at home, he may feel unjustly persecuted (Horney, 1950). This example clearly illustrates the subtlety of neurotic claims. Since the claim is not based on real attributes, its fulfillment may be presumed just as magically by the neurotic, compounding the illusion. *The implicit desire for an easy solution underlies all neurotic claims.*

How to Deal with Claims

As we have noted, Horney held that the basis for claims is the identification of the self with the idealized self-image. The best preventive measure is not to allow the real self to make the transformation. One should strive continually for self-knowledge and exploration. Since it is easy to convert a need to a claim, one should frequently examine his basic needs and expectations. Horney (1942) held that the self is highly complex: it is analogous to a large city which one could explore for years before finding all the major and minor points of interest. Learning about one's claims is like learning about the city's governing agencies.

Even the most balanced person will discover some claims behind his behavior. Expectations may be set too high, given present accomplishments, or they may be set too low. An examination of the means necessary to reach desired goals will guard against insidious conversion of needs to claims. One must also develop effective ways of dealing with the frustration that inevitably accompanies goal pursuit.

3. THE TYRANNY OF THE "SHOULDS"

One characteristic of the search for glory, it will be recalled, is the need for personal perfection. Personal perfection, which helps to sustain a godlike image of self, is brought about through a system of inner dictates or expectations which Horney designated "the tyranny of the 'shoulds.'" Like claims, shoulds are intended to suit the individual to the level required by his ideal self (Table 11–2). The difference is that while claims are unrealistic demands of people and things outside the person, shoulds are unrealistic expectations of oneself.

TABLE 11–2 METHODS OF MAINTAINING THE IDEAL SELF

Claims	Shoulds
Feels entitled never to be criticized, doubted, or questioned	Should be the epitome of honesty, generosity, justice, dignity, courageousness, unselfishness
Feels entitled to blind obedience	
Feels entitled to fool everyone	Should be the perfect lover, husband, teacher
Feels entitled to immunity and exception	Should overcome difficulties easily
Expects to be loved by all he meets	Should overcome bad moods simply by willing
Claims to impress all	
Claims to be honored by all	Should be able to endure everything
Claims to be close to others	Should be able to like everyone
Claims to live in peace; deplores combat	Should be able to love his parents, country
All needs must be fulfilled	
Feels self-sufficient (does not want to be bothered by others)	Should be spontaneous
Disdainful of others' rights	Should know and understand everything
Requires admiration	Should never be tired or ill
Claims to be openly aggressive and ambitious	Should be able to work endlessly and productively
Claims to be allowed to maintain his distance	Should be all things to all people
	Should be above pleasure
Claims not to have any problems	Should control his feelings
Claims to be better than anyone else and recognized for it	Should never feel hurt
	Should always be serene and unruffled
Claims to be exempt from illness	Nothing should matter to him
Claims to be pleased by others all the time	

Note: Both claims and shoulds follow the individual's major personality orientation; self-effacing, expansive, or resigned. Claims may be contradictory and create serious inner conflicts: e.g., expecting to be both loved and feared. Shoulds, too, may be contradictory and produce inner conflicts: e.g., being composed and dynamic at the same time.

Horney's concept of the shoulds applies to everyone to a greater or lesser degree. The task of dealing with personal expectations is universal. "How much should I demand of myself? When am I falling short of or exceeding my potentialities? How generous, or moral, or considerate, or hard-working, or humble should I be?" These are constant concerns of the healthiest of people. One should frequently examine his shoulds and attempt to bring them into line with his real self.

Shoulds Versus Realistic Self-Demands

The realistic expectations that the normal person imposes upon himself — those which take account of real assets and liabilities and prevailing circumstances — are the product of the real self. Shoulds, on the other hand, are grandiose and unattainable expectations of the real self that result from the influence of the idealized self. The justification for shoulds is obviously erroneous. Because one has attained superiority in one field, for example, he expects to be superior in all. Another individual assumes that work should be easy for him, for if he wills something, it should come to pass. Obviously the shoulds place the individual in great jeopardy and vulnerability. The uncompromising quality of a system of shoulds insures failure. One of the most devastating consequences of a system of shoulds is self-hate, because fulfillment is impossible.

To summarize briefly: the identification with the idealized self causes a hatred and contempt for the real self. This point is necessary for an understanding of Horney's conception of neurosis. The idealized self is endowed with false pride and becomes the *pride system.* The pride system, by means of shoulds and claims, has as its objective the obliteration of the hated and despicable real self. The seemingly contradictory observation that neurotics often display both pride and self-contempt makes sense in Horney's system. The *pride* stems from the ideal self and the *contempt* from the inadequacy of the real self.

4. AUXILIARY PROTECTIVE STRATEGIES

The auxiliary protective strategies can best be considered in outline form.

Mechanism	Description
Blind spots	Ignoring the conflict Being oblivious to the true situation Being "stupid" in certain areas of one's life Example: a husband who will not consider his inefficiency as a possible cause of family money problems
Compartmentalization	Segregating contradictory roles Behaving inconsistently without conscious awareness Solving conflicts by freely expressing both alternatives at different times

Mechanism	*Description*
	Example: a person who regularly attends church on Sundays but is unscrupulous in his business dealings
Rationalization	Self-deceiving by reasoning Minimizing or remodeling conflicting factors so that conflict is diminished Example: a person who calls his efforts to take advantage of others "a matter of good business"
Excessive self-control	Exertion of restraints over certain emotions and thoughts which are in conflict with opposite tendencies Resistance against distractions and personal motives Example: one who holds under control certain emotions such as enthusiasm, sex, rage, tenderness
Arbitrary rightness	Eliminating doubt from within and influence from without Regarding doubt and indecision as the worst evil Settling conflicts once and for all by declaring arbitrarily and dogmatically that one is invariably right Example: the politician who interprets all issues from the standpoint of the party line
Elusiveness	Avoiding being pinned down to any statement Choosing to remain undecided rather than resolve a conflict in favor of the wrong decision Considering all ramifications, consequences, and alternatives, then postponing a decision Example: the lawyer who refuses to give a definite opinion on the outcome of a case, but details all the possibilities instead
Cynicism	Denying and deriding moral values Not forming any values because there are none that are worthwhile Finding most things and people uninteresting Being overly discreet in tastes Example: the tired old man who wants to be left alone because there is nothing much left for him in life

CRITICAL EVALUATION

Horney was one of the first psychiatrists to call attention to cultural factors as major determinants of personality growth and functioning. Like Freud, she perceived the significance of the home environment, but she took a wider view and included the cultural forces: economic, social, political, educational, and the like. She saw that cultural practices could foster the development of abnormal trends. While Freud attempted to identify common factors that were universal in man, Horney focused upon the specific conditions of the culture and even subculture.

Horney was a master at deriving implications from a key concept. She would rival any medieval scholar in her deductive skills. In reading her work one is easily drawn away from the original assumptions and postulates and is caught up in the many ramifications and elaborations that she derived from them. Furthermore, it is difficult to separate empirical observation from inference because her only support is testimony from her own clinical experiences. Although her hypotheses have a common sense appeal, they must be tested empirically if they are to gain the status of behavioral principles. While she has a number of practicing disciples, it does not appear that her views are inspiring the necessary research support.

Nevertheless, the reader can certainly profit from the richness and depth of Horney's insights into man's deepest motivations. It should be possible to apply her ideas in promoting mental health. She devoted her entire career to this problem although, like other clinicians, she had more experience with the abnormal than with the normal. She was quite optimistic about the natural potential for growth and healthy functioning both in mankind in general and in each individual: "My own belief is that man has the capacity as well as the desire to develop his potentialities and become a decent human being, and that these deteriorate if his relationship to others and hence to himself is, and continues to be, disturbed. I believe that man can change and go on changing as long as he lives. And this belief has grown with deeper understanding" (1950, p. 22). To Horney, man's best hope for realizing his potential lies in positive support of his own constructive forces by the social environment.

INSIGHTS FROM HORNEY'S VIEWS ON NEUROSIS AND NORMALITY

In 1942, Horney wrote a book entitled *Self Analysis*. It was an attempt to provide the layman with insights from psychoanalysis that could be applied by everyone. She discussed free association, dream analysis, resistance, and transference. While the book is not a guide to mental health, it contains many valuable suggestions for improving one's life. We will consider some of these ideas.

ONE PROBLEM AT A TIME

Horney suggested that one should begin his self-analysis by identifying one problem area that is unmistakable. Undesirable traits or trends which are doubtful should not be taken up in the early stages of self-analysis. These problems will emerge as the analysis proceeds, if they are truly problems.

RATIONAL AND INTUITIVE APPROACH

Horney maintained that an approach which is both rational and intuitive should be applied. One basic step in analysis is to discover all aspects of a problem area. In looking at actual behavior, consider the various ways in which the problem is manifested. To achieve this objective, one can rely on Horney's views of neurotic trends. Is the major difficulty social relationships? Is it a matter of inflexibility in seeking to be loved, or to dominate, or to withdraw from others? Is the particular trend so compulsive that it rules the personality?

To Horney, one of the problem areas with which everyone must deal is the search for glory:

For his well-functioning, man needs both the vision of possibilities, the perspective of infinitude *and* the realization of limitations, of necessities, of the concrete. If a man's thinking *and* feeling are primarily focused upon the infinite and the vision of possibilities, he loses his sense for the concrete, for the here and now. He loses his capacity for living in the moment. He is no longer capable of submitting to the necessities in himself, "to what may be called one's limit." He loses sight of what is actually necessary for achieving something. . . . If, on the other hand, a man does not see beyond the narrow horizon of the concrete, the necessary, the finite, he becomes "narrow-minded and mean-spirited." It is not, then, a question of either-or, but of *both*, if there is to be growth. The recognition of limitations, laws, and necessities serves as a check against being carried away into the infinite, and against the mere "floundering in possibilities" (1950, p. 35).*

In addition to the manifestations of the undesirable trait, Horney suggested that one should look for interrelation of the trait with other characteristics. For instance, a trait of helplessness may be linked with a more general orientation of dependency. The dependency, in turn, may be associated with a profound fear of self-assertiveness. One should ask the question: How is the particular personality trait or trend embedded in the total structure of the personality?

One must also inquire about the scope of a trait—its centrality in the personality structure. Is the trait or trend a troublesome quirk which is occasionally set off, or is it a way of life?

Insight into the nature of a neurotic trend is often promoted by an understanding of the origins of the trend. Such analysis requires that one probe into his past. The probing should be done leisurely and without producing too much anxiety. If one begins to experience resentment, or hostility, or undue self-pity, it should be dropped until another time. One more point is salient here: Horney advised us to follow thoroughly one problem area rather than attempt a complete coverage of personality difficulties. As one gains insight into one problem area, other problems will emerge. But more importantly, personality functioning will begin to improve, and other problem areas will become easier to analyze.

DISCOVERY OF CLAIMS AND SHOULDS

Horney made a significant contribution to our knowledge of the psychodynamics of abnormal personality formations through her brilliant insights into the nature of neurotic claims and shoulds. We have already discussed the nature of both of these, but here we are concerned with the means of detecting them. Whether neurotic or not, everyone harbors some neurotic claims and shoulds, and their existence hampers the full development and functioning of personality. Table 11–3 contrasts normal and neurotic growth and summarizes the changes that take place in personality with the development of a neurosis.

---

*© 1950 by W. W. Norton and Co., Inc. Reprinted by permission.

TABLE 11-3 NORMAL VERSUS NEUROTIC GROWTH

Normal Growth Includes	*Neurotic Growth Includes*	
Actualizing self	Unrealistic claims	
Growth	Host of "shoulds"	
Self-realization	Neurotic striving for perfection	
Maturity	Unrealistic ambitions	
Fulfillment	Triumph over others	
Spontaneity	Pride, self-hate, contempt, self-accusations	
	Results:	
	Neurotic solutions: self-effacing or	
	expansive or resigned	
	Supported by one or more protective structures:	
	Blind spots	Arbitrary Rightness
	Compartments	Elusiveness
	Rationalization	Cynicism
	Excessive self-control	
	Alienation from real self	
	Striving to actualize ideal self	

It will be recalled that neurotic claims are unrealistic or unwarranted expectations or demands of people and things outside the person, whereas shoulds are unrealistic demands or expectations of oneself. A claim is an undeserved or unearned title that the person believes he has, while a should is a perfectionist demand that is applied to oneself. By their very nature claims and shoulds cannot be satisfied; thus one who possesses them will experience needless suffering—anxiety, resentment, disappointment, and anguish (in the case of unfulfilled claims)—and needless torture—self-accusation, self-contempt, self-hatred, negativism, and resistance against doing anything for oneself (in the case of shoulds).

Horney pointed out that shoulds are not simply ideals or high moral standards, but rather are glamorous and grandiose expectations. If anything, they are immoral because they are based on an inflated sense of self. Consider some of the following points:

1. One approaches a task with the attitude that he should be able to do it easily. When he fails, he begins to find excuses for himself. His approach to life is counterfeit.

2. One may expect himself to be consistently serene and calm, even in situations in which emotions are appropriate. This attitude may produce a blunting of emotional responses, and in fact the person may begin to lose touch with his emotions, so that he does not feel them when they occur.

3. Frequently there are contradictory shoulds, and the ensuing conflict may be extremely intense. "I should be all-loving, but also dynamic and aggressive." In such instances there may be sudden shifts of mood.

4. People often deal with the problems of aging, or attractiveness, or the other inevitables in life by converting them into shoulds. "It is unfair and totally unjust for this to be happening to me." "I hate the thought of growing old, so I simply won't allow it to happen; thus I am not getting old." Such thinking can become highly irrational and lead to reckless behavior to support the should.

5.   Shoulds may result from erroneous inferences. Because a person happens to be intelligent, he assumes that he should be able to write, or play the piano, or do almost anything — and furthermore, do these things easily and without too much work.

6.   If a particular should is especially powerful, the entire personality is made over. Real feelings, emotions, and desires are not experienced but are replaced with fictitious ones which suit the character of the should. One who is dominated by the inner dictate that he should love everyone is incapable of genuine love for certain persons because he has killed off this potential in himself. Instead, he experiences a pseudo, sham, or illusory love. His unreal love neither benefits him nor convinces others. He becomes progressively more unreal and shallow. The examination of such inner dictates to discover their grandiose and fantastic nature is absolutely essential to mental health. Horney said of the shoulds:

> We are less aware of the harm done our feelings by these pervasive shoulds than of other damage inflicted by them. Yet it is actually the heaviest price we pay for trying to mold ourselves into perfection. Feelings are the most alive part of ourselves; if they are put under a dictatorial regime, a profound uncertainty is created in our essential being, which must affect adversely our relations to everything inside and outside ourselves. We can hardly overrate the intensity of the impact of the inner dictates. The more the drive to actualize his idealized self prevails in a person, the more the shoulds become the sole motor force moving him, driving him, whipping him into action (1950, p. 84).*

Shoulds are interrelated with each person's style of life. Since these trends in the personality can only block the use of real abilities and the satisfaction of genuine needs, one should vigilantly question the bases of his assumptions, expectations, and demands, with respect to both himself and others. As one rids himself of neurotic trends, the potentialities of his real self begin to emerge.

TACKLING PROBLEM AREAS

The study of the self need not be an intensively critical self-scrutiny. There are degrees of self-exploration, and not everyone should attempt to plumb the depth and breadth of his inner life. But one certainly can tackle problem areas which are obvious. Taking Horney's analogy of the self as a large city, one might ask: What are the most important landmarks (traits or tendencies) in my self? Consider a typical problem: "People do not like me." Horney might suggest posing the following questions to oneself: Is it true that no one likes you? Do you think that you are more likable at some times than others? In your own opinion, are you not likable? What particular behaviors do you think are most unattractive about you? What is the simplest first step you can take to change a particularly undesirable behavior? Can you work out a simple program to change this behavior? Answers to such questions can set positive tendencies toward growth and mastery to work for everyone, Horney believed. We all have both destructive and constructive tendencies. The constructive ones must be supported and fostered if they are to operate spontaneously.

Horney believed that man can reduce or even eliminate his inner conflicts, though the process may be painful:

---

*© 1950 by W. W. Norton and Co., Inc. Reprinted by permission.

To experience conflicts knowingly, though it may be distressing, can be an invaluable asset. The more we face our own conflicts and seek out our own solutions, the more inner freedom and strength we will gain. When conflicts center about the primary issues of life, it is all the more difficult to face them and resolve them. But provided we are sufficiently alive, there is no reason why in principle we should not be able to do so. Education could do much to help us to live with greater awareness of ourselves and to develop our own convictions. A realization of the significance of the factors involved in choice would give us ideals to strive for, and in that a direction for our lives (1950, p. 27).*

SIGNIFICANT QUOTATIONS FROM HORNEY

Horney believed that the normal person is one who can integrate the three orientations to life—moving toward, against, and away from people:

From the point of view of the normal person there is no reason why the three attitudes [orientations to life] should be mutually exclusive. One should be capable of giving in to others, of fighting, and of keeping to oneself. The three can complement each other and make for a harmonious whole. If one predominates, it merely indicates an overdevelopment along one line (1945, pp. 45–6).

Her description of the work involved in self-improvement and integration parallels Maslow's concept of self-actualization (Chap. 14) and Carl Roger's picture of the fully functioning person (Chap. 13):

Putting the work to be done in positive terms, it concerns all that is involved in self-realization. With regard to himself it means striving toward a clearer and deeper experiencing of his feelings, wishes, and beliefs; toward a greater ability to tap his resources and to use them for constructive ends; toward a clearer perception of his direction in life, with the assumption of responsibility for himself and his decisions. With regard to others it means his striving toward relating himself to others with genuine feelings; toward respecting them as individuals in their own right and with their own peculiarities; toward developing a spirit of mutuality (instead of using them as a means to an end). With regard to work it means that the work itself will become more important to him than the satisfaction of his pride or vanity and that he will aim at realizing and developing his special gifts and at becoming more productive (1950, p. 364).*

Horney held that neurosis does not develop if the child is given the opportunity to grow and to actualize his inner nature. Neurosis is a thwarting of the constructive inner forces that are basic to man's nature. Conflict is not inherent but is created:

. . . the person who is likely to become neurotic is one who has experienced the culturally determined difficulties in an accentuated form, mostly through the medium of childhood experiences, and who has consequently been unable to solve them, or has solved them only at great cost to his personality. We might call him a stepchild of our culture (1937, p. 290).

Horney's concept of the basic discrepancy between the real and ideal selves is succinctly summarized in a passage which she cited from the poet Christian Morgenstern on the power of self-hate when the ideal self is dominant:

---

*© 1950 by W. W. Norton and Co., Inc. Reprinted by permission.

I shall succumb, destroyed by myself
I who am two, what I could be and what I am.
And in the end one will annihilate the other.
The *Would-be* is like a prancing steed
(*I am* is fettered to his tail),
Is like a wheel to which *I am* is bound,
Is like a fury whose fingers twine
Into his victim's hair, is like a vampire
That sits upon his heart and sucks and sucks
                        (1950, pp. 113–4).*

SUMMARY

1.   A pattern of unfavorable circumstances in the home produces in the child a condition which Horney termed basic anxiety: a feeling of being isolated and helpless in a potentially hostile environment. Healthy patterns of growth are blocked, and deviant ones are allowed to flourish.

2.   The child is forced to seek recourse in defensive strategies, the nature of which depends upon the circumstances of the home and his individual personality.

3.   The unwanted child who is both dominated and treated cruelly by his parents may be forced into a role of continual compliance and submission. He learns to avoid asserting his desires and even his rights. He gets along best in his world by a self-effacing orientation.

4.   The child who has a naturally high energy output and parents who are somewhat compliant orients to social relationships by moving against people. He fights down opposition and wins his way by overpowering others. His total orientation to life may be expansive, with the major motive being mastery.

5.   The child who is sensitive and passive by nature but who has dominant parents may learn that moving away from people is his best strategy for dealing with social relationships. He may develop a general orientation of detachment and resignation and do little to better his lot in life. He may avoid involvement with people and deal with his needs by denying them or lowering his level of aspiration.

6.   The child forms an idealized image of self because his real self is inadequate to deal with his circumstances. He gradually becomes his idealized self. Horney termed this process the alienation from self. The real source of growth is blocked and the major motivating force is the actualization of the ideal self.

---

*"Entwicklungsschmerzen" ("Growing Pains"), Caroline Newton, trans. From a collection of poems, *Auf Vielen Wegen.* Munich: R. Piper and Company, 1921.

7. The idealized self creates neurotic pride, which leads to immoderate self-regard. The demands of the ideal self with accompanying neurotic pride convert existing needs into neurotic claims and imperfections of the self into impossible "shoulds." The claims make over the outside world, while the shoulds make over the personality.

8. Needs which are compulsive, exaggerated, indiscriminate, and insatiable block the fulfillment of other needs and tendencies, producing conflicts. Horney termed the central conflict the continuing opposition of the ideal self and the real self.

9. Neurotic pride exaggerates both self-love and self-hatred. These attitudes also foster inner conflicts.

10. The neurotic solution—which takes the form of moving toward, or against, or away from people—produces conflict between the individual and the outside world. The direction of social relationships becomes part of a wider orientation, which may be described as self-effacing, expansive, or resigned.

11. The normal person keeps his image of self in close harmony with the abilities and accomplishments of his real self. He orients to people by moving toward them, or against them, or away from them, when he deems it appropriate to do so. He is neither overly self-effacing, nor driven to dominate and master, nor unduly resigned to conditions as they are. While he may have difficulties with certain needs, and while one need may be strong, he is flexible in his approach to life. He can moderate his demands and desires and accept substitutes when need gratification is blocked.

SUGGESTED READINGS

Horney, Karen. The Neurotic Personality of Our Time. New York: W. W. Norton and Company, 1937.
  Horney presents her sociopsychological view of neurosis, which holds that cultural influences, rather than the thwarting of sexual instincts, set the climate for neurosis. She stresses the striving towards security and away from anxiety.

New Ways in Psychoanalysis. New York: W. W. Norton and Company, 1939.
  In this book Horney brings out clearly her differences with the traditional Freudian views. She attempts to correct the one-sided stress on instinctual determinants by her analysis of the cultural determinants.

Self Analysis. New York: W. W. Norton and Company, 1942.
  The book is an attempt to convey to the layman some of the methods and concepts of psychoanalysis. Horney suggests that everyone could apply them with some benefit. The book deals with self-exploration and understanding.

Our Inner Conflicts. New York: W. W. Norton and Company, 1945.
  In this book Horney presents her three social orientations: moving toward, away from, and against people. She discusses the role of conflict extensively. She details the differences between normal and neurotic social relationships.

Neurosis and Human Growth. New York: W. W. Norton and Company, 1950.
  Horney rounds out her theory of neurosis by introducing the concept of the idealized self.

She stresses the alienation from the real self through the pursuit of the idealized self. She coordinates the three social orientations with more generalized orientations to life: the self-effacing, the expansive, and the resigned. She views the neurotic as one who abandons his real potentialities and attempts to actualize his idealized version of himself.

REFERENCES

Allport, G. W. Pattern and Growth in Personality. New York: Holt, Rinehart and Winston, 1961.

Horney, K. The Neurotic Personality of Our Time. New York: W. W. Norton and Company, 1937.

Horney, K. New Ways in Psychoanalysis. New York: W. W. Norton and Company, 1939.

Horney, K. Self Analysis. New York: W. W. Norton and Company, 1942.

Horney, K. Our Inner Conflicts. New York: W. W. Norton and Company, 1945.

Horney, K. Neurosis and Human Growth. New York: W. W. Norton and Company, 1950.

Jourard, S. M. Personal Adjustment: An Approach Through the Study of Personality, 2nd ed. New York: The Macmillan Company, 1963.

Maslow, A. H. Motivation and Personality, 2nd ed. New York: Harper and Row, 1970.

May, R. Man's Search for Himself. New York: W. W. Norton and Company, 1953.

Singer, J. L. Daydreaming: An Introduction to the Experimental Study of Inner Experience. New York: Random House, 1966.

Temerlin, M. K. On choice and responsibility in a humanistic psychotherapy. In Severin, F. T., ed. Humanistic Viewpoints in Psychology. New York: McGraw-Hill, 1965. Pp. 68–89.

Turner, R. H., and Vanderlippe, R. H. Self-ideal congruence as an index of adjustment. J. Abnorm. Social Psychol. 57:202–6, 1958.

PART VI

The Good Life: Ideal Models of Human Living

One of the most intriguing questions that can be posed about human nature concerns what might be termed "the good life." The inquiring minds of great men could not fail to ask this question. For most people, if not for all, life seems so imperfect; and yet the desire to live more perfectly is one of man's greatest motivations. One can recall the past with regret and recognize that it cannot be relived, and that its mistakes cannot be undone. The developing child, the adolescent, and even the adult, lacking the experience of a variety of situations and a full appreciation of their capabilities and values, are frequently confronted with disappointment and failure. One often wonders about which course to take. Should he be more bold and assertive, or socially oriented and acquiescent? Should he strive for wealth and power over others, or should he attempt to follow his deepest wishes, whatever they may be? What are the things he truly values, over and above the necessities of life? Life is filled with so many uncertainties. Man is expected to take his place in society, but he is not at all clear about what that place is or should be. He may turn to religion to find answers and, like many others, find direction and unity in its dogma. Many different desirable ways of life are presented to him; the culture offers glamorous choices which promise fame, fortune, popularity, and above all happiness. Religion portrays a different life, one which may be quite divergent from the ones offered by the culture. In stressing more concern about the afterlife, it may subordinate actual living to something beyond death.

Prescriptions or recipes for the good life have come from many sources, ranging from the personal revelations of prophets to the wisdom of "common folks." The precepts have also varied, from simple admonitions against certain practices to highly complex ceremonial codes. Carl Rogers, whose views we will consider in this section, makes some pertinent observations about these varied views of the good life:

The "good life" has had very different meanings for different groups and in different ages. For some it has meant a life given over to meditation — the holy man on the mountaintop. In sharp contrast, to others it has meant a life of achievement — gaining wealth, status, knowledge or power.

For many it has meant strict adherence to a creed, a set of rules or principles — whether found in the Bible, the Koran or emanating from a religious leader. For still others it has meant selfless dedication to a cause outside of themselves — Christian missionary work, communism or Hitler's German youth. For some it has been the indulgence of every pleasurable appetite, with the slogan "Eat, drink, and be merry, for tomorrow we die."

These examples indicate that the "good life" is not some known, fixed, timeless goal, the same for all, but is a matter of choice.*

Each of the five chapters that follow highlights the thinking of an outstanding personologist on the model of the good life. The reader may wonder about the diversity of models of the ideal life. He might observe that if we truly understand the nature of man or humanness, then could we not specify exactly what that nature should be when it is fulfilled? If this view is correct, there should be only one model of the ideal life. This argument is quite valid and deserves some consideration.

Human nature is so plastic that it can take many different forms in individual lives. The more complex a class of objects is, the greater the number of variations that are possible. The number of variables that constitute an apple, for instance, are relatively few, as compared with the number of ways in which humans may vary. We might be able to grade apples on largeness, smoothness of skin, number of blemishes, texture of the fruit, taste, degree of juiciness, and possibly a few more dimensions, but consider the number of variables that make up a human being. Furthermore, when we deal with apples, we do not have to consider the culture in which they exist, but when we deal with humans regarding the ideal life, the culture must be taken into account. Cultures vary greatly, and to live in a particular culture requires the learning of many skills, attitudes, and practices. To be self-actualized, or productive, or fully functioning, or mature, or individuated in America must be somewhat different from what it would be in Samoa. The point is that given man's highly complex nature, it is unlikely that there could be one ideal model of living. All models would have similarities because there is a basic human nature common to all men. Everyone has to have correct perceptions of his world, or survival would be impossible. The good life would not be possible unless basic biological needs were met easily and efficiently. Furthermore, one could not hope to attain the fullness of growth and functioning without being able to control his environment in some ways.

The reader will probably find that one particular personality model is more applicable to himself than the others. One model may appear more appealing and suitable to one's style of life. While all the models promote highly effective living, the emphases are different. Rogers's man enjoys rich experiences. He is quite introspective and emotional. Allport's man is more controlled and sober, and perhaps a bit less happy. Fromm stresses an active orientation to life with work and love as highly significant. Jung sought the fullest development and integration of all aspects of the personality. Maslow was concerned with living rich experiences, but he did not make thinking about life as important as does Rogers.

In reading the personality theorists, the writer has observed a major problem area that each theorist finds most significant for man and at the same time most difficult to solve. For each theorist, the ideal model of living depends upon both the major problem of man and the manner with which it is dealt. It might be instructive to consider them briefly here.

For Allport the major problem in life seems to be opportunistic living: living without goals or values. The solution he proposes is to have both short-term and long-term goals.

For Fromm the major problem in life is loneliness and feelings of isolation. The solution is productive work and productive love.

For Maslow, the major problem seems to be need gratification. His solution is to seek higher need gratification rather than more lower need gratification.

For Rogers, the major problem of life appears to be lack of authenticity. To overcome the feeling of being artificial and pretentious, one should strive to be his most complete self—to be what Rogers calls congruent.

Jung saw the major problem as lack of complete personality differentiation and growth. The solution is to pay attention to every aspect and tendency within personality and allow each full expression and development.

Several of the personality theorists tell us *what* is wrong with man, and in turn *why,* and *what* should be done about it. Rogers tells us that what is wrong with many of us is that we are not authentic, not our real selves. One outstanding explanation is that we try to meet conditions imposed by others so as to gain acceptance by them. What we should do is uncover the man behind the mask: discover the real self. Fromm proposes that most of us experience contradictions in our lives; thus we are unsettled and confused much of the time. The explanation is that our very nature creates problems for us: we can know the world and ourselves through our intelligence, but we can also see how imperfect it and we are; we have the remarkable ability to project into the future, but the same ability informs us of our own end; we can appreciate and desire the perfect, and know that our lives will be highly imperfect. What can we do about this situation? The solution, only partial at best, is to work productively and to relate harmoniously with others in brotherly and other types of love. Jung believed that the major difficulty for many of us is that our lives are one-sided, that our personalities remain undeveloped and unfulfilled. The reason is that we tend to limit our concerns to the conscious aspect of personality, to the development of the ego and the social personality in meeting the requirements of social living.

We might read each of the theorists with the view of obtaining insights into the particular problem that is considered most significant and the solution that is offered. Furthermore, we should be able to better deal with our particular difficulties in living by attempting to discover ways of dealing with them. Consulting the ideas of the particular theorist should be helpful.

Most of us have difficulty appreciating the vast range of possible styles of life. Allport continually called attention to the complexity and uniqueness of each individual. Consider how different an Amish farmer's life style is from that of a neurosurgeon in a modern urban hospital. Compare the coal miner's work with that of a research physicist in a large university. Compare the life of the busy corporation executive with that of the eighty year old woman who survives on a welfare check. How different is the life style of the young mother who spends most of her day caring for her young baby from that of her husband who is a professional airline pilot. There are literally thousands of occupations and life styles. Could it be possible that the same model of ideal living would be suitable for everyone?

CHAPTER 12

On Maturity

Gordon W. Allport

Gordon W. Allport (1897–1967)

This chapter will consider the views on maturity of the late Gordon W. Allport. The purpose of the writer is not merely to present Allport's observations on maturity, but rather to elaborate on and extend the seminal ideas he has proposed. First, general considerations regarding maturity will be presented, followed by Allport's seven specific "criteria of maturity." It should be noted that these concepts apply to Western culture and probably most specifically to American culture.

GENERAL CHARACTERISTICS OF MATURITY

A CONTINUING PROCESS

Maturity is not a state that one reaches and then maintains. It should be thought of as an ongoing process. When a person is described as "mature," the reference is to psychobiological functioning that promotes health and soundness. Each period of life presents new obstacles that must be overcome, and needs vary from period to period. Allport (1955) believes that maturity is difficult to attain before adulthood, since the equipment with which the person copes with life is not fully developed until then. Obviously, age in itself is not a guarantee of maturity. The basic point here is that maturity involves a becoming, a forward thrust, a continual working toward goals. Once one goal is reached, energy is invested in something else (Hunt, 1965). The dream of the young to somehow reach a level of grownupness, which is supposed to be the final outcome of the struggles in school, is of course a fiction. Accomplishments do not leave a person satisfied for long. The opposite of this forward thrust is stagnation, or backward orientation, or preoccupation with security, or in pathological cases, an inordinate focusing on drives.

The following chart presents Allport's criteria of maturity. These are compared with the goals of psychotherapy proposed by a group of psychiatrists.

Goals of Psychotherapy*
1. To remove unwanted symptoms
2. To adjust the person to the society in which he lives
3. To enhance the experience of well-being
4. To encourage mental health which includes the following characteristics:
   a. Cheerfulness
   b. Optimistic serenity
   c. Ability to enjoy work
   d. Ability to enjoy play
   e. Capacity to love
   f. Ability to achieve goals
   g. No extreme show of emotion
   h. Self-insight
   i. Social responsibility
   j. Appropriate reaction to situations

Allport's Criteria of Maturity
1. Extension of self
2. Warm relating of self to others
3. Emotional security
4. Realistic perceptions
5. Skills and assignments
6. Self-objectification
7. Unifying philosophy of life

MATURITY NOT THE SAME AS HAPPINESS

Allport (1955) takes an interesting stand on the relationship between maturity and happiness. He does not believe that happiness is a necessary attribute of the mature person, although what is commonly referred to as happiness may be a by-product of mature behavior. A person may study hard in order to train for a position that he feels is worthwhile. The specific goal is job advancement, not a search for happiness as such. There are many whose lives, through no fault of their own, are filled with sorrow, pain, and ill fortune, and yet they may possess maturity to a high degree. Healthy personalities are not necessarily bubbling over with euphoria. Life for many is grim and trying. A person may even be depressed or despondent much of the time and still be considered mature. For one thing, if his behavior does not interfere with the rights of others, or if he does not play out his moods on others, he may be considered emotionally mature, and this constitutes a significant part of total maturity.

---

*Note: The conditions for happiness as seen by psychotherapists are insufficient to the state of maturity as recognized by Allport.

All of us must anticipate an unknown future, with aging and death as an ultimate end. Because man faces suffering, insecurity, and many unknowns, some thinkers have stressed the more serious and sober aspects of man's behavior such as self-control, personal and social responsibility, democratic social interests, and ideals. The existentialists, with whom Allport is in sympathy, stress also the serious side of maturity: the search for meaning, a natural acceptance of the human situation, the courage to be, and taking responsibility for making something of one's life (e.g., Tillich, 1952).

What then is maturity if it is not the same as happiness? Allport offers seven criteria of maturity that will be discussed later, but for the present we might say that maturity involves self-fulfillment, self-actualizing, and the best development and functioning of the individual within the circumstances of his life.

NO ONE BEST WAY TO LIVE

Each person is unique in personality structure and there are ultimately as many ways to live properly as there are individual humans. Allport, more than any other personality theorist, focuses upon this uniqueness. General statements about man must be cautiously accepted. Each person is a modus vivendi, a unique form of life. No one can prove that being an extrovert is more desirable and fulfilling than being an introvert, although an extrovert in a culture such as ours may have an advantage (Rinder, 1964). The possession of wealth, status, and power may be highly prized in our culture; however, having or not having these things cannot be demonstrated to be more or less desirable. While we may accept the point that the unique pattern of characteristics that comprise the individual renders impossible a prescription for living based on the attributes of "human nature," Allport nevertheless recognizes that certain qualities such as extension of self, although expressed in a highly individual way, can be proposed as criteria of maturity.

GOAL-SEEKING MORE SIGNIFICANT THAN DRIVE SATISFACTION

Although failure to satisfy one's physiological drives may be disastrous to life. to ascribe man's total motivation to drives provides a wholly inadequate view of man. In a normal, healthy child one can see the powerful role of motives other than physiological drives in the form of play, curiosity, general activity, all of which may take precedence over hunger, for example (unless, of course, this drive is very strong). Only "sick" people are tied to drives. After dinner and rest, the normal person seeks something to do; he has energy to invest in activities.

The mark of maturity for Allport (1961) is setting and striving to fulfill goals.

The most basic quality of man is not his drives but his goals, not the past but the future, not so much his limitations but his possibilities. This picture of man, in contrast to Freud's, is optimistic. The opportunist, the roué, the drifter, the thrill-seeker are all instances of faulty personality development. Goals and values configurate a life and give it stability and direction. Such goals may, of course, take many forms, such as interests, preferences, values, attitudes.

MATURITY MORE THAN THE ABSENCE OF ILLNESS

A man may protest that nothing is particularly wrong in his life, yet he finds himself chronically dissatisfied and generally discontented. Probably the answer in this case, and in many like it, is a lack of positive factors. The individual who does not want for food, shelter, and the other biological necessities may lack what has been termed "the priceless unessentials," such as a unifying philosophy of life, participation in some activity that is ego-relevant, and an intimate and warm human relationship. A sound personality is characterized by a zest for living, a forward thrust, always having "irons in the fire." Warding off ill health and relieving tensions are necessary, but only a base for attaining maturity. Of course, many would do well if they could handle their tensions more efficiently, let alone set into action positive measures to enhance their lives. Yet for Allport (1961) maturity is more than being normal or not being sick.

MATURITY INVOLVES NOT MERELY LACK OF TENSION BUT ALSO CREATING TENSION

This point is related to the preceding one. Some would equate lack of tension with effective living; Freud seemed to hold this position, which in effect implies that the ideal tensionless state is death itself. Allport (1955) rejects this view and instead holds that tension is a necessary condition for maturity. The mature person actually creates tensions. While the tensions resulting from conflicts, frustrations, and pressures of day-to-day living are unpleasant and impel one to remove them as quickly as possible, certain types of tensions are not only pleasurable but have a tonic effect on everyday living. For example, a father may give up leisure time activity to join an investment club for the long-term purpose of building a financial reserve to aid his son through college. Simply having this goal creates tension since it motivates and controls behavior, not to mention the tensions that result from the risks. Tension is not avoided but deliberately instigated. Thus one manifestation of a mature personality is tension-seeking, which takes the form of short- and long-term goals. When one goal is reached, a new one is projected to replace it, tying up the available energy. If this energy is not invested in goal-seeking, it may be used in destructive ways such as self-pity, complacency, and jealousy of the good fortune of others.

MATURITY REQUIRES THE ESTABLISHMENT OF A FIRM SENSE OF IDENTITY

Each person is born into a culture which forces upon him many impositions and restrictions, shaping him according to the cultural molds. A girl in our culture is expected to behave quite differently from a boy, and each age level and class of the society has its own behavior expectations. At the same time, each individual has his own inner nature which asserts itself within the cultural setting. This inner nature, which on a psychological level may be thought of as the self, is something that develops, grows, and changes from birth onwards. Allport (1961) maintains that the self plays a large part in the maturity process. The experiences of self are diverse and complex, including a sense of one's body, a sense of self-esteem or pride, and a more or less stable sense of the core identity.

The establishment of a stable sense of identity does not come automatically, as many young people can attest (Goethals and Klos, 1970). It requires self-examination, profiting from experience, a variety of role-playing experiences, and even frustrations, failures, and disappointments. Yet without such a stable, well-established sense of identity maturity is impossible.

A WELL-FORMED SELF-IMAGE WHICH IS BEING FULFILLED

The self-image refers to the picture one has of himself, which is more or less correct, but it also includes a picture, more or less clearly defined, of what one would like to become. This aspect of the self-image, the self which is desired, is a significant motivating factor in the mature personality (Allport, 1961). Those who have no goals flowing from their unfulfilled self-image, or who are vague in their aspirations, are not mature. Rather than being pushed by drives, the mature personality is pulled or enticed by goals. What he was is not nearly so important a force as what he is becoming.

In studying Allport's characteristics of the mature personality, one should keep in mind that even the sturdiest of humans depends a great deal upon the environment for support. An extremely stressful environment makes stability and balance almost impossible. Such things as death, failing health, and the physical and psychological changes attendant upon aging tax even the strongest of personalities. On the other hand, satisfying human experiences in significant spheres of life such as marriage, career, recreation, religious belief, and life philosophy are salutary for vigorous personality growth and functioning. Pain, sorrow, and frustration do seem to play a part in promoting maturity; an easy life does not automatically pave the way. A sine qua non of maturity is being able to tolerate and meet frustration and to continue reaching and striving even in the face of defeat and discouragement. The noblest qualities of a man are often brought out in adversity.

THE SEVEN CRITERIA OF MATURITY

It is important to remember that despite its general characteristics, maturity to Allport is not a general factor but a series of continuing attainments. The normal adult is highly complex, with many facets of involvement. All through life one must interact with others in varying degrees of intimacy; one must fix upon a stable self-identity. Goals must be worked out, both long-term and short-term, and appropriate means to attain these goals must be learned. Methods must be developed for dealing with frustration, failure, disappointments, losses, and the many adversities which beset even the most gifted. Thus for Allport maturity involves a *multidimensional series of continuing attainments,* all of which necessitate continual attention and flexibility.

Now we come to the specific criteria of maturity proposed by Allport (1961). It should be noted that each individual expresses the criteria in a unique manner: for instance, my self-extensions may be quite different from yours, but mine are just as necessary for me as yours are for you. Table 12–1 briefly summarizes the criteria, giving examples of each.

1. SELF-EXTENSION

As the self grows and develops, it reaches out to more and more things. At first, the major focus of concentration is the organism itself. Then the surroundings of the home life are perceived and brought into relation with the self. As the child grows older, and if development is "normal," the self extends beyond the home to playmates, school, sports, and clubs. Still later, self-involvement includes members of the opposite sex, church, country, career, and a host of other attachments. These attachments and involvements, though changing from period to period throughout life, are absolutely essential to the pursuit of maturity.

Allport (1960) makes an important distinction between participation and activity; one may be quite active without participating in what he is doing. A man may work busily all day on an assembly line doing a routine assignment without participating in his work at all. Participation, rather than mere activity, occurs when the activity is ego-relevant. It must mean something or count for something in relation to the self. An example of this is the person who believes his job is important, likes to do it, and is reasonably good at it. The job is more than a means of earning a living. Unless these requirements are satisfied, the work is not ego-relevant and hence does not promote maturity. This does not preclude the possibility, of course, of authentic participation in some other significant way, as in one's family life, through an avocation, or in one's recreational activities.

The whole point of the requirement of self-extension is that there is vastly more to life than simply surviving and satisfying drives. Self enters into drive

TABLE 12-1 ALLPORT'S CRITERIA OF MATURITY

Criteria	Descriptions	Examples
Self-extension	Active and passive participation Task involvement Ego involvement	A young boy joins the Boy Scouts A mother quits a good job to care for her family A man devotes his energies to combating the drug problem in his community
Warm relating of self to others	Intimacy Compassion Tolerance Smooth sociability	A nurse spends extra time with a frightened patient A young man and woman decide to marry A man joins a Big Brother group
Emotional security	Self-acceptance Cooperation with inevitables Control	One who does not display his moods freely One who resists affectations One who lives harmoniously with his emotions
Realistic perceptions	Correct knowledge of people and things Perceptual soundness	One who is not driven by his inner attitudes and traits to misperceive events A man who understands the requirements of his job (knowing the rules of the game) A student who perceives that he cannot cope with college work, after having made a sincere effort to succeed
Skills and assignments	Competencies and worth-while tasks to perform	One who identifies with his work and profession and is proud of his skills The dedicated teacher who works beyond the call of duty The medical man who gives up a promising private practice for a research career
Self-objec-tification	Insight into oneself Deriving humor from one's pretenses and mistakes	A man who can admit that he is wrong in an argument A student who can see poor test scores as the result of lack of study rather than a bad test
Unifying philosophy of life	Guiding goals and values Religious faith Directedness	Valuing knowledge or learning for its own sake Striving to make money Valuing beauty Working for others Striving for power Valuing religious experiences

satisfaction, particularly when a drive is deprived for some length of time, but such a condition does not promote the attainment of maturity. One whose energies are entirely devoted to just "getting on" cannot fulfill his other potentialities, and life for him must necessarily be routine and drab.

A safecracker may be more integrated and satisfied in his work, though it be antisocial and criminal, than a bank president who unhappily carries on the tradition of the family simply because he inherited the position. If participation implies ego-relevant activity, and if such activity is closely identified with interests and preferred patterns of behavior, it would seem that, for the purpose of living more effectively, one should take pains to assure that some of his activities, at least, are what he wants to do rather than what he has to do. Gradually one should increase the ratio in favor of ego-relevant activities.

2. WARM RELATING OF SELF TO OTHERS

Allport holds that the social adjustment of the mature personality is character-ized by two types of warmth: the capacities for intimacy and for compassion. Warm human experiences of a social nature, as in a successful marriage or in a strong friendship, add zest to life and are tonic to personality growth and functioning. Intimacy is a form of self-extension which deeply binds one per-son with another. The welfare of the loved one becomes a major focus of ego involvement. Human attachments are as potent a motivational force as any motive can be. The power of a woman's love has caused many a man to leave his family and home, forsake everything he had, and even commit murder or other criminal acts. Though different in nature from heterosexuality, human attachments with the same sex are, of course, also highly motivating.

If one follows the development of affiliative behavior in children, he will ob-serve that the capacity for intimacy is a late acquisition that many never attain at all. A necessary condition for the formation of intimate relationships is the establishment of a stable sense of self-identity, which under favorable condi-tions occurs in late adolescence. The person needs not only to know himself but also to be able to know others and to see their points of view. To see an-other person as a mirror image of oneself, a fellow human who despite differ-ences shares a basic human nature, is probably the foundation of empathy and also the root source of intimacy. It may be objected by some that an in-timate relationship is frosting on the cake, not really necessary for effective liv-ing. Some people, such as the self-sufficient husband who relates to his wife only to the extent of caring for her needs, seem not to require any but superfi-cial relationships. However, in this case at least, the psychological well-being of the person may be questioned. One can survive without intimate human relationships, but maturity is not mere existence; rather it entails an ideal type of existence. An intimate relationship provides the participating parties with profound experiences that have no substitute (Dahms, 1972).

Compassion stems from an appreciation of the human condition of all men. If one understands his own limitations, weaknesses, sufferings, and the many in-evitables and unknowns in life, and is able to perceive those of others in the same light, he possesses compassion. Despite wide differences in life situa-tions, natural gifts, and liabilities, all men have much in common. No one is the complete master of his destiny; no one is without adversity and suffering; all must face an unknown future. No one really understands completely the riddles of life. Man's most penetrating questions have never been answered to his complete satisfaction. The mature person, seeing and appreciating these conditions of human life, experiences a sense of oneness with all humans. Even if the great religions had not placed high value on brotherly love, the mature personality would become aware of this aspect of his relations with other humans. The noblest qualities of man are based on this emotion. Its expression ranges from the selfless generosity of a parent toward his children to a host of charitable and altruistic acts that often return nothing except the feeling that one has helped a fellow mortal.

Another quality that flows from the previous ones is tolerance. One learns to respect the rights of others, recognizing that they are no less valid and important than one's own. Certain rights come from the fact of being human, irrespective of natural advantages or disadvantages. The mature person can tolerate weaknesses and foibles in others because he has seen and accepted some of these in himself.

3. EMOTIONAL SECURITY

A number of qualities, particularly self-acceptance, are covered under this heading. Acknowledging inherent imperfections but always striving to better himself with a genuine self-regard, the mature person appreciates the fact that no one is all that he would like to be. Our culture often presents us with the beguiling image of the perfect man or woman. The mature person comes to recognize, sooner or later, the fictional and unrealistic character of such ideal roles and bends his efforts toward fulfilling his individual potential. The difference between what he is and what he wishes to become is not as large as for the unhappy, anxiety-ridden, self-hating neurotic. When they are first formed, the dreams and self-image of the mature individual, like those of the immature person, are quite unrealistic and unattainable, but unlike his immature counterpart, the mature individual continually monitors the relation between aspirations and performance and moderates his aspirations if they are too far beyond his capacities for achievement. The self-accepting person is neither totally satisfied nor totally dissatisfied with himself, but most of the time he is on the satisfied side of the continuum and moving in the direction of complete self-acceptance, though he probably never reaches it fully.

Another aspect of emotional security is accepting emotions as a normal part of the self. In this regard the culture may be a hindrance; men are expected to hold back on emotional expression, whereas women are given much more freedom of outlet. Most people have a great deal of difficulty harmonizing their natural emotional reactions with cultural models. The mature person accepts his emotions as a part of himself, neither allowing them to rule his life nor rejecting them as alien to his nature. He not only learns to live with his emotions but also uses them for constructive purposes, as when a man who is angry with his employer turns the energy into more vigorous efforts in his work. One of the most significant aspects of emotional control is not allowing the emotions to take charge to the point of interference with others. The infantile and neurotic individual easily plays out his emotions. He wears his heart on his sleeve, so to speak. When he is in a bad mood, everyone knows it and is affected by it. In contrast, the mature person in the same state may not even be noticeably different in demeanor, though some become quieter in mood (Wessman and Ricks, 1966).

Another quality related to emotional security is frustration tolerance—the ability to continue functioning even under conditions of stress. One of the most obvious manifestations of personality disturbance is disruption of ongoing behavior. The person who receives bad news and reacts with a depression so severe that he cannot work or do much of anything for a long period of time is such an example. There are many degrees of frustration tolerance, and everyone probably has a breaking point. Most people are not confronted with catastrophic stress, although everyone faces the inevitable frustrations of life. No one has control of his environment or of his future. Living entails taking risks, being rejected, falling short—a host of frustrating events. Somehow the mature person lives with these frustrations and learns to carry on (Hutt, 1947). He learns to "cooperate rather than continually fight with the inevitables of life."

One more quality that relates to emotional security should be mentioned: confidence in self-expression. The mature person is not afraid of his emotions because he accepts and has control over them. He has developed a good sense of proportion in the order of his values. He is not afraid to be himself in most situations. His emotions are as much a part of himself as his intelligence or anything else about him. Immaturity in this respect takes many forms, for instance, failure to develop emotionally, being tied to segmental drives such as sex or eating, timidity and shyness, inability to control emotional expression, and emotional underreaction.

4. REALISTIC PERCEPTION

One of the most basic requirements of maturity is keeping in touch with reality, seeing things as they are. Often events and situations are complex and difficult to perceive correctly on that account alone. Add to this needs and ego defenses, and distortion becomes commonplace (Bruner and Goodman, 1947). Into every situation a person brings a whole history of experiences that may interfere with a correct perception of reality. The mature person cooperates with reality; he does not try to bend it to meet his needs and purposes. The not-so-sound individual creates events through perceptual distortion to suit his expectations and desires.

The habit of misperceiving may be the outcome of a general set as, for instance, a generally pessimistic person who chooses to fix upon the gloomy, discouraging, and unpleasant aspects of events rather than upon the optimistic, hopeful, and encouraging elements. Allport (1961) places much stress upon the motivating and controlling power of sets. In fact, he believes that the superstructure of personality consists of sets of various types. A set may be general, such as an optimistic or pessimistic way of viewing events in one's life. It may be highly specific, such as a liking for a certain type of person. Or it may be short-term and limited, for example expecting a phone call from a friend at six o'clock. Sets may interact, for instance the need for status and the need to earn a large income. The term "set," as used in this sense, stands for many components of personality. Motives, attitudes, preferences, aversions, and even general orientations to living may be considered as sets. Underlying perceptions are sets; the healthy person's sets assist him in obtaining a correct representation of his surroundings, while the neurotic's sets lead him to see things that are not there. He reacts to a world that does not exist.

5. SKILLS AND ASSIGNMENTS

Allport believes that mature people possess skills and competencies in one or more areas of their lives. Without basic skills, a person cannot establish the kind of security that is necessary for the building of a mature approach to living. An outstanding psychologist, R. W. White (1959), holds that competence is a major motive of life. Everyone strives to master his circumstances. A child learns to care for himself by mastering simple skills. Later, he extends his competence to school work and little chores around the home. Still later, he trains for some kind of work. Cutting across all these forms of competence-seeking are the social skills that he must acquire. Successful living is highly contingent upon an individual's competencies.

The person who has skills usually experiences the need to express them by doing some task. The concepts of task absorption and ego-relevant activity are applicable in this context. The psychological as well as the physical machinery needs activity. If the activity is not guided and channeled appropriately, there may be degeneration and even self-destruction. Freud recognized the power of self-destructive tendencies and even postulated the existence of death instincts that can work havoc on the individual. Allport, while not accepting the death instincts, recognizes the devastating effects of idleness. One needs to lose himself in a task. Some existentialists (e.g., Boss, 1963) have expressed this point in the notion that one should seek rather than avoid responsibilities. Having a duty to perform gives most people meaning in life. A father who takes seriously his duties of supporting his family, bringing up his children properly, and doing these tasks as well as he can, experiences unity and integration of personality, and his life will have meaning for him.

6. SELF-OBJECTIFICATION (KNOWLEDGE OF SELF)

Closely allied with realistic perception is a quality which Allport designates self-objectification; by this he means knowledge of oneself. Self-awareness is a concern that begins early and continues throughout life. There are wide individual differences in the degree of attainment. The mature person possesses it to a high degree; the immature person is as much baffled by this aspect of his life as he is by other major aspects. He is a mystery to himself. His behavior frequently does not make sense, or he does things that in retrospect seem completely ludicrous and irrational. Knowing oneself involves three qualities: knowing what one can do, knowing what one cannot do, and knowing what one ought to do. A person may aspire to goals that are far beyond his possibility of attainment or, of course, he may set his aspirations lower than they should be. In both instances, frustration is inevitable. Learning about one's limitations is as essential an ingredient of self-knowledge as is learning about possibilities.

Certain desirable characteristics of personality seem to be associated with a high degree of self-insight. Allport (1961, Chap. 12) cites several studies which support the following assertions: (1) The person with a high degree of self-knowledge is usually a good judge of others, as compared with the person who is low on this dimension. (2) He is usually more aware of his own short-comings and is less likely to ascribe them to others or to blame others for what is happening to him. (3) Acceptance by others is also associated with a high degree of self-awareness. (4) There is also evidence that those who have high self-awareness are on the average quite high in general intelligence. (5) Another quality of persons with good self-insight is a sense of humor. This is to be distinguished from a sense of the comic, which almost everyone possesses. Sex and aggression play a large part in ordinary comedy, but a sense of humor centers around laughing at oneself, the discrepancy between pretense and actuality, being able under certain conditions to see humor in serious pursuits. A child has a sense of the comic but not a sense of humor and, it might be added, the same is true for many adults. They cannot laugh at themselves.

7. UNIFYING PHILOSOPHY OF LIFE

Previously, goal-seeking was mentioned as one of the outstanding characteristics of maturity. This point is closely related to what may be called a unifying philosophy of life. In this expression Allport wishes to embody the notions of guiding purpose, ideals, goals, or values. The mature person has an intelligible theory of life in terms of which he finds meaning and direction. He has something to work for or toward. In contrast, the immature or infantile person has only momentary desires and often no clear-cut reason for living. Nothing may count with him — neither family nor work, nor religion, nor recreation. He is not working toward anything; he has no real self-extension. An individual with this deficiency may suffer an existential depression, which results from having nothing to live for and to extend one's life into. A woman may define her roles as a faithful wife and good mother, and so identify with the fulfillment of those roles that she experiences the inevitable benefits of living with a purpose. Many women in the middle classes of our society no longer identify with these traditional roles and perform their tasks grudgingly and superficially (Fromm, 1947). The inevitable outcome is lack of purpose and meaning with the attendant unpleasant consequences of role confusion, lack of self-fulfillment, and general dissatisfaction with living. The same remarks may apply to one's work, which constitutes for many the major unifying activity of their lives. A group of 300 well-educated persons, half of whom were in *Who's Who,* were asked to list the constructive factors leading to creativity in their lives; the most frequently identified was interest and satisfaction in work for its own sake (Allport, 1961, Chap. 12). The second most popular was the desire to know and understand. But significantly, work was first. This factor may be due to the nature of the group, who appear to be highly motivated to attain success; their work would naturally be the major vehicle.

Allport cautions against a common misconception pertaining to goal attainment. Ordinarily the attainment of a goal, like the satisfaction of a drive, is pleasurable. The pleasurable outcome is a strong incentive and may be the only aspect people think about as they attempt to set and reach goals. Yet from the standpoint of personality functioning and integration, the pleasurable outcome is not as valuable as the striving activities, the working toward the goal (May, 1967). Striving requires an investment of energy in a variety of activities, ranging from perception through problem-solving and direct coping behavior. Along with all this activity go many emotional states that may enhance and support the ongoing processes. The attainment of the objective does little to bind energy. It may tie up some energy in a celebration and tie up some more in pride and pomposity, but such activities really do not lead anywhere. Unless a new goal enters the picture, the person will experience the personality disturbances that stem from a lack of goals. It may be objected that a continual replacement of one goal or achievement by another is a sign of (or stems from) general malcontent. Malcontent differs from maturity in that it involves capricious and restless formulation and abandonment of goals.

The mature person views his goals with a balanced perspective. There is an order of priorities: some goals are more basic and necessary than others. Failure to attain a highly prized goal does not result in severe or long-continued malfunctioning. Other goals are readily adopted to take the place of the banished one. Even failure itself is viewed from a balanced perspective. The mature person does not hang everything on one peg, and therefore, if this peg breaks, he still maintains his equilibrium. This point is summed up in Kipling's admonition that one should allow neither triumph nor disaster to rule one's life.

More general than goals, and probably the basis for them, are values. One may organize his life around a system of values. These may be constructed by the individual, or one may accept a ready-made set of standards such as Christianity, communism, or democracy. Spranger (1928) proposed six major directions that values may take, and each individual has a different amount of involvement in all six, with one usually predominating. Such value orientations are highly integrating and give direction to life. One is more likely to find strong value orientations in mature people than in disturbed personalities. The six value orientations are discussed briefly here.

1. The Theoretical. The ideal type has an intense desire to know and understand the world within and around him, although his interest may be focused on a specific area of study. He seeks to comprehend, predict, and control events; thus he may be a philosopher, a scientist, or a mathematician.

2. The Economic.   The ideal type is strongly oriented toward utility, earning wealth, succeeding in the business world. Wealth is a dominant theme in his life, and the things that money can buy are highly cherished. Beauty and art may be identified with the cost of the object.

3. The Aesthetic.   The aesthetic person organizes his activities around the pursuit of rich psychological experiences. He may find these in meditation or in a variety of other ways, for example in the beauty of the country.

4. The Social.   The "social man" values other people as ends. His relations with others are often tinged with love. He possesses a high degree of compassion and respect for mankind.

5. The Political.   This individual seeks power and domination over others. Politics is but one of many outlets for the expression of this value. The state of discontent until one has the boss's job exhibits the power orientation.

6. The Religious.   Those who possess the religious orientation to a high degree strive for unity and oneness with a divine power. The person who gives up everything to become a mystic displays this orientation.

According to Allport, intrinsic or mature religion provides an all-embracing direction for many who are not quite so one-sided in this respect as is Spranger's religious type. While many, if not most people who profess religious affiliation do not make it a central part of their lives, others find in it the ultimate unifying force. According to Allport (1961), religious sentiments need not be pathological, artificial, regressive, or an infantile carryover, but may be a total response involving knowledge, and even more importantly faith, resulting in an intelligible theory of the meaning of life.

Another important directive factor is conscience. A set of imperatives and guidelines by which thought and behavior are regulated certainly provides life with unity and direction. Conscience, like all other aspects of personality, grows with increased development, but the changes may not occur as they should. The person who possesses a childish conscience carries with him many absolutes, restrictions, and prohibitions over his behavior. He usually does not know why he feels guilty or why he does what he must do. He does or does not do things because he is afraid of the law, his boss, or the Divine Power. The mature conscience is characterized by "oughts" rather than "musts." One ought to work harder because he wishes to upgrade his position, not because he is afraid of the boss. He takes on responsibilities because he can fulfill his self-image in this way. Mature conscience may include pervasive religious sentiments that constitute the major source of unity, but conscience may be centered around other values. A man may assume the duty of working hard to support his family without questioning his basic motivation. In this case, even though his philosophy of life is not clearly articulated, he is strongly directed by his self-imposed obligation. Yet perhaps the conscience that is centered about religious sentiments gives the believer a greater sense of meaning and total purpose than is afforded by any other value.

CONCLUSIONS

The criteria of maturity are not possessed by all people. Many conditions are unfavorable and hinder personality growth and functioning. Everyone is caught in a conflict between cultural expectations and personal requirements. Some are blocked from the very beginning of life from ever attaining fulfillment. Just as a plant requires an intact seed and favorable elements in the environment for the attainment of full growth, so also does a human being depend upon heredity and nourishing surroundings, probably to an even greater degree. However, many more can live mature lives if educators (including parents) and behavior scientists utilize the knowledge about personality growth that is now available. Of course, this power to improve life will also increase with new discoveries in the science of human behavior.

CRITIQUE OF ALLPORT'S CRITERIA OF MATURITY

On the plus side, Allport's criteria of maturity have a common sense appeal about them. They seem to square with everyday observation and experience. Superficially it seems better to participate in one's world than to be inactive or withdraw into oneself; it seems better to have warm and intimate associations with others than to be a loner and an isolationist; it seems better to be accepting of oneself than chronically dissatisfied with one's nature and accomplishments; it certainly seems better to have realistic perceptions, well-developed skills, and meaningful tasks to do than the opposite of these. Life appears to run more smoothly if one knows himself, his limitations and possibilities. Finally, it seems more sound to have direction in the form of guiding values, a philosophy of life, or a religious view of things than to wander through life aimlessly. Allport does admit that these criteria apply more to Western cultures than to others. Yet he has also argued for the essential uniqueness of each individual. Of course there are species characteristics, but their combinations are so vast that each configuration has its own qualities. But what is the justification for offering criteria of maturity? Could it be possible that one does not enjoy or need other people? Has this ever been proved one way or the other? Is it not really an assumption based on a presupposition about the nature of man? It is true that many neurotic people experience disturbed social relationships, but that fact does not warrant the conclusion that warm social relationships are essential for healthy living. Why should a person have values or a unifying philosophy of life? Are we really better off knowing ourselves than living according to some delusion? One would have to demonstrate that Allport's criteria of maturity are not only valid for all men but also provide the best possible life. There is no way to demonstrate this scientifically. In fairness to Allport, we would have to conclude that his criteria of maturity are often found among those who are judged to be psychologically and physically healthy. The reader can profit from an understanding and application of them.

INSIGHTS FROM ALLPORT'S VIEWS ON MATURITY

HABITS, ATTITUDES, AND TRAITS (PERSONAL DISPOSITIONS)

Allport believes that we can understand a person best by a knowledge of his pattern of values. Are there any guidelines to help one identify these major values? Allport adopts the six value orientations proposed by Spranger which we have previously discussed. We will now consider the difference between habits, attitudes, and traits (or personal dispositions) as a means of understanding the central role of values.

Habits.   A habit may be thought of as a relatively automatic stimulus-response unit. A person approaches his front door; he automatically reaches for his key. It should be noted that (1) the response does not occur unless the stimulus is encountered; (2) the proprium is not involved because the response is reflexlike; (3) the response occurs to a particular stimulus, or to a limited range of similar stimuli. How much can you learn about a person from a knowledge of his habits? Allport argues that habits are on the periphery of personality. One needs to go deeper to secure a true picture of a personality.

Attitudes.   An attitude is more complex than a habit. It includes a particular way of perceiving something, specific expectations (or sets), emotional reactions, and behavior. One may have a specific attitude toward education, or the government, or religion, or members of the opposite sex, and so on. Attitudes usually involve more of the personality than habits; thus knowledge of another person's attitudes (or our own) will offer a better personality picture than habits will. It should be noted that an attitude is like a habit in that it is set off by a stimulus, but unlike a trait, which usually activates behavior without any apparent external stimulus.

Traits.   We are closer to describing the uniqueness of another's personality when we identify his traits. It will be recalled that a trait or personal disposition has three elements: (1) a core tendency or disposition (such as a mothering tendency); (2) a range of stimuli that are perceived as relatively equivalent as a consequence of the influence of the core disposition (such as young animals, old people, children, someone who is ill); (3) a range of responses that are all expressive of the same disposition (as comforting, feeding, bathing, caring for, and so on). Many situations are treated as if they were the same, and many responses are also expressive of the same goal. While a trait may be activated by numerous stimuli, it can also be an internal cause of behavior, as when a talkative person seeks out someone with whom to converse. Values would bring together central traits.

We will now consider Allport's requirements for maturity from the standpoint of fostering them in ourselves. Unfortunately, like so many other personality theorists, Allport does not give us much in the way of implementation; thus some of the suggestions will be derived from his works and some from other sources.

SELF-EXTENSION

Ideally one should participate at an ego level in all the major areas of living. Thus one should be involved with vocation, learning, recreation, the community, religion, and home. One might begin by considering these six aspects from the standpoint of authentic participation. For instance, one can learn simply for the pleasure of learning. Again, doing a job well does in fact bring satisfactions, and Allport would advise us to value our work as an extension and expression of ourselves. Community living can be a richer experience if one participates in and is aware of the life of the community. With respect to religion, Allport distinguishes between extrinsic and intrinsic religion. He holds that a mature intrinsic religion can give meaning and direction to life. We live with many unknowns, and despite the great accomplishments of science, the meaning of life has not become any more evident to modern day man than it was to the ancient Greek philosophers. Allport disagrees sharply with Freud, who held that religious concerns are a manifestation of neurotic illness.

One more point about self-extension: Allport holds that the best form of involvement is ego involvement, but he does point out that simply doing something is involving to a degree. Many people report that they are happiest when they are active. Absorption in a task ties up energy and wards off self-preoccupation. With respect to participation in the various spheres of life Allport points out that:

> It is probably too much to expect even the mature person to become passionately interested in all these spheres of activity. But unless autonomous interests have developed in some of these areas — unless our work, our study, our families, hobbies, politics, our religious quest becomes significantly propriate — we cannot possibly qualify as mature personalities.

> True participation gives direction to life. Maturity advances in proportion as lives are decentered from the clamorous immediacy of the body and ego-centeredness. Self love is a prominent and inescapable factor in every life, but it need not dominate. Everyone has self love, but only self extension is the earmark of maturity (1961, pp. 284–285).

WARM RELATING OF SELF TO OTHERS

According to Allport if a person is given sufficient love in childhood, he will be socially receptive. But one may have difficulty finding someone who is mature enough to affiliate with. Furthermore, one may lack some of the basic skills required for harmonious social relationships. Here are some suggestions. First, certain behaviors hamper relationships with others. Don't be overly concerned about winning every point or argument. Remember that the desire to impress everyone is very tempting but is quite unrealistic. Avoid imitating the apparently successful social techniques of one who seems to be liked. Being a jokester, a hearty extrovert, always loving and pleasant, a powerful and masterful person may be highly appealing, but if it does not express your real self, it will not be suitable. Secondly, although most people respond to indications of liking or loving, there are some who are not adept at reacting to demonstrations of concern. Take a tolerant attitude toward others. Being human, no matter how favorable one's life situation seems to be, confronts everyone with unsolvable problems and dilemmas such as fear of the future, growing older, suffering pain and disappointment, inconsistencies between what is and what should be, and the like. Thirdly, learn social skills by watching others and by observing the consequences of your own behavior. Be willing to adopt new approaches and to vary your roles with different people. Fourthly,

Allport is the champion of the idea that each person is a unique creation of nature. You should strive to perfect *your* style of life: discover
your assets and bring them out more fully; work continually to improve
your shortcomings; avoid fixed poses and artificial roles.

Allport tells us some attitudes to avoid and also some to cultivate if we
would relate warmly with others:

> Both intimacy and compassion require that one not be a burden or nuisance to
> others, nor impede their freedom in finding their own identity. Constantly
> complaining and criticizing, jealousy and sarcasm are toxic in social relation-
> ships. A woman of marked maturity was asked what she considered the most im-
> portant role of life. She answered "Do not poison the air that other people have
> to breathe" (1961, p. 285).

EMOTIONAL SECURITY

In the following passage Allport details some of the negative and positive qualities related to mature self-acceptance:

> Irritations and thwarting occur daily. The immature adult, like the child, meets
> them with tantrums of temper, or with complaining, blaming others, and self
> pity. By contrast, the mature person puts up with frustration, takes the blame on
> himself (by being "intropunitive") if it is appropriate to do so. He can bide his
> time, plan to circumvent the obstacle, or, if necessary, resign himself to the inev-
> itable. It is definitely not true that the mature person is always calm and serene,
> nor is he always cheerful. His moods come and go; he may even be temperamen-
> tally pessimistic and depressed. But he has learned to live with his emotional
> states in such a way that they do not betray him into impulsive acts; nor interfere
> with the well-being of others (1961, p. 188).

It may be of some assistance in promoting self-acceptance and emotional security to consider Allport's descriptions of the neurotic and the
normal. (1) The neurotic frequently avoids or escapes anything which
involves pain; the normal confronts the requirements of his world and
attempts to satisfy his needs. (2) The neurotic habitually represses his
difficulties, but since the repressions are ineffective, they continually
cause difficulties for him. The normal person can effectively repress
certain matters and not be troubled by them: for instance, he may simply
determine not to think about death. (3) The neurotic is characterized
by many personality splits. His goals and values may be conflicting.
Many trends oppose each other. The normal person is characterized by
integration and unity. (4) Self-deception is another prominent characteristic of the neurotic; the normal person has insight into his motivations and behaviors. (5) The neurotic is characterized by fixations in
personality growth. His emotions may have a primitive quality; his motives may be childish. The normal person thinks, feels, and acts in accordance with his age expectancies. (6) The neurotic suffers from uncontrolled impulsiveness. He behaves in ways which are a mystery to
himself. The normal person can postpone gratification, tolerate frustration, and accept substitutes—or nothing at all when no outlet is possible. (7) The neurotic's involvements are quite narrow and tied to the immediate situation; the normal person can think about things and
remove himself from the here and now. He can take charge of his own
thoughts and reactions in many situations. Refer to Table 12-2 for a
summary of the traits associated with abnormality, normality, and maturity.

TABLE 12-2 COMPARISON OF NEUROTIC, NORMAL, AND MATURE ORIENTATIONS

Toward Abnormality	Toward Normality	Toward Maturity
Escapism	Reality testing, confrontation	Extension of self
Ineffective repression	Effective repression	Warm relating of self to others
Self-deception	Self-insight	Emotional security
Dissociations	Integration and progressive organization	Realistic perceptions
Narrowed thinking	Skills and assignments	Abstraction, self-reflection
Uncontrolled impulsiveness	Impulse control, frustration tolerance	Self-objectification
Fixation at juvenile level	Behavior appropriate to age and experience	Unifying philosophy of life

Note: For Allport, maturity is a step beyond normality. Maturity means more than the absence of symptoms; it is a state of fulfilled potentials and continued striving toward positive goals. (Adapted from Allport, *Pattern and Growth in Personality.* Holt, Rinehart and Winston, 1961.)

REALISTIC PERCEPTION, SKILLS AND ASSIGNMENTS

Allport groups as important qualities of maturity the ability to perceive the world realistically, the development of functional skills, and working on worthwhile tasks. These qualities need not go together, but they usually do. Certainly one can neither meet his world head on nor employ his skills correctly without a realistic perception of things.

Skills are valued possessions, no matter how humble they might be. One should guard against devaluating his accomplishments and skills because they seem less spectacular than someone else's. He should cultivate the attitude that "My skills are more important to me than whatever someone else can do." Improvement and not evaluation and comparison should be the goal. One might think of the confidence and poise of the skilled painter, carpenter, teacher, or surgeon performing his craft easily, smoothly, and seemingly without effort. Performing a skill well can be experienced as pleasurable in itself. One also experiences a sense of security and competence. One should view his skill and work as an absolute value rather than fit it into the cultural mold. Bear in mind that what is highly payed for or valued in a particular culture is not necessarily intrinsically valuable. According to Allport's notion of self-extension, what one is and what one can do are closely identified. One has a right to feel pride in his skills, just as one needs to feel positively about himself.

Allport offers a caution about economic expectations, which are so often unrealistic among the young:

Here we should add a word concerning "economic maturity." For most people the struggle to earn a living, to remain solvent, to meet fierce economic competition is a major demand of life. It causes strain and begets crisis often more devastating than the crisis of sex and self identity. College students do not always estimate correctly the challenge they will face when they enter into competition for the dollar. Youthful personalities sometimes seem relaxed (even serene) prior to their ordeal of the market place. To be able to support oneself and one's family (in America with an ever advancing standard of living) is a frightening demand. To meet it without panic, without self-pity, without giving way to defensive, hostile, self deceiving behavior is one of the acid tests of maturity (1961, p. 290).

SELF-OBJECTIFICATION: INSIGHT AND HUMOR

Allport asks this question:

How is the psychologist to tell whether or not an individual has insight? (Insight in the psychiatric sense means self knowledge.) According to an old adage, Everyman has three characters:

1. that which he has
2. that which he thinks he has
3. that which others think he has (1961, p. 291).

To elaborate: self-knowledge is clouded by over estimation of self. Look for pretense, false masks, and exaggeration of self-worth. Of course, one may err in the opposite direction by chronic self-devaluation and self-contempt. One should be able to laugh at oneself and one's foibles. Many people take themselves much too seriously for their own good. Do not be afraid of the truth about yourself because there is more positive than negative in most lives.

UNIFYING PHILOSOPHY OF LIFE

Values are more characteristic of adults than of children and of the mature than of the average or the psychologically disturbed. If you are not certain of your values, begin by looking at your interests. If you are not clear about your interests, you might look at your preferences and aversions, and ultimately at your typical behavior patterns. In this way you may arrive at a pattern of values which was not previously formulated.

Allport agrees with Spranger that the religious sentiment, if it is mature, is the most comprehensive value. Here are some points to think about regarding religious belief. (1) Mature religious beliefs are not pathological or a sign of personality weakness. (2) The religious sentiment may be one's response to the problems of living, and it may be a guide for future behavior. (3) Religion can offer the most complete explanation for living. (4) Important values often have to be sacrificed or cannot be attained. A religious sentiment can make even this fact acceptable. (5) Religious sentiment offers an optimistic approach to life. If a belief cannot be disproved, then we are justified in harboring it as long as it promotes a positive approach. (6) Allegiance to any cause is a form of directedness. Surrender to religion can be the most compelling form of directedness. (7) Most religions foster social and humanistic values.

SIGNIFICANT QUOTATIONS FROM ALLPORT

Allport considers the existential problem of commitment in the following passage:

Fortunately we have the capacity to make commitments and to take risks. We can, if we wish, gamble our life on the value of some personal project, even though we cannot prove its worth, or be assured of its success. Our faith in a project may be only half sure, but that does not mean that we will have to be halfhearted. To be able to make a life wager is man's crowning ability (1961, p. 558).

He takes up the question of freedom of action by relating freedom of choice to the number of skills one possesses:

A person whose stores of experience and knowledge contain many "determining tendencies" is freer than a person who has only a meager store. If I have only one relevant skill, or if I know only one solution, I have only one degree of freedom. I act in the only way I can. But if I have much relevant knowledge, a broad education, and have wide experience with the kind of problem I face, then I can select "on the whole" the most appropriate solution, or create a new one. A many channeled mind is freer than a one-track mind (1961, p. 562).

He also offers us a guide to the normal development of conscience, if we bear in mind that conscience is a major component of the proprium and a major determinant of behavior:

A mature person has a relatively clear self-image by virtue of which he can imagine what he would like to be and what he ought to do as a unique individual, and not merely as a member of his tribe, or as the child of his parents. He says to himself in effect, "I ought to do the best I can to become the sort of person I partly am, and wholly hope to be." This type of conscience is not the obedient "must" of childhood (1961, p. 303).

Finally, he poses an interesting question regarding the good life. Is maturity the ultimate goal? Can there be other goods?

Is maturity the only ultimate "good" value for personality? Do we not all know immature people who are highly creative, heroic in special ways, and possessed of other desirable attributes? It seems that especially the value of creativity is present in many lives that are otherwise warped, retarded, even neurotic and psychotic. And the world needs creativity. We must concede this point, and admit that there are many good things in life besides soundness and maturity of personality. We can yield on this matter, but still maintain as a generally desirable goal the development of personalities toward the highest attainable level of maturity. We shall always fall short of this goal, but when we do so, fortunately, many sound values remain (1961, p. 305).

SUMMARY

1. Maturity is an ideal state that is never attained. It is accompanied by physical and psychological well-being, but happiness is not a necessary condition for or of maturity. Maturity involves the best development and functioning of an individual within the circumstances of his life.

2. Allport stresses the uniqueness of each individual, and there are as many ways to live properly as there are individual human beings. For Allport, the outstanding quality of a mature person is the ability to set and continually

strive toward the fulfillment of goals. Goals rather than drives are the most distinctive characteristic of humanness. Goals and values provide organization, stability, and direction to personality and life. Allport believes that maturity is possible only for those who have innate and learned tendencies to live comfortably within a given environment.

3.   Warding off ill health and relieving tensions are necessary but not sufficient conditions for attaining maturity. The mature person actually creates tension, since it motivates and controls the types of behavior that secure goals, and goals themselves produce tension.

4.   Allport considers the self as continually developing throughout life, but its major components are formed by age 20. The proprium of each individual grows, develops, and changes in a unique manner through the combined determinants of heredity, environment, and eventually the proprium itself. Maturity is not possible without a stable, well-established sense of identity.

5.   A complex self-image is gradually formed. It includes one's perception of oneself as well as the perception of what one wishes to become. The image of the ideal self may be a significant motivating factor in promoting maturity because it embodies the ideals toward which the person is aiming. For the mature person the past influences the becoming process but does not completely determine or limit the future.

6.   Allport does not view maturity as a single general factor but rather as a series of attainments which follow a process fashion. Continuous attention and flexibility are required to meet the demands of maturity.

7.   The following are Allport's criteria of maturity. Remember that each individual attains and expresses them in a unique manner.
   a. Extension of the self
   b. Warm relating of self to others
   c. Emotional security (self-acceptance)
   d. Realistic perception
   e. Skills and assignments
   f. Self-objectification (insight and humor)
   g. Unifying philosophy of life (having a value orientation to life)

8.   For Allport, the basic units of building blocks of personality are habits, attitudes, and traits. Traits that constitute the proprium are the most important determinants of personality. Such traits may be major values.

9.   Allport follows the value schema of Spranger as a means of identifying the major directions of living. These values are:

   a. Theoretic
   b. Economic
   c. Aesthetic
   d. Social
   e. Political
   f. Religious

Individuals possess differing degrees of involvement in all six, with one usually predominating.

REFERENCES

Allport, G. W. Becoming. New Haven: Yale University Press, 1955.
Allport, G. W. Personality and Social Encounter. Boston: Beacon Press, 1960.
Allport, G. W. Pattern and Growth in Personality. New York: Holt, Rinehart and Winston, 1961.
Boss, M. Psychoanalysis and Daseinsanalysis. New York: Basic Books, 1963.
Bruner, J. S., and Goodman, C. C. Value and need as organizing factors in perception. J. Abnorm. Social Psychol. *42*:33–44, 1947.
Dahms, A. M. Emotional Intimacy. Boulder, Colorado: Pruett Publishing Company, 1972.
Fromm, E. Man for Himself. New York: Holt, Rinehart and Winston, 1947.
Goethals, G. W., and Klos, D. S. Experiencing Youth: First-Person Accounts. Boston: Little, Brown and Company, 1970.
Hunt, J. McV. Intrinsic motivation and its role in psychological development. *In* Levine, D., ed. Nebraska Symposium on Motivation. Lincoln: University of Nebraska Press, 1965. Pp. 189–282.
Hutt, M. L. "Consecutive" and "adaptive" testing with the revised Stanford-Binet. J. Consult. Psychol. *11*:93–103, 1947.
May, R. Psychology and the Human Dilemma. Princeton, New Jersey: Van Nostrand, 1967.
Rinder, I. D. New directions and an old problem: The definition of normality. Psychiatry *27*:107–15, 1964.
Spranger, E. Types of Men. Pigors, W., trans. Halle, Germany: Niemeyer, 1928.
Tillich, P. The Courage to Be. New Haven: Yale University Press, 1952.
Wessman, A. E., and Ricks, D. F. Mood and Personality. New York: Holt, Rinehart and Winston, 1966.
White, R. W. Motivation reconsidered: The concept of competence. Psychol. Rev. *66*:297–330, 1959.

CHAPTER 13

The Fully Functioning Person

Carl R. Rogers

Carl R. Rogers (1902–   )

BIOGRAPHY AND OVERVIEW

In his work as a psychotherapist, Carl R. Rogers became increasingly convinced that those coming to him for help with their personal problems were actually searching for their real selves. Although he had ruled out the possibility of the self as an explanatory concept, he was forced to re-examine its place in his own life and in the lives of his clients. He made a complete turnabout, so that his name is currently associated with self theory. He now holds that psychological imbalance and disharmony results from a discrepancy between the conception of self and the real self, and that congruity between self and self-awareness promotes healthy personality growth and functioning. Speaking of his position on the self, Rogers says:

I began my work with the settled notion that the self was a vague, ambiguous, scientifically meaningless term, which had gone out of the psychologist's vocabulary with the departure of the introspectionists. Consequently, I was slow in recognizing that when clients were given the opportunity to express their problems and their attitudes in their own terms, without any guidance and interpretation, they tended to talk in terms of the self. . . . It seemed clear. . . that the self was an important element in the experience of the client, and that in some odd sense, his goal was to become his real self (1959, pp. 200–01).

Carl Rogers was born in 1902 in Oak Park, Illinois. He came from a family with strong Protestant convictions. After graduating from college he attended Union Theological Seminary, but he transferred to Columbia to study clinical psychology. He received an M.A. in psychology in 1928 and a Ph.D. in 1931. For the first ten years of his professional career, Rogers worked at a child guidance clinic. During this period, he came under the influence of several

364

outstanding neo-Freudian psychoanalysts, such as Theodore Reich and Otto Rank. In 1940, he made a radical change in his life by accepting a professorship in psychology at Ohio State University. He formulated many of his clinical insights and presented them in a book which was written in 1942, *Counseling and Psychotherapy.* In 1945, Rogers moved to the University of Chicago where he headed the counseling center and taught psychology. Many important research projects came out of this experience. He developed the technique of recording counseling sessions and worked out elaborate methods for studying the responses of his clients. In his 1951 book, *Client-Centered Therapy: Its Current Practice, Implications, and Theory,* Rogers presented his ideas on counseling and also attempted to formalize a theory of personality. In 1957 he went to the University of Wisconsin, his alma mater, to hold a joint appointment as Professor of Psychology and Psychiatry. In 1964 he accepted a position as Resident Fellow at the Western Behavioral Sciences Institute in La Jolla, California. He is currently a fellow at the Center for Studies of the Person, also in La Jolla.

Rogers has applied his client-centered concepts and practices in a wide range of situations. For many years he has been personally involved in individual counseling. He has also applied his concepts and methods to family life (Rogers, 1961), to education and learning (1969), and to group tension and conflict (1959). He is currently interested in encounter groups and is steadily becoming the leader in this area (Rogers, 1970).

Mowrer (1969) has divided Rogers's work into two periods, one focusing upon client-centered counseling and the other reflecting his interest in group dynamics. Mowrer has also observed a shift in Rogers's approach from tender loving care to tough loving care. The shift reflects the increasing responsibility which is required of the participant.

Rogers has long held the conviction that every person has powerful constructive forces within his personality that need to be allowed to operate. Growing things do not need to be grown but rather given the conditions that will permit growth, for they have an inherent tendency for growth and actualization. He expresses this conviction with a vivid observation in the following passage:

During a vacation weekend some months ago I was standing on a headland overlooking one of the rugged coves which dot the coastline of northern California. Several large rock outcroppings were at the mouth of the cove, and these received the full force of the great Pacific combers which, beating upon them, broke into mountains of spray before surging into the cliff-lined shore. As I watched the waves breaking over these large rocks in the distance, I noticed with surprise what appeared to be tiny palm trees on the rocks, no more than two or three feet high, taking the pounding of the breakers. Through my binoculars I saw that these were some type of seaweed, with a slender "trunk" topped off with a head of leaves. As one examined a specimen in the interval between the waves it seemed clear that this fragile, erect, top-heavy plant would be utterly crushed and broken by the next breaker. When the wave crunched down upon it, the trunk bent almost flat, the leaves were whipped into a straight line by the torrent of the water, yet the moment the wave had passed, here was the plant again, erect, tough, resilient. It seemed incredible that it was able to take this incessant pounding hour after hour, day after night, week after week, perhaps, for all I know, year after year, and all the time nourishing itself, extending its domain, reproducing itself; in short, maintaining and enhancing itself in this process which, in our shorthand, we call growth. Here in this palmlike seaweed was the tenacity of life, the forward thrust of life, the ability to push into an incredibly hostile environment and not only hold its own, but to adapt, develop, become itself (1963, pp. 1–2).

Rogers attempts to detail the general nature of healthy growth in his theory of personality. He says his theory "pictures the end-point of personality development as being a basic congruence between the phenomenal field of experience and the conceptual structure of the self—a situation which, if achieved, would represent freedom from internal strain and anxiety, and freedom from potential strain; which would represent the maximum in realistically oriented adaptation; which would mean the establishment of an individualized value system having considerable identity with the value system of any other equally well-adjusted member of the human race" (1951, p. 532).*

This chapter will draw heavily from Rogers's ideas about "the good life" or the fully functioning person. His definite stand on this question is based upon his many years of experience as a psychotherapist. His theory of personality developed as a result of his therapeutic experiences, rather than vice versa; thus it has a strong empirical and experiential basis.

CLIENT-CENTERED THERAPY

Rogers, as a clinician, recognized that his therapeutic techniques rested on certain assumptions about personality. We will now examine the system of concepts he thus formulated regarding man's psychological make-up and functioning.

RESPECT FOR INDIVIDUALITY

A high regard for individuality underlies client-centered therapy. Although the individual may be judged irritable and obnoxious by common social standards, he must be treated with respect and accepted as a human being who has difficulties and problems that impede his fulfillment as a person. The individual merits positive regard, even when, in a social sense, he does not deserve it. Every person has a genuine need for such positive regard. Sometimes this need is so distorted that the person who has been deprived of regard may not know how to deal with it when he does experience it. At first he may look upon it as a threat, but in the warm, accepting relationship of nondirective

---

*For Rogers, the phenomenal field of experience is the total realm of psychological experiences. He defines the unconscious as psychological experiences which are not symbolized, or in other words, not available to the conscious self. When all psychological experiences can be consciously experienced, the person is in a state of congruence. He will also have a conception of self which coincides with his real self.

therapy, he gradually comes to accept and welcome the warmth of another person. It should be noted that the warm, accepting, nonjudgmental relationship between therapist and client is as important as any therapeutic procedure, if not more so, in promoting the therapeutic effects (Rogers, 1951).

The Self-Structure

The major focus of client-centered therapy is upon the self-structure. The primary source of disturbance is postulated to be centered about this self. The self-structure should be considered the real or actual self. Distinguished from the real self is the *phenomenal* self, by which is meant the self of awareness or the self which is experienced. The two selves make up the core of personality and determine behavior. Sometimes a particular behavior may be more the result of one self than the other. If the self is distorted or malformed, as it inevitably is in those who seek therapy, the person's full potentialities are severely blocked, leading to psychological or physical disorders. If a person believes that he is basically unlovable and inferior, this conception of self will limit behavior of an affectional type. Experience which goes counter to the self-conception will be distorted in such a manner as to fit the image of self as unlovable and inferior. The person may reason that the interest of another is not really genuine or is intended only to lead him on. More will be said in a later section about the incongruence between the conceptual or phenomenal self and the real experiences and needs that exist.

Regularly associated with psychological disturbances is a profound dislike of self. Since the person does not really know who he is, he may complain of not being in control, of being trapped and confused. Often there is the complaint of being evil, or basically selfish, or downright hateful. To a great extent, the culture reinforces the idea that one should not be self-satisfied. One should not really enjoy being himself because such self-appreciation might lead to complacency and hinder further attempts at improvement.

Rogers (1951) reports that in successful therapy the self-concept is modified to include the *totality of sensory and visceral experiences.* In other words, the senses are utilized and trusted fully. Material is not censored or altered to conform to the distorted self-concept. Visceral experiences are feelings and desires associated with vital psychobiologic needs, and these too are experienced freely and are accepted as a part of the real self. After successful therapy, clients report an exuberantly positive self-feeling, a genuine liking for the self that they are or have newly discovered. This is similar to what Maslow has called "peak experience," a rich and direct feeling of great joy and satisfaction. The person, for the moment at least, may be totally accepting of his "whole self" without qualification. One of Rogers's clients described this experience as a childlike delight and awe, as with a new and exciting discovery. The real self is a joyful thing to discover and to be.

BASIC GOODNESS OF MAN'S NATURE

Some religions assume that man is born with a nature tainted with antisocial and destructive tendencies, and that the growing child must be socialized and civilized. One must tame the wild beast. The cliché "Spare the rod and spoil the child" embodies the view that strict discipline is essential in child-rearing. Freud (1927) expressed this idea when he made the id the locus of the most powerful motivation in the personality: inherently selfish, antisocial, and primitive. If the id had full reign over the personality, individual survival would be reduced to the law of the jungle. Survival and civilization are made possible by channeling the tendencies of the id into socially oriented forms of expression. The power of conscience from within and the fear of punishment from without keep the basically animalistic individual in line with the standards of social living. When man is behaving "naturally" he is at his worst; witness the old aphorism "Evil comes on by natural bent, while virtue needs encouragement."

Departing sharply from Freudian theory, Rogers (1961) believes that one of the most basic principles of human nature is that man's motivations and tendencies are positive. Even our primitive impulses are not animalistic, egocentric, or antisocial. We are essentially forward-looking, sensitively humane, and "good." Rogers agrees with Maslow (1970) that our negative emotions — hatred, destructiveness, jealousy, and the like — are merely by-products of the frustration of such vital desires as security, acceptance, love, and self-fulfillment. Negative emotions are not in themselves the core of man's nature.

Incongruence

The person suffering from a personality disorder may be particularly prone to displaying negative emotions. As we have seen, he has, in Rogers's view, a distorted self-concept, a view of himself which is incomplete or grossly out of tune with the rest of his personality. This state is called *incongruence* (Rogers, 1959). If the self-concept is incongruent with the *real* needs of the self, frustration results. In such cases, negative emotions and antisocial behavior are common occurrences.

All too often, children are brought up to believe that they are "bad" or "immoral." In impressing upon the child that he constantly needs to improve, many parents and teachers convey the notion that the child is unworthy, bad, or undesirable as he is. In the process of stressing a negative self-evaluation, they frequently discourage positive feelings toward the self, treating such feelings with scorn and even punishment. Praise and recognition must come from others, never from oneself. "The meek shall inherit the earth." Humility is a virtue which the child is encouraged to adopt as a guiding principle. This leads to a one-way evaluation process: the person can be only bad, or at best neutral. Perceiving himself as bad or inferior, the child interprets, filters out, and distorts sensory inputs to support this self-conception. In therapy, or under certain other conditions such as warm human relationships, he may gradually experience positive self-feelings, and if he incorporates this aspect of his personality into his self-concept, his concept of self will be expanded. He will learn to like and genuinely approve of certain aspects of himself and to dislike and disapprove of other aspects. In other words, he will gain a more realistic picture of his personality. His conception of self will become more congruent with his real self.

INTROJECTION

A common form of self-distortion results from introjection, which is the taking over of the values, beliefs, or behaviors of another—usually one who has authority over the person—and accepting them as if they were truly one's own (Rogers, 1951). This process may lead to incongruity between one's real needs and the desires which are consciously sought. A child may introject the idea that his mother must always be liked, or on the negative side, that one should not have any feeling of hostility towards her, that one should always like her no matter what she does. The feelings the child actually experiences may be incongruent with this introjected value. In order to preserve the self-concept, the real feelings must be denied or distorted to be somehow acceptable. Sometimes the defenses break down and the person does experience his true feelings, with a resulting catastrophic reaction, such as an anxiety attack. For example, a child who has always been taught to love his mother may experience extreme hatred for her when she punishes him unfairly.

Another common distortion of the self-concept is the introjected belief that no one can care for me, that I am unlovable. When this attitude comes about, it limits the information-gathering functions. The person may fail to see genuine affection when it occurs. He may by his actions preclude a close, intimate human relationship. He may have to blunt his own positive feelings toward others to maintain his distorted self-concept. His personality growth and functioning is then greatly limited, for *a person cannot function fully when his phenomenal self, or self of awareness, is a poor approximation of what he really is.*

Conditions of Worth

Rogers's concept of conditions of worth denotes certain basic processes in the formation of the self which exert profound effects upon personality development and functioning (Rogers, 1959). Conditions of worth take the form of prescriptions (dos and don'ts) that must be followed in daily conduct if one is to be acceptable to or valued by others. The child cannot eat his food in any way he pleases; he must learn to adhere to certain standards of etiquette. Furthermore, the requirements are variable: he does not have to follow the same strict manners with his age-mates as at a formal dinner, but conditions of worth are always present. As a matter of fact, knowledge of and adherence to conditions of worth in all the varied situations one encounters is considered an indication of good adjustment. According to Rogers (1972), indiscriminate conformity has detrimental effects on the operation of the self. In other words, in order to conform to conditions of worth, the person may have to sacrifice his spontaneity and his personal desires, and in general fit himself to a pattern which may not correspond to his true nature. A man is not considered truly masculine if he cries as a means of emotional expression and outlet; this is a condition of worth which defines masculinity in our culture. It is a limitation on personality functioning, on individuality. Yet most men accept this standard as absolutely infallible. Thus if one were to object, he would be fighting not only against something external but against something in which he really believes. The fact that conditions of worth may not be at all attuned to the individual's true nature does not change the consequences of failure to meet them. The sensitive man will be judged (and will judge himself) as deviant, no matter how masculine he is, if he expresses his emotions through crying, whether alone or in the presence of others.

Need for Positive Regard

In addition to the rewarding and punishing power the parents and other significant people naturally possess, there is another aspect which is a part of the nature of the child that promotes the formation of conditions of worth, namely, the child's need for positive regard (Rogers, 1959). The normal child behaves in a way that reveals a strong need for acceptance, respect, and love from those who care for him. Giving and withholding positive regard can have profound effects upon behavior. Early in the child's life the parents, or parent substitutes, are the "biggest" happening in the child's experience. They can play with and fondle the child and provide a warm, accepting surrounding, or they can punish, reject, mistreat, and in general make life very difficult and unpleasant. The growth of the child is best promoted by positive regard because eventually the child will come to regard himself as he has been regarded by others (Rogers, 1961).

Imposing conditions of worth on the child's behavior is tantamount to telling him: "If you want to be in my good graces, you should think, feel, and act the way I want you to." Imposing such requirements upon the child is making positive regard conditional: "You are acceptable only if you behave in certain prescribed ways." Rogers (1959) advises the parent who wishes to rear a psychologically healthy child to give unconditional positive regard—to accept and respect the child as he is. For example, disapproval should be registered in a manner which communicates that the child himself is not disapproved of, only his objectionable behavior. If the child takes a toy from his brother, the parent may indicate disapproval and even take the toy away from him and return it to the other child—and do this without a great deal of emotion. The child can still feel that he is respected. But if the parent uses such expressions as "You are bad; you are terrible; you are naughty and selfish," the stress changes from disapproval of a particular behavior to disapproval of the child.

One last point: parents are important people in the child's life (and this is true of other significant people as well) and what they desire can influence the child a great deal. If the parents disapprove of something, the child should be informed so that he can weigh this fact with the existing configuration of material; thus the child can take action on the basis of a full awareness of all his perceptions, motives, and possibilities, among which are the parents' wishes. The value of conditions of worth can best be appreciated if one considers the spirit or intent of the concept, namely the imposition of a variety of preconditions for accepting another person.

AWARENESS AND BECOMING THE REAL SELF

One key factor in the discovery of the real self is awareness—awareness of sensory and visceral experiences. With awareness, the person knows what is going on in his environment and within himself. His experiences are not screened and transformed to suit a distorted self-concept. As Rogers says: "The person comes to be in awareness what he is in experience." He may thus become a complete and fully functioning person (Rogers, 1961).

The remainder of this chapter will deal with the fully functioning person as viewed by Rogers. It may be helpful to obtain an overview of the main directions that personality growth takes. Table 13–1 depicts both negative and positive directions in this growth process.

TABLE 13–1   NEGATIVE AND POSITIVE DIRECTIONS CHARACTERISTIC OF THE FULLY FUNCTIONING PERSON
(Largely derived from statements of clients)

Negative Directions (Moving Away From)	*Positive Directions (Moving Toward)*
Away from shells, facades, and fronts	Being in a continual process of change and action
Away from a self that one is not	Trusting intuitions, feelings, emotions, and motives
Away from "oughts" (being less submissive, less compliant in meeting standards set by others)	Being a participant in experience rather than being its boss or controlling it
Away from disliking and being ashamed of self	Letting experience carry one on, floating with a complex stream of experience, moving toward ill-defined goals
Away from doing what is expected, just for that reason alone	Moving toward goals behaviorally, not compulsively planning and choosing them
Away from doing things for the sake of pleasing others at the expense of self	Following paths which feel good
Away from "musts" and "shoulds" as motives for behavior	Living in the moment (existential living); letting experience carry one on
	Possessing greater openness to experience
	Being more authentic, real, genuine
	Moving closer to feelings and self (more willingness to yield to feelings and not to place a screen between feelings and self); journey to the center of self
	Accepting and appreciating the "realness" of self
	Increasing positive self-regard (a genuine liking and sympathy for self)

GETTING BEHIND THE MASKS

When Rogers uses the term "mask," he is referring to artificial or unauthentic roles which are either self-imposed or imposed from without. If major aspects of personality are in conflict as a result of opposed role expectations, a firm sense of identity will not occur. The person may complain of being trapped, or of not knowing who he is, or of instability. He cannot take a stand on anything, nor can he make a decision on his own.

For many persons, roles are difficult to perform in the prescribed way. One may not like the assigned role of father; he may have his own definition of that role. A man may desire to be married but reject the role that his wife and the culture in general expect of him. The manner of performing one's assigned roles may vary from a complete redefinition of the role to grudging, perfunctory performance of it, to a whole-hearted acceptance and identification with the role. In this last instance, the role may be practically identical with the real self (Gergen, 1971). A woman may love being a woman as defined in her cultural setting. The role expectation is congruent with her real self, and she can carry out the role without denying or distorting her real self. She does not experience conflict among her various roles, a factor which would itself hinder the discovery and full development of self.

The basic problem of the growing individual is to *discover and express his real self within the roles that are imposed upon him.* The child comes into the world as a member of a preformed culture. He is "fitted" to the culture, not the culture to him. His parents demand that he learn many things, among which are the roles he is expected to perform. He is rewarded and punished for his knowledge and performance of these roles. No matter how permissive the home environment, a variety of roles must be learned. Conformity to expectations is as much a part of successful living as is individuality. One-sided development is a major source of psychopathology. But the person who is so immersed in his culture that he does not dare to be his real self will experience a sense of emptiness and lack of identity. On the other hand, the person who rejects most or all of his culture will experience alienation and estrangement, a sense of not being a participant in life. He will have nothing with which to replace his lost cultural roots. Obviously, neither extreme is a desirable way of life.

Rogers describes the changes that have taken place in one of his clients in the following passage:

I find that many individuals have formed themselves by trying to please others, but again, when they are free, they move away from being this person. So one professional man, looking back at some of the process he has been through, writes, toward the end of therapy: "I finally felt that I simply had to begin doing what I wanted to do, not what I thought I should do, and regardless of what other people feel I should do. This is a complete reversal of my whole life. I've always felt I had to do things because they were expected of me, or more important, to make people like me. The hell with it! I think from now on I'm going to just be me — rich or poor, good or bad, rational or irrational, logical or illogical, famous or infamous. So thanks for your part in helping to rediscover Shakespeare's 'To Thine Own Self be True' " (1961, p. 170).

FLEXIBILITY OF CULTURE AND GOODNESS OF SELF

Although the culture prescribes certain roles for its members to perform, with persistent pressures (rewards and punishments) designed to encourage compliance with these prescriptions for living, a great deal of flexibility is permitted. The role expectations for being a father are quite general, with considerable latitude; not all fathers who are considered good parents play baseball with their children. Not all doctors have a pleasing bedside manner. Not all football coaches are hardboiled, and so on. The prescriptions for roles are so general and flexible that the role one "must" follow, as for example being a man or a woman, can fit within the nature of the real self. In other words, one can still be a vibrant, unaffected, genuinely warm teacher, doctor, or policeman. Carrying out the roles thus need not be a hindrance to the growth of self. The person who assumes the role of being a good teacher, the best he knows how, makes a contribution to the children he teaches and ultimately to the whole of society. If each is doing his best (functioning at the peak of his potentialities), generally all benefit (Rogers, 1961).

Many young people conceive of themselves as possessing culturally favored attributes to a high degree. Their conception of self fits a cultural stereotype. Because such roles are or appear to be highly rewarding, the developing young person clings to them with everything he has. He strongly desires to be a lover, a man-about-town, wealthy, and famous. He works diligently to structure his self to suit these goals. He blocks off experiences which tell him a different story about himself. His defenses keep such information out, unless he encounters a situation which is totally unexpected and beyond his defensive measures. Then, of course, the awful truth may come home to him in a most painful manner. Yet even this realization of the truth about the self does not usually produce personality change. The distorted self-structure and its defenses are firmly established, and habitually the disturbing experience is quickly glossed over as a bad experience, and the distorted self-structure is maintained (Coopersmith, 1967).

A person may, of course, be unrealistic in the opposite sense: his conception of self may include attributes of inferiority and of being incompetent and unlovable. This distortion of self is also quite common because there are so many ways in which one may feel inadequate. A culture which offers such glamorous and alluring possibilities to the young person necessarily sets the stage for failure and disappointment. The high-school boy who does not make the football team and thus is not sought after by the girls may needlessly experience a terrible sense of inferiority.

A conception of self as inferior or unlovable is also firmly structured and resistant to change. Defenses are erected to maintain this erroneous self-conception. A person who believes he is inferior may actually disregard or minimize contrary evidence. This may explain the depression that sometimes accompanies the achievement of a highly prized goal. A young graduate student who had a profound feeling of inferiority stayed up the whole night after he received his doctorate in a state of deep depression. His concept of self would not allow him to experience a justifiable sense of accomplishment, even over an event for which he had worked several grueling years.

Rogers (1966) has found that a permissive, warm, accepting attitude, which enables one to explore gradually his deep and unrecognized feelings without fear of censorship, is the best atmosphere for the discovery and acknowledgment of the real self. Discovering emotions such as hatred for one's parents when only love is acceptable is indeed a painful experience. Giving up false ideals and roles is also painful. But the result of the process is a new person, or better, a new self which is more in keeping with the person who was potentially there all the while. The process of discovery and the abandonment of the old conception of self move along gradually, step by step. The client gains one insight after another about his true nature. Like a child just learning to walk, he finds the process difficult but the benefits great. Some of these benefits will be considered in the next section.

TO BE THAT SELF WHICH ONE TRULY IS

MOVING AWAY FROM FACADES AND OUGHTS

The fully functioning person easily recognizes and definitely avoids putting on a facade or demeanor which does not fit his real self (Rogers, 1961). Being an extrovert may appear to be a highly desirable personality trait, but for the fully functioning person, such a trait, if it did not fit him, would be a perversion of his self and thus highly distasteful. Many young persons, and older people who should know better, cling to the belief that outgoing, talkative, humorous qualities make for popularity and success in social and vocational endeavors. Under the influence of this erroneous idea, they misshape their behaviors and selves to fit the cultural model. Our culture does place a premium on appearance. One puts on personality traits just as one might put on clothing for different occasions (Goffman, 1959). But even when appearance is stressed, success is ultimately based upon real, not merely apparent, qualities.

Moving away from parental or cultural expectations is another indication of becoming a fully functioning person. As we have seen, many values and goals are simply taken over and accepted uncritically as one's own, even though in actuality they are incongruent with one's real needs. A high school student may believe that he wants desperately to go to college and that if he does not finish college, life will be filled with hardships and disappointments. This view was common among the children of many European immigrants who saw in education the glorious way to successful living. However, intellectually and emotionally a student may not be suited for college work. He may feel constrained to go and actually make it through, but all the while he will feel tense and uneasy. He may feel that he is trapped. He is doing something he does not really believe in and this is the cause of his distress, although he may not recognize it. Many people complain that their lives are regulated from without rather than from within. They are slaves to certain things, such as money, prestige, or power.

TOWARD SELF-DIRECTION

As we have just implied, the fully functioning person takes responsibility for the main directions of his life. Although the move toward self-regulation and autonomy is a gradual and painful process, self-direction yields great satisfaction. To be dependent requires less of the person than to be independent. To accept ready-made standards of conduct, values, and goals requires less effort and poses less threat than to work these out for oneself. The person who introjects the values of his culture or his parents subjects himself to the likelihood of incongruity between what he believes he wants and his real needs, which must be denied or distorted in the process. While breaking away from dependence is terribly painful and arriving at personally determined goals is highly frustrating at times because one must inevitably make mistakes, the outcome of self-direction is ultimately the best approach to life. *One functions most fully when he is fulfilling himself in his own way* This can be accomplished only by self-direction (Rogers, 1961).

It should be noted that to take charge of one's life by examining the appropriateness of values for oneself does not imply that the culture should be rejected. To Rogers, becoming a fully functioning person does not mean breaking away from tradition and espousing an unconventional movement. Being a person means being autonomous, formulating or choosing one's own style of life. The culture is broad and flexible, and most people can function as individuals within it.

WILLINGNESS TO BE A PROCESS

By willingness to be a process, Rogers (1961) means spontaneity, creative living, flexibility, and a dynamic and changing orientation to life. It is the opposite of adjusting by attaining a static and adequate manner of dealing with one's needs and pressures, of achieving a "state" of adequate functioning. The static view of adjustedness (Lindner, 1952) reminds one of a machine which is functioning properly because all the parts are in good working order; one takes his lawn mower to be adjusted — tuned, sharpened, greased — and that's that. It runs properly. According to this view, a person who recognizes and accepts the cultural limitation of his activities and who is able to satisfy his needs without interfering with those of others — without violating their rights — is a well-adjusted person. He has a fixed set of standards and attitudes; his self-structure is firmly established; he holds a conservative point of view; and generally he is civilized and gets on well in his social setting. Rogers's different view of the matter is based upon his therapeutic experiences with those who have seemed to make the most movement in the course of therapy. From their experiences, he has derived the notion of "process living."

The person who is willing to be a process accepts inner and outer experiences as they are, without imposing requirements and standards. He flows with his experiences. He does not rule out certain things or set boundaries regarding what needs and sensory elements will be recognized. In other words, his self is not fixed and static. Rogers sees the ideal state as a fluid, changeable, unstructured, moment-by-moment existence. Like Allport (1961) with his view of becoming, he believes that the person who lives successfully is constantly moving in one direction or another, never reaching a fixed state. This is not to be taken as advocacy of a reckless, carefree, chaotic, and directionless existence. Anything but. In process living, all the needs of the person are clearly perceived, and there is a balanced attempt to meet them. Also, all sensory and organismic information is freely registered, enabling the individual to be in tune with his environment and his organism.

The notion of being a process is difficult to describe. Other aspects of the fully functioning person will help to make the notion clearer, since all of the qualities interact and support one another. The notion, however, is similar to what has been termed existential living. By this is meant living as fully as possible in the present moment. One should not regret the past, or be highly anxious about the unknown future, or attempt to fully comprehend or structure the present, but live the present as fully as possible.

Rogers is quite clear about what the good life is *not*. It is not a fixed state, a glorious state of virtue, contentment, nirvana, or happiness. The process of living is not attaining homeostasis, or tension reduction, or equilibrium. Rogers even rejects the notion that those who are fully functioning are "actualized," a term used by several outstanding personologists to describe the ideal human living. The good life is not a destination but a process or direction in which the person is participating fully according to his true nature. An essential feature of this process is inner freedom, continuing flexibility to select the direction of living.

Openness to Experience

To live fully requires that one fully know what is really going on within and without oneself. Openness to experience is the opposite of defensiveness. All organic experiences and sensory inputs are freely relayed through the nervous system. The person can sense his deepest emotions, even if they are quite negative, but at the same time he does not rule out positive ones. All of his emotions are permitted to pass into the self-structure. In fact, the openness quality rules out false masks, leaving the self-structure mobile and fluid. The person does not feel comfortable being someone other than himself. He is at his worst when he is play-acting. He does not cling to culturally determined expectations and allurements. His judgments, choices, and decisions are natural outcomes of his own evaluation of experience, both internal and external. He can live with experiences fully because he is open to them and refuses to force them into an artificial order.

Listening to Oneself. An integral aspect of openness to experience is "listening to oneself" (Rogers, 1972). This is recognized in Eastern cultures, which place much stress on becoming acquainted with one's deepest nature. In Western cultures, however, the focus is outside the person, and there seems to be a taboo against introspection. The child is admonished to keep busy, to always be doing, or looking, or listening, or playing with something. This external orientation and avoidance of inner experiences produce a one-sided development which in the long run is harmful because it blocks out a major source of knowledge. An individual faced with a decision finds that he cannot make it because he really does not know himself, and hence does not know what he wants. Obviously one cannot predict the future, and certain critical decisions which may change one's course in life cause hesitation and doubt. Yet in many instances the difficulty lies with the lack of self-awareness. The person is aware of a self and of certain goals, but these may be vague and conflicting, and the self which is experienced may seem unreal. According to Rogers's view of the nature of the self, it may well *be* unreal. The self is not what the organism is. Listening to oneself is one way in which everyone can discover his real self (Moustakas, 1972).

Existential Living

Rogers (1961) believes that a person should let his experiences tell him what they mean rather than force a meaning upon them. One is living existentially if he can react flexibly to the total complex of internal and external experiences without imposing general constructs on his perceptions of events. The self should emerge from the complex of momentary experience rather than determine it. Rogers cannot mean that there are no psychological structures or preformed ideas affecting the pattern of stimulation which is perceived, because obviously one brings into every situation the complex of attitudes, experiences, and dispositions which are an integral part of his personality. But the person who lives existentially continually evaluates the constructs which affect his style of life, allowing them to change under the influx of experience.

Rogers quotes a client who began to live existentially. "I haven't finished the job of integrating and reorganizing myself, but that's only confusing, not discouraging, now that I realize this is a continuing process.... It's exciting, sometimes upsetting, but deeply encouraging to feel yourself in action, apparently knowing where you are going even though you don't always consciously know where that is" (1961, p. 122).

Trusting One's Organism

Using his own experiences, Rogers attempts to convey what he means by trusting one's organism:

One of the basic things which I was a long time in realizing, and which I am still learning, is that when an activity feels as though it is valuable or worth doing, it is worth doing. Put another way, I have learned that my total organismic sensing of a situation is more trustworthy than my intellect. All of my professional life I have been going in directions which others thought were foolish, and about which I have had many doubts myself. But I have never regretted moving in directions which "felt right," even though I have often felt lonely or foolish at the time (1961, p. 22).

By trusting one s organism Rogers seems to mean being able to act upon momentary impulses, not being afraid to behave as one feels like behaving. The opposite of trusting one's organism is to act in accordance with guiding principles which are immediately applied to situations demanding decisions or judgments. Another example is to follow a set pattern of behavior based on prior experience: "I have never accepted an invitation without talking to my wife about it." "We do not buy anything important without discussing it for several days." "My parents have acted conservatively about taking risks, and I have taken this line also."

Rogers does not mean that one should act rashly and on the whim of the moment change his whole course of life. His meaning appears to be more in the nature of acting spontaneously, freshly, and freely, without too many constraints. His reasoning goes something like this: The person who is open to all his experiences can consider all the components because at least they are all available. Obviously if part of the evidence is missing, behavior which is based on the existing evidence may be undesirable for the person. In a particular situation, such as leaving home for a promising job, all the elements are inspected and evaluated. One may dislike leaving his parents and friends. He may fear starting a new life in a strange environment. At the same time, he sees the value of the opportunity and some exciting challenges to his creative talents. He may also appreciate that the decision does not have to be binding for life. All these elements are brought together; a judgment or several judgments emerge, and finally he fixes upon a decision. The decision, when it arrives, may feel like an intuition, but it is not. It is more like a conclusion based on premises which are not totally in awareness. If one is open to experience, he can feel confident that his choices are rational at the time he makes them, even though they may lead to behavior which must be re-evaluated later.

Many people are fearful of expressing themselves freely because they fail to trust their spontaneous actions or reactions. They are careful to censor what they say and do, and usually they are quite uncomfortable and tense (Laing, 1967). Rogers has observed that persons who have profited most from therapy are able to trust their emotions and behave on what appears to the observer to be the impulse of the moment. But one does not arrive at this point only through therapy. Learning about oneself and testing the insights that have been gained can lead to a trust in one's organism. One's emotions can be acted upon with favorable results. When the person is fully functioning, he begins to see that his total organism is often wiser than his awareness. He can come to rely upon "intuition" for certain matters.

A SENSE OF FREEDOM

The fully functioning person experiences a feeling of freedom, a sense of self-determination (Rogers, 1961). He can choose to move in a direction of growth or stagnation, to be himself or a facade, to open himself to his experiences or shut them out. On the other hand, the person who holds to strict cultural standards or the expectations of others feels that his behavior is determined by forces over which he has no control (Rotter, 1971). A man, for example, complained that he was like an automaton. He had gone through the same daily routines so frequently and mechanically that he began to accept the idea that there was no other way for him. He expressed his sense of being trapped by comparing himself to a wind-up toy that is programmed for a certain sequence of movements and executes them exactly according to the program.

One young woman complained that her life was so permeated with "shoulds" and "oughts" that she felt she had no real desires of her own. Her decisions were virtually foregone conclusions. She had to earn good grades, take a college prep course in high school, and attend college with a major in teaching. All this and much more was determined for her by her parents. She began questioning her religious beliefs, which she felt did more to block her growth and functioning than to promote it. She seemed to have an excessive amount of guilt and complained of feeling that she was basically an evil person. Her environmental circumstances and internal controls engendered a style of life which did not permit freedom of choice. It should be noted that by the time the person reaches an age at which he can begin to make choices for himself, he may have already internalized (introjected) the standards of conduct which were forced upon him, with the consequence that he cannot violate these standards without experiencing a profound sense of guilt. He ties himself up and blocks his own channels of expression.

There are two points regarding the subjective sense of freedom which may cause the reader some confusion: (1) the relation of conscience to freedom: Does the fully functioning person have a conscience? and (2) freedom versus determinism: Is not man's nature subject to the laws of causality?

Freedom and Conscience

The question of conscience is somewhat complex. The fully functioning person does not have a conscience in the Freudian sense of an unconscious set of principles which have a censorship function. Yet he can certainly be described as a man of principles. There may appear to be a paradox or contradiction here. The fully functioning person has values, moral standards, and a host of other determining sets. But for the most part these guiding tendencies and sets are conscious. The person is aware of having them, or he can bring them to awareness if he is pressed to do so. They do not operate (as they do in the rigid, compulsive, guarded individual) as a mysterious inner force, a split off superego that oversees the doings of the ego. The guiding principles and values of the fully functioning person are his own; although they may have come from his parents or friends, they are now an integral part of his real self. A man may work diligently at a task not because he is driven to do so by an inner compulsion to succeed, but because he consciously desires a particular end. He knows what he wants and takes steps to secure it.

In addition to the factor of awareness of sets, there is also the factor of flexibility. The fully functioning person's constructs, values, and so forth are not compulsively held or immutable. He is open to experiences and can modify his sets accordingly. He has a "set to change his sets." A young man may value making money, but if he finds that this goal is not satisfying his genuine desires, he changes his valued objective. Rather than allowing his sets to order experience, he governs his sets by his experience. His constructs are fluid and easily adjusted; thus he can accommodate himself to a changing world or to change in himself. Aging, for example, does not become a dreaded specter, because he changes his constructs to suit the changes in his total organism. He has *guiding sets*, and these are consciously apprehended and easily modifiable.

From these considerations it might be inferred that if one wishes to function more fully, he should examine the constructs underlying his behavior so that he can become aware of why he is doing what he is doing. Knowing the constructs is only the first step, however, and in itself cannot lead to personality change. One must be willing to discard or change his constructs. One should adopt the attitude that nothing is so sacred that it cannot be scrutinized critically, and that no behavior, aside from the inevitables in life, is beyond one's ability to change. Living is a dynamic process. Both the individual and his circumstances alter. A fixed style of life can only produce rigidity and a disordered personality.

Freedom Versus Determinism

If there is a significant movement on the part of the client undergoing psychotherapy, the result is a greater sense of freedom. The person feels more control over his life, but whether he has increased what might be termed his actual freedom is difficult to answer and involves philosophical questions beyond the scope of this book. Some observations may aid the reader in thinking through the issue. In a sense, one is freer because more potentialities are open to him. However, the fully functioning person is also subject to the laws of causality. His behavior, including his sense of subjective freedom, is determined by antecedent conditions. But the point which Rogers seems to make is that such a person is giving expression to much more of his real organismic self when he is fully functioning and thereby satisfying his needs effectively.

TABLE 13-2   TRAITS OF THE FULLY FUNCTIONING
AND INCONGRUENT SELVES

The Fully Functioning Self	The Incongruent Self
Self-aware	Out of touch with the self
Creative	Lacks firm sense of identity
Spontaneous	Introjects
Open to experience	Frustrated impulses
Self-accepting	Negative emotions
Self-determining	Distorted self-structure
Free from constraints	Antisocial behavior
Lives in his "now"	Puts forth masks
Allows full outlet of potentials	Unrealistic appraisal of potentials
Trusts his organism	
Possesses firm sense of identity	
Avoids facades	
Has sense of free choice	
Moves from introjection	
Moves toward self-direction	
Willing to be process	
Lives existentially	

Note: Represented here are the *extremes* of a continuum on the potentials of self, as considered by Rogers.

What he chooses is what he really needs; what he consciously wants mirrors what he needs.

One of the attributes of functioning fully is a sense of self-determination, because the organism is operating properly throughout. An engine which is out of tune and one which is in tune are both "determined" to function the way they do, but the one which is functioning properly maintains a certain heat level and power efficiency, whereas the malfunctioning one overheats and is highly inefficient. Aside from the philosophical difficulties involved, the fact remains that the fully functioning person *feels* a high degree of inner freedom, and this attribute is greatly valued. Freedom from constraints, whether internally or externally imposed, is an essential condition of being one's real self. In common with other humanistic psychologists, Rogers (1969) now goes beyond his earlier view that the fully functioning person feels free, believing that in a real sense he *is* more free.

Table 13-2 summarizes the traits of Rogers's fully functioning person and of the incongruent person; Figure 13-1 depicts the two selves graphically.

CREATIVITY AND SPONTANEITY

When a person is open to his internal and external experiences, when he does not fear being himself and gives up facades, when his constructs are flexible and can change with experience, the person is both spontaneous and creative (Rogers, 1961). He can conform to the requirements of the setting when this

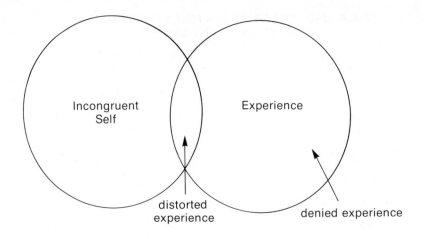

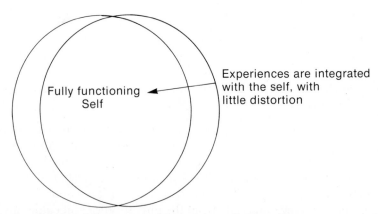

Figure 13-1 A major aim of client-centered therapy is to eliminate distortion and denial by encouraging the individual to consolidate "into one consistent and integrated system all his sensory and visceral experiences" (Rogers, 1951, p. 520). (Adapted from *Client-Centered Therapy*, Houghton Mifflin, 1951, p. 527.)

suits his needs, but he can resist the pressures placed upon him if these compel him in directions which are opposed to his self-picture.

Creativity requires a freedom from constraints. The person who must do things in a certain way, or who must meet certain standards, limits his freedom and consequently hampers his creative forces. Rather than seeking to make his life predictable, safe, orderly, and tensionless, the fully functioning person, confident in his ability to meet life head on, relishes new experiences, challenges, immediacy, stimulation, and excitement. He does not have to compulsively maintain a fixed style of living; thus he is mobile psychologically, and this is a quality which makes for creativity (Bloomberg, 1971).

The Greater Richness of Life

Rogers believes that man is truly a rational animal. When he is functioning properly, his behavior is not fearsome, not antisocial, not self-destructive. Most people are not rational to the degree that they could be. Rogers says:

When man's unique capacity of awareness is thus functioning freely and fully, we find that we have, not an animal whom we must fear, not a beast who must be controlled, but an organism able to achieve, through the remarkable integrative capacity of its central nervous system, a balanced, realistic, self-enhancing . . . behavior as a resultant of all these elements of awareness. To put it another way, when man is less than fully man—when he denies to awareness various aspects of his experience—then indeed we have all too often reason to fear him and his behavior, as the present world situation testifies. But when he is most fully man, when he is his complete organism, when awareness of experience, that peculiarly human attribute, is most fully operating, then he is to be trusted, then his behavior is constructive (1961, p. 105).

Many people are driven by the quest for unattainable goals, or they hold rigid standards of conduct that cramp and imprison them. The good life should involve a wide range of experiences. It is possible to live sensitively, with a greater variety, richness, and depth of experience than most people enjoy. One can be "a trustworthy instrument for encountering life." Rogers believes that the *good life itself* is described not by terms such as happy, blissful, content, enjoyable (although a *person* who is functioning fully can be characterized by these terms), but rather by terms such as enriching, exciting, rewarding, challenging, meaningful. The good life is not for the timid because it involves the courage to be, to stretch and grow in one's potentialities. It means having to tolerate uncertainty, ambiguity, and even pain, but it also means freedom to be oneself, to live in the moment and enjoy rich experiences freely.

CRITICAL EVALUATION

Rogers's views have been extremely influential in the field of psychology. During the 1950's and early '60's he held the position that Skinner occupies today, and he continues to be influential. His client-centered approach to counseling has spread outside of psychology to diverse fields, such as nursing, business, industry, and the ministry. It has become fashionable to respect the rights of the client, whether he be the patient in a nurse-patient relationship, the employee in a management-labor dispute, or the child in a parent-child relationship (Ginott, 1965). Even employee evaluations are sometimes presented to the employee by his supervisor, so that both may discuss the evaluation. Currently, Rogers is involved with group dynamics and the "growth" movement, but his concepts are essentially the same as they were when he was primarily a client-centered counselor, a factor that attests to the flexibility of his formulations.

Rogers has made a significant contribution to the scientific study of counseling and psychotherapy through his analysis of therapist and client responses. By recording therapy sessions, he has opened this field to scientific investigation (Rogers and Dymond, 1954). Nevertheless, his view of a benign, unfolding self that requires simply to be accepted has been criticized as naively optimistic. He offers few direct suggestions either for self-improvement or for promoting personality change in others. Although he spends far more time discussing the great benefits which result when a person attains a state of congruence, he really does not tell us how to get that way, except in rather abstract and general terms. To be a fully functioning person may require the learning of specific attitudes and skills of daily living, something that is overlooked by Rogers in his preoccupation with openness to experience and self-exploration. All the self-exploring in the world will not give the person a course to follow; no amount of self-acceptance will bring into being the kinds of skills required to satisfy needs. The behavior modification movement is a reaction against the kind of thinking that Rogers's theory represents.

One more point should be noted: there is a danger in freely exploring one's inner world. Like so many other good things, self-study can become self-preoccupation; introspection may degenerate into morbid egocentricity, which many experts hold to be the most outstanding characteristic of a disordered personality. A neurotic, for instance, is overly concerned with himself; he is acutely aware of his own needs, his emotions, his problems.

Rogers has stressed openness and expressiveness in human relationships. He maintains that we should acknowledge our feelings and emotions rather than bury them. If we feel angry with a friend, this should be communicated, not as a criticism but as a statement of an impression or feeling that the friend has been unfair, or unreasonable, or whatever may be the case. Unacknowledged feelings are potentially dangerous. They may disrupt a friendship in subtle ways if they are not perceived and confronted. On the other hand, relating to others on an emotional level can be quite risky. In many instances, it might be better to inhibit feelings and assume instead a neutral posture.

Acute sensitivity to one's feelings and emotions may endow them with a reality which they do not have: that is, emotions may be experienced more intensely by focusing on them. This condition may result in frequent fluctuations and mood changes. The person who experiences such changes makes a poor social partner, and frequently a very poor working associate as well. Allport (1961) holds that the emotionally mature person does not "poison the air that others breathe" by expressing his bad moods freely.

In this issue we are of course dealing with a matter of degree. Total emotional inhibition and control is dangerous and unhealthy. But unrestrained and indiscriminate expression and overpreoccupation with emotions is also unhealthy. With some people we may be more open than with others; under certain conditions we may be more expressive than under others. It would be extremely unwise to be emotionally expressive in all situations and with all people.

Furthermore, as Jourard (1963) points out, being our "true" selves in relationships with others may produce highly inappropriate behavior. We should take our various roles seriously and live them out fully. The roles which sons and daughters assume in relation to their parents are quite different from an intimate relationship with a member of the other sex. Many problems arise from inadequate role awareness and participation. Jourard holds that we are more ourselves with certain people and in certain situations than in others. Being oneself in every role would appear to be an impossibility, according to Jourard's view. The reader might ponder the difference between playing out roles well (Jourard) and being one's real self (Rogers).

Despite Rogers's dire warnings against extremes of morbid introspection and free emotional expression, his views on self-awareness, openness to experience, self-acceptance, and freedom can convert a dully normal life into an exciting adventure. They can enable us to become *fully functioning* rather than simply normal individuals.

INSIGHTS FROM ROGERS'S SELF THEORY

LISTENING, REFLECTION, CLARIFICATION, AND POSITIVE REGARD

We can look to Rogers's ideas and practices in his client-centered therapy for some guidance in improving social relationships.

Being a Good Listener. Rogers found that his clients wanted very much simply to talk about their problems to someone who would listen. The emphasis is on the word listen, not criticize, judge, advise, or console. A client would often report that he felt much better after an hour or so, during which time Rogers had offered no directives or advice, but had listened attentively in a warm, permissive manner. Rogers (1951) points out that the major hindrance to being a good listener is the compulsion to assert or express oneself. One does not really listen to the other because he is so busy preparing his next utterance. Most people respond positively to a sympathetic listener.

Reflection. Rogers found another procedure extremely valuable in conveying to his clients that he had a positive regard for them. He termed this technique "reflection" (Rogers, 1942). It involves acknowledgment of the other person's thoughts and feelings through verbal repetition of them, through calling attention to them, and through talking about them.

Clarification. By listening attentively and utilizing the technique of reflection, one can enable the other person to experience a clarification of his ideas and feelings. The specific ideas which one selects to reflect can also promote the process of clarification. The important factor of insight, which is so potent in bringing about personality change, is fostered through clarification. Difficulties in a personal relationship may be reduced if one person uses the techniques of listening, reflection, and clarification judiciously. Hearing an attitude or thought expressed by someone else sometimes makes it appear more vividly irrational or unrealistic.

Positive Regard. Positive regard from another, however it is expressed, is usually welcomed by anyone, particularly one who is having psychological problems. One can use his power to give positive regard to help another discover his true self, but he can also use it to promote a warm relationship. Rogers speaks of unconditional positive regard, which (as we noted earlier) is accepting the other as he is, without setting conditions. Although psychologists such as Skinner (1953) would argue that giving unconditional positive regard for neurotic behaviors constitutes a reinforcement of the very behaviors which are causing the individual difficulties, Rogers has long held that accepting the other as he is aids significantly in effecting change.

In the following passage, Rogers asks specific questions about his part in a relationship. His questions suggest the answers he has discovered in his clinical experiences. The reader may pose these questions to himself:

I should like to tell the kind of questions which my own clinical experience raises for me, and some of the tentative and changing hypotheses which guide my behavior as I enter into what I hope may be helping relationships, whether with students, staff, family, or clients.

1. Can I be in some way which will be perceived by the other person as trustworthy, as dependable or consistent in some deep sense?
2. Can I be expressive enough as a person that what I am will be communicated unambiguously?
3. Can I let myself experience positive attitudes toward this other person—attitudes of warmth, caring, liking, interest, respect?
4. Can I be strong enough as a person to be separate from the other?
5. Am I secure enough within myself to permit him his separateness?
6. Can I let myself enter fully into the world of his feelings and personal meanings and see these as he does?
7. Can I receive him as he is?
8. Can I act with sufficient sensitivity in the relationship that my behavior will not be perceived as a threat?
9. Can I free him from the threat of external evaluation?
10. Can I meet this other individual as a person who is in process of becoming, or will I be bound by his past and by my past (1961, pp. 50–55)?

Rogers presents an introspective account of his own reactions and efforts to apply the insights he has gained in his counseling and therapeutic work. Again his ideas are applicable to one's own efforts at improving mental health:

1. In my relationships with persons, I have found that it does not help in the long run to act as though I am something that I am not.
2. I find that I am more effective when I can listen acceptantly to myself, and can be myself.
3. I have found it of enormous value when I can permit myself to understand another person.
4. I have found it enriching to open channels whereby others can communicate their feelings, the private perceptual world to me.
5. I have found it highly rewarding when I can accept another person.
6. The more I am open to the realities in me and in the other person the less do I find myself wishing to rush in to fix things.
7. I can trust my experience.
8. Evaluation by others is not a guide for me.
9. Experience is for me the highest authority.
10. I enjoy the discovering of order in experience.

11. The facts are friendly.
12. What is most personal is most general.
13. It has been my experience that persons have a basically positive direction.
14. Life at its best is a slowly changing process, in which nothing is fixed (1961, pp. 16–27).

It should be pointed out that some social scientists believe that our culture has gone too far in making demands of the individual and has not allowed for his fulfillment and the expression of his individuality. One attends school and learns certain skills in order to function on the level of the culture. He marries as prescribed and has children, again as prescribed. He goes to work and pays taxes to support the institutions of the society. Meeting all these demands may leave one feeling caught in an unending series of pressures and demands, without much personality fulfillment in return. "I have paid my way by being a model member of the culture, but at the expense of not being myself."

SELF-AWARENESS

The views of Carl Rogers are quite compatible with the views of the phenomenologists. A phenomenologist is one who accepts psychological states as important determinants of behavior. As with Rogers, understanding the real self is of utmost importance. This means understanding one's values, goals, and those things which give meaning to one's life. Such understanding or awareness demands that attention be given to one's past life as it has affected the current state of being. However, because one continues to grow, such awareness is never complete but is always in process, just as one's very life is always in process. It should be noted that one does not become self-aware merely by pondering events of the day. Self-awareness is acquired most fully through observation of the self in action, particularly in social relationships, for it is then that the self is called forth actually to be what it has become.

It may be helpful at this point to draw from *Gestalt Self-Therapy,* by Muriel Schiffman, some practical suggestions for both understanding and achieving self-awareness. The Gestaltist considers much of what one does projection; the tendency to see external events from a personal frame of reference. Thus, to acquire any type of objectivity about the self and others, it becomes necessary to investigate what lies behind many of our day-to-day actions which might otherwise go unnoticed. Schiffman believes there are three principal techniques that may be used for such an investigation: (1) exploring a known fantasy, (2) playing all parts of a recurrent dream, and (3) playing an imaginary encounter with a person who has aroused any inappropriate reaction (Schiffman, 1971, p. 18).

The following five steps apply specifically to inappropriate reactions, but they may be applied to any problem areas in which one wishes to improve one's awareness.

Step 1. Recognize an inappropriate reaction. For example, a student might wonder why he becomes very angry with a certain instructor over seemingly minor matters when this does not occur with other teachers. In cases of inappropriate responses (e.g., anger), the emotion felt is often a cover for some genuine emotion that one fears to experience.

Step 2.   Feel the apparent emotion. Allow yourself to experience the anger within you. Do not be satisfied with pushing feelings aside.

Step 3.   Ask yourself what else you felt at the time. In the case of an inappropriate response or emotion, there is usually some subtle feeling which occurs just prior to the experienced emotion. For example, the angry student may recall a stab of fear felt just before the onset of anger.

Step 4.   Of what does this remind you? Recall as many situations as possible in which you responded similarly. What other authority figures, for instance, have elicited inappropriate anger from you? What did you feel toward them besides anger?

Step 5.   Look for a pattern. Try to discover what hidden emotion was being covered with what apparent one. Once you are aware of such a replacement, you may intelligently deal with the situations which precipitate such inappropriate responses. Once you recognize a pattern, you are predictable to yourself and can look forward to an opportunity to face this problem again and handle it another way.

Another technique which may prove helpful in developing self-awareness is the Q-Sort Test. The Q-Sort technique consists of a series of cards which have descriptive statements or trait names that can be used to describe the self. Begin by making a list of ways of perceiving the self, such as responsible, lazy, kind, generous, cruel, and the like. Then sort these statements into several piles, running from least to most like the way you perceive yourself. Follow this by again sorting the same topics into piles indicating how you would most like to be seen. In this manner, you may obtain a somewhat objective measure of the discrepancy between your self and your self-ideal. To support your findings, you might ask a friend or relative to sort the same statements, ranging from most to least characteristic of you. You can thus detect any discrepancy between your self-perception and the image which you project to others.

SELF-ACCEPTANCE, NOT SELF-EVALUATION

Just as Rogers stresses the value of accepting rather than evaluating others, so he insists that an acceptant attitude toward oneself is favorable to healthy personality growth and functioning. The popular view is that if one is to make steady improvements, one should be continually dissatisfied with himself. An implication of this view is that self-acceptance engenders complacency and stagnation. But Rogers believes that self-acceptance is a condition for bringing about change in personality. The self-accepting person need not fear what he discovers about himself. He can be open to his inner experiences without being overwhelmed by them. Accepting what he is essentially, he can face up to the things he dislikes about himself. Not to be underestimated is the subjective feeling of tranquility and inner harmony, which is in sharp contrast to the turmoil, anxious striving, and agitation characteristic of the person who strives furiously to be something greater than what he is. A further advantage of a basically self-accepting attitude is that it actually promotes acceptance of the individual by others.

SUMMARY

1.   A high regard for individuality underlies client-centered therapy. The individual must be treated with respect and acceptance as a human being who has difficulties and problems that impede his fulfillment as a person. The major focus in client-centered therapy is upon the self-concept. The self is the core of personality and determines behavior. In successful therapy, clients report an exuberant, positive self-feeling, a genuine liking for the self. When the realization of genuine feelings and emotions occurs, personality growth is facilitated. A key factor in the discovery of the real self is awareness of sensory and visceral experiences.

2.   According to Rogers, one of the most basic principles of human nature is that man s motivations and tendencies are positive. The core of man's nature is rational, forward-looking, sensitively social, and "good." Negative emotions result from the frustration of basic desires and tendencies. An incongruent or distorted self-structure emerges when the self is incomplete or out of touch with the rest of the personality.

3.   Introjection is the taking over of the values, beliefs, or behaviors of another and accepting them as if they were truly one's own. Thus the existing self is not the real self; one does not recognize and deal with true feelings.

4.   Conditions of worth are those prescriptions and qualifications which are imposed upon the growing child so that he may be accepted and valued by those who have authority over his life. Parents are the first and main source of conditions of worth, which take the form of dos and don'ts.

5.   Every child has a strong need for positive regard, that is, for acceptance, respect, and love. Giving and withholding positive regard can have profound effects on a child's behavior.

6.   If major aspects of personality are in conflict as a result of opposed role expectations which are either self-imposed or imposed from without, a firm sense of identity will not be established. The basic problem of the growing individual is to discover and express his real self within the roles which are imposed upon him. Yet, according to Rogers, the core self is not purely selfish and egocentric. In its purest form, the self is profoundly social as well as individual. The process of knowing and being the self is never complete.

7.   A client may best explore his deepest feelings without fear in an atmosphere which is permissive, warm, and accepting. Such an atmosphere is best for discovery and acceptance of the real self. The fully functioning person avoids putting on a facade which does not fit the real self. He moves away from parental and cultural expectations and takes responsibility for the main direction of his life. One functions most fully when he is fulfilling himself in his own way.

8.   The person who is willing to engage in process living accepts inner and outer experiences as they are, without imposing requirements and standards.

He flows with his experiences. All needs are clearly perceived and there is a balanced attempt to meet them. Sensory and organismic information is freely registered. An essential feature of this process is inner freedom, continuing flexibility to select the direction of living.

9.　The fully functioning person is open to experience. He is not defensive. All organic experiences and sensory inputs are freely relayed through the nervous system. All emotions are given free passage into the self-structure. This person listens to himself.

10.　If one trusts one's organism, one can act upon momentary impulses without fear of behaving as one feels. One will act spontaneously, creatively, freshly, and freely. Being open to all one's experiences fosters the emergence of decisions having a seemingly spontaneous quality, but which have organismic determinants.

11.　The fully functioning person possesses a feeling that he is free, a sense of self-determination, a choice in direction of growth.

SUGGESTED READINGS

Rogers, Carl R. Counseling and Psychotherapy. Boston: Houghton Mifflin, 1942.
>In this book, Rogers introduces his nondirective therapy, contrasting this with other approaches to therapy. Ultimately his concern for the client led him to change the name to client-centered therapy.

Client-Centered Therapy. Boston: Houghton Mifflin, 1951.
>Here Rogers deals with the nature of the therapeutic process and with related counseling problems. Procedures by which clients may be assisted in achieving new and more effective personality adjustments are discussed.

On Becoming a Person. Boston: Houghton Mifflin, 1961.
>Rogers has gathered many of his manuscripts into this book, which represents his major areas of interest. The book is organized to portray a developing theme from the highly personal to topics of larger social significance.

Freedom to Learn. Columbus, Ohio: Charles E. Merrill, 1969. `
>Rogers explores ways to make the classroom learning experience more meaningful to the student. Emphasis is placed upon the educator's role in creating the appropriate atmosphere for learning. Such an atmosphere has its roots in the client-centered approach to therapy.

REFERENCES

Allport, G. W. Pattern and Growth in Personality. New York: Holt, Rinehart and Winston, 1961.
Bloomberg, M. Creativity as related to field independence and mobility. J. Genet. Psychol. 118:3–12, 1971.
Coopersmith, S. The Antecedents of Self-Esteem. San Francisco: W. H. Freeman, 1967.
Freud, S. The Future of an Illusion (1927). In Standard Edition of the Complete Psychological Works, Vol. 21. London: Hogarth Press, 1963. Pp. 3–56.
Gergen, K. J. The Concept of Self. New York: Holt, Rinehart and Winston, 1971.
Ginott, H. G. Between Parent and Child. New York: The Macmillan Company, 1965.
Goffman, E. The Presentation of Self in Everyday Life. New York: Doubleday and Company, 1959.

Jourard, S. M. Personal Adjustment: An Approach to the Study of Personality, 2nd ed. New York: The Macmillan Company, 1963.

Laing, R. D. The Politics of Experience. New York: Pantheon Books, 1967.

Lindner, R. Prescription for Rebellion. New York: Grove Press, 1952.

Maslow, A. H. Motivation and Personality, 2nd ed. New York: Harper and Row, 1970.

Moustakas, C. E. Loneliness and Love. Englewood Cliffs, New Jersey: Prentice-Hall, 1972.

Mowrer, O. H. Critique of Patterson's client-centered counseling article. Counsel. Psychol. *16*: 48–56, 1969.

Rogers, C. R. Counseling and Psychotherapy. Boston: Houghton Mifflin, 1942.

Rogers, C. R. Client-Centered Therapy. Boston: Houghton Mifflin, 1951.

Rogers, C. R. A theory of therapy, personality, and interpersonal relationships as developed in the client-centered framework. *In* Koch, S., ed., Psychology: A Study of Science, Vol. 3. New York: McGraw-Hill, 1959.

Rogers, C. R. On Becoming a Person. Boston: Houghton Mifflin, 1961.

Rogers, C. R. Actualizing tendency in relation to "motives" and to consciousness. *In* Jones, M. R., ed., Nebraska Symposium on Motivation. Lincoln: University of Nebraska Press, 1963.

Rogers, C. R. Client-centered therapy. *In* Arieti, S., ed., American Handbook of Psychiatry. New York: Basic Books, 1966. Pp. 183–200.

Rogers, C. R. Freedom to Learn. Columbus, Ohio: Charles E. Merrill, 1969.

Rogers, C. R. Carl Rogers on Encounter Groups. New York: Harper and Row, 1970.

Rogers, C. R. Toward a modern approach to values: The valuing process in the mature person. *In* Bloomberg, M., ed., Creativity: Theory and Research. New Haven: College and University Press, 1972. Pp. 115–28.

Rogers, C. R., and Dymond, R. F. Psychotherapy and Personality Change. Chicago: University of Chicago Press, 1954.

Rotter, J. B. External control and internal control. Psychol. Today *5*:37–42, 58–9, June, 1971.

Schiffman, M. Gestalt Self-Therapy. Menlo Park, California: Self Therapy Press, 1971.

Skinner, B. F. Science and Human Behavior. New York: The Macmillan Company, 1953.

White, R. W. Motivation reconsidered: The concept of competence. Psychol. Rev. *66*:297–330, 1959.

CHAPTER 14

Self-Actualization

Abraham Maslow

Abraham Maslow (1908–1970)

ARE COLLEGE STUDENTS SELF-ACTUALIZING?

When Abraham Maslow, then a Professor of Psychology at Brandeis University, set out to find the most highly developed, fully evolved, fully human beings, he began by studying college students. After establishing certain criteria of what might be a self-actualizing person, he and his collaborators studied about 3000 students. To their amazement, they found that only two or three approached their requirements for self-actualization. A couple of dozen subjects could be described as promising candidates, but for a number of reasons they fell distinctly short of the criteria. There is the possibility that Maslow's standards for self-actualization were unrealistic, but significantly he did find that about one per cent of the population of men and women of middle and old age either fitted his requirements or approximated them.

Why should so few of the college students meet the requirements of self-actualization? As proposed by Maslow, self-actualization has many preconditions: many personal successes and a favorable cultural environment are involved. Self-actualization means something like fully developed, fully human, fully functioning, fulfilling one's genetic potential, growing to the fullest (Maslow, 1970). To grow and function on this optimum level requires experiences that cannot occur early in life and achievements that frequently do not come until middle age. Thus after finding that self-actualizing people are generally in their middle or older years, Maslow finally concluded that there is a distinction between *self-actualization* and *healthy growth*. In a sense, self-actualization is the end product of healthy growth. "Full" growth has not yet been defined adequately, but it is probably not attained until some time in the thirties or possibly even later, if we limit our concern to personality development. For instance, certain mental abilities, as measured by standardized psychological tests, attain a peak in the thirties (Wechsler, 1955).

392

What should be considered "healthy" growth engenders as much disagreement as the definition of "full" growth. A variety of factors, such as intellectual, emotional, and social competencies, play a part. There is much more agreement about "average" growth than about "healthy" growth (Miller, 1970). One indicator of unhealthy growth is immaturity: a ten year old who behaves like an eight year old has an unhealthy personality. At best, a ten year old cannot be a fully functioning and fully developed human being. Maturation does not run its full course by the age of ten. The ten year old also lacks the vast array of experiences which, when they occur, will profoundly alter his personality. His psychological world is dominated largely by fantasies, unrealistic perceptions, distorted cognitions, and magical ideals. He has many bouts with harsh reality ahead of him in the process of becoming a grownup. What we have said about the ten year old applies analogously to many college students; they have neither reached fullness of psychobiological development nor enjoyed certain experiences which are requisites for self-actualization (Maslow, 1970). By attending college they have postponed such basic experiences as marriage, daily routine of work, parenthood, and autonomous living. Both the normal ten year old and the college student may be growing in a healthy manner, however.

Take the average college sophomore: he may vigorously assert that he has "seen a lot" and insist upon recognition of his worldliness and sophistication, but the fact remains that his experiences have been quite restricted. He may have difficulty relating to people who are different from himself: someone of another race or creed, a little child, someone much older or younger than he, one who is uneducated, and even anyone who did not go to college. In short, he relates comfortably only to people whose experiences are similar to his own. He may have difficulty communicating with an old friend who did not go to college because their interests no longer coincide. The difference between the two friends is quite instructive because we can learn something about the conditions which must be met in order to grow up. Whereas the student is probably concerned about making a Saturday evening date, finishing his term paper in time to take a few days of vacation, or getting in shape to make the team, his friend may have a wife and child at home to worry about, a job where competition is tough, and a Saturday evening date with the insurance representative. Their lives are worlds apart in a sense; no wonder that the friend who did not go to college may be more sober, a bit quieter, and seemingly more stable than his friend who chose to be a student.

These observations about the immaturity of the college student are not intended to be derogatory. The college student may seem less mature than someone his own age who did not go to college not because he lacks the capacity for maturity nor because he is not growing properly, but simply because he lacks certain experiences. He has deliberately postponed the opportunity of having these experiences at some sacrifice to his attainment of maturity so that he may ready himself for a richer life and thus ultimately for a greater degree of self-actualization. People from primitive societies grow up at an earlier age, at least psychologically, than do people from specialized technological societies, in which preparation for adult status makes greater demands upon the young (Erikson, 1968).

What are some of the experiences which a college student ordinarily does not have that can alter a life style? Marriage is one; it implies a deep personal commitment to an intimate relationship which is unlike any other. It would be unwise to argue that marriage is always a necessary requisite for self-actualization, but it would seem to be for those who have a need for the type of relationship that it involves. Certain qualities are brought to the fore in a family setting: one must think of others who are now his responsibility; decisions can no longer be based on selfish considerations alone. A person cannot be selfish in the strict sense of the word and be a good marital partner and parent.

The college student has many ideals which need to be tempered a bit before he can hope to live effectively and productively. Most people have glamorous ideas about work, and only experience in working for several years can provide a proper perspective. One learns what he should and should not expect from his vocation. He gradually gives this aspect of his life its proper place. Work certainly can assist the self-actualization process; it is one of the most important aspects of living, but unrealistic expectations about it can also be one of the major disturbances of life. In any case, the college student has a great deal to learn about this aspect.

A student has needs and goals which cannot be met satisfactorily while he is still in college. As he moves into a better position to meet these needs and attain these goals, he will begin to look at life differently. As basic needs are gratified, other needs will take their place. According to Maslow's need hierarchy theory, the process of self-actualization can occur only when the basic lower needs (physiological, safety, love and belonging, and esteem needs) are met, and many of these are frustrated in a young person. For instance, he is forced into a dependent role; he must postpone some of his deepest desires, and postponement means frustration. Then there is the lack of knowledge about many things. He does not yet know clearly what to expect from himself, from his parents, from work, from recreation. His life may be filled with confusion and conflict. He is lacking in certain basic learning experiences; as he expands his outreach and takes over his own life, he will learn to know more about himself, to know about the harsher side of living, to take responsibility for his own actions. All this takes place after college days. Settling on a vocation, getting married, the birth of the first child are experiences that lie ahead of him. These and many others will have profound effects on his total orientation to life.

We will consider Maslow's ideas on self-actualization from a variety of angles. First we will discuss some of the methods he used to study the topic. Then we will take up the traits that he found characteristic of his healthy subjects. We will round out the picture by discussing motivation and metamotivation, metapathology, and peak experiences. Some of the ideas will be foreign to you and may contradict some of your expectations and beliefs, but bear in mind that Maslow was studying the highest levels of humanness, the superstars in the art of living. He himself was surprised by a number of his findings, and he concluded that the total life orientation of self-actualizers is of an order different from that of the average person. His study of the healthiest people also led him to the conclusion that many changes should be made in our most cherished institutions—education, economics, child-rearing, work patterns, pay incentives—so that they may promote rather than hinder personality growth and functioning. Even morality and ethics—what constitutes good and bad conduct—should be based on the nature of man. A knowledge of man's highest potentialities can help us to arrive at the true definition of the nature of man as a species. We can learn from the healthiest man what may be possible for all of us, given the optimum conditions of growth.

CHARACTERISTIC TRAITS OF SELF-ACTUALIZING PEOPLE

Maslow attempted to identify healthy human growth and functioning by studying people he knew personally, contemporary public figures, and historical personalities. Starting with a "folk" definition of self-actualization, he selected his subjects from a large sample. He then re-examined his definition in the light of his clinical studies and changed it accordingly. He made further clinical tests and observations and again modified his definition. The definition had both a positive and a negative aspect: on the negative side he eliminated subjects who showed evidence of neurosis, psychosis, and psychopathic disturbance; on the positive side he looked for signs of health and self-actualization, which was at first intuitively defined, since this is what he set out to identify: "It may be loosely described as the full use and exploitation of talents, capacities, potentialities, etc. Such people seem to be fulfilling themselves and to be doing the best that they are capable of doing, reminding us of Nietzsche's exhortation 'Become what thou art.' They are people who have developed, or are developing to the full stature of which they are capable" (1970, p. 150). Because of his subjects' resistance, he had to study them indirectly, even surreptitiously. He included such well-known public and historical figures as Albert Einstein, Franklin Roosevelt, Albert Schweitzer, and William James.

The reader should bear in mind that Maslow derived his descriptions of self-actualizers from interview impressions, biographies, autobiographies, and casual observations of behavior; they were not based on standardized tests or obtained from experimental situations. Thus they should be considered only as global impressions and first approximations to the subject. Maslow himself regarded his work as a pioneer investigation which might point out certain major directions and possible pitfalls for further study. Before attempting to obtain a more concrete and concise picture of the highest human functioning, we will study the traits that he found characteristic of self-actualizers.

1. MORE EFFICIENT PERCEPTION OF REALITY AND MORE COMFORTABLE RELATIONSHIP WITH IT

Self-actualizing people seem to have a knack for judging things correctly. They can detect fraud and sham more readily than others. Concealed and confused realities are apprehended more quickly. They demonstrate a superior ability to predict events, not as a result of intuition or extrasensory powers, but because they are able to judge situations perceptively and draw implications on the basis of facts. They are not prejudicial toward data from traits of optimism or pessimism; thus they are neutral observers. Maslow (1968c) elaborated this objective type of perception and cognition in his concept of B (Being)-cognition, which may be described as a selfless or desireless cognition. A thing, situation, or person is perceived as it is (in its being) without distorting preconceptions or wishes. Consider the case of two people conversing: the paranoid individual sees this fact as anyone else does but adds the element "they are talking about me." Most of us are prone to this tendency of putting our personal attributes into our perceptions.

Maslow found that in his healthy subjects the attitude of acceptance applied to the unknown as well as to the known: they accepted many realities for what they were and did not try to change them to suit their needs; in addition they did not feel threatened or frightened by what they did not know. In fact, they were often more attracted by it than by the known (Barron, 1968); curiosity seems more active with unknowns. Facing unknowns is for some people an extremely difficult thing, and even certain psychological disturbances, such as extreme cautiousness, compulsive ordering of things, and inordinate saving, serve the purpose of avoiding the threat of unknowns. These may develop into a catastrophic need for certainty, safety, definitiveness, or order, whereas by contrast, healthy people can tolerate uncertainty and ambiguity. Maslow put it very colorfully: "They can be, when the total objective situation calls for it, comfortably disorderly, sloppy, anarchic, chaotic, vague, doubtful, uncertain, indefinite, approximate, inexact, or inaccurate (all, in certain moments in science, art, or in life in general, quite desirable). Thus it comes about that doubt, tentativeness, uncertainty, with the consequent necessity of abeyance of decision, which is for most a torture, can be for some a pleasantly stimulating challenge, a high spot in life rather than a low" (1970, p. 155).

2. ACCEPTANCE: SELF, OTHERS, NATURE

Healthy people may be described as accepting the essence of things and people, including themselves (Maslow, 1970). For instance, a child is taken as a being in his own right and not as an inferior adult. Some people cannot understand, tolerate, or relate to children, or for that matter to anyone who is quite different from themselves. Healthy people can take things and people as they are.

The most basic form of acceptance is satisfaction with oneself. Self-actualizing people lack the shame, guilt, and doubt which are so prevalent in the general population. Falling short of ideals and perceiving their differences from and even inferiorities to others, they are nevertheless self-accepting. The self-actualizing person does not want to be someone else, although being quite realistic he does perceive his own shortcomings and is usually working to improve them.

Self-actualizing people do not put on poses. Many people, for instance, find growing older a terribly difficult and forbidding specter. Some men dislike being masculine, and many women have difficulty with menstruation or find the thought of pregnancy quite unacceptable. Healthy people are in tune with their own natures. They react to discrepancies between what is and what ought to be, but not to natural processes within themselves and others.

3. SPONTANEITY, SIMPLICITY, NATURALNESS

Healthy people may be described as spontaneous, simple, and natural (Maslow, 1970). They are not victims of cultural practices and beliefs. They tend to work out their own sets of values, and these truly influence their conduct. Yet paradoxically, they are not unconventional; indeed, they conform at least on a superficial level so as not to cause displeasure to others. Their inner lives are highly individualistic. They might be characterized as acultural or supercultural. Healthy people from different cultures are much more alike than are the average persons of those cultures (Maslow, 1968a). Such people are not afraid to be themselves because they trust their feelings and actions in relation to others. Not being themselves is highly distasteful to them; thus they express themselves freely, easily, and with an air of confidence, but not with superiority or snobbishness.

To describe the healthiest people as spontaneous, simple, and natural implies that their motivations are of a different order from those of the average person, who is typically guarded, fearful, and hesitant, and play-acts much of the time.

4. PROBLEM CENTERING

Maslow (1970) found that his healthy subjects usually have a sense of mission which is carried out in their work. They focus on problems outside of themselves. Furthermore, they are capable of approaching their own lives with a problem solving orientation: they can unemotionally make decisions which entail temporary hurt and frustration but which in the long run fulfill their goals. They have the ability to lose themselves in their work. They identify with it, and when working, they are expressing their most "selfish" motives.

5. THE QUALITY OF DETACHMENT, THE NEED FOR PRIVACY

Healthy people need and cherish privacy and solitude (Maslow, 1970). They do not have a clinging relationship with others and can therefore enjoy the richness and fullness of others' friendship. Having strong convictions about things, they can remain above the storm and are not easily swayed by a flurry of rhetoric and sophistry. The determining factors in their conduct are within rather than external to themselves; thus they are not "situationally determined." This is in sharp contrast to the attitude of self-dissatisfaction and distrust which is so common. Many people cannot be alone for very long because they do not like what they learn about themselves (May, 1953).

6. AUTONOMY

Healthy people are self-sufficient or self-contained. They can take environmental stresses because they are relatively independent of the conditions of their environment. Loss of a loved one, for instance, does not produce a catastrophic reaction.

Using his distinction between deficiency-motivated and growth-motivated people, Maslow contrasted them as follows:

Deficiency-motivated people *must* have other people available, since most of their need gratifications (love, safety, respect, prestige, belongingness) can come only from other human beings. But growth-motivated people may actually be *hampered* by others. The determinants of satisfaction and of the good life are for them now inner-individual and *not* social. They have become strong enough to be independent of the good opinion of other people, or even of their affection. The honors, the status, the rewards, the popularity, the prestige, and the love they can bestow must have become less important than self-development and inner growth. We must remember that the best technique we know, even though not the only one, for getting to this point of relative independence from love and respect, is to have been given plenty of this very same love and respect in the past (1970, p. 162).

7. CONTINUED FRESHNESS OF APPRECIATION

Maslow s subjects have the rare quality of being able to appreciate again and again the basic goods of life. The same event which to others may become commonplace and stale is for them recurrently full of beauty, inspiration, and wonderment (Schachtel, 1959). The hundredth sunset is as lovely as the first; a hike through the woods never ceases to be a joyful experience; watching a child at play uplifts the spirit. Unlike the average person, the self-actualizer does not take the mysteries of life for granted. He is continually dazzled by them.

Just as self-actualizers differ sharply from the average in their capacity to appreciate beauty external to themselves, so are they also distinguished by their continual affirmation and appreciation of what they have, by their ability to count their blessings. While they constantly strive for new things, for betterment, for change, they are not blinded into taking for granted what they already possess or have accomplished. Maslow found that many people tend to lose appreciation for and even devalue what they have in their striving for something different; thus they are in a state of dissatisfaction most of the time. Following the practice of healthy people could vastly improve the lives of everyone, Maslow believed. Value and appreciate what you have as you reach out for other things (Maslow, 1970).

8. THE MYSTIC EXPERIENCE, THE PEAK EXPERIENCE

Maslow found that his subjects could be described as religious but not in a denominational or formal sense. They have strong convictions and peak experiences like the mystics, but they are disenchanted by the ceremonial practices of the common religions. Maslow described the mystic experience in the following manner (for our purposes, peak experience may be taken as the same as mystic experience): "Apparently the acute mystic or peak experience is a tremendous intensification of *any* of the experiences in which there is loss of self or transcendence of it, e.g., problem centering, intense concentration, muga behavior, as described by Benedict, intense sensuous experience, self-forgetful and intense enjoyment of music or art" (1970, p. 165).

9. GEMEINSCHAFTSGEFUHL

Maslow (1970) borrowed the term "gemeinschaftsgefuhl" from Adler; it can be roughly translated as "older brotherly." Healthy subjects seem to identify with humans in general; being extremely human themselves, they have affection, understanding, and sympathy for others who may not be quite as highly developed as they are. They have an older brother attitude toward others. It should be kept in mind that often the healthy person feels alienated (and is treated as such by others) not because he has failed to establish a sense of identity but because he is so unlike those with whom he must live. Yet while he may long for other self-actualizers like himself, he is still able to feel sympathy and concern for all mankind.

10. INTERPERSONAL RELATIONS

Self-actualizers are capable of strongly binding relationships. They limit their friendships to a few that are highly cherished, rather than seek a wide circle of acquaintances (Maslow, 1970). Since healthy people have a warm feeling of brotherliness for all men, as if they valued humanness as a remarkable product of nature, they tend to attract admirers. This often produces a one-sided situation because they may be forced into a relationship they do not necessarily want. They cannot be unkind to the admirer.

11. DEMOCRATIC CHARACTER STRUCTURE

To Maslow (1970), the term "democratic" implies tolerance and acceptance of religious, racial, age, marital, occupational, and class differences. One of the outstanding qualities of self-actualizers is that they can relate to people in general, despite wide differences in education, age, or life style. Healthy people can learn from others; if an individual has something to teach them, Maslow's subjects will not attempt to assert their own superiorities no matter what their station in life. They can appreciate the knowledge and skills of others, even when these skills are superior to their own. This attitude might be described as a healthy humility; the superiority of the other person is appreciated, not perceived as a threat.

12. DISCRIMINATION BETWEEN MEANS AND ENDS, BETWEEN GOOD AND EVIL

Maslow's healthy subjects have a clear notion of the difference between ends and means. Means can be easily interchanged while ends tend to be permanent. These people do not operate with rigid sets and prejudged methods. Means can also be appreciated and valued, so that working toward a goal may provide as much pleasure and satisfaction as attaining it. Surprisingly, like children, they can derive pleasure from even the most routine and apparently unchallenging tasks.

Maslow also found that his subjects are quite certain of their convictions. Unlike the average person, they do not show confusion, chaos, and conflicting beliefs. They can definitely be described as ethical, according to commonly accepted standards of conduct. Maslow characterized their religious beliefs as follows:

A few say that they believe in a God, but describe this God more as a metaphysical concept than as a personal figure. If religion is defined only in social-behavioral terms, then these are all religious people, the atheists included. But if more conservatively we use the term *religion* to stress the supernatural element and institutional orthodoxy (certainly the more common usage) then our answer must be quite different, for then very few of them are religious (1970, p. 169).

One might describe the religion of self-actualizers as humanistic rather than theistic—a profound respect for human nature. They are men of principles.

13. PHILOSOPHICAL, UNHOSTILE SENSE OF HUMOR

Maslow (1970) found the humor of his subjects quite different from that of the average person. He described it as philosophical, because it is concerned with human situations such as discrepancies between what is and what should be, personal shortcomings, and peculiarities of things. For example, a self-actualizing person might laugh at his arrogant attitude when he rereads a paper he wrote years before. The typical humor centers about the release of hostility, downplaying authority, and the forbidden impulses. The humor of healthy subjects often takes an education or teaching role, but in the form of parables or fables.

14. CREATIVENESS

Maslow found in all his healthy subjects a quality which he termed "creativeness." He did not mean the remarkable accomplishments of a highly talented person, but rather inventiveness, originality, spontaneity, and freshness of approach. The drive and ability of a genius may be an isolated aspect of his personality, having little to do with healthy living:

Such talent we have no concern with here since it does not rest upon psychic health or basic satisfaction. The creativeness of the self-actualized man seems rather to be kin to the naive and universal creativeness of unspoiled children. It seems to be more a fundamental characteristic of common human nature—a potentiality given to all human beings at birth. Most human beings lose this as they become enculturated, but some very few individuals seem either to retain this fresh and naive, direct way of looking at life, or if they have lost it, as most people do, they later in life recover it (1970, p. 171).

Maslow described creativeness in terms of attitude or spirit. Being less inhibited, less bound, less restricted or enculturated, self-actualizers can be more spontaneous, more natural, more human. These vague terms are used to convey a quality which is extremely difficult to describe. We might think, for example, of the excitement of a pet dog when it sees its master coming home, the enthusiasm of children as they discover a new way of playing a game, the gleeful love play of a couple in love.

15. RESISTANCE TO ENCULTURATION, THE TRANSCENDENCE OF ANY PARTICULAR CULTURE

Are self-actualizing people well-adjusted; are they likable, easy to understand? Do they fit the image of the "hail fellow well met," the hearty extrovert whom everyone loves? The answer to all these questions is "No!" It seems that the healthiest humans are strong-willed, self-sufficient, independent of cultural norms. The stereotype of the socialized American does not fit them at all. In fact, they are considered strange, eccentric, and even antisocial by those who are incapable of appreciating them or who do not know them. There is an air of self-sufficiency about them which is offensive to some people.

Self-actualizers may be further described as (a) conventional in superficial ways but strongly self-determined when the culture violates a strongly held value; (b) nonrebels in relation to their culture but able to work diligently at bringing about change in nondramatic ways (most of them have an all-consuming mission in life); (c) selectively detached from the culture: liking and eagerly embracing certain aspects of the culture but giving up or totally ignoring others without guilt feelings; (d) autonomous because they are ruled by their own characters rather than by the rules of society. Maslow (1970) believed that self-actualizers are less "flattened out," less molded, less dominated by the culture than average people. Every culture necessarily produces certain forms of pathology. Some individuals are fortunate enough to resist the harmful effects of their culture, and this seems to be the case with self-actualizers.

16. PERSONALITY INTEGRITY

Healthy people do not experience personality fragmentation, dissociations, splits within the personality, isolated elements functioning as separate "personalities," and the like. They do not have oppositions and conflicts within them—conflicts between basic urges and conscience, between self-seeking and ideals, between childlike impulses and adult behavior. Here is the way Maslow described the failure in personality integration:

> The normal adjustment of the average, common sense, well-adjusted man implies a continued successful rejection of much of the depths of human nature, both conative and cognitive. To adjust well to the world of reality means a splitting of the person. It means that the person turns his back on much in himself because it is dangerous. But it is now clear that by so doing, he loses a great deal too, for these depths are also the source of all his joys, his ability to play, to love, to laugh, and most important for us, to be creative. By protecting himself against the hell within himself, he also cuts himself off from the heaven within, flat, tight, frozen, controlled, cautious, who can't laugh or play or love, or be silly or trusting or childish. His imagination, his intuition, his softness, his emotionality tend to be strangulated or distorted (1968c, p. 142).

17. TRANSCENDENCE OF DICHOTOMIES

Probably the one most outstanding quality of self-actualizing people is their transcendence or overcoming of dichotomies (Maslow, 1968b). In this context the term "dichotomy" indicates split or "oppositeness," the extremes of a dimension, such as work and play, being adult and being childlike, masculinity and femininity, being selfish and altruistic, self-seeking and generous, rational and emotional. The "transcendence of dichotomy" means that opposite qualities are integrated and expressed by the same behavior (not either/or, but both); for instance, a masculine man may be capable of the "feminine qualities" of compassion, empathy, and sympathy. Most people are at either one end or the other of the above dimensions; they distinguish between what is work and what is recreation, between acting childishly and acting adultlike, between being rational and being irrational. The alternatives appear worlds apart. Precisely to the degree that oppositions and conflicting elements exist within the personality do we, according to Maslow, suspect and in fact find pathology. Integrated functioning is a sign of health. Consider the carpenter who enjoys working with wood: he does good work as a matter of pride; he is acting selfishly to the limit because he loves his work, but his work also provides pleasure and joy for others. By being as good a carpenter as he can, he is benefiting both himself and others, thus transcending the dichotomy between selfishness and altruism. For him, the difference between working and playing is not sharp because his work provides him a form of recreation. He thus also transcends the dichotomy between work and play.

Many traditional views of the good life have sharply separated the so-called "animalistic" or lower nature of man from his higher nature. Interestingly, Maslow in effect did the same thing with his need hierarchy, but by complementation rather than opposition. He did not oppose "spirit" with "flesh," the higher with the lower. This is an important point in his theory of motivation: the higher needs build on, complement, and in fact transform the lower needs. One has to be gratified in his deficit needs to begin to function on the B-level of motivation. The spirit builds upon, is intrinsically dependent upon, the flesh. Indeed, to Maslow the interaction is mutual in that when a person is functioning on the higher levels of need gratification, he also functions better at the lower levels. A self-actualizing person actually enjoys his lower-need pleasures more than the one who is exclusively preoccupied with them. He does not have to overgratify these needs to find pleasure. He eats normally but enjoys food more than the glutton; he relaxes normally but enjoys the rest more than the slothful person. Again we have an instance of the transcendence of a dichotomy—between higher and lower needs.

Another way of seeing the resolution of dichotomies is by considering the structural aspects of personality. There are a variety of schemes we might consider, but Freud's system will suffice. You will recall that Freud viewed personality as made up of warring factions: id, ego, and superego; the conscious, preconscious, and unconscious; the primary and secondary processes. He considered it more effective to live on a secondary level of cognition than on a primary one; that is, seeing the world realistically and dealing with needs through rationality is more promising than fantasy, wish fulfillment, and impulse action.

In contrast to Freud, Maslow held that primitive primary processes can give breadth to living and engender creativity, spontaneity, and free expression (Wild, 1965). He believed that suppression or denial of the so-called primitive forces diminishes the personality. Part of the personality is killed off if the superego is dominant, if the ego holds complete control, or if the id is untempered. The normal person who behaves rationally, and at the same time spontaneously and creatively, is living more effectively than the person suffering from a one-sided development. Conscience, impulse, and reasoning each play a part in promoting health. The balanced person allows all aspects of personality to be expressed, as Jung held. Maslow agreed with Jung (1964), although he arrived at the same conclusion from a different perspective.

A striking example of the transcending of dichotomies (harmonizing what appear to be opposing attitudes toward life) is the philosophical principle espoused by the Shakers. The Shakers were an austere religious sect whose adherents took a vow of celibacy. They were a communal group whose Christian beliefs were organized around two principles which seem to contradict each other: "Live this day as if it were your last, and live this day as if you were going to live a thousand years." The first part of the proposition advises us to live as fully as possible each day because we do not know how long our lives will be. Living for the day has many implications, such as being concerned with immediate ends rather than overpreoccupied with means, not worrying excessively about the unknown future, not being overly ambitious, so that failure to accomplish objectives is not a tragedy, and many others. But the second part tells us to view our lives from the opposite frame of reference: to expect a long life. We are advised to plan, to look optimistically to a better tomorrow, to have hopes and dreams, not to be caught up in momentary setbacks and tensions. Actually, these are not really opposite guides to living; they both imply living as fully as possible. One may have many long-term goals and objectives but at the same time live fully in the present. Working toward goals can be need-gratifying. Having plans and goals makes the present more invigorating. We could continue with these apparent paradoxes, but the point is that what appear to be opposite and irreconcilable approaches to living can, in practice and given the appropriate level of maturity, be integrated within the style of life. The mature person accomplishes both objectives at the same time by the same behavior.

SOME BASIC QUESTIONS ABOUT SELF-ACTUALIZERS

We have been considering the attributes of self-actualizers which Maslow abstracted from his observations of those he regarded as the healthiest human beings. The reader may be having some difficulty forming a conceptual picture of self-actualizing persons as Maslow described them. We will now turn to some notions that may be of assistance: *metamotivation*, B-*values*, *metapathologies*, *peak experiences*, and *growth motivation*—all of which are related in some way to the topic of self-actualization. But before we proceed, there are some questions to answer: for instance, what are the imperfections, if any, of self-actualizers? Does every self-actualizing person have all the traits which Maslow detailed? How do we know that Maslow was not constructing a person who does not exist?

Maslow himself admitted that his findings fall far short of empirically derived principles. They are to be taken as tentative, as hypotheses to be tested. He pointed out in a recent article that the pioneer does not have the foundation of solid knowledge to conduct rigorous experimentation; he is ahead of the known; he is reaching out beyond the frontier of knowledge (Maslow, 1969). At the present level of knowledge about self-actualizing people, it is impossible to determine how much is Maslow's own projections and constructions, and how much represents "real" people. The answer probably lies somewhere between these extremes. One point in Maslow's favor is that his formulations do agree in part with those of others: with Allport's concept of maturity, with Jung's ideas on individuation, with Rogers's on the fully functioning person, and with those of theorists who have taken up the study of ideal human existence. At the present time, Maslow's hypotheses appear more thorough than the others, but ultimately the traits he has proposed must be subjected to empirical test — although the task is a formidable one — and then we will know how accurate he was.

With respect to the question of individual differences in traits, Maslow attempted to identify traits that were common to all his healthy subjects, and also to identify traits found in some, but not all, of his subjects. By doing so, he recognized the uniqueness and variability of the people he studied, but he did not deal adequately with the topic. Furthermore, he held that in many ways the traits are not irreducible, that they presuppose one another. For example, one cannot have the attribute of freshness of appreciation without creativeness. Individuality still remains a problem because the traits Maslow abstracted are general attributes and therefore approximations to individuality (Allport, 1961).

Maslow admitted the imperfections of his healthy subjects: they fell far short of the ideal humans being portrayed by novelists and biographers. They definitely had "chinks in their armor" and "feet of clay":

Our subjects show many of the lesser human failings. They too are equipped with silly, wasteful, or thoughtless habits. They can be boring, stubborn, irritating. They are by no means free from a rather superficial vanity, pride, partiality to their own productions, family, friends, and children. Temper outbursts are not rare. Our subjects are occasionally capable of an extraordinary and unexpected ruthlessness. It must be remembered that they are very strong people. This makes it possible for them to display a surgical coldness when this is called for, beyond the power of the average man (1970, p. 175).

Maslow's healthy subjects may appear heartless in their conduct. For example, a man might show few outward signs of emotion at the loss of a loved one; a young man might leave home when he makes up his mind to do so, without any of the usual doubts, fears, and conflicts, giving the impression that he has no feeling for his family; a woman might divorce her husband when she decides that this is the "only logical thing to do for their sick marriage," and do so without apparent "storm and stress."

Subjectively, the healthy subjects do experience guilt, anxiety, sadness, self-criticism, internal strife, and conflict, but these psychic states are caused by non-neurotic conditions. We might list such things as discrepancies between what is and what should be, injustices, inequalities, lack of certain perfection in the self, struggling to work out a philosophy of life. It should be kept in mind that even healthy subjects are brought up in and live in a far from perfect environment; thus some of their imperfections are undoubtedly the consequence of environmental conditions. As Horney (1937) pointed out, the culture may be "sick."

MOTIVATION VERSUS METAMOTIVATION

In dealing with the most highly evolved and fully functioning human beings, Maslow found it necessary to revise some long-standing notions about the true driving forces behind behavior. He came up with a distinction between motivation and metamotivation. He also made distinctions between *needs* and *metaneeds*, and between D-*values* (Deficit-values) and B-*values* (Being-values). To understand these distinctions, one should keep in mind that a need gives rise to a motive that is consciously experienced as a want or desire. The object of the desire is the value or incentive. Unfortunately, these words are sometimes used interchangeably. Generally, Maslow (1971) meant by motivation deficit states, and by metamotivation tendencies to seek certain growth ends, such as truth, goodness, beauty, and order. Metamotives do not involve reduction of tension; rather, they may increase tension when they are satisfied.

It has always been known, but never well understood, that some people are apparently motivated by unselfish desires, such as being altruistic, helping others, striving for goodness, seeking truth—even if doing so means self-sacrifice. These metamotives have been variously described as spiritual, moral, transpersonal, the eternal verities. Maslow, after discovering that self-actualizing people experience them, named them B-values (Maslow, 1971). They are not means to more basic motives but ends in themselves; hence the term Being-values denotes states of "being" rather than of "becoming." Freudians and many others have, of course, perceived such motives in people, but they have attempted to translate them or reduce them to more basic, selfish desires. Maslow brings some of these ideas together in the following manner:

> It is my strong impression that the closer to self-actualizing, to full humanness, etc., the person is, the more likely I am to find that his "work" is metamotivated rather than basic-need-motivated. For more highly evolved persons, "the law" is apt to be more a way of seeking justice, truth, goodness, prestige, dominance, masculinity, etc. When I ask the questions: Which aspects of your work do you enjoy most? Which gives you your greatest pleasures? When do you get a kick out of your work? etc., such people are more apt to answer in terms of intrinsic values, of trans-personal, beyond-the-selfish, altruistic satisfactions, e.g., seeing justice done, doing a more perfect job, advancing the truth, rewarding virtue and punishing evil, etc. (Maslow, 1968d, p. 39).

Maslow found a curious thing about his self-actualizers: every one, without exception, seemed to have a mission or calling, something outside of himself to live for. This was always the person's vocation or work—work not just for its own sake but because it fulfilled metaneeds. His work was a means of satisfying his metaneeds: the scientist, for instance, sought truth through his research activities. His quest for truth was an ultimate value for him. It could not be reduced to any other motive; he loved discovery, not for fame, or power, or wealth, but simply because he loved this pursuit. Another man might find order as a dominant value; he might derive great satisfaction from seeing a machine work properly. Another person might find the creation of beauty an ultimate end; he might work beyond normal retirement age because he derives this pleasure from his work. A mother's unselfish care for her child is an end in itself and cannot be reduced to a more basic, selfish need: she is expressing her very nature.

METANEEDS ARE ORGANISMIC

Maslow (1971) proposed the challenging hypothesis that metaneeds are rooted in man's biology, that they are an essential aspect of his very nature. Why, then, do most people not function on the level of metaneeds? Maslow pointed out that the major reason is that they have not taken care of their deficit motives adequately; thus their highest needs are frustrated. Moreover, it would seem that frustration of needs can produce personality disturbance, and this is precisely the case with the majority of people. They suffer from metaneed deprivation or frustration, and the resulting personality disorders are metapathologies (Maslow's own term).

In Table 14–1, the standard personality abnormalities are categorized and interpreted as frustrations of deficit needs. However, Maslow held that what some psychologists consider normal behavior may also be a form of personality disorder. He termed these disorders metapathologies because they involve the frustration of growth or metaneeds. Deprivation of a need produces some form of illness. The deprivation of the deficit needs may be clearly experienced: for instance, one is usually clearly aware of intense hunger or loneliness. Deprivation of the growth or metaneeds is not as clearly felt, but the consequences may be just as evident. One may feel uneasy and not realize that his unpleasant circumstances are producing the disturbance. To use an organic analogy, the absence of Vitamin C produces a serious disorder known as scurvy. The symptoms of the disorder are present, whether or not the person is aware of the cause. As a matter of fact, one does not experience a need for Vitamin C directly.

Some disorders occur as a result of need deprivation, and the person experiences need tensions; however some disorders, such as the metapathologies, occur without the needs even being experienced. Yet whether or not the individual experiences the metaneeds does not change the fact that their frustration hinders growth and functioning. We will now consider metapathologies in some detail. Maslow had some interesting ideas on this subject which should open up new vistas for clinicians.

METAPATHOLOGIES

Metapathologies are illnesses resulting from frustration or deprivation of higher needs (Maslow, 1971). They have been the concern of the clergyman, dramatist, novelist, poet, and biographer. Parents and teachers have had to cope with them without understanding their nature and origins. One com-

TABLE 14-1 PERSONALITY DISORDERS AND HEALTH ACCORDING TO DEFICIT AND GROWTH NEEDS

Deficit Needs		Growth Needs	
Pathology	Normalcy	Metapathology	Actualization
Psychosis:	Well-adjusted	Bored	Creative
Schizophrenia	Social	Unauthentic	Spontaneous
Paranoid reactions	Emotionally stable	Shallow	"Selfish"*
Manic-depressive	Realistic self-concept	Alienated	Insatiably curious
Involutional reactions	Positive self-image	Meaningless	Realization of potentials
	Respectful of others	Limited horizons	Functioning on level of B-values
Neurosis:	Content	Living uncreatively	Peak experiences
Anxiety			Brotherly attitude
Hysteria			Dedication to a vocation
Phobia			
Obsessive-compulsive			
Depression			
Neurasthenia			
Depersonalization			
Hypochondriasis			
Personality Disorders:			
Paranoid			
Cyclothymic			
Schizoid			
Explosive			
Obsessive-compulsive			
Antisocial			
Inadequate			
Passive-aggressive			
Narcissistic			

Note: These descriptions are not intended as an exhaustive list of pathologies found at each point along the continuum, but rather as an illustration of the role of deficit and growth needs in personality disorders and health. Within the same individual, various levels of personality functioning from pathology to actualization may exist. It should also be noted that metapathologies are found in people who are regarded as normal, but are considered abnormal by Maslow because they fall short of self-actualization.

*Self-loving or self-respecting.

mon form of metapathology is a stunting of development. The resulting disorders include the immature personality, the inadequate personality, the infantile personality, and certain other character disorders. The person may lack social feeling, or he may not develop a sufficient conscience to maintain control of his impulses, or he may fail to develop values such as generosity, considerateness, valuation of the good opinion of others.

Maslow believed that many clinicians have ignored pertinent cognitive disturbances as well. He was referring to disturbances in curiosity. Some people view passively, without any interest, everything that goes on around them. All the mysteries about them are simply ignored or taken for granted. Even when they are exposed to new ideas or facts, they may simply be indifferent to them. There is no question that cognitive stunting or disturbance is at the root of many of the traditional illness categories. Paranoid thinking is ultimately a cognitive disorder: the person fails to cognize an event correctly, either as a result of omission of details pertinent to the situation, or through the importation of material that is not a part of the picture.

Other examples of metapathology are being unable to love anyone deeply, not really enjoying anything, not being able to see the value of personal accomplishment, perceiving nothing as virtuous, and behaving immorally. The existentialists have dealt with these pathologies: although they have not named them metapathologies, they have referred to existential depression, meaninglessness, alienation, directionlessness, search for meaning. Such disorders, which are manifestations of metaneed frustration and deprivation (Kierkegaard, 1954), are often not obvious either to the practitioner or to the person who suffers from them. One may perceive that something is wrong with his life, but not know what. These ideas can alter the whole field of mental health when they are better understood, Maslow believed.

B-VALUES: EXPRESSIONS OF METANEEDS

Maslow discovered what he termed b-values in his study of "peak experiences." Peak experiences are states of being or experiencing which may be described as the highest human experiences. They are states of mind that are not means to anything else but are complete in themselves. They cannot be appreciated by anyone who has not experienced them, any more than one can taste chocolate by description. Maslow found that his self-actualizing people reported having such experiences rather frequently. He at first thought that they were a defining characteristic of such people, but later (1968c) he found that even people falling far short of self-actualization have them, though much less frequently. He also found a few self-actualizers who did not have them. Such experiences may be described as "turning on," "being inspired," "being awed." They evoke wonderment, amazement, awe, joy, inspiration, fascination, exaltation, captivation, and the like.

Need gratification is accompanied by emotion and pleasure. The type of pleasure or emotion that occurs varies with the level of need gratification. At the level of B-values there may be a lack of emotion or pleasure and instead a state of quiescence or tranquility. Usually, however, there are distinct emotions and pleasures that do occur on the B-level of gratification. It should be remembered that we are dealing here with the highest reaches of man's experiences and consciousness, and these have not been studied, although they have been reported by mystics, the religious, and even common folk for hundreds of years. The conditions leading to such experiences are not known. Maslow was the first experimentalist who attempted to illumine them. In the following passage he has given us a graphic description of the different emotions associated with his hierarchy of needs. It provides a neat summary of his theory of motivation:

At the lowest basic need level we can certainly talk of being driven and of desperately craving, striving, or needing, when, e.g., cut off from oxygen or experiencing great pain. As we go on up the hierarchy of basic needs, words like desiring, wishing, or preferring, choosing, wanting, become more appropriate. But at the highest levels, i.e., of metamotivation, all these words become subjectively inadequate, and such words as yearning for, devoted to, aspiring to, loving, adoring, admiring, worshipping, being drawn to or fascinated by, describe the metamotivated feelings more accurately (1968d, p. 61).

Table 14–2 summarizes the relation between personality functioning and the conditions of need gratification and deprivation. Note the differences in emotional states as one goes up the hierarchy.

D-Living Versus B-Living

Maslow has given us some insight into his view of the highest human potentialities by contrasting the D-life with the B-life. He has also advised us how to live on the B-plane:

I have found it most useful for myself to differentiate between the realm of being (B-realm) and the realm of deficiencies (D-realm), that is, between the eternal and the "practical." Simply as a matter of the strategy and tactics of living well and fully and of choosing one's life instead of having it determined for us, this is a help. It is so easy to forget ultimates in the rush and hurry of daily life, especially for young people. So often we are merely responders, so to speak, simply reacting to stimuli, to rewards and punishments, to emergencies, to pains and fears, to demands of other people, to superficialities. It takes a specific, conscious, ad hoc effort, at least at first, to turn one's attention to intrinsic things and values, e.g., perhaps seeking actual physical aloneness, perhaps exposing oneself to great music, to good people, to natural beauty, etc. Only after practice do these strategies become easy and automatic so that one can be living in the B-realm even without wishing or trying, i.e., the "unitive life," the "metalife," the "life of being," etc. (1968d, p. 61).

In his study of peak experiences, Maslow came to the conclusion that healthy people are on a totally different level of motivation. He believed that most people are the victims of a host of symptoms of illness, and that even some of those who set themselves up as experts in the art of living are not aware of the human potential (1968c). Since mild pathologies are so common, they overlook man's possibilities and accept as normal or even healthy standards that

TABLE 14–2 NEED HIERARCHY AND LEVELS OF PERSONALITY FUNCTIONING

Need Hierarchy	Condition of Deficiency	Fulfillment	Illustration
Physiological	Hunger, thirst Sexual frustration Tension Fatigue Illness Lack of proper shelter	Relaxation Release from tension Experiences of pleasure from senses Physical well-being Comfort	Feeling satisfied after a good meal
Safety	Insecurity Yearning Sense of loss Fear Obsession Compulsion	Security Comfort Balance Poise Calm Tranquility	Being secure in a full-time job
Love	Self-consciousness Feeling of being unwanted Feeling of worthlessness Emptiness Loneliness Isolation Incompleteness	Free expression of emotions Sense of wholeness Sense of warmth Renewed sense of life and strength Sense of growing together	Experiencing total acceptance in a love relationship
Esteem	Feeling of incompetence Negativism Feeling of inferiority	Confidence Sense of mastery Positive self-regard Self-respect Self-extension	Receiving an award for an outstanding performance on some project
Self-Actualization	Alienation Metapathologies Absence of meaning in life Boredom Routine living Limited activities	Healthy curiosity Peak experiences B-values Realization of potentials Work which is pleasurable and embodies values Creative living	Experiencing a profound insight

are far less than the highest abilities of man. They might say that everyone is depressed some of the time, that everyone gets confused about what is right and wrong, that everyone needs an outlet for his frustrations in the form of drinking, drugs, sex, or whatever. These experts on mental health gear their ideas to standards that apply to the prevailing, the average, the modal, because they have not studied the most highly evolved, healthy, mature human beings. "You can be better than you are" means that you can suffer less from mental strife, not that you can live on a higher psychobiological plane. Self-actualizers are foreign to the average person; their motivations and cognitions are on a B-level, a level which most people experience only fleetingly or not at all.

Living on the B-level may be described as temporary, metamotivated, non-striving, nonself-centered, purposeless, self-validating, an end experience, a state of perfection and of goal attainment. Maslow studied the reports of many subjects who described these being-experiences, and he also went to the literature of religion, esthetics, art, philosophy, and asceticism to round out his picture of the B-level of living. Such experiences may take the form of mystical illuminations, oceanic feelings of oneness with mankind, profound love for another person, deep appreciation of nature, and a greater response to significant events, such as the birth of a child, a religious conversion, a creative intuition, and so on. Maslow contrasted the current emphasis of psychology on deficit-living with the notion of being-living:

I call it Being-psychology because it concerns itself with ends rather than with means, i.e., end-experiences, end-values, end-cognitions, with people as ends. Contemporary psychology has mostly studied not-having rather than having, striving rather than ful-fillment, frustration rather than gratification, seeking for joy rather than having at-tained joy, trying to get there rather than being there. This is implied by the universal acceptance as an axiom of the a priori, though mistaken, definition that all behavior is motivated (1968c, p. 73).

We usually cognize and react in terms of means-value: what use do things or people have for us? Things, people, and situations are quickly labeled and given some kind of value. We automatically bring into play questions of good-ness or badness, suitability, desirability, worth. We react to things and people by judging, comparing, disapproving, valuing. The world is perceived and judged in personal terms, usually with the attitude of seeking means to ends, and when these are attained, they become means to other ends. We are in the process of becoming; we are not just being. B-values, or cognizing on this level, are intrinsic ends. A mother loves her baby; a teacher loves to teach; an architect loves to draw building plans, because each activity enables the person to attain B-values, and these values are the highest human ends, not reducible to any of the so-called lower needs.

Enumeration of B-Values

Maslow attempted to specifically identify the B-values by listing 14* of them (Table 14–3). In considering these B-values, bear in mind that although they are presented in highly abstract form, in actual life situations they are quite concrete and specifiable. For instance, the person who derives joy or pleasure from the "wholeness" value may be the business executive who delights in the integrated functioning of all the departments he supervises. Every unit does its part to manufacture the product. One might also think of each member of a baseball team contributing effectively. Fortunate is the manager who has such a team; he is satisfied not just because he is winning games but also because of his own role in bringing about the orderly functioning of the team members.

---

*Later, in *The Farther Reaches of Human Nature* (1971), he increased the number to 15. See Table 14–4.

TABLE 14–3   MASLOW'S LIST OF B-VALUES

Value	Characteristics
1. Wholeness	Unity, integration, tendency to oneness, interconnectedness, simplicity, organization, structure, dichotomy transcendence, order
2. Perfection	Necessity, just-rightness, just-so-ness, inevitability, suitability, justice, completeness, oughtness
3. Completion	Ending, finality, justice, "it's finished," fulfillment, destiny, fate
4. Justice	Fairness, orderliness, lawfulness, oughtness
5. Aliveness	Process, non-deadness, spontaneity, self-regulation, full functioning
6. Richness	Differentiation, complexity, intricacy
7. Simplicity	Honesty, nakedness, essentiality, abstract, skeletal structure
8. Beauty	Rightness, form, aliveness, simplicity, richness, wholeness, perfection, completion, uniqueness, honesty
9. Goodness	Rightness, desirability, oughtness, justice, benevolence, honesty
10. Uniqueness	Idiosyncrasy, individuality, noncomparability, novelty
11. Effortlessness	Ease; lack of strain, striving, or difficulty; grace, perfect functioning
12. Playfulness	Fun, joy, amusement, gaiety, humor, exuberance, effortlessness
13. Truth, honesty, reality	Nakedness, simplicity, richness, oughtness, pure and unadulterated beauty, completeness, essentiality
14. Self-sufficiency	Autonomy, independence, not-needing-other-than-itself-in-order-to-be-itself, self-determining, environment transcendence, separateness, living by its own laws

From *Toward a Psychology of Being* by A. Maslow. Copyright 1968. Reprinted by permission of D. Van Nostrand Company.

Maslow's list of B-values may be viewed from the standpoint of positive need tensions and from the standpoint of B-value incentives. A person may actually experience tension from the need to produce order, or create beauty, or bring about integration, or organize things into an articulate structure. In such instances, the need tensions are felt as positive emotions, such as anticipation, delight, yearning, and zestful risk-taking. The values are also incentives which satisfy the metaneeds. When attained, the incentives produce certain pleasures and emotional states. There are delights and pleasures associated with the contemplation or creation of beauty, order, perfection, wholeness, unity, balance, and so on. The metaneeds can be powerful

TABLE 14–4 B-VALUES AND SPECIFIC METAPATHOLOGIES

B-Value	Pathogenic Deprivation	Specific Metapathologies
1. Wholeness, unity	Chaos, atomism, loss of connectedness	Disintegration, "the world is falling apart," arbitrariness
1A. Dichotomy transcendence	Black and white dichotomies; loss of graduations, of degree; forced polarization; forced choices	Black-white thinking, either/or thinking; seeing everything as a dual, or a war, or a conflict; low synergy; simplistic view of life
2. Perfection	Imperfection, sloppiness, poor workmanship, shoddiness	Discouragement, hopelessness, nothing to work for
2A. Necessity	Accident, occasionalism, inconsistency	Chaos, unpredictability, loss of safety, vigilance
3. Completion, finality	Incompleteness	Feelings of incompleteness with perseveration, hopelessness, cessation of striving and coping, no use trying
4. Justice	Injustice	Insecurity, anger, cynicism, mistrust, lawlessness, jungle world view, total selfishness
4A. Order	Lawlessness, chaos, breakdown of authority	Insecurity; wariness; loss of safety, of predictability; necessity for vigilance, alertness, tension, being on guard
5. Aliveness, process	Deadness, mechanization of life	Deadness, robotizing, feeling oneself to be totally determined, loss of emotion, boredom, loss of zest in life, experiential emptiness

From *The Farther Reaches of Human Nature,* by Abraham Maslow. Copyright © 1971 by Bertha G. Maslow. Reprinted by permission of The Viking Press, Inc.

(Table continued on opposite page.)

"movers"; their gratification can occupy most of a person's waking behavior provided that his deficit needs are comfortably gratified. Table 14–4 relates Maslow's B-values to deprivation and metapathologies.

One might ask how a person feels when he is functioning on the B-level. How does this person impress others? The subjects studied report that they feel at the peak of their powers, able to operate smoothly, effectively, and effortlessly. They report feeling more intelligent, more perceptive, wittier, stronger, more graceful than at other times; they do not waste effort fighting and restraining themselves; inhibitions are dropped. They feel themselves fully responsible, creative, in total control. They appear to others more effective, decisive, strong, single-minded, able to overcome opposition, self-assured. To the observer they look more trustworthy, reliable, dependable. They seem to be people with a mission that will be accomplished (Maslow, 1968c).

TABLE 14-4 *Continued*

B-Value	Pathogenic Deprivation	Specific Metapathologies
6. Richness, totality, comprehensiveness	Poverty, coarctation	Depression, uneasiness, loss of interest in the world
7. Simplicity	Confusing complexity, disconnectedness, disintegration	Overcomplexity, confusion, bewilderment, conflict, loss of orientation
8. Beauty	Ugliness	Vulgarity; specific unhappiness, restlessness, loss of taste, tension, fatigue; philistinism; bleakness
9. Goodness	Evil	Utter selfishness; hatred, repulsion, disgust; reliance only upon self and for self; nihilism, cynicism
10. Uniqueness	Sameness, uniformity, interchangeability	Loss of feeling of self and of individuality; feeling oneself to be interchangeable, anonymous, not really needed
11. Effortlessness	Effortfulness	Fatigue, strain, striving, clumsiness, awkwardness, gracelessness, stiffness
12. Playfulness	Humorlessness	Grimness, depression, paranoid humorlessness, loss of zest in life, cheerlessness, loss of ability to enjoy
13. Truth	Dishonesty	Disbelief, mistrust, cynicism, skepticism, suspicion
14. Self-sufficiency	Contingency, accident, occasionalism	Dependence upon the perceiver; it becomes his responsibility
15. Meaningfulness	Meaninglessness	Meaninglessness, despair, senselessness of life

ENVIRONMENTAL INFLUENCES ON SELF-ACTUALIZATION

One of the differences among humans that has preoccupied philosophers and psychologists is the wide range in the development of the peculiarly human qualities of empathy, sympathy, identification, guilt, shame, embarrassment, and similar states which seem to involve the operation of conscience and the self (e.g., Hoffman, 1970). There are people who demonstrate by their behavior that they do not experience such emotional and motivational states. They range from the bizarre psychopathic rapist and murderer to the unscrupulous businessman, professional, or politician who cheats his clients through legal loopholes. What causes one person to be thoughtful, considerate, nonaggressive, and another to be just the opposite? Are some people by nature antisocial, and do they still bear the imprint of their animalistic origins, as many great philosophers and psychologists have held? Maslow believed that the answer might be a simple deprivation of appropriate human love during the time when it is essential for the healthy development and growth of a child—during the first 18 months of life. Harlow (1965) has demonstrated that even monkeys need mothering or "contact comfort," and that when they are deprived of this they develop abnormally. Furthermore, the longer the deprivation and the earlier it occurs, the more enduring and damaging are its effects. Common sense tells us that babies also need mothering, and that when deprived of it they develop badly.

In animals, early learning in the form of imprinting may result in the permanent alteration of inborn behavior patterns. An unnatural object may replace the natural object of affection (Lorenz, 1965). A duckling may be brought to prefer an artificial model, or a human, over its natural mother if during the critical period (from three to six weeks after birth) the model is present instead of the mother. Talking birds fail to learn permanently if they are not taught during a short period in their early life. There is reason to assume that imprinting takes place in humans, and that certain abnormalities in personality growth are caused by faulty or inappropriate imprinting, or the lack of it. An absence of love during the earliest months may permanently hamper the need and expression of love in the growing child. When they reach adulthood, such people may be blocked from fulfilling their fullest potentialities as human beings; they continue to bear the marks of their early childhood neglect. Not having received love, they can neither respond to it nor express it themselves. The result may be a severe distortion in conscience development, culminating in lack of social and ethical values; the total behavior is adversely affected.

Maslow held that environmental circumstances may either promote or retard self-actualization. As he viewed current cultural practices and institutions, he found them based on a distorted model of human nature (Maslow, 1968a).

CRITIQUE OF MASLOW'S IDEAS ON SELF-ACTUALIZATION

The most obvious objection to Maslow's ideas on self-actualization is that the traits and characteristics he discovered are his own constructions rather than true qualities of living people. Maslow did admit that the traits that have emerged from his investigation are his clinical impressions. In his favor is the observation that his characteristics of self-actualizing people resemble those proposed by other mental health experts.

There is an optimistic tone in Maslow's formulations, and one may be beguiled by his confidence in man's prospects into thinking that self-actualization is merely a matter of self-reflection and exploration, once one knows the traits of self-actualizers. One might be tempted to conclude that all one has to do is make the traits of the self-actualizers a part of one's own personality.

Students are often quite interested in the traits of geniuses because they think or hope that they can foster the same traits in themselves. This is wishful thinking. There is value in knowing the qualities of genius and healthy personality, but knowledge alone is insufficient to engender such qualities in oneself.

According to Maslow, self-actualization can best occur when all the lower needs are met; thus one should be comfortable with his physiological needs, his yearnings for security and order, his needs to be loved and accepted by others, his needs for self-esteem and reputation, and his cognitive and esthetic needs. The environment must provide just the proper balance between gratification and frustration. It is obvious that the possibility of self-actualization as Maslow defined it is highly limited for multitudes of people. In fact, one might go so far as to say that Maslow was an elitist in the matter of personality growth and functioning.

Maslow recommended that in keeping with man's true nature there should be radical changes in all the major social and cultural institutions. Child-rearing practices should promote growth; education should foster creativity and spontaneity in the child; religion should stimulate man's innate positive tendencies and responses; work should permit gratification of the highest needs for self-esteem and the pursuit of meaningful personal goals. The good things in life should be available to all. But how can parents be made need-gratifying rather than punitive; how can unpleasant jobs be made fulfilling to anyone; how can all of us learn high levels of skills so that we can comfortably satisfy our needs? Perhaps the objective should indeed be to create conditions that would allow more people to attain the fullness of their potentialities. But Maslow's approach is more descriptive than functional: he told us what should be the case, but he did not reveal the methods of attaining his ideals.

INSIGHTS FROM MASLOW'S GROWTH AND HEALTH PSYCHOLOGY

In this section we will attempt to distill a "technology" for promoting Maslow's ideals of the good life.

BEING AS SELFISH AS POSSIBLE

Maslow repeatedly reminded his students of the cardinal principle of his brand of growth psychology: being as selfish as possible. He meant that one should respect himself enough to want to be his most developed self. Furthermore, if one is engaging in an activity that meets his needs, he will perform the work better and benefit both himself and others. For example, if a professor uses his lectures to clarify his thinking on a research project, the students will profit from his knowledge and enthusiasm, and he may learn something from their questions. The point is that one should take his life seriously enough to live as fully as possible.

BEING CHILDLIKE

Maslow often likened self-actualization to the genuineness and natural-ness of a child. One is reminded of this same analogy used by Christ in the Bible: "Unless ye be like little children, ye shall not enter into the kingdom of heaven." The child or healthy adult expresses his needs and abilities spontaneously and creatively (Chukovsky, 1968). Growth is promoted through using one's powers. We may gain many delights from exploring, manipulating, experiencing, being involved, being in-terested, exercising choice, knowing, liking, loving — without filling any deficits or hungers. Frequently we are so occupied with the satisfaction of our deficit needs (physiological, safety, love, and esteem) that we overlook many easily available gratifications. It may be useful to con-sider the many ways of deriving pleasure from growth-promoting activi-ties without paying a heavy price. Some of these are so obvious as to appear trivial: reading a good book, enjoying the beauties of nature, cultivating a genuine appreciation for other people, making good use of all the senses both for pleasure and utility, enjoying one's feelings and emotions, appreciating cognitive experiences such as insights, in-tegrating ideas, and logical order. Perhaps the old saying "The best things in life are free" may acquire new meaning in the light of Maslow's concepts of growth.

NEEDS AS ACTIVE DETERMINANTS AND ORGANIZERS OF BEHAVIOR

If one studies his own behavior, one can usually identify some of the needs that are active. A lower need is active because there is insuf-ficient gratification. A higher or growth need may be active because its gratification results in a positive emotional experience. The lower or deficit needs are experienced as unpleasant tensions. By using this dif-ference in feeling tone, one can identify and emphasize behaviors as-sociated with the higher needs. For example, if it "feels good" to write poetry, one should enjoy this activity, regardless of lack of remunera-tion or recognition. Growth experiences are self-validating: they are ends in themselves, and the emotions which accompany them are en-joyable.

BEING VERSUS BECOMING

Maslow pointed out that there are many occasions which produce B-pleasures, moments of highest happiness and fulfillment. Furthermore, we may identify the conditions that create these peak experiences in us. Examples of such experiences are a feeling of love; a sense of brother-liness, of aesthetic perception, of intellectual insight; a nature experi-ence, and a religious experience. These experiences have no purpose, usefulness, expediency, or means value. They produce awe, wonder-ment, amazement, humility, reverence, exaltation, and similar emo-tional states. As a result of the popular use of drugs, much attention has been directed to the value of altered states of awareness, but peak ex-periences can be had without drugs (Slater, 1970). Unlike drugs, which usually have undesirable side effects, peak experiences promote self-actualization. If peak experiences are possible, why not deliberately create them?

MORE HUMAN, LESS AMERICAN

Maslow suggested the challenging idea that in order to become more human we might have to become less American. He meant that the more we identify with basic human experiences, the less we are German, Italian, Mexican, or any other nationality or cultural type. We ought not to espouse our culture at the expense of fulfilling our individual natures. Being one of the herd is not conducive to self-actualization, according to Maslow.

FEAR OF POTENTIAL GREATNESS

Maslow believed that many people fear their own potential greatness. Everyone is, according to Maslow, both worm and God. We may fear our potential because it places upon us a heavy burden to act in ways counter to the expectations of the culture and of significant people in our lives. We may easily emphasize security, the good opinion of others, and material success over self-fulfillment. It should be noted that Maslow equated the highest levels of need gratification with self-actualization, not with physical health, or material well-being, or social effectiveness, though all of these to a degree are preconditions for attaining self-actualization. Maslow would exhort us to "dare to be great."

ABSENCE OF PSYCHOLOGICAL SYMPTOMS

The absence of psychological symptoms, when one should have them, is unhealthy. Our symptoms tell us that all is not well. Denying or suppressing symptoms frustrates the normal response of the organism to abnormal conditions. Personality problems, apparent or not, may be "loud protests against the crushing of one's psychological bones" (Maslow, 1970). Many symptoms should not be denied and are to be interpreted not as personal failings and weaknesses, but rather as the result of an unfavorable life situation: unreasonable parents, stressful school requirements, forced dependence, unnatural surroundings.

PERSONAL GROWTH

Maslow suggested that although we may not be able to rid ourselves of severe neurotic conditions, there are always some things about ourselves that we can improve. He gave us an additional guideline in his observation that during peak experiences we can often perceive and understand things about ourselves and the world with a high degree of clarity. We may actively question and probe during these experiences, and thereby open ourselves to new insights. Small growth steps are possible in every life; we must be willing to endure the fear of change resulting from the pull of the safety needs when growth-promoting change is attempted.

EXPANDING AWARENESS THROUGH NEED SATISFACTION

A deprived need occupies attention and actually limits the possibilities of expanding awareness. As one satisfies his needs, his attention is freed to apprehend other aspects of himself and the external world.

PROGRESSION AND REGRESSION

Maslow pointed out an important conflict in everyone, no matter how healthy he is: the growth forces versus the coasting and regressive forces. It will be recalled that the lower needs are prepotent and are always present as a potential hindrance. In the midst of a peak experience, we must still meet our basic physiological requirements. We all get tired, discouraged, fearful, tense, angry, and confused. Yet, Maslow believed, many conflicting elements can be transcended. Rather than accept either one alternative or the other, we can be both mature and childlike, both emotional and intellectual. Higher and lower needs can be integrated and can complement each other.

SAFETY COGNITION VERSUS GROWTH COGNITION

Maslow offered the insight that knowing can take place on various need levels, with quite different consequences. He used the example of a man who hears a loud noise downstairs and discovers to his great relief that it is only a loose screen. This type of knowing serves the safety needs. On the other hand, cognition can be an expression of one's natural growth tendencies, in the same way that a healthy apple tree bears fruit. A new discovery, a sudden insight, a novel way of viewing an old problem—all promote an expanded outreach. Maslow (1968a) compared such illuminating experiences to an increase in sensory acuity: seeing things more keenly, hearing things more acutely, feeling things more intensely. One can, of course, utilize his cognitive talents in growth-promoting ways and experience some of the greatest joys of living.

RATING SCALE FOR SELF-ACTUALIZERS

Psychologists have long used rating scales and check lists to assess personality. The items vary with the intention or purpose of the test, but they typically include significant areas of life: work habits, promptness, social qualities, motivation level, assessment of abilities and capacities, and so-called character traits such as honesty, trustworthiness, reliability, and self-centeredness. Consider Maslow's traits of a superior human being with an eye to a rating scale: spontaneity, expressiveness, innocence, guilelessness, naivete, candidness, ingenuousness, childlikeness, artlessness, unguardedness, defenselessness, naturalness, simplicity, responsiveness, unhesitant manner, plainness, sincerity, unaffectedness, immediateness, primitiveness (in an open sense), uncontrolledness, freely flowing outwardness, automatic behavior, impulsiveness, instinctiveness, unrestrainedness, unselfconsciousness, thoughtlessness (in the sense of lack of censuring), unawareness. In order to construct a rating scale to measure these qualities, the foregoing terms would have to be operationally defined. Allowing for the vagueness and overlapping of meanings of the various terms, the difference between these dimensions and those typically used is quite striking. Such descriptive categories may be the personality rating scales of the future, when we know more about the highest human potentials.

SUMMARY

1. Self-actualization implies the full use of talents, capacities, and potentials. A most outstanding quality of the self-actualizing person is the transcendence or overcoming of dichotomies, so that opposite qualities are integrated and expressed by the same behavior. Such a person enjoys his lower need pleasures more than one who is exclusively preoccupied with them. Maslow formulated the following list of traits belonging to the self-actualized:

A. More efficient perception of reality and more comfortable relationship with it. The unknown is readily accepted and indeed arouses the greatest curiosity.
B. Acceptance of self, others, and nature.
C. Spontaneity, simplicity, naturalness. Self-actualizers work out their own sets of values which truly influence their conduct. Their inner lives are highly individualistic.
D. Problem centering. Decisions leading to goal fulfillment are made unemotionally. Work is the expression of the most "selfish" motive and is a source of identification to the self-actualized.
E. The quality of detachment, the need for privacy. Factors determining conduct come from within rather than from the external world. Self-actualizers are self-movers who view free will as an active process rather than as a static force.
F. Autonomy. Self-actualizers are self-sufficient, being independent of environmental conditions.
G. Continued freshness of appreciation. Pleasures do not diminish with repetition.
H. The peak experience. Self-actualizers repeatedly report intensified experiences involving loss or transcendence of self.
I. Gemeinschaftsgefuhl. Healthy people identify with humans in general. Affection, understanding, and sympathy are given freely.
J. Interpersonal relations. Friendships are limited but strongly bound.
K. Democratic character structure. Self-actualizers accept all types of people.
L. Discrimination between means and ends, between good and evil. Self-actualizers are certain about their convictions and lack confusion, chaos, and conflicting beliefs. Means are easily interchanged while ends remain fixed.
M. Philosophical, unhostile sense of humor.
N. Creativeness. Self-actualizers are inventive, original, and spontaneous.

    O. Resistance to enculturation, the transcendence of any particular culture.

    P. Personality integrity. Healthy people do not experience personality splitting or fragmentation.

    Q. Transcendence of dichotomies.

2.   Healthy individuals do experience guilt, anxiety, sadness, strife, self-criticism and conflict, but these states are not caused by neurotic conditions.

3.   A need is a deficit state, a lack of something that is required. Needs give rise to unpleasant tensions which serve as part of the motivational force. A metaneed is a lack of something that promotes growth. Metaneeds induce tensions that are experienced as positive. The search for truth, goodness, and beauty is motivated by the tensions of metaneeds. Unlike needs, metaneeds may increase tension when satisfied, rather than reduce the state of tension.

4.   Metaneeds are rooted in man's biology, yet most do not function on this level since insufficient attention is given to deficit motives. Metaneed deprivation can result in personality disorders or metapathology, which may be considered a stunting of development. Metapathologies include chronic boredom, a sense of alienation, lack of involvement, routine living, cognitive disturbances, failure to enjoy anything, lack of direction, and existential depression. Immoral behavior is also thought to stem from the frustration or deprivation of metaneeds.

5.   Metamotivation involves b-values, which are not reducible to any lower need. A list of b-values follows:

wholeness	richness	effortlessness
perfection	simplicity	playfulness
completion	beauty	truth
justice	goodness	self-sufficiency
aliveness	uniqueness	meaningfulness

6.   Persons living on the level of these b-values feel at the peak of their powers, are able to operate effectively, and feel intelligent, witty and strong, because inhibitions are non-existent.

SUGGESTED READINGS

Maslow, Abraham. Religions, Values and Peak Experiences. New York: Viking Press, 1964.
    In this brief work, Maslow proposes that the religious experience be considered scientifically. He believes a better understanding of the need for spiritual expression, as manifested in peak or religious experiences, can be obtained through science.

Toward a Psychology of Being, 2nd ed. New York: D. Van Nostrand Company, 1968.
    As a pioneer in psychology's movement away from the negativistic view of man, Maslow presents his theories of b-values, peak experiences, and self-actualization.

Motivation and Personality, 2nd ed. New York: Harper and Row, 1970.
    This is the best known of Maslow's books. It presents his theory of personality, with special attention to the need hierarchy and self-actualization.

The Farther Reaches of Human Nature. New York: Viking Press, 1971.
   This book integrates Maslow's views on creativity, biology, cognition, synergy, and the
   need hierarchy with the role of science in the study of human nature.

REFERENCES

Allport, G. W. Pattern and Growth in Personality. New York: Holt, Rinehart and Winston, 1961.
Barron, F. Creativity and Personal Freedom. Princeton: Van Nostrand, 1968.
Chukovsky, K. From Two to Five. Morton, M., trans. Berkeley: University of California Press, 1968.
Erikson, E. Identity: Youth and Crisis. New York: W. W. Norton and Company, 1968.
Harlow, H. F., and Griffin, G. Induced mental and social deficits in rhesus monkeys. *In* Osler, S. F., and Cooke, R. E., eds. The Biosocial Basis of Mental Retardation. Baltimore: The Johns Hopkins University Press, 1965.
Hoffman, M. Moral development. *In* Mussen, P. H., ed. Carmichael's Manual of Child Psychology, 3rd ed., Vol. 2. New York: John Wiley and Sons, 1970. Pp. 261–359.
Horney, K. The Neurotic Personality of Our Time. New York: W. W. Norton and Company, 1937.
Jung, C. G. Man and His Symbols. New York: Doubleday and Company, 1964.
Kierkegaard, S. The Sickness unto Death. Lowrie, W., trans. New York: Doubleday and Company, 1954.
Lorenz, K. Evolution and Modification of Behavior. Chicago: University of Chicago Press, 1965.
Maslow, A. H. Human potentials and the healthy society. *In* Otto, H., ed. Human Potentials. St. Louis: Warren H. Green, 1968a.
Maslow, A. H. Some educational implications of the humanistic psychologies. Harvard Educ. Rev. *38*:685–96, 1968b.
Maslow, A. H. Toward a Psychology of Being, 2nd ed. Princeton: Van Nostrand, 1968c.
Maslow, A. H. A theory of metamotivation: The biological rooting of the value-life. Psychol. Today *2*:38–9, 58–62, July, 1968d.
Maslow, A. H. Toward a humanistic biology. Am. Psychol. *24*:724–35, 1969.
Maslow, A. H. Motivation and Personality, 2nd ed. New York: Harper and Row, 1970.
Maslow, A. H. The Farther Reaches of Human Nature. New York: Viking Press, 1971.
May, R. Man's Search for Himself. New York: W. W. Norton and Company, 1953.
Miller, D. R. Optimal psychological adjustment: A relativistic interpretation. J. Consult. Clin. Psychol. *35*:290–95, 1970.
Schachtel, E. Metamorphosis. New York: Basic Books, 1959.
Slater, P. The Pursuit of Loneliness. Boston: Beacon Press, 1970.
Wechsler, D. Wechsler Adult Intelligence Scale Manual. New York: The Psychological Corporation, 1955.
Wild, C. Creativity and adaptive regression. J. Pers. Social Psychol. *2*:161–69, 1965.

CHAPTER 15

The Productive
Orientation

Erich Fromm

Erich Fromm (1900–   )

BIOGRAPHY AND OVERVIEW

A rich fund of suggestions for ideal living can be found in the writings of the philosophers, particularly in the field of ethics. The content of ethics is guides to living, which have some similarity to principles of mental health. One significant difference is in the degree of perfection in living: mental health principles frequently consider what is sufficient to allow one to "get by," to avoid being hurt, to adjust to one's circumstances, whereas the principles of ethics usually stretch man's strivings to the ultimate of perfection, to the best that man can attain. In some ethical systems, even mental health and well-being are sacrificed for the sake of ideal human functioning. Proper human conduct may be defined by the state, or the majority of the people, or a formalized moral code.

Because of this lack of concern for the well-being of the individual, many scientific psychologists refuse to accept ethics as a source of knowledge of the ideals of human conduct. Then too, the ethician is more concerned with ends than with means: he prescribes the ideals of the good life but does not deal with the ways of attaining them. For example, one might argue for the absolute indissolubility of marriage on the basis of the so-called natural law or on the grounds of the benefit of society as a whole, but disregard difficulties in individual cases that might justify divorce. One of the major problems in ethics is the application of universal laws, or principles based on human nature in general, to the specific individual (Brandt, 1959). Thus most psychologists and psychiatrists have turned away from philosophical speculation as a means of learning about man's behavior—both as it is and as it should be. Erich Fromm, a well-known psychoanalyst and author, is an exception: he holds that ethics can teach us much of value about the ideal life, if it is brought into line with scientific findings. For him ideal human existence is healthy existence: the two are one and the same. He believes that what is objectively right must also be good for man. This proposition represents an attitude toward the good life that deserves a hearing.

Fromm's books are likely to be quite popular on a college campus because his ideas are pertinent to several subject areas in the typical college curriculum: sociology, philosophy, psychology, and even psychoanalysis. His *The Art of Loving* is required reading in many courses. Fromm is a noted lecturer, professor, and psychotherapist. He was born in 1900 in Frankfort, Germany, and received his education in several of Europe's outstanding universities: Frankfort, Munich, and Heidelberg (where he received his Ph.D. in psychology). In 1922 he undertook instruction in psychoanalysis as a lay analyst at the Berlin Institute of Psychoanalysis. He came to the United States during the Depression and is currently living in Mexico.

FROMM'S FIVE HUMAN NEEDS

Fromm disagrees with Freud about the role of sex in man's life. It is not sexual frustration that is our biggest problem, but rather the simple fact that we are human beings. According to Fromm, the very qualities which make us human — the ability to know and reason about the things of the world; the ability to reflect upon our own thoughts, feelings, and activities; the ability to project into the future; the ability to perceive contradictions, injustices, and discrepancies, and so on — also present us with difficulties and challenges. To be human means to have a specific make-up with specific needs and specific problems to solve. We are unlike any other creature in the world. We are aliens who are not linked to nature by instincts. We must depend on our abilities to reason correctly, to develop skills, and to love productively as the best means of dealing with the problems associated with being human. If we do not meet our specifically human needs adequately, we either die or become insane. These needs are, according to Fromm (1955), relatedness, transcendence, rootedness, sense of identity, and a frame of reference. Each person must deal with these needs. They are the basic psychological requirements for living effectively.

1. Relatedness. The feeling of loneliness and isolation is common to all humans, according to Fromm. The only means of overcoming this feeling is some type of relatedness to others. But not every form of relatedness will promote happiness. Submission and dominance are forms of relatedness, but these are harmful to man. Man should use his ability to love productively in dealing with others. There are several forms of productive love: maternal love, paternal love, erotic love, brotherly love, and love of self. Productive love is the only way to overcome the feeling of aloneness and isolation common to all people.

2. Transcendence.   Relating to the world in a passive manner is contrary to the nature of man. Although there are wide differences among people, everyone has the capacity for knowledge and skills. When these capacities are not used, or are used incorrectly, personality development and functioning are impaired. Because man is not guided by his instincts, he must solve his problems by means of his own resources, including the culture in which he lives. Man, and each individual person, must create his own world.

3. Rootedness.   The desire for rootedness may be interpreted as a need for meaningful ties with one's immediate surroundings and past. One might think of Maslow's belonging and acceptance needs. One should be a part of his community, of his job, of his school. Man needs traditions, customs, and rituals that stand for things or beliefs that are greater than the individual. In a rapidly changing world, the need for rootedness becomes strongly felt (Lifton, 1970).

4. Sense of Identity.   Fromm agrees with Erikson on the need for identity. We may also think of Maslow's esteem needs in this respect. Everyone has a need to identify his place in the world.

5. Frame of Reference.   Each person has the need to make sense of his life and to understand his world. Fromm holds that even an incorrect picture of the world is better than none at all. To be in a state of chaos and confusion is highly frustrating to most people.

The reader should note that Fromm often speaks of mankind in general rather than of the individual person. It is easy to misinterpret his ideas as being highly abstract, but the reader should bear in mind that what applies to mankind also applies in some form to him. For Fromm, every person has a profound feeling of aloneness and isolation. Every person has contradictory elements within himself. Every person in one degree or another has to deal with certain problems of existence. Whenever the term "man" is encountered, it might be more effective to substitute the term "I."

VALUES AS GUIDES

Many psychologists have rejected value judgments on the ground that they cannot be tested. For example, some people believe that being charitable is a better way of living than being selfish, or that being free is more desirable than being a slave, or that self-directed behavior enhances mental health more than being ruled by an authoritarian force. To apply the empirical test of validity to value judgments appears impossible to many behavior scientists; certainly the test is fraught with difficulties. Ultimately there is the question of just what is desirable: what is an adequate measure of healthy functioning. Yet despite these objections, Fromm (1960) maintains that value judgments are the basis of our actions, and that these actions in turn have much to do with our mental health. Most of our basic expectations and significant choices are rooted in values. Whether a man chooses to marry or to remain single is a value judgment; so also is his choice to engage in gainful employment because this way of earning a livelihood is valued over others. The values may thus be his own or they may be forced upon him, a significant difference which will be discussed in detail later.

Numerous psychologists argue that values are a matter of personal preference. For them there are many ways to live, and many different values which justify these diverse modes of living. Fromm holds to norms and value judgments which apply to all men because they are based on the very nature of man—a nature which despite the uniqueness of each individual is the common inheritance of all. The person who suffers from neurosis has failed to meet certain requirements of his own nature. Fromm would say that his failure is a moral one, even though the fault may not be totally his own. To be human means to have certain problems and requirements that transcend the particular characteristics and circumstances of each life. In many instances the neurosis is the outcome of the inability to resolve conflicts of values.

SOME ETHICAL PROBLEMS

Ethics is an applied discipline, which means that it is concerned with actual behavior. It is functional in that it offers guides to living. The principles of ethics deal with decisions having a direct bearing on conduct. For the reader who has not studied ethics formally, it may be instructive to examine some questions of an ethical nature.

Consider abortion. Should a woman have the right to determine whether a fetus is to be aborted? Does the unborn child have rights, even though he cannot take up his own case? What about the welfare mother who is already overburdened with children, or the unwed pregnant teenager, or the rape victim? What place should the state have? Certainly the laws governing abortion have traditionally been quite strict. If abortion is allowed, how far on in the pregnancy should it be permitted before it is considered illegal? Should it be a matter of personal preference, scarcely different from choosing one's clothing, or type of food, or recreation? Does it violate the best interests of mankind, both as a whole and as individuals? Or is it really in the child's best interest to permit him to be born hopelessly retarded, or deformed, or into a family that will not care for him? These questions have puzzled the greatest minds. Is there anything in the nature of man that can tell us the answers? Fromm holds that man's reason can find solutions. Just as man has made sound judgments about physical nature which have resulted in marvelous achievements, so man ought to be able to make sound judgments about his own best conduct. Reason is man's only hope. Knowledge of human nature is the foundation of valid ethical judgments (Fromm, 1947).

Consider another ethical issue. A young woman with a widowed father may be tormented by a conflict between his expectations of her and the concerns both of herself and of her husband-to-be. Her father exerts pressure to keep her home, and she has a profound sense of obligation to him. At the same time, she wants to marry and have a family of her own. Is there a solution to this dilemma? The young woman may have difficulty weighing one value against another, but there is an order of priority here. She may believe that her obligation must take precedence over her "selfish" desires for marriage, but her own rights are really more important and outweigh her duty to her father. To affirm the priority of her rights is not to imply that her obligations to her father are nonexistent. His expectations of her are unjust, but there is some middle ground. She can still be a vital part of his life, while living her own. The solutions to such problems are not arbitrary, nor are they simply a matter of cultural practice. There are definite rights and wrongs which transcend cultural beliefs.

These are but two examples of the literally hundreds of ethical issues. Every aspect of life involves value judgments, and one cannot really treat the good life psychologically without considering values and their bases. Fromm believes that the norms for ethical conduct have their source within human nature itself. In his view, ethical conduct is equivalent to health. The mature, integrated, and happy person is virtuous. Vice, on the other hand, is self-mutilation. The productive orientation to life is ethical; nonproductive orientations are unethical.

AUTHORITARIAN VERSUS HUMANISTIC ETHICS

One may question the source of the guiding principles: who determines the "oughts" for man? We may also inquire about the justification or validity of the source. In authoritarian ethics some authority imposes the laws or rules (Fromm, 1947). It may be the government, parents, teachers, religion, or even the culture. There must be compliance without questioning the validity of the norms. Fear of the authority's power keeps the followers in line. It should be pointed out that authoritarian ethics may harmonize with humanistic ethics if the authority imposes controls and rules that promote human living, but most often this is not the case. The norms may be injurious to the ones who must follow them.

The rights of those subject to authority are minimized. Rewards and punishments are determined by the authority, with no participation by the subject. In the slave-master relationship, the slave has rights which are given him by the master, and no rights from his own nature. While most people are not slaves, authoritarian controls are a part of everyone's life. The parents are the authorities for the infant and young child. They make all the rules and set the conditions for rewards and punishments, often exercising their power despotically. In the early grades, the teacher also has great power, imposing conditions for success and failure that greatly affect the child's development. Like parents, many teachers do not give adequate consideration to the rights of children and young adults. They expect them to perform all requirements and tasks uniformly and neglect to acknowledge individual differences in talent, motivation, home circumstances, and the like. The failure of the system to bend to the individual often produces the learning casualty in school (Holt, 1964).

In contrast to authoritarian ethics, humanistic ethics is based on the requirements of man's nature (Fromm, 1947). What is right and wrong is at the same time good or bad for man. Fromm believes that life should be lived fully. Failure to attain fullness is a capital crime in humanistic ethics. Irresponsible living which squanders talents and fails to actualize potentialities constitutes vice.

Everyone seeks joy and happiness, but these are scarcely found in the lives of most people. According to Fromm, "man's happiness consists of 'having fun'. . . . The world is one great object for our appetite, a big apple, a big bottle, a big breast; we are the sucklers, the eternally expectant ones, the hopeful ones—and the eternally disappointed ones" (1956, p. 87). Certain values are sought after as the means for attaining happiness, but these are often the wrong values, or the means are confused with ends. Making money is a necessary requirement for survival in Western civilization; money buys the necessities and luxuries of life. But valuing money for its own sake, or judging one's worth by one's earning power, is a confusion of means with ends. Fromm points out that a man works hard to make money, and then, instead of using it to promote happiness, invests it to make more money.

For many people, what money can buy is the definition of happiness. Fromm describes the haven of this personality type as

a vision which would look like the biggest department store in the world, showing new things and gadgets, and himself having plenty of money with which to buy them. He would wander around open-mouthed in this heaven of gadgets and commodities, provided only that there were ever more and new things to buy, and perhaps his neighbors were just a little less privileged than he (1955, p. 135).

THE HUMAN SITUATION

According to Fromm (1947), every individual faces distinct problems by virtue of the fact that he is human. Although each person is unique as a living being, the tasks and difficulties that he must confront are frequently similar to those of others. All the circumstances of two people's lives may be different, but the nature of certain problems is the same. Fromm terms the state of man the human situation.

Fromm attaches considerable importance to the condition of being human. He holds that man is a freak of nature, an anomaly in the world by comparison with other animals. His very nature confronts him with conflicts which can never be totally resolved. Each man must work out some expedient way of living with the human situation. Fromm describes these peculiarly human conditions as existential and historical dichotomies.

EXISTENTIAL AND HISTORICAL DICHOTOMIES

Existential Dichotomies

To say that man is confronted with existential dichotomies means that he must face unsettling and unavoidable discrepancies, double-horned dilemmas (Fromm, 1947). For example, you did not choose to be born, but suicide is highly disapproved socially and repugnant psychologically. You have many potentialities which you know can never be fulfilled. You must live with the fact that injustices which you cannot right will plague you. You must also live as fully and completely as possible with the recognition, acute at times, that death is inevitable. As you go about satisfying your needs, you know that you can never reach a state of complete harmony and tranquility. Whenever a certain level is reached, there is renewed striving for improvement. With the greatest brain evolved, man is nevertheless the eternal wanderer. There are always new things to be known, gaps in knowledge to be filled. While man can appreciate the role of happiness in his life, he knows that he cannot attain it as a permanent condition. He strives for perfect relatedness with others, and he is doomed to failure in his attempts. Man is the only creature who can be bored, who can be discontent, who can project a better life but cannot always achieve it. It is man's lot to find harmony within himself and between himself and nature through the use of reason. Man does not discover harmony; he must create it. *He must make his own world because the world he finds is not suited to him* (Fromm, 1947). The existential dichotomies present each person with insoluble contradictions, unlike the historical dichotomies, which are contradictions that might not have taken place.

Historical Dichotomies

The historical fact that wealth is unevenly distributed is a matter that could have been otherwise. That certain people were and are treated as inferior is another incomprehensible aspect of human life. Reason dictates that this does not have to happen. The use of valuable knowledge and resources for war, and for defense against war, is another historical enigma. These are dichotomies that could be resolved through reason. Some people have a vested interest in explaining such problems as inequities in wealth as a natural outcome of the inferior status of certain groups. An authoritarian leader may have the power to convince the masses that inequities are a fact of life, but the consequences remain to plague society. Many problems which appear to be existential dichotomies are really historical dichotomies instead.

Man's only answer is to face his problems and realize that he must find solutions. For the unsolvable problems, the answer is to try to develop all one's potentialities and live productively. Fromm's unproductive orientations are unsuccessful means of dealing with the human situation. Productive love and productive work are the best remedies to the human condition. Table 15–1 lists some of the most outstanding existential and historical dichotomies. In his writings Fromm enumerates others.

TABLE 15-1   EXISTENTIAL AND HISTORICAL DICHOTOMIES

Existential Dichotomies

1. Life-Death: man desires immortality yet possesses knowledge of his imminent death.

2. Man is the bearer of vast human potentials, yet his life span does not permit their realization.

3. Each man is alone in his unique identity, and due to this uniqueness he remains dissimilar to other men. Yet no man can remain alone, unrelated to his fellow man: i.e., I want to be an individual, but I must conform in order to be related to others.

4. Man desires security and predictability, but conditions of life make for insecurity and unpredictability.

5. We desire to know truth yet are confronted with partial truths, misrepresentations, and limitations of knowledge.

6. Man desires health and freedom from accidents but is subject to both ill health and accidents.

7. Man desires to control things but is subject to many factors over which he has no control.

8. Man must make binding decisions but with uncertainty of outcome and only partial evidence.

9. Man strives for freedom but cannot cope with it once it is attained.

10. Man strives for perfection and improvement, yet mistakes are inevitable and often irreparable.

Historical Dichotomies

1. Abundant technical means for material satisfaction exist, yet there also exists the incapacity to use them exclusively for peace and the welfare of mankind.

2. Man desires long-lasting peace yet has a history of war.

3. Discrimination exists among mankind despite purported equality.

4. Wealth is unequally distributed in the face of poverty.

5. The benefits of science and technology are available to relatively few.

Fromm (1955) believes that the human situation creates a need for passionate involvement in something. For some the devotion and involvement are centered about a supernatural being. In Western culture there is a passionate pursuit of wealth, power, and prestige. One must be involved in something to a high degree, and both the type of attachment and the nature of the object which is sought have much to do with the quality of living. Neurosis may be considered an irrational religion, an immature passionate pursuit which is an attempt to find meaning. One person may strive to be loved by everyone. Another may believe that he can be happy only if he is successful in sports. Another looks for romantic love as the answer and falls in love indiscriminately. One cannot just live; there must be meaning to life.

CONSCIENCE

Conscience is a regulating agency within personality, an attribute of self-awareness which enables one to observe, reflect on, and evaluate his own conduct. The judgments of conscience may stem from internalized prescriptions which have little to do with a person's major aims or needs. They may also represent self-evaluations based on one's own ideals and values. These in turn may be the products of the real self, playing a part in meeting the needs of the person and the demands of the environment. Whether conscience consists of internalized authority (what Fromm [1947] calls the *authoritarian conscience*) or of self-imposed prescriptions (what he calls *humanistic conscience*) has much to do with productiveness. The authoritarian conscience hinders growth and functioning: it leads to conformity, lack of spontaneity, and suppression of the real self. Humanistic conscience promotes growth, freedom, spontaneity, and the fulfillment of the self's potentialities. Both types of conscience will be discussed in some detail because everyone has within himself a measure of each.

AUTHORITARIAN CONSCIENCE

Fromm's concept of authoritarian conscience is similar to Freud's concept of superego conscience, but Fromm adds some significant ideas. The basic concept is that the dictates of the principal external authorities — such as parents, teachers, tradition, and cultural expectations — are internalized and constitute the values entering into the judgments and decisions one makes. Fear and admiration are at the root of the internalization process. The source of the authority is idealized (as when a child believes that his parents are the most perfect humans), and this in turn adds further weight to its authority. When the internalization factor goes to work to form conscience, its strength is still greater because the conscience represents the authorities in idealized form.

Any opposition to conscience produces a sense of guilt. Guilt in turn creates a need for atonement. The will is weakened, and submission becomes the most comfortable means of obtaining inner harmony.

Fromm stresses that the source of authority behind authoritarian conscience may be the significant people in a child's life, but it may also be anonymous and impersonal institutions such as science, common sense, tradition, and public opinion. How many people feel guilty because they are not successful, or because they have not achieved greatness, or because they are not popular? Because one cannot attack an impersonal authority, curious things happen: the hostility which is generated has to go somewhere, so it is directed toward oneself. The person hates himself, feels unworthy, depressed, discouraged, and so on.

The authoritarian conscience makes the person feel duty-bound. Violation of duty, even in thought, produces guilt. Instead of questioning the conscience, the person questions himself. He must make sense out of what is happening to him, so he reasons that he feels guilty because he is unworthy. Again he questions his behavior rather than the conscience or that which produced the conscience in the first place.

One more important point regarding authoritarian conscience: just as authoritarian ethics may not be based on the nature of man, so also the conscience resulting from such ethics may lead to irrational behavior. The child is often forced into an impossible dilemma: his basic drives may be associated with prohibitions. Thus he commits unavoidable transgressions. Sexual desires are soon laden with guilt feelings. For example, many parents highly disapprove of masturbation as a form of sexual outlet for young people. Toilet training and cleanliness training can be other sources of guilt feelings. All sorts of natural desires are surrounded with disapproval. One must be successful in school; one must be obedient to parents and other authorities. When the child rebels—and his ego does indeed assert itself in self-defense—he experiences guilt, if not actual punishment. By the time the child is five or six, he already has a heavy load of guilt. Many of his recurring natural impulses have brought him into conflict with the authorities in his life. His conscience rules supreme; it keeps him under control. Many people in our culture are lifelong victims of their authoritarian consciences. Unable either to dispense with their impulses or to moderate their authoritarian controls, they are early victims in the fight for freedom and independence (Alper et al., 1964). Fromm describes such people as follows: They suffer from lack of spontaneity, weakness of will, automation conformity, a perpetual sense of guilt, and above all, the feeling of not really being themselves. "Man thus becomes not only the obedient slave but also the strict taskmaster who treats himself as his own slave" (1947, p. 151).

HUMANISTIC CONSCIENCE

Humanistic conscience, according to Fromm, consists of the formation within the personality of values and aims that exert a directive and restraining influence on conduct, but are based on the individual's nature and not on the precepts of external authority. The primary capacities involved in the development of humanistic conscience are the powers to reason and to love (Hoffman, 1970). The conscience is the *voice of the real self*. It points to the goals which can help a man to become his real self. It tells us what is morally good for us (moral in this sense means what is healthy and productive). It embodies not only our major aims in life but also the principles (know-how) by which these may be achieved.

While the authoritarian conscience issues orders that are supported through fear (I must do this or that because I am afraid of the law, or my parents, or my teachers), the humanistic conscience rules through precepts based on obligations to oneself. One might say: I owe it to myself to study diligently in school, to make good grades in order to prepare for a career. I owe it to myself to keep physically and psychologically fit, to rest adequately, to make my life as enjoyable as possible. The reader might use the expression "I owe it to myself" as a means of identifying the demands of his own humanistic conscience which, Fromm believes, is the real self. If the conscience is a dominant force, it keeps the person to his objectives. Because he has worked out these objectives himself, they exert considerable strength against competing desires, such as the desire not to work, or the desire for recreation, or even the crippling effects of self-doubt.

Conformity to humanistic conscience is congruent with fulfillment of the real self. The voice of conscience is in a sense a commentary upon success or failure in fulfilling oneself. A machine which is functioning properly has identifiable characteristics: it makes a certain sound; there may be a particular output, and so forth. When it is out of order, it also produces definite indications. Similarly, conscience can indicate success or failure in living productively. The "bad conscience," experienced as guilt, depression, or fear, is a sign that one is not living productively, while the "good conscience," experienced as a sense of well-being, of inner and outer harmony, is a sign of productive living. The humanistic conscience can be a good guide for judging success or failure in the art of living, and *only the humanistic conscience* can serve this function. The authoritarian conscience is active or inactive only in relation to whether one obeys or disobeys the precepts of an authority. A general sense of well-being or of guilt may not be trusted in this case. In fact, a person may be comfortable in his state of conformity to the authority but actually be living unproductively. Psychologically he may have a sense of tranquility while suffering physically from some dysfunction. Usually both body and mind are affected. But the point is that the authoritarian conscience cannot be trusted as an indicator of good living (Fromm, 1947).

Table 15–2 summarizes Fromm's views on the humanistic and authoritarian consciences. It should be noted that aspects of both forms of conscience may be operating in the individual simultaneously.

If humanistic conscience is the voice of the real self, pointing the way to successful living, then why does it so often go unheard? Fromm believes there are a number of reasons: first of all, many are so controlled by an authoritarian conscience that they distrust their own thoughts and desires. In fact, they identify the dictates of the authorities as their own, as when a man believes that successful living requires the attainment of wealth and fame. Another reason is that our culture emphasizes an outer orientation; it promotes the idea that one should always be busy doing something—reading, working, socializing. Fromm says:

In order to listen to the voice of our conscience we must be able to listen to ourselves, and this is exactly what most people in our culture have difficulties in doing. We listen to every voice and to everybody but not to ourselves. We are constantly exposed to the noise of opinions and ideas hammering at us from everywhere; motion pictures, newspapers, radio, idle chatter. If we had planned intentionally to prevent ourselves from ever listening to ourselves, we could have done no better (1947, p. 161).*

Closely related, Fromm believes, is our phobia of being alone. Any kind of company is preferable to none at all: being with ourselves is undesirable because we are afraid of what we may discover. The positive aspects of con-

---

*© 1947 by Erich Fromm. Reprinted by permission of Holt, Rinehart and Winston, Inc.

TABLE 15-2 HUMANISTIC VERSUS AUTHORITARIAN CONSCIENCE

Humanistic Conscience

1. Is independent of external sanctions and rewards.

2. Is listening to the true self.

3. Consists of a response of the total personality, being both cognitive and affective in character and involving the productive use of abilities.

4. Is a reaction of the self to the self.

5. Summons one to live fully and productively, and to realize one's potentials.

6. Is the "Voice of our loving care for ourselves" (Fromm, 1947, p. 159).

7. Is an expression of self-interest and integrity.

8. Possesses the goal of productiveness.

Authoritarian Conscience

1. Consists of prescriptions of authorities which are internalized.

2. Is "good" or unfelt when there is adherence to the prescriptions of authority and/or to internalized rules; is "bad" when guilt is experienced as a result of displeasing the authority: i.e., "If I obey, my conscience is quiet or good, and if I disobey, my conscience is felt or bad."

3. Involves a sense of inner security as a result of a symbiotic union with a figure who is perceived as more powerful. (Obedience means benefits from the authority.)

4. Depends upon love and approval from authority; thus pride and self-satisfaction are experienced when there is total compliance.

5. Is a submission of the self, as a result of fear, to the will of others who are regarded as morally superior.

6. Fromm says of the authoritarian conscience: "Paradoxically, the authoritarian guilty conscience is the result of feelings of strength, independence, productiveness, and pride, while the authoritarian good conscience springs from the feelings of obedience, dependence, powerlessness, and sinfulness" (1947, p. 150).

7. May involve self-destructive strivings which are perceived as virtuous.

8. Results in the formation of a pseudo-self which is an embodiment of the expectations of others.

---

science are not experienced strongly. More often, we encounter conscience in its negative aspects, as feelings of guilt, anxiety, depression, and lack of meaning. "The paradoxical—and tragic—situation of man is that his conscience is weakest when he needs it most" (Fromm, 1947, p. 160).

According to Fromm, three inordinate fears stand out as consequences of ignoring the real conscience: fear of (1) death, (2) growing old, and (3) disapproval of others. Not having fully experienced the present and past, we fear the future, especially old age. Not having lived fully, we find death totally unjust and incomprehensible. Not being satisfied with ourselves, we continually look for approval from others. Everyone, of course, has some difficulty with these three fears, but for some persons they become insurmountable and constantly plaguing concerns that interfere with living.

CONSCIENCE AS A GUIDE TO PRODUCTIVE LIVING

Fromm (1947) holds that conscience can foster or hinder productive living. It hinders when it blocks and suppresses the expression of the real self. The authoritarian conscience, for instance, often requires conformity to norms of conduct that may actually produce illness, as when a soldier is commanded to kill innocent victims of war. When the conscience is an expression of the real self (the humanistic conscience), complying with its dictates should be conducive to joy and happiness, if environmental conditions are favorable.

Consider the same behavior from the standpoint of the humanistic and the authoritarian conscience. Masturbation may cause guilt feelings in one with a strong authoritarian conscience, because he is violating a precept of an external authority which proclaims that such behavior is wrong. A person with a humanistic conscience may also feel guilty for practicing masturbation, but his guilt stems from his own personal conviction that he ought to be satisfying his sexual needs in a more fulfilling manner. His guilt tells him that he is not living as productively as he could; this is what Fromm holds is the essence of the humanistic conscience.

Fromm makes another important point about the authoritarian and humanistic consciences that might easily be missed. He does not hold that all external codes are arbitrary and contrary to man's nature. The great religions of the world and the systems of the moral philosophers foster ethical principles that harmonize with the human condition. Most of the precepts of the Old and New Testaments, for instance, can be the foundation of a humanistic conscience, the commandment against stealing should be taught to every child. As one acquires the ability to understand the reasons for his precepts, traditional beliefs should be re-examined to determine whether they are arbitrary and merely ritualistic, or important guides to living. One could make a case for the authoritarian conscience being gradually replaced by the humanistic. We have stressed the negative aspect of conscience, the consequences of not paying attention to it. How do we know when conscience is functioning properly, or what constitutes signs of good conscience? Fromm believes that we can be guided by certain emotional states, both positive and negative. He has some interesting modifications of the hedonistic notion.

ETHICS AND HEDONISM

Hedonism holds that pleasure and pain are the final test of the worth of values and norms. If a guiding principle promotes positive emotions, it is a valid guide to living. If it causes pain and distress, it is bad or undesirable for man and should not be applied.

One difficulty with using emotions as a final test of values is that pleasure and pain may arise from the characteristics of a person. A man with a neurotic character may actually enjoy being hurt, criticized, or subjugated to the will of others, even though this orientation hinders the fulfillment of his potentialities. What he finds pleasurable is not good for him. Just as overeating is injurious to health although the person who indulges himself enjoys it, so many other apparent pleasures retard healthy living. Indeed, what is considered painful may actually promote health. Giving birth to a child is fraught with pain, but the joy far outweighs the suffering.

Antihedonists can point to many instances in which emotions are very poor guides to follow. They consider emotions harmful because they interfere with man's highest functioning, the vigorous utilization of reason. All of us have experienced the deleterious effects of uncontrollable emotions in the face of a crisis. We cannot think clearly; alternatives all seem the same; maladaptive emotions such as hate, revenge, and pride distort the rational functions of the ego. The antihedonists may even go so far as to counsel against pleasure. The most important things are difficult and often unpleasant, while that which produces pleasure is suspect and detrimental: "What I like is either illegal, immoral, or fattening." Fromm (1970) disagrees with this view. He proposes a modified hedonism which recognizes that there are different types of pleasure — satisfaction, joy, happiness — which are not equally important to man.

PLEASURE AND PAIN AS NORMS

What does a good conscience feel like? What emotions accompany a bad conscience? Here good and bad do not refer to a moral evaluation of conscience in any absolute sense, but to the subjective feeling associated with conscience. Good or bad conscience results from conformity or lack of conformity to the authoritarian conscience. If one obeys the authoritarian dictates, although his behavior may not necessarily be growth-promoting, he will at least feel subjective tranquility and the security of support from an external force. Disobedience produces bad conscience and feelings of guilt, anxiety, and unworthiness. What about the humanistic conscience: can we use our emotions as indicators of good or bad conscience? If an activity produces pleasure, is it good or moral for man? If it produces displeasure, is it bad and immoral? Absolute hedonism, maximizing pleasure and minimizing pain, is not a valid guide to productive living. But Fromm (1947) believes that joy and happiness can be valid indicators that one is living a good life, if one remembers that not all pleasure is joy and happiness. He holds that to crave that which is harmful to self or to others is the essence of mental illness. The masochist, for example, actually derives pleasure from being hurt. The criminal who cheats another may feel elation and derive pleasure from his ill-gotten goods, but he does not experience real joy and happiness.

Happiness: A Total Organismic Response

In Fromm's view happiness is not merely a subjective state but a total organismic response, manifested in increased vitality, physical well-being, and utilization of potentialities. Unhappiness, whether conscious or unconscious, also affects the organism, producing such conditions as chronic lethargy, low energy output, headaches, backaches, and a host of psychosomatic disorders. Fromm believes that a person may consider himself happy but have bodily symptoms which suggest that his happiness is an illusion or a form of pleasure which is not happiness. A sadistic boss may not only fail to recognize his enjoyment of the suffering of those whom he controls, but may also rationalize his behavior and turn it into a virtue. He may believe he is helping his employees to work at their best so that they will receive promotions. He wants to help them, but sometimes this means hurting them temporarily. He wants his department to be the best in the company. He is deriving pleasure from his sadistic activities, but he is not aware of it. Because sadism is an unsatisfactory mode of living, he will experience deleterious consequences—if not psychologically (since he has effectively rationalized his behavior), then in some bodily dysfunction such as chronic fatigue. Here we have a person who feels pleasure but whose total organismic response reveals that he is unhappy.

Another form of pleasure-craving stems from irrational psychological needs. Although these needs do not always affect physiological functioning, they may be as abnormal as sadistic activities and can thus exert a distorting or crippling influence upon the personality. Usually having their source in fear, insecurity, or loneliness, they include possessiveness, envy, and jealousy, and the cravings for power, domination, or submission to authority. Often they result in lack of productiveness, in an inability to work or love spontaneously. Unlike physiological needs, which follow a rhythmical sequence of arousal and satiation, irrational psychological needs are often intensified but rarely satiated. How much does it take to satisfy the miser, to please the distrusting mate, to quiet the fame seeker, to quell the passions of one who seeks revenge? Even when they are satisfied, such needs produce only irrational pleasure, not true happiness.

Psychological Scarcity and Abundance

Fromm (1947) makes an interesting distinction between psychological scarcity and psychological abundance. This distinction is similar to Maslow's distinction between deficit and growth motivation. Scarcity refers to a deficiency or lack: physiological needs fit this model; so also do neurotic cravings. In each case the pleasure is derived from relief of tension. But while the tensions resulting from physiological needs provide motivation for the maintenance of life, the tensions resulting from neurotic needs are rooted in nonproductive traits such as insecurity, anxiety, and fear, and lead to detrimental emotions such as hatred, envy, and possessiveness. Abundance pleasure, which Fromm equates with joy and happiness, derives from the productive use of man's capabilities—activities which go beyond the level of necessity and tension relief. To live abundantly is to use one's abilities in a creative and constructive manner to achieve what one wants to do rather than what one must do. There are many pursuits which have no practical significance in the maintenance of life yet add zest and sparkle to living: literature and the arts are examples. The greatest achievements of man are products of abundance rather than of scarcity motivation.

Sex is a tension state, which can provide genuine pleasure when there is relief of tension, but Fromm believes that there is a great deal more to sex than tension, a mistake which Freud made. Aside from the manner of preparation, the manner of performing the sexual act, and the mechanics of satisfying this need, there are other factors such as feelings which the partners have for each other, moral considerations, and a host of others.

Abundance pleasure, in contrast to tension relief, requires active efforts. A father may derive great joy from having his son in medical school: what tensions are at the root of this pleasure? A distinction between joy and happiness is relevant: joy is the pleasure of single situations, whereas happiness is an enduring state punctuated by moments of joy. It should be noted that according to Fromm, joy and happiness are not goals in themselves but rather byproducts of the productive use of abilities.

Happiness and Conscience

According to Fromm (1947), productive living is associated with joy and happiness. The humanistic conscience, if it holds a dominant role in a person's life, will react positively or negatively depending on whether or not behavior is productive. Fromm does not elucidate the specific relationships between conscience and happiness or unhappiness, but it would seem that the operation of conscience plays an important role in both. Furthermore, the subjective state of happiness, as we noted previously, is not necessarily a valid indicator of true happiness; there must be a total organismic response. When the humanistic conscience prevails, the subjective states of pleasure and displeasure may be trusted.

Suppose we take the example of a man who derives great joy and pride from buying his son his first two-wheel bicycle. Why should this act produce joy, according to Fromm's views? First of all, it is a productive activity, involving productive work and productive love. The father buys the bicycle with money he has earned, not stolen. Second, he is giving to another human: brotherly love. Third, his love has no strings attached: he expects nothing in return. Fourth, his activity is motivated not by a painful tension but by the desire to make another happy, a condition which stresses abundance rather than scarcity. Consider other possible reasons for engaging in the same activity. A father buys a bicycle because he wants his son to win a race and bring honor to him as the father. Or he really hates his son and gets him things as a reaction-formation against his unfatherly feelings. Or his son may nag him incessantly, so that he complies in order to find relief. There are many other possible reasons. We can see from the preceding illustrations that there is a considerable difference between motives stemming from a productive orientation and motives of nonproductive orientations. Fromm considers the productive orientation morally good and the nonproductive orientations morally bad. Let us now examine these orientations in more detail.

THE PRODUCTIVE AND NONPRODUCTIVE ORIENTATIONS

To better comprehend the meaning of Fromm's productive and nonproductive orientations, we should consider some terms which he uses in a rather unique way. By behavior traits he means traits which may be identified by an observer and which are overt manifestations of character traits. Character traits are primarily motivational in nature and are usually more central. Economy is a behavior trait which may be due to lack of funds (external cause), or it may express the character trait of stinginess (internal cause). What appears to be ethically undesirable when judged strictly as a behavior trait (such as stealing) may be an expression of a character trait (such as a desire for conformity) and thus not a deliberate misdemeanor. For example, a child may steal in order to fit in with the gang. The character rather than the specific behavior must be judged. Furthermore, a character may be thought of as a constellation, a patterned organization of traits. One's character becomes fixed and represents habitual ways of thinking, feeling, and acting. Character types may be productive or nonproductive. The way a person perceives, thinks, feels, and acts is determined by the nature of his characer and not by rational responses to realistic situations. According to Fromm (1947), distinct character types, each consisting of a syndrome of traits, are identifiable.

NONPRODUCTIVE ORIENTATIONS

Although each person is unique, there are many factors which are similar for everyone in a culture. We have mentioned the existential dichotomies with which we all must deal as a result of our humanness. In childhood we are helpless and dependent on others for the satisfaction of needs. Each of us must gradually take over his own life and learn to accomplish the tasks which accompany specific life periods as Erikson (1963) points out. Things can go wrong all along the way. Quite often the difficulties begin early, with the parent-child relationship. If the development of certain basic functions is arrested, these frustrated processes remain as a source of problems for the individual. One's whole character may be centered about a particular mode of activity. Each of the nonproductive orientations represents a failure in one of the basic tasks of life.

The Receptive Orientation

In order to grow properly, each person must learn to receive from others and to give in return, to take things, to save a part of what he has. He must learn to follow authority, to guide, to be alone, to assert his claims and rights. In the receptive orientation, the dependence on others has not been outgrown (Fromm and Maccoby, 1970). The lesson that one must earn what he wants has not been learned. The individual's relatedness to others is one-sided: he is more comfortable receiving than giving or taking. More will be said about this and the other orientations in connection with abnormal forms of love.

The Exploitative Orientation

The exploitative orientation stems from another basic early activity: the explorative and acquisitive activities of the child. A child soon learns that having to wait to be given what he needs can produce considerable frustration, and that taking things can be a much more effective means of getting one's way. Eventually, the child also learns that there are many regulations to be followed, and that one must acquire rights to things rather than simply appropriate them. Failure to learn this lesson may result in a character structure whose dominant trait is to exploit others. The source of gratification is outside the individual; things are acquired simply by taking, irrespective of others' rights. Frequently the exploitative person harbors a harsh view of life: the only good he sees in others is their use value for him. Life is viewed as a constant struggle in which one must dominate others before they gain the upper hand. The qualities of sympathy and empathy have not developed.

The Hoarding Orientation

The hoarding orientation involves preserving and saving. There is suspicion of what is new. Frequently there is compulsive ordering of the events in one's life. Spontaneity and creativity are likely to be absent; rigidity and adherence to routine are characteristic. There is often a negative tone in the behavior of these persons toward others, but unlike the exploitative type they react not with aggressiveness and hostility, but rather with obstinacy and distrust. Fromm describes the hoarders as individuals to whom "the act of creation is a miracle of which they hear but in which they do not believe. Their highest values are order and security; their motto: 'There is nothing new under the sun'" (Fromm, 1947, p. 67).

The Marketing Orientation

While the receptive, exploitative, and hoarding orientations are elaborations of Freud's pregenital character types, the marketing orientation belongs to Fromm alone. Unlike the three orientations just discussed, the marketing orientation is not based on fixation or faulty development but rather springs from overidentification with the socioeconomic precepts of capitalistic society. The major theme of this orientation is one's value as a commodity—as a worker, as a love object, as a person in general. One is not only the product but also the seller. He must fit the demand of the marketplace with respect to his career, in his search for a marital partner, indeed in practically all spheres of living. What he really is must be subverted to the expectations set by others (Maddi, 1972). Standards of value are defined by external authorities. The person may conceal his real qualities to meet the demands of the marketplace and comes to judge his worth in terms of his ability to meet these outside standards. He thus becomes a victim instead of a master of his circumstances. There is always a sense of insecurity and inferiority because his status, being outside his control, is constantly threatened.

Fromm holds that in a capitalistic society one's sense of self-identity is also impaired. Identity is related to the individual's abilities and to what he does with them. Fromm points out that "Both his powers and what they create become estranged, something different from himself, something for others to judge and use; thus his feeling of identity becomes as shaky as his self-esteem; it is constituted by the sum total of roles one can play: 'I am as you desire me' " (Fromm, 1947, p. 73). There may be no market for a man's abilities, not because they are useless or without value in themselves, but because they are not in demand at the time. Social relationships are also colored by the demands of the market.

Blending of Orientations

Fromm (1947) introduces the idea that character orientations may be blended: no person is totally unproductive, or exclusively centered in a single orientation. As a matter of fact, even the nonproductive orientations are styles of living which range on a continuum from extreme nonproductiveness to at least a moderate degree of productiveness. All the unproductive orientations can be moved toward the positive end of the continuum if the constructive trends in the personality are sufficiently strong. The stubbornness characteristic of the hoarding orientation, for example, can be shaded into tenacity and persistence in achieving goals; the deadening passivity of the receptive orientation can become adaptability. The positive and negative qualities of each orientation, as Fromm listed them, are given in Table 15–3. The orientations may also be described as (1) accepting, (2) taking, (3) preserving, and (4) exchanging.

Although Fromm does not make the point clearly, we might picture the productive orientation as a properly balanced blending of all the desirable traits of the nonproductive orientation. Each trait adds something useful to the personality, although no one ever acquires all of the positive traits, and no one has just the proper balance.

THE PRODUCTIVE ORIENTATION

The productive orientation is a mode of relatedness to the world in which one develops and utilizes his potentialities as fully as possible (Fromm, 1947). Two basic modes of dealing with the world are knowing and loving. Through knowledge one becomes aware of people and things; through love one experi-

TABLE 15-3 POSITIVE AND NEGATIVE ASPECTS OF NONPRODUCTIVE ORIENTATIONS

Positive Aspects	Negative Aspects
Receptive Orientation	
Accepting	Passive, without initiative
Responsive	Opinionless, characterless
Devoted	Submissive
Modest	Without pride
Charming	Parasitical
Adaptable	Unprincipled
Socially adjusted	Servile, without self-confidence
Idealistic	Unrealistic
Sensitive	Cowardly
Polite	Spineless
Optimistic	Wishful thinking
Trusting	Guillible
Tender	Sentimental
Exploitative Orientation	
Active	Exploitative
Able to take initiative	Aggressive
Able to make claims	Egocentric
Proud	Conceited
Impulsive	Rash
Self-confident	Arrogant
Captivating	Seducing
Hoarding Orientation	
Practical	Unimaginative
Economical	Stingy
Careful	Suspicious
Reserved	Cold
Patient	Lethargic
Cautious	Anxious
Steadfast, tenacious	Stubborn
Imperturbable	Indolent
Composed under stress	Inert
Orderly	Pedantic
Methodical	Obsessional
Loyal	Possessive
Marketing Orientation	
Social	Unable to be alone
Experimenting	Aimless
Undogmatic	Relativistic
Efficient	Overactive
Curious	Tactless
Intelligent	Intellectualistic
Adaptable	Undiscriminating
Tolerant	Indifferent
Witty	Silly
Generous	Wasteful
Purposeful	Opportunistic
Able to change	Inconsistent
Youthful	Childish
Forward looking	Without a future or a past
Openminded	Without principle and values

ences relatedness. Fromm distinguishes two forms of knowing: *reproductive comprehension* and *generative comprehension*. Both are essential to knowledge. Through reproductive comprehension one becomes aware of reality, but exclusive attention to literal reality creates sterility and narrow-mindedness. Generative comprehension involves active working over of the incoming impressions, enabling one to see relationships which are not obvious, to penetrate to the essence of things, to project possibilities for action which are not given in the original perception.

There are parallels between some of Fromm's characteristics of productiveness and Allport's characteristics of maturity; for example, ego involvement in the activity (Allport), and concern and respect for objects (Fromm); warm relating of self to others (Allport), and brotherly love (Fromm). The basic idea of productiveness is activity, not compulsive work that is directed toward making something tangible, but rather activity which fosters the development of all one's potentialities. Fromm quotes a passage from Ibsen's *Peer Gynt* that brings out the essence of frustrated productiveness. Laziness is an enemy of productiveness, but so also is compulsive work.

The Threadballs (on the ground)
    We are thought   You should have thought us;
    Little feet, to life   You should have brought us:
    We should have risen   With glorious sound;
    But here like threadballs   We are earth-bound

Withered Leaves
    We are a watchword;   You should have used us;
    Life, by your sloth,   Has been refused us.
    By worms we're eaten   All up and down;
    No fruit will have us   For spreading crown.

A Sighing in the Air
    We are songs;   You should have sung us;
    In the depths of your heart   Despair has wrung us.
    We lay and waited;   You called us not
    May your throat and voice   With poison rot!

Dewdrops
    We are tears   Which were never shed.
    The cutting ice   Which all hearts dread   We could have melted;
    But now its dart   Is frozen into   A stubborn heart.
    The wound is closed;   Our power is lost.

Broken Straws
    We are deeds   You have left undone;
    Strangled by doubt,   Spoiled ere begun
    At the Judgment Day   We shall be there
    To tell our tale;   How will you fare?*

It might be interesting to relate the productive orientation to the humanistic and authoritarian consciences. The individual who has a strong authoritarian

---

Eleven Plays of Henrik Ibsen. New York: Modern Library, Act 5, Scene 6. Quoted in Fromm, 1947, pp. 94–96.

conscience may enjoy a sense of pride because he has not violated the laws of his community, the precepts of his religion, the rules of his household, the regulations of his work setting. However, because he has been so busy avoiding certain behaviors, he has not really done anything positive. He has used his abilities and talents to protect himself against the power of the authorities in his life, but at the cost of limiting the use of his abilities and potentialities. In contrast, the person in whom the humanistic conscience is dominant not only avoids certain behaviors but also engages wholeheartedly in self-expression. His conscience operates most fully when he is functioning productively — actively meeting his goals and using his abilities. He is attempting to "get to heaven" by positive achievements, rather than by backing away from hell. There is surely more joy and happiness in using one's abilities to produce things than in simply avoiding punishment and censure. Often the best way to avoid doing something wrong appears to be to do nothing, but thereby one gains nothing. For the humanistic conscience, sins of omission are just as serious, if not more so, than sins of commission. What one can do, one ought to do.

PRODUCTIVE LOVE

If you were asked to reveal the most basic and most personal striving you have, it would probably be the desire to be part of an intimate love relationship. Fromm holds that union with others, particularly erotic love between man and woman, is one of the strongest human motives. One can hardly attend a movie, a play, an opera, or become acquainted with a person without encountering the theme of unrequited love. The craving for love is the major theme of the vast majority of popular songs. Why is love so significant in human life? Fromm holds that the craving for love, whether normal productive love or the many distortions of it, is one of man's basic strivings because it points to the answer to the human situation: it is the only way that we can truly solve our condition of separation and aloneness. "In the experience of love lies the only answer to being human, lies sanity" (Fromm, 1947, p. 33). In a recent lecture, Fromm stated that love is potentially the greatest power on earth.

It will be recalled that by virtue of being human, one experiences harmony and oneness with nature. Man is separated, a stranger in his world. His sense of separation and isolation is the basic cause of his anxiety. To overcome this painful state, many means are used. Alcohol and drugs dull the realization of alienation and estrangement. In the intoxicated state, one cuts off the outside world and thus temporarily feels euphoria because he has blocked out the problem of isolation. His internal state of awareness is his only world. But the relief is temporary, and the only way to cope again with the problem is to use more intoxicants. Some drugs, such as mood elevators, enhance participation and union with the outside world by increasing sensory acuity and energy expenditure, but this again is a transitory and artificial means of solving man's basic problem. The only real and lasting solution is productive love (Fromm, 1955).

Fromm believes that many people deal with the requirement of loving in the wrong way. They seek to be loved rather than to love. They view love as an intensely emotional experience, as an involvement with a highly appealing person that simply happens when the appropriate partner is encountered. According to Fromm, "they are starved for [love]; they watch endless numbers of films about happy and unhappy love stories, they listen to hundreds of trashy songs about love—yet hardly anyone thinks that there is anything that needs to be learned about love" (1956, p. 1). Fromm portrays some of our other mistaken notions about love: "Love and affection have assumed the same meaning as that of the formula for the baby, or the college education one should get, or the latest film one should 'take in.' You feed love, as you feed security, knowledge and everything else—and you have a happy person!" (1955, p. 200). He goes on to say that many individuals "take the intensity of the infatuation, this being 'crazy' about each other, for proof of the intensity of their love, while it may only prove the degree of their preceding loneliness" (1956, p. 4).

Loving involves much more than emotional reaction; it is an active process of the total personality that brings into play thought, feeling, and behavior. The highest forms of human love do not "just happen" in the presence of another person. Romantic love is often confused with true erotic love; the sexual component is quite prominent, but romantic love is based on sudden discovery, on physical attraction, on hormonal changes; it is only an allurement to a deeper form of love (Harlow, 1971). Romantic love is not the highest form of love, if it is love at all. There are motherly love, brotherly love, love for oneself, love for God (Table 15–4). All types of productive love are rooted in activity of the total personality and involve caring, responsibility, respect, and knowledge of the loved one. Through a deliberate striving to love, the ability to love can be developed. Loving can become an enduring trait of personality—like generosity, truthfulness, promptness—that exerts a continuing influence on human relationships. Love does not happen to a person; it must be cultivated (Fromm, 1956).

Since being human means to feel alone and separated, there is a strong motivation to unite with others. This may be seen in a great variety of behaviors. Conformity to the standards set by the culture (or by subgroups within the culture) is an expression of the need for relatedness. Despite the plea that everyone wants to be different and unique, the fact remains that the urge to conform is much more conspicuous than is individualism (Fromm, 1941). The rebellious young person who joins a militant radical group may actually be more of a conformist than those he criticizes. His feeling of alienation and aloneness impels him to unite in a common cause almost to the exclusion of his individuality. If a member of such a group becomes involved in a productive love relationship with another person, the sense of relatedness and security provided by the affiliation with the radical group may be replaced by the intimate personal relationship; one may see a total change in life orientation.

TABLE 15-4 FIVE OBJECTS OR TYPES OF PRODUCTIVE LOVE

1. Brotherly love: Care for, responsibility for, respect for; and knowledge of another human being; a love between equals.

2. Motherly love: Unconditional affirmation of a child's life and needs; care and responsibility for the child's life and growth.
   a. Motherly love is an attitude which instills love for life.
   b. Motherly love is by nature a love of inequality: the mother gives and the child takes.
   c. Fatherly love is conditional: it is acquired or earned by the child's performance of duty, by his obedience, or by his fulfillment of the father's expectations.

3. Erotic love: A craving for complete fusion, for union with one other person.
   a. Erotic love is directed toward one person of the opposite sex with whom oneness and fusion are desired.
   b. Without brotherly love, erotic love is mere sexual desire and not true love.

4. Self-love (love of self): Not selfishness, not narcissism.
   a. Love for oneself is inseparably connected to love for any other being.
   b. Love of self is a prerequisite for brotherly love ("Love Thy Neighbor as Thyself").
   c. According to Fromm, love of self is a loving, affirmative, friendly attitude toward oneself.

5. Love of God: The highest value, the most desirable good to which man aspires and represents by the concept "god."

LOVE AND THE NONPRODUCTIVE ORIENTATIONS

Love is such a significant function of the total personality that any personality defect will affect the ability to love. The disturbance will produce a distortion of one or more of the aspects of loving: dominating rather than giving, demanding rather than accepting, dictating rather than reciprocating, loving as satisfaction of tension rather than as expression of regard for the other (Fromm, 1956).

Love and the Receptive Orientation

The person with a receptive orientation finds the source of all good things outside himself. One might think of the infant who can do little for himself; he depends on others for the satisfaction of his needs and appetites. The good things of life are external to him; others have the power to bestow or withhold the desirable objects. The receptive person feels inadequate to obtain what he wants; thus he hopes to receive the love of others through his submission to and compliance with them. (Note the striking parallel here to Horney's compliant individual; see Chapter 11). Paradoxically, however, if love is given to him, he never feels secure with it, but desires repeated demonstrations and proofs of the affection of the other. Because of this insistence on reassurance, and because he is much more willing and able to receive than to give love, he usually does not succeed in any type of love relationship. One who has a receptive orientation to life cannot truly love, and in fact cannot even be an appropriate object of love. A common belief held by people of this orientation is that ideal love between a man and woman is a total blending of the two lives, with each becoming totally immersed in the life of the other. As appealing as this may appear, Fromm believes that such a relationship (which cannot exist for long) is far from ideal. It may be a temporary escape from the sense of aloneness, but the preservation of individual identity is an absolute requirement for productive love. The most productive kind of love is that which allows the fullest development of individuality.

Love and the Exploitative Orientation

To take another's partner or fiancé may seem particularly desirable to the exploitative person. In fact, he may be attracted only to those who are attached. He is more interested in what he can get out of a relationship than in what he can give. Often a relationship is terminated when he ceases to get what he wants, or he may easily change to another love object if there is promise of getting something better. The loyalty of the exploitative type is highly questionable. He may tire easily of one who expects love in return for love. If he is required to make any sacrifice (for instance, remaining loyal to a chronically ill wife), the shallowness of the love relationship may become apparent. Like the spoiled child, the exploitative type sets his own conditions for love, irrespective of the needs and desires of the other person. Productive love cannot stem from a relationship in which one uses the other. A hidden aspect of the values of the exploitative type is the overvaluation of what others have and the underestimation of one's own possessions. This leads to a restless searching for new things and people, a factor which does not make for stable relationships.

Love and the Hoarding Orientation

As the label implies, the hoarding type tends to keep what he has and at the same time to suspect what is new and unknown. He builds up a wall between himself and the outside world and keeps his possessions in his sanctuary. His love relationships are characterized by two extremes, remoteness and jealous possessiveness (Fromm, 1947). Like the receptive type, he wants more to be loved than to love; the difference is that he is much more authoritarian over those who are under his influence. A husband may totally dominate his wife by controlling the flow of money, by keeping close tabs on her friends, or by imposing many tasks upon her. He may deliberately act in an obnoxious manner in the presence of her friends in order to drive them away; thus he increases his control over her. Of course, a woman of the hoarding orientation may do the same to her husband. Often the hoarding person's life is permeated by a fear of losing what he has—a desperate attempt to bring about security, order, and control. Obviously, such possessiveness blocks the unfolding and growth of individuality, and one cannot love fully unless one has developed fully as a person. Just as one cannot utilize his rational faculties when he is not free, so also one cannot love productively under rigid controls and imposed conditions.

Love and the Marketing Orientation

In the marketing orientation, the person views himself as a package to be displayed. Fromm (1947) distinguishes between the *use value* and the *exchange value* of an object. The exchange value is what the object will bring in the marketplace; the use value is its real worth. The real worth may have little to do with the actual exchange value. A man may value a woman because she fits a cultural image. In our culture that might include being physically beautiful (and standards of beauty are also defined by the culture; in some cultures the fatter the woman, the more beautiful she is thought to be). Love based on exchange value rather than real value is superficial and temporary; it is founded on qualities that are bound to change. The marketing type has a terrible dread of growing old because he then loses the value that he had as a young person. What is valued is a persona, a social mask which makes for the "good package." The relationship between two such people is thus rooted in an artificial involvement. There is even the idea that one can buy a new package if the old one loses the qualities which were a part of the original package. The marketing orientation, so common today, creates terrible stresses for the young person. He must keep in style, but not everyone fits the expected pattern; hence there is a great deal of self-depreciation (Hirsch and Keniston, 1970).

LOVE AND THE PRODUCTIVE ORIENTATION

Freud, when asked to indicate the qualities of the mature person, answered that one should be able to work and to love. Certainly, neurotic people commonly suffer from an inability to do either. The love of one who suffers from a nonproductive orientation to living is one-sided, distorted, and not conducive to the mutual development of each of the parties. What then characterizes productive love, and how does it differ from other forms?

Fromm's description of productive love resembles the popular notion of intense liking. Consider the attraction between a man and a woman: she may describe him as cute, sharp, exciting, smooth, groovy, and the like; he may describe her as doll-like, heavenly, sweet, lovable, or neat. In both instances one gets the impression of physical attraction, but there is more, there is an infatuation with personality traits. One may be especially attracted to the smile, the voice, the laugh, the wit, and so on of the other. The attraction is often due more to what the person is or has than to what the person does. Whatever this is called, Fromm does not consider it love. The qualities which make for physical and psychological attraction are merely preconditions which may set the stage for the formation of a love relationship. Productive love is not a mysterious quality which descends on a person when the appropriate object is present and available; there must be certain activities, namely, (1) care, (2) responsibility, (3) respect, and (4) knowledge of each other (Fromm, 1947).

Many young people are concerned about being attractive to members of the other sex. Fromm would counsel them to work at loving. To be loved means to be loving, just as to be interesting means being interested. A loving person will be attractive to others. People are lonely and quite eager to form close relationships: this is one of man's answers to the human situation. Man, whose plight is to feel alone, seeks relatedness, but he also needs to be independent. To be intimately related with someone or something, and at the same time remain an independent individual, one must love productively. Although there are many other forms of relatedness, they fail to satisfy these seemingly contradictory needs.

1. Care.   Care for the loved one involves activity, giving of oneself, doing something, working for another. When one works to produce something, it becomes a part of him. Two people who love each other and care for each other produce something new which neither has alone. A growing thing, the relatedness between them, is created. Again, the reader may comprehend the idea if he keeps in mind that Fromm means by love what others call intense liking.

2. Responsibility.   The notion of responsibility also implies activity. Responsibility to another does not mean domination, control, or depriving another of his autonomy. It means answering to the needs of the loved one. One of the highest forms of loving is a mother's love for her child. She expects nothing in return for her care; she responds to the child's needs, desiring only his growth and development. The mother's love is unconditional, at least during infancy. In a productive love relationship, each accepts the needs of the other as genuine, rather than attempting to change them, and strives to gratify those needs. The integrity and autonomy of the loved one must be guarded; otherwise the love may deteriorate into domination.

3. Respect.   Respect implies concern for the rights of the loved one. A relationship based entirely on an idealized image of the other is bound to falter. The relationship should be based on the real attributes of the person and not on imagined qualities which are projected onto him. If there is a desire to remake the other person, although the one desiring the change may plead strongly that he really loves, the love cannot be real. Some imperfections must be tolerated; some change is always taking place. The two create a new thing, their relationship.

4. Knowledge.   Knowledge can occur on different levels. In loving, one should penetrate to the core of the other, get to the essence of his nature. Here knowing requires experiencing the other in his totality. Knowledge should be objective, not colored by desire and distortion. One must get to know the other as he is.

All four aspects of productive love are interrelated. Self-love, care and responsibility for oneself, self-respect, and self-knowledge are also conditions of productive love.

CRITIQUE OF FROMM'S PRODUCTIVE ORIENTATION

Fromm has been quite bold in attempting to identify specific traits of the various orientations to life. In the case of the nonproductive orientations, he presents the traits in bipolar form, so that we have both the positive and the negative traits associated with each orientation. He is not clear whether the productive orientation includes all the positive traits of each of the nonproductive types, but it appears that this is the case because he does not specify the traits of the productive orientation. Fromm does not really tell us how to move from the negative to the positive traits, except in a highly general manner. We have attempted to concretize some of his ideas in this regard in the Insight section.

Fromm's distinction between the authoritarian and humanistic consciences is a valuable one, but there are problems which he does not deal with adequately. While the nature of the authoritarian conscience is depicted quite clearly, the humanistic conscience seems quite vague and even mystical. Fromm says that the humanistic conscience is the real self. But what is this real self, and how does it come about? Does it include needs, abilities, interests; and are not these subject to learning? What part does culture play? Can we really rely on joy and happiness, defined by Fromm as psychobiological well-being, as valid indicators of the humanistic conscience?

Fromm's idea of humanistic ethics as a guide to healthy living is still more a hope than an actuality. No one has yet solved the perennial problems of birth control, abortion, euthanasia, premarital and extramartial sexuality. Are these good or bad for man? Can we really establish values which are equally good for all people because they are based on human nature?

INSIGHTS FROM FROMM'S IDEAS ON PRODUCTIVENESS

THE PRACTICE OF LOVE

Fromm holds that love is an art which can be acquired through the aid of the following factors.

The Overcoming of Narcissism. In the strict sense of the word, narcissism means excessive selfishness. It may be extended to include an egocentric interpretation of events. Objective observation is not possible when narcissism is present. The person sees everything from the standpoint of his own needs, attitudes, and prejudices. No one ever succeeds completely in eliminating subjective elements, but one can more closely approximate objectivity (Elkind, 1967). Certainly, one can deliberately strive to remove the narcissistic focus. Preoccupation with oneself and distortion caused by selfish desires block the possibility of productive love (Fromm, 1947). Everyone must deal with the narcissistic aspect of his personality. It is probably the most outstanding hindrance to productive love. Self-love and selfishness for Fromm are not the same. In fact, they are opposites.

Faith.   One may distinguish between rational and irrational faith. Rational faith is grounded in sound observation and reasoning, while irrational faith is blind trust in an authority, or wish-fulfillment. Fromm believes that faith can be developed as a trait of personality. It is an essential aspect of productive love (Fromm, 1947). One must have faith that his love will create love in another. This requires faith in oneself, a conviction that one can trust his own judgments. Suspicion is the opposite of faith and can also become a general personality trait. The need for absolute certainty is detrimental to faith. Living requires a certain degree of trust in oneself and in others, as Erikson (1968) points out. One can never take full control of things: the diligent mother must have some faith in her child. She cannot protect him from every conceivable danger without reducing him to a vegetable. Obviously, she should not be foolhardy and demand from the child responsibility that is beyond his capacity. Even in the middle ground between these two extremes, there is an element of uncertainty that can be tolerated only through faith. One teaches the child some precautions, and then one must have faith that these will be followed.

An interesting aspect of faith in a loved one is that it tends to foster that which we desire in the other. If a man trusts his wife and child, they may live up to the trust, whereas if he expects them to disappoint him, they probably will. Loved ones may live up either to faith or to the lack of it; thus faith is more productive than its opposite. Again there must be a rational basis for faith: one would not trust a two year old with a large sum of money she received as a gift. Through practice one can increase his ability to have faith in himself and others. Fromm would counsel us to look for instances in ourselves of lack of faith and to try to understand the reasons for them. Consider qualities within yourself that make you distrustful or doubting. If you have to choose between having faith in an unknown future and assuming a gloomy outlook, since you are dealing with unknowns anyway, it would seem much more beneficial to proceed with faith. You may question the meaning and value of going to college and become discouraged and depressed, but if you have faith that the benefits will come, the work will get done without as much pain.

Fromm believes that man has a social, loving nature, but it can be brought out only under certain cultural conditions. No culture exists which fits man well. Capitalism, for example, at best stresses fairness rather than love. A business deal is good if each party gets something and maybe gives in to the same degree: one does not benefit at the expense of the other. But loving goes further than fairness: it implies care and concern for others. Society should promote a sense of brotherly love in all. Men should work harmoniously with a sense of mutual concern. Caring for one another should be a widespread condition in a society. This is the only hope in the face of human loneliness and alienation. The development of greater communal spirit is Fromm's (1955) answer to man's situation.

FREEDOM FROM VERSUS FREEDOM TO

Fromm (1941) offers us an interesting insight into an important human concern through his distinction between freedom from and freedom to. This distinction refers to the negative and positive aspects of freedom. There is a significant difference between being free *from* external controls, regulations, or restrictions and being free *to* use our capacities, abilities, and resources. Being able to make productive use of capabilities is the most liberating type of freedom for meeting the problems associated with being human. To be free from submission to authority does not guarantee that the positive freedom will occur. Freedom to do things is an outcome of the productive orientation.

MEETING FROMM'S FIVE HUMAN NEEDS

1. Relatedness. How can we satisfy our need for relatedness? Fromm tells us to cultivate the art of loving. Love, and hence relatedness, can be encouraged through a concentrated effort to get to know another person. A loving attitude is strengthened by caring enough for the other to do things for him. Love is also fostered by being sensitive to the other's needs, likes, and dislikes and adjusting one's behavior to them. Finally, love is promoted by respecting the other—giving him positive regard, accepting him as he is respecting his individuality and uniqueness. These are the attributes of true love, productive love as Fromm terms it. This type of relatedness cannot help but engender love in return from at least some others. Just as hate begets hate, so love begets love.

2. Transcendence. How can we overcome dependency, passivity, the pressures of immediate circumstances? Fromm suggests that we use all our abilities productively. He agrees with Maslow's problem orientation to life in his own notion of intelligence, by which he means the use of our abilities to solve the problems of living. This implies profiting from past mistakes, looking at all possible alternatives before making a decision, and dealing unemotionally with personal challenges. We should use our ability to reason, according to Fromm, as a means of perceiving things as they really are. We may contrast and compare, analyze and synthesize, integrate and coordinate the impressions we receive. Agreeing with Kelly (1955), Fromm holds that we should take the scientist's approach by forming tentative constructs of the events in our world, and then testing these through the deductions derived from them. In brief, we can use our abilities to meet our needs, if we develop these abilities as fully as possible. Like other personality theorists, Fromm places great stress on active and skilled participation in one's world.

In characteristic fashion, Fromm emphasizes the role of productive love as a means of overcoming the feeling of being trapped and victimized by the environment. Thus transcendence is achieved by productive use of reason, intelligence, skills, and emotions. The whole person is involved through thought, feeling, and action.

3. Rootedness. How can we promote a sense of belongingness? Fromm suggests involvement (similar to Allport's idea of self-extension) in something bigger than oneself. Examples might be one's church and religion, a social or civic organization, one's family, a cause. One should especially appreciate the importance of customs, traditions, places that one enjoys. Cherishing friends and acquaintances can help to satisfy the need for rootedness. Establishing one's own traditions and customs can also help to satisfy this need: for example, a family dinner together every Sunday. In an unfamiliar environment, such as a new job, one may gain a sense of rootedness simply by bringing some familiar objects to his place of work: a set of pipes, a plant, or a book rack. However it is accomplished, rootedness is one of man's requirements for productive living.

4. Identity.   How can we develop a sense of identity? Fromm says that we gain a sense of identity through creative and productive activities. We may become identified by our skills, our accomplishments, our professions. He also points out that productive love helps to foster identity because it provides for an intimate and enjoyable union between two people and at the same time fosters a sense of individuality and uniqueness. I experience vital powers in myself when I demonstrate love for another, and the love I receive affirms my identity and sense of worthiness. It should be noted that an act of loving in itself has value for personality functioning, even if it is not reciprocated.

5. Frame of Reference.   How can we promote better understanding of ourselves and of the world? Fromm would agree with Frankl (1955) on the importance of meaning in man's life. There are some things about which we are quite clear. Understanding and meaningfulness would be enhanced if we periodically reminded ourselves of those things which are important to us. Counting our blessings is one means of doing so. We may count our blessings in a negative way by considering all the things that could have happened but did not: "I cried because I had no shoes, until I met a man with no feet." A more positive approach is to affirm the value of the things we consider desirable: reviewing our achievements and instances of good fortune. Another way to foster understanding is to cultivate patience with ambiguities and deficiencies of knowledge. Learning about ourselves and our world is an ongoing process. The mysteries of life may never be known, but there can be a continual improvement in understanding and meaning. Again, we can look to science as a guide with the expectation that the same techniques and safeguards applied to the study of the universe can be applied to our own lives.

SIGNIFICANT QUOTATIONS FROM FROMM

Indeed, to be able to concentrate means to be able to be alone with oneself—and this ability is precisely a condition for the ability to love. If I am attached to another person because I cannot stand on my own two feet, he or she may be a life saver, but the relationship is not one of love. Paradoxically, the ability to be alone is the condition for the ability to love (1956, p. 112).

The deepest need of man, then, is to overcome his separateness, to leave the prison of his aloneness. The *absolute* failure to achieve this aim means insanity because the panic of complete isolation can be overcome only by such a radical withdrawal from the world outside that the feeling of separation disappears—because the world outside, from which one is separated, has disappeared (1956, p. 9).

Objectivity requires not only seeing the object as it is, but also seeing oneself as one is, i.e., being aware of the particular constellation in which one finds oneself as an observer related to the object of observation. . . . Objectivity does not mean detachment, it means respect; that is, the ability not to distort and to falsify things, persons, and oneself (1947, p. 105).*

Happiness and unhappiness are so much a state of our total personality that bodily reactions are frequently more expressive of them than our conscious feeling. The drawn face of a person, listlessness, tiredness, or physical symptoms like headaches . . . are frequent expression of unhappiness, just as physical feelings of "well-being" can be "symptoms" of happiness. Indeed, our body is less capable of being deceived about the state of happiness than our mind (1947, p. 181).*

In the following passage, Fromm affirms the frequently overlooked principle that violation of psychological laws can be just as injurious as violation of physical laws:

While a person may succeed in ignoring or rationalizing destructive impulses, he—his organism as it were—cannot help reacting and being affected by acts which contradict the very principle by which his life and all life are sustained. We find that the destructive person is unhappy even if he has succeeded in attaining the aims of his destructiveness, which undermines his own existence. Conversely, no healthy person can keep from admiring, and being affected by, manifestations of decency, love, and courage; for these are the forces on which his own life rests (1947, p. 225).*

SUMMARY

1.   Fromm holds that ethics can teach us much of value about the ideal life, if it is brought into line with scientific findings. For Fromm, ideal human existence is healthy existence. Value judgments are the basis of our actions and expectations. Neurosis is the inability to resolve conflicts of values. The source of norms for ethical conduct lies within man's nature; thus good conduct is equivalent to health. Fromm holds that the productive orientation to life is ethical; nonproductive orientations are unethical.

2.   In authoritarian ethics, some external power figure imposes laws and rules. Compliance stems from fear of authority. In contrast, humanistic ethics is based on the requirements of man's nature. Failure to develop potentials and fullness is the capital crime of humanistic ethics.

3.   Hedonism holds that pleasure and pain can be the final test of the worth of values and norms. Emotions are indicators of what is good and bad for us. Antihedonists point to instances in which emotions are poor guides to follow. Emotions interfere with reason. Fromm proposes a modified form of hedonism which recognizes different types of pleasure.

4.   One of the requirements of being human is the passionate pursuit of something; man is driven to find meaning in what he does and believes. Man must face unsettling and unavoidable discrepancies in life. For example, he desires immortality, yet recognizes his imminent death. Such a condition is

---

*© 1947 by Erich Fromm. Reprinted by permission of Holt, Rinehart and Winston, Inc.

termed an existential dichotomy. The dichotomy lies in the very nature of man. Problems such as war and the uneven distribution of wealth are termed historical dichotomies. They are seen by Fromm as soluble, manmade difficulties.

5. Conscience is a regulating agency within personality, founded in man's ability to observe, reflect, and evaluate himself. In an authoritarian conscience, the dictates of external power figures (such as parents, teachers, and government authorities) are internalized. Submission to authority creates a condition of security for the individual possessing an authoritarian conscience. A humanistic conscience stems from the ideals and values of the real self rather than from some external source. The basis for such a conscience is one's obligation to oneself. Conforming to such a conscience is equivalent to being the real self. An inordinate fear of death or of growing old, or of others' disapproval arises from ignoring the humanistic conscience, because the person has not lived his own life.

6. Happiness and unhappiness may be unconscious as well as conscious. These states entail a total organismic response. They are indicators of right and wrong behavior. Productive living accompanies joy and happiness.

7. Behavior traits are identified by an observer while character traits are primarily motivational in nature, being more central to the personality. A character type is a constellation of traits. One's character becomes fixed and represents habitual ways of thinking, feeling, and acting. Character types may be productive or nonproductive.

8. The following are nonproductive orientations to life, representing a failure in one of life's basic tasks:

Receptive orientation   Hoarding orientation
Exploitative orientation   Marketing orientation

There may be a blending of such character orientations. All nonproductive orientations may move toward the positive end of the continuum if constructive trends in the personality are sufficiently strong.

9. The productive orientation is a mode of relatedness to the world in which one develops his potentials as fully as possible. Two basic modes of dealing with the world are knowing and loving. Productivity does not mean working compulsively. Activity which fosters development of potentials is productive.

10. The craving for love is a basic striving of man, as it solves his condition of separation and aloneness. Love is an active process of the total personality. All types of productive love are rooted in activity and involve caring, responsibility, respect, and knowledge of the loved one. Any personality defect affects the ability to love.

11. According to Fromm, every person possesses five peculiarly human needs that must be met if insanity is to be avoided. These are the needs for relatedness, transcendence, rootedness, identity, and frame of reference.

SUGGESTED READINGS

Fromm, Erich. Escape from Freedom. New York: Holt, Rinehart and Winston, 1941.
    Considered Fromm's most important work, this book is an exploration of the causes of man's submission to tyranny.

Man for Himself. New York: Holt, Rinehart and Winston, 1947.
    In this work, Fromm inquires into the psychology of ethics, considering the role of morality in the world today.

Psychoanalysis and Religion. New Haven: Yale University Press, 1950.
    Both priests and analysts are summoned to respond to the challenges of technocracy's spiritual wasteland.

The Sane Society. New York: Holt, Rinehart and Winston, 1955.
    Both a psychoanalytic and socioanalytic work, The Sane Society considers the effects of contemporary Western culture on the mental health of Western people.

The Art of Loving. New York: Harper and Row, 1956.
    In this popular book, Fromm presents tangible steps for fostering the ability to love productively. Many of his major ideas are introduced briefly: it represents a good introduction to Fromm.

REFERENCES

Alper, T. G., Levin, V. S., and Klein, M. H. Authoritarian vs. humanistic conscience. J. Pers. 32:313–33, 1964.

Brandt, R. B. Ethical Theory. Englewood Cliffs, New Jersey: Prentice-Hall, 1959.

Elkind, D. Egocentrism in adolescence. Child Dev. 38:1025–34, 1967.

Erikson, E. Childhood and Society. New York: W. W. Norton and Company, 1963.

Erikson, E. Identity: Youth and Crisis. New York: W. W. Norton and Company, 1968.

Frankl, V. The Doctor of the Soul. New York: Alfred A. Knopf, 1955.

Fromm, E. Escape from Freedom. New York: Holt, Rinehart and Winston, 1941.

Fromm, E. Man for Himself. New York: Holt, Rinehart and Winston, 1947.

Fromm, E. The Sane Society. New York: Holt, Rinehart and Winston, 1955.

Fromm, E. The Art of Loving. New York: Harper and Row, 1956.

Fromm, E. Values, psychology, and human existence. In Coleman, J. C., Personality Dynamics and Effective Behavior. Chicago: Scott, Foresman and Company, 1960, Pp. 522–27.

Fromm, E. The Crisis of Psychoanalysis. New York: Holt, Rinehart and Winston, 1970.

Fromm, E., and Maccoby, M. Social Character in a Mexican Village. Englewood Cliffs, New Jersey: Prentice-Hall, 1970.

Harlow, H. F. Learning to Love. San Francisco: Albion Publishing Company, 1971.

Hirsch, S. J., and Keniston, K. Psychosocial issues in talented college dropouts. Psychiatry 33:1–20, 1970.

Hoffman, M. L. Conscience, personality, and socialization techniques. Hum. Devel. 13:90–126, 1970.

Holt, J. How Children Fail. New York: Pitman Publishing Corporation, 1964.

Kelly, G. A. The Psychology of Personal Constructs, Vols. 1 and 2. New York: W. W. Norton and Company, 1955.

Lifton, R. J. History and Human Survival. New York: Random House, 1970.

Maddi, S. R. Personality Theories: A Comparative Analysis, rev. ed. Homewood, Illinois: Dorsey Press, 1972.

Nietzsche, F. W. Beyond Good and Evil. Chicago: Henry Regnery Company, 1955.

CHAPTER 16

The Individuated Man

Carl Gustav Jung

Carl G. Jung (1875–1961)

BIOGRAPHY AND OVERVIEW

Born in Switzerland in 1875, Carl Gustav Jung was one of the pioneers of modern psychiatry. He made significant contributions to personality theory and psychotherapy, particularly with respect to the role of the unconscious in the life of man. Early in his medical career, he was influenced by the ideas of Sigmund Freud and for several years was one of his disciples. But his interest in the deeper layers of the unconscious—the *collective unconscious*—together with his rejection of the extreme position which Freud assigned to sexuality in man, eventually separated them; as a result Jung formulated his own school of psychology, *analytical psychology.*

Jung explored many aspects of man that others had not yet considered. Like Freud, he studied his own dreams, fantasies, experiences, and behaviors. He sought to discover the fundamental origins of the psyche. For more than 60 years he studied his patients. He examined such diverse phenomena as the mythology of primitive people, the religious and ceremonial practices of ancients and moderns, the dreams and fantasies of psychotics, and medieval alchemy. He even investigated the occult: prophetic dreams, mediums, flying saucers, and extrasensory perception. Although he had been trained in the biological and physical sciences, he was not afraid to tackle things that were apparently outside the science of his day. He died in 1961, working until the very end. His last work was finished just 10 days before his death.

One of the recurrent themes in Jung's writings is modern man's loss of contact with the unconscious foundations of his personality. Although Jung certainly had a profound respect for the achievements of science and for the human reasoning capacities that have made them possible, he felt that man nevertheless remains an enigma. Many complain that their lives are empty and meaningless. Much of the wonder and awe that the primitive mind found in his world is missing in contemporary life. Jung believed that contemporary man needs explanations, beliefs, and mysteries that will make his life meaningful.

Jung also introduced the term *individuation* to designate the full differentiation and integration of personality. As one matures, one undergoes the process of individuation during which potentials are fulfilled, experiences expanded, and self-realization is attained. When selfhood is achieved, ego and self become identical and self becomes the core of the psyche (1964). To achieve individuation, certain basic tasks must be accomplished in sequence. (A person undergoing Jungian therapy would be aided in dealing with the same tasks.) The individual may be informed both about his progress and about the direction he should follow by changes in the characters and occurrences of his dreams and in the events of his environment. One of the basic tasks of the individuation process is the acquisition of self-knowledge. All the components of the personality must be allowed as complete a development as possible (Jung, 1954b). Any one-sided emphasis will produce personality disturbances.

Self-knowledge begins with an exploration of the *persona,* which for now may be taken simply as the sum total of social roles *(social masks).* All too frequently we believe that there is nothing more to personality than these social roles. Jung pointed out that masks, although essential for effective living, are not the full personality; indeed, they are not even the most important part.

A further analysis of the personality requires an exploration of the *shadow.* The shadow comprises the undesirable aspects of personality. We are all aware of some of our faults, but many others are kept out of awareness. We cannot become individuated persons unless we learn about these shadow elements. They are a vital part of the personality and they must be dealt with, either by changing them, or by accepting them as part of the self, or by integrating them into the mainstream of life.

After one becomes acquainted with his social personality and with his shadow side, he can take the next step, which is to become acquainted with and deal with his opposite-sex qualities. Jung held that every man has an *anima,* composed of feminine traits, in his personality make-up. Every woman has an *animus,* which consists of masculine traits. An individuated man must know his feminine traits and integrate them with the other components of his personality: the ego, the persona, and the shadow. A woman must similarly perceive and integrate her masculine traits. A complete person is a balance of male and female qualities; or at least, while the male or the female qualities may predominate, they are tempered by the opposite attributes.

As one learns about his social personality, his shadow personality, and his feminine or masculine personality, he is becoming more and more knowledgeable of his unconscious. His personality is expanding; his awareness is increasing. The ego is no longer the center of the personality, and the self emerges as the new center of control. The person has become his real self. He is more in touch with his inner nature and can better meet his *archetypal needs*. Archetypes are inborn predispositions that must be satisfied: for instance, to worship power, to relate to members of the opposite sex, to experience a god-image. The individuated person expresses his archetypes in his daily affairs.

In addition to the tasks noted above, one should strike a balance between one's extroverted and introverted orientations. Furthermore, one should avoid being too intellectual, too sensitive and evaluative, too literal-minded, or too intuitive. The key word is balance among all the systems of personality.

Because of the vital role that personality plays in adaptation and growth, there is much we can learn from Jung's elaborate system of personality concepts. What are the components of personality and how do they operate? How are they related to one another? What conditions cause faulty development and other disturbances? What is healthy growth? What should the ideal of personality growth be? Let us now examine the answers to these questions in more detail.

THE INFLUENCE OF THE UNCONSCIOUS UPON CONSCIOUSNESS

Much goes on "underneath the surface," and what appear to the individual as conscious thoughts, desires, and emotional responses to specific situations are often the end products of unconscious processes. Ideas and images which cannot be traced to immediate happenings are striking examples of the operation of the unconscious. A person may visualize a scene or draw a picture resembling typical mythological events of which he has no knowledge. Jung traced these parallels assiduously. He took dream images and showed their resemblance to images in the Old and New Testaments and a great number of other sources, including primitive religious ceremonies. How can he account for the similarity between the production of a contemporary city dweller and the symbolic expression of people removed by centuries and great distance? Certainly the phenomenon cannot be explained on the basis of the specific contents of consciousness or learning built up in the individual's lifetime. Usually the person who creates the drawing or the artistic representation or the dream fantasy has no idea of what it signifies (Jung, 1959a). Jung believed that the contents and operations of the unconscious deserve serious consideration, because so much of conscious content and activity is influenced by the unconscious. He proposed the intriguing concept of a collective aspect of the psyche, shared by all men and manifesting itself in behavior, irrespective of culture. What we experience consciously comes from the experience of our senses, our personal unconscious, and this collective unconscious; often conscious contents have no discernible relation to any experiences in the individual's history.

THE TOPOGRAPHY OF THE UNCONSCIOUS

The unconscious layer may be divided into the personal unconscious, with *complexes* as the primary structures, and the collective unconscious, with *archetypes* as the primary structures. The total personality includes all layers of consciousness and unconsciousness.

Complexes

The personal unconscious is accumulated through individual experiences after birth. For the most part, it consists of unacceptable impulses, wishes, memories which cannot be integrated by the ego, and experiences which have registered psychologically but not consciously. In the broadest sense, the personal unconscious includes all stored impressions, accessible or not. One of the significant components of the personal unconscious is the complex.

A complex may act like a personality within the personality. It may be thought of as a network of thoughts, feelings, and attitudes held together by a nuclear idea or *core disposition* (Jung, 1960). Jung referred to this network of ideas and feelings as the *constellating power* of the complex. Complexes vary in scope and in the extent to which they are a determining force in the personality. Jung (1918) developed a test to identify complexes, known as the *word association test.* He gave his subjects a list of words and asked them to respond with the first word that came to awareness. The nature of the response could reveal something about the nature of the complex. If the *response latency* (the time for the response to occur) was slow, Jung believed that the word was connected with a complex. If the response was *rare* (not the usual response made to the word), again it would indicate the presence of the complex.

Complexes may be easily aroused by a certain class of stimuli. Many ideas are usually linked together by the core of the complex. For instance, a man may have a woman complex: almost anything can set it off; a great many of his activities are in the service of this complex; no matter what the conversation, he finds a way of getting back to the subject of women. A complex may be so powerful that it resembles a distinct personality that operates outside the control of the ego when it is activated. Even when a person knows that he is the victim of a complex, he has little control over it. Most often the core is unconscious, and therefore doing something to overcome it is very difficult. A complex disrupts ongoing behavior; the person finds himself doing or saying things that he did not intend.

The reader may be assisted in understanding the notion of complex by recalling Allport's concept of the central trait. But while Allport is concerned with core dispositions that are conscious, Jung stressed the unconscious dispositions.

The Nature and Origin of Archetypes

The collective unconscious consists of thought-forms that are inherited by each individual. These thought-forms are archetypes, predispositions to have certain experiences (Jung, 1959a). Consider your view of God; each person has a different view of what the Almighty Being is, although he has never seen Him. Take another notion: each man has had many experiences with women, and each man has a different idea of the "perfect" woman who can never be encountered in real life. Each woman, of course, also has some idea of the "perfect" man. Such images are not based exclusively on one's personal life experiences, although they are dependent on them; they are found universally. Other human beings with widely varied life experiences at other times and places have had similar images. Just as the mind is tied to sensory inputs, so also the structure of the psyche affects the types of experiences one is capable of having.

Under certain conditions, archetypes may act as complexes and function as separate identities. One instance is the complete takeover of a man's personality by his feminine self or anima, so that his ego ceases to function in its normal roles. The individual in such instances is "possessed" by an archetype and thinks, feels, and behaves in accordance with the nature of that archetype.

The collective unconscious, unlike the complex, is inherited. Jung proposed the bold hypothesis that there are two sources of experiences: one outside, reaching the person through his senses, and the other within, coming through the mediation of the preformed collective unconscious. Just as we inherit a physical structure that has a long history of evolution and takes a certain form, so also we inherit psychic structures which have a definite form. An archetype is like an "idea-form" which is actualized when a person has an appropriate experience.

Jung (1959a) seems to have viewed the archetypes in two senses: as *predispositions* to have certain experiences and as *idea-forms* that can become a part of *actual experiences*. In the first sense, archetypes do not have a concrete existence. A disposition to believe in a deity is only a potentiality until it is given an actual imaginal form, but conversely, one must have the disposition before one can have the "God" experience. One can play any combination of tunes on a piano, but it never sounds like an organ. One cannot have experiences for which there is no potentiality: learning depends upon pre-existing potentials. One cannot teach a chimpanzee to use speech meaningfully because he does not have the structures necessary for such activity. Even when the structures are present, actual experiences are needed to give the predisposition concrete form. The mother archetype requires an actual mother experience to take a definite shape.

The child views his parents not as they are objectively, but as a result of the combination of his experiences of them and the archetypes that are brought into play. The parents are the most important people in the child's life, and their effects on the child greatly determine his future course. An experience is interpreted within the framework of archetypes, but the archetypes cause a distortion of external reality if the experience does not correspond with the external object. A child gradually learns what his parents are really like as persons. For many people the influence of the parents long outlives their actual control, and this is the result of the parent archetype. For some the image of the parents even lives an independent existence in the personality, and this can cause many disturbances in relationships with others. A man may have difficulty accepting the authority of his boss because his resentment of his father lives on, as if he were still a child and his boss were really his father. This irrational behavior is due to the persistence of the father archetype, which operates outside the influence of the ego and is not easily controlled. Until the operation of projection is reduced—that is, until the man recognizes his projection and deals with his boss more objectively—the ego will not be in control and the victim will be dominated by an archetype. The more limited a man's consciousness, the more likely it is that he will encounter archetypes which are projected onto others, making other people seem superhuman, extraordinary, and endowed with magical qualities. He may feel that everyone is better than he is; everyone has more charm, can deal with problems more effectively, lives a happier life. Certain people are endowed with great power and mystery: the doctor, the priest, members of the other sex, even older members of the same sex. In this context, projection should be understood as attributing qualities to others which they do not possess, and which arise from within the individual who projects them.

In their second sense of idea-forms, the archetypes may be understood as *universal thought-forms* when they play a greater part in a person's ideas or images than they should, that is, when experiences in a real world are inadequately formed.

Jung was quite emphatic about the distinction between pre-existing ideas and pre-existing idea-forms. Archetypal images or ideas do not simply emerge spontaneously, but rather are aroused by experiences with events in the external world which are fit into idea-forms. The resulting image or concept is at first an overgeneralized or inadequate representation of the external event. The image depicts more an archetype than the real event. With further learning, the image is modified, and more closely approximates the real event. The child eventually comes to perceive significant people as they are. If the learning experiences are abnormal, the concept does not undergo the appropriate change. Thus the person is dominated by an archetype. He may, for example, overvalue authority. In Jung's system, reality orientation is essential to effective living.

Table 16–1 demonstrates the manner in which a particular concept is formed, as a combination of archetypes and actual experiences.

The archetypal image may so dominate the perceptual and interpretive functions of the ego that it seriously distorts judgment. The father archetype, as we have seen, may distort a man's perception of his boss, primarily through the mechanism of *projection* (see also p. 480). He does not really see him as the person he is, but adds elements embodied by the father archetype which dominates his ego. Adaptation to the environment obviously requires perception that approximates real events; thus real experiences can lessen the power of the primitive archetypes. When the archetypes are properly modified, they as-

TABLE 16-1   ROLE OF ARCHETYPES IN EXPERIENCE AND BEHAVIOR

Some General Roles Assigned to Women by Men	One Man's Specific Concept of Woman, Based on His Experiences of the Feminine Role as Nurturant Companion
Temptress	Care from devoted mother
Successful career woman	Solace and comfort when troubled
Nurturant person	Praise for accomplishments
Companion	Physical demonstrations of affection
Lover	Good human relationship with mother
Sexual partner	Mother perceived as perfect woman
	Maternal behavior as ideal feminine quality

Psychologists have long noted the tendency to stereotype and overgeneralize people and events. The image of the family doctor is generalized to all doctors. The stereotype which results when the archetype is activated does not really correspond to any doctor. Where does it come from? It is a generic image or archetype that was formed in man's racial past—the experience with healing persons. The perception of one's own mother becomes a stereotype for all mothers. Policemen may be regarded as all alike. The generalizations or stereotypes are subject to modification through learning, although stereotypes are remarkably resistant to change; e.g., prejudices toward members of the opposite sex, different races, and the like (Stouffer et al., 1949). Jung would explain the tendency to stereotype and overgeneralize in terms of archetypes.

The feminine archetype is easily activated by a woman who makes an impression on the particular man in the table. He is likely to find that aspect of a woman most attractive and most characteristic of femininity. One who had different experiences with his own mother and sisters would have a different stereotype of women.

sist in the process of perceiving correctly. Under normal conditions, for instance, the father archetype helps a man to understand and accept authority; he does not lose his autonomy and feeling of worth. It is significant that archetypes produce abnormalities in experience and behavior in two ways: (1) if they are not moderated by real experiences, and (2) if they are not given adequate expression.

The Operation of Archetypes.   The operation of archetypes is analogous to the operation of conscious recognition. Suppose you meet someone you like. You pay special attention to his appearance. The next time you meet him, you easily recognize him. A memory trace has been brought into play, and it helps to make the identification. If it were not present, you obviously would not recognize the person. In the case of archetypes, there is an inherent predisposition which serves as the memory trace. Consider belief in an almighty being, which has existed all over the world from time immemorial. Why did this occur? Because its occurrence was easy; there was a kind of memory trace that could be easily activated by certain conditions. A man does not have to learn to love a woman. As he gets to know her, he may love her more and more, but the knowledge is not the cause; it is a condition which is necessary. A readiness to respond to woman is within man's nature. Men have always followed leaders eagerly, but there would be no leaders unless there were a tendency to follow them on the part of some people. Each species of animal has certain characteristic tendencies which are not learned; man should not be excluded.

The Frustration of Archetypes. Events of the world activate a child's primitive archetypes; thus his world is fully of mystery, magic, fantastic events, and highly idealized characters. As the ego functions develop, and with increasing experience with the objects and events of the real world, the archetypes are modified to correspond to reality. Parents and teachers are eventually perceived as ordinary mortals. But if the child's learning experiences are abnormal, the archetypes may persist and interfere with ego activities.

The same pattern applies to the adult as to the child. A man ordinarily replaces his need for a father by his boss and company and by his patriotism. A woman replaces her need for a father by a husband who can provide the security which her father once supplied. Under normal conditions we do not acutely experience the operation of archetypes. As long as our needs are being met and there is harmony between the conscious and unconscious spheres of our psyches, with all aspects of personality given the opportunity to develop and function, we attain individuation and live effectively. But when important activities and requirements are not carried out, the effects of the archetypes are felt as symptoms of illness. Some problems that are widespread in our day may be seen as failures to find adequate expression for archetypes. We are experiencing a loss of trust and faith in our leaders. The government no longer holds its authority for many. The consequence of the lack of a "father" is the sense of meaninglessness that is so common among the young (Keniston, 1965). The father archetype may attach itself to political and philosophical movements that seem to offer a great hope for the future and for individual fulfillment.

Thus though archetypes are most strikingly present in those pathological conditions in which they completely take over the psyche, they also underlie the lives of "normal" people. Jung believed that complete individuation is an ideal state that takes many years to attain, and that few civilized people ever even approximate.*

THE CULTURE AND THE COLLECTIVE UNCONSCIOUS

As we have seen, the most important task of the growing organism is to become an individual. The biggest danger is that of being smothered—both by the requirements of social living, which demand and reward conformity, and by the collective unconscious, which can overwhelm and take over the ego. Individuation means freedom from these oppressive forces. Such freedom can be achieved through a strong ego and a realm of consciousness that includes all significant aspects of the personality.

---

*Jung's archetypal needs—the needs for meaningfulness, belief in something greater than man, guidance, authority, mothering and fathering, belief in something that makes our lives intelligible—may remind us of Fromm's five basic human needs and Maslow's metaneeds.

The environment, by means of the culture, forces the growing child into certain prescribed patterns. The child has little choice in his early years when all his decisions are made for him. When he does acquire the power of decision and judgment, he still must give up his freedom to a great extent in order to keep out of trouble and, more importantly, to meet his needs. It is much easier to conform than to be an individual; thus most people are swallowed up by their cultures. The ego must also adjust to the pressures of the collective psyche. If one is captured by the God archetype, and if it takes the form of an "ism," such as communism or capitalism or whatever, he becomes a revolutionary and gives up everything (all his potentialities for satisfying living) under the power of this archetype. Whereas the power of the culture is visible, the force of the archetypes is quite invisible. Neither culture nor the archetypes should hold sway. When development is smooth, neither is in command, but rather the ego deals with each satisfactorily.

The archetypes are instinctive requirements: they are promptings from within ourselves. Failure to take account of them, like lack of knowledge or attention to external forces, endows them with power over us. A man who has not outgrown his childlike dependence upon his mother is, without realizing it, the victim of a force that can ruin his most important relationships. Jung believed that a woman who gives up the prospect of marriage for a career may be violating an inner requirement and becomes a victim of this force. (Jung's own wife, to whom he was devoted, bore him five children and yet was a practicing analyst.) She may experience a great deal of unhappiness in later life. The archetypes may take over the ego when they are not being satisfied in behavior. They cannot be ignored without damage to the personality. The ego must master both external and internal forces. Ignoring the demands of the two sources of influence is the surest way to bring about an unhealthy state.

COMPENSATION

Jung believed that the collective unconscious and the personal unconscious make up for or correct the excesses or omissions of the conscious; it is in this sense of a *corrective* that compensation is to be understood in Jung's (1953) usage. The collective unconscious contains the "wisdom of the ages" and is often communicated in dreams. The dream reveals the problem as well as the solution. The unconscious serves as a regulatory mechanism to curb the conscious. In the waking state, a period of intense emotional activity may be followed by a state of quiescence during which emotional reactivity is deadened. Dreams are compensations for conscious disturbances.

If the conscious aspect is one-sided, as when a man identifies so completely with his persona that he does not look within for anything else, the unconscious will help to correct the defect. In his dreams the man will play an introverted role. The dream actually draws attention to the one-sided slant in his life, and although he does not necessarily recognize its meaning, it does its work, just as a medicine may work to cure an illness, whether we understand how or not.

Jung held that compensation occurs if there is moderate overdevelopment of one component of personality. The unconscious works harmoniously with consciousness by exerting a corrective counterforce. Certain physiological reactions of the body, for instance, compensate for a state of disequilibrium: when the skin is broken, fluids are localized at the site of the injury to permit the restorative and generative processes to occur. Sometimes the reaction is ineffective and causes more damage than the original injury. The unconscious ceases to compensate and actually becomes highly destructive if there is an extreme overemphasis on conscious aspects.

While the unconscious normally compensates for the one-sided character of the conscious, the intervention of the ego is usually required. Without such intervention, the operation of the unconscious may be insufficient or may become destructive rather than compensatory. The person may experience a loss of desire: nothing seems worthwhile. Or there may be an intensification of desire, but for the wrong things. Forces in the unconscious interfere with the operation of the ego: this is experienced as mild suffering in its moderate form, and in its extreme as a total collapse of the personality, possibly culminating in suicide. For example, a devoted husband, in his forties, might break up his home by running off with a secretary who is half his age. The cause might be a shadow aspect of his personality that was never properly expressed.

What one is consciously, he is the opposite unconsciously. The introvert wishes that he could be more involved with people and things, but he is also afraid, or he may assume a superior air in relation to those who need people. The intellectual is in danger of emotional upheaval because he has not done much with his emotional side. Again Jung stressed the idea of balance. One should be both extroverted and introverted, sentient and intuitive, rational and emotional. Imbalance hinders enjoyment and productivity at best, and may destroy the personality at worst.

THE ANIMA AND THE ANIMUS

The anima is the feminine aspect of a man, while the animus is the masculine aspect of a woman. Jung seems to have used the terms in two senses: to denote the masculine or feminine qualities in man or woman, and to describe archetypal images of femininity and masculinity. Unlike the sociologists, who make femininity and masculinity cultural products *Jung* (1953) *held to clearly delineated traits for the sexes.* The psychology of man is radically different from the psychology of woman. Jung's views of masculinity and femininity coincide pretty well with the traditional notions: for example, he saw men as decisive and rational and women as emotional and intuitive; men are aggressive while women are passive (Garai, 1970). Cultural inversions, such as homosexuality and mixing of roles, are distortions of human nature.

THE DEVELOPMENT OF THE ANIMA

The anima in a boy is an inborn disposition to respond to women. The mother is the first woman in the boy's life and thus receives the projection of the anima. Both in her caring and motherly role and in her role as a disciplinarian, she is greatly overestimated. Thus there is an ambivalence toward her: both love and fascination, and fear and hatred. The qualities which her son perceives are those he has assigned or projected onto her; no human could possibly be or fulfill the image the boy has. Gradually the anima is withdrawn from the mother, although never completely, and the child changes his evaluation of his mother as superhuman. If this process occurs normally, the anima image will assist the boy in knowing and dealing with women. If there is a disturbance in the boy's relation to his mother, however, the anima will exist as a disposition to misperceive women, remaining in readiness to be attributed to any woman who makes an impression. The attributes which are perceived are those of the anima—a stereotype of woman—but the man does not know it. He has entered an enchanted state by falling in love with the anima representation of a woman. His response is not to her real qualities but to what he has projected onto her. If the contact with the mother is highly unpleasant, the negative image of the anima will be personified, and the result will be a harsh view of women. The man may distrust women; he feels uncomfortable with them and does not understand the feminine personality. He always does things which go against the woman's natural expectations, as when a husband does not know how to be sentimental and responsive to his wife.

A man who is dominated by his anima is in a state of discontent and spreads discontent all around him, like a petulant child. It should be noted that Jung distinguished not only between masculine and feminine traits but also between desirable and undesirable masculine and feminine traits. He did *not* demean the role of woman. An overemphasis on the persona (a supermasculine front) may impede the normal functioning of the anima, with a resulting loss of vitality, flexibility, and responsiveness. In fact, Jung (1959a) believed that for a man after age 35, failure to be in touch with the anima produces such traits as premature rigidity, crustiness, stereotypy, stubbornly unyielding one-sidedness, or stodgy conservatism. There may also be a flattening out of the personality, a loss of humanness. Thus, after the middle of life, a man should allow his previously submerged feminine tendencies an adequate opportunity to find outlets.

In Jung's view (1953), the anima of a man is derived from three sources: (1) the feminine inheritance (some men are by nature more feminine than others), (2) actual experiences with girls and women (of particular importance is the experience with the mother, who is the first source of attachment), and (3) the primordial deposits of the collective unconscious (all the potential images of the roles women have taken in relation to men). The manner in which an individual woman is regarded depends not on her actual qualities alone, but on what is brought to the relationship from these three sources.

According to Jung, the roles in which men have cast women are quite varied, and include such images as the harlot, the temptress, the witch, the spiritual guide, the goddess, the nurturing mother, the loving sexual companion, and others. Whether a particular woman appears to a man as a goddess or she-devil or whatever, depends upon his early experiences with girls and women. Abnormal experiences can result in the persistence of an archetypal image or a stereotype of women, and can create many problems in heterosexual experiences. What we have said here applies also to the formation of the image of man in a woman, as we shall see.

THE ANIMUS

Much of what has been said about the anima applies also to the animus, or masculine aspect of a woman's personality. Just as a boy may project his anima onto his mother, so the animus may be projected onto a man with the effect of deifying him. It may have other effects, such as making a woman opinionated and encouraging her to rival men. It may cause her to establish a man as a hero, only to pick at his weak points and tear him down. On the other hand, the animus can function to promote healthy living and satisfactory relationships with men. It can serve to temper the feminine personality traits. It can become a stimulus to the anima of a man, promoting his creativity and spontaneity. But in order to attain this level of maturity, the animus must be recognized and given a hearing. The denial of masculine traits by a woman, like the suppression of feminine traits by a man, only strengthens the force of the anima or animus.

The animus also produces in woman the image of man. It helps or hinders her response to men. A particular woman has her own notion of men, and this may be applied despite the actualities of the particular man with whom she is involved. The various roles which man has taken in the life of woman are potentially available, and one may predominate. She may think of man as a seducer, not to be trusted. She may have an image of man as a conquering hero; this role is often established by her father. And of course, the man may not at all correspond to her image of him. She may view him as a magic helper who has all the answers to her problems and frustrations. She may see him as a knight errant and expect him to bow down before her in awe and wonderment. Her animus archetype may be so primitive as to hamper any real relationship with men. Men and women who have difficulty understanding the other sex are probably not in tune with their anima or animus nature. Just as the mother and sisters have much to do with the formation of the anima image in a boy, so also the father and brothers have much to do with the development of the animus in a girl.

MASCULINE VERSUS FEMININE PSYCHOLOGY

Masculine and feminine psychology are distinctly different, Jung believed. The purest form of man (what might be termed "raw masculinity": brutishness, combativeness, savagery) is disagreeable to women and is dangerous. It needs to be tempered by some of the positive emotions of femininity. Likewise, the purest form of womanhood (fickleness, emotional volatility, hypersensitivity to any supposed insult) is unappealing to men and usually creates a neurotic existence for the woman. It must be tempered by the logic and rationality of masculine traits. These *tempering influences* exist in the unconscious and normally do their work unnoticed. But when the anima and animus remain in a primitive state and intrude into consciousness, they create psychological disturbances. A man may become effeminate or a woman overly masculine. Once again, balance and moderation are the keys. A man must recognize his feminine qualities and accept them as a real part of his personality. A woman must similarly recognize her masculine traits and accept them as a part of her nature. The anima of a man adds a dimension of humanness to his masculine role, and the animus of a woman anchors her persona in rationality and control.

One might ask: is there an anima type of woman, and is there an animus type of man? Are there women who are especially attractive to men, and likewise are there men who are particularly attractive to women? We all know a man or a woman of whom everyone says: "How could he fall for her, or what could make such a fine young girl fall in love with a good-for-nothing like him?" Even the individual involved in such a romantic relationship often recognizes its irrationality as well as his own helplessness. He may say: "I know this whole thing is crazy, and my head keeps telling me no, but my heart says yes." What he sees in the other are extraordinary powers and attributes, not what is objectively there, and this is painfully obvious to those who are not captivated. Projection is at work: qualities are ascribed to the other that are projections of the anima or animus, depending on whether it is a man or a woman who is smitten.

Who are these women who seem by nature to attract anima projections? According to Jung (1959a), they may be described as sphinxlike. They are equivocal and elusive: there is always an intriguing uncertainty about them. They are not an indefinite blur that offers nothing, but have an indefiniteness that seems full of promises. A woman of this kind embodies opposite qualities: she is both old and young, mother and daughter, childlike and yet endowed with an extreme cunning that is disarming to men.

What about the man who is by nature highly attractive to women? According to Jung, he is a real master of words—words with a great deal of meaning that also create intrigue by leaving a great deal unsaid. In popular language he might be described as "having a good line." He is one of those who is "misunderstood" or in some manner at odds with his environment: he might be someone from another country. He may create the illusion that he is capable of great self-sacrifice. He is regarded as an undiscovered hero, recognized only by the woman who loves him. These are the men who capture the heart, even though the head says no.

STAGES OF DEVELOPMENT OF THE ANIMA AND ANIMUS

The anima of a man undergoes changes throughout his life. There are at least four different images of woman, each of which characterizes a man's *growing relationship* with the opposite sex. In the first stage the woman is pictured as sensual, an attractive physical being who can tantalize a man: the sexual aspect is most outstanding. The woman who exemplifies this image is Eve: she was the greatest thing that happened to Adam after his creation. The next stage is that of the romantic woman. Helen of Troy, with "the face that sank a thousand ships," is a good representative of this stage. The woman is idealized and captures a man's passions and love. The sexual component remains quite prominent. The third stage is that of the virgin; woman is depicted as simple, beautiful, warm, innocent, and capable of great love for only one man. In the fourth stage she becomes a spiritual guide — a source of stability, comfort, and wisdom. In normal development, a man's relationship with women follows this course. If a marriage is successful, the husband acquires a sincere respect for his wife as a person in her own right, and the bonds between them increase on the spiritual level.

The animus of a woman also goes through four stages, each depicting man in a characteristic masculine role. The first portrays him as powerful, sensual, animalistic, and sexually attractive. This image may be termed the "power man." In the second stage man is depicted as a lover, an attractive gentleman who has power over the woman's emotions; this image is the "romantic man." The third stage is that of the "action man." Man is seen as competent, masterful, authoritarian. Of course, the woman has a role to play in this through her support and encouragement: man has power over her only if she endows him with it. In the fourth stage, man is viewed as "a wise old man." He is the spiritual guide to woman. He gives her support, stability, and inspiration. In a healthy relationship between a man and a woman, the anima of the man complements the animus of the woman; they work harmoniously together, cooperating with their conscious aspects.

The reader may be assisted in understanding and remembering the meanings of anima and animus by connecting the term "animation" with anima and the term "animosity" with animus. Jung (1933b) often referred to the anima in a man as the soul or spirit. He did not use the term in its religious or metaphysical sense; rather he meant the tender emotions that are associated with femininity. A man who lacks spirit or soul suffers from a disturbance of his anima. The animus implies strength, courage, and aggressiveness. One who is capable of animosity can deal actively with the people and things of her environment. Of course, animosity can lead to destructive behavior and can be a source of disturbance in the personality, just as animation can be uncontrolled emotionality.

TABLE 16-2   ANIMA AND ANIMUS TRAITS

Anima

Normal	*Abnormal*
Keeps a man in touch with his emotions	Causes a man to be petty and picayune
Helps him to be creative and spontaneous	Makes him cynical and bitter about his lot in life
Makes him more intuitive	Makes him moody and overly concerned with interpersonal matters
Helps him to be sensitive to the needs and feelings of others	Makes him gossipy and intrusive in the affairs of others
Makes him a gentleman in his relationships with both men and women	Makes him effeminate and insecure in social relationships

Animus

Normal	*Abnormal*
Makes a woman reality-oriented	Makes a woman emotional and irrational
Makes her problem-oriented	Makes her morbidly introspective
Produces a balanced orientation	Produces uncontrolled emotions and fragmentation of the personality
Makes for goal-directed behavior	Causes disorganized and dissociated behaviors
Makes a woman capable of inspiring the anima in a man to be creative	Makes a woman highly opinionated and competitive with men
Helps her to establish a sense of identity and integrity	Makes her attempt to divest a man of his role, causing problems with her sense of feminine identity
Makes her stable	Makes her argumentative, negativistic, moody, irrational
Gives her self-assurance and backbone	Makes her feel inferior and insecure

Like other forms of abnormality, abnormality of the anima and animus may follow a pattern either of excess or of deficiency. The animus in a woman may cause her to castrate men as she attempts to assert her power and independence. Or it may take the form of spinelessness and an inability to be autonomous. The anima in a man may make him overly emotional and sentimental, but it may also result in a bland and shallow personality. Again, the element of balance is essential to a healthy personality, according to Jung's view of man.

Table 16–2 depicts the normal and abnormal manifestations of the anima in man and the animus in woman. It should be noted that abnormality in this sense may take the form of a deficiency or excess in required behaviors.

Jung found support for his concepts of the anima and animus in the Chinese principles of the yin and the yang. The yin embodies being receptive, yielding, withdrawing, turning inward, enclosing, containing, giving birth. It values feelings, nurturing, seduction, and emotions such as ecstasy, reverence for beauty, and sensuality. The yang emphasizes the active, outgoing, aggressive, unfeeling aspects of living. Specific behaviors are heroism, abstract spirituality, disciplined morality. It is reality-oriented and restrictive.

INTROVERSION AND EXTROVERSION

PSYCHOLOGICAL TYPES AND FUNCTIONS

Though he did not deny the uniqueness and complexity of each individual, Jung nevertheless felt that people could be categorized into definable types. He proposed two major types or attitudes: introversion and extroversion (Jung, 1933b). The extrovert focuses his interest on objects outside himself; the introvert attends more to his inner life, his self. Obviously, such orientations vary in degree, but an individual tends to organize his psychic structures in either one direction or the other.

In addition to the two orientations, there are various psychological functions that also vary in strength in each person. One might consider these functions as powers or faculties which enable a person to deal with his environment. Jung (1933b) named only four: thinking, feeling, sensing, and intuiting. At any single moment one may engage in one or more of these activities. Combining the orientations and the functions, we may distinguish eight major types of people. Depending upon the priorities of the various functions (which is dominant, which auxiliary, which inferior), there are many, many variations (Mann et al., 1972).

A word should be said about typologies. Some psychologists, as we have seen, believe that typing human personalities does an injustice to the remarkable individuality of each person. The argument is that the typology forces very different people into a neat category. The type says both too much and too little. It says too much by ascribing all of the attributes of the type to the particular individual, without specifying degree. It says too little because the specific characteristics of the person are not delineated. To say that John and Mary are both introverted does not tell you much about the unique set of traits that constitutes each personality. It should be pointed out that with present knowledge, thorough description of personality is far beyond the achievement of psychology. Yet one may discern generalities and approximations. There are relatively few styles of homes — Colonial, Tudor, Cape Cod, and the like — but each specific home has its own particular character, size, color, contents, and location. There is no good reason why personalities cannot be examined from the same point of view. The notion of types does not require that all the members be identical, only that there is enough similarity to apply a designation or label.

Jung's two types may be considered from the standpoint of attitudes toward objects: the introvert resists the power of objects and draws life energy away from them and toward himself; the extrovert invests energy in objects and finds his greatest value in objects external to himself. The introvert, as a consequence of his inward orientation, tends to be shy, quiet, and difficult to know. The extrovert tends to be in touch with the world; he is open and eager to participate in his surroundings. All classes of society have these two characteristic types; whether a man is educated or not, whether he is a highly gifted musician or a day laborer, does not obliterate the two life orientations. Furthermore, the two types are found in both men and women (Cattell, 1957). Jung believed that the basis must be native biological factors. The extrovert adapts by expanding his contact with the environment, the introvert by making himself impregnable.

There is a natural inclination to think of the extrovert as more "normal" or healthy than the introvert. The reason may be the identification of action with extroversion: in an action-oriented culture, the extrovert seems to fit better. Jung held that the two orientations are *natural* types of humans; to attempt to convert a naturally introverted person to an extrovert usually creates psychophysiological disturbances. A child who is forced into an attitude which is not suited to his nature will usually become neurotic. Jung (1933b) believed that just as femininity and masculinity are distinctive qualities, so there are introverts and extroverts, and their respective orientations to life are quite different.

Usually some components of personality are more highly developed, and more energy is employed for their operation than for others. Thus there are superior and inferior functions. If a person is an extrovert consciously, his introvertive tendencies are inferior and unconscious. The extrovertive tendencies are under conscious motivation, but there may be intrusion from the unconscious introvertive tendencies. For example, a cooperative extrovert may at times display a childish obstinacy and resist the suggestions of his friends. Since the introvert in him is not under conscious control, at times it takes on a childish, destructive aspect and constitutes a serious weakness in his personality. Recognizing his introvertive side and directing attention inward would bring such tendencies under control. A lopsided wheel does not run smoothly. If the dominant conscious orientation is organized around introvertive traits, the extrovertive tendencies are unconscious, and also are not under ego control. They too may create difficulties for the person when they intrude into the ego. The introvert may strongly desire to be more popular, to be more comfortable with people, and to develop rich friendships. But these motives may be pushed into the background and not given much attention. For example, an introverted professor who always seemed self-sufficient and content with his quiet life apparently longed for companionship. His attempts to relate to others were rather primitive and crude; he was usually left out of things. He was driven to seek companionship with an unsavory crowd, and almost ruined his reputation. With them he felt comfortable: he could let his guard down and be more himself. Thus Jung's idea that undeveloped tendencies are dangerous is applicable to both introversion and extroversion. An individual may be by nature predominantly extroverted or introverted, but allow adequate expression for the opposite attitude in himself. It should be borne in mind that Jung meant by *inferior function* an underdeveloped function.

Jung's theory of psychological types is so complex that to develop it extensively would go far beyond the scope of this book. Since the purpose of this chapter is to highlight the individuation process, Jung's idea of one-sided development and disequilibrium will be considered.

To appreciate Jung's notion of the individuation process, one must take into account both the general qualities of introversion and extroversion and the four functions of the psyche: thinking, feeling, sensing, and intuiting. One of these is usually overemphasized and overdeveloped, while the others are not expressed adequately. In such instances, a person is handicapped because he is not using all his abilities as completely as possible. The extroverted intellectual may be so intent on making an impression on others that he neglects his own feelings and emotions. Likewise, the intuitive introvert may focus so much on his inner life that he loses vital personal contacts. Jung held that there should be full expression of all the functions, so that a person fully uses what he has. Any one-sided emphasis (being too extroverted or too introverted, being overly intellectual or overly intuitive) hampers normal growth and functioning.

SYMBOLS AND THEIR FUNCTIONS

One of Jung's most significant contributions to our understanding of man's behavior is his emphasis on the role of symbols in human life. We are all familiar with the symbolic nature of language; the words of a language, which of course vary from language to language, stand for or represent things, names, complex relationships, and even situations which do not actually exist, as for example a negative number in mathematics. Words and phrases are symbols because they stand for something else; they do not have meaning in themselves but are assigned meaning. A word represents some other thing, or person, or situation, or relationship. The ability to symbolize events is a powerful tool for man (Werner and Kaplan, 1963).

There are many other symbols besides words. Certain gestures and facial expressions, certain customs and rituals, have acquired meaning and serve as symbols: a smile and handclasp to greet a friend, the giving of gifts as tokens of love. Symbols express what may be difficult to communicate in other ways, or what cannot be easily expressed, such as the love of a mother for her child, or of a man for his wife, or of people for their homeland. A man sends his beloved flowers which say things that he could not say as effectively: "I want you to care for me." "I think a lot of you." "Please forgive me—I really did not want to hurt you."

Many people do things that apparently have a great deal of meaning for them, because they repeat the practices again and again without knowing why. A great many customs have arisen—the Christmas tree, the Easter rabbit, the cap and gown, the wedding ring—and such customs have much meaning, yet those who are touched by these symbols usually cannot give an explanation of their origin. Interference with the exercise of the symbolic activities produces a disturbance: "How can you have a wedding without a wedding ring, or a graduation without cap and gown?" A woman may be terribly distressed if she has to forgo a wedding ring, even though she recognizes quite clearly that the ring is "just a matter of custom," a frill that she could just as well do without. The ring touches her in some mysterious way which she herself cannot explain. Jung held that symbols and symbolic practices give meaning to life and are absolutely essential for effective living.

Jung also proposed the challenging idea that we behave first and question later. Men have done things for centuries without knowing why they do them. Systems of theology and philosophy followed rather than preceded beliefs and ceremonial practices. Reasoning and consciousness are late evolutionary developments in man's psyche. Even in ordinary day-to-day living we do things first and find explanations later, particularly if we are required to justify our behavior (Johnson, 1968). Symbolic practices express man's nature, and often one uses reason to suppress so-called primitive behavior. Jung (1964b) believed that one of the major ills of our times is that many men attempt to order their lives in accordance with logic and reason rather than acting on impulse, and there is thus a lack of harmony between conscious and unconscious tendencies.

Certain rituals and ceremonies have had a remarkable persistence. They have occurred in many diverse places and times throughout man's history. Although the practices have varied in specific content, the forms they have taken and the responses of the peoples are often strikingly similar, even when no contact was possible, a factor which precludes imitation.

Beliefs and practices are acknowledged and used by many people, suggesting that they satisfy something important in personality. Jung held that symbols have given man a way of dealing with his problems, a way of making the human condition more bearable and comprehensible. Difficulties such as disease, loss of loved ones, the erratic character of nature, aging, and personal death can all acquire meaning and therefore be made more acceptable through religious practices, symbolism, and beliefs. Symbols are the expression or products of archetypes. The symbolic rituals surrounding such experiences as birth, marriage, and death are universal.

A failure to find expression for the archetypes necessarily leaves unsettled certain requirements of living. One needs some form of religion (a set of beliefs to explain the unknowns in life) in order to live fully, just as one requires a warm temperature to be comfortable. Life is possible at lower temperatures, but one experiences tension. Lack of gratification of archetypes involves a similar persistence of tension. For primitive people, myths were a mental therapy for suffering and dealing with the unknown, but modern-day man also has myths: for instance, that science will solve everything. *The impotence of the ordinary man is banished by the power of his prayers, rituals, beliefs, and practices* (Jung, 1933a).

When a person isolates himself from his archetypal requirements, serious consequences ensue. Becoming more and more conscious and rational has cut man off from his own inner nature; giving up ritualistic practices and beliefs has made his life less rich. He experiences depression, tension, restlessness, a feeling of alienation. Symbols touch man's deepest core tendencies; they provide for what Jung called *numinous experiences*—experiences that impart spiritual power or special significance to those who are affected by them.

Consider the flag of a country. It stands for the ideals that are cherished by the people. The flag serves as a source of security and strength. It stands for my country, of which I am an important part. My country is greater than I am, and I can find courage and strength from being a part of it. The flag is a concrete physical object that can have considerable meaning. It can become a focal point for the expression of many archetypes. Jung would say that it has a numinous quality. We feel a sense of awe in the presence of nationalistic symbols, such as the flag. We honor them and treat them with great reverence. A great deal of ritual and ceremony surrounds them, creating the numinous tone. When the flag or any symbol loses its numinous quality, then something is lost for the individual. He is left without the support he needs. Modern man's symbols—wealth, power, prestige, security—have proven unfulfilling and must be replaced, Jung (1964b) believed.

Symbolic activity may be regarded in two ways: (1) as the product of a need that has been blocked, or (2) as one means of satisfying a need. Dancing is symbolic behavior which many psychologists regard as an outlet for frustrated sexual tensions, but it may also express man's longing for freedom, for instance, those dances in which physical contact is not present. Progressive art forms seem to bring to the fore man's deepest longings: for wholeness, or rebirth, or freedom from constraints. They not only are the products of frustrated impulses, but they also point to the solution, to the goals toward which man is striving. The symbol reveals its *origins* on the one hand and demonstrates the *solutions* on the other (Jung, 1917).

The advancement of scientific understanding has changed man's relation to his world, and in many respects has blocked the expression of significant unconscious tendencies. For instance, for the urban man an empty field may be simply an empty field, but for one who derives his livelihood from the fertile soil, the same field is endowed with mystery and wonder. The responses of the two men are very different: for one the experience touches upon nothing significant, while the other has a numinous experience, a sense of appreciation of the source of his existence.

According to Jung, modern man should discover new symbols to replace those that were significant to life during more primitive eras. Although he spoke of the futility of relying on science to solve all of our problems, he did not mean that the discoveries of science and the achievements of technology must necessarily remove the wonder, mystery, and numinosity which characterized man's prescientific status. The scientist and technical specialist do not create the laws of nature; they discover and apply them. A scientist did not produce the fact that mercury rises and falls in a tube with changes in temperature; he merely discovered it. The common gadgets of a middle-class home are "miracles of nature" and can produce numinous experiences in those who will take the time to contemplate them. The contemporary automobile is a marvel of scientific achievement that captivates many. One of the pitfalls of modern science is that we may overvalue the power of the scientist and overlook the mysteries he is utilizing. Indeed, science may have an almost religious impulse, for as G. Stanley Hall, an early American psychologist, once said: "it seeks to think God's thoughts after Him" (quoted in Misiak and Sexton, 1966).

THE INDIVIDUATION PROCESS

As we have suggested, the individuation process is the development and growth of the person. Given the proper conditions, there is a natural unfolding. Just as a seed needs light and moisture to grow into a particular plant or tree, so also a human being requires favorable conditions to become what he can become. With man, however, there is a difference: the ego must participate if fullness of growth is to be achieved (Jung, 1964b). Growth occurs naturally only in part. A man with a talent for music does not perfect it—or develop it at all—if he does not recognize it and, recognizing it, deliberately work to express and improve it.

One of Jung's students recounts the story of a woman who complained that she had never done anything worthwhile in her life. She was told about a carpenter who complained to his assistant that a certain large oak tree was not good for anything, and that was the reason why the tree had not been cut for lumber. The tree appeared to the carpenter in a dream and told him that had it been useful it would not have grown to be what it now was. It would have been put to use. The person who gears his life only to productive skills or compulsive striving for success may overlook his inner potentialities. He may force himself to become what he is not by nature meant to be. Specific occupational accomplishments are much less important, Jung believed, than realizing one's psychobiological potentials.

THE PERSONA

An important aspect of individuation is the recognition and dethroning of the persona or social personality, the mask that is worn for the sake of others

(Jung, 1953). In a sense, the persona is the ideal self, but in a social sense rather than from the standpoint of the individual's own ideals. An arrogant, tough, poised air may be the persona a man attempts to express: he believes that he is behaving at his best when he acts in this manner. The persona, of course, is determined largely by cultural expectations: a man is expected to behave in a prescribed manner, and this is different from the expectations placed upon a woman. Doctors have a persona different from that of teachers, and so on.

Jung pointed out that one's profession may contribute materially to the formation of the persona. A man may take on the characteristics of his office. His ego is inflated by the attributes of his status. As a professor, he becomes the stereotype assigned to that profession. At work, his behavior may be tinged with solemnity, pomposity, and an air of great importance. But to those who really know him outside the academic setting, he may be an empty shell with no real substance of his own. Like an actor who plays a character totally different from himself, he uses his role to take over the attributes but not the qualities of the person. Although he becomes his role, it is not him; therefore he gives it up as easily as he puts it on. In real life, the person who strives to fit a self-image which is not himself suffers the consequences of this sham existence (Pervin, 1968).

The persona, like Freud's superego, regulates and controls behavior to bring about effective adjustment to one's circumstances. Many compromises with individualistic desires and requirements are usually made. The person who likes his persona and shapes his entire life in accordance with its ideal (for example, the lawyer who strives to be the best in the world 24 hours a day, seven days a week) necessarily gives up much of what is really himself. The cultural model does not perfectly suit any particular individual, and when one takes over the expectations fully, there is usually an extreme quality about the personality. Being an extrovert is an expectation of American culture, but one who adopts extroversion as a way of life, especially if this role does not fit his real nature, becomes a shallow, artificial, and dwarfed personality. Yet unless one comes to know his persona, he cannot become his real self. Getting behind the persona and coming to terms with it are necessary steps in the individuation process. Effective personality development and functioning requires a balance.

THE SHADOW

Jung believed that each person has a shadow, which is the "evil" aspect of his nature (1959a, 1959b). The term itself is quite descriptive: the shadow is the shaded aspect of personality, darkened because one attempts not to recognize it. In its most primitive form, it includes animalistic impulses: for example, cannibalism, incest, destructiveness, utter selfishness. The shadow is in opposition to and always conflicts with the persona (Jung, 1959a). "I do not want others to see anything but my best behavior; the shadow is my worst side;

therefore it must be covered up as much as possible." In fact, the covering up is usually done so well that the person himself is unaware of his shadow. Most of us, even those who claim to be objective about themselves, have a good self-opinion (Scott, 1963). Paradoxically, the person with a profound sense of inferiority is overidentifying with his persona and is no more aware of his shadow than anyone else. We think that we are reasonable and considerate, more than most people, anyway. It is extremely rare to find a person who knows his most undesirable qualities. Yet for the purpose of the individuation process, it is necessary to discover the shadow, to become aware of one's negative and animalistic tendencies and desires. One can hardly do anything about improving his development and functioning if he fails to recognize his weaker aspects. Whether one changes such qualities or is simply aware of their existence without doing anything about them, from the standpoint of the individuation process, this is certainly preferable to lack of awareness or a false belief that one possesses only desirable qualities. Knowing one's evil tendencies may give one great power over his personality. Jung believed that the shadow imparts dimension to personality: angels may be suitable for heaven but not for earthly existence. An all-perfect being would be unbearable for most of us, for we do recognize our own shortcomings in part and welcome others with theirs (Fig. 16–1).

Much of the shadow is unconscious. Though excluded from the ego, however, the shadow material is nevertheless an important aspect of the individual; it should be available to consciousness because it is part of the self. Usually the major reason for *repression* is that the material is unacceptable and too threatening to be integrated within the ego and persona. This material can also undergo *projection*. Not only does the user of projection fail to perceive his undesirable qualities; he also assigns them to others. If I can see dishonesty all around me, I can easily overlook it in myself. Consequently, what vague recognition one might have or acquire of one's own faults is muddled through the perception of these faults in others. One says in effect: "My little sins are nothing compared to those of my friends." Thus through repression and projection some very basic material is usually kept unconscious.

Figure 16–1   The individual who squarely confronts his shadow may find that its less primitive aspects give dimension and credibility to his personality. (Copyright King Features Syndicate, Inc., 1973. World rights reserved.)

Jung believed that repression and projection produce a sense of *moral inferiority:* one feels that he is unworthy or evil, but he cannot put his finger on the reasons for his feelings. He may think that the cause is lack of conformity to moral or ethical standards, but the real reason is that the vital qualities have been cut off. The personal unconscious is a kind of dumping place for unwanted aspects of the self. Therapy consists, in part, of bringing the unconscious back to consciousness. This involved for Jung an enlarging of the ego; the ego acquires more strength in the process. Certain conclusions and criticisms about the self are now accessible to the ego, and something can be done about them.

To achieve the fullest personality functioning, however, one must go beyond making the unconscious conscious. All aspects of both the conscious and unconscious areas, including the collective unconscious, must be developed completely. This involves locating the whole center of personality more nearly in the real center, which is the self.

Beneficial Aspects of the Shadow

While the shadow has a negative side, it also has a positive aspect. As we have seen, one who strongly identifies with a style of life prescribed by his profession or station in life cuts off vital aspects of his personality in his efforts to live out his persona. Allowing his shadow side to come to the surface adds a new dimension to his conscious ego. His animalistic tendencies can add vitality and zest to his life—not that the individual should become impulsive and drive-oriented, but rather that he should find acceptable outlets for his basic nature. His persona may demand dignity, composure, reserve, and so on; this pose does not allow the whole personality to be expressed. *What is "evil" in a person when uncontrolled can be channeled to good ends* (Jung, 1949b). Both Freud and Jung recognized the beneficial function of *sublimation,* a process which involves finding suitable and harmless outlets for what are considered negative tendencies.

The shadow and the persona are like two opposing poles. There is thus conflict and tension. But conflict, while painful, is not all bad. Growth is promoted by conflict; tension serves as motivation and gets things accomplished. The best solution for conflict, of course, is to take care of the opposing factions. Sometimes an activity is capable of transcending the conflict by gratifying all factions. A man may so enjoy his work that it becomes a source of pleasure. The so-called evil side of man need not be such. Only when it is unrecognized or unattended does it become a problem. Jung held strongly that the *unconscious can easily take over the conscious* if the latter does not pay heed to the requirements of the former. One cannot grow and develop normally without taking account of the shadow. The same is true of the persona. Both the persona and the shadow can constrict and misshape the ego, and both must be uncovered if the individuation process is to take place.

Becoming Aware of Anima or Animus Traits

If the process of becoming a fully developed self—the individuation process—is to take place, a man must become aware of and express his anima traits, and a woman her animus traits. If discovering one's persona or social mask is difficult, and if becoming aware of shadow elements is a task of heroic proportions, the discovery and acceptance of the opposite-sex qualities is most difficult of all. These tendencies conflict with one's conception of self even more than the shadow qualities. But as we have noted previously, the anima and animus temper the persona and are expressive of the true nature of the individual. The ego pays much attention to the persona requirements, but until the other aspects are allowed to develop and play a part in the personality, selfhood will not occur. Awareness and expression of the anima or animus is one of the most complicated steps (but an absolutely essential one) in the attainment of the good life, in Jung's view.

THE SELF AND THE INDIVIDUATION PROCESS

As we noted earlier, Jung distinguished between the ego and the self. He referred to the self in two ways: (1) the self as an archetype, and (2) the self as a controlling agent. It will be recalled that for Jung the ego is the center of consciousness and is greatly affected both by the persona and by the external world. As the person becomes more individuated—that is, as he begins to understand the nature of his persona, his shadow, his anima or animus, and his archetypal requirements—the realm of consciousness is increased to include many areas of the psyche that were previously unconscious. When this occurs, the center of personality is no longer the ego, but rather the self. Whereas the ego is the center of only a portion of the psyche, the self is the center of the whole psyche. The ego is thus replaced by the self; the ego becomes the true center of personality.

Figure 16–2 depicts the unindividuated and individuated persons. Notice how much larger is the realm of consciousness for the individuated person.

The self as an archetype is analogous to the notion of self-concept, although Jung seemed to endow the self archetype with active powers. As an archetype the self is experienced in dreams in various forms, depending upon the degree of individuation the person has attained. Jung used the dreams of his patients as a means of determining the extent to which individuation had been achieved. The self might appear as a child of the same sex who plays a helping role, or it might be a godlike image, or a wise old man or woman. Like other archetypes, the self archetype is dependent upon acquired experiences as well as innate dispositions for its make-up. Jung held that the self archetype could be a constructive force in the attainment of individuation, if the person paid attention to the messages of his dreams and was receptive to his intuitions and inner promptings.

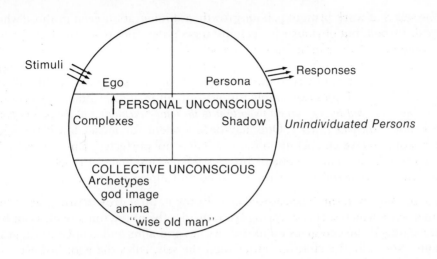

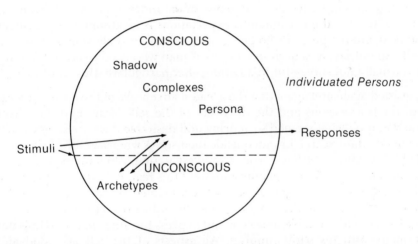

Figure 16–2 As one's comprehension of his persona increases, the conscious realm expands to incorporate many formerly unconscious areas of the psyche. There is thus a free interchange between the conscious and the unconscious in individuated persons.

The self may work at cross-purposes with the ego and create discord in the personality. It may actually take over the ego functions and cause the person to behave in antisocial and destructive ways. But Jung believed that it could also serve the personality in a positive way by communicating to the ego the requirements of the unconscious. One must be willing to listen to the self and to become sensitive to his intuitions. Promptings from the self can be extremely valuable in making important life decisions, Jung maintained. Ultimately, the self should be the true center of the personality, but this takes place only when differentiation and integration of all the components are complete.

The self is at work bringing about growth and integration even in those who are disturbed, but obviously in such instances it does not reach the fullness of its potential. A certain amount of growth occurs without any ego participation, as revealed through examining a series of one person's dreams, but ego participation, a receptivity to the self's "inner voices," is essential to the fullest growth. The self does not simply unfold and automatically attain perfection. *Consciousness and the ego are so important to the total functioning of the person that they must participate actively.* One may have a talent for music, but if the ego does not perceive and act upon it, the talent is not perfected. Inner directives from "the great man" (as one of Jung's students designated the self) must be perceived and actualized, or there can be no fullness of growth.

Ego participation can block as well as assist the natural growth processes. The inner voice which seems to spring from the depths of the unconscious can be heard only if the ego gives up its own wishes and aims and is open to suggestions. Normally the culture, rather than the self, rules the ego; however, it *should* be the self that rules, Jung believed. Because the environment presents problems, we pay attention and conform to it, but adaptation to the environment may be accomplished at the expense of an undeveloped self. Obviously, meeting cultural and environmental expectations is an absolute requirement for survival, but the person who permits his culture to swallow him cannot be himself. An old saying is pertinent here: "A man who is very successful at his work is usually not successful in anything else, particularly the art of living."

Jung insisted again and again that the greatest adventure of life is the exploration of the unconscious and the discovery of the self. Many find their lives drab and empty; what seemed so alluring and desirable does not satisfy when it is attained. Many search in vain outside themselves when actually the answer lies within. Attaining selfhood is one's greatest accomplishment; experiencing inner harmony is one of the manifestations of this feat. But whereas primitive man was in constant danger of being overwhelmed by his animal nature, civilized man has gone to the other extreme: he suffers from too many controls (Jung, 1933a). He is unable to accept and express his inner nature. He is not in harmony with his basic impulses. All aspects of the self are good and deserve recognition and an opportunity for expression. One should not be so preoccupied with the adaptive and coping functions of the ego that he does not hear the inner voice of the self.

The Transcendent Function

When selfhood is achieved, the ego becomes the true center of personality. Consciousness has expanded greatly, and the various components of the personality have become fully differentiated. Increased differentiation means that the various aspects of personality are in opposition to one another; thus there is conflict and tension. The self is confronted with the task of integrating the competing elements. The transcendent function is the *integrating activity of the self*, as it manages the personality and deals with the external environment. Jung's concept of the transcendent function is very similar to what Maslow termed the transcendence of dichotomies, which he found to be one of the outstanding characteristics of his self-actualizing people. It refers to the harmonizing of opposites. In such a state, the individual experiences a sense of unity, of well-being, of harmonious functioning.

The individuated man behaves in a manly manner, yet is not fearful of expressing his emotional nature. The feminine woman maintains her autonomy and self-assurance. They can relate socially without fearing to assert claims and personal interests. They can deal with the demands of the external world without being swallowed by it, and with their own inner requirements without becoming self-preoccupied. In short, the transcendent function allows balanced expression of the components of personality (the persona, the shadow, the anima or animus, the self, the archetypes), of the attitudes of introversion and extroversion, and of the four psychological functions (sensing, feeling, thinking, and intuiting).

CRITICAL EVALUATION OF JUNG

Many of Jung's critics accuse him of being mystical and unscientific. But his ideas are no more mystical than those of other personality theorists. Jung and his disciples have not done a good job of elucidating their basic concepts; thus many who criticize the theories do not really understand them. For example, Jung held that dreams sometimes prognosticate the future, a statement that could easily be misinterpreted as a belief in the preternatural and occult. However, Jung's explanation is quite plausible; he proposed the hypothesis that the unconscious is influenced by external events and may process information in a manner which creates a prediction of a future event through the medium of a dream. Conscious prognostication occurs frequently. Why cannot an analogous process take place unconsciously?

How different are Jung's principal constructs from those of Freud in terms of abstractness and scientific status? Freud defined id, ego, and superego by means of specific behaviors; Jung also defined his concepts of the persona, the shadow, the ego, the self, the anima and animus in terms of specific classes of behaviors. Anima behavior in men and animus behavior in women can be specified. The notions of the anima (within the man) and animus (within the woman) are no more mystical than the notions of the primitive id, or ego, or superego.

If we compare Jung with the other personality theorists on the possibility of attaining the good life, Jung is one of the most optimistic because his individuated man is man in his "natural" state. The return to, and expression of, the unconscious is within the power of everyone. Most of the other theorists—Allport, Maslow, Fromm, Rogers—set many conditions for the attainment of the good life. Only the genetically gifted and environmentally favored can become self-actualized, mature, fully functioning, or productive.

Jung did not establish such qualifications for the achievement of individuation. He would agree with the others that the individuated person is rare, but the potential for all men is great. The college professor and the coal miner alike have the potential for individuation, and perhaps Jung might hold even more promise for the coal miner. Personality weaknesses are to a great extent unnatural states, caused by life circumstances that have drawn man from his natural condition. For example, many of our problems are the result of our own intelligence, which Jung believed is a late evolutionary development in man. Consider the personality disorders associated with alcoholism, with the use of addictive drugs, with the excessive intake of manufactured foods. Modern living conditions are a product of man's ingenuity and inventiveness, but the animal in man is being perverted or denied. The diseases (arteriosclerosis, hypertension, obesity) associated with highly seasoned foods, stress, and other conditions of contemporary living, are caused directly by man. Is there any parallel in other creatures?

If man's consciousness and advanced intelligence have created problems for him, surely the same capabilities can solve them. This is Jung's creed for mankind.

INSIGHTS FROM JUNG'S INDIVIDUATION PROCESS

DEALING WITH THE SHADOW

Dealing with the shadow is like dealing with a friend who seems to have qualities which are opposite to yours. The friend deserves a hearing because his views may be just as right and valid as your own. Working with him often lessens the opposition: maybe both of you are seeking the same ends but each is too one-sided in his approach. There is usually more than one way of getting to your destination. The friend needs restriction and opposition if he interferes with your rights, but he needs love and acceptance as well. Getting along means giving and taking on both sides. The shadow is a vital part of the total self; in normal functioning it *complements* the conscious ego rather than opposes it. If it is perceived as evil or weakness, it is because the ego has not been able to bring together the opposites in personality. But opposition is the very stuff of growth: from contrasts and differences may come a higher synthesis. *The well-rounded person accepts and makes good use of everything that is within him; nothing in personality is totally bad; it is merely misused.* The shadow becomes hostile and troublesome only when it is ignored.

Everyone is conscious of some of his faults, and these are difficult enough to accept or change. Much more so are the unconscious ones. Something of the nature of these qualities may be discovered by considering those things about others that are most distasteful to you. Quite likely these are the very same qualities which you possess but have repressed in yourself and projected onto others.

FULFILLING THE PROJECTIONS OF ANOTHER

An interesting positive aspect of projection is that we tend to act in accordance with the way others treat us; that is, we tend to fulfill the expectations of those we value or who value us. Thus under certain conditions we may behave in conformity to the projections of the other (Rosenthal and Jacobson, 1968). According to Jung, many a lackluster man has soared to fame through the projections of a complex and talented, but undeveloped, woman.

DIALOGUE WITH THE ANIMA

Jung recommended that a man carry on a dialogue with his anima and a woman with her animus. The anima frequently takes the form of an emotional state—a mood of depression, for example. One may deal with this mood by treating it as if it were an *autonomous personality* and letting it state its case fully. Jung believed that this dialogue process comes rather easily, because the anima causing the disturbance has broken off from the rest of the personality and operates as a separate identity. No criticism should be made until the anima has stated its case completely; then each point can be examined critically and answered until there is a reduction of the emotional intensity. This inner dialogue is advisable, however, only when the anima makes itself felt in moodiness and dissatisfaction, an indication that it is functioning abnormally.

The reader may recall Murray's description of the ego as being like the Congress, with many factions. Murray may have obtained this idea from Jung, whom he once visited for a month. Jung personified aspects of the personality. The anima or animus, the shadow, and the self may actually be treated as if they were persons with whom one might carry on a discussion. Let the "selfish me" have its say; do not automatically rule it evil and undesirable. Let the rebellious faction have its opportunity to express itself, and so on. Like other personality theorists, Jung maintained that all aspects of the self are to be integrated and accepted as a part of the personality. Some aspects may be changed, but certainly they must be perceived as being a part of the total system.

DELIBERATELY REACTIVATING ARCHETYPES

Jung made the point that the individuation process is promoted by early recollections. These recollections may reactivate archetypes that are no longer being expressed properly. One may even attempt to activate archetypes deliberately, as when one re-examines his concept of God, or of motherhood, or of authority. Archetypes take on different forms in the course of life. A reactivation of an archetype can produce dramatic changes in personality, Jung believed. Since archetypal ideas are highly charged emotionally, they can be very disturbing when experienced. Jung says of the process of reactivating archetypes:

The recollection of infantile memories, and the reproduction of archetypal ways of psychic behavior, can create a wider horizon and a greater extension of consciousness, on condition that one succeeds in assimilating and integrating in the conscious mind the lost and regained contents. Since they are not neutral, their assimilation will modify the personality, just as they themselves will have to undergo certain alterations. In this part of what is called the individuation process . . . interpretation of symbols plays an important practical role, for the symbols are natural attempts to reconcile and reunite opposites within the psyche (1964b, p. 90).

PERSONIFICATION AND POSSESSION

Jung held that the components of the personality, when not given adequate expression, may act as autonomous agents. In dreams they take the form of characters: for instance, the anima of a man might be embodied as a beautiful woman, or one who was disreputable; the shadow might be the stranger; the self might take the form of a helping child. The nature of dream characters and the changes that occur reveal the progress toward individuation. During the waking state, the ego might be taken over by the so-called people within the personality. We might be *possessed* by our shadows. Everyone has observed that a friend is not himself today. This condition makes sense in Jung's notion of ego possession. When my shadow or anima takes over my ego, I may not know it, but everyone around me certainly does. One who allows the various facets of his personality to develop and be expressed fully is less likely to be a victim of possession.

SIGNIFICANT QUOTATIONS FROM JUNG

The individuation process is fostered by recollecting the past and examining the people and events of our dreams, Jung believed:

As the evolution of the embryonic body repeats its prehistory, so the mind also develops through a series of prehistoric stages. The main task of dreams is to bring back a sort of "recollection" of the prehistoric, as well as the infantile world, right down to the level of the most primitive instincts. Such recollections can have a remarkably healing effect in certain cases, as Freud said long ago. This observation confirms the view that an infantile memory gap (a so-called amnesia) represents a positive loss, and its recovery can bring a positive increase in life and well-being. . . . Often they [dreams] bring back a piece of life, missing for a long time, that gives purpose to, and thus enriches human life (1964b, p. 98).

In the following passage we may see Jung's concern with symbols. It should be borne in mind that symbols are ceremonial practices, beliefs, and customs, as well as designs, insignias, and the like.

Such cultural symbols nevertheless retain much of their original numinosity or "spell." One is aware that they can evoke a deep emotional response in some individuals, and this psychic charge makes them function in much the same way as prejudices. . . . It is folly to dismiss them because, in rational terms, they seem too absurd or irrelevant. They are important constituents of our mental make-up and vital forces in the build-up of human society; and they cannot be eradicated without serious loss. Where they are repressed or neglected, their specific energy disappears into the unconscious with unaccountable consequences. The psychic energy that appears to have been lost in this way in fact serves to revive and intensify whatever is uppermost in the unconscious, tendencies perhaps that have hitherto had no chance to express themselves or at least have not been allowed an uninhibited existence in our consciousness (1964b, p. 93).

Jung blamed the great upheavals of this century on inadequate expression of man's nature:

Modern man does not understand how much his "rationalism" (which has destroyed his capacity to respond to numinous symbols and ideas) has put him at the mercy of the psychic "underworld." He has freed himself from "superstition" (or so he believes), but in the process he has lost his spiritual values to a positively dangerous degree. His moral and spiritual tradition has disintegrated, and he is now paying the price for this break-up in worldwide disorganization and dissociation.

Anthropologists have often described what happens to a primitive society when its spiritual values are exposed to the impact of modern civilization. Its people lose the meaning of their lives, their social organization disintegrates, and they themselves morally decay. We are now in the same condition (1964b, p. 94).

In the following passage, Jung seems to be saying that modern man has lost contact with his original psyche. As a consequence, contemporary life is barren and empty. It lacks the wonder, inspiration, and mystery of an earlier day. The solution is to find adequate outlets for our archetypes. This does not mean that we should give up the great achievements of science, but rather that we should discover or invent new symbols to put us again in touch with our archetypes.

As scientific understanding has grown, so our world has become dehumanized. Man feels himself isolated in the cosmos, because he is no longer involved in nature, and has lost his emotional "unconscious identity" with natural phenomena. These have slowly lost their symbolic implications. Thunder is no longer the voice of an angry god; nor is lightning his avenging missile. No river contains a spirit; no tree is the life principle of a man; no snake the embodiment of wisdom; no mountain cave the home of a great demon. No voices now speak to man from stones, plants, and animals; nor does he speak to them, believing that they can hear. His contact with nature has gone, and with it has gone the profound emotional energy that this symbolic connection supplied (1964b, p. 95).

SUMMARY

1. Terms to remember:

Complex	A network of thoughts, feelings, and attitudes held together by a core disposition.
Collective unconscious	Thought-forms inherited by each individual.
Persona	The social personality; the mask worn for the sake of others and determined largely by cultural expectations.
Shadow	The aspects of personality one attempts to hide.
Personal unconscious	Impulses, wishes, and memories which the ego

	cannot integrate; accumulated after birth through individual experiences.
Archetypes	Predispositions to have certain experiences; preformed ideas that can become a part of actual experience.
Animus	Archetype of man in woman; masculine traits in woman.
Anima	Archetype of woman in man; feminine traits in man.
Self	Controlling agent in personality when individuation has taken place; core of the whole personality.
Ego	Center of consciousness, felt subjectively.
Symbols	Triggering mechanisms for an emotion or motive; enable man to have experiences which would otherwise be impossible.
Sublimation	Finding acceptable outlets for dangerous impulses.

2.   Every organism possesses a genetic destiny which reaches fullness of growth when the proper conditions are met. The process of becoming a differentiated and fully developed individual is called the individuation process. Personality at first consists of potentialities and dispositions. Growth consists of differentiation and progressive integration, proceeding from the global to the specific. The psyche is composed of a conscious and an unconscious. The center of consciousness is the ego; the unconscious layer comprises a personal unconscious, with complexes as major components, and a collective unconscious, with archetypes as primary structures.

3.   The personal unconscious consists of personal experiences that have been forgotten, overlooked, or repressed. The collective unconscious consists of inherited thought-forms or archetypes.

4.   The persona is an inborn tendency to develop a social personality. It may block the expression of inner requirements.

5.   The anima is a boy's inborn disposition to respond to women. The term also refers to the feminine traits in the male. If functioning normally, the anima will assist the boy in knowing and dealing with women. The anima of man is derived from (a) feminine inheritance, (b) experience with girls, and (c) primordial deposits of the collective unconscious. The animus is the masculine aspect of a woman's personality. When functioning properly, it helps woman respond to man. When the anima and animus intrude into consciousness, they create psychological disturbances: a man may become effeminate or a woman masculine. If ignored, the anima and animus acquire an autonomous existence, interfering with ego operations. The anima of man undergoes four image changes, seeing woman in turn as (a) sensual, physically attractive; (b) romantic; (c) virginlike, simple, beautiful, warm; (d) spiritually guiding. The animus of woman also perceives man in four stages: (a)

powerful, sensual, animalistic; (b) lover, attractive gentleman; (c) competent, masterful, authoritarian; (d) wise, spiritually guiding.

6. The shadow consists of man's animalistic tendencies and any trait a person finds undesirable and not suited to his notion of self. Much of the shadow is repressed, producing a sense of moral inferiority. Both persona and shadow constrict and misshape the ego. They must be uncovered for individuation to occur. What is "evil" in a person when uncontrolled can be channeled to good ends; one may find suitable outlets for what are considered negative tendencies. Thus the shadow complements the conscious ego when it is functioning normally.

7. When a person has attained selfhood, the self is a controlling factor, not to be confused with the early ego. Ego is the center of consciousness and is subjectively experienced. The self is not experienced directly. Normally the culture rules the ego, but optimally it should be the self that rules.

8. Symbolic practices express man's nature. Symbols give man a way of dealing with his problems, a way of making the human condition more bearable and comprehensible. Because they serve as triggering mechanisms, symbols enable man to have experiences which would otherwise be impossible. Numinous experiences impart spiritual power to those who are affected by them.

9. In projection, we see our own qualities in others but fail to recognize them in ourselves. Projection hampers self-knowledge.

10. Archetypes are innate idea-forms that are activated by actual experiences. An archetypal image may so dominate the perceptual and interpretive functions of the ego that it seriously distorts judgment. When functioning properly, archetypes aid the process of knowing the world.

11. The collective unconscious is expressed in dreams which reveal themes, characters, and plots of a primordial nature. Both the collective and the personal unconscious compensate for or correct the excesses or omissions of the conscious. Compensation occurs because so many elements of personality are in conflict.

12. According to Jung, people may be categorized into introverts and extroverts. In addition to these two definable types, there are also four psychological functions: thinking, feeling, sensing, and intuiting.

SUGGESTED READINGS

Jung, C. G. An analysis of the prelude to a case of schizophrenia. *In* Hull, R. F., trans. Symbols of Transformation. New York: Harper and Row, 1962. (Originally published in 1912.)
In this book, Jung begins to develop his own version of the unconscious. He argues for the important function of the collective unconscious: the production of symbolic material.

Studies in Word Association. London: Heinemann, 1918.
The notion of the complex is elaborated, and methods for identifying and measuring the intensity and scope of complexes are detailed.

Psychological Types. New York: Harcourt, Brace and World, 1933.
>   In this book, Jung presents the major principles of his school of analytical psychology. He also develops his theory of types (introvert and extrovert) and the four functions (thinking, feeling, sensing, and intuiting).

The archetypes and the collective unconscious. *In* Read, H., et al., eds.; Hull, R. F., trans. Collected Works of C. G. Jung, Vol. 9, Part I. New York: Pantheon Books, 1959.
>   This is an excellent presentation of Jung's theory of personality, with a discussion of such topics as the persona, the shadow, the anima and animus, the self, and the individuation process.

Man and His Symbols. New York: Doubleday and Company, 1964.
>   Written by Jung and several of his most devoted disciples, this book is probably the best introduction to Jungian psychology. Jung designed it for the intelligent layman.

REFERENCES

Cattell, R. B. Personality and Motivation Structure and Measurement. New York: Harcourt, Brace and World, 1957.

Garai, J. C. Sex differences in mental health. Genet. Psychol. Monogr. *81*:123–42, 1970.

Johnson, R. E. Smoking and the reduction of cognitive dissonance. J. Pers. Social Psychol. *9*:260–65, 1968.

Jung, C. G. Collected Papers on Analytical Psychology. New York: Moffat, Yard, 1917.

Jung, C. G. Studies in Word Association. London: Heinemann, 1918.

Jung, C. G. Modern Man in Search of a Soul. New York: Harcourt, Brace and World, 1933a.

Jung, C. G. Psychological Types. New York: Harcourt, Brace and World, 1933b.

Jung, C. G. Two essays on analytical psychology. *In* Read, H., et al., eds.; Hull, R. F., trans. Collected Works of C. G. Jung, Vol. 7. New York: Pantheon Books, 1953.

Jung, C. G. The development of personality. *In* Collected Works, Vol. 17. New York: Pantheon Books, 1954a.

Jung, C. G. The practice of psychotherapy. *In* Collected Works, Vol. 16. New York: Pantheon Books, 1954b.

Jung, C. G. The archetypes and the collective unconscious. *In* Collected Works, Vol. 9, Part I. New York: Pantheon Books, 1959a.

Jung, C. G. Aion. *In* Collected Works, Vol. 9, Part II. New York: Pantheon Books, 1959b.

Jung, C. G. The structure and dynamics of the psyche. *In* Collected Works, Vol. 8. New York: Pantheon Books, 1960.

Jung, C. G. Civilization in transition. *In* Collected Works, Vol. 10. New York: Pantheon Books, 1964a.

Jung, C. G. Man and His Symbols. New York: Doubleday and Company, 1964b.

Keniston, K. The Uncommitted: Alienated Youth in American Society. New York: Harcourt, Brace and World, 1965.

Mann, H., Siegler, M., and Osmond, H. Four types of personalities and four ways of perceiving time. Psychol. Today *6* (December, 1972):76–84.

Misiak, H., and Sexton, V. History of Psychology. New York: Grune and Stratton, 1966.

Pervin, L. A. Performance and satisfaction as a function of individual-environment fit. Psychol. Bull. *69*:56–68, 1968.

Rosenthal, R., and Jacobson, L. Pygmalion in the Classroom. New York: Holt, Rinehart and Winston, 1968.

Scott, W. A. Social desirability and individual conceptions of the desirable. J. Abnorm. Social Psychol. *67*:547–85, 1963.

Stouffer, S. A., Suchman, E. A., De Vinney, L. C., Star, S. A., and Williams, R. M., Jr. The American Soldier: Adjustments During Army Life. Princeton: Princeton University Press, 1949.

Werner, H., and Kaplan, B. Symbol Formation. New York: John Wiley and Sons, 1963.

Index

Page numbers in *italics* indicate illustrations; those in **boldface** indicate bibliographical references; those followed by a "t" indicate tabular material; those followed by a "d" indicate definitions.